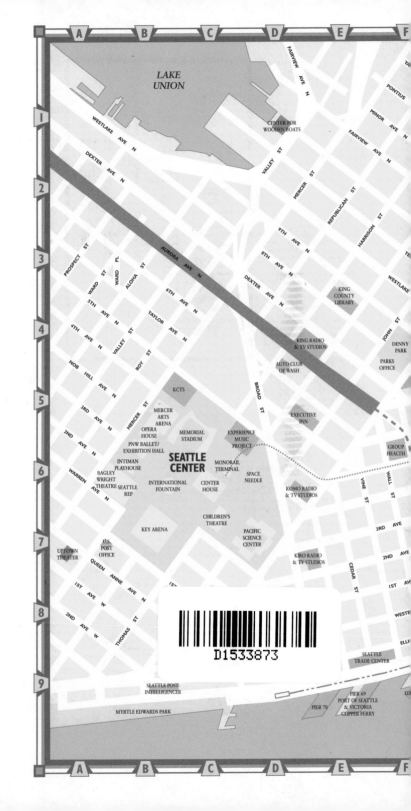

Praise for Best Places® Guidebooks

"Best Places *are the best regional restaurant and guide books in America.*"
—THE SEATTLE TIMES

"Best Places *covers must-see portions of the West Coast . . . with style and authority. In-the-know locals offer thorough info on restaurants, lodgings, and the sights.*"
—NATIONAL GEOGRAPHIC TRAVELER

"*. . . travelers swear by the recommendations in the* Best Places *guidebooks . . .*"
—SUNSET MAGAZINE

"*Known for their frank yet chatty tone . . .*"
—PUBLISHERS WEEKLY

"*For travel collections covering the Northwest, the* Best Places *series takes precedence over all similar guides.*"
—BOOKLIST

"*The best guide to Seattle is the locally published* Best Places Seattle *. . .*"
—JONATHAN RABAN, MONEY MAGAZINE

"*Whether you're a Seattleite facing the winter doldrums or a visitor wondering what to see next, guidance is close at hand in* Best Places Seattle."
—SUNSET MAGAZINE

"Best Places Seattle *remains one of the best, most straightforward urban guidebooks in the country.*"
—THE SEATTLE TIMES

"*This tome* [Best Places Seattle] *is one of the best practical guides to any city in North America.*"
—TRAVEL BOOKS WORLDWIDE

"*Visitors to Washington, Oregon, and British Columbia would do well to pick up* Best Places Northwest *for an exhaustive review of food and lodging in the region . . . An indispensable glove-compartment companion.*"
—TRAVEL AND LEISURE

TRUST THE LOCALS

The original insider's guides, written by local experts

COMPLETELY INDEPENDENT
- No advertisers
- No sponsors
- No favors

EVERY PLACE STAR-RATED & RECOMMENDED

★★★★ The very best in the city

★★★ Distinguished; many outstanding features

★★ Excellent; some wonderful qualities

★ A good place

MONEY-BACK GUARANTEE
We're so sure you'll be satisfied, we guarantee it!

HELPFUL ICONS
Watch for these quick-reference symbols throughout the book:

 FAMILY FUN

 GOOD VALUE

 ROMANTIC

 EDITORS' CHOICE

BEST PLACES®
SEATTLE

Edited by
SHANNON O'LEARY

EDITION

SASQUATCH BOOKS
SEATTLE

Printed in the United States of America
Distributed by Publishers Group West

Ninth edition
09 08 07 06 05 04 03 02   5 4 3 2 1

ISBN: 1-57061-318-4
ISSN: 1095-9734

Series editor: Kate Rogers
Cover and interior design: Nancy Gellos
Cover illustration/photograph: Paul Souders
Maps: GreenEye Design
Composition: Patrick David Barber and Holly McGuire

SPECIAL SALES

Best Places guidebooks are available at special discounts on bulk purchases for corporate, club, or organization sales promotions, premiums, and gifts. Special editions, including personalized covers, excerpts of existing guides, and corporate
imprints, can be created in large quantities for specific needs. For more information, contact your local bookseller or Special Sales, Best Places Guidebooks, 615
Second Avenue, Suite 260, Seattle, Washington 98104, 800/775-0817.

SASQUATCH BOOKS
615 Second Avenue
Seattle, Washington 98104
206/467-4300
bestplaces@SasquatchBooks.com
www.SasquatchBooks.com

CONTENTS

Introduction and Acknowledgments

Seattle is a tricky city to pin down. Depending on who's being polled, its people are either super-nice outdoorsy types kayaking every stretch of water and climbing every peak in sight, super high-achieving, fun-seeking shopaholics, or super-serious coffee-bar patrons inhaling caffeine while thinking deep thoughts. The truth is, like her famously quixotic weather patterns, there are many aspects to the city's personality, and each tends to draw a different audience.

For the big display of "play with me!" attractions, there are gleaming waterways and mountains, the Space Needle and its perky (or pugnacious, depending on your taste) sidekick, the Experience Music Project, downtown's ritzy retail and sports palaces, and the timeless Pike Place Market and Pioneer Square. Less trafficked and talked about, but no less appealing, are the micro-cultures generated by the city's urban neighborhoods. These places, from Belltown and Capitol Hill to Fremont and Ballard, are packed with a gear-stripping mix of artsy and antiques shops, tattoo parlors and dance clubs, ethnic eateries and gourmet restaurants, blue-collar businesses and designer boutiques.

Such divergent climates, of course, make a guidebook backed by a roster of know-it-all locals a particularly handy navigating tool. Thanks must go to our writers and to fact checkers Noel Cebrian, Kerrie O'Leary, and Niki Stojnic. In addition, the efforts of series editor Kate Rogers and project editor Laura Gronewold, sharp-eyed copy editor Kris Fulsaas, and proofreader Sherri Schultz were invaluable.

Whatever you're in the mood for, big-town boom or small-town novelty, Seattle is an equal-opportunity experience. Enjoy your version.

—Shannon O'Leary, Editor

Contributors

PROVIDENCE CICERO, who served as consultant for our Top 200 Restaurants chapter, is the former food editor of *Seattle* magazine. She currently writes about food and reviews restaurants for *The Seattle Times.*

CHARLES R. CROSS, author of our Nightlife chapter, is also the author of four books, including *Heavier Than Heaven: A Biography of Kurt Cobain.* He was the editor of *The Rocket,* the Northwest music and entertainment magazine, from 1986 through 2000. His writing has appeared in numerous magazines and newspapers including *Rolling Stone, Esquire, Spin, The London Times,* and many others.

ANDREW ENGLESON, who was born and raised in the Pacific Northwest, updated our Performing Arts and Lodgings chapters. He has written about books and the arts for the *Seattle Post-Intelligencer, Seattle Weekly, Publishers Weekly, Metropolitan Living, Seattle,* and *Washington Law & Politics.* He also writes about the environment and outdoors for *High Country News* and *Backpacker* magazine. When not working, he can usually be found hiking or cross-country skiing the Cascades and the Olympics.

MICHAEL HOOD, our lead reviewer for the Top 200 Restaurants chapter, was a chef and restaurateur for 25 years before starting a writing career. He is the lead restaurant critic for the *Seattle Post-Intelligencer,* where he has a weekly Q & A column, "Ask the Critic." His work was anthologized in *Best Food Writing 2000.* He's also a reporter for Agence France-Presse and has written news, food, politics, and humor stories for *The Seattle Times, Seattle, Pacific Northwest, Washington Law & Politics,* and *Tucson Weekly.*

Seattle editor and writer **MARIKA MCELROY** has spent the better part of her life rattling around the Emerald City and environs, so she was the perfect person to update the Shopping and Lodgings chapters of this edition. She is a contributing editor to *Resonance,* the local music, arts, and lifestyle magazine, and she regularly writes for *Seattle* magazine and other local publications.

KATHY SCHULTZ tracked down the details for the Planning a Trip and Lay of the City chapters. The material was not new to her—Best Places helped her plan her first trip to Seattle and has been her Bible since moving here from dry, brown, Southern California in 1997. A former editor for CitySearch.com, she writes about shopping, events, arts, and accommodations. Her articles have also appeared in *Seattle* magazine, *Seattle Bride, Lucky* magazine, *Yoga Journal,* and *Journey,* the regional magazine of AAA.

J. KINGSTON PIERCE, who wrote the Exploring chapter, was born in Portland, Oregon, but has spent most of the last two decades writing for and editing Seattle periodicals, from *Seattle Weekly* to *Pacific Northwest* and *Seattle* magazines. He's also the crime fiction editor of the literary web site "January Magazine" (www.januarymagazine.com), and the author of several books, including *San Francisco, You're History!* Pierce's writing has appeared in a wide variety of national publications, among them *Travel and Leisure, American History, People, The New York Times Book Review,* and the web magazine *Salon.*

A lifetime Seattleite and former editor of *Best Places Seattle,* **GISELLE SMITH** updated the Itineraries and Recreation chapters. Her qualifications include a dozen years editing and writing for regional magazines—and eight years of recreational rowing and hundreds of laps around Green Lake. She is currently a database editor in Seattle's high-tech industry, and is editor of the forthcoming *Best Places Northwest.*

DAVID VOLK recently took a year off to travel the world, but he still loves the Northwest best. In addition to writing the Day Trips chapter in this edition, he has written about Seattle and the region for *Alaska Airlines Magazine,* the *Puget Sound Business Journal,* and Reuters.

Seattle native **SHANNON O'LEARY** has been writing about the people and places of the Puget Sound area for a dozen years. In addition to editing this edition, her stories and reviews have appeared in numerous magazines, including *Seattle, Vancouver,* and *Horizon Airlines,* and guidebooks such as *Best Places Northwest.* She is currently editor of *Washington Law & Politics* and *Northwest Home + Garden* magazines.

About Best Places® Guidebooks

People trust us. Best Places guidebooks, which have been published continuously since 1975, represent one of the most respected regional travel series in the country. Each guide is written completely independently: no advertisers, no sponsors, no favors. Our reviewers know their territory, work incognito, and seek out the very best a city or region has to offer. Because we accept no free meals, accommodations, or other complimentary services, we are able to provide tough, candid reports about places that have rested too long on their laurels, and to delight in new places that deserve recognition. We describe the true strengths, foibles, and unique characteristics of each establishment listed.

Best Places Seattle is written by and for locals, and is therefore coveted by travelers. It's written for people who live here and who enjoy exploring the city's bounty and its out-of-the-way places of high character and individualism. It is these very characteristics that make *Best Places Seattle* ideal for tourists, too. The best places in and around the city are the ones that denizens favor: independently owned establishments of good value, touched with local history, run by lively individuals, and graced with natural beauty. With this ninth edition of *Best Places Seattle,* travelers will find the information they need: where to go and when, what to order, which rooms to request (and which to avoid), where the best music, art, nightlife, shopping, and other attractions are, and how to find the city's hidden secrets.

We're so sure you'll be satisfied with our guide, we guarantee it.

NOTE: *The reviews in this edition are based on information available at press time and are subject to change. Readers are advised that places listed in previous editions may have closed or changed management, or may no longer be recommended by this series. The editors welcome information conveyed by users of this book. A report form is provided at the end of the book, and feedback is also welcome via email: bestplaces@SasquatchBooks.com.*

How to Use This Book

This book is divided into eleven chapters covering a wide range of establishments, destinations, and activities in and around Seattle. All evaluations are based on numerous reports from local and traveling inspectors. Best Places reporters do not identify themselves when they review an establishment, and they accept no free meals, accommodations, or any other services. Final judgments are made by the editors. **EVERY PLACE FEATURED IN THIS BOOK IS RECOMMENDED.**

STAR RATINGS *(for Top 200 Restaurants and Lodgings only)* Restaurants and lodgings are rated on a scale of one to four stars (with half stars in between), based on uniqueness, loyalty of local clientele, performance measured against the establishment's goals, excellence of cooking, cleanliness, value, and professionalism of service. Reviews are listed alphabetically, and every place is recommended.

★★★★ The very best in the region

★★★ Distinguished; many outstanding features

★★ Excellent; some wonderful qualities

★ A good place

UNRATED New or undergoing major changes

(For more on how we rate places, see the Best Places Star Ratings box, below.)

PRICE RANGE *(for Top 200 Restaurants and Lodgings only)* Prices for restaurants are based primarily on dinner for two, including dessert, tax, and tip (no alcohol). Prices for lodgings are based on peak season rates for one night's lodging for two people (i.e., double occupancy). Peak season is typically Memorial Day to Labor Day; off-season rates vary but can sometimes be significantly less. Call ahead to verify, as all prices are subject to change.

$$$$ Very expensive (more than $125 for dinner for two; more than $250 for one night's lodging for two)

$$$ Expensive (between $85 and $125 for dinner for two; between $150 and $250 for one night's lodging for two)

$$ Moderate (between $35 and $85 for dinner for two; between $85 and $150 for one night's lodging for two)

$ Inexpensive (less than $35 for dinner for two; less than $85 for one night's lodging for two)

RESERVATIONS *(for Top 200 Restaurants only)* We used one of the following terms for our reservations policy: reservations required, reservations recommended, no reservations. "No reservations" means either reservations are not necessary or are not accepted.

PARKING We've indicated a variety of options for parking in the facts lines at the end of each review.

ADDRESSES AND PHONE NUMBERS Every attempt has been made to provide accurate information on an establishment's location and phone number, but it's always a good idea to call ahead and confirm. For establishments with two or more locations, we try to provide information on the original or most recommended branches.

CHECKS AND CREDIT CARDS Many establishments that accept checks also require a major credit card for identification. Note that some places accept only

BEST PLACES® STAR RATINGS

Any travel guide that rates establishments is inherently subjective—and Best Places is no exception. We rely on our professional experience, yes, but also on a gut feeling. And, occasionally, we even give in to a soft spot for a favorite neighborhood hangout. Our star-rating system is not simply a checklist; it's judgmental, critical, sometimes fickle, and highly personal. And unlike most other travel guides, we pay our own way and accept no freebies: no free meals or accommodations, no advertisers, no sponsors, no favors.

For each new edition, we send local food and travel experts out to review restaurants and lodgings anonymously, and then to rate them on a scale of one to four, based on uniqueness, loyalty of local clientele, performance measured against the establishment's goals, excellence of cooking, cleanliness, value, and professionalism of service. That doesn't mean a one-star establishment isn't worth dining or sleeping at—far from it. When we say that all the places listed in our books are recommended, we mean it. That one-star pizza joint may be just the ticket for the end of a whirlwind day of shopping with the kids. But if you're planning something more special, the star ratings can help you choose an eatery or hotel that will wow your new clients or be a stunning, romantic place to celebrate an anniversary or impress a first date.

We award four-star ratings sparingly, reserving them for what we consider truly the best. And once an establishment has earned our highest rating, everyone's expectations seem to rise. Readers often write us letters specifically to point out the faults in four-star establishments. With changes in chefs, management, styles, and trends, it's always easier to get knocked off the pedestal than to ascend it. Three-star establishments, on the other hand, seem to generate healthy praise. They exhibit outstanding qualities, and we get lots of love letters about them. The difference between two and three stars can sometimes be a very fine line. Two-star establishments are doing a good, solid job and gaining attention, while one-star places are often dependable spots that have been around forever.

The restaurants and lodgings described in *Best Places Seattle* have earned their stars from hard work and good service (and good food). They're proud to be included in this book—look for our Best Places sticker in their windows. And we're proud to honor them in this, the ninth edition of *Best Places Seattle*.

local checks. Credit cards are abbreviated in this book as follows: American Express (AE); Carte Blanche (CB); Diners Club (DC); Discover (DIS); Japanese credit card (JCB); MasterCard (MC); Visa (V).

EMAIL AND WEB SITE ADDRESSES Email and web site addresses for establishments have been included where available. Please note that the web is a fluid and evolving medium, and that web pages are often "under construction" or, as with all time-sensitive information, may no longer be valid.

MAP INDICATORS The letter-and-number codes appearing at the end of most listings refer to coordinates on the fold-out map included in the front of the book. Single letters (for example, F7) refer to the Downtown Seattle map; double letters (FF7) refer to the Greater Seattle map on the flip side. If an establishment does not have a map code listed, its location falls beyond the boundaries of these maps.

HELPFUL ICONS Watch for these quick-reference symbols throughout the book:

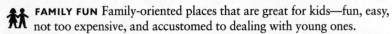 **FAMILY FUN** Family-oriented places that are great for kids—fun, easy, not too expensive, and accustomed to dealing with young ones.

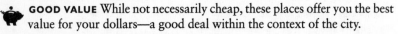 **GOOD VALUE** While not necessarily cheap, these places offer you the best value for your dollars—a good deal within the context of the city.

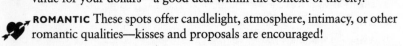 **ROMANTIC** These spots offer candlelight, atmosphere, intimacy, or other romantic qualities—kisses and proposals are encouraged!

EDITORS' CHOICE These are places that are unique and special to the city, such as a restaurant owned by a beloved local chef or a tourist attraction recognized around the globe.

Appears after listings for establishments that have wheelchair-accessible facilities.

INDEXES In addition to a general index at the back of the book, there are five specialized indexes: restaurants are indexed by star-rating, features, and location at the beginning of the Restaurants chapter, and nightspots are indexed by features and location at the beginning of the Nightlife chapter.

MONEY-BACK GUARANTEE Please see "We Stand by Our Reviews" at the end of the book.

READER REPORTS At the end of the book is a report form. We receive hundreds of reports from readers suggesting new places or agreeing or disagreeing with our assessments. They greatly help in our evaluations, and we encourage you to respond.

PLANNING A TRIP

PLANNING A TRIP

How to Get Here

BY PLANE

SEATTLE-TACOMA INTERNATIONAL AIRPORT (206/431-4444, SeaTac; map:OO6), better known as simply **SEA-TAC** (not to be confused with the city of SeaTac, sans hyphen), is located 13 miles south of Seattle, barely a half-hour freeway ride from downtown. Successful expansion, multimillion-dollar renovations to concourses in the main terminal, and a new, easily accessible parking facility have helped turn Sea-Tac into one of the most convenient major airports in the country. It now serves more than 28 million passengers a year. A high-speed computer-controlled subway system links the main terminal to two adjoining satellite terminals; allow an extra 10 minutes to reach gates in those terminals.

Travelers who need information or directions should look for roaming airport volunteers in blue jackets, or "Pathfinders" in red jackets carrying matching clipboards marked "**AIRPORT INFORMA-TION.**" These folks, available between 6am and 11pm daily, will point you in the right direction. Throughout the airport, families will find many newly renovated rest rooms with changing tables; nearly all men's and women's rest rooms, as well as the family rest rooms, have them. If you must check your e-mail, Laptop Lane, located in the main terminal across from Carvery Restaurant, provides on-line access for computers, phones, fax machines, and photocopying. Ground transportation information booths are located on the baggage level at carousels 3 and 16. **VISITOR INFORMATION SEA-TAC AIRPORT** (206/433-5218) is located in baggage claim by carousel 8, and offers trip-planning assistance regarding Seattle and the state of Washington seven days a week, along with a plethora of splashy travel brochures. Foreign visitors in need of information and services should proceed to the customs area. **OPERATION WELCOME** (206/433-5367) provides assistance in nearly 20 languages. For exhaustive information on airport services and operating conditions, call the airport information line (206/431-4444): you can listen to any of a list of recorded messages on everything from parking, paging, hotels, and customs to lost and found. Or go to the web site (www.portseattle.org/seatac/).

The newly designed **SEA-TAC PARKING** complex, which holds 10,000 vehicles, is connected to the main terminal via skybridges on the fourth floor. Exit toll booths are a thing of the past—it's self-serve when it comes to paying for parking, with automated pay stations located on the fourth floor of the garage. Machines take cash and major credit cards. Short-term parkers can pick a spot anywhere in the garage and pay $2 for up to 30 minutes and $4 for 30 minutes to one hour. General parking, located on the top four floors of the garage, costs $6 for 1 to 2 hours and $3 each hour thereafter up to $30 maximum per day. Follow the signs in the garage for valet parking, which costs $20 for up to 4 hours and $30 for 4 to 24 hours. It's drop and go only on the ticketing/departures drive. Parties can also be dropped off on the baggage claim/arrivals drive.

For less expensive long-term parking, try the numerous **COMMERCIAL PARKING LOTS** in the vicinity of the airport. The following operate 24 hours a day and offer free shuttle service for their parking and car-rental patrons: Budget Airport Parking and Car Rental (17808 International Blvd, SeaTac; 206/244-4008), Thrifty Airport Parking (18836 International Blvd, SeaTac; 206/242-7275), Park Shuttle and Fly (17600 International Blvd, SeaTac; 206/433-6767), and Doug Fox Airport Parking (2626 S 170th St, SeaTac; 206/248-2956).

AIRPORT TRANSPORTATION

One of the easiest and least spendy ways of getting to Sea-Tac Airport from downtown (or vice versa) is on the **GRAY LINE AIRPORT EXPRESS** (206/626-6088). Going to the airport, the shuttle stops every 20 to 30 minutes at downtown hotels, including the Madison Renaissance, Crowne Plaza, Four Seasons Olympic, Hilton, Sheraton, Roosevelt, Paramount, Warwick, and Westin, from about 5am until about 11pm. Going from the airport to the hotels, it runs from about 5am to midnight at the same intervals, from the north and south ends of the airport baggage claim area. Additional runs are added in the summer months. The ride is about 30 to 45 minutes between the Madison Renaissance and Sea-Tac. Cost is $14 round trip ($8.50 one way), or $10 round trip ($6 one way) for children ages 2 to 12.

SHUTTLEEXPRESS (206/622-1424 or 800/487-RIDE) provides convenient door-to-door van service to and from the airport, serving the entire greater Seattle area, from Everett to Tacoma. The cost ranges from $21.50 (from within the city) to $28.50 (from outlying suburbs) one way. Groups traveling from a single pickup point pay reduced rates. You may share the ride with other passengers, so expect to stop elsewhere en route. To ensure availability, make reservations two to three days ahead for trips to the airport. The shuttle from Sea-Tac operates 24 hours a day and requires no advance notice; the service desk is located on the third floor of the parking garage.

Thanks to a new city ordinance, **TAXIS** *to* the airport from downtown Seattle are a flat fee of $25; a ride *from* the airport to downtown runs about $30. At the airport, catch a cab on the third floor of the parking garage.

READ ALL ABOUT IT

Seattleites are bookworms. They're ranked number two in the United States in library usage and, despite their rank of 14th in population, have the sixth-biggest book market in the country. Their page-turning proclivities ensure that you don't have to go far in this town to find a store selling new or used titles, or both. Although they don't often write about the city, many well-known authors live and work in the area: Tom Robbins, Charles Johnson, David Guterson, Jonathan Raban, Rebecca Brown, Sherman Alexie, Terry Brooks, Brenda Peterson, and Pete Dexter, to name just a few. True-crime masters John Saul and Ann Rule, as well as science-fiction novelists Vonda McIntyre and Greg Bear, also live here. But it's crime novelists—from J. A. Jance to G. M. Ford to K. K. Beck—or visiting writers who seem to best capture the city.

Here's a short reading list to put you in the know about Seattle and the Puget Sound region.

Nonfiction

Northwest history is recorded by the people who lived it in A Voyage of Discovery to the North Pacific Ocean and Round the World in the Years 1790–95 (C. G. and J. Robinson, 1798) by explorer George Vancouver, and in books by early pioneers and visitors: Pioneer Days on Puget Sound (The Alice Harriman Co., 1908) by Arthur A. Denny, West Coast Journeys, 1865–1879: The Travelogue of a Remarkable Woman (Sasquatch Books, 1995) by Caroline C. Leighton, and The Canoe and the Saddle (J. W. Lovell, 1862) by Theodore Winthrop.

Skid Road: An Informal Portrait of Seattle by Murray Cromwell Morgan (University of Washington Press, 1982) is a lively, irreverent look back at some of the events and eccentrics most responsible for creating the Seattle we know today. This is the essential guide to the first 100 years of the city's history.

Walt Crowley's National Trust Guide Seattle (John Wiley & Sons, 1998) gives a wonderful overview of the city's architecture and history that both locals and visitors can enjoy. Seattle City Walks by Laura Karlinsey (Sasquatch Books, 1999) provides easy-to-use walking tours of various city neighborhoods, with historical and cultural details, directions to viewpoints, and profiles of Seattle personalities.

The Forging of a Black Community by Quintard Taylor (University of Washington Press, 1994) examines the often-troubled evolution of Seattle's Central District from the year 1870 through the civil-rights struggles of the 1960s.

Rains All the Time: A Connoisseur's History of Weather in the Pacific Northwest by David Laskin (Sasquatch Books, 1997), recounts the history of this region's relationship with its "liquid sunshine."

One of our most beloved regional books, *The Egg and I* by Betty MacDonald (originally published in 1945; reprinted by HarperCollins, 1987), is a delightfully whimsical memoir of life on a Western Washington chicken ranch.

Northwest poet Richard Hugo's work reflects the Seattle area he called home in *Making Certain It Goes On: Collected Poems of Richard Hugo* (W. W. Norton & Co., 1991). Sallie Tisdale, *Stepping Westward: The Long Search for Home in the Pacific Northwest* (HarperPerennial Library, 1992); *New York Times* correspondent Timothy Egan, *The Good Rain: Across Time and Terrain in the Pacific Northwest* (Vintage Books, 1990); and Bruce Barcott, *The Measure of a Mountain: Beauty and Terror on Mount Rainier* (Sasquatch Books, 1997), offer contemporary perspectives on the region.

Fiction

In *Catfish Café* by Earl Emerson (Ballantine Books, 1999), Seattle private eye Thomas Black is hired by a former partner to rescue his daughter, an erstwhile crackhead and an eyewitness to the recent killing of a straitlaced white schoolteacher.

Indian Killer by Native American novelist and screenwriter (*Smoke Signals*) Sherman Alexie (Warner Books, 1998) tells the story of a serial killer in Seattle who is raising racial tensions by appearing to be an Indian murdering whites in revenge for his people's treatment.

In *First Avenue* (Watershed Books, 1999), Seattle ex-cop Lowen Clausen writes about the beat on First Avenue in Belltown before recent gentrification.

River Out of Eden by John Hockenberry (Doubleday, 2001) is a thriller set against the backdrop of the Northwest, centered on the contemporary and enmeshed issues of environmental pollution, salmon survival, and Native American ways.

In *Slant* by Greg Bear (Tor Books, 1998), Seattle in the year 2050 is one of the principal settings for an innovative tale of nanotechnology and national madness.

Slow Burn by G. M. Ford (Avon Books, 1999) features Seattle private eye Leo Waterman, together with his motley cronies; Waterman tracks down the killer of an influential food critic as well as the whereabouts of a Black Angus bull destined for barbecue fame.

Snow Falling on Cedars by David Guterson (Vintage Contemporaries, 1995) is a history-based novel (made into a movie in 1999) about the murder trial of a Japanese-American fisherman working on Puget Sound; it won considerable local and national acclaim.

Lastly, the late Oregonian Ken Kesey captures the flavor of the Northwest's timber industry in *Sometimes a Great Notion* (Penguin USA, 1998), a regional classic.

—*J. Kingston Pierce*

METRO TRANSIT (206/553-3000; http://transit.metrokc.gov) offers the cheapest rides to the airport ($1.25 one way, $2 during rush hour), via two routes: the No. 174 (which can take up to an hour from downtown) and the No. 194 Express (a 30-minute ride via Interstate 5). Both run every half hour, seven days a week. The No. 194 uses the downtown transit tunnel, except on weekends, when it travels through downtown along Third Avenue. The No. 174 travels through downtown along Second Avenue, with many stops through the industrial area. Both buses stop on the baggage-claim level of the airport.

BY CHARTER OR PRIVATE AIRPLANE

Most airplane and helicopter charter companies are based at Boeing Field/King County International Airport (206/296-7380; map:KK6) south of downtown. Others are located north of the city at Snohomish County Airport (Paine Field, Everett; 425/353-2110). Services include flying lessons and aircraft rentals. Call the Seattle Automated Flight Service Station (206/767-2726) for up-to-date weather reports and flight-related information.

BY BUS

GREYHOUND BUS LINES (811 Stewart St, Downtown; 800/231-2222; map:I4) is usually the least expensive way to get to Seattle. The station is within walking distance of the downtown retail core.

BY TRAIN

The wide seats inside and beautiful vistas outside make **AMTRAK** (800/872-7245 passenger information and reservations, 206/382-4128 baggage and package express, 206/382-4713 lost and found) the most comfortable and scenic mode of transportation to Seattle. Especially eyecatching is the Portland-to-Seattle route, much of which runs along the shores of Puget Sound. The Coast Starlight leaves Seattle headed south to Portland, San Francisco, Los Angeles, and San Diego, and headed north to Vancouver, British Columbia; the Empire Builder heads east to Chicago via Spokane. The train pulls up to King Street Station (3rd Ave S and S Jackson St, Pioneer Square; map:P8) at the south end of downtown.

BY CAR

The primary north-south artery is **INTERSTATE 5**, which runs south from Seattle through Tacoma and the state capital of Olympia, to Portland, Oregon (185 miles south of Seattle), and on through California. To the north via I-5 lies Vancouver, British Columbia, just 143 miles away. More or less parallel to I-5 is the old north-south route, **HIGHWAY 99**, which becomes Aurora Avenue for a stretch through the city. Just south of downtown, I-5 meets **INTERSTATE 90**, Seattle's primary connection to all points east. From downtown, I-90 crosses a floating bridge over Lake

Washington to the eastern suburbs, then crosses the Cascades at Snoqualmie Pass before dropping down to the Columbia Plateau of Eastern Washington and curving its way toward Spokane, 280 miles east. The other link to the Eastside suburbs is **HIGHWAY 520**, which leaves I-5 just north of downtown, crosses another floating bridge, and passes near the Bellevue and Kirkland town centers before ending in Redmond. Both east-west highways connect with **INTERSTATE 405**, which runs north-south through the suburbs east of Lake Washington. To go to and from the Olympic Peninsula to the west, take a scenic **FERRY RIDE** across Puget Sound (see the "Ferry Rides" sidebar in the Day Trips chapter).

A cautionary note: Seattle's traffic can be nerve defying. It seems at any given time, on any random street, there's a crew tearing up, digging out, or jackhammering chunks of the road, from working on the earthquake-rattled Alaskan Way Viaduct of Highway 99 to laying high-tech fiber-optic cable. Road warriors need to be on the defensive. Try to plan your arrival and departure times to avoid rush hours, generally 7 to 9:30am and 4:30 to 7pm weekdays.

When to Visit

If weather is a factor in your decision of when to visit Seattle, remember that the table below shows averages; what you'll experience is unpredictable. Keep in mind that although the season from November through February may have more rain and be a little cooler, hotel rates, airfares, and admission fees are often lower at that time.

WEATHER

The toughest job in Seattle is being a weather forecaster—everyone suspects you're a liar, an idiot, or both. Between the mountains, the warm offshore currents, and the cold fronts sweeping down from the north, predicting weather here is an exercise in equivocation. Predictions are even more difficult because a torrential downpour in West Seattle might occur at the same time as blinding sunshine in Wallingford. One thing you can count on is clouds: if you don't get a glimpse of the sun for days (weeks!) on end, you may feel as though it's rained more than it actually has. If you're trying to avoid the rain altogether, July and August are the warmest and driest months, and they usually don't reach extremes of heat and humidity. Things get wet in the winter, averaging around 5 inches of rain a month from November through January, but temperatures are mild enough that snow and ice are infrequent. On those rare days when they do appear, though, watch out: the town grinds to a halt and the streets become one big roller derby.

Average temperature and precipitation by month

Month	Daily Maximum Temp. (degrees F)	Daily Minimum Temp. (degrees F)	Monthly Precipitation (inches)
JANUARY	45	35	5.38
FEBRUARY	49.5	37.5	3.99
MARCH	52.7	38.5	3.54
APRIL	57	41.2	2.53
MAY	63.9	46.3	1.7
JUNE	69.9	51.9	1.5
JULY	75.2	55.2	0.76
AUGUST	75.2	55.7	1.14
SEPTEMBER	69.3	51.9	1.88
OCTOBER	59.7	45.8	3.23
NOVEMBER	50.5	40.1	5.83
DECEMBER	45.1	35.8	5.9

Source: U.S. National Oceanic and Atmospheric Administration

TIME

Seattle is on Pacific Standard Time (PST), which is three hours behind New York, two hours behind Chicago, one hour behind Denver, one hour ahead of Anchorage, and two hours ahead of Honolulu. Daylight Saving Time begins in early April and ends in late October. Because Seattle is located so far north (between the 47th and 48th latitudes), residents enjoy long daylight hours in summer, with sunrises before 6am and sunsets as late as 9:45pm.

WHAT TO BRING

Given the variable nature of Seattle's weather, it's best to be ready for anything, especially if you're visiting between May and October. Bring layers that you can add or remove, with a sweater or a light jacket just in case; even summer evenings can be cool. From June through September, be sure to bring shorts and sunglasses. In the winter months, it's easy: dress for rain. If you plan to take walking tours of the city, wear water-resistant shoes and wool socks, and be sure to bring a bumbershoot—unless you want to pass for a local.

When choosing what to wear, remember that Seattle pioneered the art of dressing casual. Suits and ties are seen only on those unfortunate souls who work in the downtown business district; otherwise jeans, khakis, and T-shirts are ubiquitous. With a few exceptions, even the most expensive restaurants allow patrons to wear jeans, and only a select few require a jacket.

General Costs

The boom times have taken a dip lately with a lot of dot-coms becoming dot-gones, but don't let that fool you. Seattleites are still riding the crest of an economic wave. Where employers used to have to compete for employees, now the reverse is true, but plenty of jobs still exist and growth has not stopped. Boeing may have moved its headquarters to a less rainy, windier city, but the bulk of manufacturing jetliners remains. Microsoft is a titan to be reckoned with, and Starbucks is not only a thriving company but an international trend. Nordstrom just turned 100 and continues to turn out shoppers looking their best in classic clothes and shoes. Biotech is now one of the area's front-runners—witness Immunex and its groundbreaking medications. Amazon.com is a household name, REI. outfits a healthy number of the country's outdoor types, and Weyerhaeuser hasn't stopped making paper.

Housing costs remain high, especially in comparison to other major cities. According to the National Association of Realtors, in the first quarter of 2001, Seattle ranked ninth in the nation with a median home price of $227,300, just behind New York City and vicinity and Honolulu, Hawaii. Fortunately, costs for quotidian items are in keeping within the region and relative to any robust, big city.

Average costs for lodging and food

Double room:

INEXPENSIVE	$59–$89
MODERATE	$90–$150
EXPENSIVE	$150 AND UP

Lunch for one (including beverage and tip):

INEXPENSIVE	$8–$13
MODERATE	$13–$19
EXPENSIVE	$20 AND UP

Beverages in a restaurant:

GLASS OF WINE	$5–$7
PINT OF BEER	$4
COCA-COLA	$1.25
DOUBLE TALL LATTE	$2.70

Other common items:

MOVIE TICKET	$8
ROLL OF FILM	$5.50
TAXI PER MILE	$1.80
RAIN JACKET FROM REI	$30–$549
SEATTLE SOUVENIR T-SHIRT	$12–$15

Tips for Special Travelers

FAMILIES WITH CHILDREN

In an emergency, call 911, 24 hours a day. For questions about your child's health, growth, or development, call the Children's Hospital Resource Line (206/526-2500). If you think your child has ingested a toxic substance, call the Washington Poison Center (206/526-2121 or 800/732-6985). A local publication, *Seattle's Child,* serves as a resource for parents and is available free at many coffee shops, newsstands, and newspaper boxes. It's produced by Northwest Parent Publishing (206/441-0191).

The majority of downtown hotels cater heavily to business travelers. This means that family-oriented amenities such as swimming pools, game rooms, and inexpensive restaurants are more readily found at hotels outside the downtown area. Many hotels allow kids to stay free when traveling with their parents, so ask when you make reservations. Most major restaurants have children's menus.

 Watch for this icon throughout the book; it indicates places and activities that are great for families.

SENIORS

Senior Services of Seattle/King County (1601 2nd Ave, Ste 800, Downtown; 206/448-3110; map:J7) runs a referral service for seniors, offering information about health and welfare resources and transportation and mobility services. It also publishes a newsletter called *ACCESS* that lists upcoming events for seniors including fairs, opportunities for flu shots, and some happenings at neighborhood senior centers. For public transit, senior bus passes are $3 for people 65 and older. They are good for life, and reduce the fare to 25 cents on all buses. Senior passes can be purchased in person either at the downtown Metro office (201 S Jackson St, Pioneer Square; 206/553-3060; map:O8) or in the transit tunnel station underneath Westlake Center (map:J6).

PEOPLE WITH DISABILITIES

For information about using public transportation, call the Metro Accessible Services Offices (206/689-3113). After registering for services, riders can then call ACCESS for reservations (206/205-5000 or 206/749-4286 TTY). For faster or more personalized transportation, Pierce-King Cabulance (253/838-3522) operates a wheelchair-accessible taxi service. For tour companies and other private companies offering mobility services, call the Seattle/King County Convention and Visitors Bureau (206/461-5840). The Deaf/Blind Service Center (206/323-9178) offers volunteers who help deaf or blind Washington State residents take walks, go grocery shopping, or go to the bank. Visitors can contact the center in advance of their trip for a list of volunteers to call directly for assis-

OUR HUMOR'S ALL WET

After a brief visit to Seattle some years back, comedian Bill Cosby worked up a skit about the rarity of good weather here. When the sun manages to claw out from behind gray clouds, he said, natives bound from their homes and run about frantically yelling, "What have we done? What have we done?"

Maybe he overstated things just a tad. Yes, the city's favorite event is a Labor Day festival called Bumbershoot, after the British term for "umbrella." Yes, a lot of visitors would take issue with the old TV theme song from *Here Come the Brides* that claimed "The bluest skies you've ever seen are in Seattle." But this place doesn't really deserve its reputation as the wetness capital of the United States. The rain that drenches Seattle every year is typically less than what falls on Miami, New York, Boston, or Atlanta.

Yet Seattle's drippy rep hasn't been all bad. It has kept weather wimps away and even inspired a wealth of dry humor.

"What comes after two straight days of rain in Seattle?" runs one popular riddle. The answer? "Monday." The most popular movie in Seattle? *The Sound of Mucus.* Or "It's so wet in the Northwest you can watch people walk their fish." To the query "Whaddya do around here in the summer?" Northwesterners are said to reply cheerfully, "Well, if it falls on a weekend, we go on a picnic."

The rain joke is the local equivalent of the Chicago wind joke, the Michigan black-fly joke, and the Texas brag. It's a corny spill of overstatement that unites a diverse people because they all understand the exaggeration. Humor also helps fend off dampened spirits. Nobody wants to listen to somebody else whine about the rain—too depressing. But if they tell you they were knocked unconscious by a huge raindrop and that it took six buckets of sand in the face to bring them around, that makes it all right.

More surreptitious motives may be behind this brand of humor, of course. Residents who want to keep Seattle all to themselves use the rain—and the rain joke—as their first line of attack.

—J. Kingston Pierce

tance. The Washington Talking Book and Braille Library (2021 9th Ave, Downtown; 206/615-0400; map:G4) has thousands of recorded and Braille titles available for loan.

WOMEN

Seattle is known as a relatively safe city but, as in most cities, women travelers should take extra precautions at night, especially in downtown, Belltown, and the Pioneer Square neighborhood. The University of Washington Women's Center (4014 University Wy NE, Cunningham Hall, University District; 206/685-1090; map:FF6) is open to students as well as the general public and offers an extensive library, job listings, community bulletin board, and class information. For health and reproductive services, call Planned Parenthood (2001 E Madison St, Central District; 206/328-7700; map:HH6). Although primarily geared toward gay/lesbian culture, Bailey/Coy Books (414 Broadway Ave E, Capitol Hill; 206/323-8842; map:HH6) carries a wide range of books on women's issues and also supports a community bulletin board.

PET OWNERS

Travelers with pets will find themselves welcome in the most surprising places—including downtown Seattle's four-star Four Seasons Olympic Hotel. Refer to guidebooks such as *The Seattle Dog Lover's Companion* by Steve Giordano for other places your dog or cat is welcome to share your room.

If Seattle has one militant, vocal political force, it's dog owners. When the City Council discussed whether to allow pets to roam free in designated areas within some city parks, those were the best-attended and most passionate council meetings in many years. The hard-fought right to unfetter your critter comes with certain responsibilities, though: owners must make sure their dogs don't jump on other people, and they must pick up their dogs' waste—which is also true of all dog owners, whether their dogs are leashed or not. For information on Seattle's off-leash areas, listed below, call the Seattle Parks and Recreation Department (206/684-4075). Outside Seattle, area off-leash parks include Mercer Island's Luther Burbank Park (206/236-3545; map:II4) as well as Marymoor Park (206/296-2964; map:FF1) in Redmond.

GENESEE PARK (46th Ave S and Genesee St, Columbia City; map:JJ5) has doggie runs in the upper park.

GOLDEN GARDENS PARK (8498 Seaview Pl NW, Ballard; map:DD9) has an off-leash area in the eastern portion of the park.

I-90 BLUE DOG POND PARK (Martin Luther King Jr Wy at Massachusetts St, Central District; map:II6) has dog runs in the park's northwest corner.

MAGNUSON PARK (6500 Sandpoint Wy, View Ridge; map:EE5) has dog-friendly areas along the park's eastern and northern boundaries, with some water access to Lake Washington.

WESTCREST PARK (8806 8th Ave SW, West Seattle; map:KK8) has a dog area along the southern border of the reservoir.

WOODLAND PARK (N 50th St and Aurora Ave N, Wallingford; map:FF7) has a dog area in the park's northeastern portion, west of the tennis courts.

GAYS AND LESBIANS

Seattle is well known for being a gay-friendly city. Its large gay community is mainly centered around the Capitol Hill neighborhood, with a variety of gay-focused bars, dance clubs, bookstores, and bed-and-breakfast inns. The *Seattle Gay News* (1605 12th Ave, Ste 31, Capitol Hill; 206/324-4297; www.sgn.org; map:GG7) and *Seattle Gay Standard* (605

29th Ave E, Capitol Hill; 206/322-9027; www.gaystandard.com; map:GG7) are both weekly community newspapers, available at many shops, bars, and bookstores around Capitol Hill. There are two guides to the businesses and services of the community: the *GSBA Guide & Directory*, available at stores in the area or by contacting the Greater Seattle Business Association (2150 N 107th, Ste 205, Northgate; 206/363-9188; map:DD7) and the *Pink Pages* (800/929-7465), also available in stores or from the business office. Two community bookstores, Beyond the Closet (518 E Pike St, Capitol Hill; 206/322-4609; map:K2) and Bailey/Coy Books (414 Broadway Ave E, Capitol Hill; 206/323-8842; map:HH6), offer community bulletin boards and have staffs who are knowledgeable about local resources and events. The Lesbian Resource Center (2214 S Jackson St, Central District; 206/322-3953; map:HH6) provides business referrals, therapy and physician referrals, and housing and job information. For information on the city's many gay clubs and bars, see the Nightlife chapter.

FOREIGN VISITORS

Seattle hosts a number of foreign exchange brokers and foreign banks. Thomas Cook (400 Pine St, Downtown; 206/682-4525; map:I6; 10630 NE 8th St, Bellevue; 425/462-8225; map:HH3; and various Sea-Tac Airport locations) is a foreign exchange broker. Foreign banks with branches in Seattle include Bank of Tokyo (1201 3rd Ave, Ste 1100, Downtown; 206/382-6000; map:L7) and the Hong Kong Bank of Canada (700 5th Ave, Ste 4100, Downtown; 206/233-0888; map: N6).

A multitude of services are available for the foreign visitor who does not speak English as a first language. The American Cultural Exchange (200 W Mercer St, Ste 504, Downtown; 206/217-9644; www.cultural.org; map:GG8) offers language classes and arranges for summertime exchanges and visits by foreigners to American homes. ACE's Translation Center (206/281-8200) provides interpreters and written translations. Yohana International (425/771-8465) and the Language Connection (425/277-9045) provide document translation as well as interpreters in dozens of languages, including those of Asia, Africa, and Europe. The Milmanco Corporation (651 Strander Blvd, Ste 100, Tukwila; 206/575-3808; map:OO5) can help those involved in international business and in need of technical written translations (from and into foreign languages); rates vary. The Red Cross Language Bank (206/323-2345) provides on-call interpretive assistance at no charge.

Seattle's importance as a port city has brought it many foreign consulates.

AUSTRIA, 1111 3rd Ave, Ste 2626, Downtown; 206/633-3606

BELGIUM, 2200 Alaskan Wy, Ste 470, Downtown; 206/728-5145 (call for appt)

BOLIVIA, 15215 52nd Ave S, Tukwila; 206/244-6696

CANADA, Plaza 600, Ste 412, Downtown; 206/443-1777

ESTONIA, 2200 Alaskan Wy, Ste 470, Downtown; 206/467-1444

FINLAND (not open to the public), 425/451-3983 (call for appt)

FRANCE, 2200 Alaskan Wy, Ste 490, Downtown; 206/256-6184 (call for appt)

GREAT BRITAIN, 900 4th Ave, Ste 3001, Downtown; 206/622-9255

ICELAND, 5610 20th Ave NW, Ballard; 206/783-4100

JAPAN, 601 Union St, Ste 500, Downtown; 206/682-9107

MEXICO, 2132 3rd Ave, Belltown; 206/448-3526

NETHERLANDS, 4609 140th Ave NE, Bellevue (not open to the public); 425/861-4437 (call for appt)

NEW ZEALAND (not open to the public); 360/766-8002 (call for appt)

NORWAY, 1402 3rd Ave, Ste 806, Downtown; 206/623-3957

PERU, 3717 NE 157th St, Ste 100, Shoreline; 206/714-9037

RUSSIA, 2001 6th Ave, Ste 2323, Belltown; 206/728-1910

SOUTH KOREA, 2033 6th Ave, Ste 1125, Belltown; 206/441-1011

SWEDEN, 1215 4th Ave, Ste 1019, Downtown, 206/622-5640

TAIWAN, 2001 6th Ave, Ste 2410, Belltown; 206/441-4586

WEB INFORMATION

In a city as wired as Seattle, it's little wonder there's a wide range of web sites operated by private as well as government organizations, nonprofits, and for-profit ventures. The following sites are helpful to both visitors and locals. Some point the direction to the best seafood in town and others give live-cam views of the traffic on the floating bridges. See listings within other chapters for specific site addresses, where available.

WWW.CITYOFSEATTLE.NET History, tours, city parks, employment.

WWW.HISTORYLINK.ORG Seattle and King County history.

WWW.SEATTLE.CITYSEARCH.COM In-city entertainment guide with reviews on restaurants, shopping, hotels, movie times, arts, and more.

WWW.SEATTLE.NET Community, business, information, and entertainment.

WWW.SEATTLEINSIDER.COM Classified ads, jobs, events, restaurants, news.

WWW.SEATTLE-PI.COM *Seattle Post-Intelligencer.*

WWW.SEATTLETIMES.COM *The Seattle Times.*

WWW.SEESEATTLE.ORG Seattle/King County Convention and Visitors Bureau.

WWW.WASHINGTON.EDU University of Washington.

LAY OF THE CITY

LAY OF THE CITY

Orientation

Seattle is a city defined by water. Contrary to popular myth, however, it's not what falls from the sky that is most important when you're getting to know this city. Situated on a narrow isthmus of land between **PUGET SOUND** and **LAKE WASHINGTON,** bisected north from south by **LAKE UNION** and the Lake Washington Ship Canal and east from west by the Duwamish River, Seattle is surrounded by the wet stuff. The city's distinct neighborhoods developed in relative isolation, cut off from one another by the many canals and lakes—and bridges—and by the forested hills that tumble down to the water's edge.

Water is also a critical element of Seattle's awe-inspiring natural beauty, attracting droves of tourists and residents to this growing city of more than 500,000 people. Across Puget Sound to the west loom the Olympic Mountains. East of Lake Washington, the Cascades stretch in a jagged line just 50 miles away; Mount Rainier plays hide-and-seek 40 miles south of downtown, and on clear days, Glacier Peak can be glimpsed 50 miles north.

Within the boundaries of these imposing geographic landmarks lies a rapidly growing urban area. The major city landmarks of Seattle are tightly contained in a small, bustling area centered around downtown. At its heart stands the famous **PIKE PLACE MARKET** (Pike St and 1st Ave; map:J8), an authentic smorgasbord of food, flowers, and art that has served local residents and visitors for nearly a century. Taking the steps down the steep hill just west of the market leads you to the Seattle waterfront, brimming with shops, restaurants, and the always-busy **FERRY DOCKS** (map:M8) that link the city to **BAINBRIDGE ISLAND** and other points west. Directly east of the market is an ever-growing shopping district anchored by **WESTLAKE CENTER** (Pine St and 4th Ave; map:I6) and fanning out in all directions. Seattle's major office and financial district lies south of the shopping area.

At the southern end of downtown lies historic **PIONEER SQUARE** (along 1st and 2nd Aves, between Yesler Wy and S King St; map:N8), the first area of Seattle to be rebuilt after the great fire of 1889. In February 2001, a 5.9 earthquake that shook this part of town (which is built on a landfill) caused a rain of bricks from crumbling facades and considerable damage to some of the oldest buildings. But most were left intact, including the many shops, bars, and galleries in the area. Just east of Pioneer Square is **CHINATOWN/INTERNATIONAL DISTRICT,** and just south of Pioneer Square is the newly energized industrial area often called **SODO** (South of the Dome or South of Downtown), where in place of the defunct Kingdome (imploded in 2000) is a brand-new football stadium

HOW TO PASS FOR A LOCAL

Every city has its own set of idiosyncrasies. Visitors who want to mesh more naturally with the locals might benefit from these insights into Seattle's native style.

Umbrellas: Despite the city's rep, it doesn't rain buckets here daily (Miami has more rain annually). A sure way to spot a newcomer is to see an unfurled umbrella during a light shower.

Shades: Residents have to combat cloud glare more than unfettered sunshine; as a result, sunglasses are de rigueur nearly year-round.

Attire: Varies widely by neighborhood. For example, while the Capitol Hill crowd favors black ensembles, body piercings, and Doc Martens, Green Lakers sport spandex, bare midriffs, and Nikes. The main thing is, Seattleites are flexible when it comes to degrees of formality. A night at the opera here can mean evening gowns or Gap wear.

Coolness: This isn't a climate reference but an attitudinal one. Frankly, natives aren't an effusive lot—just ask any touring actor waiting for a standing ovation. Rumor has it that it takes two years to make a real friend here (unless, of course, the new friend is another lonely newcomer). It's not that we're unfriendly—we're just politely reserved.

Vocabulary: "Yeah" is as common a part of Seattle speech as "Oh my gawd!" is to a suburban teenager. Not to be confused with the intimidating interrogative "Oh yeah?!" favored by East Coasters, Seattle's "Yeah" is simply a laid-back form of assent or agreement. (In the more heavily Scandinavian sections of the city, "Ya sure, you betcha" can be used as a synonym.)

Jaywalking: That crowd on the corner isn't making a drug deal, they're simply waiting for the crosswalk sign to change. Natives are notorious sticklers for obeying these signs—and so are the police. Newcomers blithely crossing against lights may find themselves ticketed, at about $38 a pop.

Bicyclists: Some days they seem to outnumber cars. Observing the traditional politeness of the city, locals resist the urge to bump off cyclists who unconcernedly hold up traffic.

Travel espresso cups: They're everywhere. Isn't that why car cup holders were invented? Besides, a swig of caffeine takes drivers' minds off dawdling cyclists.

—Shannon O'Leary

(Occidental Ave S and S King St; map:Q9) set to open in 2002. Nearby neighbor to this monolithic sports venue is Safeco Field, a ballpark with old-time style, a state-of-the-art retractable roof, and a winning team.

Traveling north from Pike Place Market through the trendy **BELL-TOWN** neighborhood (between Virginia St and Denny Wy, between Western and 5th Aves; map:G7), one comes upon the **DENNY REGRADE**, a former hill leveled along Denny Way from I-5 to the waterfront, and across the Regrade is the sprawling **SEATTLE CENTER** complex (between Denny Wy and Mercer St, between 1st Ave N and 5th Ave N; map:B6). It's home to the Pacific Science Center and a wide variety of festivals and fairs, as well as Seattle's best-known landmark, the **SPACE NEEDLE** (Broad St and 5th Ave N). Seattle Center is on the lower slopes of **QUEEN ANNE** hill; to the west is Magnolia, and in between Queen Anne and Magnolia is the area called Interbay, along 15th Avenue W. To the east of Seattle Center, on the northern reaches of downtown, is the South Lake Union area, aka Cascade; other neighborhoods surrounding the lake are Westlake and Eastlake.

A few blocks east of downtown, First Hill (Yesler Wy to E Union St, east to 12th Ave) and, to its north, **CAPITOL HILL** rise steeply from I-5; the latter is a neighborhood of hip stores, coffee shops, and nightspots. In addition to its main thoroughfares of Broadway and 15th Avenue E, Capitol Hill encompasses many residential neighborhoods with small business districts: northeast, toward the ship canal, Montlake lies at the northern foot of the hill; southeast toward Lake Washington are the Central District, Madrona, Madison Valley, Madison Park, and Leschi neighborhoods, a microcosm of the city's diversity.

West of downtown, across the Duwamish River, is **WEST SEATTLE**, with many residential areas and thriving commercial centers such as the West Seattle Junction. In the **SOUTH END** are the Rainier Valley—including Columbia City and Rainier Beach—Beacon Hill, and Georgetown east of the Duwamish; South Park and White Center are west of it. South of Seattle are the suburban cities of Burien, Tukwila, and Renton; farther south are SeaTac, Des Moines, and Kent; farthest south are Federal Way and Auburn.

North of the Ship Canal, Lake Union, Portage Bay, and the Montlake Cut, you'll find **BALLARD** to the west, **FREMONT** and **WALLINGFORD** due north of downtown, and the **UNIVERSITY DISTRICT** and **LAUREL-HURST** to the east. Just to the north of Fremont and Wallingford is the **GREENWOOD/GREEN LAKE** area. In Seattle's expansive residential **NORTH END**, Crown Hill and Bitter Lake are north of Ballard in the west; Northgate, a busy commercial area, and Haller Lake lie north of Greenwood/Green Lake; heading east from the Green Lake area you'll find the Roosevelt, Ravenna, and Sand Point neighborhoods, north of the University District. Maple Leaf, Wedgwood, and View Ridge are residential areas to the north of Roosevelt/Ravenna, and Lake City lies north of Wedgwood. North of Seattle are the suburban cities of Shoreline in the west, Mountlake Terrace along I-5, and Lake Forest Park and Kenmore to the east on the north shore of Lake Washington. Farther north are Edmonds, Lynnwood, and Everett.

The Eastside is a growing part of the Seattle metropolitan area. East of Lake Washington are Mercer Island, Medina, **BELLEVUE**, and Issaquah; to the north lie **KIRKLAND**, Juanita, **REDMOND**, Bothell, and Woodinville.

Visitor Information

Ever since the Klondike gold rush, Seattleites have been known to lend a helping hand to travelers. If people on the street can't point you in the direction of gold, or whatever else you seek, try the administrative office of the **SEATTLE/KING COUNTY CONVENTION AND VISITORS BUREAU** (520 Pike St, Downtown; 206/461-5800; www.seeseattle.org; map:J4). It's open from 8:30am to 5pm Monday though Friday. The main visitors bureau is located on the first floor of the recently expanded Washington State Convention & Trade Center (800 Convention Pl, at 8th Ave and Pike St, Downtown; 206/461-5840; map:J4), open Monday through Friday 8:30am to 5pm and weekends 10am to 4pm. An additional information booth in **PIONEER SQUARE** (corner of Occidental Ave and Main St; map:O8) is staffed from Memorial Day to Labor Day, and another is located at the foot of the **SPACE NEEDLE** (Seattle Center, Downtown; map:C6). Free maps of Seattle can be picked up at any of these locations or requested over the phone.

Downtown shoppers can also pick up maps and information at the **CONCIERGE DESKS** in the Bon Marché (1601 3rd Ave; 206/506-6000), Nordstrom (500 Pine St; 206/628-2111), and Pacific Place (600 Pine St; 206/405-2655).

For more information about Seattle, or anything else you could possibly think of, call the research wizards at the **SEATTLE PUBLIC LIBRARY QUICK INFORMATION LINE** (206/386-INFO). The *Seattle Survival Guide* by Theresa Morrow is a thorough, reliable resource for newcomers and longtime residents alike—as is the *Newcomer's Handbook for Seattle*.

Getting Around

BY BUS

It is exceptionally easy to get around downtown Seattle without a car. **METRO TRANSIT** (201 S Jackson St, Downtown; 206/553-3000; http:// transit.metrokc.gov; map:O8) operates more than 200 bus routes in Seattle and surrounding King County. Many of the coaches are wheelchair-accessible, and all are equipped with bike racks (mounted on the front of the bus) for bike-and-bus commuters. Bus stops have small yellow signs designating route numbers, and many have schedules posted. The fare is $1.25 in the city ($1.50 during peak commuter hours—6 to 9am and 3 to 6pm), $1.25 if you cross the city line ($2 peak). Exact fare is required. Seniors, youths, and handicapped riders are eligible for discount cards. All-day passes ($2.50) are available from drivers on the weekends and holidays only. Printed schedules and monthly passes are available at Metro headquarters and the Westlake Center bus tunnel station. You can also buy passes at many Bartell Drug Stores, at the Federal Building branch of the Northwest Federal Credit Union (915 2nd Ave, Downtown; 206/682-7622; map:M7), and by phone (206/624-PASS). Bus schedules are also available at a number of downtown office buildings, including the main U.S. Post Office (301 Union St, Downtown; 206/748-5417; map:K6) as well as the ferry terminal (Pier 52, 801 Alaskan Wy, Downtown; map:M8).

One of Metro's most valued services is the **RIDE FREE AREA** in downtown's commercial core. In the area bordered by the waterfront, I-5, Jackson Street to the south, and Battery Street to the north, you can ride free on any Metro bus from 6am until 7pm. Avoid above-ground traffic snags by catching a bus in Metro's sleek, L-shaped transit tunnel within the Ride Free Area; it has five underground stations, from near the Washington State Convention & Trade Center at Ninth and Pine to the Chinatown/International District at Fifth and Jackson.

Metro also operates the **WATERFRONT STREETCAR**. The vintage 1927 Australian mahogany-and-white-ash trolleys run from Myrtle Edwards Park along Alaskan Way on the waterfront to Main Street, then jog east through Pioneer Square to Fifth and Jackson. They depart at 20-minute to half-hour intervals from 7am weekdays (around 10:30am weekends) until 6pm, with extended hours in summer. The ride takes 20 minutes from one end to the other and costs $1 (exact change only), $1.25 during Metro peak hours. The cash fare entitles riders to a transfer that allows them to disembark and sightsee for up to 90 minutes, then continue the ride. Metro monthly bus passes and discount cards are good on the streetcar.

The **MONORAIL,** which connects Seattle Center to the downtown retail district, was a space-age innovation of the 1962 World's Fair. The 90-second, 1.2-mile ride—presently the only stretch of rapid transit in town—is a great thrill for kids and passes through the Experience Music Project attraction. A smart way to avoid the parking hassle at Seattle Center is to leave your car downtown and hop on the monorail at Westlake Center (3rd floor, Pine St and 4th Ave, Downtown; www.seattle monorail.com; map:I6); the station is on a platform outside, just east of the top of the escalator. Adults pay $1.25 one way; seniors and children ages 5 to 12 pay 50 cents. Trains leave every 10 minutes Monday through Friday from 7:30am to 11pm and weekends from 9am to 11pm.

For trips from as far north as Darrington in Snohomish County, **COMMUNITY TRANSIT** (800/562-1375; www.riderlink.gen.wa.us) runs buses on a regular schedule. Fare is $3 per adult to Seattle from any point outside the city; fare within Snohomish County is $1.

GRAY LINE OF SEATTLE (4500 W Marginal Wy SW, West Seattle; 206/624-5077; www.graylineofseattle.com) has the largest fleet of charter buses and competitive prices for sightseeing tours of the city. The company also offers organized tours to destinations such as Mount Rainier, Vancouver, and the San Juan Islands. (For other bus information, see Motor Tours under Organized Tours in the Exploring chapter.)

BY CAR

Despite ongoing efforts to make mass transit accessible to more people, sometimes it takes a car to get around Seattle. Most large **RENTAL CAR COMPANIES** have offices at Sea-Tac Airport, in downtown Seattle, and in downtown Bellevue. Some larger ones, such as Enterprise (800/325-8007 out-of-town reservations) and Budget (800/527-0700), have locations in other suburbs and in various Seattle neighborhoods. Hertz (800/654-3131) is the preferred rental car company of **AAA WASHINGTON** (330 6th Ave N, Downtown; 206/448-5353, 425/462-2001 or 800/AAA-HELP emergency road service). Visitor information centers operated by the Seattle/King County Convention and Visitors Bureau offer free **ROAD MAPS** of Seattle (see Visitor Information in this chapter). One cautionary note: the fine for blocking an intersection is $71.

Centrally located **PARKING** lots charge between $15 and $20 a day; lots on the fringes of downtown—Chinatown/International District, Belltown, and Alaskan Way on the waterfront, for instance—are usually less expensive. In downtown, most of the meters have a maximum of 30 minutes, and many are off limits to all but delivery trucks, but if you're lucky enough to get one after 6pm or on Sundays and holidays, they're free. Most parking tickets cost $28; parking illegally in a space reserved for the disabled costs $250. Large facilities such as Safeco Field, Seattle Center, and Husky Stadium in the University District generally have their own parking areas. Meters cost 60 cents to $2 an hour throughout town. In an attempt to draw shoppers to the city's retail core, the Pacific Place parking garage (6th Ave and Pine St, Downtown; map:I5) charges only $7 for up to 4 hours during the day. Evenings are just $2 for up to 4 hours after 5pm, and weekends before 5pm are $5 for up to 4 hours.

For **LOST CARS**, begin by calling the Seattle Police Department's Auto Records Department (206/684-5444) to find out whether your car is listed as towed and impounded. If there's no record, it may have been stolen; call 206/625-5011, or in an emergency call 911.

BY TAXI

Most cabs are directed by dispatchers, but it's easy to hail one near major attractions or downtown hotels. Call ahead and one will meet you at most downtown locations within 5 to 10 minutes. A cab from the airport to downtown costs about $30, but from downtown to the airport it's a flat rate of $25. The standard drop is $1.80, with the meter running at $1.80 per mile or 50 cents per minute. Local companies include Farwest Taxi (206/622-1717), Graytop (206/282-8222), and Yellow Cab (206/622-6500).

BY BICYCLE

Seattle is a relatively bicycle-friendly city. Depending on the weather, between 4,000 and 8,000 bikers commute to work each day. **BIKE LANES** on arterial streets throughout the city are fairly safe routes for cyclists, and bike trails offer a reprieve from huffing and puffing up Seattle's steep slopes. For both commuting and recreation, the **BURKE-GILMAN TRAIL** is the bicycling backbone of Seattle. Extending approximately 15 miles from Kenmore at the north end of Lake Washington through the University of Washington campus to Ballard, and connecting to downtown Seattle via either the Ballard Bridge and 15th Avenue, or the Fremont Bridge and Dexter Avenue, the Burke-Gilman Trail is essentially flat as it follows a former railroad line. The trail connects in Kenmore with the Sammamish River Trail, which takes riders around the north end of Lake Washington and through Woodinville to Redmond's Marymoor Park on the north edge of Lake Sammamish.

The **ELLIOTT BAY TRAIL** is a scenic 2.5-mile spur running northwest from downtown along the waterfront through Myrtle Edwards and Elliott Bay Parks. The recently rebuilt **ALKI TRAIL** stretches along Alki Beach in West Seattle and will soon connect with the 11-mile **DUWAMISH TRAIL**, which roughly follows the west shore of the Duwamish River south to Kent (where you can pick up the Green River Trail). Recreational riders especially enjoy the bike trail in Seward Park, which circles the wooded peninsula jutting into Lake Washington. The **I-90 TRAIL** takes cyclists from just east of downtown across Lake Washington to Mercer Island. The city's **MAP OF BIKE ROUTES** in Seattle, *Seattle Bicycling Guide Map,* shows these trails and cyclists' street routes, including across the West Seattle Bridge and south to Sea-Tac Airport; call the City of Seattle Bicycle and Pedestrian Program (206/684-7583). Maps include in-depth insets on difficult-to-navigate areas, but they become scarce during summer, so call ahead if you can. For bike maps of Bellevue, call the City of Bellevue Transportation Department (425/452-2894).

If in your travels you come upon a hill or body of water that looms too large, hop on a bus or ferry. All Metro buses come equipped with bike racks on the front, and using them is free, though they hold only two bikes per bus, first come, first served (http://transit.metrokc.gov/bike/bike.html). The only restriction is that you can't load or unload bicycles in the downtown Ride Free Area between 6am and 7pm, except at the Convention Place and International District bus tunnel stations. For more information, call Metro's Bike and Ride program (206/553-3000). Taking a bike on most local ferry routes costs about 90 cents on top of the regular passenger fare. For more ferry information, see the next section.

BIKE RACKS for securing your two-wheeler are conveniently located outside the Washington State Convention and Trade Center (800 Convention Pl, Downtown; map:J4), Key Tower (700 5th Ave, Downtown; map:N6) on the Cherry Street side, and in the City Centre parking garage (1420 5th Ave, Downtown; map:J5). In addition, racks can usually be found within a block of most bus stops in commercial areas.

To **RENT A BIKE,** try Gregg's Greenlake Cycle (7007 Woodlawn Ave NE, Green Lake; 206/523-1822; map:FF7), Al Young Bike and Ski (3615 NE 45th St, University District; 206/524-2642; map:FF6), across the street from the busy Burke-Gilman Trail, Blazing Saddles (1230 Western Ave, Downtown; 206/341-9994; map:K8), or Ti Cycles (2943 NE Blakely St, University District; 206/522-7602; map:FF6).

BY FERRY

In the Puget Sound area, ferries are commuter vehicles, tourist magnets, and shortcut alternatives to driving around large bodies of water. You can take a ferry from the downtown terminal at Pier 52 on the waterfront (801 Alaskan Wy; map:M8) across the Sound to semiresidential/rural Bainbridge or Vashon Island (many people who live on the islands or the Kitsap Peninsula catch daily ferries into the city), or hop one from Anacortes, 90 miles north of town via I-5, to the San Juan Islands or even Vancouver Island, British Columbia. Travelers headed for the Olympic Peninsula use them as a scenic way to cut across the Sound; some passengers just go for the ride—people have even gotten married on them. For complete schedule and route information, call **WASHINGTON STATE FERRIES** (206/464-6400, 800/84-FERRY, or 888/808-7977; www.wsdot.wa.gov/ferries/). Schedules vary from summer to winter (with much longer lines in summer); cash or traveler's checks only. For more information on ferry routes, see the "Ferry Rides" sidebar in the Day Trips chapter.

Essentials

PUBLIC REST ROOMS
There's much ado about public toilets in Seattle. It was resolved by the City Council in 2001 to spend $638,000 on five high-tech, self-cleaning

PLACES OF WORSHIP

Houses of reverence vary widely in Seattle, from classical grandeur to eclectic jumble to tumbledown storefront. Here are a few noted for their architecture, community importance, and welcoming attitudes.

In Islam, the oldest set of doctrines are those of the Sunnis. North Seattle contains a small, attractive home for local adherents in the form of the **Idris Mosque** (1420 NE Northgate Wy, Northgate; 206/363-3013; www.idrismosque.com; map:DD6). The compact dome and minaret-evocative tower, topped with a crescent, routinely slow down traffic.

Synagogues in Seattle serve Reform, Conservative, Orthodox, and Sephardic communities. Freestanding fluted columns lend a Hellenistic air to **Temple de Hirsch Sinai** (1511 E Pike St, Capitol Hill; 206/323-8486; map:HH6), an airy, modern Reform complex. An extensive library includes more than 500 films with Jewish themes.

The twin towers of **St. James Cathedral** (804 9th Ave, First Hill; 206/382-4874; map:N4) announce an elegant and solidly impressive Roman Catholic church that boasts the city's oldest classical New Year's Eve concert and celebration, held at 11pm, featuring cathedral musicians and a chamber orchestra. The cathedral choir sings Sundays at 10am, the women's choir Sundays at 5:30pm.

St. Mark's Episcopal Cathedral (1245 10th Ave E, Capitol Hill; 206/323-0300; www.saintmarks.org; map:GG6), designed along traditional Gothic lines in the late 1920s, was never finished due to the Depression. After one of many renovations, the interior is now filled with pastel light streaming from a new rose window. A popular compline mass is held Sundays at 9:30pm.

Spacious under its central dome, the **First United Methodist Church** (811 5th Ave, Downtown; 206/622-7278; www.firstchurchseattle.org; map:M6) is a calm oasis on a frenetic corner. Music concerts presented by Earshot Jazz and Seattle Public

toilets. Possible locations for the pricey commodes include high-traffic (and high homeless) areas such as Pike Place Market, Pioneer Square, Ballard, University District, and Chinatown/International District. For now, public rest rooms are located at the base of the ramp in the Main Arcade of Pike Place Market (Pike St and Western Ave, Downtown; map:J8), at Freeway Park (6th Ave and Seneca St, Downtown; map:L5), and on the Main Street side of the Pioneer Square fire station (corner of 2nd Ave S and S Main St; map:O8). Public buildings are another option (e.g., Seattle Public Library, King County Courthouse, and the Federal Building, all downtown). Many larger parks, such as Volunteer Park on Capitol Hill and Gas Works Park in Wallingford, also have public facilities (although most are open only until dusk).

Library—organized readings by visiting authors such as Isabel Allende are often packed.

The white stucco curves of **Plymouth Congregational Church** (1217 6th Ave; 206/622-4865, Downtown; www.halcyon.com/plymouth; map:L5) are both intriguingly intricate and refreshingly simple. Black-and-white abstract crosses dance in starry columns down the sides of the building, inviting passersby in to lunchtime jazz services on Wednesday at noon.

The lofty central dome of the **St. Demetrios Greek Orthodox Church** (2100 Boyer Ave E, Capitol Hill; 206/325-4347; map:GG6) is home to Eastern Christianity. It stages a Greek Festival with everything from dancing to baklava in the fall.

First Covenant Church (400 E Pike St, Capitol Hill; 206/322-7411; map:K1), with its gold-tipped dome surmounting a heavy classical front, is a roomy space smack in the middle of nightlife-loving Capitol Hill. The long-running, cheeky live-comedy show *Late Nite Catechism* is performed here, complementing the neighborhood tone.

First Presbyterian Church (1013 8th Ave, First Hill; 206/624-0644; www.first pres.org; map:L4) is a streamlined sculptural complex dating from the 1960s; the modern architecture hides the fact that, for more than 130 years, this is one of Seattle's oldest congregations.

Look for the Buddhist festival held every July at **Seattle Buddhist Church** (1427 S Main St, Central District; 206/329-0800; www.seattlebetsuin.com; map:R4). The long brick building with upturned roof corners sits across from a park displaying the temple bell (under a canopy) and a statue memorializing the founder of Jodo Shinsu Buddhism.

Red, white, and blue upside-down triangles along the edge of the roof make **Mount Zion Baptist Church** (1634 19th Ave, Central District; 206/322-6500; map:HH6) easy to spot, and the church draws congregants from five counties.

—*Caroline Cummins*

MAJOR BANKS

Money-changing facilities are available at almost every major downtown bank. All of Seattle's larger banks also provide the full range of services, and you can locate neighborhood branches by contacting their downtown headquarters: Washington Mutual (national headquarters located in the neoclassical Washington Mutual Tower, 1201 3rd Ave; 206/461-6475; map:L7), Wells Fargo (999 3rd Ave; 206/292-3415; map:M7), US Bank (1420 5th Ave; 206/344-3795; map:K6), and KeyBank (1329 4th Ave; 206/447-5768; map:L6).

POLICE AND SAFETY

In emergency situations, dial 911. In nonemergencies, call the Seattle Police Department (206/625-5011). Seattle is known as a relatively safe city. There are fewer violent crimes here than in many large cities, although pickpockets are a problem in crowded areas such as Capitol Hill and Pike Place Market. As in any large city, be particularly aware of your surroundings when walking around downtown at night. (A fun bit of trivia: Seattle was the first city in the nation to have bicycle cops and, along with Los Angeles, the first in the nation to employ female police officers.)

HOSPITALS AND MEDICAL/DENTAL SERVICES

Seattle has so many hospitals located near the heart of the city that the First Hill neighborhood just east of downtown is known to locals as Pill Hill. One of the best facilities is Harborview Medical Center (325 9th Ave, First Hill; 206/731-3000 info or 206/731-3074 emergency; map:P4). Owned by King County and managed by the University of Washington, Harborview is home to the leading trauma center in a four-state region. Other hospitals include Swedish Medical Center (747 Broadway Ave, First Hill; 206/386-6000 info or 206/386-2573 emergency; map:N2) and the University of Washington Medical Center (1959 NE Pacific St, University District; 206/548-3300 info or 206/598-4000 emergency; map:FF6).

Doctors Referral and Appointment Service (206/622-9933 or 800/622-9933) can put you in touch with a doctor 24 hours a day. The Seattle/King County Dental Society offers a Dentist Referral Service (206/443-7607) that refers callers to a dentist or a low-cost dental clinic. HealthSouth Medical Clinics (walk-in health clinics) have numerous locations around Puget Sound, including one downtown at Denny Way and Fairview Avenue N (1151 Denny Wy; 206/682-7418; map:G3).

POST OFFICE

Downtown Seattle's main U.S. Post Office (301 Union St; 206/748-5417; www.usps.com; map:K6) is open weekdays 7:30am to 5:30pm. Hours at neighborhood branches vary, and some are open on Saturdays, so call ahead.

GROCERY STORES

If you can't find what you need in the recesses of Pike Place Market, the closest major grocery stores to downtown are the Harvard Market QFC (1401 Broadway Ave; 206/860-3818; map:L1), at the corner of Broadway and Pike, and two stores on the western edge of Seattle Center: Larry's Market (100 Mercer St, Downtown; 206/213-0778; map:A7) and QFC (100 Republican, Downtown; 206/285-5491; map:A7).

PHARMACIES

Bartell Drug Stores is the biggest local chain in the area, and most locations have prescription departments. Downtown stores are at Third Avenue and Union (1404 3rd Ave; 206/624-1366; map:K6) and at Fifth Avenue and Olive Way (1628 5th Ave; 206/622-0581; map:I6). The branch on Lower Queen Anne (600 1st Ave N; 206/284-1354; map:A7) is open 24 hours a day. Other 24-hour pharmacies are located in Walgreen Drug Stores in Ballard (5409 15th Ave NW; 206/781-0056; map:EE8) and Kirkland (12405 NE 85th; 425/822-9202; map:EE3). Two local alternatives are Medicine Man (323 N 85th St, Greenwood; 206/789-0800; map:EE8), which carries homeopathic remedies and nutritional supplements, and Rainbow Remedies (409 15th Ave E, Capitol Hill; 206/329-8979; map:HH6), a naturopathic clinic with a large selection of holistic remedies.

DRY CLEANERS AND LAUNDROMATS

Several dry cleaners operate throughout the city, and many hotels have in-house services. A couple to consider: Fashion Care Cleaners (1822 Terry Ave, Downtown; 206/382-9265; map:I3), which has an express service, and Ange's French Cleaners (2000 9th Ave, Downtown; 206/622-6727), a fixture for more than 50 years that will pick up and deliver.

Have a beer at the 5 Point Café while your clothes dry at the adjacent 5 Point Laundromat (417 Cedar St, Belltown; map:E7), patronized by an eclectic crowd 24 hours a day. An added bonus: Zeek's Pizza (419 Denny Wy, Belltown; 206/448-6775; map:E7) is kitty-corner from the laundry just past the dry fountain and statue of Chief Sealth, Seattle's namesake. Also in totally hip Belltown is the unusual Sit & Spin (2219 4th Ave; 206/441-9484; map:G6), where you can listen to live music, eat dinner, play board games, or admire the art on the walls while you do your wash. It's open Sunday through Thursday 9am to midnight, and Friday and Saturday 9am to 2am.

LEGAL SERVICES

Lawyer Referral Services (206/623-2551) puts clients in touch with lawyers who are members of the King County Bar Association. The call to the service is free; lawyers charge $30 for 30 minutes for consultations, with pro bono and low-fee programs for low-income clients. Columbia Legal Services (206/464-5911) is a federally funded program that provides free consultation for clients with very low incomes. Northwest Women's Law Center (206/621-7691) provides basic legal information and attorney referrals, as well as advice on self-help methods.

BUSINESS, COPY, AND MESSENGER SERVICES

Business Service Center (1001 4th Ave, 32nd floor, Downtown; 206/624-9188; map:M6) rents office and conference space for periods of three to 12 months; open weekdays only. Another option is Globe Secretariat (2001 6th Ave, Ste 306, Belltown; 206/448-9441; map:H5). Services available include word processing, typing, tape transcription, résumés, 24-hour dictation, copying, and faxing. Or try Key People (1904 3rd Ave, Ste 336, Downtown; 206/223-1579; map:I7), a company offering busi-

NAMING NAMES

Most people know that Seattle was named in honor of Chief Sealth, the peace-loving leader of two local Indian tribes (the Suquamish and the Duwamish) at the time when the first white settlers landed at Alki Point in 1851. But the sources of names for other landmarks, streets, and sights are less well remembered.

Denny Way. This busy street near Seattle Center recalls David Denny, one of the town's pioneers, who arrived here in 1851 with 25 cents in his pockets and eventually made a fortune with his investments—before losing it all during the Panic of 1893.

Elliott Bay. Today's harbor was christened by Lieutenant Charles Wilkes, who commanded an 1841 exploration of Pacific Northwest waterways. The bay was supposedly named after one of three Elliotts in his party. But whether it was the Reverend J. L. Elliott, Midshipman Samuel Elliott, or 1st Class Boy George Elliott is open for debate.

King County. The area containing Seattle was originally dubbed King County in honor of William Rufus DeVane King, Franklin Pierce's vice president. But it was renamed in 1986 to honor the slain civil rights leader Martin Luther King Jr.

Mercer Island. There's some doubt as to which of two pioneering Mercer brothers gave his name to this lump of land in Lake Washington. The probable honoree was Thomas Mercer, who arrived here in 1852 with a team of horses to become Seattle's first teamster and later its first judge. But it could also have been Asa Mercer, first president of the Territorial University (now the University of Washington) and the man who brought the famous "Mercer Maidens," a cargo of potential brides from the East Coast, to this virgin territory in the 1860s—an entrepreneurial feat immortalized in the 1960s TV show *Here Come the Brides*.

Puget Sound. Our "inland sea" was named after Peter Puget, a second lieutenant under British Captain George Vancouver, who commanded an exploration of the Sound in 1792.

Starbucks Coffee. Our best-known latte purveyor takes its moniker from Mr. Starbuck, a java junkie in Herman Melville's *Moby Dick*.

Yesler Way. In the early 1850s, Henry Yesler built the town's first steam sawmill on Elliott Bay. The Pioneer Square street that bears his name was originally a path down which logs were skidded from surrounding hills for processing.

—J. Kingston Pierce

ness services such as word processing, typing, transcription, dictation, copying, and faxing, as well as desktop publishing and scanning. Kinko's (1833 Broadway Ave, Capitol Hill; 206/329-7445; map:GG6; and branches), with its myriad locations, is open 24 hours every day and offers copying, in-house IBM and Macintosh computer rentals, and Internet access (on rental computers).

Elliott Bay Messenger (206/340-9525) is considered the best and fastest bicycle courier service downtown: downtown rush deliveries within 15 minutes, standard delivery within an hour, and more economical rates available for less rapid service. Elliott Bay is open weekdays only and does car deliveries to the entire Puget Sound area. Fleetfoot Messenger Service (206/728-7700) has quick-service, radio-dispatched bicyclists delivering packages downtown Monday though Friday, as well as vehicle delivery of packages up to 250 pounds—or whatever fits—statewide. And there's always Federal Express (800/463-3339) and United Parcel Service (800/742-5877), better known as UPS.

PHOTOGRAPHY EQUIPMENT AND SERVICES

Seattle's professional photographers swear by Cameratechs (5254 University Wy, University District; 206/526-5533; map:FF6). The shop services all makes and models, usually within 24 hours, and is open Monday through Saturday. For developing, custom printing, and digital outputting, the pros take their film to Photobition Seattle (424 8th Ave N, Downtown; 206/623-8113; map:D3). Another good option downtown is Ken's Cameras (1327 2nd Ave; 206/223-5553; map:K7), where you can have almost any brand of camera repaired or have your film developed in as little as one hour; it's also open Monday through Saturday.

COMPUTER REPAIRS

Uptime (2408 N 45th St, Wallingford; 206/547-1817; map:FF7) has been serving Seattle since the '80s repairing PCs and laptops. In-shop repairs are $80 an hour, or for house calls, they'll dispatch a technician for $110 an hour. According to those in the know, Westwind (510 NE 65th St, University District; 206/522-3530; map:FF6) is "head and shoulders above the rest" for Macintosh repair. The shop does laptops and desktops, has a priority service for $80, and is open Monday through Friday 9am to 6pm.

PETS AND STRAY ANIMALS

If you spot a stray animal or lose your pet in Seattle, call Seattle Animal Control (206/386-4254; www.cityofseattle.net/rca/animal/default.htm). They hold animals for three working days before putting them up for adoption, so make sure Rover has a legible license. For veterinary services, the Elliott Bay Animal Hospital (2042 15th Ave W, Interbay; 206/285-7387; map:GG8) is highly recommended by local vets. If your pet needs immediate attention after hours, contact the Emerald City Emergency Clinic (206/634-9000).

Local Resources

NEWSPAPERS AND PERIODICALS

Seattle's two daily morning papers share their business functions under a joint operating agreement, but retain entirely separate editorial operations. **THE SEATTLE TIMES** (1120 John St; 206/464-2111; www.seattletimes.com; map:F2) maintains its editorial and administrative offices downtown but has moved its production facilities to a Bothell location, where tours (reservations required) are offered Thursdays (19200 120th Ave NE, Bothell; 425/489-7000). The waterfront offices of the **SEATTLE POST-INTELLIGENCER** (101 Elliott Ave W; 206/448-8000; www.seattle-pi.com; map:B9) are home to one of the city's most eye-catching landmarks: a rotating, neon-enhanced world globe high atop the building. On the Eastside, the daily **EASTSIDE JOURNAL** (1705 132nd Ave NE, Bellevue; 425/455-2222; www.eastsidejournal.com; map:GG2) provides a local voice and a hedge against the hegemony of *The Seattle Times*. Want more local flavor? Most neighborhoods have their own weekly newspapers, usually available free at grocery stores.

Weeklies abound here. The free **SEATTLE WEEKLY** (1008 Western Ave, Ste 300, Downtown; 206/623-0500; www.seattleweekly.com; map:M8) provides coverage of politics, the arts, and civic issues. Another free alternative weekly, **THE STRANGER** (1535 11th Ave, 3rd Floor, Capitol Hill; 206/323-7101; www.thestranger.com; map:HH7), offers irreverent editorial comment and concise day-by-day music and dance-scene listings. Both are available beginning on Thursday of every week. Two other weeklies focus on Seattle's gay community: the 25-year-old **SEATTLE GAY NEWS** (1605 12th St, Capitol Hill; 206/324-4297; www.sgn.org; map:HH6), which costs a quarter and comes out on Fridays, and the free upstart, the **SEATTLE GAY STANDARD** (605 29th Ave E, Capitol Hill; 206/322-9027; www.gaystandard.com; map:GG7), which arrives on newsstands on Thursdays.

In the glossy pub department, **SEATTLE MAGAZINE** (423 3rd Ave W, Queen Anne; 206/284-1750; www.seattlemagazine.com; map:A8), a colorfully designed monthly magazine packed with insider information about the people and places of the city, can be purchased at newsstands and bookstores.

PUBLIC LIBRARIES

Public opinion is divided over Pritzker Prize–winning Dutch architect Rem Koolhaas's design for the new Seattle Public Library, scheduled for completion in the fall of 2003. Renderings of the $159 million library depict a gratelike exterior of glass, copper, and steel that some have likened to a structure in a *"Blade Runner* megalopolis." Like a phoenix rising from the ashes, the new facility will be built on the same site as the recently demolished '70s-style library. The 355,000-square-foot, 11-story library promises to be ultra-high-tech and state-of-the-art, with an amazing four-story spiral constructed within to house the nonfiction collection.

In the meantime, the **SEATTLE PUBLIC LIBRARY**'s temporary quarters are in the expanded Washington State Convention & Trade Center (800 Convention Pl, Pike St entrance, Downtown; 206/386-4636; www.spl.org; map:J4). Hours are Monday through Thursday 9am to 9pm, Friday 10:30am to 6pm, Saturday 9am to 6pm, and Sunday 1pm to 5pm. The same friendly and extremely helpful librarians are there, as are the 20-plus computer terminals where the public can reserve time to surf the Internet. The main branch also hosts the Quick Information Line (206/386-INFO), for answers to almost any question you can think of. Though only two-thirds of the lending materials are on-site, patrons can ask for stored items; expect a 24-hour wait. Besides lending books, video and audio recordings, and even artwork, the Seattle Public Library system offers lectures, films, and many other events in 24 branch libraries around the city. Call the individual branches for specific events. Mobile library service is also available (206/684-4713). The **KING COUNTY PUBLIC LIBRARY** system has 41 branches countywide and an answer line (425/462-9600 or 800/462-9600).

MAJOR DOWNTOWN BOOKSTORES

Seattle's population is legendarily literary, so it's not surprising that the city is filled with bookstores. The Elliott Bay Book Company (101 S Main St, Pioneer Square; 206/624-6600; map:O8) is the best locally owned bookstore in town. The downtown branch of the University Book Store (1225 4th Ave; 206/545-9230; map:K6) features a vast selection of technical and computer titles. Large chains with downtown branches include Borders Books & Music (1501 4th Ave; 206/622-4599; map:J6) and Barnes & Noble at Pacific Place (7th Ave and Pine St; 206/264-0156; map:I5). For more bookstores, see the Shopping chapter.

RADIO AND TV

Amid the usual horde of stations offered by the usual huge, nationwide radio conglomerates lie some gems. The University of Washington–owned, student-run 90.3 FM KEXP recently received a chunk of funding from Paul Allen, but it retains its cutting-edge music and no-commercials format. For a quick introduction to the issues and politics of Seattle, nothing beats the University of Washington's National Public Radio affiliate, 94.9 FM KUOW, and its daily *Weekday* program, running every morning from 9am to 11am. Here's a quick guide to the local radio dial.

Radio Stations

TALK RADIO	570 AM	KVI
NEWS/TALK	710 AM	KIRO
SPORTS	950 AM	KJR
MORNING TALK	1000 AM	KOMO
PACIFIC LUTHERAN UNIVERSITY, NATIONAL PUBLIC RADIO, JAZZ	88.5 FM	KPLU
UNIVERSITY OF WASHINGTON, ALTERNATIVE	90.3 FM	KEXP
BELLEVUE COMMUNITY COLLEGE, JAZZ, FOLK, WORLD MUSIC, BLUES	91.3 FM	KBCS
TOP 40, R&B	93.3 FM	KUBE
COUNTRY	94.1 FM	KMPS
UNIVERSITY OF WASHINGTON, NATIONAL PUBLIC RADIO	94.9 FM	KUOW
OLDIES	97.3 FM	KBSG
CLASSICAL	98.1 FM	KING
OUTRAGEOUS TALK	100.7 FM	KIRO
CLASSIC ROCK	102.5 FM	KZOK
ADULT ALTERNATIVE	103.7 FM	KMTT
ALTERNATIVE	107.7 FM	KNDD

TV Stations

ABC	4	KOMO
NBC	5	KING
INDEPENDENT	6	KONG
CBS	7	KIRO
PBS	9	KCTS
UPN	11	KSTW
FOX	13	KCPQ
WARNER/INDEPENDENT	22	KTZZ

INTERNET ACCESS

Many major HOTELS now offer the option of Internet access for their guests, with double phone lines in rooms or sometimes even computers and business centers (see the Lodgings chapter). And though it can get crowded at times, the downtown SEATTLE PUBLIC LIBRARY (see Public Libraries, above) has more than 20 computers available to the public with free Internet access.

Seattle is also home to several CYBERCAFES where, for a fee, you can log on and surf—or just check your email. At the Capitol Hill Internet Café (219 Broadway Ave E; 206/860-6858; map:HH6), using the PCs will cost you $6 an hour; hours are 10am to midnight daily. Other Capitol Hill establishments include Aurafice Internet and Coffee Bar

(616 E Pine St; 206/860-9977; www.aurafice.com; map:HH6), a hipster joint decked out in red walls and black leather chairs from the '70s. It's open daily 8am to 2am and costs 10 cents per minute, $6 per hour, or, if used for more than 2 hours, $5 an hour. Online Coffee Company (1720 E Olive Wy; 206/328-3731; www.onlinecoffeeco.com; map:HH6) is a comfy place with corner-office-style polished desks, open Monday through Friday 7am to midnight, Saturday and Sunday 9am to midnight. Cost is 12 cents per minute, 20 minutes free with purchase of coffee or tea, and one hour free with coffee or tea before 9am.

UNIVERSITIES AND COLLEGES

The University of Washington (Visitor Information Center: 4014 University Wy NE, University District; 206/543-2100; www.washington.edu; map:FF6) is the largest of the Washington State public universities and has one of the biggest university bookstores in the country (4326 University Wy NE, University District; 206/634-3400; www.ubookstore.com; map:FF6). Seattle Pacific University (3307 3rd Ave W, Queen Anne; 206/281-2000; www.spu.edu; map:FF8) is a private college associated with the Free Methodist Church. Seattle University (Broadway and Madison, First Hill; 206/296-6000; www.seattleu.edu; map:N1) is a private Jesuit school. Seattle Community Colleges (206/587-4100; www.seattlecolleges.org) operate three separate campuses in the city.

Important Telephone Numbers

AAA WASHINGTON	206/448-5353
AAA EMERGENCY ROAD SERVICE (24 HOURS)	800/AAA-HELP
AIDS HOTLINE	206/205-7837
ALCOHOLICS ANONYMOUS	206/587-2838
AMBULANCE	911
AMTRAK	800/872-7245
ANIMAL CONTROL	206/386-4254
AUTO IMPOUND	206/684-5444
BETTER BUSINESS BUREAU	206/431-2222
BIRTH AND DEATH RECORDS	206/296-4769
BLOOD BANK	206/292-6500
CHAMBER OF COMMERCE	206/389-7200
CHILDREN AND FAMILY SERVICES (TO REPORT ABUSE/NEGLECT)	206/721-6500
CITY OF SEATTLE INFORMATION	206/386-1234
CITY PARKS INFORMATION AND SCHEDULING OFFICE	206/684-4075
COAST GUARD 24-HOUR EMERGENCY	800/982-8813
COMMUNITY INFORMATION LINE	206/461-3200

CUSTOMS (U.S.)	206/553-4676
DIRECTORY INFORMATION (60 CENTS PER CALL)	206/555-1212
DOMESTIC VIOLENCE HOTLINE	800/562-6025
EMERGENCY RESOURCE CENTER (ACTIVATED DURING	
EMERGENCIES SUCH AS EARTHQUAKES)	206/684-3355
FBI	206/622-0460
FEMA (FEDERAL EMERGENCY	
MANAGEMENT AGENCY)	800/462-9029
FIRE	911
GREYHOUND BUS LINES SEATTLE TERMINAL	206/628-5508 OR
	800/231-22222
IMMIGRATION AND NATURALIZATION SERVICE	800/375-5283
LOST PETS	206/386-7387
MARRIAGE LICENSES	206/296-3933
METRO TRANSIT RIDER INFORMATION LINE	206/553-3000
MISSING PERSONS	206/684-5582
PASSPORTS	206/808-5700
PLANNED PARENTHOOD	206/328-7700
POISON CENTER	206/526-2121
POST OFFICE INFORMATION	800/275-8777
RED CROSS	206/323-2345
SEATTLE AREA TRAFFIC REPORTS	206/368-4499
SEATTLE/KING COUNTY	
CONVENTION & VISITORS BUREAU	206/461-5840
SEATTLE/KING COUNTY	
DEPARTMENT OF PUBLIC HEALTH	206/296-4600
SENIOR INFORMATION CENTER	206/448-3110
SEXUAL ASSAULT RESOURCE LINE	206/632-7273
STATE PATROL	425/455-7700
SUICIDE PREVENTION	206/461-3222
TICKETMASTER	206/628-0888
WASHINGTON STATE FERRIES	206/464-6400
WEATHER	206/526-6087
ZIP CODE INFORMATION	800/275-8777

TOP 200 RESTAURANTS

Restaurants by Star Rating

★★★★
Campagne
Canlis
Dahlia Lounge
The Herbfarm
Lampreia
Le Gourmand
Rover's

★★★⯪
Brasa
Cafe Juanita
Flying Fish
The Georgian
Harvest Vine
Nishino
Saito's Japanese Cafe & Bar

★★★
Andaluca
Anthony's Pier 66
Cafe Ambrosia
Cafe Campagne
Cafe Lago
Carmelita
Cascadia Restaurant
Cassis
Chez Shea
El Gaucho
Elliott's Oyster House
Etta's Seafood
Eva Restaurant and Wine
    Bar
Fandango
Fireside Room
Geneva
gypsy
The Hunt Club
Il Bistro
Il Terrazzo Carmine
Imperial Garden Seafood
    Restaurant
India Bistro
Kaspar's
La Medusa
Le Pichet
Market Street Urban Grill
Matt's in the Market
Mistral Restaurant
Monsoon
Morton's of Chicago
Nell's
Osteria La Spiga
The Painted Table
Palace Kitchen
Ponti Seafood Grill
Raga

Restaurant Zoë
Salumi
Sans Souci
Sapphire Kitchen & Bar
Shanghai Garden
Sostanza Trattoria
Stumbling Goat
Swingside Cafe
Szmania's
Szmania's (Kirkland)
Tango
Third Floor Fish Cafe
Tulio Ristorante
Typhoon!
Wild Ginger Asian
    Restaurant and Satay Bar
Yarrow Bay Grill

★★⯪
Al Boccalino
Assaggio Ristorante
Avenue One
Axis
Bandoleone
Barking Frog
Blue Onion Bistro
Cactus
Cafe Flora
Cafe Nola
Dulces Latin Bistro
Earth & Ocean
El Greco
The Four Swallows
Galerias
Greenlake Bar & Grill
I Love Sushi
Isabella Ristorante
Kingfish Café
Lush Life
Macrina Bakery & Café
Madison Park Cafe
Marco's Supperclub
Maximilien in the Market
Metropolitan Grill
Mona's
Palisade
The Pink Door
Place Pigalle
Roy Street Bistro
Salumeria on Hudson
Sazerac
Seattle Catch Seafood
    Bistro
Shallots Asian Bistro
Shea's Lounge
Shiro's

611 Supreme Creperie
    Cafe
Six Seven Restaurant &
    Lounge
St. Clouds
Tempero do Brasil
Tosoni's
Toyoda Sushi
Union Bay Cafe
Waterfront Restaurant

★★
Afrikando
Agua Verde Cafe & Paddle
    Club
Atlas Foods
Bell Street Diner
Bick's Broadview Grill
Bis on Main
Bistro Pleasant Beach
Bizzarro Italian Cafe
Black Pearl
BluWater Bistro
Boat Street Cafe
Burk's Cafe
Burrito Loco
Chinoise Cafe
Chinook's at Salmon Bay
Chutneys
Coastal Kitchen
Cyclops
Daniel's Broiler
Doong Kong Lau
Dragonfish Asian Café
El Camino
Figaro Bistro
5 Spot Cafe
Fremont Classic Pizza &
    Trattoria
Il Bacio
Il Gambero
JaK's Grill
Jitterbug Cafe
Kabul
Kaizuka Teppanyaki &
    Sushi Bar
King Ludwig's Tyrol
    Restaurant
Malay Satay Hut
Maple Leaf Grill
Marina Park Grill
Medin's Ravioli Station
Moonfish
Noble Court
Panos Kleftiko
Pontevecchio

Queen City Grill
Racha Noodles
Ray's Boathouse
Ray's Cafe
Ristorante Buongusto
Saigon Bistro
Sand Point Grill
Sanmi Sushi
Sea Garden
Sea Garden of Bellevue
Serafina
Shamiana
Siam on Broadway
Sky City at the Needle
Snappy Dragon
Spazzo Mediterranean Grill
Supreme
Taqueria Guaymas
Tia Lou's
Tup Tim Thai
21 Central
Wasabi Bistro

Wazobia
Yanni's Greek Cuisine
Yarrow Bay Beach Cafe

★★
Calcutta Grill
Chandler's Crabhouse &
    Fresh Fish Market
Coho Café
El Puerco Lloron
Fleming's Prime
    Steakhouse & Wine Bar
Gravity Bar
Hilltop Ale House
Jitterbug Cafe
Luau Polynesian Lounge
Moghul Palace
Six Degrees
Ten Mercer
Union Square Grill
Winslow Way

★
Anthony's Fish Bar
Belltown Pub
Bimbo's Bitchin' Burrito
    Kitchen
Calypso Caribbean Kitchen
Crabpot Restaurant and Bar
Filiberto's Ristorante
    Italiano & Deli
Gorditos
Hilltop Ale House
Himalayan Sherpa
    Restaurant
Luna Park Cafe
Mae's Phinney Ridge Café
The Original Pancake
    House
Rosita's Mexican
    Restaurant
Siam on Lake Union
13 Coins Restaurant
Triangle Lounge

Restaurants by Neighborhood

BAINBRIDGE ISLAND
Bistro Pleasant Beach
Cafe Nola
The Four Swallows
Moonfish
Winslow Way Cafe

BALLARD/SHILSHOLE
Burk's Cafe
India Bistro
Le Gourmand
Market Street Urban Grill
Medini's Ravioli Station
Ray's Boathouse
Ray's Cafe

BELLEVUE
Bis on Main
Calcutta Grill
Crabpot Restaurant and Bar
Daniel's Broiler
I Love Sushi
Moghul Palace
Noble Court
Sans Souci
Sea Garden of Bellevue
Spazzo Mediterranean Grill
Tosoni's

BELLTOWN
Afrikando
Assaggio Ristorante
Avenue One
Axis
Belltown Pub

Brasa
Cascadia Restaurant
Cyclops
El Gaucho
Etta's Seafood
Fandango
Flying Fish
Il Gambero
Lampreia
Lush Life
Macrina Bakery & Cafe
Marco's Supperclub
Mistral Restaurant
Palace Kitchen
Queen City Grill
Restaurant Zoë
Saito's Japanese Cafe
Shallots Asian Bistro
Shiro's
Tia Lou's
Wasabi Bistro

BURIEN
Filiberto's Italian
    Restaurant

CAPITOL HILL
Bimbo's Bitchin' Burrito
    Kitchen
Cassis
Chutneys Grill on the Hill
Coastal Kitchen
El Greco
Galerias
Gravity Bar

Kingfish Café
Monsoon
Osteria La Spiga
Siam on Broadway
611 Supreme Creperie
    Cafe
Tango
Taqueria Guaymas

CHINATOWN/
   INTERNATIONAL
   DISTRICT
Kaizuka Teppanyaki &
    Sushi Bar
Malay Satay Hut
Saigon Bistro
Sea Garden
Shanghai Garden

COLUMBIA CITY
La Medusa
Salumeria on Hudson

CROWN HILL
Burrito Loco
Rosita's Mexican
    Restaurant

DOWNTOWN
Andaluca
Dahlia Lounge
Dragonfish Asian Cafe
Earth & Ocean
Fleming's Prime
    Steakhouse & Wine Bar

37

The Georgian
Isabella Ristorante
Le Pichet
Metropolitan Grill
Morton's of Chicago
The Painted Table
Sazerac
Tulio Ristorante
Typhoon!
Union Square Grill
Wild Ginger Asian
    Restaurant and Satay Bar

EASTLAKE
Bandoleone
Cafe Ambrosia
Serafina

FIRST HILL
Fireside Room
Geneva
The Hunt Club

FREMONT
El Camino
Fremont Classic Pizza &
    Trattoria
Pontevecchio
Ponti Seafood Grill
Seattle Catch Seafood
    Bistro
Swingside Cafe
Triangle Lounge

GREEN LAKE
Eva Restaurant and Wine
    Bar
Greenlake Bar & Grill
Luau Polynesian Lounge
Mona's
Nell's
Rosita's Mexican Restaurant
Six Degrees
Tacos Guaymas

**GREENWOOD/PHINNEY
    RIDGE**
Bick's Broadview Grill
Carmelita
Gorditos
Mae's Phinney Ridge Café
Stumbling Goat
Yanni's Greek Cuisine

ISSAQUAH
Coho Cafe
JaK's Grill
Shanghai Garden

KENT
Imperial Garden Seafood
    Restaurant

KIRKLAND
Cafe Juanita
Marina Park Grill
The Original Pancake
    House
Raga
Shamiana
Szmania's
Third Floor Fish Cafe
21 Central
Yarrow Bay Beach Cafe
Yarrow Bay Grill

LAKE UNION
BluWater Bistro
Chandler's Crabhouse
    and Fresh Fish Market
Daniel's Broiler
I Love Sushi
Siam on Lake Union
13 Coins Restaurant

LESCHI/MADRONA
Daniel's Broiler
Dulces Latin Bistro
St. Clouds
Supreme

LYNNWOOD
Taqueria Guaymas

**MADISON PARK /
    MADISON VALLEY**
Cactus
Cafe Flora
gypsy
Harvest Vine
Madison Park Cafe
Nishino
Rover's
Sostanza Trattoria

MAGNOLIA / INTERBAY
Chinook's at Salmon Bay
Palisade
Sanmi Sushi
Szmania's

MONTLAKE
Cafe Lago

NORTH END
Doong Kong Lau
King Ludwig's Tyrol
    Restaurant
Taqueria Guaymas
Toyoda Sushi

PIKE PLACE MARKET
Cafe Campagne
Campagne
Chez Shea
El Puerco Lloron
Il Bistro
Matt's in the Market
Maximilien in the Market
The Pink Door
Place Pigalle
Shea's Lounge

PIONEER SQUARE
Al Boccalino
Il Terrazzo Carmine
Salumi
Wazobia

QUEEN ANNE
Canlis
Chinoise Cafe
Chutneys
Figaro Bistro
5 Spot Cafe
Hilltop Ale House
Kaspar's
Racha Noodles
Ristorante Buongusto
Roy Street Bistro
Sapphire Kitchen & Bar
Ten Mercer
Tup Tim Thai

RAVENNA/WEDGWOOD
Black Pearl

REDMOND
Coho Cafe
Il Bacio
Typhoon!

RENTON
Taqueria Guaymas

ROOSEVELT/MAPLE LEAF
Calypso Caribbean Kitchen
Maple Leaf Grill
Snappy Dragon

**SANDPOINT/
    LAURELHURST**
Sand Point Grill

SEATTLE CENTER
Panos Kleftiko
Sky City at the Needle

UNIVERSITY DISTRICT
Agua Verde Cafe & Paddle
    Club
Atlas Foods
Blue Onion Bistro

Boat Street Cafe
Himalayan Sherpa
    Restaurant
Tempero do Brasil
Union Bay Cafe

WALLINGFORD
Bizzarro Italian Cafe
Chutneys
Jitterbug Cafe
Kabul

WATERFRONT
Anthony's Fish Bar
Anthony's Pier 66
Bell Street Diner
Crabpot Restaurant and Bar
Elliott's Oyster House
Six Seven Restaurant &
    Lounge
Waterfront Restaurant

WEST SEATTLE
JaK's Grill
Luna Park Cafe
Taqueria Guaymas

WHITE CENTER
Taqueria Guaymas

WOODINVILLE
Barking Frog
The Herbfarm

Restaurants by Food and Other Features

AFGHAN
Kabul

BAKERY
Macrina Bakery & Café

BARBECUE
Burk's Cafe

BREAKFAST
Andaluca
Atlas Foods
Cafe Campagne
Chinook's at Salmon Bay
Coastal Kitchen
Dragonfish Asian Café
Earth & Ocean
5 Spot Cafe
The Georgian
Gravity Bar
The Hunt Club
Imperial Garden Seafood
    Restaurant
Jitterbug Cafe
Luna Park Cafe
Mae's Phinney Ridge Café
Maximilien in the Market
The Original Pancake
    House
The Painted Table
Saigon Bistro
Sazerac
Six Seven Restaurant &
    Lounge
Snappy Dragon
Third Floor Fish Cafe
13 Coins Restaurant
Tulio

BREAKFAST ALL DAY
Atlas Foods
Coastal Kitchen
5 Spot Cafe
Jitterbug Cafe

Mae's Phinney Ridge Café
The Original Pancake
    House
13 Coins Restaurant

BRUNCH
Atlas Foods
Bistro Pleasant Beach
Bizzarro Italian Cafe
Boat Street Cafe
Cafe Campagne
Cafe Nola
Chandler's Crabhouse
    and Fresh Fish Market
Coastal Kitchen
Coho Cafe
El Greco
Etta's Seafood
5 Spot Cafe
The Georgian
The Hunt Club
Kingfish Café
Macrina Bakery & Café
The Original Pancake
    House
Palisade
Ponti Seafood Grill
Sapphire Kitchen & Bar
Six Degrees
611 Supreme Creperie
    Cafe
Sky City at the Needle
St. Clouds
Supreme
Szmania's (Kirkland)
Yarrow Bay Grill

BURGERS
Belltown Pub
Luna Park Cafe
Maple Leaf Grill

CAJUN/CREOLE
Burk's Cafe

CHINESE
Black Pearl
Doong Kong Lau
Imperial Garden Seafood
    Restaurant
Malay Satay Hut
Noble Court
Sea Garden
Sea Garden of Bellevue
Shallots Asian Bistro
Shanghai Garden
Snappy Dragon

CONTINENTAL
Boat Street Cafe
Canlis
El Gaucho
Geneva
The Georgian
Kaspar's
Roy Street Bistro
Szmania's
13 Coins Restaurant
Tosoni's

DELIVERY
Black Pearl
Malay Satay Hut
Snappy Dragon

**DESSERTS
  (EXCEPTIONAL)**
Cafe Ambrosia
Cafe Campagne
Dahlia Lounge
Earth & Ocean
Eva Restaurant and Wine
    Bar
Figaro Bistro
Geneva
The Herbfarm
The Hunt Club
Kaspar's
Lampreia

Le Gourmand
Le Pichet
Palace Kitchen
611 Supreme Creperie
  Cafe
Szmania's
Tulio

DINER
5 Spot Cafe
Jitterbug Cafe
Luna Park Cafe
Mae's Phinney Ridge Café

DINING ALONE
Cafe Campagne
Carmelita
I Love Sushi
Kaspar's Wine Bar
La Medusa
Marco's Supperclub
Matt's in the Market
Nishino
Place Pigalle
Saito's Japanese
  Restaurant
Sazerac
Shiro's
Szmania's

EDITORS' CHOICE
Brasa
Cafe Campagne
Cafe Juanita
Campagne
Canlis
Cascadia Restaurant
Chandler's Crabhouse
Chez Shea
Cyclops
Dahlia Lounge
Elliott's Oyster House
Etta's Seafood
Fireside Room
Flying Fish
Gravity Bar
Harvest Vine
The Herbfarm
The Hunt Club
Lampreia
Le Gourmand
Matt's in the Market
Ray's Boathouse
Ray's Cafe
Rover's
Salumi
Shea's Lounge

Six Seven Restaurant &
  Lounge
Sky City at the Needle
Swingside Cafe
Third Floor Fish Cafe
13 Coins Restaurant
Wild Ginger Asian
  Restaurant and Satay
  Bar

FAMILY
Agua Verde Cafe & Paddle
  Club
Anthony's Fish Bar
Anthony's Pier 66
Atlas Foods
Bell Street Diner
Bick's Broadview Grill
Black Pearl
Blue Onion Bistro
Burk's Cafe
Burrito Loco
Chinook's at Salmon Bay
Coho Cafe
Crabpot Restaurant and
  Bar
El Puerco Lloron
Elliott's Oyster House
Filiberto's Ristorante
  Italiano
Gorditos
Greenlake Bar & Grill
Kaizuka Teppanyaki & Sushi
  Bar
King Ludwig's Tyrol
  Restaurant
La Medusa
Luna Park Cafe
Mae's Phinney Ridge Café
Medin's Ravioli Station
The Original Pancake
  House
Ray's Boathouse
Ray's Cafe
Rosita's Mexican
  Restaurant
Sand Point Grill
Snappy Dragon
St. Clouds
Taqueria Guaymas
Winslow Way

FIREPLACE
Avenue One
Cafe Juanita
Canlis
Dulces Latin Bistro

Filiberto's Italian
  Restaurant
Fireside Room
The Hunt Club
Ponti Seafood Grill
Raga
Ristorante Buongusto
Rover's
Sostanza Trattoria

FISH-AND-CHIPS
Anthony's Fish Bar
Bell Street Diner
Chinook's at Salmon Bay

FRENCH
Avenue One
Bis on Main
Cafe Campagne
Campagne
Cassis
Chez Shea
Figaro Bistro
Le Gourmand
Le Pichet
Maximilien in the Market
Mistral Restaurant
Place Pigalle
Rover's
611 Supreme Creperie
  Cafe
Shea's Lounge

GERMAN
King Ludwig's Tyrol
  Restaurant
Szmania's

GREEK
Panos Kleftiko
Yanni's Greek Cuisine

GRILL
Bick's Broadview Grill
Greenlake Bar & Grill
JaK's Grill
Maple Leaf Grill
Metropolitan Grill
Ponti Seafood Grill
Queen City Grill
Six Degrees
Triangle Lounge
Union Square Grill
Yarrow Bay Grill

HEALTHY
Afrikando
Cafe Ambrosia
Cafe Flora

Carmelita
Gorditos
Gravity Bar

INDIAN
Chutneys India Bistro
Moghul Palace
Raga
Shamiana

INVENTIVE ETHNIC
Axis
Cafe Flora
Cafe Nola
Chinoise Cafe
Coastal Kitchen
Dahlia Lounge
Etta's Seafood
5 Spot Cafe
Kingfish Cafe
Luau Polynesian Lounge
Maple Leaf Grill
Marco's Supperclub
Marina Park Grill
Matt's in the Market
Mona's
Monsoon
Roy Street Bistro
Sapphire Kitchen & Bar
Sazerac
Shallots Asian Bistro
Shamiana
Shea's Lounge
Szmania's
Wild Ginger Asian
  Restaurant and Satay
  Bar
Yarrow Bay Beach Cafe
Yarrow Bay Grill

ITALIAN
Al Boccalino
Assaggio Ristorante
Bizzarro Italian Cafe
Cafe Lago
Filiberto's Ristorante
  Italiano
Il Bacio
Il Bistro
Il Gambero
Il Terrazzo Carmine
Isabella Ristorante
La Medusa
Lush Life
Medin's Ravioli Station
Osteria La Spiga
Pontevecchio
Ristorante Buongusto

Salumeria on Hudson
Salumi
Sans Souci
Serafina
Sostanza Trattoria
Swingside Cafe
Tosoni's
Tulio Ristorante

JAPANESE
I Love Sushi
Kaizuka Teppanyaki &
  Sushi Bar
Nishino
Saito's Japanese Cafe &
  Bar
Sanmi Sushi
Shiro's
Toyoda Sushi
Wasabi Bistro

KITSCHY
Armadillo BBQ
Bizzarro Italian Cafe
Blue Onion Bistro
Cyclops
5 Spot Cafe
Galerias
Luna Park Cafe
The Pink Door

LATE-NIGHT
Bandoleone
Campagne
El Gaucho
5 Spot Cafe
Flying Fish
Queen City Grill
Sea Garden
13 Coins Restaurant
Union Square Grill
Wazobia

LATIN
Dulces Latin Bistro
Fandango
Tempero do Brasil

MEDITERRANEAN
Andaluca
Bistro Pleasant Beach
El Greco
La Medusa
Lush Life
Madison Park Cafe
Mona's
Ponti Seafood Grill
Sapphire Kitchen & Bar

Spazzo Mediterranean
  Grill
Tango
Tulio Ristorante

MEXICAN
Burrito Loco
El Puerco Lloron
Galerias
Gorditos
Rosita's
Taqueria Guaymas
Tia Lou's

NORTHWEST
Brasa
Cafe Juanita
Campagne
Cascadia Restaurant
Chez Shea
Dahlia Lounge
Earth & Ocean
Eva Restaurant and Wine
  Bar
Flying Fish
The Georgian
The Herbfarm
Kaspar's
Lampreia
Le Gourmand
Market Street Urban Grill
Nell's
The Painted Table
Palace Kitchen
Ray's Boathouse
Ray's Cafe
Shea's Lounge
Stumbling Goat
Third Floor Fish Cafe
Union Bay Cafe

OUTDOOR DINING
Anthony's Pier 66
Assaggio Ristorante
Bistro Pleasant Beach
Cactus
Cafe Campagne
Cafe Flora
Cafe Nola
Carmelita
Chandler's Crabhouse
Chinook's at Salmon Bay
El Camino
El Puerco Lloron
Elliott's Oyster House
Filiberto's Italian
  Restaurant
The Hunt Club

Il Terrazzo Carmine
Luau Polynesian Lounge
Madison Park Cafe
Maggie Bluffs
Marco's Supperclub
Palisade
The Pink Door
Place Pigalle
Ponti Seafood Grill
Ray's Boathouse
Ray's Cafe
Rover's
Serafina
Six Seven Restaurant &
Lounge
Sostanza Trattoria
Triangle Lounge
Union Bay Cafe
Yarrow Bay Beach Cafe
Yarrow Bay Grill

OYSTER BAR
Chandler's Crabhouse
Elliott's Oyster House

PAN-ASIAN
Chinoise Cafe
Dragonfish Asian Cafe
Malay Satay Hut
Shallots Asian Bistro
Wild Ginger Asian
Restaurant and Satay
Bar

PERSIAN
Kabul

PIZZA
Fremont Classic Pizza &
Trattoria

PRIVATE ROOMS
Cafe Juanita
Cascadia Restaurant
El Gaucho
Flying Fish
The Georgian
Kaizuka Teppanyaki and
Sushi Bar
Kaspar's
Metropolitan Grill
Nishino
Palace Kitchen
Ponti Seafood Grill
Ray's Boathouse
Sea Garden
Szmania's

Third Floor Fish Cafe
Tulio
Yarrow Bay Grill

ROMANTIC
Al Boccalino
Andaluca
Avenue One
Bandoleone
Bis on Main
Bistro Pleasant Beach
Boat Street Cafe
Brasa
Cafe Campagne
Cafe Juanita
Cafe Lago
Campagne
Canlis
Carmelita
Cascadia Restaurant
Cassis
Chez Shea
Dahlia Lounge
Dulces Latin Bistro
Eva Restaurant and Wine
Bar
Fireside Room
The Four Swallows
Geneva
The Georgian
gypsy
Harvest Vine
The Hunt Club
Il Bistro
Il Gambero
Il Terrazzo Carmine
Isabella Ristorante
La Medusa
Lampreia
Le Gourmand
Le Pichet
Lush Life
Madison Park Cafe
Marina Park Grill
Mona's
Osteria La Spiga
The Painted Table
The Pink Door
Place Pigalle
Pontevecchio
Ponti Seafood Grill
Ray's Boathouse
Ristorante Buongusto
Rover's
Roy Street Bistro
Sans Souci

Sapphire Kitchen & Bar
Seattle Catch Bistro
Serafina
Shea's Lounge
Sostanza Trattoria
Stumbling Goat
Swingside Cafe
Third Floor Fish Cafe
Tosoni's

SEAFOOD
Anthony's Pier 66
Bell Street Diner
Chandler's Crabhouse &
Fresh Fish Market
Chinook's at Salmon Bay
Coastal Kitchen
Coho Cafe
Crabpot Restaurant and
Bar
El Gaucho
Elliott's Oyster House
Etta's Seafood
Flying Fish
Matt's in the Market
Nishino
Palisade
Ponti Seafood Grill
Ray's Boathouse
Saito's Japanese
Restaurant & Bar
Sea Garden
Sea Garden of Bellevue
Seattle Catch Seafood
Bistro
Third Floor Fish Cafe
Waterfront Restaurant

**SOUP/SALAD/
SANDWICH**
Luna Park Cafe
Macrina Bakery & Café
Salumeria on Hudson
Six Degrees

SOUTH AMERICAN
Fandango
Tempero do Brasil

SOUTHERN
Burk's Cafe
Kingfish Café

SOUTHWESTERN
Cactus

STEAKS
Daniel's Broiler

El Gaucho
Fleming's Prime
    Steakhouse & Wine Bar
JaK's Grill
Marina Park Grill
Metropolitan Grill
Morton's of Chicago
Palisade
21 Central
Union Square Grill

SUSHI
Chinoise Cafe
Dragonfish Asian Café
I Love Sushi
Kaizuka Teppanyaki &
    Sushi Bar
Mona's
Nishino
Saito's Japanese Cafe &
    Bar
Sanmi Sushi
Shiro's
Toyoda Sushi
Wasabi Bistro

TAKE-OUT
Cafe Campagne
Macrina Bakery & Café
Salumeria on Hudson
Salumi
Taqueria Guaymas

TAPAS
Bandoleone
Fandango
Harvest Vine
Mona's
Spazzo Mediterranean
    Grill
Tango

TAVERN
Belltown Pub
Hilltop Ale House
Maple Leaf Grill
Six Degrees
Triangle Lounge

THAI
Racha Noodles
Siam on Broadway
Siam on Lake Union
Tup Tim Thai
Typhoon!

VALUE, GOOD
Agua Verde Cafe & Paddle
    Club
Atlas Foods
Bimbo's Bitchin' Burrito
    Kitchen
Black Pearl
Burk's Cafe
Burrito Loco
Chinoise Cafe
Chinook's at Salmon Bay
Chutneys
Cyclops
Doong Kong Lau
El Puerco Lloron
Filiberto's Ristorante
    Italiano
Galerias
Gorditos
Himalayan Sherpa
    Restaurant
Il Gambero
Imperial Garden Seafood
    Restaurant
India Bistro
Kaizuka Teppanyaki & Sushi
    Bar
King Ludwig's Tyrol
    Restaurant
Kingfish Café
Luna Park Cafe
Malay Satay Hut
Medin's Ravioli Station
Moghul Palace
Noble Court
The Original Pancake
    House
Osteria La Spiga
Racha Noodles
Raga
Ray's Boathouse
Ray's Cafe
Rosita's Mexican
    Restaurant
Saigon Bistro
Salumeria on Hudson
Sand Point Grill
Shallots Asian Bistro
Shamiana
Siam on Broadway
Siam on Lake Union
611 Supreme Creperie
    Cafe
Snappy Dragon
St. Clouds
Taqueria Guaymas

Tup Tim Thai
Union Bay Cafe
Wazobia

VEGETARIAN
Cafe Ambrosia
Cafe Flora
Carmelita
Gravity Bar

VIETNAMESE
Chinoise Cafe
Monsoon
Saigon Bistro

VIEW
Anthony's Pier 66
Avenue One
Bell Street Diner
BluWater Bistro
Calcutta Grill
Canlis
Chandler's Crabhouse
Chez Shea
Chinook's at Salmon Bay
Crabpot Restaurant and
    Bar
Daniel's Broiler
Elliott's Oyster House
I Love Sushi
Matt's in the Market
Maximilien in the Market
Palisade
Ponti Seafood Grill
Ray's Boathouse
Ray's Cafe
Sanmi Sushi
Shea's Lounge
Six Seven Restaurant &
    Lounge
Third Floor Fish Cafe
Waterfront Restaurant
Yarrow Bay Beach Cafe
Yarrow Bay Grill

WEST AFRICAN
Afrikando
Wazobia

WINE BAR
Boat Street Cafe
Eva Restaurant and Wine
    Bar
Fleming's Prime
    Steakhouse & Wine Bar
Kaspar's

43

RESTAURANTS

Afrikando / ★★

2904 1ST AVE, BELLTOWN; 206/374-9714

On a Belltown corner, Jacques Sarr offers a detour to French West Africa. The menu may recall his native Senegal, but the double storefront reverberates to the music of the world, and is warmed by exotic spices and renowned African hospitality. Start with *akra*, light fritters of black-eyed peas in a spicy tomato sauce with bay shrimp. Mesclun greens in the *salade* Afrikando may be of dubious African-ness, but toasted cashews and a great vinaigrette highlight the French influence on Sarr's homeland. Best-sellers include *debe*, grilled lamb chops with spicy onion mustard sauce, and couscous; *thiebu djen*, the national Senegalese dish of fish in rich tomato sauce with vegetables and *jollof rice*; and *poisson frite* (French for "fried fish"), a whole fried tilapia served with rice and tomato sauce. There's a small list of craft beers, but try the Senegalese juices—hibiscus, ginger, or tamarind; or try the bitter, dark Ataya tea served with sugar and mint. Sarr's mango tart is a delightful dessert, perfect with a cup of hot ginger tea. *$; MC, V; checks OK; lunch Mon–Fri, dinner every day; beer only; reservations recommended; self parking; map:G8* &

Agua Verde Cafe & Paddle Club / ★★

1303 NE BOAT ST, UNIVERSITY DISTRICT; 206/545-8570

Visiting Agua Verde is like escaping to a beach on Baja—and there'll be plenty of other escapees vying for a place in the sun on Portage Bay. Even waiting can be a pleasure here: just rent a kayak downstairs and tool around Lake Union before joining the young, blue-jeaned neighborhood crowd for dinner in this colorful, noisy, fun place. The cafeteria-style lunch gives way to full service at dinnertime. Choose from seven kinds of tacos, plus *tortas* (sandwiches) and all manner of side dishes—all vegetarian. The tacos are what you're here for—try the *meros*, halibut with avocado; *carnitas* with shredded pork; or *carne* with sliced flank steak, onions, and peppers. Vegetarians enjoy the *hongo*: meaty portobellos sautéed with tomatoes, onions, *guajillo* chiles, and soft, mild *cotija* cheese. Four salsas come on a cart, including smoky chipotle and a three-alarm tomato. *Camarones borrachos*—"drunken" prawns cooked in curaçao, tequila, garlic, and chiles—please among entrees, and sides include a zesty *ensalada de maiz y nopalito*, a chunky salad with corn, mild chiles, nopal cactus, and plenty of cilantro. Of course, there are sundry Mexican beers and *grandes* margaritas, as well as fresh-squeezed juices. You'll need to paddle a kayak after polishing off desserts such as the slab of Kahlúa-pecan pie or rich chocolate flan. Sunday you can only order takeout. *$; MC, V; checks OK; lunch, dinner Mon–Sat; full bar; reservations recommended; valet and self parking; www.aguaverde.com; map:EE7* &

Al Boccalino / ★★½

1 YESLER WY, PIONEER SQUARE; 206/622-7688

Smells of herbs and garlic greet the diner a block away—fragrant harbingers of delights to come in this pretty place in a historic brick building just off Pioneer Square. *Boccalinos*, the namesake wide-mouthed Italian wine pitchers, are offered for sale in the foyer of the intimate triangular dining room trimmed in dark wood and stained glass. Sure-to-please offerings include antipasti such as the *vongole oreganate*, clams baked in the half shell with oregano and bread crumbs, or *polenta ripiena con gorgonzola*, creamy polenta custard stuffed with sweet Gorgonzola heady with fresh sage. There are plenty of good pastas, too, including angel hair with sun-dried tomatoes, creminis, pine nuts, pecorino, and a surprising touch of chile oil. Seafood takes a major role here, as in the seared large scallops with pesto and white wine. Northern dishes are a specialty—try the saddle of lamb with a piquant sauce of Cognac, tarragon, and Dijon mustard. Downtown denizens love the lunches in this hideaway, with its complement of pastas and reasonably priced sandwiches, such as the grilled chicken with caramelized onions, roasted red peppers, and pesto served with a simple salad. Expect immaculate old-world service in a romantic setting. *$$; AE, DC, MC, V; checks OK; lunch Mon–Fri, dinner every day; beer and wine; reservations recommended; street parking; map:N8* &

Andaluca / ★★★

407 OLIVE WY (MAYFLOWER PARK HOTEL), DOWNTOWN; 206/382-6999

Rosewood booths, fresh flowers, eclectic murals, and textured walls in deep reds, earthy browns, and orange make Andaluca a romantic refuge for lovers with an appetite. Begin your meal with a glass of sherry at the small half-moon bar gleaming with crystal and the perfect teeth of the smart bartenders. Chef Wayne Johnson's lively menu pays tribute to the Mediterranean but always with a seasonal bent and a focus on regional seafood and produce. What could be more intimate than sharing a few small plates from the lengthy tapas menu along with a bottle of wine from the extensive list? Try the crispy duck cakes served with apricot chutney and cucumber yogurt; roasted mussels fragrant with garlic and rosemary; the polenta cakes with almonds, pecorino, and oyster mushrooms; or the spicy calamari with saffron aioli. Andaluca's paella, made with arborio rice, is loaded with prawns, clams, mussels, chicken, and chorizo cooked in a saffron broth. The *cabrales*-crusted beef is a heartbreakingly rare tenderloin with grilled pears, blue cheese, and marsala glaze. Vegetarians love the ratatouille risotto, with artichokes, tomatoes, zucchinis, and cremini mushrooms. Expect pampering from the competent, light-hearted staff. *$$$; AE, DC, DIS, MC, V; checks OK; break-*

fast every day, lunch Mon–Sat, dinner every day; full bar; reservations recommended; valet parking; map:I6 &

Anthony's Pier 66 / ★★★
Bell Street Diner / ★★
Anthony's Fish Bar / ★

2201 ALASKAN WY/PIER 66, WATERFRONT; 206/448-6688

This handsome trio of restaurants at the Bell Street Pier is designed to suit any mood, appetite, or budget. Pier 66 upstairs has the most jaw-dropping view of Seattle's working waterfront, and the Asian-inflected menu of local and regional seafood is priced accordingly. Ginger Penn Cove mussels steamed with sake will get you off to a good start, as will the Potlatch, an impressive collection of Northwest steamer clams, mussels, split snow crab legs, and half shell oysters. Planked wild chinook salmon or Alaskan halibut are always reliable entrees. Pier 66 is open for dinner only. For lunch or casual dining by Elliott Bay, the boisterous Bell Street Diner downstairs is a good choice, offering a wide selection of seafood, chowders, burgers, generous salads, rice bowls, and fish tacos. You'll enjoy the same view of the marina as the Harbormaster, whose watchtower is right next door. For a quick, no-frills bite, take the kids and join the sea gulls waterside at Anthony's Fish Bar and chow down on fish-and-chips, chowder, blackened-rockfish tacos, or bay shrimp caesar salads. *$$, $, $; AE, MC, V; checks OK; dinner every day at Anthony's Pier 66, lunch, dinner every day at Bell Street Diner and Anthony's Fish Bar; 2 full bars; reservations recommended; valet and validated garage parking at Seattle Art Institute; map:H9* &

Assaggio Ristorante / ★★★☆

2010 4TH AVE (CLAREMONT HOTEL), BELLTOWN; 206/441-1399

It's always a party at Assaggio, a slice of Rome in downtown Seattle, and in warm weather the party spills out onto the sidewalk. Owner Mauro Golmarvi is the consummate host; almost everybody who walks through the door of this frescoed hotel trattoria gets a hug, a kiss, or at least a handshake. The downtown business bunch keeps this place full even at lunch, where they are likely to show up for a light meal such as *brodetto*, a seafood soup served with rustic Tuscan bread. Golmarvi and chef Iram Macias offer a comprehensive menu of traditional Italian favorites. Particularly pleasing is the pasta with bolognese sauce, lamb shanks braised in red wine; veal saltimbocca; and penne pasta with pancetta, peppercorns, and vodka. You'll find plenty of Italian offerings among the wines, of course, but also some from Washington and Napa, with at least a half-dozen offered by the glass. *$$; AE, DC, DIS, MC, V; checks OK; lunch Mon–Fri, dinner Mon–Sat; beer and wine; reservations recommended; valet, street, and self parking; map:H7* &

Atlas Foods / ★★

2820 NE UNIVERSITY VILLAGE PL, UNIVERSITY DISTRICT; 206/522-6025
Neighborhood restaurant maestros Jeremy Hardy and Peter Levy (Jitterbug Cafe, 5 Spot Cafe, Coastal Kitchen) have another hit on their hands in this lively U-Village shopping mall stop. As in all their joints, the menu is witty and large. Breakfast is served every day 'til 3pm (with a few items offered at dinner). They not only do eggs any style, but also offer omelets and creative scrambles (called "Rumbles"), such as the Uncle Barry's Backyard Breakfast Brawl with andouille sausage, crayfish, corn, and Monterey Jack cheese. At lunch there's the nearly legendary Reverend Livingston Memorial Pork Shoulder Barbecue, a pulled pork sandwich with a whiskey barbecue sauce, or the shrimp-, cheese-, and pepper-packed *quesadilla fresca*. Dinner is all over the place, from cumin-laced Baja Marimba Fish Tacos to squash raviolis to great roast chicken. Kids love choices such as fish sticks or Honey Stung Fried Chicken, while parents appreciate the grown-up mood at the bar and wines by the bottle that are only $15 above the wholesale price—meaning the pricier the wine, the better the value. *$$; MC, V; checks OK; breakfast, lunch, dinner every day; full bar; reservations recommended; free lot parking; map:EE6* &

Avenue One / ★★★

1921 1ST AVE, BELLTOWN; 206/441-6139
What was once a turn-of-the-19th-century mortuary (you can still see the ornate choir loft on the west wall) has been transformed into a handsome 1930s-era Parisian bistro. Just ask, and the bartender behind the curved, copper-topped bar will tell tales about the ghosts that inhabit the peach-tinted dining room; better yet, ask him to pour you the cocktail of the moment as you wait for a seat in one of the lusciously upholstered booths awash in the buttery glow of vintage fixtures. A fireplace lures diners desiring intimacy to the small back room, which has a glimpse of Puget Sound. The menu has more hits than misses. Among the delights: seared Hudson Valley foie gras, balanced with the fruitiness of grenadine-marinated citrus, tart vanilla-scented rhubarb, and a brusque black pepper scone; confit of poussin made with ham hocks, leeks, and peas; and honey-and-lavender-glazed duck breast with lentil ragout and truffled peaches. Chef Charles Walpole also takes some creative risks with dishes such as the chorizo-crusted escolar with a citrus and watercress salad. The wine list has been much improved and broadened, and has won some awards of late. *$$$; AE, DC, MC, V; no checks; dinner every day; full bar; reservations recommended; street parking; map:I8* &

Axis / ★★☆

2214 1ST AVE, BELLTOWN; 206/441-9600

This sleek, soaring, multilevel space would be a drafty warehouse if it weren't for the warm lighting, giant art, and swarm of Belltown social bees buzzing around the busy bar drinking or feasting from the large menu. The long starter list is a great way to eat in this place. It's a global synthesis that ranges from fabulous fried pickles dusted in cornmeal, to Hawaiian poke salad, to pizza puttanesca, to *lumpia*, Filipino spring rolls. The dinner menu includes prime rib with mashed Yukon potatoes; perfect pan-seared Chilean sea bass with sake-butter; crispy duck salt-cured with ginger and fragrant with star anise; and chicken fried with Sichuan peppercorns and served with an exotic dipping sauce of Chinese black vinegar and housemade steamed buns. For dessert, go for the outrageous banana cream pie. *$$; AE, DC, MC, V; no checks; dinner every day; full bar; reservations recommended; valet and street parking; map:G8* &

Bandoleone / ★★☆

2241 EASTLAKE AVE E, EASTLAKE; 206/329-7559

The *bandoleone* is a small accordion that sings its sad, passionate voice and rhythm to the tango. Capturing the passionate Latino spirit is what proprietor Danielle Philippa aims for in her romantic little taverna. Certainly the dark, mellow ambience haunted by primitive Caribbean paintings sets just the right mood. Bandoleone is more laid-back and less trendy than its newer sibling, Tango (see review), but it's a well-established neighborhood standby with a loyal following. There are tapas of course; try the clams steamed in housemade blue corn beer and bacon—they're sensational. Build your own tacos with tortillas by ordering the *carnitas* with pulled pork and a tangy salsa verde. Among favorite entrees is Ternéra en Xeres, a veal shank soaked and braised in Spanish cream sherry and served with a rich rice spoonbread. Finish off the night with the *torta de cerezas*, a bittersweet chocolate cake with marinated cherries and vanilla whipped cream, or the *helados y nieves*, housemade sorbets and ice creams made with seasonal fruits. *$$; MC, V; checks OK; dinner every day; full bar; reservations recommended; bandoleone@earthlink. net; street parking; www.earthlink.net/~bandoleone; map:GG7* &

Barking Frog / ★★☆

14580 NE 145TH ST (WILLOWS LODGE), WOODINVILLE; 425/424-2999

The ambitious restaurant in the new luxury hotel Willows Lodge has more than its share of high-profile neighbors. The Columbia Winery, Chateau Ste. Michelle, and the celebrated Herbfarm Restaurant all share this short stretch of highway that winds through what is being touted as "Western Washington Wine Country." The room is comfortably rustic with elegant tabletop appointments, and the kitchen, with some personnel changes, is finding its footing. The warm Maine lobster salad is delightful—perfectly cooked lobster claws arranged on "summer-colored" couscous with melon and warm passion-fruit vinaigrette. Sicilian pistachios encrust a generous slice of foie gras served with rhubarb compote. The cassis and pinot noir sauce–roasted duck is cleverly accompanied by browned *panko*-encrusted mashed potato in the shape of a pear with a stem of cinnamon bark that tastes as good as it looks. Lobster consommé bathes the shellfish and swims in a seafood melange served with snow peas and zucchini. The wine list is an appropriate showcase for Washington wines, and its unconventional arrangement by style rather than by varietal means you'll be browsing for bottles under headings such as "Loud & Wooly," "Lush & Jammy," and "Tart & Lucid." Dreamy desserts include warm Valrhona chocolate cake with pistachio ice cream and fresh berry mousse cake with apricot and raspberry coulis. *$$; AE, DC, DIS, MC, V; checks OK; lunch Mon–Fri, dinner every day, brunch Sat–Sun; full bar; reservations recommended; free lot parking; map:BB2* &

Belltown Pub / ★

2322 IST AVE, BELLTOWN; 206/728-4311
Pub food with an Italian bent is the draw at this brightly lit Belltown hangout, where people-watching from a sidewalk table is part of the fun in fine weather. Inside, sit in high-backed wooden booths or on tall stools and eat huge burgers on house-baked bread, such as the classic favorite bacon and cheddar burger made with pepper bacon and sharp cheese. Grilled eggplant with smoked mozzarella and three-herb pesto is sure to gratify vegetarians. The salads are all bodacious—especially the gigantic spinach salad with Gorgonzola and toasted pecans. Bolognese sauce for fettuccine isn't just a ground beef affair, but spicy with pancetta ham and fennel sausage. Pesto mussels fettuccine—a pile of basil-smothered mussels over a plate of garlicky fettuccine sprinkled with Parmesan and pine nuts—is another specialty. You'll find lots of local craft beers on tap and a good list of bottled imports as well. *$; AE, MC, V; no checks; lunch, dinner every day; beer and wine; reservations recommended; street parking; map:G7* &

Bick's Broadview Grill / ★★

10555 GREENWOOD AVE N, GREENWOOD; 206/367-8481
Bick's Broadview Grill opened to serve Seattle's north end in 1997, and they've been lining up at the door ever since. Built into an old Greenwood house, Bick's feels like a ski lodge, though the food harkens more to the water-ski cultures of the Gulf of Mexico, Hawaii, and the Caribbean Islands. Start with smoked-duck spring rolls with a chipotle dipping sauce or creamy Dungeness crab cakes. For dinner, try the sesame-crusted halibut on a coconut rice cake or the signature Flattop Flattened Chicken, a boneless marinated half chicken cooked on a griddle with a steak

weight, and garnished with basil oil and goat cheese. Nightly specials are always a hit. Save room for dessert—the warm broken chocolate torte with vanilla ice cream is luscious. *$$; MC, V; no checks; dinner every day; full bar; reservations recommended; self parking; map:DD8* &

Bimbo's Bitchin' Burrito Kitchen / ★

506 E PINE ST, CAPITOL HILL; 206/329-9978

A neighborhood taco joint with great food and a sense of humor, this tiny place is filled with Day-Glo Hawaiian decor, loud indie rock, and Mexican wrestler black velvet paintings. It's popular, so expect to wait alongside the young Cap Hill hipsters, who can't get enough of the humongous burritos, tacos, quesadillas, or nachos paired with sensational cumin-lime sour cream. If you have a complaint, tell it to the customer comment card safely imbedded under the glass tabletop. Bimbo's is attached to the equally get-down Cha Cha Lounge, where the same crowd hangs in a cigarette haze. It's got the same mood and music as Bimbo's, plus it serves great margaritas with Patron tequila, no bottled mixes, and no processed ingredients. *$; MC, V; no checks; lunch, dinner every day; full bar; no reservations; street parking; map:J1* &

Bis on Main / ★★

10213 MAIN ST, BELLEVUE; 425/455-2033

A warm host well known from his years at Pioneer Square's Il Terrazzo Carmine, Joe Vilardi has his little 15-table bistro in Old Bellevue just the way he wants it: sleek, tasteful, consistent—a *soupçon* French, *un poco* Italian with burgers and a tuna melt available at lunch. With its putty-colored walls and good art, this is a neighborly respite from the franchised places so typical of the Eastside—and it's drawing a well-dressed, well-off business and social crowd. Nothing on the dinner menu is too challenging, but everything is perfectly executed and expertly served, such as lamb roulade stuffed with spinach, hazelnuts, and mushrooms braised in red wine and finished with mustard. Mr. V's generous and crisp Dungeness crab cakes take you fondly back to the late 20th century when this dish was on every dinner menu in town. The accompanying garlic tartar sauce and coleslaw tossed with apple cider vinaigrette are especially good. Dredge enough crusty bread through the brandy peppercorn sauce bathing pan-seared veal sirloin, and dessert becomes irrelevant. *$$; AE, DC, DIS, JCB, MC, V; checks OK; lunch Mon–Fri, dinner Mon–Sat; beer and wine; reservations recommended; self parking; www.bisonmain.com; map:HH3* &

Bistro Pleasant Beach / ★★

241 WINSLOW WY W, BAINBRIDGE ISLAND; 206/842-4347

Mediterranean, Moroccan, and Northwest flavors mesh at Hussein and Laura Ramadan's classy landmark for islanders that's a destination for mainlanders too. Flower boxes edge the brick patio, doubling the dining space and providing the most sought-after fair-weather tables on the island. Inside, it's sort of postmodern Bedouin: pretty and casual, done in shades of olive, mango, and deep red and filled with contemporary art. For appetizers, try Mediterranean mussels in a creamy sauce infused with lemongrass, Thai basil, cream, and Moroccan spices. Dip tender skewers  of lamb in rich curried peanut sauce fragrant with coriander. Gourmet pizzas fired over applewood in the open kitchen's brick hearth come with toppings such as buffalo mozzarella, lamb sausage, pears, Gorgonzola, or sweet onions. Fresh seafood frolics in a provençal-style tomato-based stew infused with pepper, saffron, and orange zest. Honey and cracked pepper glaze succulent boneless smoked country chicken. The shareable-size desserts, such as the tiramisu parfait—cake, mocha mousse, and whipped cream drizzled with Kahlúa and chocolate sauce—are hard to pass by. *$$; AE, MC, V; checks OK; lunch, dinner Tues–Sun; beer and wine; reservations recommended; self parking* &

Bizzarro Italian Cafe / ★★

1307 N 46TH ST, WALLINGFORD; 206/545-7327

The atmosphere gets more bizarre every year, but the food and service have gotten better. The deliberately clap-trappy, unavoidable decor has always separated this place from the herd of neighborhood Italian joints. The rooms are jammed with framed crazies and eccentric kitsch, such as the red dining table with silver and glassware hanging upside down from the ceiling. The food, always a little uneven, is more reliable these days, as if the mad Italian with the nutty hair in the ads is mellowing with age. Well loved are the steamed mussels in white wine and fresh oregano, as well as the sesame-crusted seared tuna salad with citrus mint vinaigrette. The large lamb shank, served with baked polenta triangles, is falling off the bone. Order the Forest Floor Frenzy and you'll get a melange of shiitakes, portobellos, walnuts, and roasted garlic tossed with rigatoni in sherry cream. The most bizarre thing about Bizzarro may be that the locals who used to come with out-of-towners to show off the wacky interior now also come for the food. *$$; AE, DIS, MC, V; checks OK; dinner every day, brunch Sat–Sun; beer and wine; no reservations; street parking; map:FF7* &

Black Pearl / ★★

7347 35TH AVE NE, WEDGWOOD; 206/526-5115
14602 15TH AVE NE, SHORELINE; 206/365-8989

This is one of the busiest neighborhood restaurants in the city. Many local folks don't wait for tables—takeout and home delivery accounts for about 60 percent of the Pearl's business. One of the cooks madly pumping groceries is Marlene Chang, who, with husband Ray, opened the Black Pearl as Panda's with partners more than 10 years ago. They've been going strong ever since. The housemade, hand-rolled noodles that distinguish this place shouldn't be missed. Special Chow Mein's plump and plentiful signature noodles are tossed with shrimp, chicken, beef, and seven different vegetables. The oolong tea–steamed sea bass slices are aromatically steamed with squiggles of tea leaves, served knee deep in their own fragrant juices. Another house specialty is shrimp-stuffed tofu; these plump, golden brown, fried tofu pillows are full of shrimp cake in an oyster sauce with green onions: a thin, soft wrap of tofu outside, crispness saturated with saucy, savory shrimpness inside. The diverse bunch of young servers are helpful in guiding the newcomer. *$; AE, MC, V; checks OK; lunch Mon–Sat, dinner every day; full bar; reservations for 6 or more recommended; street parking; map:EE6* &

Blue Onion Bistro / ★★★☆

5801 ROOSEVELT WY NE, UNIVERSITY DISTRICT; 206/729-0579

Lodged in a 1950s tchotchkes–filled 1930s-era gas station, chef Scott Simpson and co-owner/chef Susan Jensen cook imaginative American food and serve it with verve at this U District bistro. The menu is filled with items such as Plain Jane Salad and Some Kind of Soup or smart-aleck admonishments including "No Crying Over the Small Wine List. Eat More!" But the jokes stop when the food arrives. It's full-flavored, imaginative New American fare with classic dishes that don't take themselves too seriously. The Blue Salad, a meal in itself, combines romaine, smoked chicken, tart apples, and blue cheese. Chicken, glazed with a citrusy hibiscus sauce, is served with braised cabbage and warm potato salad. Dr. Scott's Maple Duck is medium-rare breast with a sweet maple syrupy sauce flavored with Cajun sausage and a pillar of fresh cooked spinach. The creamy tuna casserole is a rich affair, the kind you wish your mother could've made. The chicken pot pie comes in a fluffy housemade puff pastry with smoked chicken. Jensen is an accomplished baker and pastry chef—her robust herbed dinner rolls are served warm in an Easter basket and her desserts, posted on a blackboard, change regularly. *$$; MC, V; checks OK; lunch Tues–Fri, dinner Tues–Sun; beer and wine; reservations recommended; self parking; map:FF7* &

BluWater Bistro / ★★

1001 FAIRVIEW AVE N, LAKE UNION; 206/447-0769

By night this Lake Union waterside bistro draws a youngish bar crowd—it reportedly has the latest last call on the lake. Lunch and dinner hours are jumping too, with nearby office workers and well-heeled neighbors who go for the reasonably priced American bistro menu served on the lakeside patio or by the fire in drippy weather. Chef Peter Levine adds innovative touches to familiar foods: glazing barbecued baby back ribs with a chipotle-spiked honey; brushing salmon with ancho chile, lemon, and honey; and rubbing chicken satay with jerk seasonings and pairing it with pineapple jicama relish. Salads are fresh and large—the crab Louis–style seafood salad is loaded with not only crab but bay shrimp and/or grilled fish of the day. Steaks are a specialty and, when matched with a zinfandel demi-glace and housemade mashers, well worth ordering. *$$; AE, DC, MC, V; no checks; lunch, dinner every day; full bar; reservations required for large parties; pay lot parking; www. bluwater.com; map:D1* &

Boat Street Cafe / ★★

909 NE BOAT ST, UNIVERSITY DISTRICT; 206/632-4602

It looks like an old shed and though it's not easy to find, this is no Seattle secret—people line up to get in, especially for weekend brunch. Don't be fooled by the slate-topped tables, bare concrete floors, wax-dripped wine bottles, and work lights clamped to wires overhead. The bright, airy room was once a machine shop, but the menu is sophisticated country French, and when the windows are open to the flowering courtyard garden, it's easy to picture yourself in Provence. For lunch or brunch, there are summery provençal salads and sandwiches made with crusty baguettes from Le Fournil filled with thick slices of chicken, fresh basil, and smoked mozzarella or roasted sweet red peppers and caramelized onions. French hard-cooked eggs are baked *en casserole* with fresh spinach, herbed bread crumbs, and Parmesan. Come early for the soufflé-like red bell pepper, basil, and cheese *strata*, made only once and served until it's gone. For dinner there may be herb-rubbed pork tenderloin with a complex blackberry wine sauce or boneless Normandy chicken breast in a hard-cider cream sauce. For a sweet finish there's amaretto-soaked bread pudding with rum butter cream. *$$$; MC, V; checks OK; lunch Tues–Fri, dinner Wed–Sun, brunch Sat–Sun; beer and wine; reservations recommended; street parking; boatstreet@yahoo.com; map:FF7* &

Brasa / ★★★⯨

2107 3RD AVE, BELLTOWN; 206/728-4220

Brasa, translated from Portuguese, means "live coals," and you'll see why with its wide-open view of the kitchen and lively dining area. Owners Tamara Murphy and Bryan Hill have created one of the loveliest spaces and delicious kitchens in town. Dual-tiered and large at 170 seats, the restaurant's earthy decor is understated in dark woods, a gorgeous iron gate, and walls in warm pinks and oranges. Hill is a hardworking host who has seen to it that the service level is high without being obtrusive. The magic works: despite the formality usually associated with restaurants of this price range, diners are relaxed and the mood is joyful. Murphy is creating some of the most imaginative food and liveliest menus in town. The heady fragrance of Penn Cove mussels with curry, coriander, and coconut milk turns heads, as does hearty exotica such as suckling pig with chorizo, clams, and smoked hot paprika; or scallops with braised sweet Walla Walla onions, chive potato cake, a perfect little poached quail egg, and house-cured bacon. Hill's very readable wine list is global and well considered, with lots of bottles no one else has. The bar is a great stop for a glass of wine from the formidable by-the-glass list and affordable bar menu of tapas-like bites. *$$$; AE, DC, MC, V; checks OK; dinner every day; full bar; reservations recommended; self parking; seattle@brasa.com; www.brasa.com; map:F6* &

Burk's Cafe / ★★

5411 BALLARD AVE NW, BALLARD; 206/782-0091

Me-o-my-o! It's been nearly 20 years and this family-owned restaurant in Old Ballard remains not only a neighborhood favorite, but also a destination for outlanders hungry for shrimp étouffée, blackened fish, and real Cajun sausages. Owners "just-call-me-Burk" and wife Kay's little place easily survived the fading of the 1980s-Cajun if-it's-meat-let's-blacken-it madness mainly because their food's authentic and tasty. Three years ago, Burk added a smokehouse out back, sending the aromas of southern bayous—wood smoke and roasting meat—wafting into Ballard's Scandinavian sensibilities. He makes his own sausages—including the Cajun chaurice and Texas hot links. The stout, meaty ribs are not to be missed, and the barbecue combo lets you combine them with your choice of sliced beef, chopped pork, or sausage. The Dungeness crab filé gumbo is an aromatic melange that honors that venerable local shellfish, but the shrimp gumbo more than suffices if crab's out of season. Get such down-home staples as fried catfish, smoked chicken, and shrimp jambalaya in stultifying portions with slaw, red beans, and rice. *$; MC, V; checks OK; lunch, dinner Tues–Sat; beer and wine; no reservations; street parking; burk@burkscafe.com; map:EE8* &

Burrito Loco / ★★

9211 HOLMAN RD NW, CROWN HILL; 206/783-0719

Though it's hooked onto a Shell station, the old joke "Eat here—get gas" doesn't work with this wonderful Mexican family restaurant. The burritos are certainly some of the best in town. The huge Burrito Loco is jammed with meat, guacamole, salsa, cheese, rice, and beans; and there's also a *machaca* (shredded) beef burrito. Soups are a specialty, particularly menudo, the tripe-laden morning-after therapy, or the wonderful meatball soup. It's a sign of authenticity in any Mexican place to see tongue tacos—good even if your yuck-threshhold is too low to actually eat them. They're here, as are such specialties as *pipian*, chicken in a sauce made of crushed seeds (sesame, sunflower, pumpkin), a specialty from the owners' native Cuautla, Jalisco. There are numerous vegetarian possibilities, including quesadillas, fat chiles rellenos, and huevos rancheros available anytime. *$; DIS, MC, V; checks OK; lunch, dinner every day; beer and wine; no reservations; self parking; map:DD8* ᴋ

Cactus / ★★⯪

4220 E MADISON ST, MADISON PARK; 206/324-4140

If you show up around mealtimes, especially on weekends, they'll hand you a beeper to signal when they're ready to seat you. The wait's worth it, and the Madison Park neighborhood is a charming stroll. Cactus owes its popularity to the consistent quality, variety, and originality of its Mexican and Southwestern food. Bright painted tables and hanging peppers make it festive. It's fun to do just tapas for dinner. Order from the long list or opt for the daily assortment plate, which makes a great starter. Among the favorites are char-grilled asparagus spears with smoked Fresno chile mayo; empanadas stuffed with guava and Spanish cheese; and ceviche made with local salmon and *pico de gallo*. The usual Mexican entrees such as fajitas, enchiladas, and tacos are worth doing, but this is the place to try the more unusual dishes, including goat-cheese pollo relleno Chimayo enchilada—blue corn tortillas layered with chicken, chorizo, and green chile sauce; Jamaican chicken in a novel banana jerk sauce; or pork chunks roasted in banana leaves with spicy achiote, corn tortillas, and sizzling habanero escabeche. To put out the heat, there are plenty of fruit drinks, margaritas, and beers, but the wine list is limited. Three-milk Cuban flan is the must-have dessert. *$$; AE, DC, DIS, MC, V; checks OK; lunch Mon–Sat, dinner every day; full bar; reservations recommended; street parking; www. cactusrestaurant.com; map:GG7* ᴋ

Cafe Ambrosia / ★★★

2501 FAIRVIEW AVE E, EASTLAKE; 206/325-7111

Before carnivores dismiss this seriously vegan lakeside restaurant altogether, they should consider the yin and yang of entrees such as the Asian Napoleon, a layered stack of sugar snap peas, shiitake mushrooms, and shaved carrots sandwiched between phyllo sheets alongside a sesame-oiled bean pâté all sitting in a puddle of Thai basil–lemongrass sauce and scarlet swirls of beet oil. Just taste how creamy a soup can be, made with a purée of fennel and raw cashews, a leafy vine painted on its smooth surface with a drizzle of green fennel oil. The attention to detail is impressive and the food so delicious you may be tempted to eat vegan every day, especially if you can have desserts like the decadent chocolate fantasy, a layer cake with hazelnut filling and sluiced in chocolate ganache and cassis. And if you can't imagine Sunday brunch without bacon and eggs, you should taste the veggie faux sausages, scrambled tofu omelets, and waffles served here. *$$$; AE, DC, DIS, MC, V; no checks; dinner Mon–Sat, brunch Sun; beer and wine; reservations recommended; info@cafeambrosia.com; self parking; www.cafeambrosia. com; map:GG7* &

Cafe Flora / ★★½

2901 E MADISON ST, MADISON VALLEY; 206/325-9100

Cafe Flora's become a mecca for vegetarians and a comfortable experience for their carnivorous friends. The place has loosened up from its earlier fervid, boozeless self-righteousness, and the garden patio atmosphere makes for a lovely and casual place to dine. The portobello Wellington, with mushroom-pecan pâté wrapped in puff pastry, is still here, as are the Oaxaca tacos—corn tortillas stuffed with spicy mashed potatoes, cheddar, and smoked mozzarella. Salads, like everything here, reflect the seasons— a summer offering might be an organic nectarine salad with toasted pecans, orange marmalade dressing, and Bleu de Basque cheese. Vegans have items to choose from, and the kitchen will also adapt items on the menu. The short wine and beer list has plenty of domestics and imports that pair well with the lightness of the vegetarian fare. Never hesitate when the dessert tray makes the rounds. *$$; MC, V; checks OK; lunch Tues–Fri, dinner Tues–Sun, brunch Sat–Sun; beer and wine; reservations recommended; self parking; www.cafeflora.com; map:HH6* &

Cafe Juanita / ★★★½

9702 NE 120TH PL, KIRKLAND; 425/823-1505

Holly Smith bit off a big one. She bought Peter Dow's creekside Kirkland destination and promptly set about making a good restaurant great. She took down the chalkboards, expanded the menu, and made it her own. The quality's still here, but Smith's brought everything into the 21st century. Her training in the kitchens at Dahlia Lounge and Brasa shows in her carefully calculated seasonal menus that pay homage to the Mediterranean but are rooted in the Northwest. To create her simple, elegant cuisine, she gets the best regional ingredients or makes her own, as in Penn Cove mussel tagliatelle with her own bacon and sweet cicely—wild anise grown in the new kitchen garden outside the dining room windows. She features a different whole-roasted fish daily, and a rib-eye chop with a Reggiano Parmesan fonduta as rich as one of her desserts—for example, the Valrhona Chocolate Truffle Cake with espresso gelato and butterscotch. The carefully considered wine list has lots of Italian bottles, with a fair Northwest representation and a range for varied pocketbooks and tastes. *$$$; AE, MC, V; local checks only; dinner Tues–Sun; full bar; reservations recommended; street parking; map:DD4* &

Cafe Lago / ★★★

2305 24TH AVE E, MONTLAKE; 206/329-8005

The warm, bustling little gem near the Montlake Bridge is filled every night by locals who have come to expect some of the most consistently wonderful, unpresumptuous Italian fare in town from chef/owners Jordi Viladas and Carla Leonardi, who share cooking and child-rearing duties night by night. Start with the antipasto plate, stacked with eggplant, bruschetta with *olivata* (a purée of black olives), goat cheese, roasted peppers, mozzarella, roasted garlic bulbs, prosciutto, and Asiago cheese (the plate is also available meatless). City of Seattle Eggplant—grilled eggplant wedges marinated in olive oil, tomato, *balsamico*, and garlic, with a wedge of Gorgonzola—is served with thick slices of country Italian bread from La Panzanella. Also fine is the caponata, a compote of eggplant, olives, capers, and garlic served with grilled bruschetta. The lasagne is so popular, it's suggested you order it before 8pm to make sure it isn't already sold out. Made with pasta sheets so thin they are almost transparent, layered with ricotta and béchamel, the effect is so surprisingly light it's like a soufflé. Try one of the thin-crust wood-fired pizzas, perhaps one with *salsiccia*, roasted red peppers, marinara, and fontina. Jordi's wood-fired grill turns out a New York steak marinated in *basalmico* and herbs, covered with Gorgonzola, grilled onions, and radicchio. Finish up with a slice of Carla's chocolate truffle cake served in a puddle of espresso *crema inglese*. *$$; AE, DC, DIS, MC, V; checks OK; dinner Tues–Sun; full bar; reservations recommended; street parking; map:GG6* &

Cafe Nola / ★★☆

101 WINSLOW WY E, BAINBRIDGE ISLAND; 206/842-3822

Popularized by sisters Melinda Lucas and Mary Bugarin, Cafe Nola is now run by spouses Kevin and Whitney Warren, who bought the small, sunny corner cafe in 1999. Customers haven't suffered from the change of ownership. Formerly a sous-chef at Marco's Supperclub in Seattle,

Kevin creates pleasingly eclectic dishes. Popular with lunch crowds are hearty soups—from roasted eggplant to black bean portobello—and the grilled salmon sandwich dressed with seasonal greens and sturdy Essential Bakery bread. Dinner hour brings forth such fare as Sichuan ribs basted with hoisin-pineapple sauce and sweet potato fries; pan-seared scallops served over yellow corn grit cakes with roasted pepper–garlic sauce; and not-to-miss desserts, such as the triple-layer chocolate hazelnut torte. *$$; MC, V; checks OK; lunch Mon–Fri, dinner Wed–Sun, brunch Sat–Sun; beer and wine; reservations recommended; street parking* &

Calcutta Grill / ★☆

15500 SIX PENNY LN, BELLEVUE; 425/793-4646

Calcutta is a golfing term, so it will come as no surprise (to golfers at least) that this isn't a curry house but, rather, the clubhouse restaurant at the spectacular Golf Club at Newcastle. The stunning view from high atop a bluff southeast of Seattle includes Lake Washington, the downtown skyline, and the jagged Olympic Mountains. The food in this castle-like edifice is adequate and a little pricey—everything is well prepared, with no postmodern dinner-house cliché left unturned—such as steamed sea bass with soy-ginger vinaigrette, seared rare ahi with wasabi mashed potatoes, or vegetable risotto. The smoky prime ribs or the lamb rack, served with the requisite garlic mashers or polenta, respectively, are as good as it gets. As one reviewer put it, "The disappointments aren't fatal." The regular wine list carries mostly domestic bottles, with quite a few under $30 and several poured by the glass. A reserve list has prices in the three figures for its premium selections. Kids are catered to at the popular Sunday brunch buffet, complete with carved meat, crepe, and omelet stations. The Wooly Toad Cigar Bar has a dress code—no blue denim permitted, and check with management for collar regs and proper pant and skirt lengths. *$$$; AE, DC, DIS, MC, V; checks OK; breakfast Tues–Sun, lunch, dinner every day, brunch Sun; full bar; reservations recommended; self parking; cammyshepard@newcastle.com; www.newcastlegolf.com; map:JJ3* &

Calypso Caribbean Kitchen / ★

7917 ROOSEVELT WY NE, MAPLE LEAF; 206/525-5118

Here's a happy little neighborhood joint that tries (mostly successfully) to reflect the Caribbean colonizers and immigrants whose cultural threads are woven together in the food of these islands. To the backbeat of *soca* music and reggae—and even calypso—chef/owner Paul Decker puts out such favorites as Cuban black bean soup and Jamaican jerked meats and seafood. Decker's grandmother was from Trinidad, and though he honors her with some of the recipes she handed down, his kitchen sails around the archipelago to Jamaica, Cuba, Curaçao, Puerto

Rico, and all over the West Indies. He serves bright red conch chowder when the shellfish is available, which is often, though conch is a rare find in restaurants in this clam and crab town. If he's got it, go for it—it's spectacular with vegetables and a fragrant layer of sherry. Another interesting starter is Keshy Yena, a baked-to-bubbling dish of Edam cheese, shrimp, raisins, and olives, which arrives with toasted rounds of French bread for dipping. The preplated dinner salad, lettuce with some uninspired veggies such as grated carrots, is disappointing, but mango-champagne dressing nearly makes up for it. As a main dish, jerk-spiced mango chicken breast finished with a fiery mango chutney and coconut milk sauce is a big favorite with regulars. *$; DIS, MC, V; checks OK; dinner Tues–Sun; beer and wine; no reservations; self parking; map:FF7* ⅁

Campagne / ★★★★
Cafe Campagne / ★★★

86 PINE ST (INN AT THE MARKET), PIKE PLACE MARKET; 206/728-2800
1600 POST ALLEY, PIKE PLACE MARKET; 206/728-2233

Linen tablecloths, tiny vases of flowers, and wall space dedicated to wine bottles sets the French countryside mood in a very urban setting. In a courtyard near Pike Place Market, Campagne takes its cue from the cuisine of southern France. Owner Peter Lewis (one of the city's most gracious hosts) and very capable servers ensure that you dine with grace *and* gusto. Chef Daisley Gorden's large menu is a sunny French canvas using Northwest pigments from the palette of the market. Northwest and French influences meet amorously in dishes such as steamed halibut with fingerling potatoes, sweet Walla Walla onion, and artichokes on a salad of *picholine* olives; or the grilled king salmon on an English pea and basil risotto. Housemade charcuterie includes a skillfully made lamb sausage. The dessert chef haunts the market as well, gathering local fruits and berries for tarts, ice creams, and granités; chocolate lovers can count on such delectables as twice-baked chocolate gâteau with white chocolate–mint ice cream. Not the least among the many joys of dining here is the inspired, carefully wrought wine list. A short late-night menu is served in the bar—which, not unlike France, is smoky and romantic.

Cafe Campagne, located just below its stylish sibling, offers patrons a slice of French cafe life morning, noon, and night in a newly expanded setting warmed by lots of cherry wood and dominated by an elegant counter. Breakfast and lunch run from *boeuf 'n' oeuf*, a Gallic steak and egg combo; bourbon-battered brioche French toast; and croque monsieurs to elegant salads and heartier entrees. Dinner might start with fabulously garlicky calamari persillade or lamb crepinettes, sausages roasted with fennel, red peppers, and rosemary. Try bistro favorites such as steak *frites* or succulent halibut with oyster mushrooms and sautéed escarole. *$$$, $$; AE, DC, MC, V; no checks; breakfast, lunch, dinner Mon–Sat,* *brunch Sun (Cafe Campagne), dinner every day (Campagne); full bar; reservations recommended; street parking; map:I7* &

Canlis / ★★★★

2576 AURORA AVE N, QUEEN ANNE; 206/283-3313

This old establishment steak house was literally and spiritually aloof from the Seattle restaurant scene for decades. Cantilevered above Lake Union on Queen Anne Hill, it has the best views of the lakes and the Cascades of any nonrevolving joint in town. A generation passed it by before Chris and Alice Canlis brought the restaurant into modern times by giving it a $1. 5 million revamp and hiring author and mega-chef Greg Atkinson. He's gradually transformed it into an exciting regional restaurant, pulling down lots of national acclaim—including a Top 50 rating from Gourmet magazine in 2001—in the process. Atkinson has kept the older clientele happy by retaining much of the old menu while attracting a younger bunch by reworking and seasonally enhancing the classic pan-Asian Canlis fare. The Dungeness crab cakes with orange butter sauce are perfect and spicy with fresh ginger; the fat Alaska weathervane scallops are barely cooked and set into little singing scallop shells with lime. There are wonderful salads here—we love the classic, oil-free Mrs. C. Salad with greens, strawberries, and fresh basil; and the famous copper broiler yields salmon, ahi, and New York cuts of Kobe beef. Atkinson has long cultivated local producers, so you'll find broiler items inventively balanced with kabocha squash with ginger and soy; roasted garlic flan; or the mighty baked potato that the Canlis menu shall forever include. Sommelier Shyn Bjornholm presides over the massive and much-lauded wine list which ranges from a $1,000 bottle to many options in the $30 range. The dress code of yore has eased a bit, but men are still asked to wear jackets. Expect to be treated like royalty and to pay accordingly in this beautifully delicious anachronism. *$$$$; AE, DC, DIS, MC, V; checks OK; dinner Mon–Sat; full bar; reservations required; valet parking; map:GG7* &

Carmelita / ★★★

7314 GREENWOOD AVE N, GREENWOOD; 206/706-7703

Kathryn Newmann and Michael Hughes transformed a dilapidated retail space into a theatrically lit, art-filled haven of color and texture (be sure to look up at the ceiling) and introduced vegetarian fine dining to the north end. Neighbors from Greenwood and Phinney Ridge embraced Carmelita from the beginning, and the sophisticated, seasonal vegetarian menu remains enticing. Chefs have come and gone, but the food quality rarely wavers. Start with the eggplant Rockefeller, a vegetarian version of the classic oyster dish with eggplant purée in little ramekins baked on rock salt and served with a spicy tomato marmalade. The little pizzas are great—especially grape pizza with goat cheese, blue cheese, grape halves, and walnuts. The wine list is short but interesting, as well as moderately priced with few bottles over $30. Teas, tisanes, juices, and a refreshing tamarind-ginger lemonade are best enjoyed in warm weather on the charming, plant-filled deck. *$$; MC, V; local checks only; dinner Tues–Sun; beer and wine; reservations recommended; street parking; carmaveggy@earthlink.net; www.carmelita.net; map:EE8* &

Cascadia Restaurant / ★★★

2328 1ST AVE, BELLTOWN; 206/448-8884

It's an elegant, spare, but luxurious setting in cherry-wood accents. An etched-glass wall between the dining room and kitchen has water sluicing through it like rain against a window in our soggy clime. Eat with French flatware from Limoges china and sip out of handblown glassware. Chef-owner Kerry Sear uses indigenous foods and flavors of "Cascadia," the region he defines as between the Pacific Ocean and Montana and as far south as northern California. Prepare to spend a bundle here on such exotica as wild salmon on cedar fronds or white-truffled partridge baked in hay. Washington beefsteak in a tart crab-apple glaze is served with mustard vegetables and garlic fries. Food presentation can border on the precious, with such kitsch as "Kerry's Designer Soup in a Can," soup du jour such as roast tomato bisque in a little Campbell's soup can with a house-made cracker for a lid. Choose from four menus—"Wild & Gathered," "Decidedly Northwest," etc.—or from one of the seven-course tasting menus. Sear has installed a lower-priced cafe menu, which is served in the bar or outside on the busy First Avenue sidewalk. The wine list has mostly premium bottlings; there's a fair representation from the Northwest. The sommeliers are especially helpful. *$$$$; AE, DC, DIS, MC, V; no checks; dinner Mon–Sat; full bar; reservations recommended; valet parking; (allison, stacy, or jake)@cascadiarestaurant.com; www.cascadiarestaurant. com; map:G7* &

Cassis / ★★★

2359 10TH AVE E, CAPITOL HILL; 206/329-0580

This comfortable and romantic nook on the north side of Capitol Hill hums with a strong neighborhood following, but the moderately priced, well-executed French bistro fare is worth a trip across town. Dressed in warm yellows and browns, the room is thoughtfully portioned for privacy. Gallic classics including cassoulet, coq au vin, boeuf bourguignonne, calf's liver, pan-roasted capon, and steak with a tall haystack of perfect frites will put you in mind of the last time you strolled the Left Bank, or at least allow you to imagine that you once did. Desserts range from kid pleasers such as oeufs à la neige, floating islands of poached hazelnut meringue in a nutty custard, to a very grown-up goat-cheese tart in a port-kissed rhubarb coulis. P. S. There's a nifty little wine list and a small bar just made for sipping pastis. *$$; AE, MC, V; local checks only;*

dinner every day; full bar; reservations recommended; self parking; reservations@cassisbistro.com; www.cassisbistro.com; map:GG6 &

Chandler's Crabhouse and Fresh Fish Market / ★★☆

901 FAIRVIEW AVE N, SOUTH LAKE UNION; 206/223-2722

Chandler's is quintessential Seattle, due in part to the view of Lake Union with its boats and seaplanes coming and going, the lights of Queen Anne Hill in the distance, and the cross section of Seattle types and tourists at the bar and in the dining room. Though not terribly imaginative, the menu offers an old-fashioned gastronomic geography lesson on Puget Sound with a variety of local oysters, clams, and mussels, not to mention the wide selection of fresh fish. There's a sizable fresh sheet every day with a decent choice of salmon, such as the cedar-planked ginger smoked king. Crab? They've got it: Dungeness, king, blue, stone, rock, and sometimes even giant Tasmanian. It's served in crab cakes, sushi, salads, stuffed into other seafoods, in soup with whiskey, or simply cracked. The service is impersonal but highly adequate. The extensive wine list is heavy on the Northwest labels. Even the desserts have a local tang, with fruits in season. *$$$; AE, DC, MC, V; local checks only; lunch Mon–Fri, dinner every day, brunch Sat–Sun; full bar; reservations recommended; valet parking; jmesler@schwartzbros. com; www.chandlers.com; map:D1* &

Chez Shea / ★★★
Shea's Lounge / ★★★☆

94 PIKE ST, 3RD FLOOR, PIKE PLACE MARKET; 206/467-9990

Romance is always on the menu at this Seattle gem tucked on the top floor of the Corner Market Building, allowing a view through the grand arched windows of Elliott Bay and beyond. Dinner at Chez Shea is a prix-fixe affair, with three of the four courses preset and a choice of five entrees. As they have since Sandy Shea opened the place in 1983, the menus reflect the bounty of the season, employing ingredients fresh from the market stalls below. A summer meal might begin with a savory tart that brings together Walla Walla sweet onion, ricotta, Oregon blue cheese, and peach vinaigrette on a lighter-than-a-cloud pastry. The soup course may be a bisque of roasted corn tangy with ancho chiles and lime crème fraîche, or butternut and kabocha squash hinting of coconut milk and lemongrass, crowned with a Kaffir lime gougère. Entree selections usually include fish, meat, game, and a vegetarian option along the lines of pan-roasted wild king salmon with blueberry salsa; herb-crusted rack of lamb served with big white cannellini beans; or semolina gnocchi with parmigiana and a smooth saffron tomato sauce. Service is always sure and gracious. Shea's Lounge is a sexy bistro wed to Chez Shea by a common door. The menu offers about a dozen Mediterranean-accented dishes. A layered chicken and mushroom gâteau and herb crepes with creminis and fontina stand out, as do the superb pizzas and vivid salads. The perfect place to meet a friend for a little something before or after an evening on the town. *$$$, $$; AE, MC, V; no checks; dinner Tues–Sun; full bar; reservations recommended (Chez Shea); valet and self parking; map:J8*

Chinoise Cafe / ★★

12 BOSTON ST, QUEEN ANNE (AND BRANCHES); 206/284-6671
Chinoise makes lots of people happy in the upper Queen Anne Hill restaurant vortex—not an easy crowd to please. Eclectically but assuredly Asian, it's a place for Vietnamese salad rolls, Japanese sushi, Thai stir-fries, Chinese pot-stickers, and noodles from all of the above. The synthesis of cuisines and quality of the food quickly fill up tables nightly, despite the speedy—some say rushed—service. The starter *tara kasu*—black cod marinated in sake lees and broiled—is rich and savory; the spicy shrimp–green papaya salad with tomato lime fish sauce is tangy and exotic. Have the generous chicken Moshu (usually known as mu-shu), a wonderful stir-fry to be rolled up in little Chinese tacos with plum sauce for salsa. The sushi is a little more primitive than at some of the more upscale bars in town, but it's good and the price is definitely right. Chinoise on Madison (2801 E Madison St, Madison Valley; 206/323-0171) is calmer, reflecting that quieter neighborhood. It has a somewhat larger menu that ventures farther into the "pan" part of pan-Asian. Try the broiled five-spice Cornish hen or the sensational fish of the day, served with Chinese long beans in a tangy tamarind-basil oyster sauce. The Chinoise Cafe (610 5th Ave S, Chinatown/International District; 206/254-0413) is in the new Uwajimaya Village, an Asian food and import mall. It has an enlarged sushi list and some Korean dishes, and serves baseball fans before and after games at nearby Safeco Field. *$; AE, DC, DIS, MC, V; no checks; lunch Mon–Fri, dinner every day; full bar; no reservations; street parking; map:GG8* &

Chinook's at Salmon Bay / ★★

1900 W NICKERSON ST, INTERBAY; 206/283-4665
It's big, busy, and formulaic, but the Anthony's folks (see review) are using the right bait here at their showplace in the heart of Fisherman's Terminal. The light-industrial decor—high ceilings, steel countertops, visible beams, and ventilation ducts—is secondary to the bustle of the working marina outside the big windows. The Anthony's group owns its own wholesale fish business, so count on the fish being immaculately fresh. And count on the menu-standard oyster stew being creamy, with wonderful chunks of yearling Quilcene oysters throughout. The daily special sheet is the place to be, with offerings such as wild king salmon charred with sun-dried tomato-basil butter; perfectly cooked ling cod; or garlic-baked prawns with lemon and gremolata. There's a great all-you-

can-eat tempura bar—don't miss the fat, tender *panko*-coated onion rings. For dessert, try the warm wild-blackberry cobbler if you haven't already overdosed on the warm focaccia brought to you in baskets by friendly servers. *$$; AE, MC, V; checks OK; breakfast Sat–Sun, lunch, dinner every day; full bar; no reservations; self parking; chinook@ anthonysrestaurants.com; map:FF8* &

Chutneys / ★★

519 1ST AVE N, QUEEN ANNE (AND BRANCHES); 206/284-6799
Chutneys has a menu that can suffer from being too large and trying to please too many people. In these reliable neighborhood restaurants, head for the steady and hearty Indian dishes and stay away from the salads. Two reliable choices are the toasted coriander-and-paprika-dusted calamari with coconut/tamarind chutney and the curried mussels with cashew curry–wine sauce. Entrees can be ordered with varying degrees of heat, to be chased with an Indian beer; a mug of milky, cardamom-infused tea; or a mango lassi, a sweet smoothie. Try the lamb medallions marinated in saffron yogurt and roasted in the tandoori, the superhot vertical clay oven, or the spinach mushroom chicken breast and the tandoori chicken in brilliant pomegranate curry. Don't forget the Indian breads, such as the Kabuli naan stuffed with nuts, raisins, and cherries. Chutneys Grille on the Hill (605 15th Ave E, Capitol Hill; 206/726-1000) is a more laid-back sister than the Queen Anne branch or the bustling Chutneys Bistro (Wallingford Center, 1815 N 45th St; 206/634-1000). *$; AE, DC, DIS, MC, V; checks OK; lunch, dinner every day; full bar; reservations recommended; street parking; map:GG8* &

Coastal Kitchen / ★★

429 15TH AVE E, CAPITOL HILL; 206/322-1145
Peter Levy and Jeremy Hardy—of University Village's Atlas Foods, Queen Anne's 5 Spot Cafe, and Wallingford's Jitterbug Cafe (see reviews)—always invent restaurants with humor and an interesting idea. Coastal Kitchen's idea is coastal foods in general, but southern American ones in particular. This provides almost unlimited possibilities, though they're far from all being explored here—as a matter of fact, there are a few less coastlines represented since we last visited. We're still swept away to the Louisiana Gulf with Satchmo's Red Beans and Rice or the andouille sausage sandwich, or to Baja with the fried yuca (cassava) puffs stuffed with Manchego cheese. Neighbors flock in for breakfast, served all day with smoked salmon omelets, hash browns, and corn griddle cakes, as well as for the beer, pupus, and Key lime pie. *$$; MC, V; local checks only; breakfast, lunch, dinner every day; full bar; reservations recommended; street parking; www.chowfoods.com; map:HH6* &

Coho Cafe / ★★☆

8976 161ST AVE NE, REDMOND; 425/885-2646
6130 E LAKE SAMMAMISH PKWY, ISSAQUAH; 425/391-4040

This fish-themed restaurant in a suburban mall is long on ambition, if somewhat short on inspiration. The formula of adequate-to-competent food, a generous, well-priced drink, and speedy table service, however, seems to be clicking. This joint is jumping—you may be handed a beeper for a wait of up to 45 minutes at peak dinner hours. Cute metal cutouts of happy fish and crooked forks are everywhere, and the food is fetched by a perky, young, well-trained waitstaff. The fresh sheet, changed weekly, is a good place to start—a piece of wild sockeye is crusted with porcinis and served with a good toasted walnut spaetzle. The featured wood-grilled skewer of prawns with soba noodles is in a soy-sake vinaigrette. Desserts here are deliciously frivolous, such as the chocolate peanut butter tart with shortbread and caramel sauce. *$$; AE, MC, V; local checks only; lunch, dinner every day, brunch Sun (Redmond only); full bar; reservations recommended; self parking; map:EE1, JJ1* &

Crabpot Restaurant and Bar / ★

1301 ALASKAN WY/PIER 57, WATERFRONT; 206/624-1890
2 LAKE BELLEVUE DR, BELLEVUE; 425/455-2244

It's not exactly Big Easy–authentic, but Crabpot restaurants all serve up, well, pots of fresh seafood and above-average cooking with a pleasantly low-key Cajun twist. Try a special, such as a fish burger or a crab cake sandwich and a bowl of clam chowder, or, if you've really got a seafood jones, one of the "Seafeasts," prix-fixe seafood extravaganzas for two or more for which these joints are famous. There are combinations with varied prices and amounts of clams, mussels, crab, oysters, shrimp, lobster, andouille sausage, red jacket potatoes, and corn on the cob. Whichever one you choose will be dumped on your butcher paper–covered table. You strap on a bib, grab a mallet, and have at it. This can be great fun, especially with larger parties and children (kids get their own menu). The Eastside location is on Lake Bellevue (more pond than lake), and the deck is where you want to be. *$$; AE, DC, DIS, MC, V; no checks; lunch, dinner every day; full bar; no reservations; street parking; map:J9, HH3* &

Cyclops / ★★

2421 IST AVE, BELLTOWN; 206/441-1677

We were afraid we'd lost the Cyclops when the building it was located in was bulldozed in favor of a luxury apartment complex, but artists-cum-restaurateurs Gina Kaukola and John Hawkley successfully transposed the feel of the hallowed artists hangout into its new digs in Belltown, fashioned in glittered Naugahyde and Formica-ed American Primitive. The

BURGERS, PIZZA, BAKERIES, AND BBQS . . . OH, MY!

Burgers

Burgers are an important institution in American dining, and Seattle, being a town of implicit taste, has a noble history of covering the bun with relish and aplomb. Phinney Ridge's **Red Mill Burgers** (312 N 67th St; 206/783-6362 and 1613 W Dravus St; 206/284-6363) is the recognized leader of the pack with its smoky, housemade mayo, awesome onion rings, and real ice cream shakes. On the other hand, the local fast-food icon is the citywide **Dick's Drive-in** (six locations, including the University District and Capitol Hill), with their instant service, legendary fries, and low prices. **Bing's Bodacious Burgers** (4200 E Madison St; 206/323-8623) in Madison Park and the **DeLuxe Bar & Grill** (625 Broadway Ave E; 206/324-9627) on Capitol Hill are for-sure stops where you can get grown-up burgers and a beer. **Scooter's Burgers** (5802 24th Ave NW; 206/782-2966) are big and juicy in Ballard. You won't find fries at Belltown's **Two Bells Tavern** (2313 4th Ave; 206/441-3050), but their fat and famous burger on sourdough has a cultish following. On the Eastside, add a fried egg or more cheese to the huge patty at Magic Johnson's **Fatburger** (17181 Redmond Wy, Redmond; 425/497-8809).

Pizza

Pizza lovers (and who isn't one?) are very subjective—usually loyal to the pies we ate growing up. Seattle pizza represents a lot of people's 'hoods. **Pagliacci's** Philadelphia-style pizza continues to be the city's all-around favorite—great whether you're into gourmet with sun-dried tomatoes and artichokes or plain with cheese and pepperoni. A call to their central delivery line (206/726-1717) will get you a pizza from the closest outlet. Hugely popular (for good reason) are two purveyors of thin-crust New York–style: Capitol Hill's **Piecora's NY Pizza & Pasta** (1401 E Madison St; 206/322-9411) and Maple Leaf's **New York Pizza Place** (8310 5th Ave NE; 206/524-1355). Get Chicago deep-dish pizza at Wallingford's **Pizza House** (2109 N 45th St; 206/547-3663), formerly My Brother's Pizza. Get gourmet thin-crust or deep-dish at Ballard's **Madame K's** (5327 Ballard Ave NW; 206/783-9710), in olden days a brothel. **Atlantic Street Pizza** (5253 University Way NE; 206/524-4432) serves thin-crust, gourmet pies to rock stars and long lines of other humans in the U District. On the East-

Jell-O molds of the original building are nowhere to be seen, but there's great art—a touching but mystical collage on a baking sheet pulled from a Cyclops oven in 1996 bearing the image of Elvis imprinted in carbon. Icons reign—Lava lamps, a Wilbur Hathaway portrait of Malcolm X in plastic breadbag clips, tikis, Buddhas, Our Lady of Guadalupe. A bald, middle-aged drag queen busses tables. They cook colorful dishes too, including pappardelle with wild mushrooms and duck confit or steamed

side, **Coyote Creek Pizza** (15600 NE 8th St, Bellevue; 425/746-7460) is in Cross-roads Mall, but its Southwest/Mediterranean pies have a rabid following with mall-rats and discriminating Kirklanders and Bellevue-ites.

Bakeries

Seattle bakeries aren't just bakeries anymore. They are lopping off slabs of their bread to make sandwiches and serving soup and luncheon fare. Even celeb chef Tom Douglas has opened **Dahlia Bakery** (2001 4th Ave; 206/682-4142) in Belltown, which serves walk-ins as well as his restaurants (Dahlia Lounge, Etta's Seafood, Palace Kitchen; see reviews). His crew makes sandwiches, dynamite chocolate chip cookies, and his famous coconut cream pie. The fine bread bakers at **Essential Baking** (1604 N 34th St; 206/545-0444) now serve soup, salads, and desserts in their Fremont cafe. **Le Fournil** (3230 Eastlake Ave E; 206/328-6523) is a classic French patisserie in Eastlake with incredible croissants. In Ballard, **Larsen Brothers Danish Bakery** (8000 24th Ave NW; 206/782-8285) has one of the largest cookie collections in town. In the Pike Place Market, **Le Panier Very French Bakery** (1902 Pike Pl; 206/441-3699) is where the French buy French bread, while **Three Girls Bakery** (1514 Pike Pl; 206/622-1045) is known for their cheese croissants and hearty sandwiches on Russian rye. And in Kirkland, **Hoffman's Fine Pastries** (226 Park Place Center; 425/828-0926) gets raves for its cakes.

BBQ

There are all kinds of barbecue, from the South to the Southwest, and each has its avid devotees. The debate never stops even in a Northwest town, but here are some of the undisputed top of the pits. SoDo's **Pecos Pit BBQ** (2260 1st Ave S; 206/623-0629) has weekday lunches with huge five-napkin BBQ sandwiches. Rainier Valley's **Jones BBQ** (3216 S Hudson St; 206/725-2728) is an adored hole-in-the-wall with Arkansas-Texas–style ribs, and there's great brisket and boneless pork at **Backdoor BBQ & Catering** (6459 California Ave SW; 206/932-7427) in West Seattle. On the Eastside, the popular **Dixie's BBQ** (11522 Northup Wy, Bellevue; 425/828-2460) serves up famous ribs and chicken and a hot sauce not for the faint of heart called "The Man," while **Armadillo BBQ** (13109 NE 175th St, Woodinville; 425/481-1417) has a funky decor and dry, smoky meats. *—Michael Hood*

trout with Thai red curry. The food can be inconsistent, however; stick with simpler fare such as pork verde enchiladas with a poblano chile sauce and you'll be happy. The lively bar with its martini culture and unyuppified crowd is definitely where it's at here. *$$; MC, V; no checks; breakfast Sat–Sun, lunch Tues–Fri, dinner every day; full bar; reservations recommended; street parking; www.cyclopsseattle; map:G8* &

Dahlia Lounge / ★★★★

1904 4TH AVE, DOWNTOWN; 206/682-4142

The trademark dining landscape of crimson, gold brocade, and papier-mâché fish lanterns hasn't changed in Dahlia's new dining room. It's part of chef/owner Tom Douglas's philosophy of keeping guests in comfortable zones while never letting them forget they're on the cutting edge. He succeeds in keeping an exuberant, informal, but global approach with finesse and consistency. The results make for predictably unpredictable menus and the most lighthearted serious food in town. Service reflects Douglas's democratic personality—knowledgeable and professional, never servile or snotty. Expect familiar dishes with innovative ingredients, such as a Tuscan bread salad with fresh mozzarella, luxurious lobster hot pot soup with rice noodles, or a rib-eye steak with acorn–fava bean succotash and squash blossom fritter. Dessert can be such down-to-earth yet cosmic delectables as a bag of doughnuts fried to order with mascarpone and raspberry, plum, and apricot jams or his signature coconut cream pie. Dahlia's move and the release of Douglas's long-awaited cookbook have put him and his restaurants—the others are Etta's Seafood and Palace Kitchen (see reviews)—into an even higher stratum. This is a Best Place that should be visited again and again by locals and visitors alike. *$$; AE, DC, DIS, MC, V; local checks only; lunch Mon–Fri, dinner every day; full bar; reservations recommended; valet parking; map:I7* &

Daniel's Broiler / ★★

809 FAIRVIEW PL N, SOUTH LAKE UNION (AND BRANCHES); 206/621-8262

This luxurious Schwartz Brothers reformatting of Benjamin's at the southernmost shore of Lake Union is a classic steak house, where we "meat" again in a masculine and well-appointed setting with copper, wood, and windows with splendiferous lake views. There's some seafood, such as an Australian lobster for $100 or artichoke heart-encrusted halibut, but the deal's definitely the meat. For example, the 2½-pound porterhouse, the huge bone-in herb-encrusted prime rib, or the 15-ounce veal chop with herbed jus. The beef's Midwestern corn-fed, selected from the top 2 percent of all U.S. graded beef, and priced accordingly. The New York cut with green peppercorn and Cognac sauce is quite good. Expect your meat to be cooked expressly to order in the space-age 1,800°F broilers. It's all accompanied by choice of garlic mashers or a baked potato the size of your shoe. If you can stand it, follow all this up with a warm, housemade apple tart with caramel sauce and vanilla ice cream. All three of these restaurants—the other two are in Leschi (200 Lake Washington Blvd; 206/329-4192) and in Bellevue's Seafirst Building (10500 NE 8th St; 425/462-4662)—serve big meat, done well—even if it's well-done. The great water views are very Northwest, the service is luxurious (though poor acoustics can discourage table talk), and the large and praiseworthy wine lists have a wide variety of prices. *$$$; AE, DC, DIS, MC, V; checks OK; lunch Mon–Fri, dinner every day; full bar; reservations recommended; valet parking; map:HH6* &

Doong Kong Lau / ★★

9710 AURORA AVE N, NORTHGATE; 206/526-8828

The Hakkas are called the "gypsies of China." Despite having been displaced and wandering throughout the world since the third century B.C., they've kept their food, language, and customs intact. Thankfully, Henry and Cindy Chen ended up on Aurora Avenue, opening their delicious restaurant in 1990. On the huge menu, the Hakka dishes are clearly marked and mixed in with a hundred or two from those of Sichuan, Hunan, and Canton Provinces. Even in familiar dishes, the flavors are a little different, a little surprising. The Hakkas preserve vegetables and combine them with meat as in *kau yuek*, sliced pork with preserved mustard greens, or stir-fried side pork (uncured bacon) with pickled cabbage and five-spice stuffed into little buns. Sautéed long beans are cooked perfectly—with pickled cabbage and garlic sauce. Chen achieves his flavors by using not only the pickled and preserved vegetables but also strong stocks, special seasonings, and no MSG or peppers. Northern dim sum is served every day, with the most choices on weekends. *$; AE, DC, DIS, MC, V; no checks; breakfast Sat–Sun, lunch, dinner every day; beer and wine; reservations recommended; self parking; map:DD7* &

Dragonfish Asian Café / ★★

722 PINE ST (PARAMOUNT HOTEL), DOWNTOWN; 206/467-7777

Dragonfish, the appealing hotel cornerstone across the street from the Paramount Theatre, caters to hotel guests, who may be stage stars, or their entourages, from shows playing the Paramount. The menu and format are amiable pan-Asian. Walls are colorfully hung with Japanese cartoons and baseball posters, and whimsically lined with *pachinko* machines. Two exhibition kitchens—a wok station and a robata grill—are part of the energetic ambience, and the menu specializes in small shareable plates. There's sushi, chicken pot-stickers, roasted-duck spring rolls, and crispy tofu pillows with dipping sauces of spicy peanut, sweet hot mustard, and caramel ginger. A favorite is the almond-crusted halibut tempura with its sesame-garlic aioli and black soy dipping sauce. The proximity of the Paramount draws an early dinner trade before performances, but the after-theater crowd sampling the late-night dinner menu gives the place its Broadwayesque energy. *$$; AE, DC, DIS, MC, V; checks OK; breakfast, lunch, dinner every day; full bar; reservations recommended; valet parking; www.dragonfishcafe.com; map:J4* &

Dulces Latin Bistro / ★★☆

1430 34TH AVE, MADRONA; 206/322-5453

Dulces, which means "sweets," is appropriately named. This sweet, romantic, nuevo Latino bistro with its tables set with crystal and napery is popular in its own zip code, but also lures diners from all over the city. "Latino" is rather broadly defined by chef Julie Guerrero—provincial French, Spanish, Italian, and regional Mexican flavors and dishes are featured and fused. Yes, there are green chicken enchiladas (green is the color of the tomatillo sauce, not the chicken), raviolis could come stuffed with red pepper or chorizo, the fat chiles rellenos have both Montrachet and Manchego cheeses, and sometimes you'll even find New England clam chowder. The Prawns Diabla are spicy with a scent of oranges; the paella Valenciana has fresh fish, plus a plethora of shellfish, chicken, and sausage, with a fragrant saffron rice. The Guadalajara-style carne asada, a marinated skirt steak served with quesadillas, is admirable. There's a place for cigar smokers thoughtfully distanced out back. And they didn't name this place "sweets" for nothing—try the extraordinary pecan pie, the *cajeta* (Mexican caramel) and chocolate tart, or the bread pudding of the day. *$$; AE, DC, DIS, MC, V; no checks; dinner Tues–Sat; full bar; reservations recommended; street parking; map:GG7* &

Earth & Ocean / ★★★

1112 4TH AVE (W SEATTLE HOTEL), DOWNTOWN; 206/264-6060

New downtown hotels nowadays have to be as designed as all get-out, have staff that look like supermodels, and have a serious restaurant on the ground floor. Or at least that's the style at the W Seattle Hotel, replete with sexy rooms and E & O, with award-winning chef Johnathan Sundstrom. He's great with regional and seasonal seafood and game, and has planetary sense and great buying power. The Yukon Gold potato soup is a simple and hearty blend of those superior potatoes and cream. For starters try the ragout of sweetbreads and bacon, the seared foie gras with salt-roasted white peach and savory herb madeleines, or the thin tuna carpaccio with its salty blob of paddlefish caviar. An entree of roasted squab with its juicy little legs and breasts is crusted with porcini dust and piled with morels and baby beets. Lunch features many items from the dinner menu, but don't miss; the lipidinous but gooey-good grilled three-cheese sandwich. The desserts by Sue McCown never miss; she loves the tussle of sweet and sour, as in her whimsical Snap Crackle Pop Cherry Pop Tart: tangy cherries in a crispy crust with lemon crème fraîche sorbet. The food can be brilliant, but sometimes it doesn't live up to the corporate public relations with tough meat or the occasional over-the-hill vegetable. Same with the service, which can be nice and pampering or snooty and absent. *$$$; AE, B, DC, DIS, JCB, MC, V; checks OK; breakfast*

every day, lunch, dinner Mon–Fri; full bar; reservations recommended;
valet parking; www.whotels.com; map:L6 &

El Camino / ★★

607 N 35TH ST, FREMONT; 206/632-7303

This little Mexican bar and grill in laid-back Fremont isn't so laid-back.
The bar jumps all night because of the hip location (and, in summer, its
packed deckside seating), reliably smart food from south of the border,
and, of course, the superb fresh-juiced margaritas. The dining room has
the requisite ceiling fan, ceramic tiles, wrought iron, and sequined saints
to go with the retro-schlock feel of this arty but rapidly changing neighborhood. Try the salmon with tamarind sauce or the fish tacos with green
rice. The grilled pork with pasilla chiles is succulent and spicy, as are the
mussels in a creamy ancho sauce. The ever-changing dessert menu will
probably include the signature pecan tart with Kahlúa, or coconut flan.
Both are great, but the traditional postprandial margarita is de rigueur.
$$; AE, MC, V; no checks; dinner every day; full bar; reservations rec-
ommended; street parking; map:FF8 &

El Gaucho / ★★★

2505 IST AVE, BELLTOWN; 206/728-1337

El Gaucho is a retro-swank Belltown remake of the '70s-era uptown
hangout with mink-lined booths, flaming shish kebabs, and blazing baked
Alaskas. The current version has dark, wide-open spaces where cooks
scurry at a wood-fired broiler and servers deliver impaled conflagrations
of meat to the well-heeled clientele. The bar crowd sips martinis as a piano
player noodles jazz riffs on a baby grand. It's a ripe spot in which to see
and be seen. Patrons seated at comfy banquettes in the theater-in-the-
round-style dining room share chateaubriand for two or custom-aged
steaks and honking baked potatoes with all the trimmings. Equally rich
menu offerings include an ostrich fillet, veal scaloppine, and venison
chops. Seafood lovers don't get short shrift either: they can dredge garlic
bread in buttery Wicked Shrimp, or suck saffron-scented broth from an
artful bouillabaisse. Bananas Foster is a decadent and anachronistically
sublime capper to the evening. The wine card is formidable, supplemented
by a premium reserve list. Serious imbibers will be heartened by the
lengthy single-malt Scotch list, and there are two (count 'em) coed cigar
lounges. The Pampas Room downstairs, open for dancing and drinking
on Friday and Saturday, offers the full El Gaucho menu. *$$$; AE, DIS,*
MC, V; checks OK; dinner every day; full bar; reservations recom-
mended; valet parking; www.elgaucho.com; map:FF8 &

El Greco / ★★☆

219 BROADWAY AVE E, CAPITOL HILL; 206/328-4604

Warm colors, linen napkins, and fresh flowers make this Mediterranean bistro a calm oasis amid the see-and-be-seen bustle of Broadway. Thomas Sokakas is Greek, and his menus draw heavily from his native land with such delectables as Greek salads, tzatziki, chicken souvlakia, and moussaka. Expect pleasing hummus and baba ghanouj, as well as fabulous dishes like the creamy, fennel-spiked arborio rice with five perfectly cooked prawns steamed in anise-laced ouzo or a wild mushroom ragout, an earthy mix of mushrooms and vegetables served with crisp, smoked-mozzarella potato cakes. There's also French coq au vin and sautéed crispy penne from Italy. The broad-windowed storefront is a popular place to be for brunch, served five days a week. And no wonder: its menu covers standard breakfast fare like eggs and pancakes as well as exotica like frittatas and feta scrambles. *$$; AE, MC, V; local checks only; dinner Tues–Sat, brunch Wed–Sun; beer and wine; reservations accepted; street parking; map:GG6* ⅋

El Puerco Lloron / ★☆

1501 WESTERN AVE, PIKE PLACE MARKET; 206/624-0541

This delicious-smelling place is as about as authentic as you might want to get when it comes to Tex-Mex restaurants in Seattle. There are pink and aquamarine walls, cutout tin lamps, and a lady handmaking tortillas in the dining room. The salsa is as good on the jukebox as it is on the tables. Pick up your food at the serve-yourself cafeteria line—then fight for a table along with the neighboring workers who line up for the inexpensive and tasty fare (and, in nice weather, jostle for the outside tables). Eat the tamales—they're always freshly steamed; the *taquito* plate with its sliced steak and soft tortillas is the most popular dish, though the *machaca* beef comes in a close second; the chiles rellenos are fat and juicy. Most everything is served with rice and beans. Grab a Mexican beer, and it's easy to pretend for a moment you're back in San Antone. *$; AE, MC, V; business checks only; lunch, dinner every day; beer and wine; no reservations; street parking; map:J8*

Elliott's Oyster House / ★★★

1201 ALASKAN WY/PIER 56, WATERFRONT; 206/623-4340

Here's classic fish-house fare with lots of innovative seafood alternatives served up in a sparkling redo of an old Seattle waterfront favorite. Designers envisioned a classic yacht when they spent $2 million on the remodeled setting best described as nautical but nice. The ferries pull out of the terminal next door, wowing not only tourists but locals who know Elliott's for its slurpable oysters, outside dining, and mastery of fresh seafood. Try one of the rich chowders—the creamy, pink-tinged Dungeness crab chowder with a touch of cayenne is fantastic. The iced shellfish extravaganzas serve two, four, or six people. There's a safe but seafood-friendly wine list that allows the undecided to select a trio sampler for tasting. The center-cut swordfish is firm yet tender, with a butter–macadamia nut sauce that's subtly perfect with this mild fish. The mesquite-grilled ahi tacos at lunch are kicked with mango, lime, and wasabi and wrapped in thick tortillas. It wouldn't be Seattle without Dungeness crab cakes, and these are exceptional, with rock shrimp and a crab beurre blanc blended with the juice of blood oranges. The Northwest cioppino includes cracked crab, scallops, salmon, Manila clams, Alaskan side-striped prawns, and Penn Cove mussels submerged in a dense herb- and saffron-scented tomato broth zingy with cayenne and red pepper. Dining at Elliott's is an inner-city pleasure cruise without leaving the dock. *$$$; AE, DC, DIS, MC, V; checks OK; lunch, dinner every day; full bar; reservations recommended; street parking; www. elliottsoysterhouse.com; map:H8* &

Etta's Seafood / ★★★
2020 WESTERN AVE, BELLTOWN; 206/443-6000
Flamboyant chef/entrepreneur Tom Douglas created this exuberant, hip seafood house and named it after his equally effervescent daughter. Etta's is in the same freewheeling style as its notable siblings, Dahlia Lounge and Palace Kitchen (see reviews). Seafood is perhaps what Douglas does best, and he does it with originality and a respectful light touch—nothing too weird or too precious. For starters there are small half-shelled oysters—*kumomotos* or Snow Creeks; mussels or clams in broth zesty with chorizo; and house-smoked salmon. Douglas's Dungeness crab cakes spiked with green tomato relish and his spice-rubbed pit-roasted salmon are Seattle's signature versions of these dishes. Lush desserts come from dessert central in the Dahlia Bakery. Lunch can be as simple as fish-and-chips with red cabbage slaw or something more complicated, such as chilled peanut noodles with lemongrass chicken skewers. Expect to wait for a seat in the small, conversation-friendly dining room or the other larger and much noisier noshery with bar and counter seating. *$$$; AE, DC, DIS, MC, V; local checks only; lunch, dinner every day, brunch Sat–Sun; full bar; reservations recommended; self parking; www.tom douglas.com; map:I8* &

Eva Restaurant and Wine Bar / ★★★
2227 N 56TH ST, GREEN LAKE; 206/633-3538
James Hondros took his inheritance from his beloved grandmother Eva and blew it on the old Brie & Bordeaux space in the Green Lake neighborhood across from the Luau Polynesian Lounge. He and his wife, chef Amy McCray, transformed that well-windowed room with warm wood and wall stencils into a bistro that'll hopefully be around for a while. It's not the decor that will keep you coming back, it's the food. McCray spent

years honing her skills at the Dahlia Lounge and Chez Shea, where she was lead chef. She also lured pastry chef JoAnna Cruz away from Sandy Shea, and the resulting kitchen chemistry is captivating palates across the city. Panfried oysters rolled in the crumbs of pappadams (Indian flatbread) and served with a raita sauce and cilantro pesto typifies the simplicity and originality of the menu. Or the light, smooth *cabrales* flan, a blue cheese blast offset with a tangy-sweet pear relish and anchored to the earth with a buttery walnut cracker. There are basic bistro entrees as well: grilled and roasted fish, steaks, and poultry. Cruz's desserts are flawless, and Hondros's well-chosen wine list has lots of bottles in the $35 range—and nearly a dozen good half-bottles. *$$; AE, MC, V; checks OK; dinner Tues–Sun; full bar; reservations recommended; street parking; map:FF7* ♿

Fandango / ★★★

2313 1ST AVE, BELLTOWN; 206/441-1188
Chef Christine Keff of Flying Fish (see review) went on one of her exotic trips—this time south of the border—and came home inspired enough to start another restaurant. Fandango, with its bright colors and sun-drenched-even-in-February decor, is a visually and culinarily capricious tour of Brazil, Colombia, Peru, Argentina, and Mexico. The kitchen's in the middle of the room and you can watch as a cook turns the tortillas that'll be brought warm to your table. There are enough *antojitos* (appetizers) for tapas dining, with choices including shrimp tostadas with avocado and habanero salsa, steamed Manila clams with linguiça and pasilla chiles, and Argentinean carpaccio with *chimichurri* sauce. There's hearts of palm or squash blossom soup and a salad with beets, chayote, watercress, and sausage. The entrees, such as roast suckling pig, seared duck, grilled tenderloin, and a fish taco platter with rockfish and good guac, are as macho as you'd want. There's also lighter fare: perfectly cooked sea scallops with almonds, oranges, and capers. The streetside bar has 50 tequilas, *mojito* that'll make you think you're Hemingway in Havana, and a late-night menu. Sit in the front dining room with its partial waterfront view and expect to be well taken care of by the friendly, well-trained staff. *$$; AE, DC, MC, V; checks OK; dinner every day; full bar; reservations recommended; street parking; www.fandangoseattle.com; map:G8* ♿

Figaro Bistro / ★★

11 ROY ST, QUEEN ANNE; 206/284-6456
With all the faux bistros around town, here's a real one. Co-owners Philippe Bollache, a native of Lyon, and Laurent Gabrel, a Parisian, are true Frenchmen, and Figaro Bistro has aptly become a haunt of opera and ballet aficionados before or after performances at the nearby Opera House. Try the wonderful baked Swiss-cheesy onion soup and the veal

Normandy—veal scallops with cream, apples, and Calvados. There are steak *frites*, of course, and coq au vin with wild mushrooms and fresh thyme. The Magret de Canard is a succulent duck breast pan-seared and finished with the fruitiness of crème de cassis and fresh black currants. The seafood here is not to be disregarded. *Au contraire*, the bouillabaisse is full of swimmers and shellfish in a hearty fish fumet. Coquilles St. Jacques, a classic cliché in lesser joints, is served here over angel hair pasta in an intensely flavored, creamy sauce with oyster mushrooms and leeks. And don't miss the crème brûlée—it seems to be pure cream. *$$; AE, DC, MC ,V; local checks only; dinner Tues–Sun; full bar; reservations recommended; valet parking; map:A6* ♿

Filiberto's Ristorante Italiano & Deli / ★

14401 DES MOINES MEMORIAL DR, BURIEN; 206/248-1944
This south-end treasure has been around since 1975. Mina Perry, the sixtysomething sister of the founder, does the cooking and runs the place with her husband, Ron. Old-timers flock in to play boccie ball in the court out back or to eat from the comforting and familiar menu featuring every mid-20th-century Italian American standard. The flavors are all here, and it's clean and cheery, if a little worn around the edges. Pizzas and calzones from the wood-fired oven are the best things from the kitchen. But try the Bucatini Amatriciana, housemade hollow spaghetti noodles with tomato, bacon, onions, and hot peppers, the veal Parmesan, or the housemade sausages with sautéed sweet peppers. A wall is racked with a large, well-priced, help-yourself selection of Italian wines. All in all, a tasty slice of Italo-Americana. *$$; AE, MC, V; local checks only; lunch Tues–Fri, dinner Tues–Sat; full bar; reservations recommended; self parking; map:NN7* ♿

5 Spot Cafe / ★★

1502 QUEEN ANNE AVE N, QUEEN ANNE; 206/285-7768
It always seems as if a party's going on at longtime neighborhood restaurateurs Peter Levy and Jeremy Hardy's places: Atlas Foods, Coastal Kitchen, and Jitterbug Cafe (see reviews). Indeed, food festivals celebrating cuisine of different global regions change the focus every three months or so. Visit the 5 Spot during the summer Baja! Festival and you'll find creative Mexican-style dishes that, if not exactly authentic, are scrumptious: tortilla soup with chicken and fresh-squeezed lime, for instance. Vegetarians will be happy with the Patata Torta starter, a wedge of baked, layered potato slices with onions and jalapeños served with a grilled corn salad and fantastic red pepper mayo. Favorites include the pork ribs with tamarind/garlic and the marlin tacos with lime-kissed guacamole. Regular lunch fare—burgers, Reuben sandwiches, halibut fish-and-chips—is also served. Breakfast, served until 3pm daily, is very popular. Don't miss standards such as huevos rancheros with black bean

chili or Red Flannel Hash with corned beef, potatoes, and, of all things, beets (don't knock it till you've tried it!). The flavors and fun of this place make up for the infernal cuteness of the language on the menus. *$; MC, V; local checks only; breakfast, lunch, dinner every day; full bar; reservations recommended; street parking; www.chowfoods.com; map:GG8 &*

Fleming's Prime Steakhouse & Wine Bar / ★★☆

1001 3RD AVE, DOWNTOWN; 206/587-5300

This is a national chain steak house—stray too far from steaks and you may be in trouble, as we were when we ordered the lobster and the swordfish—both were overcooked. The steaks are technically faultless, cut from corn-fed beef and skillfully cooked to order over very high heat. This southern California group's strategy is to appeal to women and couples in the steak-house segment of the restaurant market. They have mostly succeeded by keeping the prices lower than their downtown meat-pushing neighbors, and by softening the clubby masculine decor. Other than steaks, favorites are the tuna mignon cooked rare with a tomato vinaigrette and the luscious veal chop. But it's hit-and-miss with the salads and sides, which are sized for sharing—for example, potato choices include good garlic mashers and poor lyonnaise. Desserts are mundane, but all 100 wines on the list are available by the glass. *$$$; AE, DC, MC, V; checks OK; lunch Mon–Fri, dinner every day; full bar; reservations recommended; street parking; www.flemingsteakhouse. com; map:L6 &*

Flying Fish / ★★★☆

2234 1ST AVE, BELLTOWN; 206/728-8595

Flying Fish is a foodie's dream come true. That's because chef/owner Christine Keff not only knows and loves seafood but has created a place where everybody seems to want to be at the same time. At this popular spot, ultrafriendly staffers haul platters and plates to exuberant wine-imbibing diners. Order the small starter plates, two or three of which can make a meal. Entree choices range from lobster ravioli with yellow-foot mushrooms in a puddle of lobster velouté to a pile of crispy fried calamari with a hot-sweet honey jalapeño mayonnaise, from shrimp and chicken rice noodles with Thai green curry and shiitakes to grilled scallops in a creamy herb polenta served with sautéed mixed greens. Everything is achingly fresh and artistically presented. Keff encourages large parties to opt for the large sharing platters that are sold by the pound, such as the whole fried rockfish or her famous Sister-in-law Mussels with chile-lime dipping sauce. The wine list is expansive and accessible, with lots of Northwest and California offerings as well as tons of mid-range bottlings from around the world. This is where Seattle goes for seafood without the distraction of a waterfront view and all that goes with that—it's a place for travelers, not tourists. *$$; AE, DC, MC, V; local checks* *only; dinner every day; full bar; reservations recommended; street parking; www.flyingfishseattle.com; map:G8* &

The Four Swallows / ★★☆

481 MADISON AVE N, BAINBRIDGE ISLAND; 206/842-3397

The historic William Grow farmhouse, within walking distance of the ferry landing, houses the charming Four Swallows. Owner Mike Sharp manages the service in the eclectic dining room, while partner Gerry Ferraro does the cooking. The warren of mismatched rooms with funky floors, primitive antiques, and comfy rural tchotchkes is a very pleasant place to sit, and the efforts of the chef, with their Mediterranean overtones, are stellar. The starter list is varied enough to graze as dinner with glasses of wine. Mussels with saffron, leeks, tomatoes, and cream are magical, as are the braised artichokes and the beef carpaccio, while the antipasto plate is a generous collection of goat cheese; roasted garlic, pepper, and beets; mushrooms; and crostini. Entrees meet expectations, too. The rack of lamb with a rosemary port sauce comes with roasted figs and mashed potatoes. The crab cakes are served with a tangy lemon aioli; the clam linguine is a flavor blast with pancetta and lots of garlic. Large parties, couples, or singles (who might prefer the privacy of the clubby black-and-ivory bar) are equally at home in this elegant yet easygoing island eatery. *$$; AE, DC, DIS, MC, V; local checks only; dinner Tues–Sat; full bar; reservations accepted; street parking* &

Fremont Classic Pizza & Trattoria / ★★

4307 FREMONT AVE N, FREMONT; 206/548-9411

On any given night, this Fremont neighborhood classic, known for thin-crusted pizzas and simple pastas, has folks lined up for tables or takeout. It's easier getting a table than it used to be—owners Paul and Erin Kohlenberg, who opened their place in 1988, have expanded, doubling seating capacity with a second dining room and an easygoing patio. Unchanged is the casual romance of the place that works as well with families as it does with couples on dates. The service is friendly—many of the servers are longtime employees on a first-name basis with the patrons. Chef Paul has enlarged his menu, too, adding seasonal dishes such as fettuccine with fresh morels, grilled ahi skewers, and simple grilled chicken served on perfect al dente penne with pine nuts and golden raisins. *$; AE, DC, DIS, MC, V; checks OK; dinner every day; beer and wine; reservations accepted for parties of 6 or more; street parking, really small lot; map:FF8* &

Galerias / ★★☆

210 BROADWAY AVE E, CAPITOL HILL; 206/322-5757

Galerias is like a Zorro movie set in a cathedral. Papier-mâché lilies, niched Madonnas, angels (both sweet ones and fierce ones wielding swords), gilded mirrors, and wrought-iron everything that is pure Castilian baroque decorate this Mexican restaurant. Campy decor and flamboyant waitstaff aside, the food is very good. Quesadillas, brown pockets of flour tortillas, are stuffed with salad shrimp and mozzarella-like *asadero* cheese, served in a tasty puddle of cilantro pesto. Vol-au-vent de Salmon al Chipotle is smoked salmon baked in pastry in a sauce with smoky peppers and ground peanuts. The Flores de Doña Elba was created (as is everything on the menu) by owner Ramiro Rubio's mother, Elba Galvan, Galerias' creative director. The broiled top sirloin steak is served over a grilled cactus leaf, with a 12-chile sweet sauce, colored with pink hibiscus petals, and topped by a bundle of sweetened tortillas filled with housemade corn ice cream. Margaritas and piña coladas are served in glass vats that could double as aquariums. Be sure to make reservations for a seat overlooking Broadway. *$$; AE, DC, MC, V; no checks; lunch, dinner every day; full bar; reservations recommended; self parking; www.galeriasgourmet.com; map:GG6* &

Geneva / ★★★

1106 EIGHTH AVE, FIRST HILL; 206/624-2222

To the strains of Mozart, Geneva's Hanspeter Aebersold (longtime Rainier Club chef) and wife Margret quietly make people happy in their little jewel box. Beneath the gorgeous old-world crystal chandelier hanging from the domed ceiling, classical European cuisine is presented by pampering servers. You can begin with such delicious continental anachronisms as escargot cooked on mushroom caps and signature entrees such as *Jägerschnitzel,* lightly crusted pork medallions with a bacon–wild mushroom sauce and buttered spaetzle, or Veal Bernoise, a ragout of veal in a wine and cream sauce loaded with mushrooms. There's also panfried calf's liver with sautéed onions, apples, bacon, and potato pancakes. Desserts are Hanspeter's specialty: try the warm apple strudel with caramel sauce and vanilla ice cream, the raisin-studded bread-and-butter pudding with vanilla brandy sauce, or the bittersweet chocolate mousse served over raspberry sauce in a Florentine cookie basket. The wine list is a mix of the old world and the new—with plenty to interest serious bibbers and lots of familiar labels and modestly priced bottles. *$$$; AE, MC, V; no checks; dinner Tues–Sat; full bar; reservations recommended; parking validated in Virginia Mason garage in back; map:L4* &

The Georgian / ★★★⯪

411 UNIVERSITY ST (FOUR SEASONS OLYMPIC HOTEL), DOWNTOWN; 206/621-7889

This grand old space for grand old occasions got a grand old face lift in 2001. A more vibrant color scheme done in shades of yellow—from ivory to sunflower—combines with new mismatched china and stemware and new upholstered chairs and settees for a brighter disposition overall. The idea was to make The Georgian (which also got an updated name) less formal and more accessible. Her high ceilings, ornate chandeliers, gleaming silver, and high prices are still here, but the dress code is not, and executive chef Gavin Stephensen has modernized the menu and made it more seasonal. The service remains uncompromisingly high however: a smiling, impeccably uniformed, and well-trained professional waitstaff tends to your every need, and a pianist tickles the ivories in the center of the room. Each dish is an objet d'art, beginning with the Dungeness crab salad with capsicam dressing, and a jumbo prawn with caviar. The intense, earthy flavors of baby beets and lentils, seared duck liver, and rosemary–honey mustard give a broad flavor to crispy, rare-cooked duck breast; buttered Canadian lobster with roasted potato ravioli fairly sings of the sea. A vegetarian prix-fixe menu and à la carte selections are also available. The wine list includes Northwest and domestic selections, as well as imports from France, Germany, Italy, and Chile. A short list of desserts ranges from milk chocolate–topped polenta pound cake with Jack Daniels ice cream to a black-and-white soufflé. The Garden Terrace is a very civilized spot for a cognac and a cigar. *$$$; AE, MC, V; checks OK; lunch, dinner every day; full bar; reservations for large groups only; street parking; map:EE7* &

Gorditos / ★

213 N 85TH ST, GREENWOOD; 206/706-9352

The name means "fat boys," and Tomas and Marlene Ramirez, the owners of this popular neighborhood place, are used to feeding ranch hands in their native Michoacán. Indeed, their burrito grande is the size of a small poodle, with an acre of meat, fish, or tofu (your choice) on two giant flour tortillas with black beans. They come "wet" (with lots of sauce) or dry . . . take the wet. There are plenty of vegetarian options—beans are made with no lard or oil, rice without meat stock. Served in an ambience best described as "busy," the mighty enchiladas are bubbly with cheese and red or green salsa; quesadillas are large flour tortillas with guacamole. The fajitas are huge, sweaty piles of meat, tofu, or prawns and roasted peppers. And there are Pacificos or Coronas to go with them all. There are a salsa bar, everything's reasonably priced, and, with lowered fat content, it's allegedly healthy, though the portion sizes may mitigate that a bit. *$; AE, DIS, MC, V; checks OK; breakfast,*

*lunch, dinner Wed–Sun; beer and wine; no reservations; self parking;
map:EE7* &

Gravity Bar / ★★☆

415 BROADWAY AVE E, CAPITOL HILL; 206/325-7186

It's Seattle's coolest juice bar and vegetarian restaurant. Its tables of con-
ical, galvanized steel and glowing green glass are where Bauhaus meets
Star Trek—in Broadway Market. A pierced, excruciatingly hip-in-black
crowd meets each other for shots of wheatgrass juice grown on the premises, or other drinks from the "pharmacy," such as Liver Flush (grape-
fruit, lemon, garlic, olive oil, and cayenne), Mayan Ruin (orange,
pineapple, yogurt, and spirulina), or Mr. Rogers on Amino Acid
(pineapple, orange, banana, yogurt, and amino acids). Plenty of the lesser
chic congregate here too—drawn by healthy food that will actually challenge taste buds. The menu offers lots of salads, soups, sandwiches, and
vegan dishes. Tofu, tempeh, quinoa, and brown rice are coupled with a
variety of sauces and vegetables. There are roll-ups and sandwiches such
as the Beso de Queso, with black bean spread, sliced avocado, sun-dried
tomatoes, and melted provolone cheese on rustic whole wheat bread, or
the barbecue onion and mushroom vegan burger with tomatoes, avo-
cado, and provolone on an herb and onion bun. *$$; MC, V; local checks
only; lunch, dinner every day; no alcohol; no reservations; self parking;
map:HH6* &

Greenlake Bar & Grill / ★★★☆

7200 E GREEN LAKE WAY N, GREEN LAKE; 206/729-6179

John Schmidt took eight years to build the Taco del Mar burrito chain,
then stepped away to open this little laid-back place with his brother
James. It's obviously a labor of love. The decor is out there—yellow light
boxes centered on mole-colored walls, unfinished plywood tables with
weird rubbery tops. But this comfortable Green Lake eatery is about
good grilled seafood, chicken, and steaks, and big salads. These are
served with such reasonable prices and genteel atmosphere that the place
is well inhabited by families and singles alike. The flavors here are widely
varied, and dishes are well constructed. The soup du jour might be
roasted yams and ginger. A chunk of summer halibut is slathered with
pesto and sun-dried tomato drizzle; a piece of perfectly cooked salmon
may have a pickled ginger peppercorn crust. The grilled vegetable sand-
wich is a neighborhood lunch favorite—a tasty pile of sliced assorted
peppers, summer squashes, and portobellos are grilled and stuffed into a
bollo roll with a sun-dried tomato spread. A brief wine list has choices
under $30, most of which are available by the glass. *$$; AE, MC, V;
checks OK; lunch, dinner every day; full bar; reservations for large
groups only; street parking; map:EE7* &

gypsy / ★★★

2805 E MADISON ST, MADISON PARK; 206/709-8324

Caterer Peter Neal, owner of CaterArts, boldly opened gypsy in the already restaurant-rich neighborhood of Madison Park. However, all the elements for Seattle restaurant success seem to be here: low-lit decor in reds, oranges, and yellows, attractive art on the walls, table tops with white linen and butcher paper, and a sweet bar along one wall. With long-time chef Carrie Duncan installed in the kitchen, gypsy's short menu reveals dishes that are simultaneously homey and upscale. A bread salad is an intense melange of house-smoked chicken breast, nubbins of fresh mozzarella, cubes of French bread in figgy balsamic, sweet peppers, grilled red onions, radicchio, kalamatas, arugula, and oven-dried tomatoes. The barbecued pork tenderloin is thick-sliced over Chinese fermented black beans with sautéed peppers, sweet baby bananas, smudges of ginger/orange/citrus sauce, and crisp fried plantains. A well-priced wine list is judiciously balanced between California, Northwest, and good-valued imports, with many by-the-glass choices. An imaginative and seductively rich dessert list, featuring the espresso pot de crème in a chocolate cookie crust, brings couples in late for a sweet nightcap. *$$; AE, MC, V; checks OK; lunch, dinner Tues–Sat; full bar; reservations recommended; street parking; map:GG5* &

Harvest Vine / ★★★½

2701 E MADISON ST, MADISON VALLEY; 206/320-9771

It's hard to re-create the leisurely gusto with which the Spanish eat and drink—especially in Seattle, with its soggy clime and endemic earnestness. But Joseph Jimenez de Jimenez and his crew do it every night in this tiny, rustic shoebox of a place where it's standing room only for tapas and paella. This is a grazing place. Get a bottle or glass of wine and start ordering *platitos* from the more than two dozen tapas that make up most of the menu. Everything is shareable, including the salad of grilled escarole and black truffles circled by a slice of delightfully subtle smoky salmon or the gratin of cardoons with a tomato sauce and mild but rich *idiazabel* cheese. We enjoyed the skewered venison chunks, grilled bloody rare and tender, resting in a mess of garlicky oyster mushrooms. Sweet *piquillo* peppers stuffed with herbed Dungeness crab lie in a dish-lickable puddle of shellfish sauce. The most fun is to sit at the copper-clad tapas bar and watch the action as Jimenez presides with precision, humor, and charm. Even sitting at one of the few tables, you'll meet fellow diners in a dinner-party atmosphere—with everybody comparing dishes, pointing and yelling, "Give me one of those!" This is one of the most inviting and warm restaurant experiences in town—don't miss it. *$$; MC, V; checks OK; dinner Tues–Sat; beer and wine; no reservations; street parking; map:GG7* &

The Herbfarm / ★★★★

14590 NE 145TH ST, WOODINVILLE; 206/784-2222

The Herbfarm is a must-experience place for anyone who loves serious food and formal service, and can pay the freight. The nine-course prix-fixe dinner with accompanying wines costs around $175 per person. After a devastating fire followed by a short time in a temporary location, Ron Zimmerman and Carrie Van Dyke moved their foodie shrine to brand-new, gorgeous digs in the Woodinville "wine country," near the Ste. Michelle and Columbia wineries, on the property of the posh Willows Lodge. Nationally renowned chef Jerry Traunfeld presides over menus that change with the seasons of local produce and herbs—much of which is grown in the Herbfarm's own substantial gardens. The food is immaculately presented and carefully explained. This is the fastest five hours you'll ever spend. A night's repast could typically encompass tempura squash blossoms stuffed with goat cheese; crab salad with fennel and chives; pea flan with caviar; sweet corn soup with smoked mussels and chanterelles; salmon smoked in basil wood; herb-crusted lamb; cheeses; desserts such as a roasted Italian plum tart and a caramelized pear soufflé with rose geranium sauce; and a selection of small treats— miniature s'mores with cinnamon and basil, chocolates, or lemon-thyme espresso truffles—to go with your coffee. Every service detail is seen to by the army of staff, wiping your brow, pouring your wines, and clearing away the Christofle flatware and crystal as you use it. The rooms are filled with a tasteful mass of framed art and memorabilia. Arrive a half hour before dinner for Van Dyke's tour around the gardens. This is a coveted, one-of-a-kind destination—reservations usually need to be booked months in advance, especially for holidays. *$$$$; AE, MC, V; checks OK; dinner Thurs–Sun; full bar; reservations required; self parking; www.theherbfarm.com; map:AA2* &

Hilltop Ale House / ★

2129 QUEEN ANNE AVE N, QUEEN ANNE; 206/285-3877

This Queen Anne Hill watering hole has pub food that's a cut above the usual burgers and frozen deep-fried tidbits. There are cool little nibbly things such as the oven-roasted curried cashews. But most everything else is big enough for an entire meal: a huge cilantro pesto quesadilla, a so-called starter, is crammed with roasted peppers, Monterey Jack cheese, cilantro pesto, and grilled chicken if you so choose. The half salads (baked goat cheese or caesar) can be dinner with a cup of soup or the spicy Hilltop Gumbo, full of shrimp, chicken andouille sausage, and veggies. The chicken breast sandwich is a handful oozing with mozzarella and cream cheese served on toasted rye. This is a noisy, popular joint run by the same owners as the Columbia City Alehouse (4914 Rainier Ave S, Rainier Valley; 206/723-5123) and the 74th Street Alehouse (7401

Greenwood Ave N, Greenwood; 206/784-2955). The creative fare is but a worthy accompaniment to the real business at hand: the 15 beers and ales on tap. *$; MC ,V; checks OK; lunch, dinner every day; beer and wine; no reservations; street parking; www.seattlealehouses.com; map:GG8* &

Himalayan Sherpa Restaurant / ★

4214 UNIVERSITY WY NE, UNIVERSITY DISTRICT; 206/633-2100

Here's another cuisine heard from as Seattle leaps to planetary diversity. Japanese in a past life, the restaurant is now hung with Tibetan prayer flags and pictures of the Dalai Lama and famous Sherpas. The menu's divided between Sherpa, Indian, Nepalese, and Bhutanese dishes. The *momos*, Sherpa steamed dumplings, come stuffed with ground meat or vegetables and served with a delicious tangy *achar* (sauce). *Kothay* are *momos* except they're fried on one side like pot-stickers. The Sherpa chow mein is jammed with chicken, sweet peppers, and housemade whole wheat noodles. The Sherpa stew is just that—beef, potatoes, onions, carrots, and whole wheat pasta in a savory, unthickened soup. These dishes are uncomplicated, hearty (some would say heavy), and full-flavored. Phone ahead to see if there's yak, a lean red meat served in stir-fries when available. *$; AE, DC, MC, V; no checks; lunch, dinner Tues–Sun; full bar; reservations recommended; self parking; www. himalayansherpa.com; map:EE7* &

The Hunt Club / ★★★
Fireside Room / ★★★

900 MADISON ST (SORRENTO HOTEL), FIRST HILL; 206/343-6156

The Hunt Club, ably helmed by chef Brian Scheehser, is fully prepared for the 21st century, though the burnished mahogany and weathered-brick room looks like a men's club from the 19th. Scheehser produces a short, Mediterranean-accented menu while employing superb Northwest ingredients. Especially fine is his way with meats: trimming and cutting them beautifully and marinating them in olive oil and herbs. His prime-grade New York steak is wondrous, arguably the best in town. Look for pink, tender, flavorful duck and the lamb chops, too, but start with terrific house-cured salmon. Don't miss the frothy mussel bisque (or one of the other fabulous soups). Fish receive respectful medium-rare treatment. Desserts rise to nearly the same standard. The wine list runs deep and broad. Savvy patrons take dessert, coffee, and Cognac in the octagonal, wood-paneled Fireside Room off the lobby, where piano music and card and board games frequently draw crowds and a light menu is available day or evening. In summer, half the hotel's circular, fountain-centered driveway (lined by palm trees that are heated from underground) becomes a civilized but traffic-noisy alfresco cafe. *$$$, $; AE, DIS, MC, V; checks OK; breakfast, lunch, tea, dinner every day, brunch Sat–Sun;*

full bar; reservations recommended; valet parking (Hunt Club); www.hotelsorrento.com; map:L4 &

I Love Sushi / ★★☆

1001 FAIRVIEW AVE N, SOUTH LAKE UNION; 206/625-9604
11818 NE 8TH ST, BELLEVUE; 425/454-5706

Don't let the have-a-nice-day name put you off. Chef Tadashi Sato has created a pair of bustling, bright, high-energy sushi bars with immaculately fresh fish. The staff at both restaurants are friendly and helpful—making them a good place for those unfamiliar with Japanese food to learn, though Sato and his army of chefs attract many Japanese customers who know a good thing when they eat one. The sushi combinations are a veritable bargain (particularly at lunch), while such traditional Japanese specialties as sea urchin, abalone, and fermented bean paste may raise the stakes somewhat. The à la carte dishes, such as flame-broiled mackerel or salmon, the ubiquitous tempura, or geoduck *itame* sautéed with spinach, are excellent. *$$; AE, MC, V; no checks; lunch Mon–Fri, dinner every day (Seattle); lunch Mon–Sat, dinner every day (Bellevue); full bar; reservations recommended; self parking; ilovesushi.com; map:GG7, HH3* &

Il Bacio / ★★

16564 CLEVELAND ST, REDMOND; 425/869-8815

Despite its Redmond strip-mall setting, an old-fashioned ambience—neoclassical statuary and faux flora, tables set with maroon-on-white napery, tux-shirted servers—imbues this popular Italian bistro. Italian-born chef Rino Baglio does his part to complete the picture by creating authentic dishes: antipasti such as good old chopped salad with cheese, salami, and mushrooms or clams sautéed with garlic, white wine, and fresh tomatoes. A specialty is the tenderloin of buffalo wrapped in prosciutto, with a demi-glace of barolo wine. Try the herbed veal chop served with wild mushrooms or the Risotto di Novara, a peasant dish of Italian arborio rice, sausage, Tuscan beans, sage, and fresh tomato sauce. There are plenty of great pastas here, including penne puttanesca with olive oil, tomato, olives, capers, and anchovies, or Baglio's angel hair pasta with lobster meat in a fresh tomato sauce. *$$; AE, DC, DIS, JCB, MC ,V; no checks; lunch Mon–Fri, dinner every day; full bar; reservations recommended; self parking; ilbacioredmond@aol.com; www.ilbacio.com; map:EE1* &

Il Bistro / ★★★

93-A PIKE ST, PIKE PLACE MARKET; 206/682-3049

 It's one of the most enduring stars in the expanding Seattle universe of small Italian restaurants. Tucked away under the eaves of the market, it is low-ceilinged and candle-lit, a perfect place to tryst again the way you did last summer. You can go for all the courses or pick and choose. Try the Penn Cove mussels, fragrant of garlic and basil, or the crostini with roasted garlic and goat cheese for starters and then go from there. While you're at it, take some time to order wine from the daunting list that runs to more than 500 choices. If you're still hungry after the antipasti, a sizable pasta list includes housemade gnocchi in tomato-cream, cheese tortellonis (lavishly sized tortellinis) in a garlic cream reduction, or a sumptuous pile of linguine in spicy tomato-basil sauce with frutti di mare, fresh seafood from the market. For *secondi*, the rack of lamb is heady with rosemary and a sauce sweet with Sangiovese wine. Save some space for either the lemon-glazed, almond-crusted cheesecake or the Marquis, a chocolate mousse cake so rich it ought to be a controlled substance. Though longtime owner Tom Martino recently sold Il Bistro to out-of-town investors, we're hoping the quality remains the same—stay tuned. *$$$; AE, DC, MC, V; no checks; dinner every day; full bar; reservations recommended, required Fri–Sat; valet parking; map:J8* ⅃

Il Gambero / ★★
2132 1ST AVE, BELLTOWN; 206/448-8597
It's all about romance—and garlic—at this rustic trattoria owned by seasoned restaurateurs Gaspare Trani and his wife, Dianne, who are also proprietors of Gaspare's in Maple Leaf. Il Gambero means "the shrimp" in Italian, and you'll do well by taking the hint and ordering the jumbo black tiger shrimp grilled with rosemary and olive oil. You won't go wrong either with the zesty red cioppino with mussels, clams, squid, shrimp, and scallops or the Pollo Diplomatico, a chicken breast layered with prosciutto and smoked mozzarella in white wine and rosemary. The saltimbocca, veal and prosciutto with a dry marsala wine sauce, is stellar, as is fat Ravioli Rustico stuffed with spinach in a sensational sauce that blends mascarpone and green pea purée. Share a glass of wine from the value-oriented wine list or the calories of the ice-cream-filled truffle called *tartuffo*. *$$; AE, MC, V; no checks; dinner Mon–Sat; full bar; reservations recommended, required Fri–Sat; street parking; map:H7* ⅃

Il Terrazzo Carmine / ★★★
411 1ST AVE S, PIONEER SQUARE; 206/467-7797
Carmine Smeraldo's handsome and romantic restaurant is nestled in an urban-renewed alley with entrances through the historic lobby on First Avenue or through the back courtyard. The airy room and small terrace outside are a perfect environment for the kind of romantic but decisive tête-à-tête it requires to navigate the formidable and tempting menu. For a lusty starter there's calamari in *padella* (Italian frying pan), tender squid in a heady tomato garlic sauté, or fresh spinach sautéed with lemon and garlic. The creamy soup of prawns and roast peppers is rich and unusual. Cannellonis are creamy and bubbly with ricotta and filled with veal and spinach; the fettuccine is tossed with in-house smoked salmon, mush-

rooms, and peas. The osso buco is oh-so-good-o, braised in red wine and served with buttered fettuccine. The prime-cut tenderloin is roasted and served with a brusque wine and pancetta sauce. Tiramisu and crème brûlée are appropriately decadent and well crafted, but so are the ever-changing choices such as cheesecakes, cannolis, or housemade gelati that showcase local fruits in season. A guitarist plays classical music most nights, adding to the dreamy escapism of this exceptional restaurant. *$$$; AE, DC, DIS, MC, V; no checks; lunch Mon–Fri, dinner Mon–Sat; full bar; reservations recommended; valet parking; map:O8* &

Imperial Garden Seafood Restaurant / ★★★
18230 EAST VALLEY HWY, KENT; 425/656-0999
Off-putting to urbanites who consider even the north end of Kent as distant as Beijing, Imperial Garden is easily worth the trek to darkest suburbia—or, in this case, the Great Wall Mall, the Asian shopping center south of IKEA. Arguably the best Chinese food south of British Columbia, the restaurant has linen, full service, and an impressive menu. Usually kitchens need 24 hours' notice to prepare Peking duck. Not here; it's served every day in two ways. Order it both ways; the duck is carted to the table, the delectable, nearly fat-free skin cut into little patches to

be eaten with little pancakes and sauces. The denuded duck is taken back to the kitchen, reappearing boneless and braised in a delicate broth of wine, more spices, and mushrooms. If duck doesn't do it for you, try the panfried black cod, whole fish steamed in clay casseroles, one of the many noodle dishes, or vegetables with roasted nuts. Dim sum served weekends is a movable feast that never stops. There are lobster dumplings, almond shrimp balls, pork buns with airy pastry as delicate as any strudel in Vienna. The pork shiu mai with black mushrooms are little satchel bombs of flavor, as are the panfried vegetable dumplings or shrimp-stuffed tofu. *$; DIS, MC, V; no checks; breakfast, lunch, dinner every day; full bar; reservations recommended; self parking* &

India Bistro / ★★★
2301 NW MARKET ST, BALLARD; 206/783-5080
The exotic smells of the Malabar Coast or Kashmiri Province come from an unlikely corner in Seattle's old Norwegian neighborhood. Run by three partners—manager Mike Panjabi, chef Gian Jaswal, and his assistant, Gurmohan Singh—India Bistro is one of the best-reviewed and most enduring Indian restaurants in the city. This speaks not only to the demographic and ethnic sea changes happening in Ballard, but also to the quality of this small, well-appointed place. The long menu has curries, vegetarian dishes, Indian breads, or meats from the tandoori, the superhot, traditional vertical clay oven. Start with *samosas*, fried pastries stuffed with mildly spiced potatoes and peas, or *pakoras*, little bundles of vegetables, chicken, or fish fried in a lentil batter, before seguing to

entrees such as the spicy Goan vindaloo curries in lamb, chicken, or fish with a hint of vinegar or Mughlai biryani, an ornate rice dish with lamb, yogurt, nuts, and raisins. From the tandoori, don't miss the delectable and inexpensive lamb rack or the fish cooked amazingly moist at 800°F. India Bistro is the destination of frequent pilgrimages by Indian nationals and other locals knowledgeable of Indian food and craving the authentic. *$; AE, DC, DIS, MC, V; no checks; lunch Mon–Sat, dinner every day; beer and wine; reservations recommended; street parking; map:FF8* &

Isabella Ristorante / ★★★

1909 3RD AVE, DOWNTOWN; 206/441-8281
Towering carmine walls, Prussian blue columns, a dining room decked in brocaded booths, and the warmth emanating from the imported blue-tiled wood-burning brick oven combine to give Isabella a subdued European romance. The large menu holds forth with selections such as Panzanella Mariella, a cucumber, bread, and tomato salad with fat cannellini beans and fresh mint that is a must; the Ravioli Bosco, fresh spinach pasta stuffed with four cheeses and sautéed with wild mushrooms, fresh tomatoes, and artichoke hearts; and osso buco, the signature lamb shanks braised with shiitakes and other vegetables and dressed in a rosemary-infused demi-glace. The tempting pizzas include one with the housemade Italian sausage or another with mild Parma ham. Pasta dazzlers range from linguine with Dungeness and king crab in a creamy lemon saffron sauce and fresh basil to lobster raviolis with egg-and-black pepper pasta, and the sauce has leeks and fresh tomatoes. Finish it all off with the tiramisu or the strawberry and white chocolate torte. *$$; AE, DC, DIS, JCB, MC, V; local checks only; lunch Mon–Fri, dinner every day; full bar; reservations recommended; street parking; map:I7* &

JaK's Grill / ★★

4548 CALIFORNIA AVE SW, WEST SEATTLE; 206/937-7809
14 FRONT ST N, ISSAQUAH; 425/837-8834
For a no-baloney steak house that serves good corn-fed Nebraska beef that they dry-age themselves, JaK's (the annoying typography stands for owners Jeff Page and Ken Hughes) is the place. Don't wander too far from steak and you'll be a very happy carnivore. There aren't any real appetizers anyway, just some salads, side orders of skewered veggies, fries, baked potatoes, and garlic mashers. The bourbon and brown sugar–marinated double-cut pork chops in a honey peppercorn glaze also work, as does the perfectly grilled prime grade porterhouse, which comes big as your car and paired with the crispy-on-the-outside potato pancakes. Both locations are nearly identical and very popular. *$$; AE, MC, V; checks OK; dinner every day; full bar; no reservations; self parking; map:II8* &

Jitterbug Cafe / ★★

2114 N 45TH ST, WALLINGFORD; 206/547-6313
This little sliver of a place is another neighborhood gem-ette from the minds of Peter Levy and Jeremy Hardy of Atlas Foods, Coastal Kitchen, and 5 Spot Cafe fame (see reviews). Typically large menus are a little heavy on the shtick, but are supplemented every few months with a loosely interpreted ethnic menu. Fending off boredom seems to be the intent, and it works. Breakfast is a high point: gingerbread waffles and great omelets such as one with serrano ham, cannellini beans, pecorino Romano, tomatoes, and asparagus. There's pub food, too (though it's tricked out as 1950s diner fare), such as a thick-fried bologna sandwich with bacon, onions, and mayonnaise or the rib-eye steak croissant with mozzarella cheese and horseradish sauce. Its location across the street from an art-house theater, the Guild 45th, makes the Jitterbug a popular place to grab a pre- or post-picture bite. *$; MC, V; checks OK; breakfast, lunch, dinner every day; full bar; reservations recommended; street parking; www.chowfoods.com; map:FF7* &

Kabul / ★★

2301 N 45TH ST, WALLINGFORD; 206/545-9000
In Afghanistan, cooks marinate meats and infuse them with mint, coriander, cilantro, and dill. There's lots of cooling yogurt, scallions, and basmati rice. Chef Sultan Malikyar, who emigrated from Afghanistan in the late '70s, shares his family's recipes, which include his father's kebab and his mother's *chaka* (garlic-yogurt sauce). He and partner Wali Khairzada make fragrant, elegant food such as crisp *bolani* (scallion-potato turnovers with *chaka* for dipping), *ashak* (delicate scallion dumplings with either beef or vegetarian tomato sauce), and kebabs served on perfumed piles of basmati. The dining room's simple decor is as soothing as the cardamom-and-rose-water custard *firni* (sometimes known as Turkish Delight) served for dessert. On Tuesday and Thursday, live sitar music adds to the exotica. *$; AE, DIS, MC, V; local checks only; dinner every day; beer and wine; reservations required; street parking; www.cuisinenet.com; map:FF7*

Kaizuka Teppanyaki & Sushi Bar / ★★

1306 S KING ST, CHINATOWN/INTERNATIONAL DISTRICT; 206/869-1556

Mount Baker and Madrona residents consider this homey little teppanyaki and sushi place their best-kept secret. Mom-and-pop roles are filled by owners Jeff and Lisa Kaizuka. Tucked into the subterranean space long occupied by the original Nikko, you'll find well-crafted standards including tempura and teriyaki. There's a separate sushi bar and four tatami rooms. The sushi service itself (less expensive here than elsewhere) offers generous cuts of maguro, hamachi, and saba folded over sticky rice. The star attraction, however, has to be the six hot-top tables reserved for teppanyaki, the Japanese restaurant art of flashing knives, blazing spatulas, whooshing flames, explosive sizzles, and flying eggs—as much martial arts as cooking. Jeff Kaizuka flash-sears beef, chicken, and fish; he's a rock star with a gleaming grill for a stage. Offstage, Lisa Kaizuka works the floor, making this a very friendly experience. *$$; AE, DC, DIS, MC, V; no checks; lunch Tues–Fri, dinner Mon–Sat; beer and wine; reservations recommended; self parking; map:II6*

Kaspar's / ★★★

19 W HARRISON ST, QUEEN ANNE; 206/298-0123

The pre-theater/opera/ballet crowd loves Kaspar's because the staff always gets them seated, sated, and out the door in time for an opening curtain. Lodged in a cool, multitiered building just west of Seattle Center, Swiss-born Kaspar Donier imaginatively couples classic European cooking styles with fresh Northwest ingredients. An easy, intimate room with bamboo accents and shoji screens in shades of brown and green has a lattice-shaded solarium on the lower level—the favored seats. Some just stop by to duck into the cozy wine bar, with outstanding wines-by-the-glass drawn from a broad list of mostly West Coast labels. Well-trained servers make you feel welcome and well cared for. Order the sampler tower with its selection of appetizers that changes daily—such as the Asian "antipasto," with Dungeness crab wrapped in a lettuce roll, tuna sashimi, and boiled prawns in sheer rice-paper rolls. Though seafood gets the royal treatment, don't overlook the meats, such as the huge Chianti-braised lamb shank. For years Donier has been serving variations on his signature dish, Duck Prepared Two Ways: pink-fleshed, roasted Muscovy duck breast with a crispy bone-in duck leg confit served with licorice or chanterelle sauce; ours came with carrot purée, braised broccoli hearts, and mashed potatoes. Desserts are sublime: don't turn down anything you're offered that's chocolate. *$$$; AE, MC, V; no checks; dinner Tues–Sat; full bar; reservations recommended; valet and self parking; info@kaspars.com, www.kaspars.com; map:A8* &

King Ludwig's Tyrol Restaurant / ★★

8501 5TH AVE NE, NORTHGATE; 206/524-3100

This brightly lit dining room is dotted with Tyrolean tchotchkes: fancy beer steins, gaudy clocks, and potted plastic philodendrons. The hills are alive with the sounds of taped men's choirs singing drinking songs and women yodeling. Never mind the kitsch, though: chef Agnes Rideg's German kitchen is redolent with the smells of warm buttery things. She and husband Karoy are Hungarians, so the menu features goulashes and cabbage rolls. The rotisserie-roasted fresh pork hock crackling on the outside is all paprika-ed and crispy, the meat inside succulent and rich. It comes with mild sauerkraut with caraway seeds; sweet-sour kraut spiced with cinnamon and applesauce; and a warm potato salad. Try the falling-off-the-bone Hungarian Paprika Chicken with its foothills of buttery spaetzle (tiny butter dumplings). Agnes Rideg bakes housemade bread, including sturdy white and caraway rye. There's also game on weekends, such as tender rack of venison or wild boar chops. The wine list has both sweet and dry Hungarian tokays, and the popular red vin ordinaire called Bull's Blood. There are also some German imports—Liebfraumilch, Rieslings, Piesporters, and German beers on tap and in bottles. *$$; MC, V; local checks only; dinner every day; full bar; reservations recommended; free lot parking nearby; www.kingludwigs.com; map:DD7* ⚹

Kingfish Café / ★★⯪

602 19TH AVE E, CAPITOL HILL; 206/320-8757

The Coaston sisters have their restaurant just the way they want it—busy. It's a stylish, casual, contemporary space with blown-up sepia-tinted photos from the family album on the walls, including one of distant cousin Langston Hughes. They don't take reservations, so expect long lines of people waiting for a taste of sassy Southern soul food. It's kind of a party waiting at Kingfish, wine in hand—regulars, we're told, look

forward to it. The buttermilk fried chicken is a huge favorite, as is Big Daddy's Pickapeppa Skirt Steak or the velvety pumpkin soup, crab and catfish cakes with green-tomato tartar sauce, or seafood curry with coconut grits. Lunch is a bargain: try the pulled pork sandwich with peach and watermelon barbecue sauce. At Sunday brunch, those crab and catfish cakes are topped with a poached egg and hollandaise. *$$; no credit cards; checks OK; lunch Mon, Wed–Fri, dinner Mon, Wed–Sat, brunch Sun; beer and wine; no reservations; street parking; kingfish cafe@aol.com; map:HH7* ⚹

La Medusa / ★★★

4857 RAINIER AVE S, COLUMBIA CITY; 206/723-2192

Sherri Serino and Lisa Becklund opened La Medusa in 1997 in a cozy storefront, serving what they call Sicilian soul food in the Rainier Valley's gently gentrifying Columbia City neighborhood. Start with the house-smoked trout salad tossed with arugula and avocado or the seasonal Grandma's Greens braised with pignolia, kalamatas, and golden raisins served in broth in a bowl with tiny corn muffins. The *spaghetti con le sarde* (which would be the national dish if Sicily were a nation) is a rich heap of pasta, fresh sardines, fennel, raisins, pine nuts, olives, and tomatoes. Their manicotti are crepes (*crespelle*) stuffed fat with fluffy herbed ricotta and baked with fresh mozzarella and marinara. There are thin-crusted pizzas and entrees such as roast quail with pancetta or grilled tenderloin with Gorgonzola. A kids' menu has Sicilian versions of spaghetti, pizza, and mac and cheese. Desserts are housemade—particularly good is the cannoli (it would hardly be a Sicilian place without one), a crispy pastry tube filled with ricotta and chocolate bits surrounded with marsala-soaked fruits. Medium-priced wines mainly hail from Southern Italy. *$$; MC, V; no checks; dinner Tues–Sat; beer and wine; reservations recommended; street parking; map:KK6* &

Lampreia / ★★★★

2400 1ST AVE, BELLTOWN; 206/443-3301

He's young, he's grumpy, he's a genius, and his restaurant is not for everyone. Scott Carsberg has a cultish following, and in his restaurant, he does it his way. If you want it another way, Carsberg may suggest "the highway." Raised in West Seattle when it was still a blue-collar neighborhood, he made his way to the East Coast and was mentored by a master Tyrolean chef who took him to Italy. Carsberg returned to open his spare ocher dining room, which is not unlike like his minimalist creations. For appetizers there's garden vegetables and pesto in a *cocotte* (little French iron casserole) with a poached egg, a silky sweet squash soup, or the Walla Walla onion tart with *osetra* caviar, sweet and salty in a thin, buttery crust. The Intermezzo courses include such offerings as creamy whipped potatoes set on a crispy, crepelike "tulip" of Reggiano Parmesan and piled with spot prawns, those Alaskan shrimp so tasty they rival Atlantic lobsters, and covered in *tartufi bianchi*, the rare Piedmontese white truffles. Carsberg features fresh truffles of all kinds in their fall and winter seasons on a "fresh sheet." Main courses include his famous veal chop with fonduta cheese sauce that has diners sucking the bones. Other triumphs are the matsutake, a prized wild mushroom, with grilled smoked salmon or the five-spice duck breast with fruit mustards and chanterelles. Servers bring a selection of handcrafted local cheeses, which make a fine end to a meal or an even better prelude to a chocolate delectable or delicate lemon tart. Service, as directed by Carsberg's wife, Hyun Joo Paek, is seamless and reverential. *$$$; AE, MC, V; no checks; dinner Tues–Sat; full bar; reservations recommended; street parking; map:F8* &

Le Gourmand / ★★★★

425 NW MARKET ST, BALLARD; 206/784-3463

Bruce Naftaly is one of the seminal purveyors of Northwest regional cooking. He combs the region for ingredients, and in his French kitchen uses vegetables and flowers from his own garden and from producers he's cultivated for many years. With the advent of the Italian-joint-on-every-corner era, his unlikely French storefront on the edge of Ballard has endured and matured into fine-honed perfection. Service is personal and capable in this quiet, romantic room with its ceiling painted like a clear spring day and a trompe l'oeil wall of trees, hollyhocks, and lupines. His prix-fixe menu includes appetizer choices, entrees, and *salade* après. Naftaly's fortes are sauces, such as the creamy one with local caviars gracing the sole or the huskier one with shiitakes, Cognac, and fresh sage accompanying the loin of rabbit. Naftaly married Sara Lavenstein, a pastry chef, a fortunate coupling for us all. Try her profiteroles with Naftaly's housemade ice cream, if you doubt what the power of love can do. Here's a chef who's reached his full stride, and Seattle diners are the winners. The wine list features a notable collection of French, California, and Northwest bottles, with plenty of good mid-range price options. *$$; AE, MC, V; checks OK; dinner Wed–Sat; beer and wine; reservations recommended; street parking; map:FF8* &

Le Pichet / ★★★
1933 1ST AVE, DOWNTOWN; 206/256-1499

Don't judge the immensity of the flavors or the largess of the menu by the size of this tiny storefront *café à vin* near the market. Owned by chef Jim Drohman, late of Cafe Campagne, and business partner Joanne Herron, this *café la nuit* features a collection of housemade charcuterie—pâtés, sausages, and confits—that lesser places would buy from France. The sleek, tasteful Parisian ambience with warm overhead lighting and wood-framed mirrors puts tables together so couples are seated with strangers—you'll find yourself chatting with the couple next door, trading bites of the potted duck for forkfuls of the pork confit. Try the salad of Belgian endive with walnuts and Roquefort; the *Pâté à Albigois*, a country-style pork pâté with walnuts in a little pool of honey; the mighty gratin lyonnaise; or onion soup that can be an entire meal. The potted duck on its salad of celery root creamy with a little horseradish is tangy with vinaigrette and dried cherries. The wine list has about 50 labels, mostly French, and most under $25 and available by the glass, *pichet* (two-thirds of a bottle), or *demi-pichet* (two glasses). *$$; MC, V; no checks; breakfast every day, lunch, dinner Thurs–Mon; full bar; reservations recommended; street parking; map:I8* &

Luau Polynesian Lounge / ★★☆
2253 N 56TH ST, GREEN LAKE; 206/633-5828

During warm weather, locals lounge at the Luau under umbrella-shaded tables, partaking of exotic tropical potables such as coconut martinis or vats of Trader Vic's classic Zombies. There's a good list of bottled, imported beers or local microbrews on tap. Inside, the bar is hot and the food fun, with a menu that roams from the Pacific Rim to Hawaii and Japan for pulled pork, pupu platters, pot-stickers, sticky rice, and stir-fries, and ambles down to the Caribbean and nods at Mexico and Jamaica, yet still manages to serve a darn good burger. Try the smoked Hawaiian-style baby back ribs served with serrano chile corn bread or the ancho- and caramel-glazed rib-eye with spicy black-eyed peas and greens. *$$; AE, MC, V; checks OK; lunch Tues–Fri, dinner every day; full bar; reservations recommended; street parking; jessicaluau@msn. com; map:FF7* &

Luna Park Cafe / ★

2918 AVALON WY SW, WEST SEATTLE; 206/935-7250

Decked out in old neon and memorabilia, this West Seattle beanery is named after the "Coney Island of the West," the amusement park that glittered on the northern tip of West Seattle from 1907 to 1913. Nobody remembers this brief landmark these days, but it's celebrated here with tableside jukeboxes loaded with Top 40 hits and retro foods mostly from the 1950s: burgers, real shakes, grilled sandwiches, meat loaf, and roast turkey. Proportions are equally old-fashioned. When they say jumbo hot fudge sundae, they mean it. The diner will flood you with memories of those bygone days, even if you never lived them. *$; MC, V; checks OK; breakfast, lunch, dinner every day; beer and wine; reservations required; self parking; map:JJ9* &

Lush Life / ★★☆

2331 2ND AVE, BELLTOWN; 206/441-9842

Lush Life lives up to its namesake. Inspired by the sensuous strains of the Billy Strayhorn classic, its candle-lit dinner room is swathed in richly dark colors, and the intimate patio in back is perfect for couples to play footsie on a warm summer evening. The more sophisticated (and quieter) sibling to Marco Rulff and Donna Moodie's other restaurant, the nearby Marco's Supperclub (see review), Lush Life is definitely built for two. Even the servers, though attentive enough, seem to know when *not* to show up. The primarily Mediterranean menu offers up shareable fresh pastas and gourmet pizzas dressed in fresh vegetables, smoked mozzarella, roasted garlic, and fennel sausage. Other specialties include portobello mushrooms marinated in balsamic vinegar with barley risotto and a grilled pork chop marinated with juniper berries. To seal the moment, there's tiramisu, peach sorbet, or a soulful chocolate-sambuca cake. *$$; AE, MC, V; local checks only; dinner Mon–Sat; full bar; reservations recommended; self parking; map:F8* &

Macrina Bakery & Café / ★★☆

2408 1ST AVE, BELLTOWN (AND BRANCH); 206/448-4032
615 W MCGRAW ST, QUEEN ANNE; 206/283-5900

Seattle was a one-bread town until Leslie Mackie, originator of the rustic bread program at Grand Central Bakery and later with her own ovens at Macrina, transformed us into the bread lovers we are today. She's gained national acclaim as a bread baker; she and her small army of bakers can hardly keep up with the demand for her gutsy, exceptional breads, which you'll find on the tables at the city's finest restaurants. Mornings, Belltown regulars show up for warm buttery goods, bowls of fresh fruit, housemade granola, and creamy lattes to be enjoyed in the sunny Euro-chic cafe setting. Others hasten out the door with a loaf of crusty whole wheat cider bread warm from the oven. Lunch brings simple, artful soups

93

(try the corn chowder studded with Dungeness crab), salads, panini, and a classy meze trio of daily-changing Mediterranean-inspired noshes. Don't leave without one of the famous Rick's cookies—chewy with chocolate chunks, apricot, and espresso. *$; MC, V; local checks only; breakfast, lunch Mon–Fri, brunch Sat–Sun; beer and wine; reservations not accepted; street parking; map:F8,GG8* &

Madison Park Cafe / ★★☆

1807 42ND AVE E, MADISON PARK; 206/324-2626
Tables in the sun-dappled cobblestone courtyard of this charming 1920s-era clapboard house are a welcome alfresco retreat from urban surroundings. Chef Marianne Zdobysz has distinguished herself and this neighborhood landmark with a menu that's gently French but ventures into the Italian. There's an incredible chicken liver mousse with currants plumped-up with port that's smearable on the housemade crostinis. Try the lavender honey rack of lamb; the puttanesca ravioli tossed with fresh tomatoes and Greek olives; or the rich cassoulet with duck confit, pork, lamb, and andouille sausage. The northern seas meet the Mediterranean quite affably in the halibut with three-olive salsa. Host/owner Karen Binder takes outdoor reservations for the weekend brunch, which offers such temptations as huevos rancheros, sourdough waffles, and ricotta pancakes. *$$; AE, MC, V; no checks; dinner Tues–Thurs, brunch Sat–Sun; full bar; reservations recommended; street parking; madison park@aol.com, map:GG6*

Mae's Phinney Ridge Café / ★

6412 PHINNEY AVE N, GREENWOOD; 206/782-1222
Images of Holstein cows adorn Mae Barwick's north-end eggs-and-hash-browns mecca, and there always seems to be a herd out front waiting for a table. Fortunately the wait's rarely very long for the four sprawling dining areas. Portions of giant omelets and scrambles, pancakes, and French toast are huge. Farm-size servings of potatoes or grits come with every combination. For advanced carbo-loading there's the famous Spud Feast—a mountain of fried potatoes with onions, sweet peppers, cheese, sour cream, and salsa. Service is casually rushed, but you might have to flag down a server for a coffee refill. An espresso bar offers access from a walk-up window. *$; AE, MC, V; checks OK; breakfast every day, lunch Mon–Fri; no alcohol; reservations recommended; self parking; map:FF8*

Malay Satay Hut / ★★

212 12TH AVE S, CHINATOWN/INTERNATIONAL DISTRICT;
206/324-4091

The flavors of Malaysia are blended with those of China, India, and Thailand in this noisy, Formica-topped family joint set in a Vietnamese strip mall in an area known as Little Saigon. Buddhist monks, Malaysians, and Asian food fans pack this ambience-free place for fresh seafood, curries, wontons, stir-fries, and satays, of course. There's grilled *roti*, Indian flatbread served with a potato-chicken curry sauce, and Buddha's Yam Pot, an amazing stir-fry of chicken, shrimp, and vegetables in a deep-fried basket of grated sweet potato and taro root. You may want to avoid the crispy pork intestines or the fish head soup, but then again, maybe not. Definitely have Cantonese chow fun—wide noodles loaded with veggies and chicken. There are whole fish steamed or fried—the pompano is dense and intense in a black bean sauce, crispy and flaky when deep-fried. Ikan Merah is crisp snapper fillets in a sweet and pungent sauce. Neon-colored gelatin desserts are to be missed, but try a sweet drink such as the jelly ice soybean milk. *$; MC, V; no checks; lunch, dinner every day; beer and wine; reservations recommended; self parking; map:HH6* &

Maple Leaf Grill / ★★

8929 ROOSEVELT WY NE, MAPLE LEAF; 206/523-8449

Order the barbecue ribs or the cioppino and you'll wish the Maple Leaf Grill were in your neighborhood. Everybody here seems to know each other—maybe it's the conversation-friendly bar, where flannel- and denim-clad regulars gather for the oyster stew chock-full of tasso ham, portobellos, corn, peppers, and butternut squash or the fat burgers with housemade mayo. With blues on the sound system and a huge selection of hot sauces, customers are gratefully digging in or tacking their names to the waiting list while trading gibes with the convivial manager, waiter, and bartender, David Albert. Neighbors also hang here for the extensive lists of brews and selection of wines by the glass. *$$; MC, V; checks OK; lunch Mon–Fri, dinner every day; beer and wine; reservations recommended; self parking; map:DD6* &

Marco's Supperclub / ★★★

2510 1ST AVE, BELLTOWN; 206/441-7801

This lively place bursts out onto the sidewalk on warm evenings. The covered alfresco dining and jumping bar scene is an institution in the upscale renaissance that now defines Belltown. Veteran restaurateurs Marco Rulff and Donna Moodie have created a funky, sexy, noisy, warm atmosphere that attracts regulars and tourists. The kitchen is adventurous and capable—don't miss the signature starter of fried sage leaves or the shiitake-stuffed spring rolls with holy basil. Moodie's family recipe for Jamaican jerk chicken is a perennial favorite, served with sweet potato purée and sautéed greens. Other exotic entrees include halibut with a Moroccan harissa rub and couscous or pineapple-ginger pork loin served with fresh papaya sauce. An eclectic collection of European and Northwest wines is available by the bottle or glass. A bar running the length of the dining room is a great perch for those dining alone, and in the fair-weather months, a deck out back doubles the seating capacity. *$$; AE, MC, V; checks OK; dinner every day; full bar; reservations recommended; street parking; map:F8* &

Marina Park Grill / ★★

89 KIRKLAND AVE, KIRKLAND; 425/889-9000

This comfortable, spacious restaurant is another venture by Mike Brown, who owns the nearby swanky steak house 21 Central (see review). The clientele is mature, prosperous, and casually dressed. There's an easygoing feel here with romantic droplights and candles, copper-colored textured walls, wood parquet and carpets, a glowing art deco bar, and Sinatra on the sound system. The kitchen produces steaks and broiled seafood with influences from the Northwest, Louisiana, Mexico, and Asia. There's a good jambalaya with shrimp, salmon, crab, and Mexican chorizo sausage. Also worth a try are tempura baby lobster tails, Dungeness crab cakes, and an unpretentious roast chicken with Madeira butter. The wine list is mostly domestic with little imagination and few choices under $40. *$$$; AE, DC, DIS, MC, V; checks OK; lunch, dinner every day; full bar; reservations recommended; self parking; www.marinaparkgrill.com; map:EE3* &

Market Street Urban Grill / ★★★

1744 NW MARKET ST, BALLARD; 206/789-6766

The times, they are a-changin' in little ol' downtown Ballard. The rapidly transmogrifying Scandinavian neighborhood has acquired not only a Class A movie theater (the nearby Majestic Bay) but also an eatery of the same caliber. Thanks goes to savvy owners John and Kendell Sillers and Shing and Ellie Chin. Among other bright moves, they hired Frank Springmann, former chef of Flying Fish and alumnus of the Painted Table, whose menu and execution would put some Belltown posers to shame. The well-matched starter of crisp, juicy foie gras and sweetbreads is delivered on a pile of young mustard greens braised in mushroom broth. The roasted eggplant and chicken soup is full flavored and perfect. The saddle of lamb arrives with fresh pea vines and a red wine–cinnamon sauce. Watch winter menus for game, ranging from quail to venison osso buco. The owners all pull full shifts in this well-appointed food shrine— evidence of their commitment to making this place work on the ground floor of Ballard's hipification. *$$$; DIS, MC, V; checks OK; dinner Mon–Sat; full bar; reservations recommended; self parking; map:EE8* &

Matt's in the Market / ★★★

94 PIKE ST, 3RD FLOOR, PIKE PLACE MARKET; 206/467-7909

This spot in the Corner Market Building is hard to find if you're not looking for it. Our advice: look for it. Matt's is curled up in a tiny space where the old cafe's tiled counter and stools still remain. A handful of tables stand in the back of the room, looking out large-paned windows over Pike Place Market to Elliott Bay and the Olympic Mountains. The durable chef, Erik Canella, turns out food that's not only well crafted but some of the freshest, most innovative eats downtown. It's no wonder it's fresh—cooks shop the market twice a day. Seafood is the best bet here— the rare-seared albacore is a mainstay; the smoked catfish salad is pleasantly original. At lunchtime, the line of nearby office workers forms early for oyster po'boys, heady filé gumbo, or clams and mussels in an ouzo-infused broth. There's also a quirky and wonderful wine list. Owner Matt Janke does everything else in this place—waiting, greeting, busing, prepping, and washing dishes. He sometimes even manages to squeeze in musicians to play live jazz. *$$; MC, V; no checks; lunch, dinner Tues–Sat; beer and wine; no reservations; self parking; map:J8*

Maximilien in the Market / ★★★

81A PIKE ST, PIKE PLACE MARKET; 206/682-7270

Maximilien is a charming French restaurant located in the hub of Pike Place Market, owned and operated since 1997 by chef Eric Francy and frontman Axel Mace; the pair bought out their former employer, Francois Kissel, who graced the Seattle Gallic restaurant scene with various restaurants for three decades. Maximilien has the old-world charm of a Parisian hideaway but with a panoramic view of Elliott Bay, West Seattle, and the Olympic Mountains. Here are such French classics as tournedos Rossini, frog legs, and escargot but also more modern offerings, such as seared salmon served over fresh lentil salad dressed in a sensational purple vinaigrette, the color of which comes from the seed of a little-known French mustard. Game lovers should try the quail stuffed with wild mushrooms, foie gras, and port wine sauce. Lunch has great entree salads or sandwiches such as the gooey chicken and Brie. The French-centric wine list is extensive, with a wealth of mid-priced wines (wines by the glass are frequently changed) and some expensive imports. *$$; AE, DC, DIS, MC, V; no checks; lunch, dinner Tues–Sat, brunch Sun; full bar; reservations recommended; valet and self parking; www.maximilienrestaurant.com; map:J8* &

Medin's Ravioli Station / ★★

4620 LEARY WY NW, BALLARD; 206/789-6680

If raviolis are your passion, this is your place. Whether fried, steamed, or boiled, they're almost all that's served at the Ravioli Station. Bill Medin and his sisters, Lennie and Leann, cater to a steady stream of customers from downtown "Frelard," the funky anti-neighborhood that's part Ballard, part Fremont. The triangular dining room is tasteful but low-frills, and a bar at one end has an amazing water-heated handrail and stools made from train pistons. Fat dumplings filled with house-smoked salmon, grilled vegetables, three cheeses, beef, or spinach dominate the short menu. Select your favorite sauce: tomato cream, marinara, alfredo, or roasted red pepper. Other entrees include pork loin packing spinach, mushrooms, artichokes, and sun-dried tomatoes and a chicken phyllo ravioli, a large golden-brown rectangle of phyllo filled with chicken, curried apples, and Brie drizzled with a curry coconut sauce. Low prices, casual atmosphere, and most kids' love of raviolis make this a good spot for families. *$; MC, V; local checks only; lunch Mon–Fri, dinner Tues–Sat; beer and wine; reservations recommended; street parking; map:FF8* &

Metropolitan Grill / ★★★

820 2ND AVE, DOWNTOWN; 206/624-3287

Seattle loves this masculine, meaty haunt deep in the financial district, and why not? It does what it does very well, which is to serve steaks to men in suits and well-heeled tourists. Lunch comes with a floor show of financiers, power brokers, and their underlings table-hopping and networking. Dow Jones numbers are posted in the bar on a blackboard. There's a showcase out front featuring the arsenal of prime grade, corn-fed, dry-aged slabs of beef in New York, porterhouse, T-bone, and top sirloin cuts. The house specialties are an extra-thick veal chop with garlic rosemary demi-glace and, of course, prime Delmonico, a bone-in New York strip. Stick with the meat; the pastas and seafood are less well executed, so often the case in these bovine shrines. Expect to be well cared for by a well-trained waitstaff. As you'd expect, muscular red European and domestic wines dominate the lengthy list priced accordingly high. *$$$; AE, DC, DIS, JCB, MC, V; checks OK; lunch Mon–Fri, dinner every day; full bar; reservations recommended; valet parking; www.the metropolitangrill.com; map:M7* &

Mistral Restaurant / ★★★

113 BLANCHARD ST, BELLTOWN; 206/770-7799

When chef William Belickis opened his stark little luxury restaurant, it caused immediate controversy among Seattle diners and foodies. The crux of the brouhaha revolves around his rather strong opinions about what diners should and shouldn't eat (an example of the latter dictum:

bread with his food). Then there's the heavily promoted prix-fixe chef's tasting menu, designed at his whim and allegedly different for each patron. He offended reviewers and diners alike by being, they say, precious, pretentious, and pricey, but no one can deny the quality and innovation of the food nor the risks taken by this young chef. Expect first-rate treatment by an experienced waitstaff. The fare is uniformly impressive. Entrees from his "Market Menu" include the breast of Moulard duck; sablefish with brown-butter cauliflower and almond oil; and the squab with savoy cabbage and local beans. Entrees are prefaced with changing *amuse bouches*, such as a creamy goat cheese–Maine lobster quiche in a puddle of chive sauce and dollop of *osetra* caviar. Desserts can be a luscious vanilla-bean crème brûlée or a strawberry-almond tart with a nutty crust. Like it or not, Seattle, this is a food experience unlike any other in town. *$$$$; AE, DIS, MC, V; checks OK; lunch Fri–Sat, dinner Tues–Sat; full bar; reservations recommended; street parking; william@mistralseattle. com; www.mistralseattle.com; map:G8* &

Moghul Palace / ★★☆

10301 NE 10TH ST, BELLEVUE; 425/451-1909
Shah Kahn's pretty restaurant, a block north of Bellevue Square mall, has a well-stocked bargain Indian lunch buffet that's popular with shoppers and the downtown Bellevue work force alike. This place makes its own mango ice cream, all fruity and chunked up with pistachios and almonds. It's a good way to top off a meal of mango ribs, tender tandoori chicken, vegetarian or chicken dhal, lamb korma, curried mussels, plus other options. (That is, if you haven't already spoiled your appetite on the enticing Indian breads, crispy potato or chicken naan or the fragrant onion kulka.) The masala fish is spicy, though there was a problem with freshness on one of our visits. Maybe it's best to stick with the meat or vegetarian dishes, such as the vegetable biryani and the lamb vindaloo, a spicy, sumptuous melange. *$$; AE, DC, DIS, MC, V; local checks only; lunch Mon–Sat, dinner every day; full bar; reservations recommended; street parking; map:HH3* &

Mona's / ★★★☆

6421 LATONA AVE NE, GREEN LAKE; 206/526-1188
Tito Class and Annette Serrano had the *Mona Lisa* in mind when they named their Green Lake restaurant. The charm of the candle-lit dining room is due in part to art created by Annette herself, making the style of the room more (Frida) Kahlo than Leonardo (da Vinci). The food from the small Mediterranean menu continues the seduction. Mona's menu changes seasonally, paying homage to both sides of the Med with local seafood and produce. Regulars on the starter menu are baked Brie, a duck confit, and a real caesar. Scallop ceviche graced a recent menu. Entrees frequently include hearty paella, pork tenderloin, and

roasted–butternut squash ravioli. Finish with a terrific housemade dessert; the tiramisu is among the best in town. The couple annexed the storefront next door and Class converted it into an intimate conversation bar that often features live music—a great place for after-dinner drinks or dessert. *$$; AE, DC, MC, V; checks OK; dinner every day; full bar; reservations recommended; street parking; map:EE7* &

Monsoon / ★★★
615 19TH AVE E, CAPITOL HILL; 206/325-2111
Sister and brother Sophie and Eric Banh have added their chic, upscale Vietnamese jewel to the diverse Seattle restaurant scene. They cook exotic seasonal dishes in the gleaming, steamy open kitchen, which fronts a four-stool counter and a spare, elegant dining room. Don't miss the tamarind soup with tiger prawns and chicken, a sweet and tangy mix with lotus root, pineapple, and bean sprouts, though you may get side-tracked by compelling appetizers such as the cold shrimp-shiitake rolls, the *la lot* beef, or the five-spice baby back ribs. The entree portions are agreeably ample. Try the sea scallops and crispy yam with spicy chile sauce or the fresh halibut steamed with crunchy lily buds and shiitakes in a banana leaf. Vegetable dishes such as the grilled Asian eggplant with green onions in coconut sauce or snap peas and shiitakes help make the menu a very comfortable place for herbivores. The dining room can be very noisy when full. Expect a wait at the door and to be handled gracefully and democratically by the other Banh sister, Yen. *$$; MC, V; no checks; lunch Tues–Fri, dinner Tues–Sun; beer and wine; reservations recommended; street parking; www.monsoonseattle.com; map:HH7* &

Moonfish / ★★
4738 LYNWOOD CENTER RD NE, BAINBRIDGE ISLAND; 206/780-3473
The understated elegance of Moonfish is the creation of veteran East Coast restaurateurs chef David Perlman and manager Kevin Noyes. In the well-connected rooms, pale peach walls glow softly in the light of jewel-toned glass sconces, while halogen lights spotlight delicate Japanese floral arrangements. Perlman's menu is an ambitious one made up of small and large "adventures" that don't venture far from the usual dinner fare in this price range. The grilled shrimp and zucchini fritters are unusual, though—sassy with the flavor of good olives and artichoke mayonnaise. He has a list of wood-fired flatbreads—cracker-crust pizzas with such wonderful toppings as pulled chicken, eggplant, and spinach or white clam, arugula, roasted garlic, and shaved Parmesan. Entrees mostly hit, including the Asian-style slow-roasted duck breasts with a huckleberry glaze. The crusty and perfectly cooked Chilean sea bass rests in a thin soup of tomatoes, field greens, and basil-mint pesto. You can't go wrong ending an evening with the frozen chocolate Grand Marnier cake with chocolate apricot crème anglaise. *$$$; AE, MC, V; checks*

OK; lunch Tues–Fri, dinner Tues–Sat; full bar; reservations recommended; self parking; moon02@worldnet.att.net &

Morton's of Chicago / ★★★

1511 6TH AVE, DOWNTOWN; 206/223-0550

It's a chain steak house in a basement, but it does the simple, important things that steak houses are supposed to do. And it does them very well. That is: cook huge slabs of meat in a screaming-hot, 1,800°F broiler to the internal temperature you order. This lion's den is definitely masculine, done in dark wood panels, old photos, and LeRoy Nieman serigraphs. Everything is large here—the potatoes, even the asparagus. And the meat is not exactly petit, as you'll note when the cart is rolled out for you, showcasing it in all its proffered cuts—USDA prime dry-aged fillets, porterhouse, New York, T-bone, rib-eye, chicken, veal, and lamb chops—along with swordfish, salmon, and a three- or four-pound lobster. After being given a talking tour of the cart by the waiter, you make your choice and it's taken back to the broiler and properly cooked. You'll find nothing wrong with any of the straightforward, well-made food. This is big bucks for big food done well. *$$$; AE, MC, V; checks OK; dinner every day; full bar; reservations recommended; valet parking; www.mortons.com; map:J4 &*

Nell's / ★★★

6804 E GREEN LAKE WY N, GREEN LAKE; 206/524-4044

Philip Mihalski has seamlessly taken over this Green Lake institution, which was formerly Saleh al Lago. The sleek, multilevel lakeview dining room has been redecorated but it's still recognizable, and Saleh himself sometimes still greets customers at the door on weekends—a comfort to the old regulars. Mihalski, a veteran chef of such kitchens as Marco's Supperclub and Dahlia Lounge, has retained a few of the old menu favorites but has added his own twist to new and seasonally changing menus. He offers a five-item prix-fixe tasting menu and a healthy list of à la carte choices. On one visit, stellar first-course items included a sweet onion tart with Jerusalem artichokes and hazelnut butter and the porcini-dusted sweetbreads. The second-course Muscovy duck breast was rare and succulent, served with an herb bread salad and *picholine* olives, and the king salmon was perfect with oven-dried tomato risotto. Equally enthralling was the peach and blueberry crisp paired with housemade peach ice cream and the fig and honey tart topped in crème fraîche. The wine list is more or less split between French and domestic labels. *$$$; AE, MC, V; checks OK; dinner every day; full bar; reservations recommended; valet and self parking; map:EE7 &*

Nishino / ★★★☆

3130 E MADISON ST, MADISON VALLEY; 206/322-5800

Kyoto-born Tatsu Nishino apprenticed at one of Japan's renowned *kaiseki* (many-coursed, ritualized seasonal cuisine) restaurants, then spent five years working with celebrated chef Nobu Matsuhisa in Los Angeles before coming to Seattle and opening Nishino, on the fringes of moneyed Madison Park. The space is decorated with spare, Japanese elegance. In the open kitchen and in the adjacent sushi bar, Eastern traditions meet Western bravado felicitously. The voluptuous assortment of fresh seafood on display is fashioned into striking arrangements: raw, pale pink albacore tuna may anchor a crown of taro chips or support a dollop of lumpfish caviar and a drop of edible liquid gold. Look to the fresh sheet for memorable flavor combinations, such as pan-seared halibut cheeks with shiitakes and spinach in a luxurious butter sauce with bits of sea urchin, lemon, soy, and mirin. More than two dozen sushi items are listed on the menu, and while you can certainly opt for tempura or teriyaki, you would miss much of the sheer joy of dining at Nishino. A wonderful and adventurous way to eat here is *omikase* style—letting Mr. Nishino pick your dinner. The wine list features plenty of reasonably priced Washington, Oregon, and California labels. For dessert, don't miss the popular Banana Tempura—deep-fried bananas with vanilla ice cream and caramel drizzled on top. *$$$; AE, MC, V; no checks; dinner every day; full bar; reservations recommended; self parking; map:GG6* &

Noble Court / ★★

1644 140TH AVE NE, BELLEVUE; 425/641-6011

Here's a major dim sum stop that's *not* in Seattle's Chinatown/International District—it's on the Eastside. Lines of dim sum lovers—especially on Sundays—can cause waits of up to an hour or more. In fact, it may be best to avoid the crowds and go on Saturday. Steamed shrimp dumplings, pork buns, lotus seed balls, and chicken feet with oyster and black bean sauce are only the beginning of the movable feast carted to your table during lunchtime. The regular menu is massive, too. There's a live tank with Dungeness and king crabs served with choices of sauces. Other seafood specialties include whole flounder and rockfish, geoduck, and abalone. There are hot pots, sizzling platters, and lot of noodles. You can get Peking duck without 24-hour preordering. *$$; AE, MC, V; no checks; lunch, dinner Mon–Fri, dim sum Sat–Sun; full bar; reservations recommended; self parking; map:GG2* &

The Original Pancake House / ★

130 PARK PL CENTER, KIRKLAND; 425/827-7575

OK, so it's not exactly original (the first opened in Portland in 1953), but it *is* the ultimate answer to the pancake question. Expensive? For pancakes, you might think so. But it's worth a drive to Kirkland just to ponder the prodigious pancake options (including buttermilk, buckwheat, sourdough, and Swedish). There's hotcakes, flapjacks, and griddle cakes, plus fruit, nut, or bacon waffles. The baked apple pancake is a single pancake smothered with apples and cinnamon sugar that's slightly smaller than a manhole cover; Dutch babies are golden-brown, air-filled puffs served with lemon, whipped butter, and powdered sugar. There are also lots of crepes, with fruits and conserves and syrups to roll in them, not to mention the usual breakfast works of omelets, bacon and eggs, and oatmeal. Kids and grandmas love this place. *$; AE, DIS, MC, V; no checks; breakfast every day, lunch Mon–Fri; no alcohol; no reservations; self parking; flapjack@seanet.com; www.originalpancakehouse.com; map:EE3* &

Osteria La Spiga / ★★★

1401 BROADWAY AVE, CAPITOL HILL; 206/323-8881

A step off Broadway brings you to sunny Romagna. Sisters Sabrina and Sachia Tinsley and Sabrina's Romagnan husband, Pietro Borghesi, have created this very special rustic Northern Italian *taverna*. The decor is imported from Italy—long, rough-hewn tables; bisque tiles painted with black-and-white roosters; marble-topped bar; wrought-iron arches; hand-stamped floral kerchief curtains; wood and rattan stools. Start with tomato slices and fresh mozzarella with hand-torn basil and good olive oil. *Piadina*, a flatbread that's a cross between pita bread and tortillas, can be ordered plain or filled with a plethora of goodies, including prosciutto and aged mozzarella. Soups change every day—it could be *passatelli*, a light beef broth with egg, cheese, and little pastas, or a lentil soup with sour apples. Pastas are handmade—such as the tortellini with ricotta, spinach, and a sauce of tomato, cream, and smoked prosciutto. The housemade tiramisu is a dreamy puff of mascarpone with a thick layer of coarsely ground cocoa. Wines are modestly priced and aptly mostly Italian. *$$; MC, V; local checks only; lunch Mon–Fri, dinner Mon–Sat; beer and wine; reservations recommended; street parking; map:HH6* &

The Painted Table / ★★★

92 MADISON ST (ALEXIS HOTEL), DOWNTOWN; 206/624-3646

Chef Tim Kelley has been quietly putting out some of the most inspired plates, from one of the best boutique hotels, in Seattle for years now. The Painted Table may have recently gotten a brand-new look, but Kelley's talented touch with game meat and fish dishes is ever the same, as are his close ties with regional organic growers, which account for the unusual,

OODLES OF NOODLES

Slurping noodles—whether pho, yakisoba, or chow mein—is a beloved Seattle pastime. That's because they're fun for everybody (kids love 'em) and they fit every budget. **Than Brothers** (516 Broadway Ave E, Capitol Hill; 206/568-7218 and 7714 Aurora Ave N, Green Lake; 206/527-5973) can be counted upon for great pho and the free appetizer cream puffs. **Pho Bac** (1314 S Jackson St, Chinatown/International District; 206/323-4387) has some of the best pho in town. The popular Fremont Noodle House, dislodged by gentrification, has been reincarnated with an expanded menu as **Thaiku** (5410 Ballard Ave NW, Ballard; 206/706-7807). **House of Dumplings** (514 S King St, Chinatown/International District; 206/340-0774) has all manner of Chinese pasta—sui mai, pot-stickers, fried Singapore-style noodles, or chow fun. Vegans and vegetarians are well-served at **Bamboo Garden Vegetarian Cuisine** (364 Roy St, Queen Anne; 206/282-6616). Other best noodle bets: the classy **Orrapin Noodle Experience** (2208 Queen Anne Ave N, Queen Anne; 206/352-6594) and funky **Noodle Ranch** (2228 2nd Ave, Belltown; 206/728-0463). —*Michael Hood*

inventively prepared seasonal vegetables that make it to his menu. Such offerings include a starter of slow-cooked lobster with lotus root and pea shoots in a carrot-cardamom broth, a huckleberry-sauced Muscovy duck breast, or guinea hen with black truffles and roasted kabocha squash. His range is showcased in selections such as a braised venison osso buco with parsnip purée and roasted carrots, and the lighter three-clam linguine using Manila, razor, and geoduck clams. Kelley also runs five-course tasting menus (dessert included) that change weekly and reflect seasonal availabilities. Flavors are matched by gorgeous presentation and a mighty wine list. Chocolate lovers can count on several selections per menu: a recent knockout was "s'mores" with warm chocolate ganache, housemade graham crackers, and vanilla-bean meringue. Yow! *$$$; AE, DC, DIS, MC, V; local checks only; breakfast, dinner every day, lunch Mon–Fri; full bar; reservations recommended; discounted valet parking in Alexis Hotel garage; www.alexishotel.com; map:L8 &*

Palace Kitchen / ★★★

2030 5TH AVE, BELLTOWN; 206/448-2001
The palatial open kitchen and lively center-stage bar scene circulate a constant energy buzz through the Palace until closing time. Servers are capable and well-trained, and you can catch the action from various vantage points: seated at the enormous tile-topped bar, beneath a huge painting of a lusty 17th-century banquet, in a private booth, at a storefront banquette, or in the glassed-in private room. Though this is essen-

tially a bar, Tom Douglas's—yes, he of Dahlia Lounge and Etta's Seafood (see reviews)—food is always robust and innovative. To get in the convivial spirit of the Palace, order shareable selections such as the fat and spicy grilled chicken wings, bowls of clams, or crispy-fried, semolina-coated anchovies. The goat-cheese fondue with chunks of bread and apple slices is also fun for a crowd, or try Douglas's collection of Northwest artisan cheeses. Or go all out and choose one of the night's specials from the applewood grill, including the pit-roasted lamb, chicken, or whole fish. The informative wine list is the most entertaining in town. *$$; AE, DC, DIS, MC, V; checks OK; lunch Mon–Fri, dinner every day; full bar; reservations recommended; street parking; www.tomdouglas. com; map:H6* &

Palisade / ★★☆

2601 W MARINA PL, MAGNOLIA; 206/285-1000

Here's one of the most incredible waterfront settings in the area, with a splendid 180-degree view of Elliott Bay, Alki Point, and the Seattle skyline. The view's distracting, but so is Palisade's interior of huge radiating beams and Japanese garden, complete with bonsai and bubbling brook. The menu offerings are eye-catching too: go for a *pau hana* (after-work) drink and pupu platters of steamed butter clams, Whidbey Island mussels with sun-dried tomatoes and fresh thyme, or the inevitable Dungeness crab cakes. The seafood chowder is ultracreamy and loaded with crab and shrimp. Chef John Howie uses an applewood broiler, wood oven, flash-searing grill, and wood-fired rotisserie for the extensive menu of fish and meat, but his signature dish is salmon roasted on a red cedar plank (you even get to take the plank home with you). Check the daily fresh sheet for local fish such as steelhead trout, Oregon sea bass, Columbia River sturgeon, or flown-in warm-water Pacific fishes such as mahi mahi, yellowfin tuna, or the dense, rich Fijiian star, escolar. There are steaks, chicken, prime ribs, and fork-tender racks of Ellensburg lamb that are spit-roasted over applewood. The servers are friendly and particularly poetic in describing desserts, such as the white chocolate mousse tart and the Granny Smith apple tart with cinnamon ice cream and warm caramel sauce. *$$; AE, DIS, DC, MC, V; checks OK; lunch, dinner every day, brunch Sun; full bar; reservations recommended; self parking; map:GG8* &

Panos Kleftiko / ★★

815 5TH AVE N, SEATTLE CENTER; 206/301-0393

Panos Marina is the chef, host, heart, and soul of this tiny, traditional Greek *taverna* a few blocks north of Seattle Center. Bring a bunch of friends and crowd your table with *mezedes*, Panos's tapas-like "little dishes." There are four pages to choose from; they're moderately priced and best accompanied by warm housemade pita bread, hummus, or creamy tzatziki sauce and a glass or three of retsina. Try the melitzano-salata, an eggplant salad with good olive oil, tomatoes, and herbs; the baked kalamata olives; or the meatballs. There are entrees to like, too—spanakopita with fresh spinach layered in crispy phyllo dough or the tender roast lamb with rich, garlicky aioli. Arrive early if you have tickets to a show; Panos encourages lingering (if you do, sample a slice of baklava paired with rich Greek coffee) and doesn't take reservations. *$; MC, V; local checks only; dinner Mon–Sat; beer and wine; no reservations; street parking; map:B4* &

The Pink Door / ★★☆

1919 POST ALLEY, PIKE PLACE MARKET; 206/443-3241

The low-profile entrance (just a pink door on Post Alley) underscores the speakeasy style of this Italian trattoria just steps from the Pike Place Market. In winter, the dining room grows noisy around a burbling fountain. Come warmer weather, everyone vies for a spot on the trellis-covered terrace with its breathtakingly romantic view of the Sound. Inside or out, the arty, under-30 set who call the place home might be happily noshing on garlicky black-olive tapenade and quaffing tumblers of wine from the reasonably priced, mostly Italian list. The menu features hearty, generously portioned pastas, a daily risotto, excellent rack of lamb paired with mascarpone mashed potatoes, and a lusty seafood-filled cioppino. Inventive salads are composed of mostly organic local produce. Desserts are a homey affair, such as apple crisp in a cereal bowl or a rich pumpkin bread pudding the size of a paving brick with warm caramel sauce. There's often live music (and sometimes a tarot card reader) in the evenings. *$$; AE, MC, V; no checks; lunch Tues–Sat, dinner Tues–Sun; full bar; reservations recommended; self parking; map:J8* &

Place Pigalle / ★★☆

81 PIKE ST, PIKE PLACE MARKET; 206/624-1756

Place Pigalle is indeed the place—if you're looking for picture-postcard views of Elliott Bay, warmly professional service, and ambitious French-Northwest-Italian cooking from a tiny kitchen whose crew must choreograph every movement. Hidden away in the market, the bistro is the perfect spot to sip an eau-de-vie, lunch with a friend, or engage in a romantic dinner à deux. Ask for a window table and order something as simple as calamari sautéed with ginger, garlic, spinach, and creamy mustard sauce. Or try something as sophisticated as a saddle of rabbit filled with apples, spinach, and blue cheese or a soup plate of saffron broth packed with seafood, shiitakes, and roast tomatoes. There's an excellent artisan cheese list, reasonably priced and changed frequently. And, for dessert, offerings include rich pots de crème or the signature brandied apricot–almond torte. On sunny days, a small deck attracts those anxious to catch every ray, but the inside tables have the advantage of being in servers' sight lines. The little bar is ideal for dining solo—or for snuggling up to your choice of hundreds of wines, which range from Northwest to French and Australian labels. *$$$; AE, DC, MC, V; no checks; lunch, dinner Mon–Sat; full bar; reservations recommended; valet and self parking; map:J8*

Pontevecchio / ★★

710 N 34TH ST, FREMONT; 206/633-3989

If Federico Fellini had lived to discover Fremont, he'd have been a regular at Pontevecchio, where on some evenings you might have to wait until a couple dancing the tango finishes so you can get to your table. A boccie-ball toss from Fremont's famous *Waiting for the Interurban* sculpture, fewer than a dozen candle-lit tables populate Michele Zacco's hopelessly romantic Italian bistro. Zacco has the heart of an impresario and the soul of an artist—and he can cook. He simmers his tomato sauce for hours, and ladles it over the ravioli. His antipasti platter is a carnival of flavors, his panini fresh and toothsome. Though the menu seldom changes, the music does: one night a tenor singing Puccini; on another, a flamenco guitarist. It's always a little zany. *Dolce* is as simple as gelato or cannoli. A recent addition for the lunch crowd is a takeout window dispensing inexpensive, light Italian lunches. *$$; MC, V; local checks only; lunch Mon–Fri, dinner Mon–Sat; reservations recommended; street parking; www.pontevecchiobistro.com; map:FF8*

Ponti Seafood Grill / ★★★

3014 3RD AVE N, FREMONT; 206/284-3000

Ponti would be downright Mediterranean, with its canalside perch, stucco walls, red-tiled roof, and understated dining rooms, but for the passing salmon boats and the funeral parlor next door. Also, the menu borrows from an array of ethnic flavors (with more than a passing nod to Asia). Twentysomething Tom Hollywood, who was promoted to head chef in 2001, creates cross-cultural magic with combinations such as seared ahi in a ginger-jolted shoyu and sake sauce with coconut rice cake and cucumber-wasabi aioli. The test of Hollywood's star power may rest with one dish: the Thai curry penne (with broiled scallops, Dungeness crabmeat, spicy ginger-tomato chutney, and basil chiffonade) that is a long-running favorite. Savvy diners turn to the fresh sheet for the most exciting offerings of the day: grilled sea bass with tomatillo sauce; a stew of lobster and mussels in coconut broth flavored with cilantro pesto; red wine risotto with halibut cheeks, artichoke, asparagus, and chard. Tempting desserts range from white chocolate crème caramel to seasonal fruit tarts. Dine outdoors in warm weather on balconies on the Queen Anne side of the ship canal, overlooking the boat traffic and the joggers and bikers on the path below. *$$$; AE, DC, MC, V; local checks only; lunch Sun–Fri, dinner every day, brunch Sun; full bar; reservations rec-*

ommended; valet and self parking; mnger@ponti.com; www.ponti seafoodgrill.com; map:FF8 ⅙

Queen City Grill / ★★

2201 IST AVE, BELLTOWN; 206/443-0975
Peter Lamb's pioneering Belltown saloon is a chic crowd-pleaser. There's a doorman during prime hours who manipulates a velvet rope to control the traffic into this noisy restaurant/bar. Once you're inside, high-backed wooden booths come with streetside views, or park it at the bar to enjoy the work of some of the most popular bartenders in town. The kitchen seems to have straightened out some of the past inconsistencies. Meat selections, such as the mixed grill of chicken, andouille sausage, lamb, and pork chops, are capably executed. However, seafood is still the best bet here. There's a tasty mixed seafood grill with clams, mussels, and chunks of salmon or snapper. Queen City also has the distinction of being one of the first Seattle restaurants to serve Dungeness crab cakes, and they're still wonderful in a tangy remoulade. For afters, try the dense, flourless Chocolate Nemesis Cake or the mocha crème caramel. All in all, this is a classy, convivial place to enjoy a nosh. *$$; AE, DC, DIS, MC, V; no checks; lunch Mon–Fri, dinner every day; full bar; reservations recommended; valet parking; map:G8* ⅙

Racha Noodles / ★★

23 MERCER ST, QUEEN ANNE; 206/281-8883
Racha's been on lower Queen Anne for years, but recently the Thai owners took a giant step up in stature. In an enlarging remodel and menu expansion, they've taken it from neighborhood noodle house to serious Thai cuisine. An open kitchen dominates the center of the room, overseen by chef Napaporn Empremsilapa (her friends call her Meow). She's a gifted chef often sent by the owners to Bangkok to learn new skills. There's a healthy list of *yums*, those spicy wrap salads eaten rolled up in cabbage or lettuce, and the prawn rolls are golden cylinders of fried rice

paper stuffed with sausage and prawns and served with plum sauce. Other delectables include Ms. Meow's duck, which is steamed in herbs, then deep-fried, boned, sliced, and served dry, and the Ocean Wrap Curry, shrimps and scallops steamed in rice wontons in green curry sauce rich with coconut milk. Desserts can be green tea, mango ice cream, or black sticky rice rich with sweet coconut milk. The surroundings, such as large Thai murals, strike an authentic note. And on Saturday and Sunday nights, the meditational tones and civil rhythms of Thai classical and folk tunes played on traditional instruments by local ensembles add an exotic soundtrack. *$; AE, MC, V; checks OK; lunch Mon–Fri, dinner every day; full bar; reservations recommended; street parking; map:B4* ⅙

Raga / ★★★

212 CENTRAL WY, KIRKLAND; 425/827-3300

Kamal Mroke opened Raga in Bellevue in 1991, and all went well until a fire destroyed it in 2000. After 10 months, Raga relocated, this time in neighboring Kirkland, in the location of the old Bistro Provencal. The decor is pleasantly distracting. Spangled Indian fabrics adorn the ceiling and exotic musical instruments decorate the walls; a fireplace blazes incongruously in the middle of the room. The tables are set with linen; waiters put your napkin on your lap. Try the two dishes unique to this kitchen: the Malai chicken kebab is a breast marinated with cashews and cream before being flash-grilled in the tandoori; *methi* is the pungent herb

fenugreek, and Mroke uses the dried leaves, plus garlic and curry, to make a sauce for lamb, prawns, or chicken that is unforgettable. Lunch is an inexpensive all-you-can-eat buffet with a few western salads, bright red chicken tikka from the tandoori, and an ever-changing selection of meat and vegetable dishes. On Sunday, the buffet makes for a wonderful brunch, and the flirtatious and funny Mroke is in the dining room frying up fresh little potato pancakes called *aloo tiki* served in a pool of thin yogurt and tamarind sauce. These are a rare find around here, so they bring lots of Indians and their families to his door. Liquid treats include a tangy mango lassi (the Indian equivalent of a yogurt smoothie) or a selection from the short but well-rounded wine list. *$$; AE, DC, MC, V; checks OK; lunch, dinner every day; full bar; self parking; map:EE3* ⅙

Ray's Boathouse / ★★
Ray's Cafe / ★★

6049 SEAVIEW AVE NW, BALLARD; 206/789-3770

Ray's Boathouse has achieved iconic status in the annals of Northwest restaurants. And no wonder—it's a beautiful and comfortable place reminiscent of a yacht club with peerless views of Shilshole Bay and the Olympic Mountains. The service is gracious, capable, and well trained. The landmark consistently turns out such Northwest fish-house staples as whole Dungeness crabs to be steamed for you fresh out of the live tank or Manila clams in butter and dill broth from Skookum Inlet. There's also Mediterraneanata such as savory roasted garlic cheesecake. Salmon is always great (Ray's was the first restaurant to acquire its own fish buyer's license), and all fish are usually wild and always fresh. The rich black cod is a signature selection, which can be applewood smoked or marinated *kasu*-style in sake lees. Expect an extensive Northwest wine list, and a healthy mix of locals and tourists. Ray's Cafe, which occupies the upper Boathouse, serves up lighter fare, though you are welcome to order from the downstairs menu, too. Choices include fish-and-chips, burgers, or blackened red rockfish. Diehard Northwesterners sit on the outside deck, toddy in hand, any time of the night or year—there are blankets for the asking if you're chilled. The cafe serves lunch, for which you should make reservations on weekdays. *$$$, $$; AE, DC, DIS, MC, V; checks OK; dinner every day (Boathouse), lunch, dinner every day (Cafe); full bar; reservations recommended (Boathouse); valet or self parking; rays@ rays.com; www.rays.com; map:EE9* &

Restaurant Zoë / ★★★

2137 2ND AVE, BELLTOWN; 206/256-2060

Sure, the postmodern restaurant clichés, almost a prerequisite in Belltown, are here—exposed heating ducts, charred ahi tuna, beautiful young waitstaff. However, the popularity of this relative newcomer goes beyond shallow pose. For one thing, the servers are well-trained. And owner/chef Scott Staples, who made Kirkland's Third Floor Fish Cafe (see review) into a notable destination, has vision and skill. The fresh ricotta raviolo appetizer is a cheesy herbed pillow of pasta in a plate-lickable lobster sauce, festooned with leeks, shiitakes, and oyster mushrooms. Staples's signature grilled romaine salad is a must—whole hearts of romaine, grilled just enough to get a touch of smoke, then dressed with a bacon, apple, and Roquefort dressing. Staples is at his best with fish. The charred ahi is thickly crusted with Tellicherry peppercorns and served with quinoa tabbouleh and kalamata pesto. A chunk of perfectly broiled king salmon is served over a savory mess of Puy lentils, minced beets, and citrusy brown butter. No clichés in the dessert department: try the slice of brioche French toast with crème brûlée and maple syrup glaze. A flaky-crusted lemon tart with in-season fruit, ice cream, and fresh berries is perfectly Northwest. The lively bar shares the small space with diners. That and the hardwood acoustics can make this place noisy. *$$$; AE, MC, V; checks OK; dinner Mon–Sat; full bar; reservations recommended; street parking; map:G7* &

Ristorante Buongusto / ★★

2232 QUEEN ANNE AVE N, QUEEN ANNE; 206/284-9040

With a cozy fire in winter and an umbrella-strewn streetside deck for summer, this is a place for all seasons. Owner and manager Salvio Varchetta is from Napoli, but he and his chefs draw from up and down the entire Italian peninsula for their well-rounded menu. Antipasti change daily and make good use of an array of organic vegetables. Familiar dishes are done very well, such as the meaty portobellos brushed with oil and grilled with radicchio, veal scallops sautéed in butter with mushrooms and marsala, rigatoni in smooth tomato sauce with a touch of cream loaded with sausage and eggplant, or housemade raviolis stuffed with pumpkin and served in a creamy sauce with almonds and golden raisins. Order wine from the wide-ranging list of mostly Italian selections. The service is seamless and charming—designed to stay out of the way of your romance. *$$; AE, DC, DIS, MC; checks OK; lunch*

Tues–Fri, dinner every day; full bar; reservations recommended; street parking; map:GG7 &

Rosita's Mexican Restaurant / ★

7210 WOODLAWN AVE NE, GREEN LAKE; 206/523-3031
9747 HOLMAN RD N, CROWN HILL; 206/784-4132

Rosita's has been serving good old-fashioned comes-with-rice-and-beans Tex-Mex food for years. At this pair of restaurants, you won't find the trendy pan-American ceviche-cilantro-chipotle consciousness that's becoming ubiquitous in such un-Mexican neighborhoods as Belltown or Madison Park. The large dining room is simply decorated with all the usual Mexican tchotchkes, but the tables and roomy banquettes are great for large parties. Rosita's is a place your kids will actually love, especially for the *platos pequeños*—plates with tacos, tamales, burritos, and even cheeseburgers sized and priced for smaller, younger considerations. Adults do well here too. There's super nachos, a gigantic heap of corn chips layered with chicken and cheese, guacamole and beans, and a green tomatillo sauce. Avoid the seafood, but let them get fancy with the *pollo al carbon*, chicken with creamy chipotle sauce; chile verde, long-cooked chunks of pork in a green sauce; or the sizzling fajitas (the steak is best). At night, be sure to special-order the fresh housemade corn tortillas to be slathered with butter. They're so good they eclipse the forgettable salsa. The Holman Road branch is larger but serves essentially the same menu. *$; AE, MC, V; no checks; lunch Mon–Sat, dinner every day; full bar; reservations recommended; street parking; map:EE8, DD8* &

Rover's / ★★★★

2808 E MADISON ST, MADISON VALLEY; 206/325-7442

Though Rover's diminutive and fedora-wearing chef/owner, Thierry Rautureau, has won the hearts of Seattleites, half his customers are out-of-towners making pilgrimages to his charmingly decorated restaurant in a small house tucked into a garden courtyard in Madison Valley. His warmth and wit are only part of the equation. His inspired hand in the kitchen has won him national renown. Choose from three prix-fixe menus de degustation (one of which is vegetarian) served with gorgeous presentation and a generous hand. Rautureau's forte is seafood, and he's adept at finding the best-quality ingredients. He's a master of sauces, using stocks, reductions, herb-infused oils, and purées to enhance breasts of quail, slices of sturgeon, steamed Maine lobster, wild mushrooms, Russian caviar, and foie gras. One knockout regular appetizer: eggs scrambled with garlic and chives, then layered with crème fraîche and lime juice in an eggshell cut into a tiny cup and topped with white sturgeon caviar. Expect professional service from Rautureau's loyal staff, and sticker shock when perusing the carefully chosen, extensive wine list. Dining in the courtyard, weather permitting, is an enchanting experience.

$$$$; AE, DC, MC, V; checks OK; dinner Tues–Sat; beer and wine; reservations required; street parking; www.rovers-seattle.com; map:GG6 ⅏

Roy Street Bistro / ★★⅏

174 ROY ST, QUEEN ANNE; 206/284-9093

On a tree-lined lower Queen Anne street just a short stroll from Seattle Center, find the unpretentious appeal of an English village dining room. Indeed, proprietor Patrick Conlan hails from London, and as a former waiter, he brings polish and warmth to the front of the house, often tending the busy bar himself. The short, daily-changing menu puts a creative spin on classic British and Northern European fare with appetizers such as smoked salmon and cucumber tartlets, hot buttered oysters with Parmesan cheese, or sautéed shrimp with gin and lime over wilted spinach. There's bistro food including calf's liver sautéed with caramelized onions, lamb shanks with pears, fennel, and white beans, or roast chicken with rosemary and mashed potatoes. Fish can range from grilled salmon to cumin-dusted halibut. Conlan has composed a thoughtful wine list and will expertly walk you through it. Simplicity is the hallmark of desserts: for example, poached pears with chocolate and raspberry sauce. *$$; AE, MC, V; local checks only; dinner every day; full bar; reservations recommended; street parking; bistro@drizzle.com; map:A6* ⅏ *(except bar)*

Saigon Bistro / ★★

1032 S JACKSON ST, STE 202, CHINATOWN/INTERNATIONAL DISTRICT; 206/329-4939

Here is a tasty, inexpensive trip to Vietnam with a menu not too scary for the timid nor too limited for the adventurous. There's a long list of phos, those fragrant, clear-brothed, fine-noodled soups with beef, chicken, duck, or tofu, served with a heap of bean sprouts, branches of basil and mint, slices of jalapeños, and lime wedges. It's soup, salad, and entree all in one. Popular with neighborhood day-workers are the huge sandwiches bursting with grilled meats, veggies, and fresh basil and mint on a baguette for only two bucks! The wonderful *goi cuon*—summer salad rice-paper rolls with vermicelli, shrimp, pork, or tofu—and the egg rolls with shredded pork and mushrooms make for a healthy lunch, as does the Vietnamese crepe, a fluffy rice-flour pancake with turmeric, mung beans, sprouts, and green onions to wrap in lettuce. Worthy entrees include roasted coconut chicken, clay pot dishes such as spare ribs or catfish, and a delectably rich casserole of eggplant, tofu, and sea snails. Have a sweet dessert drink—navy, mung, and red beans in coconut milk over ice or a cold-brewed iced coffee with condensed milk. The branch in Uwajimaya Village (600 5th Ave S; 206/621-2085) has only the faster, more portable items from the fuller menu of the Jackson Street location. *$; MC, V; checks OK; lunch, dinner every day; beer and wine; no reservations; self parking; map:HH6* ⅏

Saito's Japanese Cafe & Bar / ★★★☆

2120 2ND AVE, BELLTOWN; 206/728-1333

On any given night in this smart Belltown place, you might see the Japanese ambassador or—more impressively—Mariners superstars Ichiro Suzuki or Kazuhiro Sasaki, who are regulars. They come for Saito-san's sushi, arguably the best in town. The fish is immaculately fresh and cut thicker than you'll usually find in Seattle. Sometimes you'll find *toro*, the fatty blue fin tuna that literally melts in your mouth. All the seafoods—crab, tuna, shrimp, spotted mackerel, steelhead, yellowtail, albacore, salmon—are here, as well as the chewy ones (the small conch, surf or yellow clams, octopus) and some that are still alive, such as the quivering geoduck and the flinching abalone. The modern Japanese mirrored dining room is served well by Saito-san's vivacious wife, Anita, and a staff of knowledgeable servers. The innovative chef, Viljo Basso, who's been given full rein by Saito, is experienced in luxury cuisine (he came from Rover's) and now has a new spectrum of ingredients to play with. You'll be fortunate if his butter *itame*, a sauté of geoduck, sugar snaps, and shiitakes, is a special during one of your visits. For example, he goes further than the traditional American Japanese restaurant with vegetable tempura, picking what's fresh: sugar snaps, squash blossoms, and matsutake, oyster, and morel mushrooms cut thin and fried delicately in tempura batter. Be sure to try the housemade Japanese ice cream sampler sporting flavors such as green tea and mango. Or, for more kick, choose from the 50-plus list of sakes. *$$; AE, DIS, E, MC, V; no checks; lunch Tues–Fri, dinner Tues–Sat; full bar; reservations recommended; street parking; www.saitos.net; map:F8* &

Salumeria on Hudson / ★★☆

4918 RAINIER AVE S, COLUMBIA CITY; 206/760-7741

Sherri Serino and Lisa Becklund, owner/operators of La Medusa (see review), opened Salumeria on Hudson in 1999. La Medusa's diurnal sister serves lunch but is also a cookery store, greengrocer, and wine shop. Salumeria (Italian for "delicatessen," pronounced sal-loo-ma-RI-a) is a bright, comfortable corner storefront with a few tables. Though you can buy pasta machines and olive oil, the open kitchen is the heart of the place. Order up the panini—grilled foccacia full of mild house-cured pork loin, marinated red onions, and fontina. The meatballs in the meatball sandwich, which are altogether too big for the split half baguette, are soaked in Sunday gravy. It takes both hands and five napkins to eat it, which is exactly the way it should be. Have the sweet Italian sausage sandwich with braised peppers and provolone. There are wonderful salads and soups to boot, such as a real chop salad full of wine salami and hearty white bean and lentil soup. *$; MC, V; lunch, dinner Tues–Sat; beer and wine; no reservations; street parking; map:KK5* &

Salumi / ★★★

309 3RD AVE S, PIONEER SQUARE; 206/621-8772

If you're thinking of going vegetarian, eat here first—you may want to reconsider. In this little wedge of Italy near the King Street train station, arias soar and the angels sing. Armandino Batali is a retired aeronautics engineer who got busy after 31 years at Boeing, dusted off his family recipes, went to culinary school in New York, worked in a salami factory in Queens, and apprenticed with butchers in Tuscany. He cures his own *coppa*, three kinds of salami, lamb or pork prosciutto, spicy finochiona, and citrusy sopressata, a lamb and orange sausage. They're cut to order and all sold cheaply by the pound for takeout, or let him slice you some to lay on a crusty baguette slathered with an anchovy-rich pesto or garlic sauce. Try the braised oxtail or the amazing meatball sandwich on rosetta rolls piled high with sautéed peppers and onions. Rotating specials are indeed special—lasagne with pork cheek, fennel bulb vinsanto, and hoji poji soup (so named because it is a hodgepodge of ingredients such as greens, pancetta, and olives). If you're still considering vegetarianism, there's Swiss chard, dandelion greens, or roman beans. Batali's weekly private dinners are booked up months in advance (reservations required for parties of 10 or more), but lunch at communal tables is for everyone right now, and we suggest you go there at once. *$; AE, MC, V; checks OK; lunch Tues–Fri, dinner Sat; beer and wine; reservations recommended; street parking; armo@rainsound.com; map:O7* &

Sand Point Grill / ★★

5412 SAND POINT WY NE, SAND POINT; 206/729-1303

From the day it opened in the middle of a little strip of businesses along tree-lined Sand Point Way, this bistro has been packing in the locals. Though circled by affluent neighborhoods, it keeps its prices in the moderate range and has an easygoing unpretentiousness. The long, narrow room has a cozy feel that's a good fit for families—especially for birthdays and special occasions. Expect well-crafted food with few misses. The seasonal all-day menu draws from diffuse cuisines: Mediterranean—a juicy roast chicken breast with sweet-corn risotto; American South—grits and hush puppies; Asian—Filipino Adobo Pork marinated in orange and chipotle; the Northwest—grilled salmon with lemon-pepper spaetzle. The short wine list includes a generous offering of by-the-glass choices. *$$; AE, MC, V; local checks only; dinner every day; full bar; reservations recommended; self parking; SPGrill@msn.com; map:FF5* &

Sanmi Sushi / ★★

2601 W MARINA PL, MAGNOLIA; 206/283-9978

You could come to Sanmi Sushi to enjoy the spectacular view of downtown across Elliott Bay. You could come here to look at Mount Rainier towering over the hundreds of pleasure craft docked on the other side of the window from your table. Or you could come here for the sushi. Here's some of the freshest raw seafood, artistically prepared by sushi master Misao Sanmi, who, after years working around town for other people, opened his own place next door to Palisade. A good sign is the many visiting Japanese scarfing the nigiri. If you're in luck, *toro*, the fatty, premium blue fin tuna, will be in season. The menu features a long list of appetizers, including black cod *kasu*-style, also available as an entree, as well as seared slices of albacore resting on a vinegary sweet onion salad and grilled *hamachi kama* (grilled yellowtail collar) and a lengthy list of soups, grilled meats and fish, combination dinners, bento box lunches, and noodles. Though it is tucked away in Elliott Bay Marina, it is worth the hunt, and the service will make you feel like family. *$$; AE, MC, V; no checks; lunch Tues–Fri, dinner Tues–Sun; full bar; reservations recommended; self parking; map:GG8* ᕋ

Sans Souci / ★★★

10520 NE 8TH ST, BELLEVUE; 425/467-9490

Sans Souci is Italian for "without worry," a good name for this, the latest venture of chef/restaurateur Luciano Bardinelli. In the 1980s, with his successful ventures Settebello and Paparazzi, he introduced Seattle to Italian food that went beyond spaghetti and meatballs. After years in California, Luciano's back, with chef Carlo Ochetti and an Italian menu with a halfhearted nod to France. The "Harry's Bar" carpaccio appetizer is a gorgeous plate of shaved raw tenderloin as served in the famous American expat hangout in Paris. On the French side, there's the Normandy-style pork chop with Calvados and fresh apples. Bardinelli's signature osso buco is revived from Paparazzi—a huge portion of marrow bone-in veal shank braised in red wine on creamy-crunchy saffron risotto. The *ravioli di zucca*, little pillows of pasta stuffed with spaghetti squash in a buttery sauce with sage, is stellar. There is also a terrific tiramisu, a lavish chocolate decadence cake, and a sophisticated wine list. Service is charming and capable—famed Settebello waiter Siro was coaxed out of retirement to head up the handsome European dining room. The only drawback is Sans Souci's location on the second floor of a second-rate Bellevue shopping mall. However, you'll be too taken with the romance, flawless food, and service of the place to remember such trivialities. *$$; AE, B, DC, DIS, MC, V; checks OK; lunch Mon–Fri, dinner every day; full bar; reservations recommended; self parking; map:HH3* ᕋ

Sapphire Kitchen & Bar / ★★★

1625 QUEEN ANNE AVE N, QUEEN ANNE; 206/281-1931

Even before you've tasted a thing, Sapphire's dramatic harem-tent decor transports you straight to Casablanca. The menu of chef Leonard Ruiz Rede, a classically trained California native, also displays his North African/Spanish roots. The *meze* plate has warm triangles of housemade pita bread for scooping the nutty hummus, or the intensely deep and smoky baba ghanouj served with minty tabbouleh in a radicchio leaf. Mussels Catalan are steamed with sherry and romescu sauce (a paste of red bell pepper thickened with almonds), a wonderful meal as well as entree. The menu changes frequently and fish dishes vary, but Rede's wild coho salmon in a traditional Moroccan *charmoula* marinade (ginger, cilantro, garlic, cumin, and olive oil) shows his mastery of fish cookery, as does the popular seafood paella with prawns, sea scallops, mussels, and chorizo in rice cooked in a saffron-scented broth. The young waitstaff is especially helpful—it doesn't take much to talk them into fetching you a chocolate-espresso torte with white chocolate mousse and a glass of 20-year-old tawny port. *$$; MC, V; local checks only; lunch Mon–Fri, dinner every day, brunch Sat–Sun; full bar; reservations recommended; street parking; www.sapphirekitchen.com; map:GG7* &

Sazerac / ★★☆

1101 4TH AVE (HOTEL MONACO), DOWNTOWN; 206/624-7755

The motto is "Serious fun—damn good food." Not the usual approach for a downtown restaurant serving a luxury hotel, but Sazerac delivers on both boasts. The room is disarming in dizzy chandeliers and Mardi Gras colors. Chef Jan Birnbaum celebrates his Louisiana homeland with a menu that's inviting in its wit and width. Appetizers truly tease: lobster cocktail with spiced peaches and toasted pine nuts or crispy dumplings with truffled pea emulsion, spinach, and a Parmesan cracker. The kitchen does well with broiler and smokehouse preparations such as the crispy rotisserie duck or the cedar-smoked salmon with corn risotto and chanterelles. If you think that's tempting, you'll be bowled over by the warm and gooey chocolate pudding cake served with its own pitcher of cream. Equally grandstanding is the Sazerac, a New Orleans–invented cocktail that's a wicked blend of rye, Peychaud bitters, and herb saint, an anise-y faux absinthe liqueur. More down to earth is the wine list with its concentration of mid-priced California and Northwest offerings. Menu poetry aside, the cooking lives up to the wordplay and the service is funny and capable. *$$$; AE, DC, DIS, MC, V; checks OK; breakfast, lunch, dinner every day; full bar; reservations recommended; valet parking; brian.reed@sazerac.com; map:K6* &

Sea Garden / ★★
Sea Garden of Bellevue / ★★

509 7TH AVE S, CHINATOWN/INTERNATIONAL DISTRICT; 206/623-2100
200 106TH AVE NE, BELLEVUE; 425/450-8833

The live tanks with crabs and lobsters at the door are a clue to what's best in this busy Cantonese eatery. In a tasteful dining room guarded by photographs of terra-cotta warriors, you can sip a Tsingtao beer while the lobster you picked is brought to the table for your approval. It'll be back soon, sliced in a black bean sauce or wearing ginger and green onion. Don't miss the oysters with roast pork or double mushroom scallops. There's a whole lot of panfrying going on here—don't miss the panfried sliced rock cod or panfried squid in shrimp paste. Meats are great too—try the pork chops fried crispy and soaked in garlic honey sauce. The boneless duck steamed with eight kinds of meat and vegetables is a signature dish. Ask for chow fun noodles when ordering the Sea Garden special chow mein; they're the thick rice noodles that good Chinese places have on request. This deluxe chow mein has vegetables, fresh roast pork, sliced fish, prawns, scallops, geoduck, and squid barrels. *$, $$; AE, DC, MC, V; no checks; lunch, dinner every day; full bar; reservations recommended; street parking; www.chinesecuisine3.com; map:HH3, Q6* &

Seattle Catch Seafood Bistro / ★★☆

460 N 36TH ST, FREMONT; 206/632-6110

Follow the neon arrows around the corner into Seattle Catch, where on a summer evening diners are seated near the large opened French windows enjoying their meals while watching the action on N 36th Street. A massive, mirrored, mahogany back bar, antique glass chandeliers, open kitchen, and several cozy high-backed booths along the west wall set a stylish tone for this Fremont eatery with its focus on seafood with an Italian accent. Owner Jill Levine has created a comfortable space with reasonably priced food and an approachable wine list. For starters, the steamed clams and mussels are first-rate, as are the salads and soups. Most pasta dishes sport seafood; many are served in a sizzling skillet, such as the signature linguine, a huge dish of Fra Diavolo with crab, calamari, shrimp, scallops, mussels, and clams in a tomato sauce. Entrees are anchored by grilled fish, four to choose from—often salmon, snapper, tuna, and halibut—simply cooked medium-rare with olive oil and fresh herbs. For dessert, there are chocolate truffles or the housemade chocolate mousse. *$$; AE, MC, V; no checks; dinner every day; full bar; reservations recommended; self parking; www.seattlecatch.com; map:FF8* &

Serafina / ★★

2043 EASTLAKE AVE E, EASTLAKE; 206/323-0807

Between the lovely dark bar by the entrance, the low, dark ceilings, the candle-lit tables, and the friendly, relaxed staff, one cannot help but be seduced by Serafina. Created by ex–New Yorkers, its ever-changing lineup of live music featuring Afro-Cuban, Latin, and jazz fuels the romantic chemistry of the place, which would feel right at home in Greenwich Village. The Italian-influenced menu changes periodically, but expect a variety of pasta dishes and entrees with seafood, beef, pork, game birds, and seasonal vegetables. Griglia Misto offers a mixed grill feast of three meats, for a cornucopia of flavors. While the dessert menu also changes, if the profiteroles are on it, order them. The kitchen has been known to drop the ball, but the romance here apparently is enough to keep this a popular trysting place. *$$; MC, V; checks OK; lunch Mon–Fri, dinner every day; full bar; reservations recommended; street parking; serafina@ wolfenet.com; www.serafinaseattle.com; map:GG7* &

Shallots Asian Bistro / ★★★

2525 4TH AVE, BELLTOWN; 206/728-1888

Pan-Asian restaurants are nearly as common as Italian bistros in this town. Among them, few are as likable as Shallots. Dark wood booths, elaborately folded napkins, tasteful Asian art, and a pleasant patio make for an agreeable ambience just steps away from the bustle of Fourth Avenue. The food is mostly Chinese with an intriguing mix of Thai, Vietnamese, Cambodian, Japanese, and Korean dishes. Portions are generous and well priced. Satays and satay roll appetizers, for example, can come as full meals with a bowl of fragrant rice and a mini-salad. Lunch choices include kung pao chicken, black bean salmon, or a wok-fry of chow fun, the wide rice noodles, plus seafood. Try the rock-candy gingered rabbit, the French Cambodian New York Steak Salad, or anything simmered in a *lu* pot. *$$; AE, DC, DIS, MC, V; checks OK; lunch Mon–Fri, dinner every day; full bar; reservations recommended; street parking; map:E7* &

Shamiana / ★★

10724 NE 68TH ST, KIRKLAND; 425/827-4902

They call what they do "From India and Beyond." Having grown up as foreign service kids in far-flung places quite a bit east of here, Eric and Tracy Larson have loaded their menu with foods from Bangladesh, Kenya, and Pakistan. Vegetarians do well with curries and such Indian veggie dishes as eggplant *bartha* or peas and cumin. Vegan dishes (without meat or dairy) are plentiful and plainly marked. There are good rice and grain dishes such as dhal with red lentils or pullao with fragrant basmati rice. There are three kinds of naan, the delicious unleavened bread plucked hot from the tandoori, the superhot Indian clay oven. Meat lovers do very well here too—there's chicken, lamb, and prawns in traditional spicy Pakistani barbecue; velvet butter chicken; or Chile Fry Lamb, chunks of lamb slow-cooked in coconut milk, chiles, and tomatoes. One of the big draws at this Kirkland institution is its good-value luncheon buffet. *$; AE, DC, DIS, MC, V; checks OK; lunch Tues–Fri, dinner Tues–Sun; beer and wine; no reservations; self parking; map:EE3* ♿

Shanghai Garden / ★★★

524 6TH AVE S, CHINATOWN/INTERNATIONAL DISTRICT; 206/625-1689
80 FRONT ST N, ISSAQUAH; 425/313-3188

Shanghai Garden owner/chef Hua Te Su and family cater to a largely Chinese clientele in this luscious pink restaurant in Chinatown/International District. Su attracts diners from every Chinese province with Shanghai dishes that change seasonally. Try the Shanghai favorite—soupy buns, the flowery little packets of delicate dough twisted at the top containing combinations of minced pork, shrimp, or crab in a spoonful of hot broth. The flavors explode in the mouth and, even when nibbled expertly, it's hard to eat a soup dumpling without leaving some on your shirt. Prepare to be wowed by anything made with pea vines or with the chef's special hand-shaved noodles. The vivid green tendrils of the sugar pea plant resemble sautéed spinach, and are amazingly tender and clean-tasting, especially when paired with plump shrimp. The noodles, shaved off a block of dough (rice, corn, or barley green), make the best chow mein you'll ever eat. The Shanghai emphasis is on seafood. Especially memorable are the pepper salted scallops or pepper salted shrimp with a thin, crunchy M&M–like shell that when chomped gives a mouthburst of the sea with the sedate heat of white pepper. This might be the only Chinese restaurant in town where desserts should not be missed. Su makes his own ice cream—try the sour plum. Su's Issaquah branch has attracted its own local following. *$; MC, V; no checks; lunch Mon–Fri, dinner every day (Seattle, Issaquah); beer and wine (Seattle), full bar (Issaquah); reservations recommended; free lot parking; map:JJ3* ♿

Shiro's / ★★★☆

2401 2ND AVE, BELLTOWN; 206/443-9844

Shiro Kashiba introduced the concept of sushi to several generations of Seattleites at his legendary Nikko, and they loved him and his seafoody perfectness for it. After 20 years, he sold Nikko to the Westin Hotel, where he presided for a year before opening Shiro's in 1995. And now Kashiba has another success on his hands. In the simple, immaculate dining room, a small menu offers full-course dinner entrees including tempura, sukiyaki, and teriyaki. The *kasu*-style black cod, that elegantly rich fish marinated and broiled, is not to be missed. The hundreds of sushi variations are the main event, and the blond hardwood sushi bar is always jammed with Shiro's regulars, an amazing mix of people:

Japanese tourists, Belltown hipsters, business types—sushi fanatics all. There's also a nice selection of sakes, a hard-liquor bar stocked with Japanese scotches, and desserts ranging from red bean ice cream to fresh peeled persimmon. *$$$; AE, MC, V; no checks; dinner every day; full bar; reservations recommended; street parking; map:F8* &

Siam on Broadway / ★★
Siam on Lake Union / ★

616 BROADWAY AVE E, CAPITOL HILL; 206/324-0892
1880 FAIRVIEW AVE E, EASTLAKE; 206/323-8101

Among Seattle's many Thai restaurants, Siam on the busy Harvard Exit theater end of Broadway wins the popularity contest, with lines out front every night. The seats at the front counter are a great place from which to watch the ballet performed by women chefs who work the woks and burners in the tiny open kitchen. While the menu doesn't stray far from Bangkok standards such as phad thai, the dishes created by the skilled hands in the kitchen are distinctive and consistent. Among other flavorful dishes is one of the city's best examples of *tom kah gai*—the chicken soup spicy with chiles, pungent lemongrass, and coconut milk. Sit at the counter and enjoy the show or wait for one of only 15 tables in the back. You won't have to wait at Siam on Lake Union, a larger outpost built into the railcar structure on a long-forgotten Victoria Station, and the huge, private parking lot offers ample space for the car you couldn't park on Broadway. Though good, the food here doesn't quite live up to its Broadway sibling's. *$, $; AE, DC, MC, V; checks OK; lunch Mon–Fri, dinner every day; beer and wine (Broadway), full bar (Eastlake); reservations recommended; street parking (Broadway), self parking (Eastlake); map:HH6, GG7* & *(Eastlake)*

Six Degrees / ★★☆

7900 E GREEN LAKE DR N, GREEN LAKE; 206/523-1600

By day this place is mellow and laid back—at night it's raucous, fun, and packed. Six Degrees achieves the owners' goals of reinventing the British pub by marrying it to the modern American tavern. They put this dream into stylish, bright colors with plenty of natural light, as would behoove a Green Lake eatery for the pretty people and jogger wannabes. There's even an off-and-on-again art gallery upstairs. They've gone back to the drawing board with their menu—once having such exotica as wild boar ribs—and now the food is standard but substantial with tasty pub fare such as fajitas, buffalo wings, and a killer barbecue pork sandwich. Don't miss the fat, *panko*-crispy onion rings served stacked on a peg or the clams with Portuguese sausage and sambuca. There are lots of bottled beers to choose from and an interesting list of craft kegs. *$$; AE, DC, DIS, MC, V; checks OK; lunch, dinner every day, brunch Sat–Sun; beer* *and wine; no reservations; valet parking; www.info@eatsixdegrees. com; map:EE7* &

611 Supreme Creperie Cafe / ★★☆

611 E PINE ST, CAPITOL HILL; 206/328-0292

It's like a crumbling-romantic Parisian dive, though the decor and food are quite intentionally fashioned by owner Margaret Edwins and her staff. There are bare brick walls, stressed wooden floors, unobtrusive art, and high ceilings. From the open kitchen with hanging pans and utensils comes an impressive list of entree crepes such as cheese, almonds, ham, roasted eggplant, and smoked salmon, all with choices of sauces; or create your own from a long list of sexy ingredients. There are some salads like the Cambazola—Bibb lettuce tossed with a creamy dressing made from that wonderful hybrid of Camembert and Gorgonzola—and an onion soup full of Gruyère and croutons. But the menu's *pièces de résistance* (yes, deliciously plural) are the desserts—an entire page of crispy dessert crepes with various garnishes such as orange butter, whipped cream, caramelized apple, shaved chocolate, or Nutella. There's a full bar with pastis, Calvados, Armagnac, and Pernod; the inexpensive wine list is all European bottlings, but even these are mostly French. *$; MC, V; no checks; dinner Tues–Sun, brunch Sat–Sun; full bar; reservations recommended; street parking; map:J1* &

Six Seven Restaurant & Lounge / ★★☆

2411 ALASKAN WY/PIER 67 (EDGEWATER HOTEL), WATERFRONT; 206/269-4575

The well-worn dining room in the Edgewater has been transformed into a forest of bark-covered posts passing as trees, limbs jointed with stainless steel, stretching through the hotel lobby into the bar and dining room. The decor could be described as "eco-tech." On one wall, video screens silently roll nature films; on another, there's a bank of holographic gas fireplaces. Here is one of Seattle's best decks—you're at water level and it seems as though you're part of the busy harbor action. Radiant heaters and a windbreak make the outdoor experience comfy year-round. The food is pan-everywhere, with an emphasis on Asia. There's a bar with middling sushi, but most menu items are winners—such as the fiery starters of clams in black bean sauce or steamed mussels in yellow Thai curry broth. Good entree choices include the alder-planked salmon, the macaroni with three cheeses, or the lamb osso buco with star anise, cinnamon, and goat-cheesy mashed potatoes. For a closer, try a slice of banana cream pie. The wine list numbers some 200 bottles and blends Northwest, Australian, South African, and Chilean vintages. Service is undertrained and inexperienced, though at press time Six Seven had been open for only a few months. *$$$; AE, DC, DIS, MC, V; no checks;*

breakfast, lunch, dinner every day; full bar; reservations recommended; valet parking; map:F9 &

Sky City at the Needle / ★★

219 4TH AVE N, SEATTLE CENTER; 206/905-2100

Being 520 feet in the air, the restaurant on the Space Needle could serve broiled hockey puck, charge the same stratospheric prices it does now, and still be packed. This famous revolving Jetsonian landmark has been shunned by many Seattleites over the years because of its reputation for mediocrity and tourist-trap ambience. With the Needle's yearlong, $20 million renovation, however, the restaurant got a bland, retro-1950s refit and, frankly, things are looking, well, up. It's a predictable menu, Northwest tried-and-true—prime rib, peppercorn New York steak, crab cakes, salmon Wellington—with nods to Asia including the inevitable seared ahi with wasabi mashed potatoes. The good news is, the food is much better than mediocre, the service is friendly and capable, and you can linger even after the restaurant turns the two-and-a-half rotations allotted your dinner visit. The fixed-price weekend brunch has a wide selection of breakfast foods, poultry or seafood courses, and desserts. The wine list offers the usual suspects of Washington wines, and desserts lean toward the standards—cheesecakes, mousses, and seasonal pies. If you have the dough and folks from out of town want a ride on an icon, it's worth a twirl. *$$$$; AE, DIS, MC, V; local checks only; lunch Mon–Fri, dinner every day, brunch Sat–Sun; full bar; reservations recommended; valet parking; www.spaceneedle.com; map:C6 &*

Snappy Dragon / ★★

8917 ROOSEVELT WY NE, MAPLE LEAF; 206/528-5575

The Maple Leaf neighborhood in Seattle's north end is lucky to have Judy Fu and her snappy, well-crafted Chinese food offered up in their quiet midst. And they know it, too. They flock to eat in at this quaint house-turned-restaurant or take out from a menu that would stand proud in any Chinese neighborhood this side of Shanghai. Don't miss the house-made noodles in the soft-noodle chow meins or in the *jaio-zi*, boiled dumplings. The crispy tea-smoked duck is aromatic, served with hoisin sauce and steamed buns. Judy rocks on specials such as the stir-fried glass noodles and minced pork she calls Ants Climb Up a Tree. Other big sellers are the spicy-sweet Sichuan favorite, General Tsao's Chicken; the clay pot stews (especially the one with shrimp); chicken meatballs; prawns; scallops; and veggies. Almond Cranberry Chicken is an unusual sweet-sour savory melange that makes something lush, complex, and very Chinese out of the simple puritanical New England sour fruit we usually equate with Thanksgiving. *$; AE, DC, DIS, MC, V; local checks only; lunch, dinner Mon–Sat; full bar; reservations not accepted; street parking; map:DD7 &*

Sostanza Trattoria / ★★★

1927 43RD AVE E, MADISON PARK; 206/324-9701

Talented chef/owner Lorenzo Cianciusi's charming trattoria at the farthest end of Madison Park's tony commercial strip is a prime dining destination in the city's galaxy of Italian stars. His strategy is simple: Use first-rate Italian ingredients and have the good sense not to mess with the centuries-old traditions of the cookery of Northern Italy. His Tuscan-style dining room has exposed beams and a big brick fireplace; he's added a full bar upstairs and a skylighted dining room that opens onto a balcony with a peekaboo view of Lake Washington. The food is straightforward and fresh—such as the pappardelle with veal sauce and wild mushroom risotto; air-dried bresaola (beef) with fennel, arugula, and a green bean–fennel salad; quail wrapped in pancetta with Chianti demi-glace; crab and prawn pasta; or halibut piccata. Desserts are equally unpretentious—a slice of warm pear upside-down cake with housemade vanilla ice cream or lemon angel food with berry sauce. Distinctive Italian bottlings join a smattering of domestic favorites on the limited but well-chosen wine list. *$$; AE, DC, MC, V; local checks only; dinner Mon–Sat; full bar; reservations recommended; self parking; map:GG6* &

Spazzo Mediterranean Grill / ★★

10655 NE 4TH ST, BELLEVUE; 425/454-8255

It's a sign of our age that downtown Bellevue's rustic Mediterranean restaurant resides atop a glass and steel tower. But then, Spazzo's not all that rustic. An upscale showplace of the Schwartz Brothers' empire, it exudes a certain sophistication and lots of polish, enticing a mixed crowd, including singles in the bar and dates in the dining room. The menu supposedly draws from wherever in the Mediterranean the olive tree grows, from Turkey to Portugal. It tends to favor the eastern end, with many choices from Greece. A local pioneer in popularizing tapas, Spazzo kicks out nearly 30 or more varieties of these shareable little appetizer plates. Order a few, and a few more, until you're full. More traditional, mostly Italian options are available for dinner, but the quality in this volume restaurant can vary. If you stick with the simple stuff—lamb chops, rigatoni—this can be fun, which, translated to Greek, is *spasso*. *$$$; AE, DC, DIS, JCB, MC, V; local checks only; lunch Mon–Fri, dinner every day; full bar; reservations recommended; self parking; kwallace@schwartzbros.com; map:HH3* &

St. Clouds / ★★☆

1129 34TH AVE, MADRONA; 206/726-1522

Friendly, upscale Madrona is blessed with quite a few great restaurants, and this is one of them. St. Clouds' menu is split between "Out for Dinner" (fancy, pricier) and "Home for Dinner" (homey, cheaper), the latter perfect for busy families. The home side typically offers herb-roasted chicken and mashers; a rice bowl with ginger-steamed vegetables; slow-roasted ribs with corn bread and collard greens; or Hoppin' John Supper, black-eyed peas in griddle cakes with a lemon–goat cheese aioli. Going "Out" entails more uptown dishes with higher prices, such as pan-roasted halibut with a peanut-soy-ginger sauce, served with sautéed whole spinach and a lemongrass noodle salad. A kids' menu features chocolate chip pancakes, mac and cheese, spaghetti and meatballs, and burgers. The dessert menu is brief, but pray for the macadamia nut brownie and vanilla ice cream drizzled with mango-caramel purée. The brunch is known for white chocolate scones and sour cream coffeecake. Live music plays nightly in the cozy bar. *$$; AE, MC, V; checks OK; lunch Mon, Wed–Fri, dinner Wed–Mon, brunch Sat–Sun; full bar; reservations recommended; street parking; john@stclouds.com; www.stclouds.com; map:HH5* &

Stumbling Goat / ★★★

6722 GREENWOOD AVE N, GREENWOOD; 206/784-3535

The husband-and-wife team of chef Craig Serbousek and Erin Fetridge-Serbousek are behind this wildly popular Greenwood bistro. The Goat's cozy rooms, painted scarlet and forest green with red velvet draperies, illuminated by cheap 1950s lamps, somehow achieve an idiosyncratic homeyness. The menu is equally eclectic. The winter menu might offer such selections as beet salad with tangy blue-veined Stilton, mesclun greens, and a light vinaigrette or truffled barley risotto cooked in a rich porcini-enhanced vegetable stock, studded with quartered creminis, and surrounded with tender pea vines. The bistro standards are done well—boneless, pan-roasted chicken served on an island of rich mashed potatoes in a pond of pan juices and roasted garlic cloves or pan-seared rainbow trout, crusty on the outside, served atop a salad of baby arugula with sweet rice vinegar, red onions, and roasted red potatoes. Desserts range from a crème brûlée trio with flavors (such as raspberry, espresso, and coconut) that change daily to warm apple tart with ginger caramel sauce and vanilla bean ice cream. The petite, though well thought out, wine list offers a number of attractive wines by the glass. The service can be laid back, but it's forgivable because all the neighbors seem to be here and loving it. *$$; MC, V; local checks only; dinner Tues–Sat; beer and wine; no reservations; street parking; map:EE7* &

Supreme / ★★

1404 34TH AVE, MADRONA; 206/322-1974

The decor is postmodern stark with a stressed, paint-spattered cement floor and exposed ductwork. A mural covering one wall depicts a farmscape on the Great Plains, apropos because the tables and pewlike benches are as stark as Kansas. The brave visuals are from former designer Tova Cubert, who co-owns Supreme with Chris Hunter, a former chef at Etta's Seafood. The food is mostly great, with some inconsistencies and reports of unevenness. By all means, get the creamy, buttery chicken liver pâté, served with a little tangle of sweet onions pickled with vinegar and red wine. The oven-roasted cod comes nicely browned in its spicy broth with whole clams and chorizo. The grilled chicken is boneless and homey with a leek risotto and sour cherry sauce. The short wine list is well written, helpful, and free of winespeak. It's a thoughtful collection of European, California, and Northwest wines, including some from Wilridge Winery down the street. *$$; AE, MC, V; local checks only; dinner every day, brunch Sat–Sun; full bar; reservations recommended; street parking; map:H3* ⌖

Swingside Cafe / ★★★

4212 FREMONT AVE N, FREMONT; 206/633-4057

Chef/owner Brad Inserra has his little place just the way he wants it. It's a romantic, cramped, funky, homey living room hung with Pittsburgh Pirates memorabilia, pictures of saints, and a staff best described as guerrilla-gracious. Most important, it's a place where Brad is comfortable bending linguine and rubbing cheeks with halibuts. He runs his sweaty, one-man kitchen in an innovative, gregarious, Sicilian way that's made his place a beloved classic. The dining room and kitchen are the only puny things here—flavors, portions, and hospitality are huge. You'll find venison, clams, veal chops, mussels, and sturgeon in pan-Mediterranean styles and aromatherapeutic sauces. Pastas are hard to pass up—especially the Aglio e Olio ("the dish that made the Swingside famous"), ordinarily simple fare with garlic and olive oil but here an elaborate plateful of linguine lavished with capers, sun-dried tomatoes, anchovies, marsala, and ground hazelnuts. There are cheesy potato gnocchi, fat housemade raviolis, and a tangy puttanesca loaded with scallops and prawns. There's a muscular wine list and a good selection of beers. Reservations are only for parties of six or more, so plot your visit cleverly—this place has never not been hot. *$$; MC, V; checks OK; dinner Tues–Sat; beer and wine; reservations recommended; street parking; map:FF8* ⌖

Szmania's / ★★★
Szmania's (Kirkland) / ★★★

3321 W MCGRAW ST, MAGNOLIA; 206/284-7305
148 LAKE ST S, KIRKLAND; 425/803-3310

Never mind the remoteness of the original Magnolia location, which Ludger and Julie Szmania (pronounced SMAHN-ya) opened in 1990. Over the years, Ludger, a German-born chef trained in Europe, has made this outpost a Seattle must. The space offers a stylish, modern feel, with warm light and artwork, expert service, and fireside tables. His seasonally changing menus offer a mix of European, Northwest, and pan-Asian cuisines with artful presentation. Homage to Szmania's Dusseldorfian roots is paid with the *Jägerschnitzel*, three thick slices of lightly crusted, crispy pork tenderloin served with red cabbage and cheese spaetzle. The Kirkland restaurant opened in 2001 in a bright, wide-open space, and has proven to be very popular with Eastsiders. The food is lighter, the decor younger—it's a good destination, with the same attention to food as the original, but a more carefree feel. There's a kitchen-side counter with stools for the audience. *$$$; AE, DC, MC, V; local checks only; lunch Tues–Fri (Kirkland), dinner Tues–Sun, brunch Sun (Kirkland); full bar; reservations recommended; self parking; ludger@zszmanias. com; www.szmanias.com; map:FF8, EE3* &

Tango / ★★★

1100 PIKE ST, CAPITOL HILL; 206/583-0382

Danielle Philippa has spawned a sexy, savory sibling to her successful dress-down Bandoleone (see review). Sex is traditional in this building, which formerly housed the Apple Theater, a 1970s porn house. The look now is Spanish hacienda, with windows reaching from the tiled floor to the high ceiling—the designers incorporated the original raw wood beams of the restored 1909 building. Unlike its older brother, Tango offers only a few entrees and almost 30 tapas: among them salads, soups, meats, seafood, vegetable dishes, olives, and cheeses. A meal can be made of several of these tapas. Philippa lets her chefs work freestyle with local ingredients and influences, so the tapas, though not strictly Spanish, are innovative and fabulous anyway. The Chinese-inspired Pato del Oriente is duck confit in a ginger-melon vinaigrette with seasonal cress; grilled tiger prawns come with green peppercorns and coriander jelly. Servers are fun and, better yet, reliably knowledgeable. Desserts assiduously avoid the mundane: the El Diablo is a dark chocolate cube (with a devilish hint of cayenne) perched on a fluff of burnt meringue, spiced almond, and cocoa nibs with a tequila caramel sauce. Dessert choices each come with a couple of drink suggestions. The animated bar scene is a good spot for a nightcap. *$$; MC, V; local checks only; dinner every* *day; full bar; reservations recommended; self parking; tango@ bandoleone.net; www.bandeleone.net; map:J3* &

Taqueria Guaymas / ★★

1622 ROXBURY ST SW, WHITE CENTER (AND BRANCHES); 206/767-4026

Happily, here's an ever-expanding family restaurant chain that serves genuine Mexican food and doesn't seem to vary in quality or authenticity no matter where the location. The food in the branch in White Center, the gritty suburb 25 minutes southwest of the city, is as simple as the decor: a small lunch counter, picnic tables, a fridge full of beer, and a TV blaring soap operas in Spanish. Tacos and burritos can come with the usual beef, chicken, or pork or jazzed up with tripe, tongue, or beef cheeks. This is more than a cafeteria-style taqueria—the enchiladas are some of the best in the area, as is the chile verde. On weekends try the menudo, a therapeutic soup for hangovers. Daily thirst-quenchers ladled from big glass jars include melon juice, rice water (*horchata*), or tamarind. Other locations (some go by the name of Tacos Guaymas) are in Renton, West Seattle, Lynnwood, and Everett, with two slightly more upscale versions on Capitol Hill and one on Green Lake—don't miss the *enchiladas de mole* in these places. *$; MC, V; checks OK; breakfast, lunch, dinner every day; beer only; no reservations; street parking; map:LL8* &

Tempero do Brasil / ★★★☆

5628 UNIVERSITY WY NE, UNIVERSITY DISTRICT; 206/523-6299

Brazilians in Seattle are few but avid. Our gray skies have traditionally discouraged emigration. The small but fierce band of assorted expats, graduate students, and samba fanatics have been heartened by this hangout. From Bahia come Antonio and Graca Ribeira, in other lives dancers and artists (their art hangs in the dining room). Their partner, sax player Bryant Urban, helps Graca do the cooking, while Antonio tends bar. Bahia's bar/beach/street food is exemplified by *tira-gustos* (appetizers). The salt cod cakes, the ubiquitous Bahian bar food, are served with fresh limes and are great with a beer, as are the fried cakes of black-eyed peas served with Antonio's shrimp hot sauce. The national dish, feijoada (pronounced fay-ZWHA-duh), traditionally available on weekends, is a stew of black beans, long-cooked with ham, garlic, sausage, and beef and served with *couve* (julienned collard greens with orange wedges). Feijoada must be accompanied by the strong Brazilian drink caipirinha, made with sugar, lime, and ice. Antonio makes his authentically with cachacha, liquor distilled from the juice of fresh sugar cane. Evenings, there's live music on the patio out front—chef Urban's been known to burst from the kitchen playing his soprano sax. Otherwise, the well-lit ambience throbs with the Brazilian pop-jazz sounds of

Caetano, Djavan—or Jobim, for the older folks. *$; DC, MC, V; no checks; lunch Sat–Sun, dinner Tues–Sat; full bar; reservations recommended; street parking; map:EE7* &

Ten Mercer / ★★☆

10 MERCER ST, QUEEN ANNE; 206/691-3723

A gorgeous place for gorgeous people. Downstairs is a lovely seat-yourself bistro with a bar filled with thirtysomethings in ostrich feather trim and faux Gucci baseball caps drinking Skyy Vodka out of frosty vats shaped like martini glasses. This is a fine-dining venture by the owners of neighboring T. S. McHugh's and Floyd's Place. There's a two-story booze bin on a rolling bookstore ladder—nimble bartenders climb up and swing limb to limb fetching bottles of Armagnac and Glenfiddich from the upper reaches. Upstairs is romantic with napery, candlelight, and a view of the street. The food is a little over the top and sometimes uneven, but try the smoked sturgeon appetizer, the crispy duck, or the whole fried sea bass. Grilled House Smoked Tenderloin is broiled medium rare and served with panfried spaetzle. Vegetarians are treated to the Rustic Vegetable Tart, a rich pie of puff pastry filled with vegetables and Stilton cheese. The service is friendly and well informed, the feeling is festive and warm. *$$; AE, MC, V; local checks only; dinner every day; full bar; reservations recommended; valet parking; map:B4* &

Third Floor Fish Cafe / ★★★

205 LAKE ST S, KIRKLAND; 425/822-3553

It's a no-expectations, office-building elevator ride to dinner, but when you get to your third-floor destination, you'll be delighted. A warm, stained-wood, nautical-but-nice set of well-windowed rooms look out on Lake Washington with views that invite lingering, especially when the sun starts to set. Chef Greg Campbell took the top toque position seamlessly when his predecessor, Scott Staples, went to Seattle to open a place of his own. Staples's signature grilled heart of romaine with apples, crispy bacon, and Roquefort is still here and a must-sample. A Yukon Gold potato soup with Cougar Gold cheddar is a hearty choice when available. But, as the restaurant's name suggests, the best option is to order fish, such as the pan-seared salmon with fennel and red onion salad. Or at least the seafood, such as sea scallops with stewed organic vegetable ragout in a tarragon broth. Campbell makes five- and seven-course tasting menus with accompanying wines that are quite good, showing off his skills beyond fish. Desserts range from an oven-roasted plum cake with plum caramel and whipped cream to a triple chocolate semifreddo. Service is unwaveringly polished and professional. The wine list of mostly domestics is carefully selected, but short at the low end, with just a bottle or two priced below $30. *$$$; AE, DC, DIS, MC, V; local* *checks only; dinner every day; full bar; reservations recommended; valet parking; map:EE3* &

13 Coins Restaurant / ★

125 BOREN AVE N, DENNY REGRADE; 206/682-2513
18000 PACIFIC HWY S, SEATAC; 206/243-9800

It will take a lot more than 13 coins to pay for the privilege of sinking into one of the cushy booths or high-backed leather seats at the counter to watch the polished work of short-order cooks at this 30-year-old Seattle dining institution. But who can resist the opportunity to choose from a menu so varied (with breakfast, sandwiches, pasta, fish, and meat dishes) and so perfectly dated (eggs Benedict and fettuccine alfredo)? Especially when it's all available 24/7? Ample portions and decades of momentum (not to mention lack of competition in their respective neighborhoods, near the *Seattle Times* and the airport) have kept this pair of restaurants popular. If you crave sweetbreads at 3am, these places are for you. *$$; AE, DC, MC, V; checks OK; breakfast, lunch, dinner every day; full bar; reservations recommended; self parking; map:F3* &

Tia Lou's / ★★

2218 1ST AVE, BELLTOWN; 206/733-8226

A newcomer to the Belltown scene, Tia Lou's opened for business in 2000 as a tribute to Eluteria Garcia Contreras, grandmother of owners and brothers Greg and Eric Contreras. Tia Lou, as she was called, was famous for creating traditional Mexican family feasts of housemade tamales, posole, enchiladas, green chile stew, and other favorite recipes. The brothers Contreras re-create these recipes with wonderful results. Clearly Tia Lou knew her way around a chile pepper; they're brilliantly used in every dish offered. The green chile stew is the stuff you'd go to New Mexico for, as is the spicy posole, a comforting soup with hominy and slow-roasted pork. *Pollo al chipotle* is a chicken breast with smoky peppers, tomatoes, and black rice (rice with a sauce made of black bean liquor). They use flank steak for the carne asada and it's served with guacamole, *pico de gallo*, and real tortillas to roll them in. All the margaritas feature top-shelf tequila; food and drink portions are generous. From the authentic food to the friendly waitstaff, this is a sleek first-class trip to Mexico. Make reservations for large groups. *$$; AE, DIS, MC, V; lunch Mon–Fri, dinner Mon–Sat; full bar; reservations recommended; self parking; word13@aol.com; www.tialous.com; map:G7* &

Tosoni's / ★★★☆

14320 NE 20TH ST, BELLEVUE; 425/644-1668

One of the Eastside's enduring treasures, Tosoni's is known to its many loyal regulars simply as "Walter's place." Look hard, or you could miss it, hidden in an Overlake strip mall. But this humble exterior belies the old-world delights awaiting inside, where chef Walter Walcher and a sous-chef work the open kitchen, presiding over a small dining room filled with antique cabinets and armoires. The menu, written out on a blackboard hung over the kitchen, tends toward the continental (Walcher hails from Austria, but feels more kinship with Northern Italy). While the garlic lamb has been retired from the menu after many years, meat eaters still find plenty to enjoy, such as venison, rack of lamb, and a nice wienerschnitzel. Also look for fresh fish and poultry dishes such as duck or chicken. It depends on the season, the night, and Walter's fancy. It's sort of like sitting in an old friend's dining room with a view to the kitchen, where one can watch the chef arrange the bounty plate by plate. *$$$; AE, DIS, MC, V; local checks only; dinner Tues–Sat; beer and wine; reservations recommended; self parking; map:GG2*

Toyoda Sushi / ★★★

12543 LAKE CITY WY NE, LAKE CITY; 206/367-7972
If you're craving sushi but you don't want to stray from the north end to fight for parking and wait in line in Belltown or Chinatown/International District, no problem. Try Lake City's very own sushi mecca: Toyoda Sushi. This place has become one of Seattle's favorite sushi destinations, offering up some delicious morsels of fresh, raw fish at affordable rates. The dining room is packed with brightly lit tables; a dozen or so seats are available at the sushi bar. As you sit at the bar pondering the delicacies refrigerated under glass in front of you, you are handed a cup of miso soup or maybe a tangy-sweet octopus salad. Nigiri, sashimi, and hand rolls are produced with skill from the freshest ingredients. Or go for one of the dinners from the hot kitchen, such as tempura or teriyaki. Everything keeps the long lines of north-enders happy, right down to the *mochi* ice cream. *$$; MC, V; no checks; dinner Wed–Mon; beer and wine; no reservations; self parking; www.toyodasushi.com; map:CC6*

Triangle Lounge / ★

3507 FREMONT PL N, FREMONT; 206/632-0880
Once a triangular hippie tavern, now remodeled into a triangular hipster lounge, the Triangle lies at the center of Fremont's self-styled Center of the Universe scene. It serves as a reminder of the old raucous Fremont that is fast disappearing as prosperity brings gentrification to the once bohemian/artist neighborhood known for presenting at least three sides to every question. The triangular dining room with hanging art of conspicuously three-sided pieces opens onto a narrow, festively lit patio that is indeed the center of the universe on a warm night in Fremont. A long bar dominates the main room with a neon sign that says "Prescriptions." Service is flaky, but the pub food—charbroiled lamb burgers, grilled chicken and hummus pitas, pasta, pizzas—is pretty darn good and well accepted by classy drinkers and the drinking class alike. *$; AE, MC, V;*

no checks; lunch, dinner every day; full bar; no reservations; street parking; map:FF8 &

Tulio Ristorante / ★★★

1100 5TH AVE (HOTEL VINTAGE PARK), DOWNTOWN; 206/624-5500

Step inside the antique revolving doors of Tulio and find yourself in a charming cosmopolitan environment in a bustling downtown hotel setting. The upstairs dining room allows space for overflow or large parties, but the downstairs main room, including the sexy little bar and the sidewalk patio tightly fitted with white-draped tables, is where the action is. The smells of roast garlic and whole prosciutto hang in the air; a wood-burning oven and an open kitchen make the room reminiscent of a graceful Tuscan villa. Service is swift and knowledgeable, and with chef Walter Pisano in charge, dinner is in good hands. Choose from a variety of dishes including orecchiette with roasted vegetables, risotto Zaffereno (made with saffron), and pepper-crusted roast loin of pork. There are great housemade pastas, from ravioli filled with smoked salmon in a lemon cream sauce served with asparagus to linguine with local mussels, garlic, preserved lemon, and olive oil in herbs. At Tulio, baked focacce, gelati, granitas, and desserts are all made fresh on the premises daily. The thoughtful and extensive wine list is about half Italian, half domestic. *$$; AE, DC, MC, V; local checks only; breakfast, lunch, dinner every day; full bar; reservations recommended; valet parking; map:L6* &

Tup Tim Thai / ★★

118 W MERCER ST, QUEEN ANNE; 206/281-8833

Form definitely follows function at Tup Tim Thai, which is sparsely decorated with a few travel posters and bright lighting. This place is all about serving inexpensive, well-prepared Thai food to as many people as possible. Some say it's the best Thai food in town (a good way to start an argument in Seattle); there's certainly no shortage of clientele. Tup Tim Thai jumps with a neighborhood mix of families, singles, business suits, and the formally dressed on their way to the theater as well as baseball-capped Sonics game-goers. Spring rolls or chicken satay are classic starters, and reliable entree choices include the slightly sweet chicken phad thai, the fragrant red and yellow curries, or sweet-and-sour pork. Tup Tim noodles are panfried rice noodles with ground beef, onions, and tomatoes rich with good oil, and the intensely flavored garlic prawns are without a doubt some of the best in town. The only dessert is sliced mango served with sticky rice that is soaked with sweet coconut milk, which somehow manages to be just the thing to end a rich meal. Be sure to make a reservation and give yourself time to park. *$; DC, MC, V; checks OK; lunch Mon–Fri, dinner Mon–Sat; beer and wine; reservations recommended; street parking; map:GG7* &

21 Central / ★★

21 CENTRAL WY, KIRKLAND; 425/822-1515

Mike Brown fired up an 1,800°F broiler in this opulent steak house with the clubby feel of a Gilded Age saloon. In the tradition of the other Seattle glam steak houses, Daniel's Broiler and Met Grill, 21 Central has a commitment to the trappings of luxury, pretentious service, and, of course, large pieces of meat cooked the way you want it. There's a menu glossary of how 21 Central defines doneness, making sure you know how you want it. The offerings are much the same as in other steak houses of this price range: oysters Rockefeller, caesar salads, premium shellfish, all manner of potatoes. Steaks come in all the usual cuts but only one size: big. There's a wine list that's mostly in the $50 range with few bargains, which doesn't matter to the crowd that frequents this house. *$$$$; AE, DC, DIS, MC, V; checks OK; dinner Mon–Sat; full bar; reservations recommended; valet parking; www.21central.com; map:EE3* &

Typhoon! / ★★★

1400 WESTERN AVE, DOWNTOWN; 206/262-9797
8936 161ST AVE NE, REDMOND; 425/558-7666

Filling the hallowed space where Wild Ginger wowed diners for so many years before moving to larger digs, the owners of this upscale Thai restaurant have preserved the basic floor plan so familiar to so many. Typhoon's chef/owner, Bo Lohasawat Kline, manages the Bangkok crew in the huge open kitchen with lightning speed and unusual skill. The appetizer Bags of Gold, fried parcels of shrimp, shiitakes, and water chestnuts, are a delight. The *miang kum*, toasted coconut, shallots, ginger, lime, peanuts, tiny dried shrimp, and Thai chile wrapped in spinach, is to be popped into your mouth for a burst of flavors that play a two-octave chord on your palate. A salad of crunchy green slivered papaya has a thin slice of lime that gives both bite and fragrance. There's a terrific version of everybody's favorite, phad thai, and such hearties as the wide-noodled *lahd nah*—with egg, mushrooms, vegetables, and the lightest of gingery gravies. Those coconut-milk curries, the mainstay of Thai restaurant cuisine, are velvety and rich but not too heavy-handed. The Redmond location in Bella Bottega Center has much the same menu but better parking. *$$; AE, DC, DIS, MC, V; checks OK; lunch Mon–Fri, dinner every day; full bar; reservations recommended; street parking; www.typhoonrestaurants.com; map:I7* &

Union Bay Cafe / ★★★

3515 NE 45TH ST, UNIVERSITY DISTRICT; 206/527-8364

For years chef/owner Mark Manley has consistently offered excellent fare from an ever-changing menu in his relaxing, gently lit restaurant on the UW edge of Laurelhurst. And every night his tables are filled with anniversaries and birthday celebrations, romantic evenings, postwork relaxations, and even a sturdy meal before or after a Husky game. The menu, while clearly leaning to the Italian side, makes good use of seasonal and regional ingredients, particularly local mushrooms such as chanterelles and morels. For starters, give the mussels a try, or the country-style rabbit pâté. Manley works well with a wide variety of meats and seafoods, and is known for his use of game meats. Look for rabbit, venison, or ostrich, for example, or try more conventional meats such as pork tenderloin or New Zealand lamb. And there will always be entrees to equally please vegetarians. A reasonably priced wine list boasts a wide variety of premium selections by the glass. All this fine dining, and without the downtown sticker shock. A courtyard offers outdoor seating in good weather. *$$$; AE, DC, DIS, MC, V; checks OK; dinner Tues–Sun; beer and wine; reservations recommended; self parking; ubscafe@aol.com; map:FF6* &

Union Square Grill / ★★

621 UNION ST, DOWNTOWN; 206/224-4321
Union Square Grill is a dependable downtown steak house for the beef and martini set. With its steak-house dark wood and oversize antique posters, there's an undeniably glitzy feel to the handsome dining room. At lunchtime the place is packed with business types, all of whom seem to be negotiating that last detail of a big deal. That is, when they're not enjoying the chowder, entree-size caesar salads, sandwiches, or a expense-account London broil. Dinner draws theatergoers taking advantage of the well-executed pretheater menu that features prime rib and the usual cuts of steak cooked on the mesquite grill and accompanied by garlic mashers or baked potatoes. À la carte sides of fresh asparagus, sautéed button mushrooms, sauce béarnaise, or wild mushroom demi-glace should satisfy just about anyone in the mood for clubby retro cuisine. There's some seafood, too, including grilled salmon or halibut, weather-vane scallops in lobster cream, and a pricey bouillabaisse. The bar is a favorite downtown watering hole, thanks to a flashy selection of martinis, single-malt scotches, and a full bar menu. *$$$; AE, DC, DIS, JCB, MC, V; local checks only; lunch Mon–Fri, dinner every day; full bar; reservations recommended; valet and self parking; map:K5* &

Wasabi Bistro / ★★

2311 2ND AVE, BELLTOWN; 206/441-6044
This handsome, ultramodern, backlit room has great service, beautiful servers, generous martinis, a lengthy sake list, and a menu priced to impress. Chef Dan Miller brings some innovation to chic eats with Japanese ingredients, though few clichés are left unturned—from the crusted ahi to the grilled portobellos to the squash dumplings. However, exceptions are in evidence: a rare-cooked ahi crusted with Japanese seven-spice in a subtle scallion sauce is an exception, as is the Hawaiian

beef *poke*, a warm, chunky salad of beef, eggplants, sweet onions, and peppers, and the barely seared sea scallops in gingery carrot sauce and scallion oil. Lunch is also well done, with some bento boxes and salads, including the seaweed and seafood one and the one with baby spinach, toasted soy nuts, and sesame dressing. The sushi is more chichi than sushi. However, this is a hot Belltown spot—and hanging at the bar is where it's at. Venture farther than that, and you may be disappointed. *$$; AE, DC, DIS, MC, V; no checks; lunch Mon–Fri, dinner every day; full bar; reservations recommended; street parking; map:F8* &

Waterfront Restaurant / ★★☆

2815 ALASKAN WY/PIER 70, WATERFRONT; 206/956-9171
Waterfront is a visual antithesis to Paul MacKay's re-created old-Seattle steak-and-cigars place, El Gaucho (see review). With partner Vicky McCaffree, who serves as executive chef, the veteran Seattle restaurateur built the Waterfront from the water up at the newly redeveloped Pier 70 complex. The restaurant has sweeping harbor views from an 80-foot serpentine bar, the 175-seat dining room with elegant and whimsical touches in bold colors, and two private glassed-in dining rooms. There's an interesting hazelnut roasted rack of lamb, but this informal but posh place mostly has good waterfront fare including grilled salmon, oven-roasted halibut, and grilled escolar, with a little Italian seafood linguine and a touch or two of Asia such as the Thai seafood stew or the salt and pepper crab. The wine list features well-priced bottlings with an emphasis on Northwest and California. *$$$; AE, B, DC, JCB, MC, V; checks OK; dinner every day; full bar; reservations recommended; valet and self parking; www.waterfrontpier70.com; map:D9* &

Wazobia / ★★

170 S WASHINGTON ST, PIONEER SQUARE; 206/624-9154
Wazobia's dark orange walls are hung with batiks, Malian mud-cloth tapestries, and Yoruba belts with trade beads and cowries. Chef/owner Jerry Emmatrice is from Lagos, Nigeria, and his restaurant serves the down-home food that is the mother of American Creole cooking. The West African hospitality is obvious here—everyone's friendly and the portions large. This is a magnet for local West Africans, and the kitchen's open till 4am on weekends with Afro-pop DJs, Congolese Soukou, or Nigerian Fuji bands. A good bet here is the Wazobia Combo Plate; you'll get *jollof* rice (a classic West African pilaf with vegetables), a huge plate of black-eyed peas, fried plantain, greens, and chicken or fish. There's a half page of vegetarian dishes such as the *egusi* soup made with ground melon seeds or the vegetarian combo with rice, greens, black-eyed peas, and *fufu*, starchy pounded yams mixed with palm oil. Lunch is a good-valued, all-you-can-eat buffet, an excellent way to explore the cuisine. *$;*

MC, V; checks OK; lunch Tues–Fri, dinner every day; full bar; reservations recommended; street parking; map:GG6 &

Wild Ginger Asian Restaurant and Satay Bar / ★★★

1401 3RD AVE, DOWNTOWN; 206/623-4450

Responsible for launching the local pan-Asian craze when it opened in 1989, Wild Ginger has moved into larger, sleeker digs but still brings the best dishes from the streets and restaurants of Bangkok, Singapore, Saigon, and Djakarta. The new space features 100 more seats, private rooms, and a second-story cocktail lounge overlooking another bar below. Ginger's owners, Rick and Ann Yoder, bought the historic and long-vacant Mann Building in 1996 and spent millions renovating the decayed structure. There are still complaints from the natives that the new place lacks the coziness and the familiarity of the old—we'll have to get used to it. The service is as professional as usual, and executive chef Jeem Han Lock has included lots of old favorites on his menu including the *laksa*, Malaysian seafood soup, and the sliced fragrant duck breast to smear with plum sauce and tuck into little pillows of housemade *bao*. At the mahogany satay bar, order from a wide array of skewers: simple seared slices of sweet onion and Chinese eggplant, tender Bangkok boar seasoned with cumin and turmeric and basted with coconut milk, or lamb tenderloin with traditional peanut sauce. The wine list carries a mix of domestic varietals from primarily West Coast producers with lots of whites, a good-size half-bottle selection, and eight or 10 wines poured by the glass. *$$$; AE, DIS, MC, V; no checks; lunch Mon–Sat, dinner every day; full bar; reservations recommended; valet and self parking; map:L8* &

Winslow Way / ★★☆

122 WINSLOW WY E, BAINBRIDGE ISLAND; 206/842-0517

This pretty island eatery is an easy walk from the ferry dock and ideal for family outings. They welcome kids, giving them their own menu of burgers, spaghetti, and pizza. Big people do well here, too. The bar's always busy with island regulars who come in for a drink and a chat to go with the steamed clams or crusted calamari. Lunch can be a crab cake salad with fresh Dungeness served with wasabi aioli and Asian slaw or a crab monte cristo with prosciutto and goat cheese. Dinner has a reasonably priced menu with some gourmet pizzas, a decent Northwest paella, and an interesting pork porterhouse steak with sweet-hot apricot chutney. A local favorite is Trixie's Pasta, penne with sausage, red peppers, tomatoes, mozzarella, and Gorgonzola. *$$; AE, MC, V; checks OK; lunch, dinner every day; full bar; reservations recommended; street parking* &

Yanni's Greek Cuisine / ★★

7419 GREENWOOD AVE N, GREENWOOD; 206/783-6945

A neighborhood staple in the Phinney-Greenwood corridor is one of Seattle's best Greek restaurants. Yanni's is a comfortable joint with the simple comforts of a Greek *taverna*. Any night you will find the place packed with locals. The deep-fried calamari, with perfectly fried, tender squid rings and skordali dipping sauce, is an appetizer big enough for an entree. Add a horiatiki salad—a huge pile of tomatoes, cucumbers, feta, kalamata olives, and a little pita—and you have a meal for two. The huge, seven-page menu lists all the classic Greek dishes including spanakopita, moussaka, or the terrific house specialty, spit-roasted chicken, which you can eat in or take home. Yanni's also offers an extensive selection of Greek wines and beers to accompany your meal. *$; MC, V; checks OK; dinner Mon–Sat; beer and wine; reservations recommended; street parking; map:EE8* &

Yarrow Bay Grill / ★★★
Yarrow Bay Beach Cafe / ★★

1270 CARILLON PT, KIRKLAND; 425/889-9052 (GRILL); 425-889-0303 (CAFE)

These sibling restaurants stacked atop one another are joined by the hip—the Eastside casual hip, that is. Upstairs, the tony grill ranks in the upper echelons of price and quality among Kirkland places, having seamlessly survived the exodus of former chef Vicky McCaffree, who was replaced by Felix Acosta. He continues the pan-seared, pan-global approach of his predecessor with such diversities as Hawaiian sea bass, Cuban pork tenderloin, New England risotto, and Bangkok barbecue chicken. Every table has a lake view, the service is quite good, and there's a solid wine list. All of this makes the Grill a worthy destination. Downstairs, the Beach Cafe has a clamorous Topsider-shod bar scene and Cameon Orel's riskier fare—get a shark quiche, tuna muffaletta, Vietnamese spring rolls with chorizo, or a burger. Delectable desserts range from the Black Bottom Banana Cream Pie in the Cafe to, if you're lucky, the Mexican Caramel Apple Flauta on the ever-changing upstairs Grill menu. *$$$, $$; AE, DC, DIS, JCB, MC, V; no checks; lunch Mon–Fri, dinner every day, brunch Sun (Grill), lunch, dinner every day (Cafe); full bar; reservations recommended; valet and validated parking; map:FF3* &

LODGINGS

LODGINGS

Ace Hotel / ★★

2423 IST AVE, BELLTOWN; 206/448-4721

The 30-room Ace is possibly the city's coolest hotel. This newcomer to the lodgings scene (opened in 1999) offers futuristic—and surprisingly affordable—respite from dowdy floral-print bedspreads and bland hotel furnishings. The location (above the Cyclops Cafe), owners (one a founder of Rudy's Barbershop), and press clips (*Wallpaper** and *Details*) all lend the place hipster cred. Rooms here are smartly stark: low beds adorned with simple wool French Army blankets, spare midcentury modern furniture, stainless-steel sinks and vanities, and funky original art. In the tradition of European hostels, standard rooms share six large bathrooms down the hall (and all have full-size beds). Those who don't dig the communal washrooms should opt for the more expensive deluxe rooms (there are 15 of these, following recent remodels) with private baths and king- or queen-size beds. Amenities include small wall TVs, phones with data ports, and—in deluxes—CD players. There's no room service, but with the abundance of good eating in the area, guests won't go hungry. Extras such as condoms and a copy of the *Kama Sutra* at the end of the bed distinguish the Ace as a grown-up getaway (although kids are welcome). For a quiet evening, avoid rooms on the noisy First Avenue side. Pets okay. *$$–$$$; AE, DC, DIS, JCB, MC, V; checks OK; self parking; reservation@theacehotel.com; www.theacehotel.com; map:F8*

Alexis Hotel / ★★★

1007 IST AVE, DOWNTOWN; 206/624-4844 OR 800/426-7033

The Alexis marries whimsy, hedonism, and elegance inside a turn-of-the-19th-century building. Even at 109 rooms (including 44 spacious suites), it has an intimate, boutique-hotel feel. (Request a room facing the inner courtyard, because rooms above First Avenue can be noisy.) Some suites include Jacuzzis or wood-burning fireplaces, but for sheer indulgence book one of the spa suites with two-person tubs. An on-site Aveda spa provides in-spa or in-room services (the hotel also has an on-call masseuse). Amenities range from voice mail, data ports, and complimentary morning tea and coffee to evening wine tasting, shoeshines, and a guest membership to the Seattle Club. Imaginative touches include in-line skating tours and a John Lennon suite, complete with original art. The Painted Table (see review in the Restaurants chapter) serves innovative Northwest cuisine; the Bookstore Bar is a cozy, though smoky, nook for libations. Pets okay. *$$$–$$$$; AE, DC, DIS, E, JCB, MC, V;*

checks OK; valet parking; seattleres@kimptongroup.com; www.alexis hotel.com; map:L7 ↸

Best Western Executive Inn / ★

200 TAYLOR AVE N, DENNY REGRADE; 206/448-9444 OR 800/351-9444

Despite its boxy, nondescript exterior, this no-nonsense 320-room motor inn welcomes guests with a surprisingly cozy lobby complete with rustic furniture and a gas fireplace. Rooms on the west side offer an in-your-face view of the Space Needle and the Experience Music Project, both just one block away. The decor is uninspiring but clean. Proximity to the Monorail at Seattle Center makes the location feasible even without a car. The inn has a Jacuzzi and workout room, as well as an informal restaurant and lounge. There's no charge for children under 17, and parking is free. Pets okay. *$$; AE, DC, DIS, JCB, MC, V; checks OK; self parking; www.exec-inn.com; map:E5* ↸

Best Western Pioneer Square Hotel / ★★

77 YESLER WY, PIONEER SQUARE; 206/340-1234 OR 800/800-5514

This genteel four-story brick hotel doesn't flaunt the fact that it's a Best Western, which is probably an attempt to maintain an air of boutiqueness. Handsome, comfortably appointed, moderately priced: this is a boon for travelers intent on staying in the heart of Seattle's bustling—and sometimes rough-and-tumble—old town. The 75 guest rooms here vary in size (some are scarcely larger than the bed), but you'll find sturdy cherry-wood furniture and, in some, small sitting alcoves. These surprisingly quiet rooms (the hotel is a block from the busy Alaskan Way Viaduct) come with a range of bed options, from a king with a queen sofa bed to two twins. Guests in search of a view will want to avoid rooms on the south side, which face the back of another building. And sleepyheads will find that the complimentary continental breakfast may be pretty picked over after 7:30am. Pioneer Square can be edgy at night, so timid travelers might opt for a more gentrified neighborhood. However, those looking for an authentic urban experience will find it here. Kids under 12 stay free. *$$; AE, DC, DIS, JCB, MC, V; no checks; self parking; info@ pioneersquare.com; www.pioneersquare.com; map:N8* ↸

Camlin Hotel / ★

1619 9TH AVE, DOWNTOWN; 206/682-0100 OR 800/325-4000

The dim, cool lobby of the Camlin invites visions of steamer-trunk-era sophistication. Charmingly slow elevators ascend and descend creakily. Built in 1926 by two bankers who embezzled the funds necessary to raise this 11-story property, the Camlin has become a sort of threadbare grande dame in the northeast corner of the downtown core (not far from the convention center and the Paramount Theatre). Unfortunately, the last time it was remodeled was in the mid-1980s, as evidenced by the

139

SPA TREATMENT

Everyone needs respite from the stresses and strains of daily life—even if you're on a vacation. Fortunately, you don't have to travel far in Seattle to get away from it all. Here are some in-and-out-of-city pampering best bets:

The energetic staff at **Spa Bellissima** (2620 2nd Ave, Belltown; 206/956-4156; www.spabellissima.com; map:E7) is almost as refreshing as the organic ingredients they harvest from Pike Place Market to use in their treatments. Owner Kristi Eyre Frambach creates everything by hand, using natural ingredients such as honey, sesame seeds, yogurt, lavender, and ginger. An organic healing facial ($75 for one hour) uses many of these edibles.

Slipped into historic Ballard is local favorite **Habitude** (5350 Ballard Ave NW; 206/782-2898; www.habitude.com; map:FF8). Opt for the "Under a Northern Rain-forest" spa package ($185), which includes a sampling of pampering for the whole body. Between services, spa-goers are treated to herbal teas and fresh fruits. A complimentary cosmetic touch-up is part of the experience; just ask.

Inside the tranquil, Asian-inspired environs, **Robert Leonard Day Spa and Salon** (2033 6th Ave, Belltown; 206/441-9900; www.robertleonard.net; map:H5) offers everything from a $25 manicure to a full day of beauty (underwater and table massage, body scrub, manicure, pedicure, facial, hair styling, makeup, and lunch) for $455. They also offer stomach-crunching, muscle-toning Pilates classes ($12 for a mat class, $50 for a private session) in the attached studio.

Owner Nina Ummel conjures a global environment at **Ummelina International** (1525 4th Ave, Downtown; 206/624-1370; www.ummelina.com; map:K6) with themed "journeys." One such journey, the Equator, makes for a romantic spa interlude where you can spend the day "au naturel" with your significant other underneath a real waterfall, a gentle rain from the "Rain Forest," and mud-caked baking in the "desert." Scrub clean with a return visit to the waterfall, all for $140 each. For less adventurous (and less expensive) treatments, choose from the "rituals" (facials, massages, or manicures starting at $35). Book early—appointments are at a premium.

One of three Juarez spas in the Seattle area, **Gene Juarez Salon and Spa** (607 Pine St, Downtown; 206/326-6000; www.genejuarez.com; map:F9) contains fountains and fireplaces that provide an opulent but cozy atmosphere. You'll move from room to room for services (there are many) for massages, facials, and pedicures. In the "envelopment" room, clients lie on a floating bed while wrapped like a burrito in a body mask (order the Signature Envelopment Therapy, which includes foot soak, steam and Swiss shower, and massage for $150). Don't miss the waterworks—the European jet spa, an underwater massage with no less than 77 jets, and the Vichy shower with overhead rain bars will wash stress right down the drain.

It's convenient—shop, drop, and get a hot-rock massage at **Spa Nordstrom** (500 Pine St, 5th Floor, Downtown; 206/628-1670; www.nordstrom.com/spanordstrom; map:J5). Within Nordstrom's flagship store lies an escape from all those pesky shopping decisions. There are services aplenty, such as body cocoons (aka wraps, $80–$90), milk whey baths ($50), eyebrow and eyelash tinting ($15–$20), and signature facials ($90). But, as one fellow spa-goer put it, "I couldn't forget I was naked in a department store."

Topnotch treatments for the digits are the forte at the very fem **Frenchy's** (3131 E Madison St, Ste 103, Madison Park; 206/325-9582; map:GG6). There are no wham-bam-thank-you-ma'am pedicures here. Sink into a cream-colored leather chair to soak your tootsies in style while staff offers coffee and tea. A deluxe manicure is $20 and a pedicure $35; both use aromatherapy exfoliating scrubs. Get a massage or one of their phenomenal facials while your nails dry.

Aestheticians dressed in no-nonsense whites take their skin seriously at **Jaroslava** (1413 4th Ave, Downtown; 206/623-3336; map K6). Trained at Carlsbad in the Czech Republic, the veritable birthplace of spas, Jaroslava Stovickova and her staff deliver deft treatments to the face and body, slathering on lots of product to soften and rejuvenate in this intimate, very European spa. Facials start at $75.

Right behind the Wild Rose, the singular nightspot for lesbians, is a clothing-optional bathhouse for (surprise!) girls only. The modern, minimalist decor at **Hothouse** (1019 Pike St, Ste HH, Capitol Hill; 206/568-3240; map:K3) makes for a soothing, relaxing, inexpensive indulgence where for only $9 gals can enjoy a deep, blue-tiled jetted tub, steam room, and sauna. Massage therapists are available by appointment.

Bio Azur (114 Central Wy, Kirkland; 425/828-9770; www.bioazurspas.com; map:EE3) is a petite spa with a perfect location for an after-treatment luncheon, followed by browsing galleries and shopping in quaint downtown Kirkland. A body steam with essential oils is only $15; add a facial, manicure, pedicure, firming treatment, underwater massage, complete new 'do (shampoo, scalp massage, hair mask, cut and style), and makeup for a full day of pampering for $435.

Just 45 minutes east of Seattle, **Salish Lodge Spa** (6501 Railroad Ave, Snoqualmie; 425/888-2556; www.salishlodge.com), with its plummeting waterfall and lavishly appointed lodge, is the quintessential Northwest retreat. Try a heated stone massage ($95), but arrive 30 minutes before to soak or sweat in the pools, sauna, and steam room for free. One design flaw: the waiting room of the spa is adjacent to the workout room, so a hotel guest may traipse by as you sit in nothing but your robe.

—Kathy Schultz

rooms' grimy mauve vinyl easy chairs and worn carpet. It's definitely due for some sprucing up. (Rumors of an extensive interior remodel have been circulating for years but, so far, no signs of action.) As a concession, management lowered room rates significantly. Large rooms have small sitting/work areas, walk-in closets, and clean bathrooms (albeit with a few chipped tiles); those with numbers that end in 10 boast windows on three sides. Avoid the Cabanas—they're small and dreary and mainly for smokers—and the room service, which can be quite slow. The top-floor Cloud Room comprises a dining room and a cocktail-and-piano bar with a rooftop deck. Kids under 18 stay free. *$–$$; AE, DC, DIS, JCB, MC, V; checks OK; self parking; map:I4*

Claremont Hotel / ★★☆

2000 4TH AVE, BELLTOWN; 206/448-8600 OR 877/448-8600

The light, airy rooms in this 1926 building situate travelers in a prime downtown location: three blocks from Pike Place Market, three blocks from Pacific Place, and a block and a half from the Monorail. Built as an apartment hotel, the Claremont underwent a mid-'90s renovation (except for the fourth and fifth floors). Today, sunny guest rooms offer one king- or queen-size bed, two queens, or two double beds, as well as a sitting area and a bathroom of white tile and marble. Artsy touches such as handmade glass pieces and framed botanicals on the walls complete the look. Junior Suites are bigger, with granite wet bars, while Executive Suites have separate living rooms and bedrooms. The hotel's yummy extras include Aveda products and complimentary copies of *Seattle Magazine*. For longer stays, a few rooms with kitchens are available. All rooms provide robes, hair dryers, irons and ironing boards, two-line phones with computer data ports, and voice mail. Upper floors boast views of downtown, Puget Sound, the Space Needle, Lake Union, and the Olympic Mountains. Room service includes a full breakfast and a 24-hour "snack" menu (a complete 24-hour menu is in the works). On the ground floor, Assaggio Ristorante (see review in the Restaurants chapter) is an excellent Northern Italian eatery. *$$$; AE, DC, DIS, JCB, MC, V; checks OK; valet parking; stay@claremonthotel.com; www.claremont hotel.com; map:I6* &

Courtyard by Marriott Seattle / ★★☆

925 WESTLAKE AVE N, SOUTH LAKE UNION; 206/213-0100 OR 800/321-2211

This latest addition to the Courtyard by Marriott series of hotels caters mostly to the business crowd, but its location near downtown and Seattle Center makes it an option for tourists, too. The sunlit lobby is bright and open, and a denlike cocktail lounge offers a place to curl up with a book. Rooms are well furnished with the usual business-hotel amenities: TVs, coffeemakers, irons and ironing boards, and hair dryers. Desks come complete with an ergonomic executive-style chair, Internet data ports, and high-speed broadband hookup available for an hourly charge. The hotel features a tiny business center, small pool, and restaurant with standard American fare and room service. A free shuttle is available to five popular downtown destinations. *$$–$$$; AE, DC, DIS, MC, V; checks OK; self parking; www.courtyardlakeunion.com; map:C2* &

Crowne Plaza Seattle / ★★☆

1113 6TH AVE, DOWNTOWN; 206/464-1980 OR 800/227-6963

This monolith crams 415 rooms into 34 stories that rise above Sixth Avenue. Although the low-ceilinged guest rooms serve as reminders of the Crowne Plaza's similarity to an egg carton, the hotel is constantly booked with repeat and corporate visitors. The enormous, banklike lobby reverberates with clicking heels, ringing cell phones, and the hiss of the espresso cart. All rooms come with one king or two double beds, and the top "Executive Floors" are corporate, comfortable, and clean, with spotlessly remodeled bathrooms and amenities such as bottled water and robes. Business travelers taking advantage of "club-level" services receive a lot of individual attention in addition to free papers, a lounge, complimentary breakfast, and evening hors d'oeuvres (for just a $25 upgrade). Lower-floor guest rooms are spacious, if not especially visually appealing. There is a full range of newly remodeled meeting facilities with high-speed Internet connections and videoconferencing capabilities. And the location is convenient: right off the freeway and about four blocks from the convention center. Some pets okay with deposit. *$$$; AE, DC, JCB, MC, V; no checks; valet parking; www.basshotels.com/crowneplaza; map:L5* &

The Edgewater / ★★★

2411 ALASKAN WY/PIER 67, WATERFRONT; 206/728-7000 OR 800/624-0670

A longtime waterfront landmark, the Edgewater is home to some of the Emerald City's most unusual claims to fame. It's the only Seattle hotel literally over the water (if watching whitecaps makes you dizzy, avoid first-floor rooms). And, in 1964, the Beatles checked in and dropped fishing lines out their hotel window (see the Fab Four photo in the gift shop). You can't fish from the windows anymore, but you can still breathe salty air and hear the ferries. And now the 238-room hotel has a flashy metal log-cabin exterior (aluminum shingles evoke silvery fish scales). The brand-new overhaul extends to the lobby and rooms (all with fireplaces), which are dressed in updated Northwest lodge: bark pillars with antler-like branches, antler furniture, and log bed frames. The sleek new Six Seven Restaurant & Lounge (named for the pier) serves Northwest cuisine with pan-Asian influences, and sports a sushi bar and an MTV-style wall of televisions (see review in the Restaurants chapter). The eatery's uninterrupted views of Elliott Bay, Puget Sound, and the Olympics now extend to a balcony over the water. It's a short walk to Bell Street Pier (Pier 66), with restaurants, the Odyssey Maritime Discovery Center, and an overpass to nearby Pike Place Market. Pets okay. *$$$; AE, DC, DIS, MC, V; checks OK; valet parking; www.edgewaterhotel.com; map:F9* &

Elliott Grand Hyatt Seattle / ★★★

721 PINE ST, DOWNTOWN; 206/774-1234 OR 800/233-1234
Seattle's newest megahotel opened in summer 2001 sporting an arsenal of high-tech extras, from bedside switches that raise and lower drapes to guest-room doorbells that change to "do not disturb" mode at the push of a button. An earth-tone Northwest motif runs from the expansive lobby to the backlit marble panels in hallways. Adjacent to the convention center, the Elliott is poised to embrace a slew of conventioneers, with 425 guest rooms and 113 suites. Since rooms begin on the 10th floor, nearly every view in the house reveals at least a sliver of lake or mountain. All rooms have one king or two full beds, cotton linens, leather desk chairs, refrigerators, complimentary high-speed Internet access, and separate glassed-in marble showers and deep cast-iron bathtubs with cascading faucets. Huge 800-square-foot suites with separate living and sleeping areas add flat-screen televisions, wet bars, and dual-head showers to the list of features. The three-tiered restaurant 727 Pine serves "eclectic Northwest cuisine," with an emphasis on seafood and a steak selection to please most red-meat aficionados. Of course, any hotel guest can indulge in 24-hour room service. Shop inside the hotel at Bellissimo Home, St. Croix Knits (for men), Flora and Henri (for kids), and the hotel florist, Flowers at the Elliott. Although the hotel's first few months weren't devoid of new-hotel wobbles (malfunctioning elevators and construction dust), the place will no doubt evolve into a well-oiled part of the Hyatt machine. *$$$; AE, DC, DIS, JCB, MC, V; checks OK; valet and self parking; www.hyatt.com; sales@seaghp.hyatt.com; map:J5* &

Executive Pacific Plaza Hotel / ★

400 SPRING ST, DOWNTOWN; 206/623-3900 OR 800/426-1165
For those who care more about location and budget than amenities, this clean-cut, midsize hotel fits the bill. Guest rooms are simple but comfortable and have small, clean bathrooms. The hotel recently underwent a $4 million renovation, updating rooms and furnishings; all rooms now feature 25-inch TVs, hair dryers, coffeemakers, irons and ironing boards, in-room movies, and two-line phones with voice mail. Rates include a generous continental breakfast. The hotel's one drawback is its lack of air conditioning (although all rooms are equipped with fans)—and opening the windows invites substantial traffic noise. *$$; AE, DC, DIS, JCB, MC, V; checks OK; self parking; reservations@pacificplazahotel.com; www.pacificplazahotel.com; map:L6*

Four Seasons Olympic Hotel / ★★★★

411 UNIVERSITY ST, DOWNTOWN; 206/621-1700 OR 800/821-8106

Guests who want to be pampered and coddled spare no expense and book rooms at the Four Seasons. Smiling maids, quick-as-a-wink bellhops, and a team of caring concierges ensure around-the-clock comfort at this posh 1920s landmark. The hotel's old-world luxury extends from the newly updated 450 guest rooms and suites—furnished with king or two oversize twin beds; baths with showers and soaking tubs and terry robes; and freshly replaced carpets, drapes, and bedding—to the venerable Georgian restaurant (see review in the Restaurants chapter). Executive suites feature down-dressed king-size beds separated from elegant sitting rooms by French doors. Several refined meeting rooms and shops flank the lobby. Enjoy afternoon tea in The Georgian (or in The Garden during the holidays), work out in the health club, or relax in the solarium hot tub and pool (a massage therapist is on call). Four Seasons' prices are steep, but this is Seattle's one world-class contender. Deposits required for cash guests. The hotel goes out of its way for kids, right down to a toy in the crib and a step stool in the bathroom. Pets okay. *$$$$; AE, DC, DIS, JCB, MC, V; checks OK; valet parking; www.fourseasons. com/seattle; map:K6* &

Hotel Monaco / ★★★

1101 4TH AVE, DOWNTOWN; 206/621-1770 OR 800/945-2240

The Monaco's brash digs cheerfully flout Seattle's penchant for earthy grays and browns. The upbeat mood is set in the lobby—with its nautical mural of dolphins—and sealed in the boldly designed rooms. All 189 are decorated in a blend of eye-popping stripes and florals that may strike some as insanely busy, others as utterly charming. All rooms come equipped with queen- or king-size beds; Mediterranean Suites feature deluxe bathrooms with two-person Fujijet tubs. As with many local hotels, views take a backseat to service and design (business travelers appreciate 6,000 square feet of meeting space). Monaco's campy principality extends to the Southern-inspired Sazerac restaurant, named for the bar's signature drink (see review in the Restaurants chapter). Pets okay (or ask for a loaner goldfish in its own bowl). *$$$$; AE, DC, DIS, JCB, MC, V; checks OK; valet parking; seattleres@kimptongroup.com; www.monaco-seattle.com; map:L6* &

Hotel Vintage Park / ★★★

1100 5TH AVE, DOWNTOWN; 206/624-8000 OR 800/624-4433

From the lobby's plush velvet settees and leather armchairs to the Grand Suite's double-sided fireplace, the Vintage Park looks like the ideal spot to break out a smoking jacket and a nice Chianti. Rooms are named after wineries, with updated Tuscany-inspired decor, and fireside wine tasting is complimentary every evening. Part of the San Francisco–based

Kimpton Group, the personable Park offers rooms facing inward or outward (exterior rooms have a bit more space, but forget about views) with two doubles or one king- or queen-size bed. Rooms come with fax machines, hair dryers, irons and ironing boards, double phone lines with data ports, and phones in the bathrooms. There's lightning-fast 24-hour room service, including lunch or dinner from the hotel's Italian restaurant Tulio, where the atmosphere is reminiscent of a Tuscan villa, and the pastas are great (see review in the Restaurants chapter). Unfortunately, a nearby busy Interstate 5 on-ramp makes lower floors a bit noisy; soundproofing helps on upper floors. Pets okay. *$$$; AE, DC, DIS, JCB, MC, V; checks OK; valet parking; www.vintagepark.com; map:L6* &

Inn at Harbor Steps / ★★
1221 1ST AVE, DOWNTOWN; 206/748-0973 OR 888/728-8910
The Inn at Harbor Steps couples an in-the-thick-of it location with quiet-getaway ambience. Tucked inside a swanky high-rise retail-and-residential complex across from the Seattle Art Museum, rooms here are shielded from the surrounding urban hubbub. The second Northwest property (after Whidbey Island's Saratoga Inn) from the California-based Four Sisters Inns, Harbor Steps offers 25 rooms with sleek, citified furnishings, garden views, fireplaces (excepting five of the rooms), air conditioning, king- or queen-size beds, sitting areas, wet bars, fridges, data ports, and voice mail. Deluxe rooms include spa tubs. Among the amenities are 24-hour concierge/innkeeper services, room service from Wolfgang Puck Cafe (4–10pm), complimentary evening hors d'oeuvres and wine, and a full gourmet breakfast. Guests have access to an indoor pool, sauna, Jacuzzi, exercise room, and meeting rooms. *$$$; AE, DC, JCB, MC, V; no checks; self parking; www.foursisters.com; map:K7* &

Inn at the Market / ★★★☆
86 PINE ST, PIKE PLACE MARKET; 206/443-3600 OR 800/446-4484
Everything about the Inn at the Market oozes quintessential Seattle atmosphere: views of Elliott Bay and the Olympics from most rooms, the proximity to the bustling Pike Place Market, and room service from country-French Campagne (see review in the Restaurants chapter). An ivy-draped courtyard wraps around its entrance amid high-end retailers and restaurants. The 70 newly updated rooms come with one or two queen-size or one king-size bed, and are handsomely dressed in a Biedermeier scheme of soft taupe, copper, and green (replacing Laura Ashley decor). All rooms above the fifth floor afford views, and those on the west have floor-to-ceiling windows that open to breezes off the Sound and unmatched vistas. (Don't fret if the weather turns gloomy; some of the most memorable views come through rain-streaked windows.) Other amenities include in-room safes and refrigerators, and oversize bathrooms. Rise early to sample the market's fresh pastries (try Le Panier

Bakery) and fruit. Or sleep late and indulge in room service from Bacco in the courtyard. In-room dinners come courtesy of Campagne (5–10pm). Campagne's bar is a snug, if smoky, spot for a nightcap. *$$$–$$$$; AE, DC, DIS, JCB, MC, V; checks OK; valet parking; info@innatthemarket.com; www.innatthemarket.com; map:I7* &

Inn at Virginia Mason / ★

1006 SPRING ST, FIRST HILL; 206/583-6453 OR 800/283-6453

The Inn at Virginia Mason works hard to let people know it's not just a place for friends and family of patients at Virginia Mason Medical Center. The location is convenient to the convention center, yet offers respite from the downtown bustle (if not from Pill Hill ambulance sirens). The standard rooms are on the small side and the paint is cracking in some rooms, but they're comfortable and feature European-style decor. It's probably worth it to splurge for a larger suite with a king-size bed— a few suites also have jetted tubs. The suite on the top floor sports a fireplace, bar, and behind-the-city view of Puget Sound. There's also a rooftop patio open to all guests. Take your meals at the pleasant Rhododendron Restaurant, or take a short walk for a good selection of downtown restaurants. *$$$; AE, DC, DIS, MC, V; checks OK; street parking; www.vmmc.org/dbAccommodations/default.htm; map:L3* &

Marriott Residence Inn Lake Union / ★★

800 FAIRVIEW AVE N, SOUTH LAKE UNION; 206/624-6000 OR 800/331-3131

With an emphasis on longer stays, this Marriott hotel isn't exactly on Lake Union; rather, it's across busy Fairview Avenue. Still, the 234 rooms, half of which are one-bedroom suites boasting lake views (request one on the highest floor possible), are spacious and tastefully decorated, and all have fully outfitted kitchenettes. Continental breakfast and evening dessert are presented in the lobby—a light- and plant-filled courtyard with an atrium and a waterfall. The hotel has no restaurant, but plenty of the lakeside eateries across the street allow guests to charge meals to their rooms. Amenities include meeting rooms, lap pool, exercise room, and sauna. If you're paying by check, do so at least seven days in advance. *$$$; AE, DC, DIS, MC, V; checks OK; self parking; www.residence inn.com/sealu; map:D1* &

Mayflower Park Hotel / ★★

405 OLIVE WY, DOWNTOWN; 206/623-8700 OR 800/426-5100

Past and present come together in a pleasing fashion at this handsomely renovated 1927 hotel set in the heart of the city's retail district (it's connected to Westlake Center). Upon entering an inviting lobby decorated with antique Chinese artwork and furniture, you have two excellent choices: to your right, you can sip one of Seattle's best martinis at Oliver's, a popular bar—or take a left, and enter Andaluca, an upscale restaurant combining Northwest and Mediterranean themes (see review in the Restaurants chapter). The 171 rooms are small, but preserve reminders of the hotel's past: lovely Oriental brass and antique appointments, elegant dark-wood furniture, deep tubs, thick walls, and double-glazed windows that trap noise. Coffeemakers come stocked with Torrefazione—a nice touch, since it's one of the finest brands available in this city of coffees. Suites offer comfortable sitting areas and most have king-size beds. The slightly bigger corner suites have better views; ask for one on a higher floor, or you may find yourself facing a brick wall. *$$$; AE, DC, DIS, JCB, MC, V; checks OK; valet parking; mayflowerpark@mayflower park.com; www.mayflowerpark.com; map:I6* &

MV Challenger Bunk & Breakfast / ★

1001 FAIRVIEW AVE N, STE 1600, SOUTH LAKE UNION; 206/340-1201 OR 800/288-7521

Rooms with water views aren't unusual in Seattle, but most don't come through a porthole. This perky red-and-white two-level 1944 tug moored on south Lake Union offers eight rooms, five with their own bath. The top-level Admiral's Cabin features a four-poster queen bed, soaking bath, and spectacular view. You won't find luxury on board; some quarters are tight, ladders between floors are steep, and the rooms are slightly worn. But this "bunk & breakfast" is filled with details that make for a charming stay: navigation charts as wallpaper, nautical brass fixtures, a comfy sitting room with a fireplace, a 300-plus videotape library. A full buffet breakfast is served in a cozy solarium, and there's 24-hour coffee and tea service. Eateries are steps away, as is the fascinating Center for Wooden Boats. Weather allowing, the tug takes a short cruise on Lake Union daily. Longer multiday trips on Puget Sound and to the San Juan Islands are also available—check the web site for a schedule. *$$–$$$; AE, DIS, DC, JCB, MC, V; checks OK; street parking; www.tugboatchallenger.com; map:GG7*

Paramount Hotel / ★★

724 PINE ST, DOWNTOWN; 206/292-9500 OR 800/325-4000

Ideally located for all sorts of diversions, the Paramount is kitty-corner from the historic Paramount Theatre, in the lap of swanky midtown retailers, and near the convention center. The Paramount's modest size— 146 guest rooms, two small meeting rooms, and a tiny fitness center— appeals to those who eschew nearby megahotels. Standard guest rooms are prettily appointed, though small, as are bathrooms. Each room includes phone with data port and voice mail, movie and game systems, coffeemaker, hair dryer, and iron. Consider splurging for an "executive king," which is always on the corner, quite a bit roomier, and outfitted with fireplaces and a whirlpool jet tub. The adjoining restaurant, pan-Asian–inspired Dragonfish Asian Cafe (see review in the Restaurants chapter), is trendy but tasty. *$$$; AE, DC, DIS, MC, V; checks OK; valet parking; www.westcoasthotels.com/paramount; map:J4* ⅋

Pensione Nichols / ★★☆

1923 1ST AVE, DOWNTOWN; 206/441-7125 OR 800/440-7125
Bohemian atmosphere, a superb location (perched above Pike Place Market), and reasonable prices set Pensione Nichols apart from the crowd. Though some might find the furnishings too well-worn, others will be charmed by the lovely antique pieces from the 1920s and '30s. Ten guest rooms share four bathrooms. Some rooms face noisy First Avenue; others don't have windows, but have bright skylights and are quieter. Also available: two spacious suites with private baths, full kitchens, and living rooms with jaw-dropping water views. A large, appealing common room on the third floor has a similarly spectacular view of Elliott Bay; it's here the bountiful breakfast—including fresh treats from the market—is served. Be warned—the stair climb from street level is a big one. No kids. Well-behaved pets okay. *$$; AE, DC, DIS, MC, V; checks OK; 2-night min summer weekends; street parking; www.seattle-bed-breakfast.com; map:H8*

Renaissance Madison Hotel / ★★

515 MADISON ST, DOWNTOWN; 206/583-0300 OR 800/278-4159
This 553-room hotel is aimed mostly to the business and convention crowd, but doesn't have the carnival atmosphere of some of the busier downtown hotels. The staff is professional—though it can be on the cool side. The color scheme is slowly transitioning from '80s teal and brass to more "modern" hues of toasted almond and cherry wood. Most rooms have great city and mountain views, but avoid rooms on the freeway side—windows are soundproofed, but noise still seeps in. Guests enjoy complimentary coffee, morning newspapers, and a rooftop pool. Amenities on the pricey Club Floors include free in-town transportation, hors d'oeuvres and a continental breakfast at the Club Lounge, and the best views. Prego, the restaurant on the 28th floor, offers a fine selection of seafood and gorgeous views. Check payments in advance only. *$$$; AE, DC, JCB, MC, V; checks OK; valet and self parking; www.renaissance hotels.com; map:M5* ⅋

Sheraton Seattle Hotel and Towers / ★★★☆

1400 6TH AVE, DOWNTOWN; 206/621-9000 OR 800/325-3535
A giant megalith looming over the downtown convention center, the Sheraton goes all out for business travelers. While its 840 guest rooms are smallish and standard, emphasis is given to meeting rooms and restaurants. On the first floor are the lobby lounge and an oyster bar, as well as the casual Pike Street Café (home to a famous 27-foot-long dessert bar) and Andiamo's, a pizza and pasta place. The Sheraton's former fine-dining

restaurant, Fullers, was converted to a private dining facility in 2001, and is available for bookings by individuals or companies. Convention facilities at the Sheraton are second to none in the city. Discriminating businesspeople head for the upper four Club Rooms (31–34), where they'll find their own lobby, concierge, private lounge, and complimentary continental breakfast and hors d'oeuvres. The 35th-floor health club features a heated pool and knockout city panorama (unfortunately, if you're not staying in the Club Rooms, you'll have to pay to use it—rates run $5 per day or $10 per stay). *$$$–$$$$; AE, DC, DIS, JCB, MC, V; checks OK; valet and self parking; www.sheraton.com; map:K5* &

Sixth Avenue Inn / ★

2000 6TH AVE, BELLTOWN; 206/441-8300 OR 800/648-6440
Catering to tourists and conventioneers, this personable motor inn is undertaking a top-to-bottom refurbishing of all of its 166 rooms—including new carpets, furniture, and refitted bathrooms—set to be completed in early 2002. The clean, simple, but spacious rooms feature TVs with pay-per-view movies and game players, and even a selection of books in some rooms. There's less street noise on the east side. Service is professional and friendly, and you'll also find room service, a bar and restaurant, free parking, and a good location, both central to downtown shopping and not too far from Seattle Center. *$$; AE, DC, DIS, MC, V; checks OK; self parking; www.sixthavenueinn.com; map:H5*

Sorrento Hotel / ★★★☆

900 MADISON ST, FIRST HILL; 206/622-6400 OR 800/426-1265
First opened in 1909, the Sorrento is an Italianate masterpiece grandly holding court on its own corner just east of downtown in Seattle's First Hill neighborhood. Evoking a classic European hostelry, the beauty of the Sorrento is in the details: rose petals left on your pillow by the evening turndown service (or hot water bottles in winter months), elegant furnishings, a softly lit and welcoming lobby. The 76 rooms are decorated in muted good taste, varying from old-world elegance to Northwest contemporary. Despite their historic feel, rooms include concessions to technology: direct TV, CD players, and dual-line cordless phones with data ports. There's also a small exercise room. Top-floor suites make posh quarters for meetings or parties—the showstopper being the 2,000-square-foot, $1,800-a-night penthouse, with a grand piano, fireplace, patio, Jacuzzi, view of Elliott Bay, and luxurious rooms. The Fireside Room off the lobby, a plush symphony of dark mahogany and deep red furnishings, is a civilized place for taking the Sorrento's high tea in the late afternoon or sipping Cognac while listening to jazz piano in the evening. The manly Hunt Club serves a carnivore's carnival of Mediterranean-influenced cuisine (see review in the Restaurants chapter). Complimentary town-car service takes guests downtown. Some travelers

consider the Sorrento's location—five blocks uphill from the heart of the city—inconvenient, but we find it quiet and removed. Small pets okay. *$$$$; AE, DC, DIS, JCB, MC, V; checks OK; valet parking; mail@ hotelsorrento.com; www.hotelsorrento.com; map:M4* &

Summerfield Suites by Wyndham / ★★

1011 PIKE ST, DOWNTOWN; 206/682-8282 OR 800/426-0670

For better or for worse, this suites-only hotel is just steps away from the convention center (and also a short walk uphill to the funky Pike/Pine neighborhood of shops, pubs, and restaurants). All rooms are commendably spacious (even the studios), with a living room and fully appointed kitchen including dishwasher, coffeemaker, microwave, and stovetop (some units have full ranges with ovens). The hotel recently underwent a $3.5 million upgrade, and the rooms are appointed with plush pillow-top mattresses, CD alarm clocks, cordless phones, desks with ergonomic Herman Miller chairs, and furnishings in subtle tans and whites. Some rooms have fireplaces, while others have jetted tubs. Expect all the amenities of a full-service hotel: conference rooms, exercise rooms (sauna and Jacuzzi, too), and laundry service. There's no restaurant, but an extensive continental breakfast buffet is included. There's even a shop in the lobby that stocks frozen dinners to pop in your microwave. Summerfield Suites is ideal for corporate clients on long-term stays or families on vacation who want a little room to spread out (each room has two TVs and there's a heated outdoor pool for the kids). *$$$; AE, DC, DIS, JCB, MC, V; checks OK; valet parking; www.wyndham.com; map:K3* &

W Seattle Hotel / ★★★☆

1112 4TH AVE, DOWNTOWN; 206/264-6000 OR 877/W-HOTELS

The W chain of hotels has brought a breath of fresh air to the predictable world of Seattle's corporate hotels. The W's see-and-be-seen lobby alone merits a cover charge—indeed, sometimes the staff pumps up techno dance music to give the place a nightclub feel. Colorful postmodern art adorns the walls, chocolate-velvet drapes run the length of the high windows, and plush modern furniture is situated between oversize chess sets and stylish magazines. Naturally, it's a magnet for black-garbed people with cell phones or froufrou drinks, as is the adjacent bar leading to the hotel's Earth and Ocean restaurant (see review in the Restaurants chapter). The staff is also clad in black, but thankfully lacks the hipper-than-thou attitude. Rooms exhibit a simpler chic than the lobby: colored in taupe and black and outfitted with stainless-and-glass-appointed bathrooms, safes, irons and ironing boards, coffeemakers, desks, and Zen-inspired water sculptures. Many rooms (particularly higher corner rooms) have impressive downtown views; all have two double or one king-size "W Signature Bed" sheathed in goose-down duvets and pillows, and 250-thread-count linens. Honor bars wittily yield mints, wax lips, and "intimacy kits." Room service is 24 hours, as is the fitness room; stylish meeting space totals 10,000 square feet. The W is also totally wired: each room comes equipped with 27-inch TV with Internet access, CD and video player, two-line desk phone with high-speed Internet connection, conference calling, voice mail, and a cordless handset. A "Pet Amenity Program" provides plush pet beds and treats for your pooch. *$$$$; AE, DC, DIS, JCB, MC, V; checks OK; valet parking; www. whotels.com; map:L6* &

Warwick Hotel / ★★

401 LENORA ST, BELLTOWN; 206/443-4300 OR 800/426-9280
From the outside, the Warwick appears to be nothing more than a dated '70s-era corporate hotel with little character. Inside, things improve. The staff is courteous, and in the small lobby you'll find free newspapers and coffee. Rooms are large and comfortable with elegant furnishings, including floor-to-ceiling windows, small balconies (reserve a room above the sixth floor for a great view), and marble bathrooms. TVs, movies, phones with data ports, hair dryers, and minibars complete the business-friendly rooms. The pool in the health club is too short for laps, but a spa and sauna will help you unwind. If you've got the bucks, splurge for the Queen Victoria Suite, with its elegant appointments and panoramic view (good for private parties, too). The hotel's restaurant, Brasserie Margaux, has decent service, serves a passable combination of Northwest and French specialties, and provides room service. Twenty-four-hour courtesy van service available for downtown appointments. *$$$; AE, DC, DIS, MC, V; checks OK; valet and self parking; res.seattle@warwickhotels.com; www.warwickhotels.com; map:H6* &

WestCoast Grand Hotel on Fifth Avenue / ★★

1415 5TH AVE, DOWNTOWN; 206/971-8000 OR 800/325-4000
Formerly Cavanaugh's on Fifth, the WestCoast Grand has changed its name, but the 297 rooms in this former office building remain much the same. Recent improvements include adding feather beds, game players, and wireless Internet access to the laundry list of standard business-traveler fare: king- or queen-size beds, televisions tucked into armoires, coffeemakers, hair dryers, and data ports. Most of the standard rooms also provide honor bars and vanity counters outside the bathrooms. If you plan to spend much time in your room, move up to one of the suites, which offer separate parlors, better views of downtown or the Sound, and bathrobes. (A Presidential Suite comes equipped with a fireplace and a dining room that seats six.) Rooms higher up are best for people who want to shut out noise from hectic Fourth and Fifth Avenues. Room service is available 24 hours. The fifth-floor Terrace Garden Restaurant serves Northwest cuisine in a light-filled space or (when the weather cooperates) on an outdoor terrace. The Elephant & Castle, a tame

British-style pub and restaurant below the lobby, serves up fish-and-chips, bangers, and mash, in addition to American burgers. *$$$; AE, DC, DIS, MC, V; checks OK; self parking; 5thavesales@westcoast hotels.com; www.westcoasthotels.com; map:K6* &

WestCoast Roosevelt Hotel / ★

1531 7TH AVE, DOWNTOWN; 206/621-1200 OR 800/426-0670
Gone is the grand skylit lobby that so distinguished the Roosevelt when it first opened its doors in 1930; the space is now inhabited by Von's Grand City Cafe (where martinis and Manhattans flow in great quantities). The new hotel lobby is small, and a piano offers jazz most nights to those who can fit into the few chairs and couches scattered about. Elsewhere, the Roosevelt's art deco sensibilities have been somewhat preserved. The hotel's 20 stories have been reconfigured for the contemporary traveler, but studios are still almost comically small. The deluxe rooms are a better choice, with adjoining sitting areas; suites each contain a whirlpool tub and a separate sitting area. Considering its proximity to the convention center and the shopping district, the Roosevelt's prices are decent. *$$–$$$; AE, DC, DIS, MC, V; checks OK; valet parking; www.roosevelthotel.com; map:J5* &

WestCoast Vance Hotel / ★

620 STEWART ST, DOWNTOWN; 206/441-4200 OR 800/426-0670
Here's another WestCoast project to save a forgotten downtown hotel. Most of the decade-old restoration, it seems, was focused on the lobby—making for a very pretty entrance. The small and spartan rooms are showing serious signs of wear: carpet stains, a slight mustiness, scuff marks, and the occasional chipped paint. Standard rooms are no bargain, as there's barely enough room to swing even a cliché cat (the bathrooms are shoehorned into former closets; claustrophobics should shower elsewhere). Service could be more polished, but the Vance's central location still makes this midrange hotel a viable choice for those looking to stay downtown. The north-facing rooms above the fifth floor are best, with a view toward the Space Needle. Room service comes from the Latin restaurant downstairs, Yakima Grill. *$$–$$$; AE, DC, DIS, MC, V; checks OK; valet parking; sales@vancehotel.com; www.westcoasthotels. com/vance; map:H5*

The Westin Seattle / ★★★

1900 5TH AVE, DOWNTOWN; 206/728-1000 OR 800/WESTIN-1
The Westin's twin cylindrical towers evoke all sorts of comparisons by local wits: corncobs, trash cans, mountain bike handlebars. Nonetheless, they do provide spacious rooms with unbeatable views, particularly above the 20th floor. The gargantuan size of the hotel (891 rooms and 34 suites) contributes to some lapses in service: the check-in counter can

resemble a busy day at Sea-Tac Airport, and the harried concierge staff may have little time for your requests. Rooms are smartly furnished, and all beds (king or double) come with pillow-top mattresses and luxurious 300-thread-count linens. Hotel amenities are corporate-minded: business center, convention facilities spread over several floors, and a multilingual staff. You'll also find a large pool and Jacuzzi with city view, and an exercise room. On the top floors are some ritzy, glitzy suites suitable for all manner of CEOs, finance ministers, and sultans. The Westin's location, near Westlake Center and the Monorail station, is excellent, as are meals at Nikko, a Japanese restaurant, and Roy's (where gooey-in-the-center chocolate soufflés are reason enough to pay a visit). *$$$$; AE, DC, DIS, JCB, MC, V; checks OK; valet and self parking; www.westin.com; map:H5* &

Capitol Hill

Bacon Mansion / ★★

959 BROADWAY AVE E, CAPITOL HILL; 206/329-1864 OR 800/240-1864

Built by Cecil Bacon in 1909, this Edwardian Tudor-style mansion is home to a classy bed-and-breakfast, with lovingly restored woodwork and common areas featuring antique rugs, a grand piano, and a library. Nine rooms in the main guest house (seven with private baths) are appointed with antiques and brass fixtures. The top of the line is the Capitol Suite, a huge room on the second floor with a sunroom, a fireplace, a pine empress bed, and a view of the Space Needle (though surrounding trees are starting to eclipse the view). The lovely Emerald Suite sports a sleigh bed, fireplace, and claw-footed bathtub with shower. The Carriage House, a separate two-story building, is appropriate for a small family or two couples. There's a peaceful rose garden in the courtyard, and the inn is a brief walk to Broadway's numerous restaurants and shops. Proprietor Daryl King is an enthusiastic, friendly host. *$$–$$$; AE, DIS, MC, V; checks OK; street parking; info@baconmansion.com; www.baconmansion.com; map:GG6*

Bed and Breakfast on Broadway / ★

722 BROADWAY AVE E, CAPITOL HILL; 206/329-8933

Conveniently located just one block north of the popular Broadway strip of shops, restaurants, and movie theaters is this distinctive house featuring beautiful stained-glass windows, hardwood floors, and Oriental rugs. Hosts and proprietors Russel Lyons—whose original paintings are on display throughout—and Don Fabian preside over four spacious guest rooms, all with private baths. The Penthouse has a private deck lined with well-tended flower pots. A generous continental breakfast, which often features homemade coffee cake, is included. No children; check in after 5pm unless by prior arrangement. *$$; AE, DIS, MC, V; checks OK; self parking; www.bbonbroadway.com; map:GG6*

Capitol Hill Inn / ★★☆

1713 BELMONT AVE, CAPITOL HILL; 206/323-1955

This is one of the most conveniently located B&Bs in the city—within walking distance of the convention center and Broadway shops and restaurants (you'll get your daily exercise on the hills). Unfortunately, you give up any charm of a neighborhood for this convenience, but the 1903 Queen Anne–style home (which was at one time a bordello) is itself a lovely place. Mother-daughter team Katie and Joanne Godmintz, who live on the premises, have beautifully restored the inn down to its custom-designed wall coverings, period chandeliers, carved wooden moldings, and sleigh and brass beds. There are four guest rooms upstairs (two with full baths, two with toilets and sinks and a shower down the hall) and three lower-level guest rooms in the daylight basement (all with private bath, fireplace, and Jacuzzi). No young children. *$$; MC, V; checks OK; street parking; www.capitolhillinn.com; map:HH6*

Gaslight Inn / ★★★☆

1727 15TH AVE, CAPITOL HILL; 206/325-3654

Refreshingly free of the antique-and-lace overkill common to B&Bs, the Gaslight mixes modern elements such as vibrant glass art with period pieces befitting its turn-of-the-last-century pedigree. Even the stuffed gazelle head over the fireplace in the living room comes off as a deft design move rather than a hunting-lodge cliché. Of the eight guest rooms (all with one double or one queen-size bed), five have private baths (shared baths are accessed by a staircase), one has a fireplace, and all are gorgeously decorated in a distinct style—some contemporary, some antique, and some Mission. Out back, sundecks smartly set off a heated swimming pool (open May through October). Suites in the annex next door (one is a studio) are targeted at businesspeople and come with private baths, wet bars, coffeemakers, microwaves, refrigerators, and phones with data ports. One suite takes up the entire top floor and has a spectacular view of downtown and the Olympic Mountains. Though the Gaslight's aesthetics are impeccable, the same cannot always be said for the people skills of its proprietors, who can be a bit gruff. No kids or pets (except the inn's dogs, Buster and Spike). *$$; AE, MC, V; checks OK; 3-day min in summer; self parking; innkeepr@gaslight-inn.com; www.gaslight-inn.com; map:HH6*

Hill House Bed and Breakfast / ★★★
Amaranth Inn / ★★

1113 E JOHN ST, CAPITOL HILL; 206/720-7161 OR 800/720-7161
1451 S MAIN ST, CENTRAL DISTRICT; 206/720-7161 OR 800/720-7161

The special touches and personal service from innkeepers Herman and Alea Foster are what make the Hill House memorable. What with fresh flowers in all guest rooms, down comforters in pressed cutwork duvet covers, crisp cotton sheets, and handmade soaps, you may find it hard to even leave your room. But be sure you do, because you won't want to miss Herman's exceptional two-course gourmet breakfasts, with entrees such as smoked salmon omelets and walnut bread French toast, cooked to order and served on china and crystal. This elegantly restored 1903 Victorian, located in the heart of historic Capitol Hill, offers guests a choice of seven beautifully decorated rooms, five with private baths. The Fosters also own and operate Amaranth Inn, a similarly appointed bed-and-breakfast housed in a 1906 Craftsman in the Central District (often called South Capitol Hill). The location is more convenient to Chinatown and Pioneer Square, and it contains spacious rooms with boatlike antique beds, some with private baths, most with gas fireplaces, and a few with jetted tubs. Children 12 and over are okay at both places. *$$$; AE, DC, DIS, MC, V; no checks; self parking; www.seattlebnb.com; www. amaranthinn.com; map:GG6, HH6*

Salisbury House / ★★★

750 16TH AVE E, CAPITOL HILL; 206/328-8682

This bed-and-breakfast in an elegant turn-of-the-19th-century Capitol Hill home is an exquisite hostelry on a tranquil residential street near Volunteer Park. Glossy maple floors and lofty beamed ceilings lend a sophisticated air to the guest library (with a chess table and a fireplace) and the living room. Up the wide staircase and past the second-level sun porch are four guest rooms—one with a lovely canopied bed, all with queen-size beds and down comforters—with full baths. The lower-level suite has a private entrance, fireplace, refrigerator, and whirlpool tub, making it a perfect home base for longer stays. Friendly innkeepers Mary and Cathryn Wiese serve a sumptuous breakfast that can be taken in the dining room or on the sunny terrace. Classy and dignified, devoid of televisions (except the suite), the Salisbury is a sure bet in one of Seattle's finest neighborhoods. No children under 12. *$$; AE, MC, V; checks OK; street parking; sleep@salisburyhouse.com; www.salisburyhouse.com; map:HH6*

University District/North End

Best Western University Tower Hotel / ★★

4507 BROOKLYN AVE NE, UNIVERSITY DISTRICT; 206/634-2000 OR 800/899-0251

When this hotel's new management chose to rename the former Edmond Meany Hotel the Best Western University Tower Hotel, they turned their backs on a name with a long and interesting history. Forgotten is Edmond Meany, a popular turn-of-the-19th-century University of Washington professor, mountaineer, and Seattle promoter. The renaming is another example of the disturbing trend that threatens to transform distinctive American cities into generic corporate-run mediocrity. That said, the recent $5 million renovation of this 15-story art deco tower designed by renowned architect Robert C. Reamer (who also did downtown's Skinner Building and a couple of grand hotels in Yellowstone National Park) has improved the place considerably. Hallways are trimmed in sunny yellows, reds, and blues and the rooms are equally stylish—complete with brightly colored contemporary decor, plush feather beds, and modern amenities such as hair dryers, coffeemakers, ironing boards, and phones with data ports. The octagonal-tower design allows every one of the 155 guest rooms (more than half of which contain king-size beds) a bay window with a view; those on the south side are sunny. The rates include a continental breakfast buffet and ample free parking. There's no longer a restaurant on the premises; however, the hotel staff will order delivery from one of many nearby restaurants. And you're just one block away from shopping on the Ave and two blocks from the UW campus. If you plan to pay by check, a credit card is still required for check-in. *$$; AE, DC, DIS, MC, V; checks OK; self parking; www.meany.com; map:FF7* &

Chambered Nautilus / ★★☆

5005 22ND AVE NE, UNIVERSITY DISTRICT; 206/522-2536

This guest house set on a woodsy hillside is run with friendliness and panache by energetic innkeepers Joyce Schulte and Steve Poole. The blue 1915 Georgian colonial atop a steep set of stairs offers six airy guest rooms beautifully furnished with antiques. All have private baths (though one bath is a few steps outside the bedroom door). Four rooms open onto porches with views of the Cascades. An annex next door houses four "University Suites"; one has two bedrooms, the remaining three have one bedroom—and all suites are appointed with full kitchens, antique iron queen beds, and sofa couches. Suites are available for long-term stays between October and May. All of the rooms at Chambered Nautilus offer welcoming touches: robes, antique writing desks, flowers, reading material, bottled water, gourmet chocolates, and resident teddy

FEELING SHELLFISH

A geoduck (pronounced "gooey-duck") is an ungainly creature, a huge, 2-pound clam with a foot-long siphon that it can't completely retract into its shell. Doesn't matter, though; geoducks inhabit deep sands in Puget Sound tideflats, from which only the tip of the siphon protrudes. They are rarely discerned, except by habitués of beaches at low tide—and by visitors to Pike Place Market, who stare in disbelief at the bizarre appearance of the limp, harvested specimens displayed on ice. Geoducks are profoundly difficult to dig from their lairs, 3 feet deep in the sand.

Luckily for anyone interested in a genuine Puget Sound experience, many shellfish species are much easier to obtain than geoducks. Native butterclams and littlenecks, and introduced species such as Manila clams, are found in shallower habitats; mussels and oysters live on subtidal rocks. If you're willing to make a day trip of it, hike a bit, and dig a little, you're sure to come back with a bucket full.

State regulations establish seasons and harvest limits for all shellfish, and you'll need a modestly priced license, available at sporting goods and hardware outlets where fishing licenses are sold. Make sure your destination is one that's open to public digging. Beginners need a tide table (you'll need at least a modest minus tide, the lower the better) and a good guide (the Audubon Society Pacific Coast Nature Guide is excellent). Call the state's Red Tide Hotline (800/562-5632), which lists any areas in which mollusks are contaminated by paralytic shellfish poison (PSP) or other marine biotoxins; in some years, much of Puget Sound is off-limits by late August.

Unfortunately, when the legendary Seattle songwriter/entrepreneur Ivar Haglund rejoiced in his "happy condition / Surrounded by acres of clams," it was a more bucolic time. Today, because of urban pollution, no beaches in the immediate Seattle area are advisable for clam digging. The nearest spots are Dash Point and Saltwater State Parks in Federal Way, south of Seattle; the best places are a ferry ride away, such as the beach at Double Bluff Park, a 3-mile-long walk-in park on Whidbey Island. Hood Canal is the place to hunt oysters: two of the best areas are Shine Tidelands and Hood Spit, both just on the west side of the Hood Canal Bridge, requiring a ride on the Bainbridge Island or Edmonds-Kingston ferry. (See Hood Canal in this chapter.)

What to do with your loot? Steam clams or mussels in a pot, or use them to make clam chowder or mussel stew (don't overcook them or they'll get tough). Real enthusiasts like to take along an oyster knife and shuck a couple of their finds right on the beach. Add a dash of lemon juice and you can have lunch on the spot. And if you somehow manage to extract a geoduck from the sand, it's excellent diced up in a stir-fry—yes, siphon and all (dip the siphon briefly into boiling water and remove the skin first). With geoducks, you need only one for a meal.

—Eric Lucas

bears (in case you forget your own). The location is a few blocks from Fraternity Row, and can get noisy during the opening of classes in early October. Other times, though, it's quite peaceful. A full breakfast is included, and complimentary coffee, tea, and cookies are always available. Make prior arrangements for kids under 8. *$$; AE, MC, V; checks OK; street parking; stay@chamberednautilus.com; www.chambered nautilus.com; map:FF6*

Chelsea Station on the Park / ★★

4915 LINDEN AVE N, FREMONT; 206/547-6077 OR 800/400-6077

The neighborhood may not be the most convenient if you're planning on hitting the city's popular tourist destinations (with the exception of the superlative Woodland Park Zoo, which is just across the street), but this charming guest house makes the extra few miles worth the effort. Situated in two 1929 brick homes in the Federal colonial revival style, the inn is thoughtfully dressed in Craftsman-style furniture to match. Each of the nine guest rooms comes with an antique king- or queen-size bed, private bath (two rooms come with shower only), and phone with voice messaging. Each room has its own appeal; the Margaret suite on the top floor offers three rooms and a view out to the Cascades, the Sunlight suite features a small kitchen, and the Morning Glory suite boasts its own in-room piano. Traffic is a little noisy on the north side, but in general this is a quiet neighborhood. Generous gourmet breakfasts of stuffed French toast, Mexican scrambles, smoked salmon hash, or banana nut pancakes are served in the sunny common area downstairs. Kids age 6 and over okay. Tip: Sometimes bookings allow for shorter-than-minimum stays April through October. *$$; AE, DC, DIS, MC, V; checks OK; 3-night min Apr–Oct; self parking; www.bandbseattle.com; map:FF7*

College Inn Guest House / ★

4000 UNIVERSITY WY NE, UNIVERSITY DISTRICT; 206/633-4441

Despite its Historic Register status, this 1909 three-level Tudor on the doorstep of the University of Washington campus is appealingly collegial. The staff is young and knowledgeable and the place has the feel of a good European hostel (even though all rooms are private). It's free of TVs and radios (but all rooms have phones), has shared "facilities" (showers are separate-sex), and can get a little noisy (there's a cafe and pub downstairs). Each of the 27 guest rooms does have a sink, a desk, and a single or double bed, and the best of the lot have window seats. A generous continental breakfast (included in the bargain rates) is served upstairs in the communal sitting area. Kids ages 5 and up okay. *$; MC, V; checks OK; street parking; c-inn@speakeasy.org; www.speak easy.org/collegeinn; map:FF6*

University Inn / ★★☆

4140 ROOSEVELT WY NE, UNIVERSITY DISTRICT; 206/632-5055 OR 800/733-3855

This is a bright, clean, well-managed establishment. Rooms in the newer south wing are more spacious; some have king-size beds, and all contain irons and ironing boards. North-wing rooms are more standard, with shower stalls in the bathrooms (no tubs). Some have small balconies overlooking the heated outdoor pool and hot tub. All rooms offer voice mail, small safes, and data ports. Other amenities include a complimentary continental breakfast, free morning paper, a tiny exercise room (the staff affectionately refers to it as the "fitness closet"), and free off-street parking. Extended-stay rooms are available. The hotel's Portage Bay Café serves up affordable if lackluster fare. The entire hotel is non-smoking. Watertown Hotel—a new 100-room hotel one block north, owned by the same company that manages the University Inn—is scheduled to open in spring 2002; check the web site for details. *$$; AE, DC, DIS, JCB, MC, V; checks OK; self parking; reservations@university innseattle.com; www.universityinnseattle.com; map:FF7* &

Queen Anne/Seattle Center

Hampton Inn & Suites / ★★☆

700 5TH AVE N, SEATTLE CENTER; 206/282-7700 OR 800/426-7866

Located within strolling distance from Seattle Center and Lower Queen Anne eateries, this clean, efficient, friendly facility houses 198 rooms and suites (all suites have balconies). This is a practical, if not an incredibly luxurious, place to lay your head. Recently updated decor features striped easy chairs and pleasant neutrals. Guests here are mostly business travelers and families with heavy tourist schedules that keep them off the premises most of the day. Standard rooms include individually controlled heating and air conditioning, hair dryers, irons and ironing boards, and voice mail. One-bedroom and two-bedroom suites also feature multiple televisions, gas fireplaces, and small kitchen units. A complimentary continental breakfast is served each morning. *$$; AE, DC, DIS, JCB, MC, V; no checks; self parking; www.hilton.com/en/hp/; map:A4* &

Inn of Twin Gables / ★

3258 14TH AVE W, INTERBAY; 206/284-3979 OR 866/466-3979

If you seek some distance from the madding crowd of downtown and Capitol Hill, consider spending time at the Inn of Twin Gables. Mother and daughter innkeepers Fran and Katie Frame have turned this Craftsman home on the west slope of Queen Anne Hill into a comfy inn. The three guest rooms are all decorated with period antiques and distinctive quilts. Two of the rooms share a bath (which is somewhat basic but adequate), and the third has its own private shower. Hearty breakfasts usually include homemade scones and dishes seasoned with homegrown herbs. The downstairs dining room is surrounded by tried-and-true B&B kitsch: collections of antique tea sets, Japanese and Chinese prints, overstuffed chairs. But the best seat in the house is in the glassed-in front porch, a great spot to curl up with a novel, sip your coffee, and watch the sun set behind the Olympic Mountains. No kids. *$$; AE, DIS, MC, V; checks OK; street parking; info@innoftwin gables.com; www.innoftwingables.com; map:GG8*

Marqueen Hotel / ★★

600 QUEEN ANNE AVE N, QUEEN ANNE; 206/282-7407 OR 888/445-3076
Entering the lobby of the Marqueen Hotel, it seems you've stepped into an Edith Wharton novel. The opulent lobby of this 1918 building is lined in dark mahogany wainscoting and stocked with graceful fin de siècle furnishings. You almost expect a lady in corsets, long dress, and feathered hat to come floating down the hotel's grand staircase. But despite its historic look, the Marqueen became a hotel during a more recent turn of the century; before its renovation in 1998, it served as an apartment building. As a result of the recent work, all of the rooms have modern amenities: TVs, mini-kitchens, coffeemakers, microwaves, refrigerators, hair dryers, and phones with data ports. Some rooms have full ranges with ovens, and a few rooms have glassed-in parlors that make a nice common relaxing spot if you're renting several rooms as a group. The cheapest standard rooms face a goofy sylvan mural painted on the building next door, but there's no disguising the fact that the rooms on the east side of the hotel are much darker than the sunlit rooms facing west. Room service is available from the nearby Ten Mercer restaurant. *$$$; AE, DC, DIS, JCB, MC, V; no checks; valet parking; info@marqueen.com; www.marqueen.com; map:A7*

Bainbridge Island

The Buchanan Inn / ★★☆

8494 NE ODDFELLOWS RD, SOUTH BAINBRIDGE; 206/780-9258 OR 800/598-3926

Close enough to Seattle for easy access but far enough to leave the city sounds behind, this beautifully renovated 1912 B&B (formerly an Odd Fellows Hall) is set in one of the island's most picturesque and sunny neighborhoods. Run by a friendly team of innkeepers, Judy and Ron Gibbs, the Buchanan features four spacious suites with large private baths and king- or queen-size beds, separate sitting areas, CD players, coffeemakers, and mini-fridges stocked with complimentary beverages; gas fireplaces are in two rooms. A short stroll away are Fort Ward State Park and the beach (ask Judy for the lowdown on other sights), and it's just steps to the inn's rustic cottage and a bubbling hot tub. Children over 16 okay. No pets (though dogs are on-site). *$$; AE, DC, DIS, JCB, MC, V; checks OK; self parking; jgibbs@buchananinn.com; www.buchananinn.com* &

Eastside

Bellevue Club Hotel / ★★★

11200 SE 6TH ST, BELLEVUE; 425/454-4424 OR 800/579-1110

From the sunken tubs in every room to original pieces by Northwest artists, the Bellevue Club's accommodations are some of the Eastside's most opulent. The 67 rooms are strikingly swathed in Asian-inspired colors—lots of soothing neutrals, browns, and grays—and furnished in cherry-wood pieces custom-made on Whidbey Island. Many overlook tennis courts; Club Guest rooms' French doors open onto private terracotta patios. There's ample opportunity to work up a sweat at the extensive athletic facilities, including an Olympic-size swimming pool; indoor tennis, racquetball, and squash courts; and aerobics classes. Oversize limestone-and-marble bathrooms—with spalike tubs—are perfect for postworkout soaks. The club offers fine dining at Polaris restaurant and casual fare at the Sport Cafe. *$$$–$$$$; AE, DC, MC, V; checks OK; valet and self parking; julias@bellevueclub.com; www.bellevueclub. com; map:HH3* &

Hilton Bellevue / ★★

100 112TH AVE NE, BELLEVUE; 425/455-3330 OR 800/BEL-HILT

The Hilton Bellevue's 179 rooms are not exactly showstoppers—the color scheme is done in 1970s oranges and browns, the bathrooms are basic. However, amenities such as use of a nearby health-and-racquet club, free transportation around Bellevue (within a 5-mile radius), complimentary room service (until midnight), a Jacuzzi, a sauna, a pool and exercise area, cable TV, and two restaurants make the Hilton a solid lodging bet. Working stiffs will appreciate the high-speed Internet access and desks in every room; computer, fax machine, and copy machine are also available. *$$$; AE, DC, DIS, MC, V; checks OK; self parking; www.hilton.com; map:HH3* &

Hyatt Regency at Bellevue Place / ★★

900 BELLEVUE WY NE, BELLEVUE; 425/462-1234 OR 800/233-1234

A platinum card's throw from Bellevue Square, this Hyatt is part of the splashy, sprawling retail-office-restaurant-hotel-health-club complex called Bellevue Place. The 382-room, 24-story hotel offers many extras:

pricier Regency Club rooms on the top three floors, some great views (particularly southside rooms above the seventh floor), two big ballrooms, several satellite conference rooms, use of the neighboring Bellevue Place Club (for $8), and a restaurant, Eques, serving Pacific Rim cuisine. *$$$–$$$$; AE, DC, DIS, JCB, MC, V; checks OK; valet and self parking; www.hyatt.com; map:HH3* &

Residence Inn by Marriott–Bellevue/Redmond / ★★☆

14455 NE 29TH PL, BELLEVUE; 425/882-1222 OR 800/331-3131
Well suited to business travelers yet also great for families, this may very well be the Eastside's best-kept lodging secret. The 120 condolike suites just off Highway 520 in east Bellevue have fireplaces and full kitchens (they'll even do your grocery shopping) with separate living rooms and bedrooms; a complimentary breakfast buffet is provided in the main building. The complex has an outdoor pool, three spas, a workout room, and a sports court; passes to a nearby health club are also provided. Other amenities include laundry facilities and a complimentary van shuttle within a 5-mile radius of the hotel. Pets okay. Travelers with smaller budgets might try the moderately priced basic hotel rooms next door at the Courtyard by Marriott (425/869-5300). *$$$; AE, DC, DIS, MC, V; checks OK; self parking; www.marriott.com; map:GG2* &

Shumway Mansion / ★★

11410 99TH PL NE, KIRKLAND; 425/823-2303
In addition to hosting retreats for the likes of Bill Gates and other Eastside tech-glitterati, this gracious 1909 estate has welcomed regular folks to its eight guest rooms since owners Richard and Salli Harris rescued the Shumway from the wrecking ball in 1985. The couple had the whole building moved to its current location. The guest rooms are furnished with antiques and stuffed animals (some might find the latter a bit cloying); public rooms overlook Juanita Bay and the lower parking lots. Common areas are decorated with period furnishings and frilly details, but also feature business-practical data ports. The ballroom downstairs, often used for weddings or meetings, opens onto a flowering patio in summer. A full breakfast buffet is served in the dining room on linen-covered tables. The beach as well as the nature trails at Juanita Bay Park are just blocks away. Children over 12 welcome; no pets. *$$; AE, MC, V; checks OK; self parking; info@shumwaymansion.com; www.shumway mansion.com; map:DD3* &

Willows Lodge / ★★★☆

14580 NE 145TH ST, WOODINVILLE; 425/424-3900 OR 877/424-3930
This spectacular destination boutique hotel opened in September 2000 to unbridled accolades. Even the *New York Times* devoted ample column inches to a glowing review. World-class wineries and voluptuous gardens

surround this 88-room luxury hotel. As the only upscale lodging in the area, its target market is twofold: nearby high-tech firms (including Microsoft, which wanted a Northwesty place to impress recruits) and romantics. The luxe lodge features a two-level lobby lined with 100-year-old reclaimed Douglas fir beams, a library, and an enormous stone-framed wood-burning fireplace. All rooms have fireplaces, king- or queen-size beds, stereo-DVD-CD systems, high-speed Internet connections, lush bathrooms (some with jetted tubs and heated towel racks), and balconies or patios with views of the gardens, Chateau Ste. Michelle Winery, Sammamish River (and its popular bike trail), or Mount Rainier (on a clear day). The poshest of the six suites ($750 per night) boasts a high-end Bang & Olufsen stereo, whirlpool bath, and flat-screen TV. Other lodge amenities include a spa, 24-hour fitness room, and evening wine tastings. The gazebo in the herb garden shelters wedding ceremonies and other momentous events. The Barking Frog restaurant (see review in the Restaurants chapter) serves Mediterranean-influenced dinners and weekend brunch. Guests also have access to nine-course meals at the renowned Herbfarm Restaurant (see review in the Restaurants chapter), which, along with its famed herb gardens, occupies its own site on the grounds. *$$$–$$$$; AE, DC, DIS, JCB, MC, V; checks OK; self parking; www.willowslodge.com; map:BB2* &

The Woodmark Hotel on Lake Washington / ★★★

1200 CARILLON POINT, KIRKLAND; 425/822-3700 OR 800/822-3700
Still the sole establishment that can boast lodgings on the shore of Lake Washington, the Woodmark has a singularity that extends beyond its location. Don't be deceived by the officelike exterior: this is one of the finest hotels in or out of Seattle. The Woodmark's 100 guest rooms, all with one king- or two queen-size beds (the best have lake views), swim in cream-color furnishings and plush extras such as minibars and refrigerators, terrycloth robes, and matchless service (from laundry to valet). Suites include the palatial Woodmark, with a lake and mountain view, dining space for six, lavish bathroom with Jacuzzi, 950 square feet of parlor space, entertainment center, and a wet bar. Smaller suites feature varying parlor sizes. All guests get a complimentary newspaper and a chance to "raid the pantry" for late-night snacks and beverages. Downstairs is a comfortable Library Bar with a grand piano and a well-tended fire. The hotel's restaurant, Waters, features Northwest cuisine; specialty shops (including a day spa) are nearby. *$$$–$$$$; AE, DC, JCB, MC, V; checks OK; valet and self parking; mail@thewoodmark.com;www.the woodmark.com; map:EE3* &

Airport Area

Doubletree Hotel Seattle Airport / ★★

18740 PACIFIC HWY S, SEATAC; 206/246-8600 OR 800/222-TREE

Guests at this enormous hotel enjoy the spoils of a well-calibrated operation and, in the east-facing rooms, a view of the Cascades. With 858 rooms and 12 suites, services here are primed to handle scores of conventioneers and business travelers. Diners can choose from two full restaurants, and two lounges provide weekend entertainment such as dancing, televised sports, and interactive video. On-site amenities include a workout room and pool. Additional services include around-the-clock airport shuttle and room service. Despite the hotel's gargantuan size, guests feel a little more at home when they're greeted with freshly baked chocolate chip cookies—a Doubletree tradition. Small pets okay. *$$; AE, DC, DIS, JCB, MC, V; checks OK; self parking; www.doubletreehotels. com; map:PP6* &

Hilton Seattle Airport Hotel / ★★★

17620 PACIFIC HWY S, SEATAC; 206/244-4800 OR 800/HILTONS

The recently completed $56 million redevelopment added about 200 rooms (for a total of 396, including seven suites), a fitness room, and a 39,000-square-foot, state-of-the-art conference center. A cool, expansive lobby leads to rooms set around two landscaped courtyards with a pool and indoor/outdoor Jacuzzi. Inside are the expected complement of desks, computer hookups, high-speed Internet access, irons and ironing boards, and coffeemakers. Meeting rooms and a 24-hour business center cater to worker bees. The hotel's restaurant, Spencer's for Steaks and Chops, serves all meals. Complimentary airport shuttle. *$$–$$$; AE, DC, DIS, JCB, MC, V; checks OK; self parking; www.hilton.com; map:OO5* &

Radisson Hotel Seattle Airport / ★★

17001 PACIFIC HWY S, SEATAC; 206/244-6000 OR 800/333-3333

On sunny summer days, the large outdoor pool at this spic-and-span 308-room airport hotel gets plenty of traffic from its littlest guests. Family-friendly accommodations are coupled with 12 meeting rooms and amenities such as in-room voice mail, data ports, hair dryers, cable TV, and coffeemakers. Rooms come with a king-size bed and sleeper sofa or two queen beds; suites are available, too. Although the gold-colored bedspreads have a plasticlike feel, the rooms are clean, and those in the newly opened wing on the hotel's south side sport a more updated decor. The restaurant serves typical hotel fare and local seafood, and the lounge is open until 11pm. Room service is available 6am to 11pm. Complimentary 24-hour airport shuttle. *$$$; AE, DC, DIS, JCB, MC, V; checks OK; self parking; www.radisson.com/seattlewa; map:OO5* &

Seattle Marriott at Sea-Tac / ★★

3201 S 176TH ST, SEATAC; 206/241-2000 OR 800/228-9290

It's no surprise that this hotel one block from the airport attracts travelers who want to get in and out of town with a minimum of stress. The swift service at this 457-room megamotel makes transfer to and from Sea-Tac Airport virtually painless. Convenience doesn't come at the expense of enjoyment, though. The lobby, with its warm Northwest motif, opens into an enormous atrium complete with indoor pool and two Jacuzzis. For slightly higher rates than the standard rooms, five more spacious, handsomely appointed suites are available, and rooms on the concierge floor include turndown service, hair dryers, irons and ironing boards, and a lounge that serves continental breakfasts and nightly nibbles. All guests have access to a sauna and well-equipped exercise room. A casual dining room offers the usual hotel fare. Pets okay. *$$$; AE, DC, DIS, JCB, MC, V; checks OK; self parking; www. marriott.com; map:PP6* &

WestCoast Sea-Tac Hotel / ★

18220 INTERNATIONAL BLVD, SEATAC; 206/246-5535 OR 800/325-4000

A no-nonsense hotel with easy airport access. Meeting facilities at this WestCoast outpost can handle up to 200 people; an outdoor pool, Jacuzzi, exercise room, and sauna are open to everyone who stays in the bright rooms here. Thirty-two limited-edition suites step up the amenities with terrycloth robes, morning newspapers, and mini-refrigerators. All 146 rooms contain hair dryers and coffeemakers. Pets okay. Free valet parking and a 24-hour airport shuttle. A slightly downscale West-Coast Gateway hotel (18415 International Blvd, SeaTac; 206/248-8200) across the street caters handily to the business traveler. *$$; AE, DC, DIS, MC, V; checks OK; valet parking; www.westcoasthotels. com/seatac; map:PP6* &

EXPLORING

EXPLORING

Top 25 Attractions

1) PIKE PLACE MARKET

Pike St to Virginia St, between 1st and Western Aves, centered on Pike Pl, Downtown; 206/682-7453 If cities have souls, then certainly Pike Place Market is Seattle's. Opened as an experiment on August 17, 1907, in response to the demands of housewives who were angry at having to pay exorbitant food prices padded by middlemen, this oldest continuously operating farmers market in the United States remains a boisterous bazaar, aggressively eschewing chain stores or franchise operations (except, of course, for Starbucks, which opened its first store in 1971—at the market).

The way to "do" the market is to spend an unstructured day meandering its crannies, nibbling from its astonishing variety of ethnic and regional foods, browsing the shops, and watching the street-corner musicians, puppeteers, and mimes. (If you visit before 9am, you can observe the place come alive as the farmers set up.)

The official entrance is at the corner of First Avenue and Pike Street, at the **INFORMATION BOOTH** (206/682-7453), where you can pick up a map and some advice on sights, or just a self-guided-tour pamphlet. (The booth doubles as a day-of-show, half-price ticket outlet, called Ticket/Ticket, Tues–Sun, noon–6pm.) **READ ALL ABOUT IT** (206/624-0140), the market's extensive newsstand and official gossip station, anchors this busy corner. So does the **DELAURENTI SPECIALTY FOOD MARKET** (206/622-0141), a beloved Italian deli—packed with eye-opening arrays of olive oils, cheeses, imported meats, and wines—that in 2001 passed out of the hands of its founding family into those of three Pagliacci Pizza co-owners. Just to the south is the **SOUTH ARCADE**, home to modern-looking shops and condos that have spread forth from the 7-acre Market Historic District (created by voters in 1971).

Walking west from here, down the covered corridor, you'll come to the elbow of the L-shaped market, home to the big bronze piggy bank named **RACHEL** and weekend crowds that delight in the salmon-throwing antics of salespeople at **PIKE PLACE FISH** (206/682-7181). This is the start of the **MAIN ARCADE**—the famous neon Pike Place Market sign and clock are just above you—where produce vendors called "highstallers" display beautifully arranged (don't touch!) international produce and lowstallers sell seasonal, regional produce. In the midst of this is a market institution: the **ATHENIAN INN** (206/624-7166), a smoky, working-class cafe that's been the favorite haunt of market old-timers ever since 1909 (and was one of the settings for 1993's *Sleepless in Seattle*).

TOP 25 ATTRACTIONS

1) Pike Place Market
2) Pioneer Square
3) Hiram M. Chittenden Locks
4) Space Needle & Seattle Center
5) Experience Music Project
6) Seattle Asian Art Museum
7) Smith Tower
8) Museum of Flight
9) Seattle Art Museum
10) Odyssey, the Maritime Discovery Center
11) Waterfront
12) Westlake Center & Monorail
13) Woodland Park Zoo

14) Klondike Gold Rush National Historical Park
15) Elliott Bay Book Company
16) Burke Museum of Natural History and Culture
17) Volunteer Park
18) Pacific Science Center
19) Fisherman's Terminal
20) Seattle Aquarium
21) Nordstrom & REI
22) Boeing Plant Tour
23) Washington Park Arboretum
24) Spirit of Washington Dinner Train
25) Green Lake Park

Engraved floor tiles throughout the market were part of a 1986 fund-raising project, which promised folks a wee bit of immortality for only $35. The Main Arcade also has two labyrinthine levels below the street, where you can find **GOLDEN AGE COLLECTABLES** (206/622-9799), featuring a wonderful trove of new and vintage comic books and the **MARKET MAGIC SHOP** (206/624-4271), where you might catch owners Darryl Beckman and Sheila Lyon demonstrating their dexterity with legerdemain. An outdoor staircase on the Main Arcade's west side leads to the **HILLCLIMB CORRIDOR**, a steep cascade of steps that connects the market (at Western Avenue) with the waterfront below.

In summer, the artists' and craftspeople's tables stretch along the Main and North Arcades all the way from Pike Place to Virginia Street and **VICTOR STEINBRUECK PARK** (see Parks and Beaches in this chapter), a splash of green that marks the market's northern border. Across Pike Place from the Main and North Arcades, you'll discover shops and ethnic eateries—including the original **STARBUCKS**—leading to a shady courtyard in the back, where covered tables are set out for **EMMETT WATSON'S OYSTER BAR** (206/448-7721), a folksy seafood joint named in honor of the late, lamented Seattle newspaper columnist and raconteur.

If you take a short detour here, up the wooden stairs to **POST ALLEY**, you'll find **THE PINK DOOR** (206/443-3241; see review in the Restaurants chapter), a funky trattoria with terrific summertime porch seating, and **KELLS** (206/728-1916), a lively, rough-hewn Irish pub and restaurant. Follow Post Alley south, back toward Pike Place; you'll pass the stylish, 65-room **INN AT THE MARKET** (206/443-3600; see review in the Lodgings chapter), Pike Place Market's only sizable hotel. In the next block you'll go by the see-and-be-seen sipping bar at **SEATTLE'S BEST COFFEE** (206/467-7700) and the entrance to a wide variety of shops and eating places—including a fine regional gift seller, **MADE IN WASHINGTON** (206/467-0788)—in the **POST ALLEY MARKET BUILDING**.

Back on Pike Place heading south, across the street from the high-stallers you'll encounter **TOTEM SMOKEHOUSE** (206/443-1710), where you can pick up smoked salmon (or arrange to have it shipped). Stop by **MEE SUM PASTRIES** (206/682-6780) for savory Chinese pot-stickers, or score balcony seating and a dish of flavorful paella at the **COPACABANA CAFE** (206/622-6359), the city's only Bolivian restaurant. **SEATTLE GARDEN CENTER** (206/448-0431) stocks many difficult-to-find bulbs and seeds. **SUR LA TABLE** (206/448-2244) is a nationally acclaimed cook's emporium.

Inside the **SANITARY MARKET** (so named because horses were not allowed inside) is a chaotic jumble of produce stands and eating places, including the **PIKE PLACE MARKET CREAMERY** (206/622-5029), which

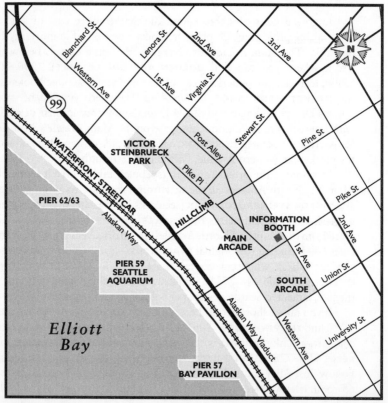

PIKE PLACE MARKET

sells delicious dairy goods; **JACK'S FISH SPOT** (206/467-0514), purveyor of steaming cups of cioppino from an outdoor bar; and **THREE GIRLS BAKERY** (206/622-1045), an excellent sandwich counter that's easily identified by its long line of regulars. Just to the south is the last building in this historic stretch: the picturesque **CORNER MARKET** houses produce and flower stalls. A couple of restaurants are hidden in its upper reaches: the tiny **MATT'S IN THE MARKET** (206/467-7909), a cozy perch from which to enjoy an oyster po'boy; and **CHEZ SHEA** (206/467-9990), perhaps the most romantic nook in town, with an adjoining bistro/bar called **SHEA'S LOUNGE** (see reviews of all three in the Restaurants chapter). Post Alley continues on the south side of Pike Street, as it dips down below street level and passes the dimly lit Italian restaurant **IL BISTRO** (206/682-3049; see review in the Restaurants chapter) and the **MARKET THEATER** (206/781-9273), home to an improvisational comedy–theater troupe.

It's almost impossible to get a parking space on congested Pike Place, so either come here by bus or splurge for a space in the spiffy 550-slot parking garage on Western Avenue, with its elevator that opens directly into the market (some merchants help defray the cost by giving out parking stamps, free with purchase, so be sure to ask). Alternatively, try one of the lots a little farther south on Western or along First Avenue to the north. *Every day; information@pikeplacemarket.org; www.pikeplace market.org; map:J8–I8*

2) PIONEER SQUARE

S King St to Yesler Wy along 1st and 2nd Aves, Downtown Like the Energizer bunny, this historic neighborhood located just south of the modern business district just keeps going and going. Originally the site of a Native American village, it was settled by white pioneers in 1852, but the Great Fire of 1889 reduced the city's original downtown to cinders. Although rebuilt according to more architecturally coherent—and less flammable—standards, by the 1960s Pioneer Square had become so run-down that conservative city officials proposed leveling it. Fortunately, wiser heads fought to save Pioneer Square and turn it into Seattle's first historic district. Accidents and disasters continue to threaten the neighborhood, however; in 2001 a semi-truck accident collapsed the square's graceful **PERGOLA**, followed by the Mardi Gras riots and the Ash Wednesday earthquake, which brought building bricks crashing down into the streets.

Encompassing almost 90 acres, Pioneer Square is one of the most extensive "old towns" in the nation. It's a busy place filled with bookstores, art galleries, restaurants, antique shops, and nightclubs. Lawyers, architects, and media folk dominate the workforce. Panhandlers and homeless transients are also drawn here by a preponderance of services (and park benches).

Seattle's earliest intersection, at First Avenue and Yesler Way, is home to triangular **PIONEER PLACE PARK**. While its 1909 iron-and-glass pergola (a holdover from the days of trolley cars) is off being repaired, the park's most prominent fixture is its totem pole—a replica of a Tlingit Indian work stolen by Seattle burghers during an 1899 visit to Alaska. Facing the park is the **PIONEER BUILDING**, designed by Elmer Fisher, a prolific Scotsman who established the architectural vernacular of post–Great Fire Seattle, synthesizing his Victorian philosophies about facades with the weighty Romanesque Revival look. The building houses a maze of antique shops on its lower level, and the headquarters of **BILL SPEIDEL'S UNDERGROUND TOUR**, an interesting subterranean prowl through the original streets of downtown (see Walking Tours under Organized Tours in this chapter).

In the mid-19th century, greased logs and trees cut in the Seattle hills were dragged down diagonal **YESLER WAY** to feed pioneer Henry Yesler's waterfront sawmill. The avenue quickly became familiar as "skid road" (often mangled into "skid *row*"), an early-20th-century insult used to describe inner-city neighborhoods that—like Pioneer Square—had fallen on hard times. Just across Yesler from Pioneer Place is **MERCHANTS CAFE** (109 Yesler Wy; 206/624-1515), Seattle's oldest restaurant. To the west, you'll find a tasty breakfast or late-night dinner at **TRATTORIA MITCHELLI** (84 Yesler Wy; 206/623-3883). **AL BOCCALINO** (1 Yesler Wy; 206/622-7688; see review in the Restaurants chapter) is a wonderful nook for a romantic (and pricier) Italian meal.

First Avenue is the main, tree-lined artery through the historic district, intersected by streets that terminate at the waterfront a block west (best chance for parking in this area is under the Alaskan Way Viaduct; bring quarters for the meters). Heading south you'll see the **NEW ORLEANS RESTAURANT** (114 1st Ave S; 206/622-2563), a Creole/Cajun eatery known for its Dixieland and R&B acts as well as its mint juleps, and **NORTHWEST FINE WOODWORKING** (1st Ave S and S Jackson St; 206/625-0542), with its continually changing exhibits of exquisite hand-crafted furniture and sculptures. On the same block is the **GRAND CENTRAL ARCADE**. Opened in 1879 by entrepreneur (and later Washington governor) Watson C. Squire, the structure housed Seattle's first real theater. It now contains two levels of upscale retail, including the excellent **GRAND CENTRAL BAKING COMPANY** (214 1st Ave S; 206/622-3644).

Immediately across from the Grand Central on S Main Street is the unusual **KLONDIKE GOLD RUSH NATIONAL HISTORICAL PARK** (see listing below), and at First Avenue S and S Main Street is the renowned **ELLIOTT BAY BOOK COMPANY** (see listing below). **GRAND CENTRAL MERCANTILE** (316 1st Ave S; 206/623-8894), a quality kitchen emporium, and the whimsical **WOOD SHOP** (320 1st Ave S; 206/624-1763), an imaginative toy shop with great stuffed animals, are a couple of other worthy stops along this stretch.

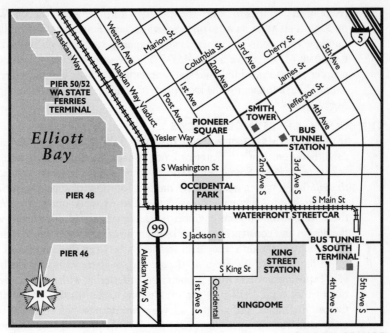

PIONEER SQUARE

OCCIDENTAL AVENUE S, a sun-dappled, brick-lined pedestrian walkway between First and Second Avenues S, is studded with galleries. On the **FIRST THURSDAY GALLERY WALKS** of every month, all of Pioneer Square fills up with art appreciators (see "Art Appeal" sidebar). Occidental Avenue S segues into **OCCIDENTAL PARK,** a Northwest attempt at a Parisian park setting with cobblestones, trees, and totem poles. The international feeling is enhanced by the occasional horse-drawn buggy or rickshaw-like pedicab. A more novel park, the **WATERFALL GARDEN,** is tucked into a corner at Second Avenue S and S Main St (see Parks and Beaches in this chapter).

South King Street is Pioneer Square's southern boundary. Look farther south and you can't miss **SAFECO FIELD** (1250 1st Ave S; 206/346-4287), the retractable-roofed home of the Seattle Mariners baseball club, as well as a new football stadium (Occidental Wy S and S King St), being built next door primarily for billionaire Paul Allen's Seattle Seahawks on the site of the old Kingdome, which was demolished in 2000. **F. X. MCRORY'S STEAK, CHOP AND OYSTER HOUSE** (419 Occidental Ave S; 206/623-4800) is the restaurant and watering hole of choice for game-goers. Just north of the stadiums is **KING STREET STATION** (2nd Ave S and S Main St; 206/382-4125). With its striking clock tower, the station opened for business in 1906 and still receives Amtrak trains. A pricey restoration promises to return the station to it former glory in 2003. West on King is **MERRILL PLACE**, once Schwabacher's Hardware, a revitalized building that conceals an enclave of apartments, and **IL TERRAZZO CARMINE** (411 1st Ave S; 206/467-7797; see review in the Restaurants chapter), an esteemed Italian restaurant with a romantic bar and a terrace overlooking a fountain—the ideal place to wind up a Pioneer Square tour. *Map:O9–M8*

3) HIRAM M. CHITTENDEN LOCKS

3015 NW 54th St, Ballard; 206/783-7059 Talk of digging a navigable canal between the fresh water of Lakes Washington and Union and the salt water of Puget Sound began shortly after Seattle's pioneers arrived in the 1850s. However, debates over the best location for such a waterway and searches for financing delayed the start of work until 1911. And there were still numerous engineering challenges ahead: the biggest was the design and construction of locks near the canal's western end, which could control the difference in water levels between the Sound and the much higher Lake Washington. (In the end, the latter was lowered by 9 feet, exposing new lakefront property and interfering with salmon migrations.) Not until 1917 was the 8-mile-long **LAKE WASHINGTON SHIP CANAL** dedicated, and another 17 years would pass before it was officially declared complete. In 1936, the U.S. Army Corps of Engineers named the locks in honor of Major Hiram M. Chittenden, who had supervised the canal project.

Today more than 100,000 pleasure and commercial boats per year go through the canal and what are colloquially known as the "Ballard Locks." Couples and families trot down to watch this informal regatta as it works its way through the "water elevator." The descent (or ascent) takes 10 to 25 minutes, depending on which of the two locks is being used. Particularly good people-watching is available during Seafair in July, when boats filled with carousing men and women crowd the locks, impatient to get through.

Across the waterway, in **COMMODORE PARK**, the **FISH LADDER** that bypasses the locks entices struggling salmon bound for spawning grounds in Lake Washington and Cascade mountain streams. You can watch the fishes' progress from a viewing area with windows onto the ladder: salmon in summer (peak viewing for sockeye is in early July) and steelhead in winter.

Call the **VISITORS CENTER** for times of tours (daily in summer, weekends only the rest of the year); there's also an interesting exhibit that explains the use and building of the locks. The green lawns and tree-lined waterside promenade of the park, along with the impressive rose display at the **CARL S. ENGLISH JR. BOTANICAL GARDENS** (see Gardens in this chapter), make grand backdrops for summer picnics. *Free; every day; map:FF9*

4) SPACE NEEDLE AND SEATTLE CENTER

Denny Wy to Mercer St, 1st Ave N to 5th Ave N, Queen Anne; 206/684-8582 More than 10 million visitors walk through Seattle Center every year. This 74-acre park north of downtown, at the base of Queen Anne Hill on the edge of the Denny Regrade, is the prized legacy of the 1962 Century 21 Exposition—Seattle's second world's fair (after the 1909 Alaska-Yukon-Pacific Exposition). The center is the arts and entertainment hub of this city—its biggest new draw being the Frank Gehry–designed **EXPERIENCE MUSIC PROJECT** museum (see listing below)—playing host to such popular annual events as the Northwest Folklife Festival (Memorial Day weekend), the Bite of Seattle (mid-July), and Bumbershoot (Labor Day weekend).

Legend has it that the city's most recognized symbol, the 605-foot **SPACE NEEDLE** (206/905-2100), originally called the "Space Cage," began as a doodle sketched on a cocktail napkin by world's fair chairman Eddie Carlson. Architects John Graham Sr., Victor Steinbrueck, and John Ridley translated that into what at the time was considered a futuristic concept in metal and glass. When King County commissioners refused to fund the project, a private corporation stepped in and completed the work in an astonishing eight months, at a cost of $4.5 million. (The Needle is still privately owned.) Anchored to terra firma by almost 6,000 tons of concrete, the tower was built to withstand winds of up to 200 miles per hour and has already survived two major earthquakes (in 1965 and 2001) unscathed. The 43-second ride up provides panoramic views on clear days for only $11 ($9 seniors, $5 kids 5–12, free for younger children). *Every day; marketing@spaceneedle.com; www.spaceneedle. com; map:B6* &

SKYCITY AT THE NEEDLE (206/443-2150), formerly the Space Needle Restaurant, is located at the 500-foot level and revolves 360 degrees every hour (thanks to two gearboxes equipped with one-horsepower motors), giving diners and slow sippers in the bar panoramic views of Puget Sound, the Olympic Mountains, and the city center. Restaurant patrons ride the elevator free of charge.

Seattle Center's visitors who arrive with children head for the dinosaurs and dynamos at the **PACIFIC SCIENCE CENTER** (see listing below). Chances are, they'll also visit the **FUN FOREST** (206/728-1585), a small-scale amusement park near the Space Needle that contains a Ferris wheel, a wild river ride, a roller coaster, and an indoor pavilion offering laser tag and video games. Ride tickets—purchased individually or in discounted packs—are available at booths within the Fun Forest. Just past the Fun Forest is **MEMORIAL STADIUM**, where high school football games and outdoor concerts are frequently held.

For surprisingly sophisticated youth entertainment, there's the **SEATTLE CHILDREN'S THEATRE**, with two stages—the 485-seat Charlotte Martin Theatre and the smaller Eve Alvord Theatre. Adults enjoy the performing arts at a string of other stages arranged along Mercer Street at the center's northern edge. The neon-adorned **BAGLEY WRIGHT THEATRE** is home to the Seattle Repertory Theatre (206/443-2210 for free tour of the theater, Sept–May). The Rep's old digs, the **INTIMAN PLAYHOUSE,** currently houses the Intiman Theatre. Normally at home in the **OPERA HOUSE,** the **SEATTLE OPERA** and **PACIFIC NORTHWEST BALLET** will perform in the nearby **MERCER ARTS ARENA** until a multi-million-dollar renovation of the Opera House is completed in 2003. (For more on all of these, see the Performing Arts chapter.)

If you'd just rather hang out—even get wet—on a sunny summer day, head to the **INTERNATIONAL FOUNTAIN,** a huge landmark near the center of Seattle Center's grounds, where enormous jets of water shoot from a metal dome into the sky, sometimes synchronized with music and lights. Just to the north is the **NORTHWEST CRAFT CENTER** (206/728-1555), displaying a variety of pottery, crafts, paintings, and jewelry for sale. Beyond them are the Northwest Rooms, where traveling exhibitions such as Bumbershoot's Bookfair are shown; to the east is the exhibition hall for larger shows; to the south is the **FLAG PAVILION,** with flags commemorating all 50 states. Should you grow hungry, stop in at the nearby **CENTER HOUSE** (206/684-8582), a cavernous structure filled with ethnic fast food, conventioneers, pre-adolescents looking to be seen, and senior citizens. On the lower level of the Center House is the world-class **CHILDREN'S MUSEUM** (see Museums in this chapter).

There is no admission charge to get onto the Seattle Center grounds (except during a few major festivals such as Bumbershoot), but parking can be a problem. The cheapest lots are on the east side. For events at the Opera House, Mercer Arts Arena, and Intiman Playhouse, the covered parking garage directly north across Mercer Street from the Opera House affords easy access, but the egress can be maddeningly slow on busy nights. One way to avoid the problem is to take the **MONORAIL** from downtown—a 90-second ride (see listing below) that drops you off at the Center House. (The Monorail stops running at 11pm, however, so you may have to hail a cab back downtown after a late show.) *Every day; www.seattlecenter.com; map:B6* &

5) EXPERIENCE MUSIC PROJECT

325 5th Ave N, Seattle Center; 206/367-5483 A great, polychromatic metal wave of a building, designed by Southern California architect Frank Gehry, the Experience Music Project (EMP) started out as a modest museum conceived by Microsoft co-founder Paul Allen and devoted to one of his boyhood idols, Seattle-born rock guitarist Jimi Hendrix. But difficulties in securing permission from Hendrix's family to use the musician's name and music helped persuade Allen to expand his vision as well as his museum, which ended up containing 140,000 square feet and costing some $240 million to construct. Like Cleveland's Rock and Roll Hall of Fame, EMP is unstinting in its celebration of modern music—mostly rock, but also blues, funk, and the culture that surrounds them all. Memorabilia scattered about the place includes Elvis Presley's motorcycle jacket, Janis Joplin's bell-bottoms, and guitars once played by Hendrix and Kurt Cobain.

Visitors tour at their own pace, clutching compact, shoulder-slung digital devices that allow them to access snippets of display interpretation and musical clips. While the glitziest draw here may be **ARTIST'S JOURNEY**, a roller coaster–like experience that immerses you in the realm of rock 'n' roll, other don't-miss attractions include the **GUITAR GALLERY**, featuring versions of the instrument that date back as far as 1770; the **HENDRIX GALLERY**, which recounts that cult guitarist's rise from his days playing teen dances in Seattle to holding forth at the original Woodstock; **ON STAGE**, where—with the help of screaming-crowd effects—you can satisfy your childhood dream to be a rock star; and **SKY CHURCH**, with its giant light-emitting diode (LED) screen on which concert videos are shown at the top of every hour. EMP also hosts rotating exhibits (such as a recent one on the man who made hips hip, Elvis Presley) and concerts by big-name musicians, from Dave Matthews to Emmylou Harris. Admission is $19.95 for adults, $15.95 for seniors and students, and $14.95 for children 7–10. *Every day; www.emplive; map: D6* ♿

6) SEATTLE ASIAN ART MUSEUM

1400 E Prospect St, Capitol Hill; 206/654-3100 Volunteer Park's Seattle Asian Art Museum is exquisite. With the opening of the downtown Seattle Art Museum in 1991, this original building (designed in Moderne style by local architect Carl F. Gould) was renovated to house the museum's extensive Asian art collections. Built in 1931 by Richard Fuller and his mother, Margaret E. MacTavish Fuller, the museum contained their 1,700-piece collection of Asian art before growing into a more eclectic institution. Now the carefully lit galleries once again hold the kind of art (the Hindu deities Siva and Parvati rapt in divine love) that draws you away from daily obsessions and expands the soul. In addition to old favorites from the collection—such as the Fullers' array of elaborate *netsuke*—don't miss the ancient Chinese funerary art and the collection of 14th- to 16th-century ceramics from Thailand. An Educational Outreach Gallery offers hands-on displays. Admission for adults is $3; free for children 12 and under; free to all the first Thursday and Saturday of each month. (Admission tickets also may be used for entry to SAM downtown—see listing below—within a week of purchase.) *Tues–Sun; www.seattleartmuseum.org; map:GG6* ♿

7) SMITH TOWER

506 2nd Ave, Downtown; 206/682-9393 Against the picket fence of sky-scrapers that currently make up Seattle's skyline, the Smith Tower looks almost puny. Yet when it was first opened in the summer of 1914, this 42-story (522-foot) terra-cotta-and-steel spire was the tallest building west of the Mississippi. It remained the highest in Seattle until 1969, when the old Seattle–First National Bank Tower (now the 1001 Fourth Avenue Building) rose to 50 stories, or 609 feet. (The 605-foot Space Needle, finished in 1962, is also taller than the Smith Tower but doesn't usually count in the record books since it isn't a "building" per se.) Even now, though, the Smith Tower is considered the most beloved of this city's cloud-kissing edifices.

It's the legacy of New Yorker Lyman C. Smith, an armaments man-ufacturer turned typewriter magnate, who commissioned the Syracuse, New York, architectural firm of Gaggin & Gaggin to design an office structure both distinctive and tall enough that it wouldn't be exceeded in Seattle during his lifetime. He got what he'd ordered, if not what he'd intended; Smith died in November 1910, before his skyscraper was finished.

Despite a recent multimillion-dollar renovation (which included upgrades that made this structure an address of choice for high-tech firms), the Smith Tower retains what are reportedly the West Coast's only manually operated elevators—eight brass-caged beauties. Its 35th-floor **CHINESE ROOM,** an elaborate space that's popular for weddings, is sur-rounded by an observation deck from which visitors can take in magnif-icent views of downtown for a couple of bucks (on weekends only, 11am–4pm). *Every day; map:O7* &

8) MUSEUM OF FLIGHT

9404 E Marginal Wy S, Georgetown; 206/764-5720 You don't have to be an aviation buff to enjoy the spectacle of 20 full-size airplanes—including a 40,000-pound B-17—suspended from the ceiling of a stun-ning six-story glass-and-steel gallery. Although it's often referred to informally as "the Boeing Museum of Flight," this institution, located 10 miles south of Seattle, has no formal affiliation with the aircraft manu-facturer, apart from its location at Boeing Field and its origination in the **RED BARN,** which was Boeing's humble first Seattle home in 1910 and now sits adjacent to the main museum structure.

The museum takes you from the early legends of flying (including a replica of the Wright brothers' original glider) through the history of avi-ation, from pioneering stages to the present, with special emphasis on Pacific Northwest flight—military, commercial, and amateur. Highlights include a 707 version of Air Force One; Apollo and Mercury space cap-sules; and the 98-foot Lockheed A-12 Blackbird, the fastest plane ever built (it has flown coast to coast in 67 minutes). The museum offers a variety of workshops, films, tours, and special programs. Children especially enjoy the hangar with three explorable planes, and hands-on learning areas with paper airplanes, boomerangs, and other toys that fly. Admission for adults is $9.50, for youths it's $5; free on the first Thursday evening of each month, 5–9pm. *Every day; www.museumof flight.org; map:NN6* &

9) SEATTLE ART MUSEUM

100 University St, Downtown; 206/654-3100 Containing 145,000 square feet of space (though only a third of it is actually gallery space), the Robert Venturi–designed Seattle Art Museum has a worldwide focus, with particular emphasis on Asian, African, and Northwest Coast Native American art. Each gallery is especially tailored to complement the collections—for example, dark, dramatically lit rooms for the ceremonial works of Africa and the Northwest Coast; tall ceilings with ornate moldings for European decorative arts; and white loftlike spaces for New York School paintings. The **JAPANESE GALLERY** features an authentic bamboo-and-cedar teahouse, where a Japanese master performs the tea ceremony for small groups of visitors two or three times a month (reservations required). A big **SPECIAL EXHIBITIONS GALLERY** houses periodic traveling shows, an occasional in-house exhibit, and events geared to mass audiences, such as the 2000 show of works by painter John Singer Sargent.

A lecture room and a 300-seat auditorium lend themselves to talks, films, music, and dramatic performances; there's a fully equipped art studio for children's and adult classes; and a good cafe faces the immense hallway connecting the First and Second Avenue lobbies. The **MUSEUM STORE** is excellent. And you can't miss sculptor Jonathan Borofsky's 48-foot mechanical **HAMMERING MAN** at SAM's First Avenue entrance. On Thursday evenings SAM stays open late, with refreshments, live music, and performances scheduled each week. General admission is a suggested $7 donation for adults, $5 donation for students, free for children 12 and under; free to all on the first Thursday of each month. (Admission tickets also may be used for entry to the Seattle Asian Art Museum in Volunteer Park—see listing above—within a week of purchase.) *Tues–Sun; www. seattleartmuseum.org; map:K7* &

10) ODYSSEY, THE MARITIME DISCOVERY CENTER

2205 Alaskan Wy/Pier 66, Waterfront; 206/374-4000 Seven piers north of the Seattle Aquarium sits a complementary museum that shifts the focus from water life to shore life. Odyssey is an interactive museum celebrating the natural and commercial uses of Seattle's marine environment, with exhibits that allow visitors to experience simulated kayaking, fishing, and freighter navigation. Geared toward children but entertaining for adults too, the educational center emphasizes technology, human interactions with the maritime environment, and an overall "you-are-there" exhibit feel. Enter a full-size crane cab and race against a clock to load containers onto a virtual ship. Use the power of your legs to spin a propeller that's 10 feet in diameter, bringing home the fact that it takes a lot of power to move ships. Learn just how significantly ocean trade routes have expanded over the last 3,000 years. In a city still known for its 1999 anti–World Trade Organization (WTO) riots, this center's promotion of international trade may seem anachronistic, but don't mention that to the kids who are dreaming of working heavy machinery on the water. Admission is $6.75 for adults, $4.50 for students 5–8, children under 4 are free. *Every day (mid-May–mid-Sept), Tues–Sat (mid-Sept–mid-May); education@ody.org; www.ody.org; map:G9* &

11) WATERFRONT

S Main St to Denny Wy along Alaskan Wy, Downtown Since the 1950s, Seattle's waterfront has been separated from the rest of the city by the controversial Alaskan Way Viaduct (Highway 99) running high overhead—some love it, some think it's ugly, some think it's unsound. However, construction of the **BELL HARBOR INTERNATIONAL CONFERENCE CENTER,** a maritime museum, and a $27 million **WORLD TRADE CENTER** and hotel around Pier 66 were all calculated to draw more visitors and maybe even locals to this still-working, but decidedly touristy, harbor.

The best way to explore Seattle's waterfront is to walk in one direction and then hop aboard the **WATERFRONT STREETCAR** (206/553-3000) for the return trip. These vintage wood-trimmed trolleys, imported from Australia, make nonnarrated, 20-minute trips from Pier 70 south along Alaskan Way, then through Pioneer Square to the Chinatown/International District. Streetcars operate daily, with extended hours in summer. The fare is $1 ($1.25 during rush hours); kids' fare is 75¢ and senior/disabled fare is 25¢.

The nonindustrial waterfront is anchored at **PIER 48** (foot of S Main St) and the pergola of the **WASHINGTON STREET PUBLIC BOAT LANDING.** The waterfront side of the pier has an excellent interpretive display of this harbor's history, and periscopes offer grand seaward views.

North on Alaskan Way is the city's main ferry terminal, **COLMAN DOCK** (foot of Marion St at Pier 52), where boats depart for Bremerton, Bainbridge Island, and (for foot passengers only) Vashon Island and West Seattle (see the Lay of the City chapter).

At Pier 54 are a couple of Seattle's most endearing landmarks. **YE OLDE CURIOSITY SHOP** (206/682-5844), established in 1899, is a mecca for trinket junkies and anyone who wants to commemorate his or her Seattle visit with a keepsake rubber slug, or maybe a shrunken head. **IVAR'S ACRES OF CLAMS** (206/624-6852), with its breezy outdoor fish bar (attracting more than a few hungry seagulls), was the first in a local chain of seafood eateries created by notorious Seattle booster and ace fish hustler Ivar Haglund.

WATERFRONT PARK, at Pier 57, offers boardwalks and elevated levels to give visitors a fine perspective on both Elliott Bay and the Seattle cityscape. Adjacent to the park is a plaque that recalls the Klondike gold rush's beginning here in 1897, when the steamer *Portland* arrived at the former Pier 58 with the first news that gold had been discovered in northwestern Canada.

Past Pier 59 and the **SEATTLE AQUARIUM** (see listing below) is **PIER 66/BELL STREET PIER,** which includes the International Conference Center, a marina (with short-term public moorage available), several restaurants that take advantage of splendid views out over the Sound, and **ODYSSEY, THE MARITIME DISCOVERY CENTER** (see listing above). The Port of Seattle, once headquartered at Pier 66, has moved to Pier 69, where it has joined the **VICTORIA CLIPPER** (see the Day Trips chapter) in a huge white whale of a building. Next door is **PIER 70,** a picturesque, barnlike structure that contains, among other things, the aptly named **WATERFRONT** (206/956-9171; see review in the Restaurants chapter), a high-end seafood restaurant with exceptional Elliott Bay views.

Finally comes **MYRTLE EDWARDS PARK** (see Parks and Beaches in this chapter), which winds north to more working piers (you'll often see container ships and auto carriers docked back here) and a huge grain elevator that has become a waterfront landmark. Keep walking north through Elliott Bay Park and you'll come to a public fishing pier. Farther north, this path leads to **ELLIOTT BAY MARINA** and the glitzy **PALISADE** restaurant (2601 W Marina Pl; 206/285-1000; see review in the Restaurants chapter), although this last is more conveniently reached by car from Magnolia. *Map:O9–A9*

12) WESTLAKE CENTER AND MONORAIL

400 Pine St, Downtown; 206/441-6038 Monorail, 206/287-0762 or 206/467-1600 Westlake Center Few places speak more clearly of Seattle's commercial complexity or the determination of its leaders to preserve the energy of downtown than does the glass-and-steel **WESTLAKE CENTER.** Developed by the Rouse Company, a Maryland-based designer of "festival marketplaces" (including Boston's revitalized Faneuil Hall), this shopping mall spikes up from what used to be a major streetcar hub. Since the 1950s, the property had been a battleground where architects (who wanted to create a commodious urban commons on the site) faced off against merchants (who wanted to retain the land for retail). In the late '80s an uneasy compromise was finally struck, giving over most of the site to a retail arcade and office building but establishing a triangular portion on the south end as Westlake Park.

Across Pine Street (once closed to traffic, but reopened in 1997 by public vote), **WESTLAKE PARK** hosts Seattle artist Robert Maki's *Westlake Star Axis/Seven Hills*, which includes a pink granite column, a granite-framed waterfall, and a granite arch from which public speeches are sometimes made. Red, gray, and white granite paving blocks (arranged in a weaving pattern familiar from Salish Indian baskets) tie this open space across Pine Street to the mall. Though low on landscaping, the park is high on citizen occupation. Warm afternoons attract a diverse mix of businesspeople on lunch breaks, street musicians, teenagers milling around trying to define "cool," and stentorian preachers telling the world exactly where it's gone wrong.

Three of the mall's four retail levels are occupied by upscale chain stores as well as some local/regional enterprises. The top floor is dominated by fast-fooderies, serving everything from pizza to Thai food to hot dogs on a stick.

The top floor of Westlake Center is also the location of one of two stations for the **MONORAIL**. Way back in 1910, a local inventor named W. H. Shephard suggested that the city construct an elevated monorail network to reduce traffic on its streets, but not until Seattle hosted the 1962 world's fair was a monorail erected here. Although it cost $3.5 million at the time, it was basically just a space-age gimmick (built by Sweden's Alweg Rapid Transit Systems) that shuttled tourists between downtown and the fairgrounds at what's now Seattle Center. Yet it was so popular that even after the fair closed down, the city continued to operate the Monorail, and—suggesting that Shephard was right all along—there has been serious talk recently of expanding the Monorail as part of an extensive mass-transit system for the city. The elevated trains presently carry about 40,000 riders each year, making this one of the world's few profitable rapid-transit operations. The Monorail travels 1.3 miles (a 90-second ride) between Westlake Center and Seattle Center. Tourists are the principal users—except during Bumbershoot and the Folklife Festival (both guaranteed to fill parking lots around Seattle Center), when many city residents prefer to park downtown and hop the Monorail to the festivities. Trains depart Westlake and Seattle Center every 15 minutes. Fare is $1.25 one way for adults, 50¢ one way for kids and seniors (double the price for a round-trip ticket). *Every day; map:I6* &

13) WOODLAND PARK ZOO

5500 Phinney Ave N, Greenwood; 206/684-4800 Occupying what was once the "country estate" of an eccentric 19th-century Canadian real estate baron named Guy Phinney, Woodland Park Zoo has been hailed as one of the nation's 10 best zoological gardens. It's evolved significantly over the last couple of decades, shedding its roots as an animals-behind-bars facility in favor of lifelike re-creations of natural habitats ("bioclimatic zones," in zoo lingo). Among these habitats are a grassy **AFRICAN SAVANNA** populated with giraffes, zebras, and hippos that wallow merrily in their own simulated mud-bottomed river drainage (the lions, though nearby, enjoy their own grassland); **TROPICAL ASIA**, with its **ELEPHANT FOREST**—4.6 acres that include an elephant-size pool, a replica of a Thai logging camp and Thai temple (this last serving as the elephants' nighttime abode), and Hansa, the most recent baby pachyderm born at this zoo; and the **TRAIL OF VINES**, an adjoining 2.7-acre exhibit that takes visitors on an imaginary voyage through India, Malaysia, and Borneo with its display of orangutans, siamang apes, Malayan tapirs, and lion-tailed macaques. The heavily planted **LOWLAND GORILLA ENCLOSURES** conceal a brooding troop of adults and their precocious offspring. And a new, $2 million **AFRICAN VILLAGE**, located on the edge of the savanna exhibit, shows visitors what life is like in a rural East African settlement.

On a tamer scale, the renovated **FAMILY FARM** (inside the Temperate Forest) is a wonderful place for human youngsters to meet the offspring of other species. The **RAIN FOREST CAFE** is an indoor-outdoor food court (and a great place to throw a birthday party); you might not love the food, but the kids, no doubt, will. The zoo also offers a rich schedule of family programming, including orientation walks, classes, special events, and lectures. Its popular **ZOOTUNES CONCERTS** series, held outdoors on summer evenings, draws from a panoply of top musicians (206/615-0076). Zoo admission is $9.50 for adults, $7 for youths 6–17, and $4.75 for children 3–5. *Every day; www.zoo.org; map:FF7* &

14) KLONDIKE GOLD RUSH NATIONAL HISTORICAL PARK

117 S Main St, Pioneer Square; 206/553-7220 "Seattle has gone stark, staring mad on gold," reported the *New York Herald* after the steamship *Portland* docked at Elliott Bay on July 17, 1897, bearing 68 ragged prospectors and what local newspapers claimed was a "ton of gold" (it was actually closer to two tons) collected from tributaries of northwestern Canada's Klondike River. Within a week, bank clerks, barbers, ferry pilots, and preachers from all over town had turned in their resignations and sailed to the Southeast Alaskan coast, from which rugged mountain trails and turbulent watercourses led them inland to Canada's Yukon and raucous Dawson City, at the heart of the Klondike valley. They were followed by tens of thousands more men and women, all anxious to find their fortunes during North America's last great frontier adventure: the Klondike Stampede.

Those wild times are still celebrated at this Pioneer Square "park"— really a storefront museum, the southernmost unit of the National Park Service's Klondike gold rush historical sites. (Other units are the town of Skagway and the famous Chilkoot Trail, both in Southeast Alaska.)

Myriad black-and-white photographs and films show steamers leaving Seattle docks in 1897 and '98, all crowded with would-be Croesuses. Exhibits highlight the use of placer-mining equipment and the decisive role newspapers played in spreading word of that subarctic mother lode. There's even a set of gold scales once owned by George Washington Carmack, the first man to stake a claim on the Klondike's richest tributary. Perhaps the most unusual display, though, shows the 2,000 pounds of provisions—from crates of evaporated apples and cans of coffee and condensed milk, to winter clothing and equipment for cooking and mining—that Canada's North-West Mounted Police required each prospector to have in tow upon entering the Yukon. Free. *Every day; www.nps.gov/ klgo; map:O8* &

15) ELLIOTT BAY BOOK COMPANY

101 S Main St, Pioneer Square; 206/624-6600 Since opening in 1973, Seattle's premier independent bookstore has grown well beyond its original one-room shop in Pioneer Square. It still offers a relaxed literary atmosphere, but nowadays you may need a map to navigate your way around. The children's section has expanded to fill a large area of the store. Travel has its own high-ceilinged room, filled with not only guidebooks but also maps, atlases, volumes of travel essays, and foreign-language references. Children's books have moved to a larger loft space. The crime-fiction department offers one of the best selections in the city. Regardless of your favorite niche, you're likely to find something interesting among Elliott Bay's more than 150,000 new and used titles. Service is smart and efficient; employees will field any question, and they'll even wrap and ship all your gift purchases. If you just can't wait to begin reading your new volumes, drop into the basement cafe for soups, sandwiches, and, of course, coffee.

Readings and signings, drawing the nation's most distinguished authors—from out-of-towners such as Amy Tan and Richard Russo to local celebs such as Sherman Alexie and David Guterson—take place here on most evenings. There's no charge for these events, but tickets are often required to ensure seating. Children's readings and events usually take place on the first Saturday morning of each month. *Every day; queries@elliottbaybook.com; www.elliottbaybook.com; map:O8*

16) BURKE MUSEUM OF NATURAL HISTORY AND CULTURE

17th Ave NE and NE 45th St, University District; 206/543-5590 Once an eccentric treasure trove of dusty relics, the Burke—named in honor of Judge Thomas Burke, an early Seattle mover and chief justice of the Washington State Supreme Court—has become a more sophisticated and attention-grabbing place in the last decade. From its collections of more than 3 million artifacts and specimens, the museum has created two permanent exhibits. **THE LIFE AND TIMES OF WASHINGTON STATE** looks back over 500 million years of regional history, examining how nature shaped the land and the life upon it. Telling that story has meant assembling prehistoric plant and animal fossils; a selection of cast dinosaur skeletons as well as the Northwest's only real dinosaur skeleton, a 140-million-year-old, flesh-eating Allosaurus; and even a glass case of native (and sometimes bizarre) Washington insects, with an accompanying interactive information center. Probably better appreciated by adults, though, is PACIFIC VOICES, which highlights the richness of cultures all over the Pacific Rim, using historic and contemporary artifacts, from Hawaiian musical instruments and traditional Korean marriage paraphernalia to wonderful potlatch masks crafted by Northwest Coast Natives and the setting for a Chinese New Year feast.

A main-floor GIFT SHOP sells curiosities from around the Pacific Rim; downstairs is the BURKE MUSEUM CAFE, an especially comfy espresso-and-pastries spot. Admission for permanent exhibits is a suggested $5.50 donation for adults and $2.50 for students; free for children 5 and under, museum members, and UW students/staff. Charges for special exhibits vary. *Every day; recept@u.washington.edu; www.washington.edu/burkemuseum; map:FF6* &

17) VOLUNTEER PARK

15th Ave E and E Prospect St, Capitol Hill; 206/684-4075 Mature trees, circling drives, grassy lawns, and lily ponds make this the most elegant of Seattle's parks—as stately as the mansions that surround its 48 acres. Designed by the distinguished Olmsted Brothers firm of Massachusetts and dedicated to Seattleites who fought in the Spanish-American War, Volunteer Park graces the top of Capitol Hill, offering sweeping views of the Space Needle, Puget Sound, and the Olympic Mountains.

At the north end of the main concourse lies the elaborate 1912 VOLUNTEER PARK CONSERVATORY (near 15th Ave E and E Galer St; 206/684-4743), boasting three large greenhouse rooms filled with flowering plants, cacti, and tropical flora. It's open (no charge) to the public; step inside for a quick trip to the tropics, complete with the humidity. At the conservatory's entrance, don't miss the monument to William H. Seward, the U.S. Secretary of State who purchased Alaska dirt cheap from the Russians in 1867. Traipse a bit farther north from the conservatory and you'll hit LAKEVIEW CEMETERY, containing the graves of numerous Seattle pioneers as well as those of father-son martial-arts stars Bruce and Brandon Lee.

At the other end of Volunteer Park's main concourse is an old 75-foot WATER TOWER (1400 E Prospect St), its observation deck featuring an excellent interpretive exhibit of the Olmsteds' park-designing history in Seattle. The SEATTLE ASIAN ART MUSEUM is also located here (see listing above). *Every day; map:GG6*

18) PACIFIC SCIENCE CENTER

200 2nd Ave N, Seattle Center; 206/443-2001 A cluster of white buildings around shallow pools and graceful, 110-foot white arches at Seattle Center, the Science Center was originally designed as part of the 1962 world's fair by Minoru Yamasaki, the architect responsible for the inverted-pencil Rainier Square tower downtown (as well as New York City's erstwhile twin-towered World Trade Center). Since then, 30 million people have trooped through the 6 acres of this recently spiffed-up complex to see hands-on science and math exhibits for school-age children as well as traveling shows aimed at all age groups.

One of several permanent exhibits, **DINOSAURS: A JOURNEY THROUGH TIME** introduces five roaring robotic creatures from Earth's Mesozoic period, including a flesh-eating *Tyrannosaurus rex* and a three-horned, herbivorous Triceratops. In the **TECH ZONE,** children can play virtual basketball, hang-glide through a virtual city, and match wits with a robot. The **SCIENCE PLAYGROUND** offers a kid-friendly introduction to physics. There are also insect and tropical butterfly exhibits. Outside the center, kids can take aim with a water cannon or explore their center of gravity on the **HIGH RAIL BIKE**. Admission is $6.75 for adults; $5.75 for kids; and free for children under 3, members, and disabled persons.

Also in this complex, an **IMAX THEATER** (206/443-IMAX) boasts a six-channel surround-sound system and a 35-by-60-foot screen on which viewers can thrill to experiences such as a trip to Alaska or a climb up Mount Everest. Admission is $6.75 for adults, $5.75 for kids, free for children under 3. Ccombination IMAX–Science Center tickets are available. *Every afternoon, Thurs–Sat evening* &

19) FISHERMAN'S TERMINAL

3919 18th Ave W, Interbay; 206/728-3395 A most authentic tourist attraction, this working terminal is the busiest of its kind in the North Pacific. Built in Ballard in 1913, it was one of the Port of Seattle's first facilities and is now home base to some 700 commercial fishing vessels (ranging in length from 30 to 300 feet), most of which head north into Alaskan waters. The terminal sits on the south shore of protected Salmon Bay, the last stretch of the Lake Washington Ship Canal before it reaches the **HIRAM M. CHITTENDEN LOCKS** (see listing above) and meets the waters of Puget Sound.

Head out to the crowded piers to inspect hundreds of gillnetters and crab boats that make up the Northwest's most active fleet. Look also for trollers (they're the ones with two tall poles stuck straight up in the air) and the big factory processors, on which fish are cleaned at sea. This freshwater terminal is an optimal choice for fishers, since their boats are protected from the corrosion and other problems associated with salt-water storage.

Revamped in 1988, the terminal includes new docks, a large public plaza (with interpretive panels detailing the development of the local fishing industry), and the **SEATTLE FISHERMEN'S MEMORIAL,** a bronze-and-concrete pillar created by Seattle sculptor Ron Petty to honor local fishers lost at sea. **CHINOOK'S** (206/283-4665) offers tasty seafood dishes and a splendid view of the waterway; or try its annex next door for quick fish-and-chips. At the **WILD SALMON SEAFOOD MARKET** (1900 W Nickerson St; 206/283-3366), mere feet from the boats, you can purchase fresh fish for your dinner table. Time your visit with an incoming fishing boat, and you might get an even fresher catch. *Every day; map:FF8*

20) SEATTLE AQUARIUM

1483 Alaskan Wy/Pier 59, Waterfront; 206/386-4320 While plans are being made for a new, much larger aquarium at Pier 62/63, the original facility continues to rake in crowds of students and travelers. Two parts of this waterfront aquarium have long earned the most attention. The **UNDERWATER DOME** is a 400,000-gallon fish tank that surrounds visitors, their heads aswivel as they try to take in the myriad king salmon, reef sharks, snappers, and other colorful Puget Sound and Pacific Ocean inhabitants whisking by. And in the topside tanks, seals and sea otters act especially clownish at feeding times.

The **SOUND TO MOUNTAINS** exhibit draws its own following with a pair of playful river otters and a "Marsh Room" where, with tadpole tanks and a rushing freshwater stream, children learn the importance of watersheds. Elsewhere, a functioning salmon ladder explains the life cycle of these iconic Northwest fish. Children enjoy the **DISCOVERY LAB,** where they can handle sea stars and hermit crabs, and marvel at the display of giant Pacific octopuses, native to Puget Sound. Admission is $9 for adults, $6.25 for youths, $4.25 for children 3–5, free for children 2 and under. *Every day during summer, call about Mondays during winter; www.seattleaquarium.org; map:J9* &

The adjacent **SEATTLE IMAX DOME** theater (206/622-1868) is a dramatic cinema-in-the-round, featuring *The Eruption of Mount St. Helens* and other IMAX spectacles in more than a dozen showings daily. Admission is $7 for adults, $6.50 for youths, free for children under 5. Combination IMAX Dome/Seattle Aquarium tickets are available. *Every day; info@seattleimaxdome.com; www.seattleimaxdome.com* &

21) NORDSTROM AND REI (RECREATIONAL EQUIPMENT INC.)

500 Pine St, Downtown; 206/628-2111, 222 Yale Ave N, Cascade; 206/223-1944 Whether you're a fashion maven or an incurable gearhead, you can worship at the cash-register altars of this city's two premier shopping destinations. In 1998 locally grown retail giant **NORDSTROM** opened its shining new department store across the street from its old location (the new building was once the flagship for the defunct Frederick

& Nelson chain). It boasts a whopping five spacious floors of clothes, shoes, accessories, cosmetics, fine jewelry, and fabled customer service. Special attractions of this Nordy's include a full-service day spa and a complimentary wardrobe consulting service; besides the customary cafe, there's the Nordstrom Grill, featuring fresh market seafood. And the shoes: 150,000 pairs (including hard-to-find sizes, 3AAAAA to 14EE for women) are spread among five departments. Befitting a store that first made its mark in shoe leather, Nordstrom has installed glass cases around the store displaying examples of footwear, ranging from turn-of-the-19th-century ankle boots to 1970s ankle-challenging platform shoes. (Nordstrom's two-week anniversary sale in late July is a bona fide Northwest event.) *Every day; www.nordstrom.com; map:J5* &

At REI, the nation's largest consumer co-op (60 stores in 24 states), you'll find basically everything you need for mountaineering, backpacking, camping, cross-country skiing, biking, and other energetic outdoor pursuits. Seattle's high-visibility, two-level location just off Interstate 5 features a 65-foot indoor climbing pinnacle, mountain bike and hiking test paths, a rain simulator in which to try out the latest Gore-Tex gear, a children's play area, a deli/cafe, and a wide assortment of fleece items, as well as maps, trail food, and outdoor books. The trip planning office of the U.S. Forest Service's Outdoor Recreation Information Center is also located here (206/470-4060).

Anyone can shop here, but members (who pay only $15 to join for a lifetime) receive at least a 10 percent yearly dividend on their purchases. Founded in 1938 by a group of Seattle mountaineers who wanted to import European equipment, the co-op was presided over for years by Everest conqueror Jim Whittaker, and it is still staffed by knowledgeable outdoorspeople. The flagship is constructed largely out of recycled building materials, featuring many playful accents: clocks in the shape of Swiss Army watches, and ice-ax door handles, to name a couple. Many lectures, events, and courses take place here; call for a current schedule. Rentals at good prices, too. Smaller branches are in Bellevue, Federal Way, and Lynnwood. *Every day; www.rei.com; map:H1* &

22) BOEING PLANT TOUR

Tour Center, Hwy 526, Everett; 206/544-1264 or 800/464-1476 An engineer and the son of a Michigan timber baron, William E. Boeing first became fascinated with flying in 1910. Ninety years later, despite some rough going, the company he created has become one of the world's aerospace giants. Boeing's magnitude is well reflected in the dimensions of its **MAIN AIRPLANE ASSEMBLY BUILDING,** adjacent to Paine Field in Everett, 30 miles north of Seattle. With almost 300 million cubic feet of space, this is the world's largest building by volume, big enough to make even 747s and 777s look small inside.

Even in the face of bad local press regarding Boeing's decision to relocate its headquarters from Seattle to tonier digs in Chicago, public tours of the company's Everett plant are expected to remain popular. These tours have been conducted ever since 1968, with annual attendance now up around 140,000 people. Lasting approximately an hour and a quarter, the escorted jaunts begin at the Tour Center with a short video presentation about Boeing airplanes and other products. Participants are then loaded onto a bus and taken to the assembly building, where a balcony gives them an exciting view of planes under construction. From there, the bus wheels out to the Flight Line, where a variety of jets are nearing completion.

A limited number of tour tickets are sold at the Tour Center for same-day use, beginning at 8:30am every weekday; during summer, visitors line up for tickets as early as 7am, so get there early too. From May through October, tickets can all vanish by noon. However, you can now make reservations at least 24 hours in advance by calling the Tour Center's 800 number. Children must be at least 50 inches tall, and visitors may not carry babies on the tour. No cameras are allowed on company property. Boeing began charging admission for the tours in 1999: $5 for adults, $3 for children under 16 and seniors; cash only at the door. *Mon–Fri; everett.tourcenter@ boeing.com; www.boeing.com/company offices/aboutus/tours*

23) WASHINGTON PARK ARBORETUM

2300 Arboretum Dr E, Madison Valley; 206/543-8800 Year-round, naturalists and botanists rub elbows with serious runners and casual walkers, for this 200-acre public park (set aside as urban wilderness in 1904 and developed beginning in the 1930s) doubles as a botanical research facility for the nearby University of Washington. The arboretum stretches from Foster Island, just off the shore of Lake Washington, through the Montlake and Madison Park neighborhoods, its rambling trails screened from the houses by thick greenbelts. More than 5,000 varieties of woody plants are arranged here by family. (Pick up maps or an illustrated guide at the visitors center if you want to find specific trees.)

From spring through autumn, the arboretum's **JAPANESE GARDEN** (1502 Lake Washington Blvd E; 206/684-4725) is well worth a visit. Just off Lake Washington Boulevard E, which winds north-south through the park, this authentic garden of pruned living sculptures was constructed in 1960 under the direction of Japanese landscape architect Juki Iida. Several hundred tons of rock hauled from the Cascades were incorporated into the design, as were stone lanterns donated by the city of Kobe and a **TEAHOUSE** sent by the governor of Tokyo. The graceful **CARP POND**, spanned by traditional bridges of wood and stone and lined with water plants, is home to countless ducks, herons, and muskrats. Though the original teahouse was destroyed by vandals years ago, it has since been replaced, and the tea ceremony is still performed on the third Saturday of the month, April through October, at 1:30pm by members of the Seattle branch of the Urasenke Foundation. Guided tours are available by arrangement for a fee. Call for admission prices, event schedules, and operating hours; closing time varies seasonally. *Every day; map:GG6*

Just across the road to the north runs **AZALEA WAY**, a wide, grassy thoroughfare that winds through the heart of the arboretum. (No recreational running is permitted on this popular route.) Azalea Way is magnificent in April and May, when its blossoming shrubs are joined by scores of companion dogwoods and ornamental cherries. Drop in on the **JOSEPH A. WITT WINTER GARDEN**, especially from November through March, which focuses on plants that show distinctive seasonal bark, winter flowers, or cold-season fruit to attract birds. Side trails lead through the arboretum's extensive **CAMELLIA AND RHODODENDRON GROVES** (the latter collection is world famous).

Follow Azalea Way to the copper-roofed **DONALD A. GRAHAM VISITORS CENTER** (2300 Arboretum Dr E; 206/543-8800), where you can find maps and arboretum guides as well as horticulture-related books, gifts, and informational displays. The arboretum also hosts an annual spring plant sale each April, a fall bulb sale each October, and guided weekend tours. *Every day, 7am–dusk; wpa@u.washington.edu; depts. washington.edu/wpa; map:GG6* &

24) SPIRIT OF WASHINGTON DINNER TRAIN

Spirit Depot, 625 S 4th St, Renton; 425/227-RAIL or 800/876-RAIL It's not exactly the Orient Express, but the Spirit of Washington Dinner Train definitely attracts diners who crave a bit of nostalgia and adventure with their meal. At downtown Renton's **SPIRIT DEPOT**, you and your fellow passengers board a train composed of Depression-era railcars and engines, all immaculately restored. From there, you're whisked north on a 45-mile, 3.5-hour round trip along the eastern shore of Lake Washington to Woodinville (all the while following Burlington Northern tracks used by freight trains six days a week). Among the highlights of the excursion is when the train passes over Bellevue's **WILBURTON TRESTLE**—at 102 feet high and 975 feet in length, the longest wooden trestle still in use in the Northwest. For the best views, pay a $10 premium to secure seats in one of the three dome cars.

And it isn't just the scenery that travelers will remember. Meals served on board are much better than you might expect. When you make your reservation for a ride, you choose one of four entrees. (A separate children's menu has options for kids.) If the meal and the gentle rocking of the coach don't put you to sleep, visit the **COLUMBIA WINERY** at the route's northern end. Take a 45-minute tour of the winery or simply retire to its tasting room for samples of fine Northwest vintages. And take that nap on the way back south, while your fellow passengers are enjoying cocktails or dessert and coffee.

During the summer, trains run once daily and twice on weekends. Dinner guests pay $59.99 for regular seating, $69.99 for dome seats. Lunch is $49.99 for regular seating, $59.99 for dome seats. For those who like to dress up and play games, the train runs "Murder Mystery Trains" on select weekdays year-round ($74.99 per person including dinner). From November through April, children 12 and under ride—and eat—for no charge in the regular parlor cars when accompanied by an adult; however, they are still charged full fare in the dome cars. *Every day (June–Sept), Tues–Sun (Oct–May); www.spiritofwashingtondinner train.com; map:NN3–CC2* &

25) GREEN LAKE PARK

Between E Green Lake Dr N and W Green Lake Dr N, and N 55th and N 79th Sts, Green Lake; 206/684-4075 When the sun shines and the joggers, tanners, and in-line skaters muster en masse, the greenbelt around Green Lake looks like a slice of Southern California that's been beamed to the temperate Northwest. Even on dreary days, the 2.8-mile paved inner circuit around the lake is likely to be crowded. For less competition (but more car exhaust fumes), runners can try the 3.2-mile unpaved outer loop. No less than President Bill Clinton used to run here (accompanied by a phalanx of Secret Service agents) when he was visiting Seattle. On any given day, however, you're much more likely to spot couples circling the water in intense conversation—some of them looking distinctly pained. So many lovers have broken up during Green Lake strolls that Seattleites are known to cringe at the very prospect of visiting there with their paramours.

The lake offers enjoyable sailing and windsurfing, as well as great people-watching. If you'd rather watch birds, they're around too, from red-winged blackbirds and the occasional bald eagle to Canada geese. Although the tennis courts, soccer field, indoor pool and recreation center, outdoor basketball court, baseball diamond, pitch-and-putt golf course, boat rental, thriving commercial district, and considerable car traffic around the lake make it feel like an urban beach resort, you can usually find one or two grassy patches for a picnic. There's a well-equipped kids' playground on the northeast side.

Limited parking can be found in three lots: the northeast lot (Latona Ave N and E Green Lake Wy N)—the most crowded, the northwest lot (7312 W Green Lake Wy N), and the south lots (5900 W Green Lake Wy N). *Every day; map:EE7*

Neighborhoods

DOWNTOWN/BELLTOWN

Between Western Ave and Boren Ave, Yesler Wy and Denny Wy Seattle's commercial district has shifted over time. Before 1900, most government and business offices huddled in Pioneer Square (see Top 25 Attractions in this chapter), at the south end of today's downtown. After the Great Fire of 1889, crowding in that historic district and the search for cheaper real estate drove the city's expansion northward.

Today's **RETAIL CORE** lies basically between Third and Sixth Avenues from Stewart to University Streets (for details, see the Shopping chapter). It's anchored by two big department stores—**THE BON MARCHÉ** (4th Ave and Pine St) and **NORDSTROM** (5th Ave and Pine St)—as well as two upscale malls. **WESTLAKE CENTER** resides at Fourth and Pine (see Top 25 Attractions in this chapter) and airy **PACIFIC PLACE,** which opened in 1998, sits two blocks east, at Sixth Avenue and Pine Street. Along Fifth Avenue you'll also find that stylish dealer in men's and women's clothes, **BANANA REPUBLIC** (1506 5th Ave), and hometown favorite **EDDIE BAUER** (1330 5th Ave).

Paralleling Pine Street is Pike Street, and at Seventh Avenue and Pike are housed video game emporium **GAMEWORKS** and **NIKETOWN.** Colorful smaller shops line Fourth and Fifth Avenues south to **RAINIER SQUARE** (4th Ave and Union St), an elegant three-story atrium at the base of **RAINIER TOWER,** a modernist box of a building that's balanced atop a tapered 12-story pedestal. Across University Street to the south is the **FOUR SEASONS OLYMPIC HOTEL** (4th Ave and University St; see the Lodgings chapter), the noble grand dame of Seattle hostelries, opened in 1924 and now girded with boutiques of international pedigree.

To see the results of Seattle's 1980s construction boom, you need only look up: downtown Seattle bristles with skyscrapers. All hope to outshine their neighbors—but few stand out in terms of architectural quality. The **1201 THIRD AVENUE BUILDING** (formerly known as the Washington Mutual Tower) is a postmodern confection with a stair-stepped profile reminiscent of the Empire State Building's and a covering of pink granite that glows at sunset. **CITY CENTRE** (5th Ave and Pike St) boasts a light-filled lobby, delightful glass sculptures, three floors of exclusive shops, and the **PALOMINO** bistro. The tallest building downtown—but also one of the least attractive—is the 76-story **COLUMBIA CENTER,** about six blocks south at Fourth Avenue and Columbia Street. For a grand view, visit its observation platform on the 73rd floor. Check in with the security desk in the lobby ($3.50 adults, $1.75 children and seniors; Mon–Fri only). More interesting are some older towers, such as

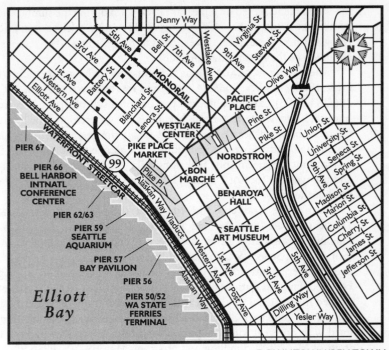

DOWNTOWN/BELLTOWN

the 1910 **COBB BUILDING** (4th Ave and University St), an elegant 11-story brick-and-terra-cotta structure, and the 1929 art deco, 26-story **SEATTLE TOWER** (3rd Ave and University St).

Walk west along University Street to reach **BENAROYA HALL** (between 3rd and 2nd Aves), the distinctive new home of the Seattle Symphony, and the **SEATTLE ART MUSEUM** (between 1st and 2nd Aves; see Top 25 Attractions in this chapter). North on First Avenue from the museum is **PIKE PLACE MARKET** (see Top 25 Attractions in this chapter), popular with both shoppers and people-watchers.

First Avenue has upscaled considerably in past years (it used to be best known for its strip clubs and pawn shops), and its shopping and entertainment opportunities now stretch north beyond Virginia Street into **BELLTOWN** (Virginia St to Battery St, Western Ave to 5th Ave). Belltown has become known for its music clubs, such as the famed **CROCODILE CAFE** (2200 2nd Ave; 206/441-5611), but also attracts with an abundance of stylish shops, such as the sleek modern furnishings of **URBAN EASE** (2512 2nd Ave; 206/443-9546), and restaurants, including the Latin-American-flavored **FANDANGO** (2313 1st Ave; 206/447-1188), **MARCO'S SUPPERCLUB** (2510 1st Ave; 206/441-7801), with a 'round-

the-world menu served on a pleasant back patio during the summer; and
DAHLIA LOUNGE (2001 4th Ave; 206/682-4142), celebrity chef Tom
Douglas's first place, recently relocated to brighter digs. (For reviews of
all three, see the Restaurants chapter.)

The **DENNY REGRADE,** home to nightspots such as sister clubs **TINI
BIGS** (100 Denny Wy; 206/284-0931) and **WATERTOWN** (106 1st Ave N;
206/284-5003), extends a block or two on either side of Denny Way from
Interstate 5 to Western Avenue; beyond is the waterfront. North of the
Regrade, between Seattle Center and I-5, is the booming South Lake
Union area and the residential/industrial Cascade neighborhood. The
eastern foot of Queen Anne Hill along Lake Union is the Westlake area,
and the western foot of Capitol Hill along Lake Union is the Eastlake
neighborhood.

East of the retail core, the **WASHINGTON STATE CONVENTION &
TRADE CENTER** (8th Ave and Pike St), a mammoth, glass-enclosed
building, sprawls atop 12 lanes of freeway and adjoins **FREEWAY PARK**
(6th Ave and Seneca St), an extraordinary park that forms a grassy lid
over thundering Interstate 5. On the east side of I-5 is the First Hill neighborhood. Five bus stations of the underground **METRO TRANSIT TUNNEL**
opened in late 1990 to ease Seattle's downtown traffic woes. From the
convention center to Chinatown/International District, each station is
lined with different kinds of public art (from sculpture to poetry), the
fruits of Metro's $1.5 million arts program. *Map:F5–N5, F9–N9*

CHINATOWN/INTERNATIONAL DISTRICT
S Dearborn St to S Washington St, between 4th Ave S and 14th Ave S
The history of white treatment of Asians in Seattle is not a pleasant one,
but you wouldn't know that to look at this peaceful and unpretentious
neighborhood southeast of Pioneer Square. Seattle's Chinatown/Interna-
tional District is a collection of distinct ethnic communities (the Chinese
have their own newspapers and opera society, the Japanese have a theater) and a cohesive melting pot (a community garden, museum, and
neighborhood playground are shared by all). The influx of Southeast
Asian immigrants and refugees in recent decades has only served to enrich
this neighborhood's long-standing mix of Chinese, Japanese, Filipinos,
Koreans, and African-Americans and given the "ID" a new vibrancy.

The southern edge of this district is marked by the handsome, barrel-
vaulted **UNION STATION** (4th Ave S and S Jackson St; 206/622-3214),
opened in 1911 for the Union Pacific Railroad and refurbished not long
ago as the headquarters for Sound Transit. A centerpiece of the neighborhood is the newly relocated and expanded emporium **UWAJIMAYA**
(600 5th Ave S; 206/624-6248), the closest thing this city has to a real
Japanese supermarket/department store—its cooking school is well
regarded throughout the region, and it also houses **KINOKUNIYA**

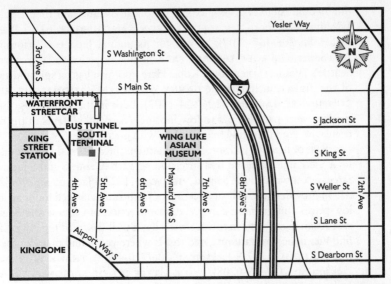

CHINATOWN/INTERNATIONAL DISTRICT

(206/587-2477), a branch of the largest Japanese bookstore chain in the United States. To get an idea of the engaging contrasts of the International District, drop in at tiny **HOVEN FOODS** (508 S King St; 206/623-6764), which sells excellent fresh tofu and soybean milk as well as take-home bags of plump, frozen pot-stickers.

If you'd rather have somebody else prepare all of the intriguing foodstuffs available in this neighborhood, note that a traditional Chinese breakfast can be had at **HOUSE OF DUMPLINGS** (512–514 S King St; 206/340-0774). Try **TOP GUN** (668 S King St; 206/623-6606) or **HOUSE OF HONG** (409 8th Ave S; 206/622-7997) for dim sum. **SHANGHAI GARDEN** (524 6th Ave S; 206/625-1689) offers the cuisines of varying regions of China and what many consider to be the best Chinese food this Pacific Rim city has to offer. The oldest continuously operated Chinese restaurant in town—which says something about its ability to satisfy—is **TAI TUNG** (659 S King St; 206/622-7372).

On Seventh Avenue is the **WING LUKE ASIAN MUSEUM** (7th Ave S and S Jackson St; see Museums in this chapter), which sensitively chronicles the experience of early Asian immigrants to the West Coast. Across Jackson Street to the north is the main Japanese district, where you'll find a real Japanese pre–World War II five-and-dime, the **HIGO VARIETY STORE** (604 S Jackson St; 206/622-7572). This is also where many of the I.D.'s Japanese restaurants are clustered, including **BUSH GARDEN** (614 Maynard Ave S; 206/682-6830) and the tiny, inexpensive **KORAKU** (419

6th Ave S; 206/624-1389). North on Sixth Avenue and then east on Washington a short way are the **NIPPON KAN THEATRE** (628 S Washington St; 206/467-6807), known for its annual Japanese Performing Arts Series, and **KOBE TERRACE PARK,** with a noble stone lantern from Seattle's Japanese sister city of Kobe. Here, too, you'll get a splendid view of the district, including the **DANNY WOO INTERNATIONAL DISTRICT COMMUNITY GARDENS** (206/624-1802). Built in the late 1970s, these gardens were parceled out to low-income elderly inhabitants of the district, who tend their tiny hillside plots with great pride.

East of here on Jackson, the Chinatown/International District takes on a Vietnamese air; the area surrounding 12th Avenue S and S Jackson Street is known as Little Saigon. **VIET WAH** (1032 S Jackson St; 206/328-3557) provides an excellent selection of fresh and packaged foods at very low prices and the most comprehensive selection of Chinese and Southeast Asian ingredients in town. Seattle has a well-deserved reputation for fine Vietnamese restaurants, and this is where you'll find many of them: **HUONG BINH** (1207 S Jackson St; 206/720-4907), **THANH VI** (1046 S Jackson St; 206/329-0208), and **A LITTLE BIT OF SAIGON** (1036-A S Jackson St; 206/325-3663). Or stop by **THE SAIGON DYNASTY DELI** (1200 S Jackson St; 206/322-3700) for spring rolls and grilled beef sandwiches. *Map:O6–R6, O2–R2*

CAPITOL HILL

From Madison St to Montlake Cut, from I-5 to 23rd Ave, centered along Broadway from E Pine St to E Roy St, and along 15th Ave E from E Denny Wy to E Mercer St Along the spine of Capitol Hill lies Broadway Avenue, Seattle's answer to the effervescent spirit of San Francisco's Castro Street. At one time a victim of urban decay, **BROADWAY** has established itself as a haven for black clothes and pierced body parts, Seattle's unofficial gay district, and one of the few areas of town where sidewalks are still busy after 10pm.

The northern end of the district is at Harvard Avenue E and E Roy Street, home to the **HARVARD EXIT** (807 E Roy St; 206/323-8986), one of Seattle's foremost art-film theaters, and the **DELUXE BAR AND GRILL** (625 Broadway Ave E; 206/324-9697), crowded with folks who want their burgers and microbrews served without chichi decor on the side. Just across the boulevard, Thai fanciers will find sufficiently tongue-searing dishes at **SIAM ON BROADWAY** (616 Broadway Ave E; 206/324-0892). Capitol Hill's free-stepping spirit is perhaps best expressed in Jack Mackie's inlaid bronze *Dancers' Series: Steps,* offbeat public art that appears at intervals as you walk south along Broadway, inviting strollers to get in step with the tango or the foxtrot.

Vintage and imported fashion, books, and home accessories are the focus of Broadway's best stores. **BROADWAY MARKET** (between Republican and Harrison Sts; 206/322-1610), featuring a florist, clothing and card shops, a movie complex, and the futuristic, vegetarian **GRAVITY BAR** (206/325-7186; see review in the Restaurants chapter), is an imposing symbol of the continuing million-dollar enfranchisement of this once-funky street. **RETROVIVA** (215 Broadway Ave E; 206/328-7451) purveys kitschy, retro fashions. On the other side of Broadway are a well-stocked newsstand, **STEVE'S BROADWAY NEWS** (204 Broadway Ave E; 206/324-7323), and a warmly eclectic bookstore, **BAILEY/COY BOOKS** (414 Broadway Ave E; 206/323-8842).

The southern end of the strip is permeated with Seattle Central Community College's diverse students; across Pine Street from the campus is a second excellent movie house, the **EGYPTIAN** (801 E Pine St; 206/323-4978), perched right on the edge of the so-called **PIKE-PINE CORRIDOR,** desperately wanting to be the hip spot of the moment. Just east of Broadway, continuing a few blocks between Pike and Pine Streets, this neighborhood is getting known for its rising housing costs, trendy little shops, and its nightclubs. Two to look out for are the graceful **CENTURY BALLROOM** (915 E Pine St; 206/324-7263) and Goth-rock club **THE VOGUE** (1516 11th Ave; 206/324-5778). Distinctly less chic—and damn

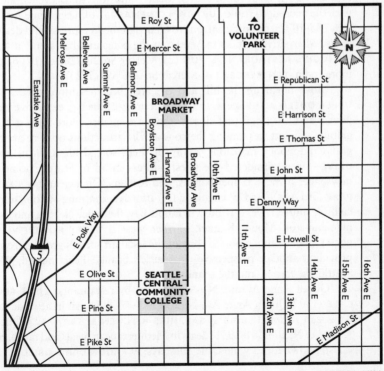

CAPITOL HILL

proud of it—is the **COMET TAVERN** (922 E Pike St; 206/323-9853), a smoky pool joint.

Capitol Hill's other main drag is the slightly less flamboyant **15TH AVENUE E**. It's lined with shops and eateries, including **COASTAL KITCHEN** (429 15th Ave E; 206/322-1145), a loud, fun diner-cum-grill-house with kickin' flavors from coastal regions worldwide. Several blocks farther north on 15th Avenue E, **VOLUNTEER PARK** drapes its grassy lawns among the stately mansions of north Capitol Hill (see Top 25 Attractions in this chapter). *Map:HH6–GG6*

QUEEN ANNE

From Denny Wy to Lake Washington Ship Canal, from 15th Ave W to Aurora Ave, centered along Queen Anne Ave N Seattle's Queen Anne is divided into two districts—Upper and Lower—joined by "the Counterbalance," the part of Queen Anne Avenue that climbs up the steep south slope and owes its nickname to the days when weights and pulleys helped haul streetcars up that incline.

LOWER QUEEN ANNE is anchored by Seattle Center (see Top 25 Attractions in this chapter). The area also boasts some fine restaurants: within a few blocks' radius you can eat Mediterranean, Chinese, Thai, fondue, or Mexican food. Seattle Center and KeyArena events, along with the neon-deco triplex **UPTOWN CINEMAS** (511 Queen Anne Ave N; 206/285-1022), disgorge patrons to fill up late-night espresso and dessert spots. Alternatively, folks may take in the congenial bar scene at **T. S. MCHUGH'S RESTAURANT & PUB** (21 Mercer St; 206/282-1910) or the more stylin' **TEN MERCER** (10 Mercer St; 206/691-3723).

Move north up the hill and the area becomes more residential. **UPPER QUEEN ANNE** seems to be the territory of the big, expensive view house (and it is), but look closely: there are smaller, more modest bungalows and cottages among the condos. Big attractions up here are the grand old-money mansions, many of them spread along **HIGHLAND DRIVE**—once considered the finest address in all of Seattle, home to newspaper owners, timber barons, and bankers. On a clear day, **KERRY PARK** (3rd Ave W and W Highland Dr) affords a smashing outlook (especially at sunrise) over downtown, Elliott Bay, the Space Needle, and even hide-and-seek Mount Rainier. Farther west is **BETTY BOWEN VIEWPOINT** (named in memory of one of the local art scene's great patrons), providing another perspective on Seattle's beauty: Puget Sound, West Seattle, the ferries, and the islands.

Queen Anne Avenue N is dominated by restaurants. The **5 SPOT CAFE** (1502 Queen Anne Ave N; 206/285-7768) is rich in attitude and American regional cuisines; **SAPPHIRE KITCHEN & BAR** (1625 Queen Anne Ave N; 206/281-1931) deals in Mediterranean meals and tapas, but is also known for its wine-table Tuesdays; **PARAGON BAR & GRILL** (2125

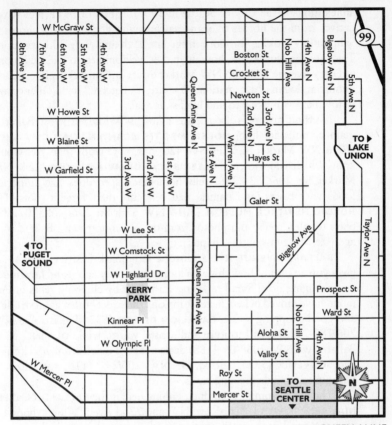

W McGraw St

8th Ave W
7th Ave W
6th Ave W
5th Ave W
4th Ave W

Boston St

Crocket St

Newton St

Nob Hill Ave
4th Ave N
Bigelow Ave N
5th Ave N
99

W Howe St

Queen Anne Ave N

2nd Ave N
3rd Ave N

W Blaine St

TO ▶
LAKE
UNION

Warren Ave N
1st Ave N

Hayes St

W Garfield St

3rd Ave W
2nd Ave W
1st Ave W

Galer St

W Lee St

◀ TO
PUGET
SOUND

W Comstock St

W Highland Dr

Bigelow Ave

Taylor Ave N

Prospect St

KERRY
PARK

Queen Anne Ave N

Ward St

Kinnear Pl

Nob Hill Ave
4th Ave N

W Olympic Pl

Aloha St

Valley St

W Mercer Pl

Roy St

Mercer St

TO
SEATTLE
CENTER
▼

N

QUEEN ANNE

Queen Anne Ave N; 206/283-4548) serves traditional American dishes with elegant or seasonal twists; the often-noisy **HILLTOP ALEHOUSE** (2129 Queen Anne Ave N; 206/285-3877) concentrates on pub grub and its wide array of beers. But a few other enterprises deserve attention, too, including **QUEEN ANNE AVENUE BOOKS** (1629 Queen Anne Ave N; 206/283-5624), strong on fiction and children's lit; **A & J MEATS AND SEAFOODS** (2401 Queen Anne Ave N; 206/284-3885), offering a diverse selection of basic cuts and prepared meals; and the tempting **MCGRAW STREET BAKERY** (615 W McGraw St; 206/284-6327). *Map:GG7*

BALLARD

From Lake Washington Ship Canal to 85th St NW, from 15th Ave NW to Shilshole Bay, centered along NW Market St and Ballard Ave NW Ballard began as an industrial burg, full of sawmills, shingle mills, and shipyards, and it has retained its distinctive character ever since (despite its annexation by the City of Seattle in 1907). Much of its current flavor derives from the hordes of Scandinavians who flocked to the shores of Salmon Bay looking for work in the late 19th and early 20th centuries. Traces of the Nordic life show up in the "Velkommen to Ballard" mural at Leary Avenue NW and NW Market Street and in the neighborhood's unofficial slogan of affirmation: "Ya Sure, Ya Betcha." In no other corner of town are you likely to find lutefisk for sale.

Its ethnic history is also apparent along NW Market Street, Ballard's main commercial hub. **NORSE IMPORTS SCANDINAVIAN GIFT SHOP** (2016 NW Market St; 206/784-9420) has more trolls than you would know what to do with, and **OLSEN'S SCANDINAVIAN FOODS** (2248 NW Market St; 206/783-8288) sells homemade specialties and imported foods with tastes (and names) that celebrate their foreign roots. The **NORDIC HERITAGE MUSEUM** (3014 NW 67th St; 206/789-5707) displays textiles, tools, and photos from the old country and Ballard long ago (see Museums in this chapter).

BALLARD AVENUE NW, a Historic Landmark District since 1976, gives you an idea of how this area looked a century ago—and how much it is changing now. Small retailers, scared off by climbing rents in Fremont, have moved in here instead, making the street both a good strolling and good shopping locale. **CAMELION DESIGN** (5335 Ballard Ave NW; 206/783-7125) sells furniture and artists' wares, while **OLIVINE** (5344 Ballard Ave NW; 206/706-4188) deals in very French women's clothing and **SOUVENIR** (5325 Ballard Ave NW; 206/297-7116) specializes in ultrahip handmade greeting cards.

The most prominent landmark along here is the **BALLARD CENTENNIAL BELL TOWER** (Ballard Ave NW and 22nd Ave NW), a cylindrical, copper-topped monument holding a 1,000-pound brass bell that was saved from Ballard's 1899 City Hall, which stood on this corner until it was torn down after a severe earthquake in 1965. Nearby **BURK'S CAFE** (5411 Ballard Ave NW; 206/782-0091) is one of the brightest spots in the Ballard dining scene, known for its Cajun and Creole eats. Farther down the street, **HATTIE'S HAT** (5231 Ballard Ave NW; 206/784-0175) may have been rediscovered by modern trendmongers, but with its imposing back bar and patrons fresh off the fishing boat, it retains a welcome seedy tone. **CONOR BYRNE'S PUB** (5140 Ballard Ave NW; 206/784-3640) schedules weekends of traditional Irish music, but if you're looking for a wider variety of tunes—from blues to rock to reggae—try the **BALLARD FIREHOUSE** (5429 Russell Ave NW; 206/784-3516), a converted 1908 fire station.

To the west, Ballard encompasses Salmon Bay and the **HIRAM M. CHITTENDEN LOCKS** (see Top 25 Attractions in this chapter), Shilshole Bay Marina, and Golden Gardens Park, a perennial favorite for beach

BALLARD

fires at sunset. One good way to get a feel for this area is to take a tour with the **BALLARD HISTORICAL SOCIETY** (206/782-6844). Call for reservations and information, or pick up a copy of the self-guided walking tour at the **BALLARD CHAMBER OF COMMERCE** (2208 NW Market St, Ste 100; 206/784-9705) or area merchants. *Map:FF8*

FREMONT/WALLINGFORD

North of the Lake Washington Ship Canal and Lake Union from 15th Ave W to I-5, centered along Fremont Ave N and N/NE 45th St Like so many of the hippies who once gave the neighborhood its funky charm, Fremont seems to have gone in for a mainstream makeover. Yes, it still boldly proclaims itself the "Center of the Universe" and not-so-secretly delights in the involvement of nude bicyclists in its summer Solstice Parade every June. But the development of new commercial and office buildings on Fremont's waterfront—including those that house **ADOBE** software com-

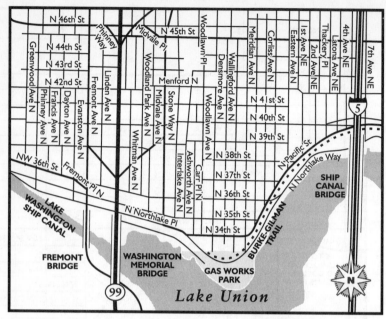

FREMONT/WALLINGFORD

pany's Seattle headquarters—is starting to clog surrounding streets and cause observers to worry for the district's soul.

Fremont boasts the city's most popular—and populist—sculpture, *People Waiting for the Interurban* (Fremont Ave N and N 34th St), which locals revel in decorating year-round. It also claims one of the most unusual art pieces, the **FREMONT TROLL** (under the north end of the Aurora Bridge), as well as one of its most controversial, a huge statue of Vladimir Lenin (Fremont Pl N and N 36th St) that only emphasizes Fremont's independent nature.

Streets here are filled with highly browsable antique, secondhand, and retro-kitsch stores that have names such as **THE DAILY PLANET** (3416 Fremont Ave N; 206/633-0895) and **DELUXE JUNK** (3518 Fremont Pl N; 206/634-2733). When you need refueling, stroll the pleasant park strip along the **LAKE WASHINGTON SHIP CANAL** to the **TROLLEYMAN**, Redhook Ale's comfortable brewpub. Or drop into the stylish but comfortable **TRIANGLE LOUNGE** (3507 Fremont Pl N; 206/632-0880), take a seat at the eclectically decorated bar, and order up surprisingly good pastas or pizzas.

To the east lies Wallingford, a more conventional but no less ingenuous sort of place—"the James Garner among Seattle neighborhoods," as one local magazine put it. While Fremont caters mostly to young singles, Wallingford is full of young marrieds—so full, in fact, that locating streetside parking here can be a nightmare. Most of the businesses hug N 45th Street. Gentrified into a warren of restaurants and jewelry, clothing, and book stores, **WALLINGFORD CENTER** (N 45th St and Wallingford Ave N; 206/632-2781) was originally a public school, one of many designed in Seattle during the early 20th century by carpenter-turned-architect James Stephen. Just across Wallingford Avenue you'll find **WIDE WORLD BOOKS** (4411 Wallingford Ave N; 206/634-3453), a great resource for both real adventurers and armchair travelers. Heading east on 45th Street, you can't miss the very Irish **MURPHY'S PUB** (1928 N 45th St; 206/634-2110); **JITTERBUG** (2114 N 45th St; 206/547-6313), a wonderfully relaxed eatery with a pan-ethnic menu; and **DICK'S DRIVE-IN** (111 NE 45th St; 206/632-5125), a Seattle classic serving up both some of the best French fries in town and a parking lot full of watchable families and teens in lust. Anchoring the south end of Wallingford is **GAS WORKS PARK** on the north shore of Lake Union (see Parks and Beaches in this chapter). *Map:FF7*

GREENWOOD/GREEN LAKE

Along Greenwood Ave N/Phinney Ave N, from N 45th St to N 85th St, and east to I-5 People who've lived in Greenwood for a while say it's "like Wallingford before it became so popular." Once considered a far-northern suburb of Seattle, barely connected to downtown by a rattling municipal streetcar line, Greenwood remains more family-oriented than commercial, with a preponderance of secondhand stores, such as **PELAYO ANTIQUES** (7601 Greenwood Ave N; 206/789-1999). But since about the mid-1980s it has been attracting many younger residents and the diversity of restaurants they crave.

The neighborhood's most interesting stretch runs south from N 85th Street along Greenwood Avenue N. The **PIG 'N WHISTLE** (8412 Greenwood Ave N; 206/782-6044) is a cozy pub and eatery offering fine ribs and ample sandwiches (try the savory meat-loaf variety). For a dollop of attitude with your latte, there's **DIVA ESPRESSO** (7916 Greenwood Ave N; 206/781-1213). The comfort-food craze rules at **PETE'S EGGNEST** (7717 Greenwood Ave N; 206/784-5348); **YANNI'S** (7419 Greenwood Ave N; 206/783-6945) is one of the top Greek restaurants in the city, for good reason; **CARMELITA** (7314 Greenwood Ave N; 206/706-7703) dispenses inventive vegetarian meals; and the **74TH STREET ALE HOUSE** (7401 Greenwood Ave N; 206/784-2955) is known for its chicken sandwiches and spicy soups. **TERRA MAR** (7200 Greenwood Ave N; 206/784-5350) offers handmade clothing, masks, and folk art from national and international makers.

Greenwood Avenue N becomes Phinney Avenue N at N 67th Street, which is also where you'll find **RED MILL BURGERS** (312 N 67th St;

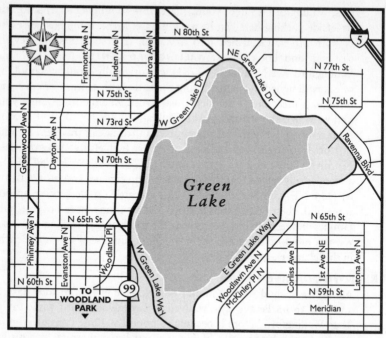

GREENWOOD/GREEN LAKE

206/783-6362), attracting crowds with its wide selection of juicy burgers. And weekends rarely fail to cause a lineup of breakfast aficionados outside **MAE'S PHINNEY RIDGE CAFE** (6412 Phinney Ave N; 206/782-1222). Continue south on Phinney, and you'll hear the trumpeting of elephants and cackling of wild birds that signals your approach to the **WOODLAND PARK ZOO** (see Top 25 Attractions in this chapter).

East of Greenwood, the **GREEN LAKE PARK** area is busy with runners as well as patrons of the many businesses that ring the water. On the lake's east side, **NELL'S** (6804 E Green Lake Wy N; 206/524-4044), in the space formerly occupied by the legendary Saleh al Lago, gives a Mediterranean accent to regional foods such as Columbia River sturgeon and Dungeness crab. **SPUD FISH 'N' CHIPS** (6860 E Green Lake Wy N; 206/524-0565) wraps up orders of flaky fish and greasy fries. **GREGG'S GREENLAKE CYCLE** (7007 Woodlawn Ave NE; 206/523-1822) stocks a wide variety of bicycles and in-line skates for sale, but also rents wheels to fair-weather athletes. *Map:EE7*

UNIVERSITY DISTRICT

From Portage Bay/Montlake Cut to NE 65th St, from I-5 to 35th Ave NE, centered along University Wy NE Just 15 minutes north from downtown on the freeway, the 694-acre **UNIVERSITY OF WASHINGTON** campus is the center of a vital and diverse community as well as the Northwest's top institute of higher learning. The university was founded in 1861 on a plot of land downtown (on University St) and moved to its present site in 1895. In 1909, the campus played host to Seattle's first world's fair—the Alaska-Yukon-Pacific Exposition—and inherited from that not only some grand buildings, but infrastructural improvements to support the neighborhood's growth. The "U-District" is the city's most youth-dominated area, with street life running the gamut from fresh-scrubbed college students to panhandling teens. The UW Visitor Information Center (4014 University Wy NE; 206/543-9198) has maps and information regarding the large, well-landscaped campus.

The university's **MAIN ENTRANCE** is on NE 45th Street at 17th Avenue NE opposite **GREEK ROW,** a collection of stately older mansions inhabited mostly by fraternities and sororities. Just inside that entrance,

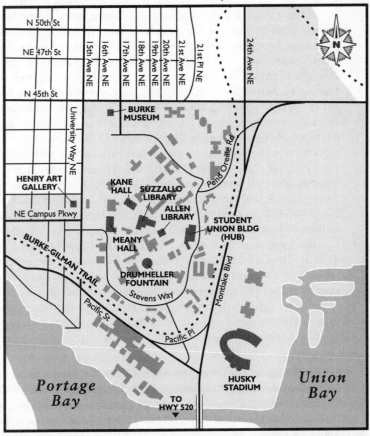

UNIVERSITY DISTRICT

to the right, is the **BURKE MUSEUM OF NATURAL HISTORY AND CUL-TURE,** displaying Native American artifacts and natural-history exhibits (see Top 25 Attractions in this chapter). Wander south past the Burke on Memorial Way to see **DENNY HALL,** the oldest building on campus (circa 1895) and the source of the hourly chimes that can be heard ringing throughout the district. Continuing south, you'll find **CENTRAL PLAZA—** aka "Red Square"—a striking marriage of Brutalist architecture with Siena's town square. Adjacent are **MEANY HALL** and the **HENRY GALLERY,** but most noteworthy there is **SUZZALLO LIBRARY** (206/543-9158), the UW's main research library, with a Gothic exterior and stained-glass windows, as well as its modern **ALLEN LIBRARY** addition (donated by Microsoft co-wizard Paul Allen). Walk south between Suzzallo and the adjacent administration building, and you'll reach **DRUMHELLER FOUN-TAIN** ("Frosh Pond"), a pleasant stopping point among rose gardens, from which (on a clear day, anyway) you can see Mount Rainier.

If the university is the brains of this district, **UNIVERSITY WAY NE,** known to all as "the Ave," is its nerve center. Though chain stores are prominent here, there are still some distinctly local and often eccentric spots. **FOLK ART GALLERY/LA TIENDA** (4138 University Wy NE; 206/632-1796) carries select art objects and exotic crafts from several continents. Across the street is the **BIG TIME BREWERY AND ALEHOUSE** (4133 University Wy NE; 206/545-4509), offering good sandwiches and beers made on the premises. Just off the street in an alley you'll find **CAFE ALLEGRO** (4214½ University Wy NE; 206/633-3030), serving excellent espresso in a counterculturish atmosphere. **BULLDOG NEWS** (4208 University Wy NE; 206/632-6397) is a browser's paradise where you can flip leisurely through hundreds of periodicals. But the real bibliophile's dream is the **UNIVERSITY BOOK STORE** (4326 University Wy NE; 206/634-3400), in perpetual rivalry with the Harvard Co-op for the title of biggest, best, and most varied university bookshop in the country.

Since you're in the area, drop by the **BLUE MOON TAVERN** (712 NE 45th St; 206/633-6267). A half-dozen blocks west of the Ave, it was where poet Theodore Roethke—and, later, novelist Tom Robbins—held court for many years, and where Jack Kerouac (according to legend) and other Beats did their inimitable thing. Heading in the other direction, west of the Ave and just north of campus is **UNIVERSITY VILLAGE,** an upscale shopping area that keeps the U District supplied. *Map:FF6*

WEST SEATTLE

From W Marginal Wy SW to Alki Ave SW, from SW Barton to Duwamish Head, centered along California Ave SW While Pioneer Square likes to be thought of as the cradle of Seattle, the city's *real* birthplace is in what's now West Seattle. It was there, on November 13, 1851, that a party of about two dozen Midwesterners led by Arthur Denny stepped off the schooner *Exact.* They dreamed of building a western version of New

York City at Alki Point, but it took only a year—including one damp, wind-whipped winter—to convince them to retreat eastward across Elliott Bay in search of more sheltered ground.

Today, however, this migration is often reversed—especially on sunny summer days, as winter-pale Seattleites head to **ALKI BEACH** (along Alki Ave SW). With its numerous in-line skaters, volleyball games, picnicking families, and body-conscious teens clad in more suntan oil than bathing suit fabric, this 2-mile-long stretch of sand is the closest thing we have to California's Venice Beach. Need a break from the bikini-and-biceps scene? Step right across Alki Avenue SW to the **LIBERTY DELI** (2722 Alki Ave SW; 206/935-8420), which serves terrific sandwiches and clam chowder, and on Friday and Saturday nights offers some better-than-expected dinner theater performances. Given the New York attitude in this deli, it's only appropriate that the place should be located right across from a 3-foot-high replica of Manhattan's **STATUE OF LIBERTY,** dedicated by the Boy Scouts in 1952. If you prefer your landmarks full-size and tourable, check out the **ALKI POINT LIGHTHOUSE** (3201 Alki Ave SW), located at the southern end of Alki Beach. Built in 1913, this 37-foot functioning U.S. Coast Guard facility offers 30-minute guided tours, during which you will learn some of the area's history. Continue farther south, on Fauntleroy Way SW, and you'll reach **LINCOLN PARK** (see Parks and Beaches in this chapter) and the ferry dock to Vashon Island.

Also worth visiting in West Seattle is an area called **THE JUNCTION** (around California Ave SW and SW Alaska St), known for its historical murals as well as the **WEST SEATTLE FARMERS MARKET,** which operates each Sunday from early June through late October. Browse through the market to find local, organically grown produce, baked goods, and plentiful flowers. While in the neighborhood, don't fail to swing by **EASY STREET RECORDS** (4559 California Ave SW; 206/938-EASY), which boasts a knowledgeable staff and expansive listening stations; the new **ARTSWEST** theater and gallery (4711 California Ave SW; 206/938-0339 box office); and **CAPERS** restaurant (4521 California Ave SW; 206/932-0371), known for its scones and quiches, and also featuring an unusually good gift shop. After running around, stop by the **HUSKY DELI** (4721 California Ave SW; 206/937-2810), famous for its homemade ice creams.

On the east side of the West Seattle ridge is the Delridge neighborhood and, to the south, South Park and White Center, home to a growing Hispanic community and South Seattle Community College. To get the best perspective on West Seattle, reach the neighborhood via **WATER TAXI** (206/684-1753). This 8-minute boat ride travels from Pier 54 on the downtown Seattle waterfront to West Seattle's Seacrest Park. The taxi runs seven days a week, from Memorial Day weekend through the end of the year. Adults pay $2 (one-way), and children under 5 ride free. *Map:JJ8*

BELLEVUE

From Lake Washington to Lake Sammamish, between I-90 and Hwy 520, centered on NE 12th St and Main St To many Seattleites, Bellevue symbolizes everything they don't like about Eastside suburbs—political conservatism, cookie-cutter houses, and a lack of identifiable community history. But this largest city on the east side of Lake Washington now rivals Seattle for its downtown skyline of hotels and office towers. And though Bellevue does seem to be mostly about shopping (one of the city's most recognizable landmarks is **BELLEVUE PLACE**, a hotel, restaurant, and chichi shopping complex downtown), little pockets of livability can be found among the malls. Past the drive-through espresso stands and parking lots full of BMWs are parks, streets lined with small shops, and a surprising variety of ethnic foods—all of which can be enjoyed without setting foot in Bellevue Square.

This is not to say there's no reason to visit the square itself. With hundreds of fashion outlets, fast-fooderies, and shops selling home decorations, the constantly metamorphosing **BELLEVUE SQUARE** (NE 8th St between Bellevue Wy NE and 110th Ave NE; 425/454-8096) is the proverbial one-stop-shopping center and a focus for the community. Some people even show up there on weekday mornings just to walk for exercise. Conclude a visit to Bellevue Square with a walk through the **BELLEVUE ART MUSEUM** across the street (see Museums in this chapter), or on nice days, take a stroll through the 19-acre **DOWNTOWN PARK**, also adjacent to Bellevue Square, where you'll find a 240-foot-wide, 10-foot-high waterfall, a canal enclosing a 5-acre meadow, and a 28-foot-wide promenade.

Art-fair lovers shouldn't miss the **PACIFIC NORTHWEST ARTS AND CRAFTS FAIR** (held the last weekend in July at Bellevue Square), which attracts hundreds of artists from throughout the West. It is said to be the largest crafts fair in the Northwest, and local legend holds that it never rains on the weekend of the fair (Eastsiders plan weddings and barbecues accordingly).

Before leaving this area, you might want to make two last stops: at **UNIVERSITY BOOK STORE** (990 102nd Ave NE; 425/632-9500 or 206/632-9500), the Eastside outlet of Seattle's famed store (minus the textbook and buy-back options), and the **ROSALIE WHYEL MUSEUM OF DOLL ART** (1116 108th Ave NE; 425/455-1116), with its diverse selection of dolls, teddy bears, and miniatures.

East of town, out SE Eighth Street, is **KELSEY CREEK PARK**, a good place for suburban kids to get a taste (albeit a tame one) of the country. A demonstration farm offers up-close contact with pigs, horses, chickens, and rabbits. Farther east lies **CROSSROADS SHOPPING CENTER** (NE 8th St and 156th Ave NE; 425/644-1111), a midsize mall where the emphasis shifts from shopping to community events and ethnic foods. Visitors can

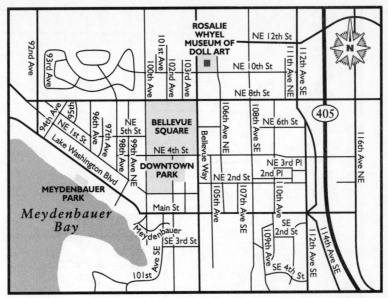

BELLEVUE

play a game of chess (with giant chess pieces) at the giant board painted on the floor, or choose from the menus of a growing number of ethnic eateries. Almost nobody passes up a visit to **THE DAILY PLANET** (425/562-1519), one of the best newspaper and magazine stands in the area. And every Friday and Saturday night, Crossroads sponsors free live musical entertainment—featuring some of the area's most talented musicians playing anything and everything, from jazz to polka (Thursday night is open mike, for those who dare). *Map:HH3–HH1*

KIRKLAND

East of Lake Washington to 132nd Ave NE, between Carillon Point/Hwy 520 and NE 116th St This town was supposed to be "the Pittsburgh of the West"—or at least that was the dream shared in the late 19th century by Leigh S. J. Hunt, publisher of the *Seattle Post-Intelligencer,* and Peter Kirk, an English industrialist. They were convinced that an iron-and-steel works could thrive on Moss Bay, just east of Seattle across Lake Washington. However, in 1893, after only a few buildings and homes had been raised in the area, the nation was struck by its worst financial depression. All that remains of Kirkland's campaign to become Pittsburgh are a few handsomely refurbished historical structures, such as the **PETER KIRK BUILDING** (620 Market St) and the **JOSHUA SEARS BUILDING** (701 Market St).

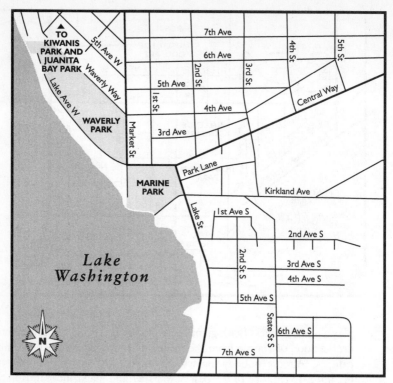

KIRKLAND

Kirkland today is a friendly, low-profile Eastside town hugging Lake Washington that offers more public access to the water than any other city on the lake's shores. One of the best ways to experience the lake is to head a bit north of Kirkland to Juanita for a visit to **JUANITA BAY PARK** (access is off Market St just south of Juanita Dr), home to great blue herons, owls, turtles, beavers, and other varieties of wildlife. Also strollable is **ST. EDWARDS STATE PARK** (take Market St north and head west on Juanita Dr), a densely forested park with a variety of trails that lead down to lakefront beaches, and **BRIDLE TRAILS STATE PARK** (116th Ave NE and NE 53rd St), laced with horse trails.

A more urban tour of the town might begin at the **KIRKLAND ANTIQUE GALLERY** (151 3rd St; 425/828-4993), with more than 80 dealers selling everything from antique tin toys to Depression-era glass. Downtown Kirkland is also replete with **ART GALLERIES**, including Foster/White Gallery (126 Central Wy; 425/822-2305), Howard Mandeville Gallery (120 Park Ln; 425/889-8212), Kirkland Arts Center (620

Market St; 425/822-7161), and Park Lane Gallery (130 Park Ln; 425/827-1462).

When you need to nourish your body instead of your soul, try the Northern Italian **RISTORANTE PARADISO** (120-A Park Ln; 425/889-8601) or, for smashing lake views, there's **ANTHONY'S HOMEPORT** (135 Lake St; 425/822-0225) or the **THIRD FLOOR FISH CAFE** (205 Lake St; 425/822-3553). If all you really want is a cup of coffee, head to the **TRIPLE J CAFÉ** (101 Central Wy; 425/822-7319).

CARILLON POINT, south of downtown proper, is a luxury waterfront complex that includes the **WOODMARK HOTEL** (1200 Carillon Pt; 425/822-3700 or 800/822-3700), specialty shops, waterfront walkways, paths, and benches. **YARROW BAY GRILL** (1270 Carillon Pt; 425/889-9052) features fancy food at fancier prices, while downstairs the **YARROW BAY BEACH CAFÉ** (425/889-0303) offers simpler fare. Fortunately, the best thing about Carillon Point is free: the view west over the lake toward Seattle. *Map:EE3*

REDMOND

East of Lake Washington, between Hwy 520 and NE 124th St, and 132nd Ave NE and 164th Ave NE Even many people who have lived in Seattle for years know Redmond as nothing more than the headquarters for two corporate giants: **MICROSOFT** and **NINTENDO**. But like neighboring Bellevue, Redmond has a bustling downtown shopping mall: **REDMOND TOWN CENTER** (near NE 74th St and 164th Ave NE; 425/867-0808), with more than 50 stores and the **REDMOND TOWN CENTER CINEMAS** arranged around plazas and a large open space used for musical performances. This city also offers some more distinctive delights, including **MARYMOOR PARK** (6046 W Lake Sammamish Pkwy NE; 206/296-2966). Located south of downtown, Marymoor comprises 522 acres of playfields, running and horseback-riding trails, tennis courts, an interpretive nature trail, and even a 45-foot climbing wall (crowded on weekends). This is also where you'll find the **MARYMOOR VELODROME** (2400 Lake Sammamish Pkwy; 206/675-1424), a 400-meter oval bicycle-racing track that attracts championship riders from around the country as well as picnickers who come to watch the spoked wheels go round and round. (Spectators pay $3 to attend Friday-night races.) For a less-active diversion, check out the **CLISE MANSION,** built by Seattle businessman John Clise in 1904 as an Eastside hunting lodge. Today that brown-shingled retreat contains the Marymoor Museum (425/885-3684), which recalls the area's history in exhibits focusing on dairy farming, Native American habitations, and turn-of-the-19th-century village life. Every Fourth of July weekend, the park hosts a **HERITAGE FESTIVAL** featuring ethnic foods, crafts, and music.

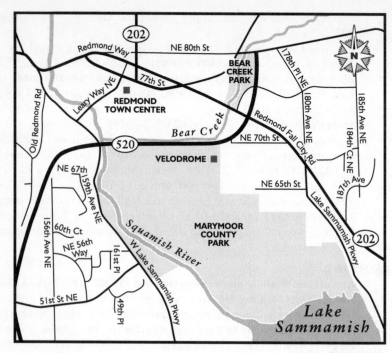

REDMOND

From Marymoor, the **SAMMAMISH RIVER TRAIL** stretches 10 miles north, skirting Woodinville, to Bothell, which lies north of Kirkland and Juanita at the north end of Lake Washington. It's a flat but circuitous route ideal for fair-weather bicyclists, runners, and skaters who enjoy views of the surrounding mountains, slow-moving livestock, and even a few wire sculptures of cows. In Bothell the trail can be linked to the Burke-Gilman Trail along the west shore of Lake Washington into Seattle. *Map:EE1–FF1*

Museums

Even as people have complained about funding shortages for cultural endeavors, Seattle has invested heavily in its complement of museums. The 1990s brought a boom in museum construction, as the Seattle Art Museum moved from Volunteer Park into fancier and larger accommodations downtown, the Henry Art Gallery at the University of Washington was expanded, and both the Frye Art Museum and the Burke Museum of Natural History and Culture were remodeled. With the more recent openings of Experience Music Project and the new Bellevue Art

Museum, Seattle Symphony conductor Sir Henry Beecham's prediction, voiced in the middle of the last century, that this city would become a "cultural dustbin," does not appear to be coming to pass. In addition to the big institutions, smaller venues—such as the **GENERAL PETROLEUM MUSEUM** (1526 Bellevue Ave E, Capitol Hill; 206/323-4789), which celebrates the era of full-serve gas stations, and the **FRISBEE MUSEUM** (206/364-9808; by appointment only)—add not only depth but a bit of needed fun to Seattle's cultural landscape. (For additional listings, see Top 25 Attractions in this chapter.)

BELLEVUE ART MUSEUM (BAM) / 510 Bellevue Wy NE, Bellevue; 425/637-1799 For years, the joke was that no other city except Bellevue—which has long promoted itself as a shopping destination—would think to house its art museum in a shopping mall. But with BAM's recent move into new high-design quarters across the street, it is even attracting Seattleites, who generally look down at anything on the Eastside. Part of the reason is the $23 million museum building itself, a three-story brick-red edifice of concrete, glass, a variety of roof levels, and high-ceilinged rooms full of light. It was designed by Steven Holl, a Northwest-born architect now living in New York, who also designed Seattle University's Chapel of St. Ignatius. The art featured at BAM—from the usual paintings to kid-engaging video-based installations—is in constant danger of being upstaged by outdoor terraces, glass expanses, and technological entertainments such as a wall that shows images from the Hubble telescope. The museum sponsors the massively popular Pacific Northwest Arts and Crafts Fair at Bellevue Square each July. Admission to the museum is $6 for adults, $4 for seniors and students, free for children under 6. The first Thursday of each month is free for everyone. *Tues–Sun; bam@bellevueart.org; www.bellevueart.org; map:HH3* &

CENTER FOR WOODEN BOATS / 1010 Valley St, South Lake Union; 206/382-2628 You can sail away with the exhibits at the Center for Wooden Boats, which has its own little harbor at the southern tip of Lake Union. This maritime museum, kept afloat financially by private donations and a contingent of volunteers, celebrates the heritage of small craft before the advent of fiberglass. Of the 75 vintage and replica wooden rowing and sailing boats in the collection, more than half are available for public use. Admission is always free. Rentals range from $10 to $25 an hour. Lessons in sailing, traditional woodworking, and boatbuilding are offered for all ages. *Wed–Mon; www.cwb.org; map:D1*

THE CHILDREN'S MUSEUM / Center House, Seattle Center; 206/441-1768 Located on the fountain level of the busy Seattle Center House, the Children's Museum has tripled in size since its opening. It's an imaginative learning center that stresses participation, with hands-on activities and exploration of other cultural traditions, and houses a number of per-

ART APPEAL

While some visitors to Seattle notice nothing in the way of arts beyond our ubiquitous totem poles, more observant types can hardly miss this city's numerous artistic offerings, both public pieces and private galleries.

Undoubtedly the most riveting landmark downtown is Jonathan Borofsky's towering black **Hammering Man** (1992) (100 University St, Downtown; map:K7), a four-story figure whose motorized arm and hammer are set to pound four beats a minute, commemorating—so the artist intends—the city's workers. Downtown also contains the city's largest art project to date: the **Metro transit bus tunnel** (Downtown; map:I3–J6) and its terminals (opened 1990), on which dozens of artists worked to create murals, benches, and clocks. Buses traveling through the 1.3-mile tunnel stop at all five stations (Chinatown/International District, Pioneer Square, University Street, Westlake Center, and Convention Place) frequently every day except Sunday, when the tunnel is closed.

Two major artworks can be found at Seattle Center's KeyArena (Thomas St and 1st Ave N, Queen Anne; map:B7): a 60-foot "rain wall," called **Hydraulis** (1995), by Trimpin and Clark Wiegman; and **In the Event** (1995), a huge video installation by Sheldon Brown. In the Broad Street sculpture garden (Broad St and John St, Queen Anne; map:C6) are Ronald Bladen's mighty minimalist welded-steel **Black Lightning** (1981) and Alexander Liberman's immense bright-red **Olympic Iliad** (1984), which consists of forty-one 40-foot-long steel cylinders.

The fanciful **Fremont Troll** is a cultural representative of Fremont's high-spirited neighborhood. Staring out from under the Aurora Bridge (north end of Aurora Bridge on N 36th St, Fremont; map:FF7), this 18-foot-tall, one-eyed concrete creature clutches a real Volkswagen Beetle in its grasp. Blocks away is Richard Beyer's **People Waiting for the Interurban** (1979) (Fremont Ave N and N 34th St, Fremont; map:FF7), arguably the city's most beloved public sculpture, featuring a gray, huddled band of cast-aluminum trolley riders whose distinctly homely figures are periodically decorated with timely garb or signage.

Other notable sculptures around town include Henry Moore's 11-ton bronze bone forms, **Three-Piece Sculpture: Vertebrae** (1968) (1001 4th Ave Plaza, Downtown; map:M6); Isamu Noguchi's stone doughnut, **Black Sun** (1968), in Volunteer Park (1400 E Prospect St, Capitol Hill; map:GG6)—look through the hole at a classic

manent features, including a play center, a mountain, and a global village with child-size houses from Japan, Ghana, and the Philippines. The variety of special programs—Mexican folk dancing, Native American games, Chinese storytelling, Japanese kite making—is impressive. The Imagination Station features a different artist every month guiding activ-

Space-Needle-in-the-sunset vista; Doris Totten Chase's handsomely holey 14.5-foot-tall **Changing Form** (1971) in Kerry Park (3rd Ave W and W Highland Dr, Queen Anne; map:GG8); Barnett Newman's elegiac column, **Broken Obelisk** (1963–67), in the University of Washington's central Red Square (NE 40th St and 15th Ave NE, University District; map:FF6); George Tsutakawa's **Naramore Fountain** (1967), a 15-foot-high piece with water forced onto curved bronze shapes (6th Ave and Seneca St, Downtown; map:L5); and, on the North Loop trail at Magnuson Park (NE 70th St and Sand Point Wy NE, Sand Point; map:EE5), and John T. Young's extraordinary **The Fin Project: From Swords into Plowshares** (1998)—a 410-foot-long environmental sculpture created from the recycled diving plane fins of decommissioned nuclear submarines.

If you'd prefer to take in an abundance of art on foot, join one of Seattle's art walks. The monthly **First Thursday Gallery Walk,** centered in downtown Seattle's historic Pioneer Square, is an arts staple, with crowds of sophisticates (and art-loving singles) cruising the area's dozens of galleries, which stay open for extended hours, 6 to 8pm.

The **Capitol Hill Arts Orbit** walk is on the first Saturday of the month, 1 to 6pm. Orbit maps are available at the Robbie Mildred Gallery in the Broadway Market (401 Broadway Ave E, Capitol Hill; 206/325-5228). On the second Saturday of the month, 1 to 5pm, galleries, working studios, and public art pieces participate in **Fremont's Art About** walk. Maps are available at the Marvin Oliver Gallery (N 35th St and Fremont Ave N, Fremont; 206/633-2468); more information is available from the Fremont Chamber of Commerce (206/633-0812). Other Seattle art rambles include the **Ballard Art Walk** (second Saturday of each month, 7–10pm) and the **Greenwood/Phinney Art Walk** (in early May).

In Kirkland, the **Second Thursday Art Walk** takes in several closely packed galleries and some quirky public art on the second Thursday of each month, 5 to 9pm. Free 4-hour parking is available at the Kirkland Library (808 Kirkland Ave, Kirkland).

To check up on what's being shown in local art galleries and museums, pick up a free copy of *Art Guide Northwest* (available in many Pioneer Square galleries and bookstores), *Arts Patron* (available at the Seattle Art Museum, the Frye Art Museum, the Bellevue Art Museum, and other select locations), or *Seattle Weekly,* which can be found in sidewalk newsboxes all over town. —*J. Kingston Pierce*

ities with various materials. The Discovery Bay exhibit is geared to infants and toddlers. Admission is $5.50 per person; annual family memberships are $55–$100. *Every day; tcm@thechildrensmuseum.org; www.thechildrensmuseum.org; map:B6* &

FRYE ART MUSEUM / 704 Terry Ave, First Hill; 206/622-9250 This once-stodgy museum, known for sentimental 19th-century German salon paintings from the collection of late Seattleites Charles and Emma Frye (who made their fortune in meat processing), underwent a dramatic expansion and remodel in 1997. Since reopening, it's become a lively hub of activities, with poetry readings, chamber music, and other perform-ances in addition to frequently changing exhibits. A new director has chosen a more liberal view of the museum's commitment to figurative art. Shows can be as diverse as the metaphorical paintings of Norwegian artist Odd Nerdrum, the art of Russian ballet dancer Vaslav Nijinsky, or a tribute—in words and imagery—to National Poetry Month. Admission is always free. *Every day; www.fryeart.org; map:N3* &

HENRY ART GALLERY / 15th Ave NE and NE 41st St, University District; 206/543-2280 After a major expansion project that quadrupled its size, the Henry is working to forge a new identity that lives up to its exemplary past. Although it hasn't yet re-created the furor caused by the Ann Hamilton and James Turrell installations in the early '90s, the new Henry is mounting some provocative shows, with a bent toward installations, video, and unusual media. The permanent collection—especially strong in photography—now has a showcase in the original galleries. Additions to the museum include an outdoor sculpture court, a 150-seat auditorium, a cafe (the food is pre-fab), and an education center for children. Located on the University of Washington campus. Admission is $5 for adults, $3.50 for seniors, free for UW students and faculty. *Tues–Sun; www.henryart.org; map:FF6* &

MUSEUM OF HISTORY AND INDUSTRY (MOHAI) / 2700 24th Ave E, University District; 206/324-1126 The rambling, amiable MOHAI is a huge repository of Americana, with artifacts pertaining to the early history of the Pacific Northwest. There's an exhibit about Seattle's Great Fire of 1889 (which started in a gluepot on the waterfront), a hands-on history of the fishing and canning industry in the Northwest, and a half-dozen immense wooden female beauties—and one masculine counterpart—who once rode the prows of ships in Puget Sound. Locally oriented exhibits change throughout the year. *Metropolis 150,* an extensive col-lection of old photographs and artifacts that celebrates the city's first 15 decades, will run through 2003. The museum is scheduled to move into a space at the Washington State Convention & Trade Center, which is occupied by the main branch of the Seattle Public Library until its new downtown facility opens in 2003. Admission is $5.50 for adults, $3 for seniors and children 6–12, $1 for children 2–5, free for kids 2 and under. *Every day; www.seattlehistory.org; map:FF6* &

NORDIC HERITAGE MUSEUM / 3014 NW 67th St, Ballard; 206/789-5707
Established in a stately restored schoolhouse, the Nordic Heritage
Museum focuses on the history of Nordic settlers in the United States,
with exhibits of maritime equipment, costumes, and photographs,
including an Ellis Island installation. Periodic traveling exhibits have
included a show of 18th-century Alaskan and Northwest Coast Native
artifacts from the National Museum of Finland, as well as artworks by
contemporary Scandinavian artists. Holidays bring ethnic festivals.
Admission is $4 for adults, $3 for seniors and students, $2 for children
6–18, free for kids under 6. *Tues–Sat; nordic@intelistep.com; www.
nordicmuseum.com; map:EE9* &

**ROSALIE WHYEL MUSEUM OF DOLL ART / 1116 108th Ave NE, Bellevue;
425/455-1116** Occupying a pink confection of a building near Bellevue
Square, this privately owned museum opened in 1992 and was an instant
hit in the insular world of doll collecting. Don't be put off by that. You'll
find more than 3,000 dolls, including everything from effigies and ancient
Egyptian burial charms to extravagantly outfitted porcelain princesses—
not to mention a few of their modern, mass-produced counterparts. A gift
shop with a pricey selection of new and antique toys caters to collectors.
Admission is $7 for adults, $6 for seniors, $5 for children 5–17, free for
kids under 5. *Every day; www.dollart.com; map:HH3* &

**WING LUKE ASIAN MUSEUM / 407 7th Ave S, Chinatown/International
District; 206/623-5124** Named after Seattle's first Chinese-American city
councilman, this lively little museum in the Chinatown/International District is devoted to the Asian-American experience in the Northwest. Particularly moving is the small exhibit of photographs and artifacts relating
to the internment of Japanese Americans during World War II. Changing
exhibits are devoted to Chinese, Korean, Filipino, Vietnamese, and
Laotian peoples and their often difficult meetings with the West. Admission is $4 for adults, $3 for students and seniors, $2 for children 5–12,
free for kids under 5. Free for everyone on the first Thursday of every
month. *Tues–Sun; folks@wingluke.org; www.wingluke.org; map:R6* &

Galleries

In a city that so much wants to be thought of as having good taste, it's
no surprise that art galleries proliferate. Or that art finds a home in the
streets as well, decorating office building plazas, public squares, even the
Metro bus tunnel running under downtown. Thanks to the ubiquity of
his iridescently hued works, local glass artist Dale Chihuly, who in 1971
helped found the world-renowned Pilchuck Glass School in Stanwood
(50 miles north of Seattle), enjoys a name recognition almost on a par

with that of the latest Mariners star. Hollywood celebrities such as Gene Hackman and Gillian Anderson have come here to prowl among the art for sale (both have been spotted at the Greg Kucera Gallery).

Although most urban neighborhoods have outcroppings of galleries, Seattle's main gallery scene is concentrated in the historic **PIONEER SQUARE** district downtown, with additional galleries sprinkled to the north along First Avenue, especially in the vicinity of the downtown Seattle Art Museum. One good way to get to know many of these galleries is to roam with the crowd in and around Pioneer Square on the **FIRST THURSDAY ART WALKS** each month (about 6 to 8pm), when new shows are previewed (see "Art Appeal" sidebar).

BENHAM STUDIO GALLERY / 1216 1st Ave, Downtown; 206/622-2480
From its roots as a photographic exhibition in a passport studio entryway, the Benham has grown into one of Seattle's finest photo galleries. The gallery represents primarily Northwest photographers, from the well-known (such as Phil Borges and Bruce Barnham) to up-and-comers, whose work is mounted here in a popular group show in December or January. *Every day; benham@benhamgallery.com; www.benhamgallery.com; map:L7* &

CAROLYN STALEY FINE PRINTS / 314 Occidental Ave S, Pioneer Square; 206/621-1888 The specialty here is fine old prints, including Japanese *ukiyo-e* woodblock prints, antique maps, and botanical prints. Staley also hosts occasional book-art shows. *Tues–Sat; staleyprints@ earthlink.net; map:O9* &

DAVIDSON GALLERIES / 313 Occidental Ave S, Pioneer Square; 206/624-7684 Geared to traditional tastes, Davidson shows landscapes and figurative works by contemporary Northwest painters, interspersed with shows by Russian, Czech, and Chinese artists. The back gallery features contemporary printmakers from around the world. Upstairs, check out the antique print department and rotating shows. *Tues–Sat; www. davidsongalleries.com; map:O8* &

ELLIOTT BROWN GALLERY / 215 Westlake Ave N, Cascade; 206/340-8000 Owner Kate Elliott has been involved with the Pilchuck School and its glass art almost from the school's beginning in 1971. In her gallery, she uses her connections in the glass world to line up shows by top international artists. One highlight of her roster was the first solo West Coast show of famed Czech glass artists Stanislav Libensky and Jaroslava Brychtova. *Tues–Sat; kate@elliottbrowngallery.com; www.elliottbrown gallery.com; map:FF8* &

FOSTER/WHITE GALLERY / 123 S Jackson St, Pioneer Square; 206/622-2833 Foster/White showcases paintings, sculpture, and ceramics—usually abstract and decorative—by Northwest artists living and dead. The gallery, which moved in 1999 to Pioneer Square, is also one of the major local dealers in contemporary glass by Pilchuck School stars, most notably Dale Chihuly. An Eastside outpost is located in downtown Kirkland (126 Central Wy; 425/822-2305; map:EE3). *Every day; ask@foster white.com; www.fosterwhite.com; map:O8* &

FRANCINE SEDERS GALLERY / 6701 Greenwood Ave N, Greenwood; 206/782-0355 In judicious operation since 1966, Seders represents some venerable members of Seattle's art community, including Gwen Knight, Robert Jones, and Michael Spafford. New additions to the stable include generous numbers of minority artists, among them painters, sculptors, and assemblagists. *Tues–Sun; www.sedersgallery.com; map:EE7* &

G. GIBSON GALLERY / 122 S Jackson St, 2nd floor, Pioneer Square; 206/587-4033 Gibson opened her cozy upstairs space in 1991, providing a much-needed venue for contemporary photography—by both well-known Americans and adventurous young Northwesterners. *Tues–Sat; ggibson@halcyon.com; www.ggibsongallery.com; map:O9*

GREG KUCERA GALLERY / 212 3rd Ave S, Pioneer Square; 206/624-0770 One of the city's top gallery owners, Kucera maintains a carefully chosen stable of artists, many with national reputations. He has a great eye for emerging talent but also shows editioned works by established blue-chip artists. Recent shows have featured prints by Frank Stella, Robert Motherwell, and Helen Frankenthaler. One thematic exhibit each year addresses a touchy topic: sex, religion, politics. The gallery has recently relocated to this new space in the same neighborhood. *Tues–Sat; staff@gregkucera.com; www.gregkucera.com; map:O7*

GROVER/THURSTON GALLERY / 309 Occidental Ave S, Pioneer Square; 206/223-0816 In the heart of the gallery district, Grover/Thurston gained considerable status when it picked up one of the region's most popular artists, Fay Jones, just before her 1997 retrospective at SAM. Otherwise, the gallery's focus veers toward the decorative. *Tues–Sat; rcthurson@worldnet.att.net; www.groverthurston.com; map:O8* &

KIRKLAND ARTS CENTER / 620 Market St, Kirkland; 425/822-7161 In a historic brick building near the waterfront, this publicly funded center puts on several shows each year by Puget Sound–area artists. A variety of art classes are open to children and adults. *Mon–Fri; www.kirkland artscenter.org; map:EE3*

LINDA HODGES GALLERY / 316 1st Ave S, Pioneer Square; 206/624-3034 Hodges shows contemporary paintings, and occasionally photography and sculpture, by artists from Seattle, Portland, and other Northwest burgs. The art ranges from fantasy to realism, with the biggest draw being the zany, countrified mythology of adored Eastern Washington painter Gaylen Hansen. *Tues–Sun; ldhgallery@aol.com; www. lindahodgesgallery.com; map:O8* &

LISA HARRIS GALLERY / 1922 Pike Pl, Pike Place Market; 206/443-3315 Amid the jostling crowds of the market, this small upstairs gallery can be an oasis of calm. Harris favors expressionistic landscape and figurative works, with several Bellingham artists forming the core of her stable. *Every day; staff@lisaharrisgallery.com; www.lisaharrisgallery. com; map:I8*

MARTIN-ZAMBITO FINE ART / 721 E Pike St, Capitol Hill; 206/726-9509 These two guys from the East Coast know more about the obscure corners of Northwest regionalism than almost anybody. And they're on a mission: to bring recognition to overlooked early artists of the area, especially women—such as photographer Myra Wiggins, whose work attracted international attention in the early 1900s and then disappeared in the shifting tides of art history. *Tues–Sat; info@martin-zambito.com; www.martin-zambito.com; map:K1* &

NORTHWEST FINE WOODWORKING / 101 S Jackson St, Pioneer Square; 206/625-0542 This cooperatively owned gallery offers one-of-a-kind tables, desks, chairs, cabinets, sideboards, screens, boxes, and turned bowls, all by local craftspeople. An Eastside gallery is in Bellevue (610 108th Ave NE, Plaza 100; 425/462-5382; map:GG3). *Every day; sales@ nwfinewoodworking.com; www.nwfinewoodworking.com; map:O8*

SACRED CIRCLE GALLERY OF AMERICAN INDIAN ART / Daybreak Star Cultural Arts Center, Magnolia; 206/285-4425 A profit-making arm of the United Indians of All Tribes Foundation, this topnotch gallery in Discovery Park features contemporary paintings, prints, and sculptural pieces, always reflecting tribal heritages, by a broad selection of Native American artists from the United States and Canada. *Every day; map:FF9* &

SNOW GOOSE ASSOCIATES / 8806 Roosevelt Wy NE, Maple Leaf; 206/523-6223 Gallery space here is filled with art and artifacts of Alaskan and Canadian Eskimos and Northwest Coast Indians. Annual shows include the fall exhibit of prints by Inuit artists from Cape Dorset on Baffin Island. Snow Goose has been in operation for almost 30 years. *Tues–Sat; sgassociates@qwest.net; map:DD7* &

WILLIAM TRAVER GALLERY / 110 Union St, Downtown; 206/587-6501 Pilchuck School glassworks are always on view at Traver, which hosts an annual Pilchuck glass show in December. The stunning second-story space at First Avenue and Union Street, near the Seattle Art Museum, showcases paintings, sculptures, photographs, ceramics, and assemblages, mostly by local artists. *Every day; www.travergallery.com; map:K7* &

WOODSIDE/BRASETH GALLERY / 1533 9th Ave, Downtown; 206/622-7243 You'll find strictly Northwest fare in the city's oldest gallery (founded in 1962): paintings by Mark Tobey, William Ivey, Morris Graves, Paul Horiuchi, and a varying selection of midcareer artists. *Tues–Sat; info@woodsidebrasethgallery.com; www.woodsidebraseth gallery.com; map:J4*

Gardens

Here's the upside to all of that rain that falls on the Pacific Northwest: the region ranks among the world's best places for gardening. The **SEATTLE P-PATCH PROGRAM** (206/684-0264), a community gardening program begun in 1973, is one of the largest in the country, with 38 sites throughout Seattle. All P-Patch sites are organic and provide gardening space for families and individuals throughout the city. And downtown rooftops and terraces are green with gardens. **FREEWAY PARK** (6th Ave and Seneca St) drapes the midcity interchanges with verdant curtains of ivy, the incessant roar of the traffic obscured by whispering stands of bamboo. The University of Washington campus is rich with trees; pick up the **BROCKMAN MEMORIAL TREE TOUR** pamphlet for a small fee at the bus shelter across from Anderson Hall (Stevens Wy). **VOLUNTEER PARK** (1400 E Prospect St) on Capitol Hill boasts magnificent specimen trees and a splendid Victorian conservatory overflowing with flowers. The Washington Park Arboretum (2300 Arboretum Dr E) offers more than 200 acres of wandering trails.

BELLEVUE BOTANICAL GARDEN / 12001 Main St, Bellevue; 425/452-2750 The botanical garden, which sits on 36 acres within Wilburton Hill Park, contains several smaller display gardens. The Waterwise Garden features descriptive signage detailing techniques to conserve water; spe-cially selected plants are well labeled to provide ideas for the home gardener. The Alpine Garden boasts a generous display of flora found in rocky alpine settings (visitors are asked not to sit or climb on the rocks). The half-mile trail that rings the botanical garden winds past several other gardens, including the Yao Japanese Garden, a well-executed garden incorporating modern and traditional Japanese features. The trail continues on to the Perennial Border—a 20,000-square-foot mixed planting of perennials, bulbs, trees, shrubs, and grasses.

Its largest event, Garden d'Lights, is a holiday light festival that extends from late November through early January nightly. The Shorts Visitor Center, open 10am to 4pm daily, houses a gift shop and provides maps. Docents are available Saturday and Sunday, March through October, and group tours can be arranged by calling ahead (206/451-

3755). No pets, bicycles, or skateboards are allowed in the garden. Admission is free. *Every day; www.bellevuebotanical.org; map:HH3* &

BLOEDEL RESERVE / 7571 NE Dolphin Dr, Bainbridge Island; 206/842-7631 Since the late 1980s, this 150-acre Bainbridge Island estate has been open to the public on a limited basis. The manse, which overlooks Puget Sound, is now a visitors center where interpretive material is available to guide one's walk through the property. The parklike grounds contain a number of theme gardens, including a Japanese garden, and nature trails lead through native woods and wetlands. A small pond attracts birds in increasing numbers as its plantings mature. Not a place for a family picnic or a romp with the dog. Reservations for entrance are required (call well in advance during the busy spring months). Guided tours can be arranged for groups, and many of the trails are wheelchair accessible (the reserve has two sturdy wheelchairs available for public use; call ahead). Admission is $6 for adults; $4 for seniors, students, and children 5–12; free for children under 5. *Wed–Sun; www.bloedelreserve.org* &

CARL S. ENGLISH JR. BOTANICAL GARDENS / 3015 NW 54th St, Ballard; 206/789-2622, ext 212 One of the region's great horticulturists, Carl English made Seattle a horticultural hotspot in the last century through his plant- and seed-collecting efforts. Here at Hiram M. Chittenden Locks, one can explore 7 acres of gardens containing more than 500 species of plants, including those that made up English's personal arboretum. The English gardens are worth a visit even in winter, when the tapestry of bark and berry and the perfume of winter-flowering plants brighten the grayest day. In summer, the Seattle Fuchsia Society's display garden enlivens the spacious lawns, where one can picnic and watch the boats make their way through the lock systems that connect Lake Washington to Puget Sound. A summer band concert series and special theme family events, such as Scandinavian Day, provide further entertainment on the weekends. Guided tours of the locks, fish ladder, and garden are held daily in summer (June 1 through September 30) and on weekends during the rest of the year; special in-depth tours can be arranged. (See also Hiram M. Chittenden Locks under Top 25 Attractions in this chapter.) Admission is free. *Every day; www.nps.usace.army.mil/opdiv/lwsc/garden.htm; map:FF9*

KUBOTA GARDENS / 55th Ave S at Renton Ave S, Rainier Beach; 206/725-5060 This Japanese garden tucked away in the Rainier Beach neighborhood at the south end of the Rainier Valley is a surprising oasis, home to such exotics as dragon trees. The large area encompasses many styles, from traditional Japanese garden to expansive lawns perfect for picnicking. The grounds are laced with winding paths that open onto ethereal views framing the many artfully trained pines and pruned plantings. A number of benches provide places for quiet contemplation. The north-central area of the garden is the site of the Necklace of Ponds, a network of waterfalls and ponds with a recirculating water system. Admission is free, and free tours are available on the last Saturday and Sunday of each month at 10am, starting in the parking lot; tours can also be arranged at any time for groups of eight or more. The Kubota Gardens Foundation holds plant sales in May and September, which are open to the public. *Every day; map:MM4*

PACIFIC RIM BONSAI COLLECTION / Weyerhaeuser Wy S, Federal Way; 253/924-5206 The corporate headquarters of the Weyerhaeuser Company, America's biggest timber business, also houses a pair of significant plant collections, both open to the public (see also next listing). Frequently changing exhibits showcase the diminutive gems of the bonsai collection, including a 1,000-year-old dwarf Sierra juniper. On alternate Sundays at 1pm, mid-April to mid-October, professional bonsai artists demonstrate pruning, propagation, and caretaking techniques. Basic bonsai care lectures are offered the second Saturday of the month, June through September. Tours are Sunday at noon or by appointment. Admission is free. *Sat–Wed (June–Feb), Fri–Wed (Mar–May); www. weyerhaeuser.com/bonsai* &

RHODODENDRON SPECIES BOTANICAL GARDEN / Weyerhaeuser Wy S, Federal Way; 253/661-9377 The Rhododendron Species Foundation's plantings encompass the largest, most comprehensive collection of rhododendron species and hybrids in the world. This is as much a preserve as a garden—more than 60 of the 500-plus species growing here on 22 acres at the Weyerhaeuser Company's corporate headquarters are endangered in the wild. A pair of study gardens are open throughout the year, so visitors can observe the rhododendron family's changing beauties through the seasons; though most are spring bloomers, others peak in winter or in summer, and many deciduous species take on magnificent fall foliage color. The garden has a gift shop and a plant sale pavilion. This is not a garden for picnicking or pets. Admission March through October is $3.50 for adults; $2.50 per person for students, seniors, and tour groups; free to children under 12 and school groups. Free to all November through February. *Sat–Wed (June–Feb), Fri–Wed (Mar–May); rsf@halcyon.com; www.rhodygarden.org/index.html* &

SEATTLE TILTH DEMONSTRATION GARDENS / 4649 Sunnyside Ave N, Wallingford; 206/633-0451 Urban gardeners find a world of practical assistance at the Tilth gardens on the grounds of Wallingford's Good Shepherd Center. Self-guided instructional walks lead visitors through the gardens and an impressive array of composting units. Travel at your own pace, absorbing information from the explanatory signs provided at each step. The thriving gardens are tended organically and are kept healthy through natural pest controls and environmentally sound horticultural practices. Edible landscaping is a specialty here, but many of the 1,200 plants grown are also ornamental (including edible flowers). This midcity oasis of living greenery serves everyone from raw beginners interested in learning how to prepare soil and sow carrots to advanced gardeners who trade heritage vegetable seeds or rare border plants. The Children's Garden, east of the demonstration gardens, lets young green thumbs practice organic and sustainable gardening too. The west end of the garden houses the Good Shepherd P-Patch. Numerous workshops and classes are offered. Tilth activities also include a spring plant sale at the end of April. Admission is free. *Every day; www.seattletilth.org; map:FF7* &

UNIVERSITY OF WASHINGTON MEDICINAL HERB GARDEN / Stevens Wy at Garfield Ln, University District; 206/543-1126 First established in 1911 by the UW School of Pharmacy on a single acre, the Medicinal Herb Garden currently occupies a little more than 2 acres on the University of Washington campus and is reportedly the largest such garden in the Western Hemisphere. It serves as an accurate specimen garden for botanists, herbalists, medics, and gardeners. (It is not meant to provide medical information, however, and none is posted.) The garden displays more than 600 species and is divided into seven areas running west to east. A centrally located office displays a map of the garden and gives descriptions of each "room." Admission is free, and free tours are available the second Sunday of every month at noon, May through October. In-depth tours can be arranged by appointment for groups of 10 or more for a fee of $5 per person. The garden is located across from the Botany Building and extends east to Rainier Vista. *Every day; map:FF6* &

WOODLAND PARK ROSE GARDEN / 5500 Phinney Ave N, Green Lake; 206/684-4863 Seattle's premier rose garden offers gardeners a chance to evaluate the regional performance of several hundred kinds of roses. Two acres of permanent plantings hold some 5,000 shrubs, both old-fashioned varieties and modern hybrids. Newest of all are the unnamed roses grown each year in the Seattle Rose Society's trial beds. Here likely candidates are tested for two years; the best of the bunch will become All-America Rose Selections. The Seattle Rose Society offers rose care and pruning demonstrations in the appropriate seasons (call the garden for information). Admission is free. *Every day; www.zoo.org/VirtualTour/ rose_garden.htm; map:EE7* &

Parks and Beaches

At last count there were 397 parks and playgrounds in the city of Seattle alone; the following are some of the best. See also Top 25 Attractions and neighborhood write-ups in this chapter for more information.

ALKI BEACH / Along Alki Ave SW from Duwamish Head to 63rd Ave SW, West Seattle; 206/684-4075 This 2½-mile strip of West Seattle beach is the spot where, in 1851, Seattle's original white settlers established their first homesteads. Now the beach has many faces, depending on the season. It's cool and peaceful in the fall, stormy in winter. But the summer months are when this sandy strand really becomes active, with volleyballers demonstrating their spiking prowess, picnickers vying for space at public tables, and young women sashaying about in bikinis that rarely fail to make a splash with teenaged male gawkers.

A private natatorium (indoor swimming pool) was installed here in 1905. And, in 1907, famed German carousel maker Charles I. D. Looff (creator of Coney Island's first carousel) built Luna Park, a 10-acre amusement center, on Duwamish Head at the north end of this strip. The park and its thrill rides are long gone, but you can walk, jog, bike, or skate along the paved path that runs beside the waterfront to find a miniature **STATUE OF LIBERTY** (61st Ave SW and Alki Ave SW), erected by the Boy Scouts in 1952, as well as the Coast Guard's automated and tourable **ALKI POINT LIGHTHOUSE** (3201 Alki Ave SW) at the tip of the point. The scenic extension of Alki Beach continues southward along Beach Drive SW past windswept **ME-KWA-MOOKS PARK** and on to Lincoln Park (see listing below). Views over the Sound are especially good from Duwamish Head and the lighthouse.

BRIDLE TRAILS STATE PARK / 116th Ave NE and NE 53rd St, Kirkland; 425/455-7010, 425/828-1218, or 800/233-0321 general information, 360/902-8500 state Parks Department headquarters in Olympia As its name suggests, this 480-acre park is a densely wooded equestrian paradise laced with horse trails (one links up with Marymoor Park) and even an exercise ring. Though you may feel like an alien if you come to do anything but ride (even the private homes in the area all seem to have stables), the park also features picnic sites. Warning: The overgrowth is so dense that it's easy to get lost on the trails; also, for obvious reasons, watch where you step. *Map:FF2*

CAMP LONG / 5200 35th Ave SW, West Seattle; 206/684-7434 West Seattle's Camp Long, run by the Seattle Parks and Recreation Department, has a variety of broader functions: a meeting/conference facility (a lodge holds 75 people in its upper room and 35 in the basement), an in-city outdoor experience for family or group use (10 rustic bunk-bed-equipped cabins sleep up to 12 people at $30 a cabin—make reservations at least two weeks in advance), and simply a 56-acre nature preserve. The park also offers interpretive programs, perfect for school or Scout groups, and family-oriented nature programs on weekends. The lodge and cabins feature 1930s-style log architecture. Climbers can sharpen their skills on a climbing rock and a simulated glacier face. *Map:JJ8*

CARKEEK PARK / NW Carkeek Rd and 9th Ave NW, Crown Hill; 206/684-4075 Carkeek Park is 186 acres of wilderness in the city's northwest corner. Forest paths wind from the parking lots and two reservable picnic areas (206/684-4081) to a footbridge spanning the railroad tracks, and then down a staircase to the broad beach north of Shilshole Bay. (Use caution around the tracks; trains run frequently through the park, and you may not hear them clearly.) Grassy meadows (great for kite flying), picnic shelters, and pretty, meandering Pipers Creek are other good reasons to relax here. *Map:DD8*

CHISM BEACH PARK / 1175 96th Ave SE, Bellevue; 425/452-6885 One of Bellevue's largest and oldest waterfront parks, Chism sits along the handsome residential stretch south of Meydenbauer Bay. There are docks and diving boards for swimmers, picnic areas, a playground, and a large parking area above the beach. *Map:HH4*

DISCOVERY PARK / 3801 W Government Wy, Magnolia; 206/684-4075 Formerly the site of Seattle's Fort Lawton Army base, this densely foliated Magnolia wilderness has been allowed to revert to its pre-metropolitan natural order. At 513 acres, it is full of variety and even a little mystery—in 1982 a cougar was discovered in the park. Self-guided interpretive nature loops and short trails wind through thick forests, along dramatic sea cliffs (where powerful updrafts make for excellent kite flying), and across meadows of waving grasses. The old barracks, houses, and training field are the few vestiges of the Army's presence. Discover the park's flora and fauna yourself, or take advantage of the scheduled walks and nature workshops conducted by park naturalists. On weekends, the park offers free guided walks and, in spring and fall, bird tours—call ahead to check the schedule, or stop by the visitors center in the east parking lot, near the Government Way entrance (206/386-4236). Groups can also arrange their own guided walks. Check the tall trees frequently; there's often a bald eagle in residence.

Two well-equipped kids' playgrounds are here, along with picnic areas, playfields, tennis and basketball courts, and a rigorous fitness trail. The network of trails is a favorite among runners; the 2.8-mile Loop Trail circles the park, passing through forests, meadows, and sand dunes. **DAYBREAK STAR CULTURAL ARTS CENTER** (206/285-4425) sponsors Native American activities and gallery exhibits of contemporary Indian art in the

Sacred Circle Gallery (see Galleries in this chapter). **WEST POINT LIGHT-HOUSE**, built in 1881, is the oldest lighthouse in the Seattle area. *Map:FF9*

FAY-BAINBRIDGE STATE PARK / 15446 Sunrise Dr NE, Bainbridge Island; 206/842-3931 or 800/233-0321 general information, 360/902-8500 state Parks Department headquarters in Olympia, 800/452-5687 camping reservations About a 15-minute drive from the Winslow ferry dock on Bainbridge Island, Fay-Bainbridge is a smallish (17-acre) park known for its camping areas and views of Mount Rainier and Seattle. The log-strewn beach has pits for fires; other features include a boat launch, horseshoe pits, and two kitchen shelters. It's a popular stop for cyclists on their way around the hilly isle.

GAS WORKS PARK / N Northlake Wy and Meridian Ave N, Wallingford; 206/684-4075 What do you do when the piece of property with the grandest skyline and lakeside view in the city is dominated by a greasy old coal-gasification plant? You turn it into a park, of course. Wallingford's Gas Works Park represents urban reclamation at its finest. A quarter-century after the Seattle Gas Company plant shut down here in 1956, landscape architect Richard Haag re-created the industrial eyesore as one of Seattle's most delightful greenswards, with a high grassy knoll for kite flying, a large picnic shelter with reservable space (206/684-4081), a wonderful play barn, and a multitude of front-row spots from which to watch sailboats bounce around on Lake Union. Climb the grassy knoll to enjoy a huge mosaic **SUNDIAL** (created by artist Charles Greening) and a view of the downtown towers just 2 miles south. The threat of lurking pollutants has led to periodic soil cleansings, but risks are few, provided you don't eat the dirt. (Parents with toddlers, beware.) Cutting east from Gas Works is the **BURKE-GILMAN TRAIL,** a wonderful 12½-mile biking and jogging path that winds clear up to Lake Washington's northern end. *Map:FF7*

GOLDEN GARDENS PARK / North end of Seaview Ave NW, Ballard; 206/684-4075 A breezy, sandy beach, nearby boat ramp, beach fire pits, and the pretty—but cold—waters of Shilshole Bay are Golden Gardens' biggest lures, although fully half of the park's 88 acres lie to the east of the railroad tracks along the wooded, trail-laced hillside. The marina here is home to a small village of sailboats. *Map:EE9*

HING HAY PARK / S King St and Maynard Ave S, Chinatown/International District; 206/684-4075 Hing Hay Park (the Chinese words translate as "pleasurable gathering") is a meeting and congregating place for the International District's large Asian community. From the adjacent Bush Hotel, an enormous multicolored mural of a dragon presides over the park and the ornate grand pavilion from Taipei. A great place to get a feel for the rhythms of I.D. life. *Map:Q6*

KIRKLAND WATERFRONT / Along Lake Washington Blvd, Kirkland; 425/828-1218 A string of parks, from Houghton Beach to Marina Park at Moss Bay, line the shore of Kirkland's beautiful Lake Washington Boulevard. Kids feed the ducks and wade (only Houghton Beach and Waverly Beach have lifeguards); their parents sunbathe and watch the runners lope by. This is as close to Santa Cruz as the Northwest gets. *Map:DD4*

LAKE SAMMAMISH STATE PARK / 20606 SE 56th St, Issaquah; 425/455-7010, 425/837-3300, or 800/233-0321 general information, 360/902-8500 state Parks Department headquarters in Olympia, 800/452-5687 camping reservations The sprawling beach is the main attraction of this state park at the south end of Lake Sammamish just off Interstate 90. Shady picnic areas, grassy playfields, and volleyball courts are excellent secondary draws. Large groups must reserve day-use areas—the place can be overrun in summer. Issaquah Creek, fine for fishing, runs through the park's wooded area.

LAKE WASHINGTON PARKS / From E Madison St and 43rd Ave E, Madison Park, to 5800 Lake Washington Blvd S, Rainier Valley; 206/684-4075 This string of grassy beachfronts acts as a collective back-yard for several of the neighborhoods that slope toward Lake Washington's western shore. Bicycle Saturdays and Sundays take place in the summer, when the route from Colman Park to Seward Park is closed to cars from 10am to 6pm. **MADISON PARK** (E Madison St and 43rd Ave E), is a genteel neighborhood park, with a roped-in swimming area and tennis courts. If you head west on E Madison Street and turn left onto Lake Washington Boulevard, you'll wind down to meet the beach again, this time at **MADRONA PARK** (Lake Washington Blvd and Madrona Dr), a grassy strip with a swimming beach, picnic tables, a (summer-only) food concession, and a dance studio. Farther south is **LESCHI PARK** (Lakeside Ave S and Leschi Pl), a handsomely manicured retreat that occupies the hillside across the boulevard. It offers great views of the Leschi Marina and the dazzling spinnakers of sailboats, as well as a play area for kids. Another greenbelt, **COLMAN PARK** (36th Ave S and Lakeside Ave S), also with a play area, marks the start of the seamless lakefront strip that includes **MOUNT BAKER PARK** (Lake Park Dr S and Lake Washington Blvd S), a gently sloping, tree-lined ravine; the hydroplane racing mecca—once a marshy slough, now a manicured park and spectator beach with boat launches—called **STAN SAYRES MEMORIAL PARK** (3800 Lake Washington Blvd S); and the lonely wilderness peninsula of **SEWARD PARK** (5800 Lake Washington Blvd S; see listing below). *Map:GG5–JJ5*

LINCOLN PARK / Fauntleroy Ave SW and SW Webster St, West Seattle; 206/684-4075 Lincoln Park, a 130-acre jewel perched on a pointed bluff in West Seattle, offers a network of walking and biking paths amid grassy forests, reservable picnic shelters (206/684-4081), recreational activities from horseshoes to football to tennis, and expansive views of the Olympic Mountains from seawalls and rocky beaches. There are tide pools to be inspected and beaches to roam, and kids delight in the playground equipment. Don't miss the (heated) outdoor saltwater **COLMAN POOL** (summer only), which began as a tide-fed swimming hole. *Map:LL9*

LUTHER BURBANK PARK / 2040 84th Ave SE, Mercer Island; 206/236-3545 Occupying a good chunk of the northern tip of Mercer Island, Luther Burbank Park is the Eastside's favorite family park. There are picnic areas, barbecue grills, a swimming area, nicely maintained tennis courts, an outdoor amphitheater for summer concerts, a first-rate playground, several playing fields, docks for boat tie-ups (the haunt of sun-worshiping teens in summer), and green meadows that tumble down to the shore. *Map:II4*

WARREN G. MAGNUSON PARK / Sand Point Wy NE and NE 65th St, Sand Point; 206/684-4075 This 194-acre park fronts Lake Washington just southeast of now-closed Sand Point Naval Station, with a mile of shoreline, a boat launch, a playing field, and six tennis courts. The Burke-Gilman Trail winds past Magnuson Park, linking it to Ballard and Bothell. Just north of the park is the National Oceanic and Atmospheric Administration (NOAA), where you'll find a series of unique artworks along the beach. One sculpture, the *Sound Garden,* is fitted with flutelike aluminum tubes that create eerie music when the wind blows. The site is open every day from dawn to dusk and is a hauntingly wonderful spot to sit on a blue whale bench, listening to the wailing wind chimes and watching the sun come up over Lake Washington. *Map:EE5*

MYRTLE EDWARDS PARK / Alaskan Wy between Bay St and W Thomas St, Waterfront; 206/684-4075 Myrtle Edwards and adjacent Elliott Bay Park provide a front lawn to the northern section of downtown. This breezy and refreshing strip is a great noontime getaway for jogging (the two parks combined form a 1.25-mile trail), picnicking on benches that face Puget Sound, or just strolling. Parking at the Pier 70 lot just south of Myrtle Edwards is at a premium, but the Waterfront Streetcar stops nearby. *Map:B9*

NEWCASTLE BEACH PARK / 4400 Lake Washington Blvd S, Bellevue; 425/452-6885 This Bellevue park takes full advantage of its waterfront location with a fishing dock, swimming area, and bathhouse facility (complete with outdoor showers). Walking paths—including a three-quarter-mile loop—weave throughout the 28 acres, and a wildlife area offers the chance to see animals and birds in their natural habitat. *Map:JJ3*

RAVENNA PARK / 20th Ave NE and NE 58th St, Ravenna/University District; 206/684-4075 This steep woodland ravine strung between residential districts north of the University District is a lush sylvan antidote to the surrounding city. At the west end is **COWEN PARK** (University Wy NE and NE Ravenna Blvd), with tennis courts and play and picnic areas. Trails along burbling Ravenna Creek lead to the eastern end of the park in the Ravenna neighborhood and more picnic areas, tennis courts, and playing fields, plus a wading pool. The whole expanse is a favorite haunt of runners, as is Ravenna Boulevard, a tree-lined thoroughfare that defines the park's southern flank and leads west to Green Lake. *Map:EE6*

SCHMITZ PARK / SW Stevens St and Admiral Wy SW, West Seattle; 206/684-4075 Just south of West Seattle's Alki Beach is this 53-acre nature preserve, full of raw trails through thickly wooded terrain. The largest western red cedars and hemlocks here are likely to be about 800 years old—seedlings back when Richard the Lionhearted was leading his troops on the Third Crusade. No playgrounds, picnic areas, or other park amenities. *Map:II9*

SEWARD PARK / Lake Washington Blvd S and S Juneau St, Rainier Valley; 206/684-4075 This majestic wilderness, occupying a 277-acre knob of land in southeast Seattle, gives modern city dwellers an idea of what this area must have looked like centuries ago. At times the park is imbued with a primal sense of permanence, especially on misty winter days when the quiet of a solitary walk through old-growth Douglas fir forest is broken only by the cries of a few birds. But at other times—hot summer Sundays, for instance—Seward turns into a frenzy of music and barbecues. You can drive the short loop road to get acquainted with the park, past the bathhouse and beach facilities; **SEWARD PARK ART STUDIO** (206/722-6342), which offers classes in the arts; some of the six reservable picnic shelters (206/684-4081); and some of the trailheads, which lead to the fish hatchery and the outdoor amphitheater, and into the forest preserve. Cyclists and runners can make an even better loop on the scenic 2.5-mile lakeside trail encircling the peninsula. *Map:JJ5*

VICTOR STEINBRUECK PARK / Western Ave and Virginia St, Pike Place Market; 206/684-4075 Pike Place Market's greatest supporter and friend is the namesake of this slice of green at the north end of the market. With the Alaskan Way Viaduct right below, the park can be quite noisy during peak traffic hours. It also tends to be a favorite hangout for street people. Despite those caveats, the park's grassy slopes and tables make a fine place for a market picnic, and the view of blue Elliott Bay and ferry traffic is refreshing. *Map:H8*

WATERFALL GARDEN / 2nd Ave S and S Main St, Pioneer Square; 206/624-6096 How many downtowns can boast a park with a 22-foot crashing waterfall, even an artificial one? The waterfall in this tiny Pioneer Square park was built to honor the United Parcel Service, which started at this location in 1907. It does crash (this is no place for quiet conversation), and the benches fill up by noon on weekdays, but the park (on the northwest corner of this intersection) makes for a marvelous little nature fix in the middle of a busy urban day. *Map:O8*

WATERFRONT PARK / Pier 57 to Pier 61 on Alaskan Wy, Waterfront; 206/684-4075 A park that spans three piers between the Seattle Aquarium and Pier 57 provides a break from the bustling activity of the rest of the waterfront. The park contains a tree-encircled courtyard, raised platforms with telescopes for a view of Elliott Bay and islands, plenty of benches, and—strange for a park in this town—nary a blade of grass. *Map:J9*

WOODLAND PARK / 5200 Green Lake Wy N, Green Lake; 206/684-4075 This 188-acre park abuts Green Lake on one side and has busy Aurora Avenue running through the middle. On the west side are the rose garden (see listing above) and Woodland Park Zoo (see Top 25 Attractions in this chapter). On the east are playfields, picnic areas, lawn bowling, and tennis courts. *Map:EE7*

Organized Tours

Strolling or busing through a city on your own will introduce you to the most obvious sights. But to get beneath the surface, to learn how the place got to be the way it is today, nothing beats a tour. Clearly fun for visitors, a tour is also a great chance for locals to learn something new about their hometown. Tours can be as informational as one of the **SEATTLE ARCHITECTURAL FOUNDATION'S VIEWPOINTS TOURS** (206/667-9186), which examine the mix of art and architecture throughout the city; as colorful as Jeri Callahan's specially tailored **DISCOVER HOUSEBOATING** (206/322-9157) tours-by-water of Lake Union's quirky houseboat neighborhoods; or as delicious as the **TASTE OF THE NORTHWEST CHEF'S TOUR** (206/340-6710), which—for just $65—lets you cruise the stalls and shops of Pike Place Market with chef Tim Kelley from the Alexis Hotel's Painted Table (see review in the Restaurants chapter), then sit down to a Northwest-inspired lunch (complete with Northwest wines) at the arty hotel restaurant. Speaking of arty, every other year in late April/early May, the **SEATTLE ART MUSEUM** (206/654-3198) sponsors a walk through the lofts and studios of some of the city's artists. When selecting your tour of the city, call ahead; some excursions are by reservation only.

AIR TOURS

KENMORE AIR / 950 Westlake Ave N, South Lake Union; 6321 NE 175th St, Kenmore; 425/486-1257 or 800/543-9595 The largest seaplane operator in the area, Kenmore Air has a fleet of 20 planes that make scheduled and charter flights around Puget Sound and to Victoria, British Columbia, from seaports on Lake Union and north Lake Washington. A one-way passage to the San Juan Islands is $85 per person on a scheduled flight ($96 May 1–June 15; $99 June 16–Sept 4), or $395 for a 1-hour charter for one to three people. A 2-hour round-trip scenic flyover of the San Juans is $50 per person; or sign up for a spring or summer daytrip package (including lunch and ground transportation on San Juan Island) for $159. Round-trip all-day excursions to Victoria are $168 per person. The company also offers a 20-minute city tour (which originates from the Lake Washington location only) for $198 for three passengers, $235 for six. Be sure to call ahead; several tours are available on a day-of-flight basis only, and advance reservations are required for other trips. *www.kenmoreair.com; map:GG7, BB5*

SEATTLE SEAPLANES / 1325 Fairview Ave E, Eastlake; 206/329-9638 or 800/637-5553 Seattle Seaplanes does its main business in charters to Canadian fishing camps, but also offers a 20-minute exhaustive airborne tour of Seattle (University of Washington, Lake Washington, the waterfront, Magnolia, the Locks, Shilshole, Green Lake, and back to Lake Union) for $57.50 per person. Consider taking a flight to and from majestic Mount Rainier ($365 for one to four passengers, $410 for five), Mount St. Helens ($730 for one to four passengers), or the San Juan Islands ($510 for one to four passengers). Call for reservations. *info@seattleseaplanes.com; www.seattleseaplanes.com; map:E1*

SOUND FLIGHT / 243 W Perimeter Rd, Renton; 425/255-6500 Up to 20 passengers can arrange their own pilot-narrated floatplane tours of Seattle, Mount Rainier, the San Juan Islands, Mount St. Helens, or the North Cascades. Prices (from $99 to $325 per person) depend on the number of people and extent of the tour. Based at Renton Municipal Airport. *info@soundflight.com; www.soundflight.com; map:MM4*

BOAT TOURS

Given Seattle's watery surroundings, it's only natural that waterborne travel is one of the best ways to get a look around the Puget Sound area. Besides customizing your own tour via one of 29 **WASHINGTON STATE FERRIES** (206/464-6400; www.wsdot.wa.gov/ferries)—seven of which leave from downtown's Colman Dock a total of 71 times daily en route to Bainbridge Island, Bremerton, or Vashon Island—there's a boatload of boat tours available. (See also the Lay of the City chapter.)

SEATTLE MICROBREWERIES

Although coffee has become synonymous with Seattle (no wonder the pace of life here seems to have sped up significantly over the last decade), many locals would prefer that the city's reputation rise and fall on the foam . . . er, fame of its beers. Not the colorless, characterless, watery brews produced in the Midwest, but noble ales, refreshing lagers, and fortifying porters that burst with flavor—the very sort produced by Seattle's increasing number of smaller craft breweries.

Once the region's most famous microbrewer, **REDHOOK** can no longer claim that title, as it currently sells more than 100,000 barrels annually—well in excess of the 15,000-barrel limit that defines the term "microbrewery." The company, founded in 1981, now produces its beers—including Ballard Bitter, Redhook ESB, and Winterhook—at breweries in Woodinville and Portsmouth, New Hampshire, and sells them nationwide. Here's a sampling of local beermeisters and tour info.

Hale's Ales Brewery (4301 Leary Wy NW, Ballard; 206/782-0737) Sit down for a glass of beer or a full meal at the comfortable pub inside this brewery, or take a free tour of the facility, which features traditional, English-style open fermenters. Open seven days a week; tours upon request.

Mac & Jack's Brewery (17824 NE 65th St, Ste B110, Redmond; 425/558-9697) The people responsible for making the savory Mac & Jack's African Amber offer free tours of their 4,000-square-foot Eastside facility on Saturday, 11am and 2pm.

Maritime Pacific Brewing Co. (1514 NW Leary Wy, Ballard; 206/782-6181) The makers of the popular Flagship Red Ale, the dark, delectable Nightwatch, and other specialty brews offer tours every Saturday in the early afternoon. There's a tap room too, called the Jolly Roger.

Pike Brewing Co. (1432 Western Ave, Pike Place Market; 206/622-3373) The makers of the celebrated Pike Place Ale have a pleasant brewing facility and pub located near the edge of Pike Place Market. Tours are available by reservation.

Pyramid Breweries (1201 1st Ave S, SoDo; 206/682-3377) Formerly Hart Brewing, this expansive pub and brewing operation near Safeco Field offers free tours and tastings of the popular Pyramid ales Monday through Friday at 2pm and 4pm and on weekends at 1, 2, and 4pm. A mere $2 buys you a souvenir glass.

Redhook Ale Brewery Redhook has two Puget Sound–area breweries: **Redhook Ale Brewery and Trolleyman Pub** (3400 Phinney Ave N, Fremont; 206/548-8000) and **Redhook Ale Brewery and Forecasters Public House** (14300 NE 145th St, Woodinville; 425/483-3232). Tours are offered daily at the Woodinville brewery only, on the hour, from noon to 5pm. Cost is $1 per person, and includes beer samples and a souvenir glass. —Jo Brown

ARGOSY CRUISES / Piers 54, 55, and 57, Waterfront; 1200 Westlake Ave N, South Lake Union; 206/623-1445 or 800/642-7816 Scheduled tours departing from Lake Union include daily, year-round, 1-hour narrated cruises along the Seattle waterfront and Elliott Bay ($16); 2½-hour tours through the Hiram M. Chittenden Locks and Lake Washington Ship Canal ($30); and a 2-hour Lake Washington excursion ($26), featuring peeks at the pricey palaces surrounding the lake—including the 40,000-square-foot Xanadu that Microsoft CEO Bill Gates has erected. Saltwater sportfishing trips on Puget Sound waters are available year-round (for about $80). On the Eastside, Argosy offers seasonal 1½-hour cruises around Lake Washington ($26) that depart from the Kirkland City Dock. Charters for private parties or special events are available for groups of 10 to 400. *sales@argosycruises.org; www.argosycruises.com; map:L9–K9, A1*

EMERALD CITY CHARTERS (LET'S GO SAILING) / Pier 56, Waterfront; 206/624-3931 A 70-foot custom-built former racing sloop, the *Obsession* cuts through Elliott Bay waters May 1 to October 15. Star of the movie *Masquerade* (along with Rob Lowe and Meg Tilly), the yacht can comfortably carry up to 49 passengers, who should count on packing their own meals for the scheduled 1½-hour trips that leave from the north side of the pier at 11am, 1:30pm, and 4pm daily. Costs for day cruises are $23 for adults, $20 for seniors, $18 for children 12 and under. A 2½-hour sunset sail leaves between 6 and 7pm daily and costs $35 for adults, $32 for seniors, and $28 for children 12 and under. Private charters are also available year-round. Call to check on sailing times and availability. *sailingseattle@qwest.net; map:K9*

MOSQUITO FLEET SAN JUAN ORCA CRUISES / 1724 W Marine View Dr, Everett; Cap Sante Marina, Float D, Space 0, Anacortes; 425/252-6800 or 800/325-ORCA Whale-watching cruises leave daily from Everett and Anacortes June through September, and on a limited basis during April, May, September, and October. The 9½-hour cruises are narrated by a naturalist, who lectures on orcas (and identifies their pods) as well as on other marine life and San Juan maritime history. Depending on the time of year, tickets range from $29.50 to $79. Call for reservations. *info@whalewatching.com; www.whalewatching.com*

RIDE THE DUCKS OF SEATTLE / 5th Ave N and Broad St, Seattle Center; 206/441-DUCK or 800/817-1116 for reservations See the city's sights by land and sea aboard amphibious vehicles (aka "ducks"). The refurbished World War II landing craft are piloted by Coast Guard–certified sea captains who motor visitors about the streets of downtown, Pioneer Square, and Fremont before launching into the waters of Lake Union for tours past Seattle's houseboats and glass artist Dale Chihuly's studio. The 90-minute rides are $20 for adults, $10 for kids 12 and under.

The ducks take off hourly throughout the year from the northeast corner of Fifth and Broad (across from the Space Needle). Drop by that same location for tickets, or call for reservations; private duck tours are also available. *info@seattleducktours.net; www.ridetheducksofseattle.com; map:C6*

SPIRIT OF PUGET SOUND CRUISES / 2819 Elliott Ave/Pier 70, Waterfront; 206/674-3500 reservations It's clear that these professionals have floating entertainment figured out. The 600-passenger luxury ship sails daily (depending on availability) for 2-hour lunch and 3-hour dinner tours of the Sound in a style akin to that of a deep-sea cruise liner: with a full-service restaurant, entertainment, and dancing. Lunch cruises run $30 to $35, dinner cruises $55 to $60. *www.spiritcruises.com; map:D9*

TILLICUM VILLAGE TOUR / Pier 55, Waterfront; 206/443-1244 A Northwest tourist staple, this 4-hour narrated voyage from downtown Seattle to nearby Blake Island (reputedly the birthplace of Seattle's namesake, Chief Sealth) has been operating for more than 35 years. The highlight of the hyped-up look at Northwest Indian culture is a salmon bake and a Native American dance ($50.25 per person). (Also accessible from Bremerton; see the Day Trips chapter.) *www.tillicumvillage.com; map:L9*

MOTOR TOURS

GRAY LINE OF SEATTLE / 4500 W Marginal Wy SW, West Seattle; 206/624-5813 This popular bus touring service offers several choice trips: Mount Rainier (summer only, $54 per person); the Boeing plant ($39 per person; see Top 25 Attractions in this chapter); the popular Seattle city tours ($39 per person for 7 hours or $27 per person for 3 hours); overnighters to Victoria, British Columbia, and more. Free pickup at several downtown hotels. *info@graylineofseattle.com; www.graylineof seattle.com; map:JJ8*

PRIVATE EYE ON SEATTLE MYSTERY AND MURDER TOUR / Windsor and Hatten Legal Investigations; 206/622-0590 Grizzled gumshoe Windsor Olson weaves his blood-red van in and out of some of Seattle's most notorious crime scenes—from the International District, site of the Wah Mee Club massacre, to downtown alleys such as one at Fifth Avenue S and S Jackson Street, where the 70-plus Olson reveals the mystery of the "unclaimed" head. Crime tours of downtown/Queen Anne and Capitol Hill/University District are both available. Be advised, these are not excursions for children or squeamish adults. Cost for the 1½-hour macabre adventure is $20 per person; group discounts are available. *jake13@foxinternet.com; www.privateeyetours.com*

SEATTLE TOURS / 206/768-1234 Ballard's Locks and downtown shops as well as Fremont, Alki Beach, the floating bridges, and more are on the itineraries for these 3-hour minicoach tours. Custom-designed coaches hold up to 20 people, and cost is $34.99 per person. Closed December 15 through January. *info@seattlecitytours.com; www.seattlecitytours.com*

SHOW ME SEATTLE / 206/633-CITY Colorfully decaled vans hit the usual Seattle hotspots—downtown, the Seattle Art Museum, the International District—and do drive-bys of the city's more distinctive neighborhoods, including Fremont, Green Lake, and Queen Anne. The *Sleepless in Seattle* houseboat on Lake Union is an oft-requested stop. Cost is $33 per person; reservations required. *www.showmeseattle.com*

WALKING TOURS

BILL SPEIDEL'S UNDERGROUND TOUR / 610 1st Ave, Downtown; 206/682-4646 Although the 2001 earthquake caused damage to the exterior of some Pioneer Square buildings, it didn't lead—as feared—to the closure of this popular attraction. These tours are mostly one story down—the level of the city before it was rebuilt after the Great Fire of June 6, 1889. (Poor drainage at the old, lower level made the higher streets imperative.) It's all pretty cornball, but you'll get a salty taste of the pioneers' eccentricities and some historical insights, with plenty of puns from the guides. The tours begin at Doc Maynard's Public House in Pioneer Square and run 1½ hours. Tour times vary seasonally. Cost is $9 for adults, $7 for seniors and students, $5 for children 7–12, free for kids under 7. *www.undergroundtour.com; map:N8*

CHINATOWN DISCOVERY / 425/885-3085 Humorous Seattle native Vi Mar conducts four walking tours of the Chinatown/International District, providing a historical and cultural perspective that, in some cases, comes with a meal. For instance, the Chinatown by Day tour features a six-course dim sum lunch; the nighttime tour is an eight-course affair. Reservations required. Rates for adults range from $12.95 to $38.95, and for children from $7.95 to $21.95. Group rates for 10 or more adults are available. *heking@juno.com; www.seattlechamber.com/chinatowntour*

SEATTLE WALKING TOUR / 425/885-3173 This 2-hour tour led by local author Duse McLean concentrates on the architecture and history of downtown. The $15 tours begin outside Westlake Center (400 Pine St) on Wednesday and Thursday at 5:30pm and Saturday at 10:30am, June through September. *dusem@aol.com; map:I6*

SEE SEATTLE WALKING TOURS / 425/226-7641 Catering to those with no time to waste finding Seattle's favorite sights on their own, Terry Seidler conducts several walking tours through Pike Place Market, the waterfront, Pioneer Square, and other downtown points of interest. Custom tours are available for groups, including mystery and scavenger hunts (perfect for parties or corporate groups). Typical cost is $10 to $15 per person. *walking@see-seattle.com; www.see-seattle.com*

SHOPPING

SHOPPING

Neighborhoods, Shopping Districts, and Malls

The Space Needle. Experience Music Project. The cash register. It's tough to say which of these is the most frequented tourist attraction in Seattle. Shopping has become as irresistible as cruising the waterfront. An abundance of retail options draws urbanites during the week, crowds of suburbanites on weekends, and hordes of visitors every day.

DOWNTOWN

Amid first-rate restaurants, cafes, and theaters, nearly every corner downtown sports an A-list retailer. **BANANA REPUBLIC**, located in the historic Coliseum movie theater building, dresses up the northeast corner of Fifth Avenue and Pike Street; **KENNETH COLE** is on the southeast corner of Sixth Avenue and Pike Street; the **WARNER BROS. STUDIO STORE** is on Fifth between Pike and Pine Streets; **NIKETOWN**, a three-story tabernacle of sneakers and sportswear, dominates the northeast corner of Sixth Avenue and Pike Street; its arch rival **ADIDAS** is just down the street on the corner of Fifth and Pike; the **ORIGINAL LEVI'S STORE** fits into the Meridian shopping/entertainment complex on Sixth between Pike and Pine; and the trendy clothing store **OLD NAVY** dropped anchor on the corner of Sixth and Pine, while its slightly more upscale sibling, **THE GAP**, is settling into gigantic new digs on the corner of Fifth and Pine. Along Fifth Avenue, **ESCADA**, **LOUIS VUITTON**, and the like share the street with **ANTHROPOLOGIE** and **URBAN OUTFITTERS**.

The biggest and brightest jewels in downtown's commercial crown are the side-by-side flagship **NORDSTROM** store and **PACIFIC PLACE** shopping center, which opened for business in 1998. Joined at the hip by a glass walkway that stretches over Sixth Avenue, they are an irresistible shop-till-you-drop combination.

THE BON MARCHÉ / 3rd Ave and Pine St, Downtown; 206/506-6000
The Bon's floor upon floor of departments almost seem an anachronism against the sleek bustle of high-end specialty stores downtown now. However, the venerable institution has been fulfilling shoppers' clothing and household needs in its present location for more than 100 years, and its annual hoisting of its 3,600-bulb Holiday Star signals the start of the holiday season. *Every day; map:I6*

CITY CENTRE / 1420 5th Ave, Downtown; 206/622-6465 (cinemas only)
Upscale clothier Barneys New York flaunts its wares on one side of this urban mall, with toy baron FAO Schwarz on the other. Ritzy retailers prevail here, from Italian handbag purveyor Furla to always appropriate

Ann Taylor. To sweeten the appeal there's the posh Palomino Euro-bistro and 1,100 underground parking spots. *Every day; www.shopcitycentre. com; map:J5*

NORDSTROM / 500 Pine St, Downtown; 206/628-2111 See Top 25 Attractions in the Exploring chapter.

PACIFIC PLACE / 600 Pine St, Downtown; 206/405-2655 If downtown Seattle is a shopping mecca, this is its most holy institution. Inside a 12,000-square-foot skylit atrium, Pacific Place shelters a wealth of retailers: Tiffany & Co., Cartier, J. Crew, Tommy Hilfiger, Ann Taylor, Barnes & Noble, Restoration Hardware, Pottery Barn, and Williams-Sonoma Grande Cuisine. To ease shopper headaches, the center has 1,200 surprisingly cheap underground parking spaces, several strength-sustaining restaurants, and a state-of-the-art 11-screen cinema, fashioned after a Northwest lodge, that caps the complex. *Every day; www.pacific placeseattle.com; map:J5*

RAINIER SQUARE / 1335 5th Ave, Downtown One of downtown's quieter malls, Rainier Square features a small but tasteful population of retailers, Barcelino and Eddie Bauer among them. *Every day; www. rainier-square.com; map:K6*

WESTLAKE CENTER / 400 Pine St, Downtown; 206/467-3044 Though this four-floor mall saw a mass exodus to nearby Pacific Place a few years ago, an influx of newcomers includes the sophisticated Galleries of Neiman Marcus, high-design gift store Chiasso, and others. Westlake offers the full range of top-of-the-line retailers, from the arty (Fireworks) to the aromatic (Aveda). An upper-level food court has more than 18 eateries. Boasting the city's largest lighted Christmas tree, Westlake is particularly appealing during the holidays. *Every day; map:I6*

HISTORIC DISTRICTS

Despite its primary renown as a tourist attraction, the **PIKE PLACE MARKET** (between Western and 1st Aves from Pike to Virginia Sts, Downtown; every day; map:J8–I8) is still a favorite among local residents and restaurants, who stock their pantries with the market's offerings. Arguably the most unusual shopping area in town, this is the spot for food—mainly fresh produce and seafood—and fun: the fish-throwing antics of the crew at **PIKE PLACE FISH** are a perennial crowd-pleaser. It's like a carnival every day here, with street performers competing for the attention of shoppers, who meander in and out of the market's labyrinthine passageways and arcades packed with vintage apparel, antiques, arts, and crafts. (See also Top 25 Attractions in the Exploring chapter.) Recent years have also brought an upscale overspill of shops, as the neighboring South Arcade (1st Ave between Pike and Union Sts, Downtown; map:J8) marches southward along First Avenue.

Another egress from the market is via an appealing lineup of retail along the **PIKE MARKET HILLCLIMB** (Pike St to Pier 59, Downtown; map:J8) toward the waterfront (Alaskan Wy from Pier 52/Columbia St to Pier 70/Broad St, Downtown; map:M8–D9). Here, during summer months, tourists outnumber the seagulls hanging about the piers, most of which have been converted into colorful emporiums that stock typical touristy items, but there are quirkier offerings. Alfred Hitchcock would be quite at home in Pier 54's **YE OLDE CURIOSITY SHOP**, which counts an authentic mummy among its bizarre decorations. The **BAY PAVILION** on Pier 57 has its own arcade, complete with a replica of a 1910 wooden carousel.

PIONEER SQUARE (between 1st and 2nd Aves, from Yesler Wy to S King St, Downtown; map:N8) is where Seattle got started in 1852; now the area boasts the Northwest's most prestigious concentration of art galleries and a dizzying proliferation of cafes, bars, and shops. The square combines upscale condominiums, office space, and retail in many of its elegantly restored brick buildings. You'll encounter a number of Oriental rug stores and good bookstores, including the **ELLIOTT BAY BOOK COMPANY**. (See also Top 25 Attractions in the Exploring chapter.)

NEIGHBORHOODS

The Ave (University Wy NE from NE 41st St to NE 50th St, University District; map:FF6), running just west of the University of Washington campus, features a concentration of book, record, and ice cream stores, plus some interesting boutiques and ethnic restaurants. Though the Ave's student/bohemian flavor is being erased by a combination of deadbeat culture, encroaching panhandlers, and advancing chain stores, the retail blocks still yield some good browsing and are slowly spreading north.

Once a sleepy shopping spot, **UNIVERSITY VILLAGE** (NE 45th St and 25th Ave NE, University District; 206/523-0622; every day; map:FF6), east down the 45th Street viaduct from the UW campus, has seen an explosion of new retail. Home to especially good gourmet and specialty food stores, the open-air shopping center, whose expansion began in 1995 with an Eddie Bauer branch and a gargantuan Barnes & Noble, has grown to include branches of Pottery Barn and Restoration Hardware.

Two neighboring districts also serve university folk with good shopping: **ROOSEVELT** (Roosevelt Wy NE from NE 55th St to NE 70th St; map:EE6), a strip offering stereo stores, vintage-clothing shops, and diverse restaurants; and **WALLINGFORD** (along N 45th St from Stone Wy N to Latona Ave NE; map:FF7). With a refurbished and converted school building, **WALLINGFORD CENTER** (1815 N 45th St, Wallingford; every day; map:FF7), as its showpiece, Wallingford caters to its constituents with funky gift shops and slightly "alternative" retail (an erotic bakery, for instance).

South of Portage Bay and the Lake Washington Ship Canal, head for CAPITOL HILL's Broadway Avenue (E Pine St to E Roy St; map:GG6), center of Seattle's punk universe and the best see-and-be-seen shopping scene in town. Vintage clothing, apparel appropriate for rock shows and art openings, espresso, and housewares dominate, as do restaurants. Five blocks east is the neighborhood commercial district of 15TH AVENUE E (E Denny Wy to E Mercer St, Capitol Hill; map:HH6), which embodies the homegrown, untrendy element of Capitol Hill's collective personality: mom-and-pop businesses, a health-food grocery, consignment shops, and several small bookstores. South of here, E Madison Street intersects 15th Avenue E on its way from downtown to MADISON PARK (along E Madison St from McGilvra Blvd E to 43rd Ave E; map:GG6). Here, the lakeside shopping/restaurant enclave reflects the family orientation and upward mobility of the neighborhood. Closer to downtown is MADISON VALLEY (along E Madison St from 23rd Ave to 32nd Ave E; map:GG6), a highly browsable retail pocket that attracts the landed gentry from the nearby Washington Park and Broadmoor residential districts.

Increasingly giving the Hill a run as the city's cool capital, BELL-TOWN (Western to 5th Ave, between Virginia St and Denny Wy, Down-town; map:G8–D8) has supper clubs that chummily mix with billiards halls and nightclubs. Retail offerings range from vintage clothing and record stores to ultramodern gift and home-furnishing shops. Being hip can be a transitory experience, however; businesses here have a habit of disappearing faster than Internet startups. And, much as in Pioneer Square and on Capitol Hill, among the retro retail, cafes, and condos you'll find panhandlers and the homeless.

To the north is QUEEN ANNE (map:GG8), a hill whose lower slopes around Queen Anne Avenue N and Mercer Street are studded with shops and restaurants. Seattleites are rediscovering the many good restaurants at the top of the hill, and new retail establishments are cropping up every-where. Past the northern slope of Queen Anne Hill and across the ship canal lies FREMONT (Fremont Ave N and N 34th St; map:FF7), a funky neighborhood known to its residents as the "Republic of Fremont" and noted for antique-and-kitsch stores, retro boutiques, and some of the city's better pubs. The neighborhood, like most Seattle environs, has seen more growth in recent years (thanks in part to Adobe's headquarters there) and higher-end eateries and stores are cropping up, as are new condos, to the chagrin of longtime residents who feel the neighborhood's gentrification is eroding its charm.

West of Fremont lies BALLARD (map:EE8). Although Ballard has been famous locally for its Scandinavian population and its excruciat-ingly slow drivers (not coincidentally, there's a large senior population), the arrival of the Bay Theaters cineplex cemented the notion of sleepy Ballard as an up-and-comer. Along cobblestoned Ballard Avenue NW, the neighborhood's old section, trendy boutiques have opened, drawing shoppers from other areas. And where shoppers go, retailers follow. The snowballing community of small upscale stores here is drawing some choice transplants from Fremont (including Second Ascent, the beloved used outdoor equipment shop formerly known as Second Bounce). Other important players in the turning of Ballard's new leaf include home accessory shop **LUCCA** (5332 Ballard Ave NW), handmade card shop **SOUVENIR** (5325 Ballard Ave NW), and Northwest chef Kathy Casey's retail store, **WHIM** (5130 and 5136 Ballard Ave NW).

Finally, Eastsiders in search of the neighborhood shopping experience head for **OLD BELLEVUE** (Main St at Bellevue Wy NE; map:HH3), where traditional shops on flower-lined streets cater to the carriage trade, or the **KIRKLAND WATERFRONT** (along Lake Washington Blvd NE from 2nd Ave S to Central Wy; map:EE4), a stretch of retail and art galleries hugging the shore of Moss Bay.

SUBURBAN MALLS

The Eastside invented shopping mall know-how, so it's not surprising that it's home to the standard-setter for the region: **BELLEVUE SQUARE**. Smaller Eastside malls include **KIRKLAND PARK PLACE** (exit 18 off I-405, Kirkland; 425/828-4468; every day; map:EE3), **FACTORIA MALL** (exit 10 off I-405, Bellevue; 425/641-8282; every day; map:II3), **TOTEM LAKE MALL** (124th St exit off I-405, Kirkland; every day; map:CC3), and **CROSSROADS SHOPPING CENTER** (NE 8th St and 156th Ave NE, Bellevue; 425/644-1111; every day; map:HH1). With its mix of retail, restaurants (24 international eateries), live music, a giant chessboard, and a 12-screen cinema, Crossroads earns its nickname of "the Eastside's living room."

Seattle's north end has **NORTHGATE**; its south-end, climate-controlled counterpart is **SOUTHCENTER** mall (off I-5 at Southcenter mall exit, Tukwila; 206/246-7400; every day; map:OO5). Just south of Southcenter, at the **PARKWAY SUPERCENTER** (17300 Southcenter Pkwy, Tukwila; every day; map:OO5), every store, from Old Navy to Shoe Pavilion, deals in discounted merchandise.

Other suburban shopping action can be found at the discount megamall **SUPERMALL OF THE GREAT NORTHWEST** (1101 Supermall Wy, Auburn; 253/833-9500; every day), at **SEA-TAC MALL** (off I-5 at 320th St exit, Federal Way; 253/839-6150; every day), and at **ALDERWOOD MALL** (off I-5 at Alderwood Mall exit, Lynnwood; 425/771-1211; every day).

BELLEVUE PLACE / 10500 NE 8th St, Bellevue; 425/453-5634 Just down the street from its fellow Kemper Freeman–designed mall, Bellevue Square, Bellevue Place boasts 20 high-end shops and a number of excellent restaurants, some of which occupy the dramatic glass-walled Wintergarden atrium. *Mon–Sat; map:HH3*

BELLEVUE SQUARE / NE 8th St and Bellevue Wy NE, Bellevue; 425/454-8096 Still the area's brightest shopping beacon, Bellevue Square recently expanded with an annex featuring home accessory bigshot Crate & Barrel, as well as Borders Books and several eateries. And, of course, you'll still find the Big Three department stores (Nordstrom, The Bon, and J. C. Penney), and an ever-expanding coterie of exceptionally high-quality shops ranging from FAO Schwarz and Pottery Barn to Guess? and Banana Republic. *Every day; information@bellevuesquare.com; www.bellevuesquare.com; map:HH3*

NORTHGATE MALL / N Northgate Wy and 1st Ave NE, Northgate; 206/362-4777 This is a no-frills shopping experience, but it had the distinction (or shame, depending on your opinion of malls) of being the first mall in the nation when it opened in 1950. Northgate (off I-5 at the Northgate exit) has the full complement of stores, including Nordstrom and The Bon Marché, as well as an excellent food court and newsstand. *Every day; map:DD7*

REDMOND TOWN CENTER / 16495 NE 74th St, Redmond; 425/867-0808 The newest mall in the area, Redmond Town Center (off SR 520 at W Lake Sammamish Pkwy) caters to Eastsiders who don't want to stray far from Microsoft. Dubbed by its operators a "lifestyle center," the open-air mixed-use mall has an impressive array of retail—Abercrombie & Fitch, the Gap, Victoria's Secret—and restaurants, plus an eight-screen movie complex. *Every day; www.shopredmondtowncenter.com; map:FF1*

Shops from A to Z

ANTIQUES/VINTAGE/RETRO

ANTIQUE LIQUIDATORS / 503 Westlake Ave N, South Lake Union; 206/623-2740 What Antique Liquidators lacks in ambience, it makes up for in sheer volume. The largest antique store in town, its 22,000 square feet of sales and storage space house a slew of practical furnishings (mostly Danish and English; lots of chairs and drop-leaf tables). Endless variety and good prices, but don't expect perfect quality. *Every day; map:D2*

AREA 51 / 401 E Pine St, Capitol Hill; 206/568-4782 A furniture selection that would make George Jetson feel right at home draws Capitol Hill urbanites and other unconventional decorators to Area 51. The expansive store's mostly 1960s, 1970s, and contemporary inventory runs to retro relics such as rotary phones in a full spectrum of colors and borderline kitsch pieces, such as 1960s stereo chairs. The staff has a knack for morphing everyday objects into design-conscious decor additions: glass lab beakers become vases, gym lockers become wardrobe space. *Every day; map:K2*

THE CRANE GALLERY / 104 W Roy St, Queen Anne; 206/298-9425
Spare and uncluttered, the Crane's selection speaks to its reputation as a
purveyor of fine Asian antiques and artifacts. Paintings, ceramics,
bronzes, ivory, jade, prints, netsuke, and furniture from the Orient are
museum quality—and priced accordingly. *Tues–Sat; map:GG7*

**DAVID WEATHERFORD ANTIQUES & INTERIORS / 133 14th Ave E,
Capitol Hill; 206/329-6533 / 1200 2nd Ave, Downtown; 206/624-3514**
This antiques-seller doesn't muck about with reproductions or second-
rate furniture. Housed in a Capitol Hill mansion, David Weatherford
sells exquisite 18th-century English and French furniture, as well as Oriental rugs, porcelain, screens, and art glass. A resident design team
advises clients on integrating antiques gracefully with their present furnishings. The downtown location in the Washington Mutual Tower specializes in commercial collections. *Mon–Sat; drw@davidweatherford.
com; www.davidweatherford.com; map:HH6, L7*

DELUXE JUNK / 3518 Fremont Pl N, Fremont; 206/634-2733 A subterranean den of whimsy, Deluxe Junk blends equal parts camp, collector's
items, and classic vintage furniture in quintessential Fremont style. Midcentury furnishings and housewares reign here, but the staggering
breadth of selection ranges from a smattering of garments to antiquated
lunchboxes and 40-year-old movie magazines. This former funeral parlor
is also a favorite of the local theater set, who regularly peruse the shelves
in search of authentic props. *Mon, Wed, Fri–Sun; map:FF7*

**FREMONT ANTIQUE MALL / 3419 Fremont Pl N, Fremont; 206/548-
9140** Owner Marc Salo collects the community's castoffs almost indis-
criminately, which yields a vast inventory of furnishings, clothing, and
tchotchkes. The tri-level store is a godsend for last-minute gift shoppers
and anyone decorating on a shoestring. Vintage toys, dinnerware, and
appliances cram the shelves, along with a record collection that has vinyl
fanatics spraining their fingers in their haste to whip out their wallets.
Every day; map:FF7

FRITZI RITZ / 3425 Fremont Pl N, Fremont; 206/633-0929 Most clothes
here are relics of the sock-hop and hula-hoop era, but fashions range
from Edwardian pumps to early '60s bowling shirts. Fritzi Ritz labels all
threads with their decade of origin, which makes creating authentic retro
looks a snap. With racks of dresses, skirts, shoes, slacks, and handbags,
plus a well-stocked jewelry case, this shop is a perennial favorite among
hard-core vintage shoppers. *Tues–Sat; map:FF7*

**GREG DAVIDSON ANTIQUE LIGHTING / 1020 1st Ave, Downtown;
206/625-0406** Greg Davidson's shop glows with artfully restored relics
from the days when Thomas Edison lit his first bulb. The cavernous shop

stocks mostly American, vintage lighting elements and a few pieces of period furniture. *Every day; map:L8*

HONEYCHURCH ANTIQUES / 1008 James St, First Hill; 206/622-1225 When out-of-towners go looking for superior Asian antiques, the Seattle Art Museum has been known to send them to Laurie and John Fairman's renowned shop—and not simply because Honeychurch stocks a few museum-quality pieces. The Fairmans' scholarly knowledge of their high-quality wares is paralleled only by their affable approachability. John's parents opened the original Honeychurch in Hong Kong more than 40 years ago, and he's been doing business in Seattle for 24 years. The store's attraction lies in its tasteful blend of Asian fine art, folk art, and furniture, which spans a time period that reaches from the Neolithic era and the Han Dynasty (206 B.C.) to early 20th-century basketry. The shop puts on occasional shows of a variety of wares. *Tues–Sat; info@ honeychurch.com; map:O3*

ISADORA'S ANTIQUE CLOTHING / 1915 1st Ave, Downtown; 206/441-7711 For about 30 years, Laura Dalesandro's shop has defied the notion of vintage clothing as frumpy and threadbare. Impeccable designer evening wear from the 1900s to the 1950s sells for gasp-inducing prices. Laura also carries her original bridal and formal designs and estate jewelry. The museum-quality gowns, tuxedos, and accessories at Isadora's embody elegance and refinement. *Every day; isadoras@earthlink.net; www.isadoras.com; map:I7*

JEAN WILLIAMS ANTIQUES / 115 S Jackson St, Pioneer Square; 206/622-1110 Jean Williams travels to Europe to handpick her inventory—and for those who can't afford the genuine antiques, she imports Seattle's only European-made reproductions. A 15-year veteran of the Emerald City's antique community, this three-floor shop showcases a distinctive collection of French, English, and American 18th- and 19th-century country to formal furnishings. Handsome fireplace mantels, mirrors, and other classic accent pieces fill the crannies here. *Mon–Sat; www.jean williamsantiques.com; map:O9*

LE FROCK / 317 E Pine St, Capitol Hill; 206/623-5339 Miu Miu, Prada, and Armani regularly beckon from the racks of this high-end vintage-to-contemporary vendor, and new designer samples sell here too. The cozy space brims with a healthy complement of men's clothes, including suits, as well as women's dresses, skirts, handbags, and shoes. Prices are moderate but fair. You need a certain amount of imagination to shop the bargain balcony, but you'll need less cash than for main-floor buys. *Every day; www.lefrockonline.com; map:K2*

PELAYO ANTIQUES / 7601 Greenwood Ave N, Greenwood; 206/789-1999 Spanish expat Pedro Pelayo has consolidated his two store locations into one. The enormous Greenwood shop is stuffed with Danish country pine furniture from the 19th and 20th centuries, as well as pieces from England and central Europe. He also stocks Scandinavian crockery, bric-a-brac, wine jugs, brass and copper accessories, and Russian religious icons. *Every day; www.pelayoantiques.com; map:EE8*

PRIVATE SCREENING / 3504 Fremont Pl N, Fremont; 206/548-0751 Mint-condition Western shirts of the hyper-embellished Roy Rogers variety adorn the walls at Private Screening, but the collection isn't limited to buckaroo apparel. Men's and women's clothing, accessories galore, and odd furnishings pack this den of 1950s and '60s style. Patient treasure hunters should take a moment to dig through the tall chest of drawers stuffed full of gloves, brooches, and scarves. *Every day; map:FF7*

RHINESTONE ROSIE / 606 W Crockett St, Queen Anne; 206/283-4605 Those who know their faux jewels turn to Rhinestone Rosie (Rosie Sayyah) to make their wrists, necks, and ears glitter. Rosie rents, buys, sells, and repairs an inventory of thousands of estate and costume jewelry treasures in all colors, shapes, and sizes. Hers is the only store on the West Coast with a rhinestone repair service; she will search her rhinestone vaults to find replacement stones, convert clip earrings to pierced, or lengthen necklaces and bracelets. She's also an *Antiques Roadshow* appraiser. *Tues–Sat; map:GG8*

STUTEVILLE ANTIQUES / 1518 E Olive Wy, Capitol Hill; 206/329-5666 A classic beacon in the hipster fog of Capitol Hill, this collection of 18th- and early 19th-century furniture owes its immaculate appearance to owner Marshall Stuteville. He restores the American, English, and occasional continental pieces here. The authenticity of every item, including the smaller silver and porcelain items, is evident. Stuteville also offers restoration, identification, and appraisal services. *Tues–Sat, and by appointment; map:HH6*

VINTAGE LAUNDRY / 1530 Melrose Ave, Capitol Hill; 206/839-0759 If shabby chic had a flagship store, this would be it. The preponderance of flaking paint and iron farmhouse relics at Vintage Laundry is enough to make Martha Stewart herself misty-eyed with joy. Piles of 1940s and 1950s drapes and textiles in bold floral designs drape the country French furniture selection, which includes washbasins, wardrobes, and motel chairs. Vintage clothing, too. *Every day; map:J2*

APPAREL

ALHAMBRA / 101 Pine St, Downtown; 206/621-9571 Named for Granada's Moorish palace and adorned with Andalusian accents, this store actually carries women's clothing and jewelry that hail from locales as diverse as Italy and Istanbul. The upscale inventory includes an exclusive (and accordingly priced) line from Turkish designer Bahar Korcan, a smattering of elegant evening wear, and gorgeous art jewelry studded with semiprecious stones. Customers help themselves to tea and linger on Saturday afternoon for live music. *Every day; alhambra@qwest.net; www.alhambra.net; map:I6*

BCBG MAX AZRIA / 600 Pine St, Downtown; 206/447-3400 / Bellevue Square, Bellevue; 425/454-7691 Parisian designer Max Azria fills his stores with merchandise that looks like stock from a couture house in his hometown, but retails at less stratospheric prices. Women who can't swing high-fashion price tags, but don't bat an expertly coiffed eyelash at $128 pants, are in their element among the suits, semiformal dresses, and backless sequin tops here. Shoe fetishists find ample distraction among the 4-inch heels and funky flats. *Every day; map:J5, HH3*

BETSEY JOHNSON / 1429 5th Ave, Downtown; 206/624-2887 Forever toeing the line between fashion forward and fashion backward, Betsey Johnson's dress-code-busting styles continue to draw women who want to be noticed. The boutique's girly profusion of little dresses, flirty shirts, and outrageous pants in vibrant pinks, chartreuses, and turquoises reflects Johnson's notoriously garish personality. *Every day; map:J5*

BROOKS BROTHERS / 1335 5th Ave, Downtown; 206/624-4400 / Bellevue Square, Bellevue; 425/646-9688 Famously synonymous with button-down upper management, Brooks Brothers has moved from its sleepy Rainier Square location to a more bustling Fifth Avenue spot. Of late, the store's casual and dress fashions for men have included a few colorful departures from the usually stoic line. Brooks Brothers' trademark depth of inventory, fine special-order system, and gracious service remain, though, as do two terrific sales a year (two weeks in June and the week after Christmas). Customers will find some decent women's wear à la Banana Republic among the oxfords here. *Every day; www.brooks brothers.com; map:K6, HH3*

BUTCH BLUM / 1408 5th Ave, Downtown; 206/622-5760 / University Village, University District; 206/524-5860 Butch Blum sees wardrobes as investments, and shies away from trendy fads in favor of classic menswear lines from venerated labels such as Giorgio Armani, and Versace. The consistent polish of the garments here sets the tone for high-end men's fashions that won't fall out of style. The University Village store carries similar quality sans the suits. *Mon–Sat (downtown), every day (University Village); www.butchblumworld.com; map:FF6, K6*

DAVID LAWRENCE / 1318 4th Ave, Downtown; 206/622-2544 / Bellevue Square, Bellevue; 425/688-1699 Both stores of David Lawrence stock brands with heavy runway presence, such as Dolce & Gabbana, Hugo Boss, and Donna Karan. The GQ set will find appropriate togs, from Versace tuxes to tattered D&G jeans, for looking smashing at occasions of

SEWN IN SEATTLE

Seattle may be 3,000 miles from the haughty haute couture of NYC's Fifth Avenue, but plenty of Emerald City designers are stitching up original creations to sell out of neighborhood storefronts.

In the very mainstream neighborhood of Green Lake is **Pearl** (310 NE 65th St; 206/729-1149; map:EE7), where owner Victoria Simons showcases one-of-a-kind handbags. Her satchels ooze rock-star cool—especially those fashioned from Fender amplifier covers, which she rescues through her musical connections (Fender won't sell the material), and most bags run a reasonable $80 to $120. Simons also spruces up homes in her spare time, including designing a Gehry-esque couch in fire engine red for a "pearl" of another kind—Pearl Jam's Eddie Vedder.

Long before Belltown was "discovered," **Carol McClellan** set up shop there in 1979, where she created rock star–worthy wear for members of Seattle duo Heart in their heyday. Her designs cater to men and women with the funding to build a wardrobe the way most people invest in real estate (her custom leather trousers average between $950 and $1,150). Now she shapes supple leathers into Michael Kors– and Yves St. Laurent–influenced jackets and pants in her studio (130 Battery St; 206/956-8484; map:F8), which is open Thursday through Saturday, or by appointment.

Designer Adam Arnold sells his own line of chic, ready-to-wear men's and women's clothing. He has outfitted local celebrities, from drag sensation Dina Martina to actor Cathy Sutherland (for whom he fashioned a Marie Antoinette–era gown equipped with a puppet theater in the skirt). The boutique at **Vain** hair salon (2018 1st Ave, Belltown; 206/441-3441; www.vain.com; map:I7), carries Arnold's line, as well as edgier limited-edition pieces from Lorna Leedy, who runs the shop, and local accessory designers' work. Prices here cater to young (read: underpaid) hipsters. Vain owner Victoria Gentry occasionally puts on fashion shows in the shop.

Darbury Stenderu (2121 1st Ave, Belltown; 206/448-2625; www.darbury stenderu.com; map:H7) is a printmaker first, who paints or prints swooping, brilliant patterns on bell-sleeved dresses, flowing skirts, pillows, and velvet quilts. Her gothic edge appeals to more than one opera diva (including Seattle's Dominique LaBelle). While Stenderu's clothes aren't cheap (dresses run about $400), they make infinitely more inventive souvenirs than those Space Needle key chains.   —*Marika McElroy*

all sorts. Smaller dimensions and approachable staff make shopping here a less intimidating experience than at some comparable retailers. *Every day; www.david-lawrence.com; map:K6, HH3*

FINI / 86 Pine St, Downtown; 206/443-0563 Fini tempts accessory hounds with credit limit–pushing eye-candy such as designer handbags (from designers such as Lulu Guinness), sophisticated (but trendy) jewelry, and precious hair accessories and sunglasses. The window displays are always arresting, never out-of-date. *Every day; map:I7*

JERI RICE / 421 University St, Downtown; 206/624-4000 Formerly Helen's (Of Course), Jeri Rice's name change heralded a few updates in inventory for this old-money magnet. The marble-paneled store now carries Jean Paul Gaultier, Sonia Rykiel, and more of the haughtiest names in fashion. Here, seasoned saleswomen minister to longtime clients, some of Seattle's worldliest—and wealthiest—fashion mavens. *Every day; map:K6*

LES AMIS / 3420 Evanston Ave N, Fremont; 206/632-2877 This tidy shop nestled in an elegantly weathered space embodies the Fremont ethos: independent, eye-catching, and out of the ordinary. Characterized by a certain whimsy and daring, these are clothes that will make the wearer stand out in a crowd, subtly. Lacy lingerie, feminine dresses, and brand-name lines, such as Krista Larson, Michael Stars, and Three-Dot tees, fill the shop. There's a nice selection of socks, bags, and other delicate jewelry, too. *Every day; www.lesamis-inc.com; map:FF8*

LIPSTICK TRACES / 500 E Pine St, Capitol Hill; 206/329-2813 Owner Jennifer Gallucci's little shop (quite possibly the coolest new addition to Capitol Hill's retail community) carries every item necessary for outfitting a well-rounded scenester girl. In addition to a few articles of clothing (some from local designers) and handbags and wallets from Olympia cult favorite Rebecca Peary, she stocks great gifts for the indie-rock girl or *Bust*-magazine reader on your list: books such as *Please Kill Me* (required punk reading), tough-but-cute jewelry, and Italian soaps, among others. Gallucci, who is well connected with the local music community, also showcases work from up-and-coming Seattle artists. *Wed–Mon; map:J2*

MARIO'S OF SEATTLE / 1513 6th Ave, Downtown; 206/223-1461 From Hugo Boss suits for men to Jimmy Choo shoes for women, Mario's maintains its position as Seattle's doyen of high fashion. The men's and women's collections here include the latest from Dolce & Gabbana, Calvin Klein, Prada, Zegna, and Giorgio Armani. The store is spacious with Mediterranean overtones, the staff courteous and skilled, and custom-tailored shoes and special orders on exclusive European merchandise are available. *Every day; www.marios.com; map:J5*

THE POWDER ROOM / 101 Stewart St, Ste 101, Downtown; 206/374-0060 The Powder Room has rescued many a cash-strapped club maven in search of a hot little number in a hurry. The mix-and-match separates here mirror trends at pricier purveyors of sass, such as Bebe, but few Powder Room items sell for more than $60. Though the clothes here may not weather more than a few seasons, they're an ideal option for a party girl in a financial bind. *Every day; map:I7*

TOTALLY MICHAEL'S / 521 Union St, Downtown; 206/622-4920 Catering to women with a penchant for luxurious fabrics and an aversion to flesh-baring styles, owners Michael Smith and Carol Baldwin have been draping their discerning clientele in timeless fashions since 1971. The store carries clothing for sophisticates at work (beautifully tailored suits and separates), at play (relaxed casuals), and after dark (evening and party dresses). You'll find local designers represented along with international talents such as Iris Singer and Tamotsu. *Mon–Sat; www.totallymichaels.com; map:K5*

URBAN OUTFITTERS / 1507 5th Ave, Downtown; 206/381-3777 / 401 Broadway Ave E, Capitol Hill; 206/322-1800 The new downtown Urban Outfitters is still popular with under-30 shoppers who cultivate a look that wavers between "found it in my grandfather's closet" and DIY design. Intentionally dirtied, slashed, and frayed clothes often find their way to the racks here, as do loads of unsullied but edgy threads, home accessories, and gifts. The relatively puny price tags occasionally reflect merchandise quality, but the selection is vast and turnover high. For scandalously low prices, check out the upstairs racks at the Broadway store, which consolidates clearance items from all West Coast stores. *Every day; www.urbn.com; map:J5, GG6*

YAZDI / 1815 N 45th St, Wallingford (and branches); 206/547-6008 The imported women's wear at the three Seattle Yazdi stores leans to batiks in bold colors that look like the products of exotic isles. Flowing dresses, laid-back pants, and shirts that let you move are its staple. The wide range of sizes is a plus and part of the reason that this store has a devoted customer base, so much so that the shop takes up two retail spaces in its flagship store at Wallingford Center. Additional locations in the Broadway Market (401 Broadway Ave E, Capitol Hill; 206/860-7109; map:HH7) and downstairs at the Pike Place Market (206/682-0657; map:J8). *Every day; map:FF7*

BODY CARE

DANDELION BOTANICAL COMPANY / 708 N 34th St, Fremont; 206/545-8892 or 877/778-4869 Dandelion's signature blue bottles of essential and perfume oils span the spectrum of Mother Nature's finest scents. The store also carries herbal remedies and will custom blend lotions and oils. *Every day; www.dandelionbotanical.com; map:FF7*

ESSENZA / 615 N 35th St, Fremont; 206/547-4895 With products from Fresh, L'Occitane, and other hoity-toity purveyors of hygiene, this airy little shop at the Center of the Universe (Fremont) is a fragrant find. Just around the corner from its sister store, Les Amis, Essenza offers all the benefits of high-end downtown stores in laid-back Fremont surroundings. In addition to body care lines, the store carries bedding, linens, precious baby clothes, and grown-up sleepwear. *Every day (summer), Tues–Sun (winter); www.essenzainc.com; map:FF7*

THE HERBALIST / 2106 NE 65th St, Ravenna; 206/523-2600 In addition to their primary inventory of herbs to cure, clean, and calm, the Herbalist offers plenty of chemical-free body care options: essential and massage oils, natural cosmetics, vitamin supplements, and a good selection of books and potpourri supplies. *Every day; www.theherbalist.com; map:FF6*

L'OCCITANE / 600 Pine St, Downtown; 206/903-6693 French soaps are the Swiss watches of body care: steeped in tradition, crafted to perfection, and geared for flawless performance. This worldwide chain (which was inspired by the herbal abundance of France's Provence region) recently arrived at Pacific Place. In addition to soaps, they carry lotions, perfume oils, and other products that make good use of Provence's lavender and verbena crops. *Every day; map:I5*

PARFUMERIE ELIZABETH GEORGE / 1424 4th Ave, Downtown; 206/622-7212 At this downtown shop, pairing people with scents is a science: Elizabeth George occasionally tests the pH content of customers' skin, but she's been in the business so long, she usually doesn't have to. Specializing in custom and hard-to-find perfumes, George matches the right fragrance to your skin and advises on how to wear it. She sells one of the top lines of designer-matched scents (less expensive copies of the originals), as well as eye-catching atomizers and a line of lotions and bath products. *Tues–Fri, Sat by appointment; map:J6*

PARFUMERIE NASREEN / 1005 1st Ave, Downtown; 206/682-3459 or 888/286-1825 Floor-to-ceiling scents fill this small perfumery off the lobby of the Alexis Hotel. Parfumerie Nasreen is the only all-perfume store in the city, stocking close to 750 different fragrances, many from exotic locales, in all price ranges. *Mon–Sat; www.parfumerienasreen. com; map:L8*

THE SOAP BOX / 4340 University Wy NE, University District (and branches); 206/634-2379 This pioneer of specialty body care has been a Seattle fixture for more than 26 years. In addition to their own line of pure-as-a-lily products, Pre de Provence, the Soap Box carries tons of other perfumed soaps, bath oils, lotions, and other novelties for the bath from all over the world. This is a lifesaving last-minute gift shop; they'll mix any scent you like into a lotion, oil, or bubble bath brew. There's a branch in Pike Place Market, as well as one in West Seattle. *Every day; map:FF6*

TENZING MOMO / 93 Pike St, Pike Place Market; 206/623-9837 From the incense cloud at the door to the herbal body-care products that line the shelves, Tenzing Momo is a hippie magnet and the oldest herb store on the West Coast. The staff is extremely knowledgeable about the properties (and mysteries) of the dozens of varieties of herbs, tinctures, and elixirs they carry, including natural remedies for PMS, dandruff, athlete's foot, or whatever ails you. *Every day; map:J8*

BOOKS AND PERIODICALS

ALL FOR KIDS BOOKS AND MUSIC / 2900 NE Blakeley St, Ste C, Ravenna; 206/526-2768 All for Kids has enough literature to keep a growing mind occupied, from the *Green Eggs and Ham* years through young adult novels. The store stocks plenty of kits, tapes, and activities as well. There's a weekly story hour on Tuesdays and lots of author events. *Every day; www.allforkids.com; map:FF6*

BAILEY/COY BOOKS / 414 Broadway Ave E, Capitol Hill; 206/323-8842 This Broadway institution stocks a selection of literature as diverse as the passersby on the famously outré street outside. Fiction and literature (including mystery and sci-fi), poetry, lesbian and gay studies, women's studies, and philosophy line the shelves. Look here also for coffee-table books, child care, gardening, cooking, and a good selection of literary magazines. *Every day; map:GG7*

BARNES & NOBLE BOOKSELLERS / University Village, University District (and branches); 206/517-4107 It's been the scourge of independent booksellers around town, and the staff is generally not a fount of literary acumen, but Barnes & Noble's reliably huge selection garners plenty of customers. The colossal U Village store has the area's best selection. Eight branches in the Seattle area include one in Pacific Place. *Every day; www.bn.com; map:FF6*

BEATTY BOOK STORE / 1925 3rd Ave, Downtown; 206/728-2665 Two large rooms sprinkled through with enticing cubbyholes make treasure hunting irresistible here. The largest general used-book store in Seattle, Beatty's huge inventory includes one of the best bibliography sections ("books about books") on the West Coast. Excellent regional, art, philosophy, military history, and cookbook sections, too. The knowledgeable staff pays well for the used books they buy and asks fair prices for the books they sell. *Tues–Sat (summer), Mon–Sat (winter); www.beatty bookstore.com; map:I6*

BEYOND THE CLOSET BOOKSTORE / 518 E Pike St, Capitol Hill; 206/322-4609 From political to piquant (and downright erotic), Beyond the Closet carries all manner of new and used books both by gay and lesbian authors and on gay or lesbian subjects. The fiction houses plenty of lesser-known authors and books from small presses, though you'll also find best-sellers if they're relevant. The requisite bookstore cat, Oscar, holds court here, too. *Every day; admin@beyondthecloset.com; www. beyondthecloset.com; map:K1*

BORDERS BOOKS & MUSIC / 1501 4th Ave, Downtown (and branches); 206/622-4599 The general collection here is respectable, but it's the broad selection of CDs that sets Borders apart. Regular events and signings complement the store's sensible, comfortable layout. A wide and varied Northwest section and small cafe give the branch credible local appeal. Branches are in Redmond (16546 NE 74th St; 425/869-1907; map:EE2), Bellevue (Bellevue Square; 425/990-8171; map:HH3), and Tukwila (17501 Southcenter Pkwy; 206/575-4506; map:OO5). *Every day; www.borders.com; map:J6*

BULLDOG NEWS AND FAST ESPRESSO / 4208 University Wy NE, University District; 206/632-6397 / Broadway Market, Capitol Hill; 206/322-6397 With one of the fiercest foreign-press selections in town, this venerable newsstand on the Ave has prevailed in the face of big-name bookstore encroachment. There's a magazine (or newspaper) for everyone here. Customers can sip espresso from the counter and surf the Web at Internet kiosks, too. The new Broadway Market branch has moved from its former kiosk location into a bona fide storefront. *Every day; info@bulldognews.com; www.bulldognews.com; map:FF6, GG6*

CHAMELEON BOOKS / 514 15th Ave E, Capitol Hill; 206/323-0154 With a growing selection of high-quality rare and antiquarian books, this Chameleon is transforming itself into a fine rare bookseller. The collection includes volumes on art and architecture, science and medicine, and illustrated books, among others. You'll find sets, fine bindings, books on books, and first editions, too. Adding to the atmosphere, owner Alan D. Frank occasionally practices jazz riffs on his upright piano. Fair prices for trades. *Every day; www.abebooks.com/home/chameleon/; map:GG6*

CINEMA BOOKS / 4753 Roosevelt Wy NE, University District; 206/547-7667 From the Silver Screen to the *Simpsons*, Cinema Books is packed with new and used books relating to movies, television, and theater. You'll also find magazines, screenplays, posters, stills, and technical books for filmmakers. This movie-lover's paradise is appropriately located downstairs from the cozy Seven Gables theater. *Mon–Sat; map:FF6*

DAVID ISHII, BOOKSELLER / 212 1st Ave S, Pioneer Square; 206/622-4719 Reminiscent of a harried professor's study, this Pioneer Square store specializes in fly-fishing and baseball books—owner David Ishii's areas of expertise. Ishii's eclectic collection of used, out-of-print, and scarce books is the region's largest on these subjects. *Every day; map:O8*

EAST WEST BOOKSHOP OF SEATTLE / 6500 Roosevelt Wy NE, Roosevelt; 206/523-3726 or 800/587-6002 Based on the East West store in

Palo Alto, Seattle's version is a good place to thumb through books on Eastern spirituality and meditation, as well as one of the most comprehensive Jungian psychology selections in town. Frequent speakers' forums in the store's roomy space focus on topics ranging from spiritual healing to near-death experiences. *Every day; www.ewbookshop.com; map:EE7*

ELLIOTT BAY BOOK COMPANY / 101 S Main St, Pioneer Square; 206/624-6600 A beloved Seattle institution, this creaky, wonderful bookstore offers a marvelous maze of books for browsing, excellent service, and one of the most respected reading series in the country. Undoubtedly a best place. See Top 25 Attractions in the Exploring chapter. *Every day; queries@elliottbaybook.com; www.elliottbaybook.com; map:O8*

FILLIPI BOOK AND RECORD SHOP / 1351 E Olive Wy, Capitol Hill; 206/682-4266 Fillipi's collection of rare general books, records of all sizes, and sheet music ranges from hard-to-find 78s and 45s (especially jazz records) to single sheets of music. The all-used inventory's prices tend to be higher than elsewhere in the city, but many an idle hour has been happily passed perusing the shelves here. *Tues–Sat; map:HH7*

FLORA & FAUNA BOOKS / 121 1st Ave S, Pioneer Square; 206/623-4727 If Mother Nature had a library, she'd stock it with books from Flora & Fauna. This Pioneer Square basement's books on natural history, gardening, birding, and the life sciences make it one of the few of its kind in the country. New, used, and rare books, from field guides to Rachel Carson's *Silent Spring*, make up the more than 25,000 titles here. Buy or sell. *Mon–Sat; map:N8*

FREMONT PLACE BOOK COMPANY / 621 N 35th St, Fremont; 206/547-5970 This cozy neighborhood bookstore is a small, well-loved bright spot at the center of Fremont. In a community where the printed word is revered, Fremont Place is an essential component. New and contemporary fiction, women's studies, gay and lesbian literature, and regional books are the areas of emphasis, along with a small but well-chosen children's section. Staff recommendations are subtly pasted to the shelves. *Every day; fremontbks@aol.com; map:FF8*

THE GLOBE BOOKS / 5220 University Wy NE, University District; 206/527-2480 / 999 3rd Ave, Downtown; 206/682-6882 This unstuffy purveyor of new and used books specializes in the humanities (especially literature and reference books) and carries a growing section of natural-science books. Don't be intimidated by the specialized inventory; this is a wonderfully down-to-earth shop. Browse through the antique maps and replicas, too. Trades are welcome. The downtown store has a great selection of automotive books. *Thurs–Tues (closed every other Fri); map:FF6, L7*

HALF PRICE BOOKS RECORDS MAGAZINES / 4709 Roosevelt Wy NE, University District (and branches); 206/547-7859 Those who happen on Half Price rarely go back to regular retail. The store sells used and new books at, well, half price. The large selection of classical literature and huge line of discounted new and used software and coffee-table books galore make for a bookworm's nirvana. They also buy used books daily. Branches in Bellevue, Redmond, Tukwila, and Edmonds. *Every day; www.halfpricebooks.com; map:FF7*

HORIZON BOOKS / 425 15th Ave E, Capitol Hill (and branches); 206/329-3586 Readers looking to wax philosophical should swing by Horizon Books, where Don Glover buys and sells used general books with an emphasis on literature, criticism, history, mystery, and philosophy. His second store (6512 Roosevelt Wy NE, Roosevelt; 206/523-4217; map:EE7) is well stocked, neatly laid out, and eminently browsable, and a third location is now open in Greenwood (8570 Greenwood Ave N; 206/781-4680; map:EE7). *Every day; map:GG6*

ISLAND BOOKS / 3014 78th Ave SE, Mercer Island; 206/232-6920 or 800/432-1640 Mercer Islanders rely on Island Books for a good general selection. Besides a fine assortment of children's books, nice touches for kids include a playhouse and story hours on Saturday throughout the year. Owner Roger Page has added a small but growing section of carefully chosen used books. Gift wrapping and domestic shipping are additional free services. *Mon–Sat; islandbooks@seanet.com; islandbooks. booksense.com; map:II4*

KINOKUNIYA BOOKSTORE / 525 S Weller St, Chinatown/International District; 206/587-2477 With Asian mega-grocery Uwajimaya's move, Kinokuniya got expanded digs and broadened their literary scope. In addition to a selection of Japanese books and magazines large enough to keep a Tokyo native endlessly occupied, the new spot inside the new Uwajimaya carries books in Chinese, English-language books relating to Asia, and a sizable selection of general books in English. Children's books, cookbooks, stationery, and Eastern medicine volumes also line the shelves here. *Every day; map:Q7*

LEFT BANK BOOKS / 92 Pike St, Pike Place Market; 206/622-0195 With undeniable leanings in the political direction its name suggests, this worker-owned bookseller distributes literature with a radical bent. The emphasis is on politics of a blackish hue; there are also good new and used sections on social science, contemporary poetry, fiction, gay and lesbian studies, and philosophy. *Every day; leftbankbooks@leftbankbooks. com; www.leftbankbooks.com; map:J8*

M COY BOOKS / 117 Pine St, Downtown; 206/623-5354 Small independent booksellers such as this one are rare in the heart of downtown.

This Pine Street store (one block east of Pike Place Market) carries a spectrum of books, with an emphasis on contemporary literature, photography, art, gardening, and interior and graphic design. Owner Michael Coy has a talent for suggesting other titles that will interest you (discuss them over a latte at the espresso bar in back). *Every day; mcoybooks@att.net; map:J8*

MADISON PARK BOOKS / 4105 E Madison St, Madison Park; 206/328-7323 This neighborhood store is a great place to while away an hour. It carries a decent general selection and a nice array of large-format coffee-table volumes, with a concentration on art and photography, and cookbooks and garden books are well represented. Kids' selections are thoughtfully chosen. *Every day; mpbooks@hotmail.com; map:GG6*

MAGUS BOOKSTORE / 1408 NE 42nd St, University District; 206/633-1800 Magus has rescued many a starving student from full-price sticker shock with its 60,000-strong used-book inventory. A staple in this student-dominated neighborhood, the store carries everything from classical literature to engineering; it has a large science-fiction selection and tons of Cliff Notes, as well as a poetry section that would do any new-book store proud. *Every day; magusbks@halcyon.com; www.magusbks.com; map:FF6*

MARCO POLO / 713 Broadway Ave E, Capitol Hill; 206/860-3736 Practical travelers and hopeless romantics find the literary incitement for wanderlust here. The extensive array of travel guides is paired with world literature from all corners of the globe. In addition to books, Marco Polo rounds out your journey preparations with travel gear, a beautiful assortment of antique globes, and a well-traveled staff who are generous with their knowledge. *Every day; travel@marcopolos.com; www.marcopolos.com; map:HH7*

MISTER E BOOKS / Pike Place Market, lower level, Downtown; 206/622-5182 Ferreted away beneath the market, this shop merits a trip into the maze under Pike Place. Mister E specializes in mystery (hence the name), fantasy, horror, and signed editions by the likes of Ray Bradbury, Harlan Ellison, and Maurice Sendak. Lots of kids' books, as well as hard-to-find collectors' volumes and an eclectic array of LPs, too. *Every day; misterE@misterE.com; map:I8*

OPEN BOOKS—A POEM EMPORIUM / 2414 N 45th St, Wallingford; 206/633-0811 Owners Christine Deavel and John Marshall (both poets) took the inspiration for their poetry-only store from Cambridge's renowned Grolier Book Shop. The pair stock volume after volume of new, used, and out-of-print poetry (as well as poetry on tape, CD, and video). Quiet and inviting, Open Books hosts poetry readings and signings (featuring such revered scribes as Nobel laureate Seamus Heaney and John Ashbury), and an adjoining wine bar increases the allure of reading and contemplation. Obscure poets are here, as well as classics and contemporary greats, but Deavel and Marshall are not too proud to carry *Poetry for Cats. Tues–Sat; www.openpoetrybooks.com; map:FF7*

PARKPLACE BOOK COMPANY / 348 Parkplace Center, Kirkland; 425/828-6546 Children's books, mystery, and fiction are all culled with expertise by book rep and co-owner Ted Lucia. He and his wife, Kathi, own this impeccably organized general bookstore, which has a friendly staff worthy of a book rep's knowledge. *Every day; map:EE3*

PETER MILLER ARCHITECTURAL AND DESIGN BOOKS AND SUPPLIES / 1930 1st Ave, Downtown; 206/441-4114 Appropriately surrounded by architectural elegance and edge, Peter Miller's shop carries the best local selection of new, used, and out-of-print architectural books (one of few such specialized outlets in the country). Frank Gehrys–in–the–making also shop here for European and Japanese gadgets and drafting supplies. *Every day; petermiller@petermiller.com; map:I7*

QUEEN ANNE AVENUE BOOKS / 1629 Queen Anne Ave N, Queen Anne; 206/283-5624 Browsing in close quarters at this neighborhood bookstore can be cozy or cramped, depending on your degree of claustrophobia. However, the staff more than make up for the squeeze with their intelligence, good recommendations, and overall geniality. Special orders are handled quickly and efficiently. *Every day; qabooks@uswest.net; www.queenanneavebooks.com; map:GG8*

READ ALL ABOUT IT INTERNATIONAL NEWSSTAND/FIRST AND PIKE NEWSSTAND / 93 Pike St, Pike Place Market; 206/624-0140 Tourists and locals buzz around the vast selection of local, national, and international papers and magazines at this colorful newsstand and Pike Place Market institution (across from DeLaurenti Specialty Food Markets). More than 100 foreign newspapers and around 1,600 publications in all make the stand a magnet for a diverse crowd of browsers and buyers. *Every day; map:J8*

SEATTLE MYSTERY BOOKSHOP / 117 Cherry St, Downtown; 206/587-5737 This 11-year-old subterranean shop attempts to answer one eternal question in thousands of different ways. Stocked entirely with new, used, and signed whodunits, the shop narrows the genre into such categories as "Forensic Detectives and Serious Killers" and "Cheap Thrills" (the 99-cent rack). From the latest releases to Sherlock Holmes, you'll find them here. Today's most popular mystery writers often drop in for signings. *Every day; staff@seattlemystery.com; www.seattlemystery.com; map:N8*

SECOND STORY BOOKSTORE / 1815 N 45th St, Wallingford; 206/547-4605 This Wallingford Center general bookstore makes for delicious rainy-day reading: good displays draw you in, and big, comfy armchairs invite you to stay. Excellent children's, regional, and fiction sections. Ask about the cassette-rental library, or come for an autograph party or kids' event. *Every day; map:FF7*

SECRET GARDEN BOOKSHOP / 2214 NW Market St, Ballard; 206/789-5006 Seattle's oldest exclusively children's bookstore outgrew its former 15th Avenue location and has expanded to include books for grown-ups, too. Today it's nearly double the size, and in addition to comprehensive parenting and children's nonfiction sections, the new space includes a solid general selection. Special events (musical performances, classes, signings, and the occasional reading) are entertaining, and the Secret Garden does programs for teachers and parents and book fairs for local schools. There are also story times twice every Thursday. *Every day; staff@secret gardenbooks.com; www.secretgardenbooks.com; map:FF7*

STEVE'S BROADWAY NEWS / 204 Broadway Ave E, Capitol Hill; 206/324-7323 / 3416 Fremont Ave N, Fremont; 206/633-0731 At any hour of the day (or night), newshounds pack Steve Dunnington's Broadway shop. From regional magazines to Australian dailies, the selection here is comprehensive. No back issues. *Every day; map:GG7, FF7*

TWICE SOLD TALES / 905 E John St, Capitol Hill (and branches); 206/324-2421 The atmosphere in this much-frequented store is nearly as captivating as the contents of its shelves: a world population counter faces the street, and signs inside list questions "guaranteed to annoy Twice Sold Tales staff." Twice Sold, which began as a one-room shop on Capitol Hill, has overflowed into the space next door and two other (separately owned) locations. The shelves offer a generous collection of fiction, poetry, and cooking titles, and a stellar history selection—and some less traditional genres ("Smut" and "Bad Self-Help" among them). The stores are known for fair prices when buying books (Wednesday through Saturday), though this is reflected in the retail prices, which some people feel are high. The John Street location, which is open all night Friday for insomniac bookworms, always keeps it interesting: a bubble machine runs constantly out a front window, cats stroll overhead on specially designed highways that bridge the bookcases, and owner Jamie Lutton never holds her opinionated tongue. Branches are in the U District (1311 NE 45th St; 206/545-4226; map:FF6) and Fremont (3504 Fremont Ave N; 206/632-3759; map:FF7). *Every day; tst@twicesoldtales.com; www. twicesoldtales.com; map:GG7*

UNIVERSITY BOOK STORE / 4326 University Wy NE, University District (and branches); 206/634-3400 Now in its second century of operation, the University of Washington's bookstore is arguably the best spot in town to find whatever you seek on the printed page: from science fiction and travel books to weighty academic tomes. One of the largest bookstores in Washington State and the largest independent college bookstore in the United States, the UW's primary bookstore has a vast selection (especially the gardening, arts, and design departments). Don't hesitate to ask for help: customer service goes far beyond expected boundaries, with free book shipping, gift wrapping, and parking validation; and in the rare event that your title is not in stock, staff will promptly special-order it. The store often sponsors large events and readings (see Literature in the Performing Arts chapter) in conjunction with the university, and if you want a computer, a camera, or a stuffed Husky dog dressed in purple and gold, you'll find them here. The smaller branch across the lake in Bellevue (990 102nd Ave NE; 425/462-4500; map:HH3) does not carry textbooks or offer the buy-back service; it does carry an extensive general literature and children's selection. In 1995 a branch opened downtown (1225 4th Ave; 206/545-9230; Mon–Sat; map:K6) with an impressive selection of business and computer titles. *Every day; ubs books@u.washington.edu; www.bookstore.washington.edu; map:FF6*

WESSEL AND LIEBERMAN BOOKSELLERS / 208 1st Ave S, Pioneer Square; 206/682-3545 Wessel and Lieberman's new digs (a couple of doors down from the original 1st Ave location) house a broader selection of rare and out-of-print volumes, first-edition fiction, Western Americana (especially Northwest and Native American history), and books on books. Their presentations of books as art objects—miniature books, take-apart books, books in cigar-box covers, and a rotating exhibit of artists' books—give bibliophiles yet another reason to visit often. *Mon–Sat; www.wlbooks.com; map:N8*

WIDE WORLD BOOKS & MAPS / 4411 Wallingford Ave N, Wallingford; 206/634-3453 or 888/534-3453 For many Seattleites, a stop at Wide World is de rigueur predeparture shopping. Aside from a vast array of travel books, you'll find a complete range of accessories, including globes, maps, language tapes, a passport photo service, and luggage. And the inventory is presided over by a staff of seasoned travelers. Now located two blocks away from its former spot on 45th, the store is close to Julia's bakery, an ideal place for poring over new guidebooks and sipping espresso. *Every day; travel@speakeasy.net; www.travelbooksand maps.com; map:FF7*

CHILDREN'S CLOTHING AND ACCESSORIES

BOSTON STREET / 1815 N 45th St, Wallingford; 206/634-0580 / 16515 NE 74th St, Redmond; 425/895-0848 Natural fibers and playful colors abound at Boston Street. Kids sizes 0 to 14 look dashing in the clothing here, much of which is locally made and one of a kind, including pretty smocks and tiny jean jackets. Boston Street also carries the colorful Cotton Caboodle label and pint-size accessories and umbrellas. Some of the best baby duds around. *Every day; map:FF7, FF1*

FLORA AND HENRI / 717 Pine St (Elliot Grand Hyatt), Downtown; 206/749-0004 or 888/749-9698 / 705 Broadway Ave E, Capitol Hill; 206/323-2928 The clothes at this high-end store might have walked off the set of a 1953 French film. The classic cotton designs for children from newborns to 12-year-olds are pricey but precious. Definitely for the child who must have everything, from lovely 100 percent cotton batiste dresses to tailored overcoats more expensive than anything found in most adult Seattleites' closets. The newly opened shop in Broadway's Loveless Building boasts more of the same. *Every day; info@florahenri.com; www.florahenri.com; map:J4, GG7*

THE KIDS CLUB / University Village, University District; 206/524-2553 / Crossroads Shopping Center, Bellevue; 425/643-5437 Both slightly pricey locations get high traffic from soccer moms who might also stop off at Banana Republic or the Pottery Barn. They have an abundance of baby paraphernalia, from car seats to bottle warmers to baby carriers. Both stores have kiddie hair salons (the Hair Chair) and TVs with videos running to divert kids while their fashion fates are determined by Mom or Dad. *Every day; map:FF6, HH1*

LI'L PEOPLE / Westlake Center, Downtown; 206/623-4463 / Bellevue Square, Bellevue; 425/455-4967 Fashions for the formative years (0 to 6) in whimsical cotton designs. Charming and practical reversible-print jumpers, overalls, sweet little sweaters, and inventive headgear, including a selection of sun and just-for-fun hats. *Every day; map:I6, HH3*

RISING STARS / 7404 Greenwood Ave N, Greenwood; 206/781-0138 No cookie-cutter kids walk out of this Greenwood shop, where local designers (some of whom live and work mere blocks away) create some of the clothing. You'll find an eclectic selection of pajamas and cotton casuals for boys and girls, plus lots of handmade dolls, art supplies, books, and a large playroom with a treehouse. *Every day; map:EE8*

THE SHOE ZOO / 1037 NE 65th St, Roosevelt (and branches); 206/525-2770 The Shoe Zoo specializes in old-fashioned service (they keep a file of kids' previous purchases so you don't have to remember your child's shoe size in a particular brand every time), with a good selection of everything from Kenneth Cole for dress-up to the latest version of kid Tevas. Branches are at the Commons (240 NW Gilman Blvd, Issaquah; 425/392-8211) and Redmond Town Center (7325 164th Ave NE, Redmond; 425/558-4743; map:FF1). *Every day; map:FF6*

ETHNIC AND SPECIALTY FOODS

DELAURENTI SPECIALTY FOOD MARKET / 1435 1st Ave, Pike Place Market; 206/622-0141 Ingredients for a truly Mediterranean diet abound at this market cornerstone. For more than 50 years, DeLaurenti has served as a failsafe source for international foodstuffs, and is nearly as well known for its great service. The narrow aisles are dense with canned goods, olives, olive oils, imported pasta, and truffles. The deli is noted for its excellent meats, and carries more than 160 kinds of cheese. The wine department is known for its Italian labels and good selection, and the baked-goods department features breads from some of the area's best bakers. *Every day; map:J8*

EL MERCADO LATINO / 1514 Pike Pl, Pike Place Market; 206/623-3240 Colorful strings of chiles signal the entrance to this store in the Sanitary Market. The fresh and preserved ingredients of Caribbean, South American, Spanish, Creole, and Thai cuisines dominate the shelves here. The greengrocer in front is stocked with vegetables and fruits, plus six to eight varieties of chiles and more dried and canned types. Many hard-to-find spices, dried edible flowers, beans, and fruit drinks are also stocked. *Every day; map:J8*

THE MEXICAN GROCERY / 1914 Pike Pl, Pike Place Market; 206/441-1147 Deliciously foreign aromas of warm tortillas and dried chiles waft from this tiny store in the market's Soames-Dunn Building. The Mexican Grocery carries authentic foods such as tamales, mole, Mexican chocolate, corn husks, and more than a dozen kinds of dried chiles, along with Mexican canned goods and fresh salsas. The grocery's own La Mexicana fresh tortillas come in corn, flour, organic blue corn, or red chile flavors, and the staff serves up fresh tamales during lunch. Call ahead for uncooked hominy for use in posole, and masa dough for tamales. *Mon–Sat; map:J8*

UWAJIMAYA / 600 5th Ave S, Chinatown/International District; 206/624-6248 / 15555 NE 24th St, Bellevue; 425/747-9012 Asian megagrocery Uwajimaya has further cemented its reputation as the center of Chinatown/International District with its move to a sparkling, sprawling retail-residence complex, called Uwajimaya Village, one block south of its old location. The store still carries a vast selection of Asian foods, small electrical appliances (rice cookers, woks), housewares, gifts, and makeup. But now it also boasts a bank, condos above the store, and a nearby pan-Asian restaurant (Chinoise Cafe, located on the southwest corner of the village). As always, the real distinctions here are the variety of canned goods, depth of choice (one aisle is wholly devoted to rice), fresh shellfish tanks, and produce department. You'll find fresh geoduck, live prawns and crabs, bitter melons, water chestnuts, and all the makings for sushi. Service is knowledgeable. Check out the yummy pastries at the Yummy House in the food court; the Bellevue store has a fine Asian bakery case. Both branches have in-store cafes with Asian food for eating in or carrying out. *Every day; www.uwajimaya.com; map:Q7, GG1*

FLORISTS, GARDENING SHOPS, AND NURSERIES

ALAMEDA ORCHIDS / 2028 2nd Ave, Belltown; 206/728-1911 Not your Aunt Sally's flower shop. The sleek, urban look of this new downtown shop is a good match for its inventory of orchids, the couture mavens of the plant world. The elegant blossoms get ample attention from the well-versed staff, and customers who can't stand to go without blooms can return plants whose prime has passed and exchange them for a discount on the next plant. Pottery and bamboo, too. *Tues–Sat; map:G6*

BAINBRIDGE GARDENS / 9415 Miller Rd NE, Bainbridge Island; 206/842-5888 A worthy destination for gardeners and tourists, this country nursery sprawls over 7 acres on Bainbridge Island. In addition to a fine selection of woody plants, there are theme gardens for herbs, perennials, grasses, water plants, and shade plants. There's also a well-stocked garden gift shop. The nursery's new partnership with renowned garden writer Ann Lovejoy includes education programs on sustainable gardening. The restored Harui Memorial Garden (begun in 1908, abandoned during World War II) showcases bonsai trees, and a nature trail loops through native woods. In November and December, customers can reserve a wreath-making machine (no fee) to fabricate their own Northwest holiday gifts (there's UPS service on-site as well). A small outdoor cafe offers beverages, snacks, and light lunches. *Every day; info@ bainbridgegardens.com; www.bainbridgegardens.com*

BALLARD BLOSSOM / 1766 NW Market St, Ballard; 206/782-4213 Traditional arrangements at this Ballard shop are FTD in nature, and the business has been family-run since 1927—its blazing neon sign is a neighborhood landmark. The friendly staff presides over a cheerful profusion of fresh flowers, silk flowers, dried flowers, potted plants, and gift items. Customers can have many selections sent anywhere in the world, while personally chosen arrangements can be delivered areawide. *Mon–Sat (every day, Dec); www.ftd.com/ballardblossom; map:FF8*

BAY HAY AND FEED / 10355 Valley Rd, Bainbridge Island; 206/842-2813 An authentically useful rural outfitter and delightfully shoppable gift spot, this shop housed in a 1912 general storefront has served the Rolling Bay neighborhood of Bainbridge Island for 22 years. There's an abundant selection of farm- and garden-related toys, gifts, books, and clothing. The garden center is ably staffed, specializes in organic gardening, and offers a full range of edible and ornamental plants, including some collectors' treasures. Rustic lawn furniture, hand tools, and unusual clay pots are specialties. The new espresso bar in the nursery features goodies from Bainbridge Bakers. *Every day*

CITY PEOPLE'S GARDEN STORE / 2939 E Madison St, Madison Valley; 206/324-0737 / 5440 Sand Point Wy NE; 206/524-1200 Truth be told, some Seattleites adore City People's for its diverse selection of garden and gift options, while others eschew it as ridiculously overpriced. No one will debate the store's excellent browsing options, though: plants (the selection of both garden plants and houseplants is very good), gifts, garden tools, books, furniture, and ornaments. Areawide delivery. The Sand Point location carries more housewares, clothing, and hardware and fewer nursery items. *Every day; map:GG6, EE5*

CRISSEY FLOWERS AND GIFTS / 2100 5th Ave, Downtown; 206/448-1100 Traditionalists appreciate Crissey's arrangements, which run to English garden and tropical hi-style (a synthesis of Dutch and Japanese traditions). And with more than 110 years in the business, Seattle's oldest established florist has plenty of experience with blooms of all varieties. From private dinner parties to corporate galas, from weddings to wakes, Crissey is a full-service florist that does everything with excellence, delivering areawide and worldwide. *Mon–Sat; www.ftd.com/crissey; map:H6*

MARTHA E. HARRIS FLOWERS AND GIFTS / 4218 E Madison St, Madison Park; 206/568-0347 Although it's mere coincidence that the proprietor bears the same first name as a certain home-decorating maven, Ms. Stewart would probably stamp her approval on this upscale Madison Park shop. Martha E. Harris often fills out her English garden–style arrangements with native evergreenery and local flowers. The florist shop here is way at the back, past fine accessories, jewelry, and accent pieces for the home. Expect extravagant, dramatic, bountiful arrangements. Parties and weddings are Martha Harris's specialties, and she maintains a bridal registry. Deliveries within greater Seattle and worldwide daily except Sunday. *Every day; map:GG6*

MEGAN MARY OLANDER FLORIST / 222 1st Ave S, Pioneer Square; 206/623-6660 The relaxed arrangements at this longtime Pioneer Square shop are a perfect complement for the shabby-chic home. Olander's loose, elegant arrangements in the European country garden style incorporate border perennials and wildflowers as well as the hothouse beauties. All flowers are available by the stem, too (the pleasant staff offers expert assistance). Olander also carries a pretty assortment of containers, French ribbon, dried wreaths, and tussy-mussies. Corporate accounts are a specialty (no weddings), but walk-ins are welcome. Deliveries areawide and worldwide. *Mon–Fri, Sat by appointment; map:O8*

MOLBAK'S GREENHOUSE AND NURSERY / 13625 NE 175th St, Woodinville; 425/483-5000 / 1600 Pike Pl, Pike Place Market; 206/448-0431 Since 1956, Molbak's has catered to Northwest gardeners with plants that thrive in the Emerald City and environs. The novice and the expert gardener will find plenty to explore among the hundreds of houseplants and the full range of outdoor plants (everything from trees to ground covers). Molbak's also offers gifts, a Christmas shop (lavish holiday displays bring visitors here in droves), a garden store, and distinctive floral designs. *Every day; www.molbaks.com; map:BB2, I8*

PIKE PLACE FLOWERS / 1st Ave and Pike St, Pike Place Market; 206/682-9797 The fresh-cut flowers that crowd this corner of the market are a sweet-smelling beacon. Inside you'll find contemporary, original, and English garden to hi-style arrangements (no carnations). Bunches of flowers cost as little as $3, and arrangements go for $10 and up ($40 minimum on deliveries, areawide or worldwide). Staff are enthusiastically helpful. *Every day; www.pikeplaceflowers.com; map:J7*

SWANSON'S NURSERY AND GREENHOUSE / 9701 15th Ave NW, Crown Hill; 206/782-2543 Five acres of annuals, perennials, trees, shrubs, and display gardens make this a great stop for serious gardeners and a decent diversion for those with undeveloped green thumbs. This excellent full-service nursery includes uncommon plants of all kinds and emphasizes choice offerings over sheer quantity. A charming cafe in the gift shop offers light meals and espresso amid European garden tools, books, knickknacks, and handsome planting containers. *Every day; garden@swansonsnursery.com; www.swansonsnursery.com; map:DD8*

WELLS MEDINA NURSERY / 8300 NE 24th St, Bellevue; 425/454-1853 Many a swanky Medina home has a landscape graced with flora from this 5-acre nursery. A favorite among perennial lovers, and regionally famed for depth and variety, this is also the place to buy choice shrubs—the selection of rhododendrons and Japanese maples is unmatched in the area. Look here for unusual vines, bulbs, and ground covers as well, and check out the long demonstration border. The excellent plant range and prices are complemented by a smart and helpful staff. *Every day; map:GG4*

GIFTS AND HOME ACCESSORIES

BITTERS CO. / 513 N 36th St, Fremont; 206/632-0886 Sisters and co-owners Amy and Katie Carson turned this stylishly simple space into a classic Fremont showplace that they liken to an eclectic general store. Scouring the United States and the world in a well-honed, no-tchotchkes-need-apply fashion, they stock their store with modern rustic furniture, such as tables, chairs, and day beds, as well as folk art, Filson clothing, Norwegian sweaters, jewelry, and gift-worthy items. The in-store wine bar is a great place to relax and browse from your seat, and live music every Friday sets the mood for lingering. *Tues–Sun; info@bittersco.com; www.bittersco.com; map:FF8*

BURKE MUSEUM STORE / University of Washington, University District; 206/685-0909 The ideal spot for gifts for nature-lovers and museumophiles, this shop (also a branch of the University Book Store) is located in the Burke Museum on the UW campus. Browse the selection of Northwest Coast Native American art, silkscreen prints, basketry, and wooden boxes, and don't miss the geological specimens, books, and dinosaur replicas. *Every day; map:FF6*

BURNT SUGAR / 601 N 35th St, Fremont; 206/545-0699 This stylish Fremont store is not for the cash-strapped. Prices are high, but so is the quality. Vintage furnishings and accessories and imaginative contemporary pieces here range from funky suitcases from the '40s and chrome kitchen tables to new couches and lighting elements. Lushly colored candles, jewelry, smashing handbags, cheery linens, and French dishes provide a modern touch. *Every day; map:FF8*

DESIGN CONCERN / 1420 5th Ave, Downtown; 206/623-4444 Functional high design reigns at this City Centre shop, where the inventory is equally suited for corporate gift giving and sucking up to rich in-laws. Pens and desktop accessories, handcrafted jewelry, watches, leather goods, and housewares and glassware from around the world make browsing a pleasure here. *Every day; map:J5*

EGBERT'S / 2231 1st Ave, Belltown; 206/728-5682 Owner Jim Egbert manages to pull off his widely variant inventory without a mishmash feeling. An Italian leather chair sets off a Scandinavian dining table in light wood; art jewelry from around the world approaches museum quality; artifacts from India and African art mix with folklore-inspired bronzes. Despite the variety, current looks and high quality are universal. *Tues–Sat; map:G8*

FIREWORKS GALLERY / 210 1st Ave S, Pioneer Square (and branches); 206/682-8707 The profusion of color and media here fairly grab passersby by the lapels and drag them in. A favorite with visitors, Fireworks displays a compelling array of ceramics, glass, and other handcrafted wares—from the wild and whimsical to the elegantly functional. A walk through the store provides an introduction to the work of choice local artisans as well as outside talent. Great art jewelry, fiber art, and woodwork. The holidays usher in a selection of surprising tree-trimming options. Other branches are at Westlake Center, Bellevue Square, and University Village. *Every day; fireworksgallery@mindspring.com; www.fireworksgallery.net; map:O8*

FRANK AND DUNYA / 3418 Fremont Ave N, Fremont; 206/547-6760 A vestige of Fremont's earthy, counterculture era, Frank and Dunya (named for the owners' departed dogs) is filled with local jewelry, whimsical artwork, and accessories—nearly all crafted locally. Everything here is a character piece—overwhelmingly so. Expensive, and well worth it. *Every day; map:FF7*

GREAT JONES HOME / 1921 2nd Ave, Downtown; 206/448-9405 Half the enjoyment of shopping Great Jones stems from the atmosphere: expansive and reminiscent of a SoHo shop, the uncluttered space, complete with a pair of cooing doves, makes for easy, unhurried shopping. The emphasis here is on European items. Small wooden frames, handmade cards, scented candles, vintage American pottery, and slipcovers and bedding round out the offerings. *Every day; map:I7*

KASALA / 1505 Western Ave, Downtown; 206/623-7795 or 800/ KASALA1 / 1014 116th Ave NE, Bellevue; 425/453-2823 or 800/418-2521 One-stop shopping for urban abode decor: Kasala's contemporary, design-conscious furniture includes trendy European furniture and home accessories—with an emphasis on lighting systems—plus glassware and gift items. *Every day; seastore@kasala.com; www.kasala.com; map:J8, HH3*

MADE IN WASHINGTON / 1530 Post Alley, Pike Place Market (and branches); 206/467-0788 The name of this market fixture is aimed like an arrow at tourists—which isn't a bad thing; merchandise here is authentic and tasteful. From smoked salmon and regional wines to local art and books, this is the place to stock up on true Northwest treats to send to friends who have the misfortune to live elsewhere. Seven stores in the Seattle area. *Every day; www.madeinwashington.com; map: J8*

MILAGROS MEXICAN FOLK ART / 1530 Post Alley, Pike Place Market; 206/464-0490 Milagros is named for the small religious trinkets that many Latin Americans use to petition saints for help (*milagros* is Spanish for "miracles"). The store carries the little metal arms, legs, and hearts, as well as an array of Day of the Dead paraphernalia, Mexican lottery games, pounded-tin-framed mirrors, and silver jewelry from Mexico. Prices are excessively more than you'd pay for these wares in their country of origin, but probably cheaper than springing for a Mexican vacation. *Every day; www.milagrosseattle.com; map:J7*

NIDO / 1920½ 1st Ave, Downtown; 206/443-1272 This tiny nook's name means "nest" in Spanish and Italian—and owner Andrea Stuber-Margelou has a knack for feathering it with an eclectic collection of one-of-a-kind home accessories. You'll find body-care products, architectural artifacts, handcrafted jewelry, candles, and Victorian and chic European furniture side by side here. Definitely not for the budget-conscious. *Mon–Sat; map:I7*

NORTHWEST DISCOVERY, ELEMENTS GALLERY / Bellevue Square, Bellevue; 425/454-1676 / 10500 NE 8th St, Bellevue; 425/454-8242 Local artists get ample representation at Northwest Discovery, which carries a fine woodwork collection of boxes, cribbage boards, and mirrors as well as handblown glass, pottery, and wall art. Fourteen-karat, faceted, and fashion jewelry are distinctive and reasonably priced. Bonnie Altenburg owns Elements; her husband, Michael Altenburg, owns Northwest Discovery. *Every day; www.northwestdiscovery.com; map:HH3*

PHOENIX RISING GALLERY / 2030 Western Ave, Belltown; 206/728-2332 Owner Steven M. Dickinson's forte is carefully chosen and beautifully displayed functional art (blown glass, local ceramics, modern jewelry, and handcrafted furnishings), works that have garnered the shop national acclaim. *Every day; www.phoenixrisinggallery.com; map:H8*

PORTAGE BAY GOODS / 706 N 34th St, Fremont; 206/547-5221 Fittingly transplanted to Fremont from its former downtown location, Portage Bay combines good taste with do-good environmental and social awareness. Many of the crafts and handmade items here are fashioned from recycled materials or bought from international cooperatives, and some display furniture is made by local artists. *Every day; www.portage baygoods.com; map:FF8*

ZANADIA / 1815 N 45th St, Wallingford; 206/547-0884 The wares in this Wallingford Center shop are uniformly classy. Zanadia carries a wide range of contemporary, moderately pricey new furniture and antiques, as well as reasonably priced kitchen and lifestyle accessories, rugs, clocks, mirrors, magazine racks, picture frames, and the requisite supply of candles. Don't miss the downstairs portion of the store. *Every day; www. zanadia.com; map:FF7*

JEWELRY AND ACCESSORIES

ALVIN GOLDFARB JEWELER / 305 Bellevue Wy NE, Bellevue; 425/454-9393 Owner Alvin Goldfarb's shop is a favorite among moneyed Bellevueites. He learned his trade as a gemologist at Friedlander, his wife's family's business. Today he provides unerring personal attention and quality. *Mon–Sat; www.alvingoldfarbjeweler.com; map:HH3*

BEN BRIDGE / 1432 4th Ave, Downtown (and branches); 206/628-6800 Ben Bridge began in Seattle in 1912. While the shop has expanded to malls nationwide, its original downtown location is still a landmark and a decent diamond-shopping destination. The stones range from inexpensive to expensive, and service is informative. Mountings are fairly traditional, but custom design work is also offered. *Every day; www. benbridge.com; map:K6*

CARROLL'S FINE JEWELRY / 1427 4th Ave, Downtown; 206/622-9191 Flanked by an ornate clock, Carroll's is one of the loveliest and most fascinating gem stores in Seattle. To add to the atmosphere, customers sip tea and nibble on complimentary homemade cookies at this 1895 establishment. In addition to new and custom jewelry (mostly traditional designs), look for unusual finds such as an antique silver picture frame or a set of antique Oriental gaming pieces. There's also a classy selection of watches, rings, bracelets, necklaces, and gemstones. *Mon–Sat; www.carrollsfinejewelry.com; map:K6*

FACÈRÉ JEWELRY ART GALLERY / 1420 5th Ave, Downtown; 206/624-6768 Jewelry hunters in search of original adornments find them at Facèré in City Centre. Proprietor Karen Lorene, one of the city's leading authorities on antique jewelry, specializes in Victorian jewelry art. Along with exquisite old pieces, some dating from the late 18th century, she offers a beautifully displayed collection of 1920s engagement rings, as well as contemporary works by local designers and jewelry artists from around the country. *Mon–Sat; facereart@aol.com; www.facerejewelry art.com; map:J5*

FOX'S GEM SHOP / 1341 5th Ave, Downtown; 206/623-2528 This is the kind of place people dress up to shop at, an elegant shop with stiff prices. The specialties: glittering gemstones and dazzling diamonds. The gift section has some silver and a large selection of clocks. Fox's carries gems from Cartier as well as Mikimoto pearls and jewelry. *Mon–Sat; map:K6*

GSS JEWELERS / 526 1st Ave N, Queen Anne; 206/284-2082 / Bellevue Square, Bellevue; 425/462-8202 GSS (formerly the Gold & Silver Shop) crafts its own designs in-house. Styles range from traditional to ultramodern, and diamonds are an especially good value because the shop buys directly from contacts in Israel. Gemstones, too. *Every day; map:A7, HH3*

PHILIP MONROE JEWELER / 519 Pine St, Downtown; 206/624-1531 For truly one-of-a-kind jewelry, this shop is the place, and the top of the line when it comes to custom jewelry (which makes up 95 percent of its business). Occasionally the lovely selection of unusual and antique jewelry hangs from the arms of exquisite Oriental figurines. Antiques and art objects, too. *Mon–Sat; map:J5*

TURGEON-RAINE JEWELLERS / 1407 5th Ave, Downtown; 206/447-9488 An ever-present guard stands at the entrance to Norman Turgeon and Jerry Raine's chichi custom jewelry store. From new classics (tension-set diamonds) to old (modern twists on antique pieces), this store sells some of the city's finest custom and designer pieces. Despite the elegant digs, the approachable sales staff will make you feel at home among the precious baubles, bangles, and beads. Expensive? Sure. Worth it? Indeed. *Every day; jewellers@turgeon-raine.com; www.turgeonraine.com; map:J5*

MUSIC (CDS, RECORDS, AND TAPES)

BOP STREET RECORDS / 5219 Ballard Ave NW, Ballard; 206/297-2232
This Ballard record shop has an enormous selection of jazz, blues, and rock vinyl. Plenty of used CDs, 78s, and cassettes are hanging around, but Bop Street's main draw is its inventory consisting of approximately 500,000 albums and 45s. If you feel a bit overwhelmed by the massive stock here, owner Dave Voorhees is more than willing to help you navigate, just as he helped the members of British mega-band Radiohead, who spent seven hours in the shop last time they were in town. *Mon–Sat; bopstreet@foxinternet.com; www.bopstreet.com; map:EE8*

BUD'S JAZZ RECORDS / 102 S Jackson St, Pioneer Square; 206/628-0445 To Seattle jazz aficionados, this Pioneer Square store's underground location is the area's music-buying epicenter. Since 1982, Chicago refugee and jazz buff Bud Young has owned Seattle's only jazz, all-jazz, and nothing-but-jazz store. It has one of the most extensive inventories in the country, with around 15,000 titles in all—making it the biggest of its kind west of Chicago. Surrounded by framed photographs of the jazz greats, musicians argue over the unlisted sidemen on old Charlie Parker records, and Bud (who's almost always on duty) keeps an exhaustive jazz library for settling such arguments. The free search service has a great track record, and Bud also hangs jazz-related art shows on the walls. *Every day; map:O9*

DJANGO'S CELLOPHANE SQUARE / 4538 University Wy NE, University District (and branches); 206/634-2280 Of Cellophane Square's three branches, the University District location maintains the best selection (likely fed by the area's population of penniless students, since the store pays top dollar for good-condition used CDs). As a group, the stores carry one of Seattle's most extensive selection of used rock CDs. Good news for reclusive types: Cellophane Square's web site (now run by Portland-based Djangos.com) lets you download the entire inventory so you can do all your shopping on-line. Branches are in Bellevue (322 Bellevue Wy NE; 425/454-5059; map:HH3) and on Capitol Hill (130 Broadway Ave E; 206/329-2202; map:GG6). *Every day; www.djangos.com/stores_seattle.asp; map:FF6*

EASY STREET RECORDS / 4559 California Ave SW, Ste 200, West Seattle; 206/938-3279 Downtown dwellers with a hankering for new and used vinyl and rare imports regularly make the trek to this West Seattle Junction institution. The store's sales list is an indie-rock barometer for the Northwest, and the bar and cafe on-site provide yet another reason to loiter. Seattle-music luminaries shop here, as do visiting bands. Easy Street carries new and used CDs and features plenty of in-store performances. A second store in Ballard is separately owned (2220 NW Market St; 206/782-2344; map:FF7). *Every day; map:JJ8*

ROCK 'N' ROLL CITY

It's a running joke that Seattleites don't know how to drive in the snow, given how infrequently the white stuff falls here. But it is even more true that we haven't a clue about dealing with earthquakes. Residents of San Francisco and Los Angeles are so accustomed to periodic shakings that they barely notice them anymore, and they're prepared when a quake of any consequence hits. Seattleites, on the other hand, will sit before their televisions for every bit of breaking news if a tremor barely strong enough to register on the Richter scale unsettles the area's equilibrium. And then, when a truly violent quake does strike, as it did in 2001, they run out into the streets (a no-no when bricks are falling all around), bewildered and waiting for somebody to tell them what to do next.

Whether you knew it or not, the Emerald City has always been on shaky ground. More than 1,000 earthquakes with magnitude 1.0 or greater rumble through Washington and Oregon every year, most of them in the Puget Sound region. (Each unit of increase in magnitude represents about a 30-fold increase in energy release; so a magnitude 6.0 quake, considered of a damaging intensity, has approximately 1,000 times as much energy as a magnitude 4.0 quake.) Few of these shivers of the earth—maybe two dozen—are strong enough to be felt.

However, the area has withstood three substantial temblors over the last half century. Most destructive was the 7.1 magnitude quake on April 13, 1949, centered between Tacoma and Olympia, which damaged 30 Seattle schools, caused local power outages, and killed eight people. Less intense, with a 6.5 magnitude and centered between Seattle and Tacoma, was the quake of April 29, 1965. It damaged almost all waterfront facilities in Seattle, cast building rubble down on parked cars, made the Space Needle sway enough that the water in its toilet bowls spilled out, and was blamed for seven deaths. More recent was the February 28, 2001, shaker—measuring 6.8 on the Richter scale and centered 11 miles north of Olympia—which substantially harmed several of Pioneer Square's historic masonry buildings, shattered windows in the control tower at Seattle-Tacoma International Airport, and forced the closure of the Alaskan Way Viaduct, a potentially early casualty of any truly serious quake.

FALLOUT RECORDS & COMICS / 1506 E Olive Wy, Capitol Hill; 206/323-BOMB In a town where indie rock still thrives, Fallout gets plenty of punk cred for riding out the last two decades and remaining fiercely independent. This small-but-well-known location has vinyl (true to punk's roots), some CDs, and a staff who know every obscure independent/punk label, band, and recording ever made. One side of the store is devoted to music, the other to indie-press books, zines, and comics (we're not talkin' Marvel here). Doing its part to compete with the pervasive

So when is "the big one" due? Seismologists wisely avoid making such predictions. But they are more than willing to say why the Seattle area is in for more bumpy rides on the earth's crust. There are three different sources of local earthquakes.

First is the **Cascadia Subduction Zone,** a 750-mile-long stretch located in the Pacific Ocean about 50 miles off the West Coast, where an eastward-moving structural plate of the ocean floor—the Juan de Fuca Plate—is being forced very slowly beneath the North American Plate, on top of which sits the land we see around us. These plates tend to shove against one another, then suddenly break apart again with a violence that can produce quakes of magnitudes 8.0 or greater anywhere along the zone.

The second source of drastic local shakings is the **Benioff Zone,** an area of faulting that radiates out from the Cascadia Subduction Zone and may cause deep quakes with magnitudes of up to 7.5.

Finally, there are shallow earthquakes—maybe the worst-case scenario for Seattle. These upheavals occur within the North American Plate, close to the ground's surface, and (especially with aftershocks) can do considerable damage to whatever rests upon that surface, be it skyscrapers or highways or people. This area's best-known weakness in the earth's crust is the **Seattle Fault,** which runs east-west through the city from Issaquah to Bremerton. Geological evidence indicates that the Seattle Fault has been quiet for something like 1,100 years. But its last convulsion was a real humdinger, provoking landslides into Lake Washington and a tsunami (or tremendous wave) on Puget Sound. Seattle's 1949, 1965, and 2001 quakes were all deep quakes, and most buildings here are designed to withstand those. However, seismologists are becoming increasingly concerned about the Seattle Fault, as small quakes occur with greater frequency along its length.

In the event of a significant quake, stay inside if you're already there and squeeze yourself under something that can protect you from falling debris, such as a sturdy desk or table. If you're outside, duck into a doorway or move into an open area, staying clear of telephone poles and overhead wires. And for heaven's sake, tell those dumbfounded Seattleites milling in the streets to take cover, too. — *J. Kingston Pierce*

Ticketmaster, Fallout also sells tickets to rock shows and hosts frequent in-store performances from local and national bands, as well as art openings. *Tues–Sun; www.falloutrecords.com; map:GG6*

GOLDEN OLDIES / 201 NE 45th St, Wallingford (and branches); 206/547-2260 Customers looking to buy the sweet sounds of yesteryear should stop by this aging Wallingford establishment. Faded and peeling, Golden Oldies has more records than other formats, and of those, many are 45s. Pick up an insert adapter and you can head straight home with your 45 and plop it on your turntable (assuming you still have one) with no delay. Well organized—CDs by genre and vinyl by artist, with a catalog stretching back to 1910—the store will buy, sell, or trade almost anything recorded since 1900. There are three branches total (others are in Renton and Tacoma). *Every day; oldies@ix.netcom.com; www.golden oldies-records.com; map:FF7*

ORPHEUM / 618 Broadway Ave E, Capitol Hill; 206/322-6370 Orpheum's smugly knowledgeable staff peddle one of the area's best selections of new releases in modern and indie rock, jazz, techno, and dance. It carries a few rarities and boxed sets, but the main draw tends to be the upstairs, mainly vinyl, loft, where DJs of all flavors converge to battle over new and used hip-hop, R&B, techno, and house records. *Every day; map:GG6*

SINGLES GOING STEADY / 2219 2nd Ave, Belltown; 206/441-7396 Punk rock in all its varying subgenres (straight edge, oi!, ska, etc.) lives at Singles Going Steady. With an impressive selection of vinyl, CDs, T-shirts, patches, buttons, studded belts, collars, and armbands, plus posters by modern graphic-art hero Lindsey Kuhn to boot, this record store has truly cornered the market on punk collectibles. Ex-punkers take note: the shop will take your old gear off your hands, and they'll pay top dollar for it, too. *Every day; orders@singlesgoingsteady.com; www.singles goingsteady.com; map:G7*

SONIC BOOM RECORDS / 3414 Fremont Ave N, Fremont; 206/547-BOOM This independent Fremont store is run by a pair of music lovers with an encyclopedic knowledge of music—especially the locally grown sort. Frequent in-store performances by local indie-rock acts complement the excellent selection of vinyl and the staff's never-pretentious helpfulness. *Every day; sonicboom@sonicboomrecords.com; www.sonicboom records.com; map:FF7*

WALL OF SOUND / 2237 2nd Ave, Belltown; 206/441-9880 Mainstream music fans, steer clear: you'll find no Top 40 dance hits here. You're in luck, however, if you're in search of off-the-beaten-path CDs and records falling roughly into the world beat, jazz, or electronica categories. The key word here is "eclectic" (in fact, it's the most common filing category in the store). From French hip-hop to Peruvian percussion, their inventory offers a round-the-world tour. One side of the store houses all the CDs, the other is a vinyl-topia (a shared space with the Mag Daddy magazine store). The store has listening stations, too, where you can relax with the store cat while perusing possible purchases. *Every day; map:G7*

OUTDOOR GEAR

ALPINE HUT / 2215 15th Ave W, Interbay (and branches); 206/284-3575 This no-frills shop outfits for fun on the water, the slopes, or the trail. This is a great place to find good deals on all kinds of ski gear in winter or in-line skates, mountain bikes, and bike wear in summer. The owner is friendly and the store aims to please. *Every day; map:EE8*

C. C. FILSON CO. / 1555 4th Ave S, SoDo; 206/622-3147 Some of the virtually indestructible wear at this centenarian Seattle outfitter hasn't altered in design since 1914. Around since the turn of the (19th) century, Filson sells rugged wearables that are enjoying something of a rebirth since the opening of a retail store just south of downtown. Heavy wool jackets and vests, canvas hunting coats, oil-finish hats, and wool pants are the style here. The original C. C. Filson sold clothes to the men headed north to Alaska during the gold rush, and today's clothes are still attractive and tough. There's a complete line of handsome luggage (including gun bags), too. At Filson they take themselves rather too seriously, but after more than 100 years in business, why shouldn't they? *Every day; www.ccfilson.com; map:R9*

CROSSINGS / 921 Fairview Ave N, Ste C120, South Lake Union; 206/287-9979 / Carillon Point, Kirkland; 425/889-2628 Nautical fashions for landlubbers and water fiends alike. Though Crossings emphasizes its sailing wear (it's the official outfitter for the Windermere Cup), the classic clothing here is suited for any boating adventure. The outerwear keeps you dry on deck, and the natural-fiber fabrics keep you looking the sailor. *Every day; www.crossings-crew.com; map:D1, EE3*

ELLIOTT BAY BICYCLES / 2116 Western Ave, Belltown; 206/441-8144 Titanium frames and shop talk rule in this Bentley of bike stores. Elliott Bay is regarded as something of a pro shop: it sells bikes to cyclists who know what they're doing and do enough of it to justify paying high prices. Among its other attributes, the shop is home base for Bill Davidson, a nationally known frame builder, whose designs include aforementioned custom titanium frames. *Every day; feedback@elliott baybicycles.com; www.elliottbaybicycles.com, www.davidsonbicycles. com; map:H9*

FEATHERED FRIENDS / 119 Yale Ave N, Downtown; 206/292-2210 Serious climbers and snow campers turn to Feathered Friends for expedition insulation. These are the top-of-the-line down products in the city; the shop's Gore-Tex and handmade down clothes have accompanied climbing expeditions for years. It specializes in sporting goods, sleeping bags (made to order), and climbing equipment, and also sells bedding and comforters. *Every day; www.featheredfriends.com; map:H1*

GREGG'S GREENLAKE CYCLE / 7007 Woodlawn Ave NE, Green Lake (and branches); 206/523-1822 Gregg's is a high-volume, high-pressure Seattle institution, perhaps (at least initially) by virtue of its location. Gregg's stocks kids' bikes, all-terrain bikes, and Japanese-, Italian-, and

American-made racing bicycles, along with Seattle's largest collection of touring bikes. If you do buy from Gregg's, you'll get good follow-up service. The Green Lake location, just yards from the lake's busy bike path, has a large clothing and accessories department and rents bikes, roller skates, in-line skates, and snowboards. Branches are in Bellevue (121 106th Ave NE; 425/462-1900; map:HH3) and at Aurora Cycle (7401 Aurora Ave N, Green Lake; 206/783-1000; map:EE7). *Every day; seattle@greggscycles.com; www.greggscycles.com; map:EE7*

IL VECCHIO / 140 Lakeside Ave, Leschi; 206/324-8148 George Gibb's Leschi shop is the bicycle equivalent of a Gucci boutique. The award-winning Weinstein-designed store is minimalist in appeal—there are very few bikes here—and maximalist in quality (and price): Italian racers De Rosa and Pinarello, and American-made Landshark. Proper frame fit is a certainty. In addition to the road and racing bicycles, the shop sells top components and cycling apparel. *Tues–Sat and by appointment; il vecchio@mindspring.com; www.ilvecchio.com; map:HH6*

MARINER KAYAKS / 2134 Westlake Ave N, Westlake; 206/284-8404 Owners and brothers Cam and Matt Broze bring years of paddling experience and sea kayak expertise to their operation—and they're always available to debate the finer points of hull shape and function. Mariner kayaks are considered by many sea kayakers as some of the best in the world. Matt developed the modern paddle float used for rescues, and has written numerous articles on sea-kayaking skill and safety. In addition to the Mariner line, which includes kayaks for sea touring and the outer coast surf, Mariner Kayaks sells the Seda, Nimbus, and Feathercraft lines, Lightning and Epic paddles, and everything else you need to get out on the water. *Tues–Sat; www.marinerkayaks.com; map:GG7*

MARLEY'S SNOWBOARDS AND SKATEBOARDS / 5424 Ballard Ave NW, Ballard; 206/782-6081 When co-owner Ian Fels took up snowboarding more than a decade ago, he never looked back at skiing. He's a friendly, talkative guy who can tell you anything you need to know about getting extreme or getting started. Marley's carries top brands that range in price from reasonable to jaw-dropping. There's a wide selection of snowboarding wear, too. In summer the emphasis switches to skateboards. *Every day; map:FF8*

MARMOT MOUNTAIN WORKS / 827 Bellevue Wy NE, Bellevue; 425/453-1515 Eastsiders heading for the snow and ice stop at Marmot. Everything for the skier, backpacker, and mountaineer is for sale or rent here, including cross-country skis, packs, tents, boots, crampons, ice axes, and more. Prices for outerwear are some of the highest around; however, deals can be found on some ski accessories, such as climbing skins for the backcountry. An excellent selection of climbing hardware. *Every day; www.marmotmountain.com; map:HH3*

THE NORTH FACE / 1023 1st Ave, Downtown; 206/622-4111 As the Ralph Lauren for the backpacking set, North Face's prices are pretty exorbitant, but the quality of backpacking equipment and design here is topnotch. North Face also carries down clothing and bags, outdoor apparel, and skiwear. The store has every mountaineering guidebook imaginable. The feeling here is of a yuppified REI, but that doesn't mean the store isn't serious about products and service. *Every day; www.the northface.com; map:L8*

NORTHWEST OUTDOOR CENTER / 2100 Westlake Ave N, Westlake; 206/281-9694 or 800/683-0637 Novice kayakers choose from a smorgasbord of beginning paddling instruction here: from Whale Searching to Whitewater. And advanced paddlers can get suitably schooled here, too. Right on the lakefront (Lake Union), NWOC is the easiest place to try out or rent a variety of kayaks—a must if you are thinking of buying. A full-service paddling shop, NWOC carries sea and whitewater kayaks, gear, and accessories. Enthusiastic staff, excellent instruction. *Every day; www.nwoc.com; map:GG7*

PATAGONIA / 2100 1st Ave, Belltown; 206/622-9700 Polar fleece with a granola conscience and a customer base planted firmly in their Birkenstocks and SUVs. Sleek-wood glamour and high-quality outdoor fashion pervade Seattle's own Patagucci Central. The signature (and ultra-engineered) fleece pieces and oh-so-politically-correct garments made with organically grown cotton are famously long-wearing and notoriously spendy. Great book selection. Staff are well versed in local environmental issues and eager to talk. *Every day; www.patagonia.com; map:H8*

PATRICK'S FLY SHOP / 2237 Eastlake Ave E, Eastlake; 206/325-8988 Patrick's Fly Shop has been reeling in anglers for more than 50 years— and justly so. Fishing enthusiasts think of this shop (the oldest fly shop in the state) as the premier source of information on area fly-fishing and fly-tying. Patrick's offers workshops as well as old-fashioned fishing stories and advice. *Every day; www.patricksflyshop.com; map:GG7*

R & E CYCLES / 5627 University Wy NE, University District; 206/527-4822 A stronghold of custom frame-building expertise (the shop has crafted bikes for one-armed customers), R&E specializes in hand-built Rodriguez frames. And owners Dan Towle and Estelle Gray include tandems, racing bikes, and wheel building in their repertoire. They also operate Seattle Bike Repair (5601 University Wy NE; 206/527-0360; map:EE7). The shop opens at noon, but is open mornings and after hours by appointment. *Tues–Sun; sales@rodcycle.com; www.rodcycle.com; map:FF6*

REI (RECREATIONAL EQUIPMENT INC.) / 222 Yale Ave N, Downtown (and branches); 206/223-1944 See Top 25 Attractions in the Exploring chapter.

RECYCLED CYCLES / 1007 NE Boat St, University District; 206/547-4491 or 877/298-4683 Old (and not-so-old) bikes get geared up for new owners here. At Recycled's pleasant Boat Street location, old bikes are taken in, cleaned up, given new parts where necessary, and put back on the market. There's a full-service repair shop, too. Though the focus is on mountain, road, and 10-speed bikes, no bike is too old, specialized, or goofy-looking—even old Schwinn cruisers, track bikes, or two-wheeled transporters that would have suited Mary Poppins. *Every day; steve@ recycledcycles.com; www.recycledcycles.com; map:FF6*

SECOND ASCENT / 5209 Ballard Ave NW, Ballard; 206/545-8810 This shop recently changed its name (it was formerly Second Bounce) to reflect its focus on outdoor gear rather than ball-related sports. Frugal adventurers turn here for a wide range of new and used quality gear for climbing, mountaineering, cycling, paddling, and general camping. The store is folksy, with excellent help, and owners know their business, carrying the right products at bargain prices. Buy, sell, trade, and consign. *Every day; www.secondascent.com; map:EE8*

SNOWBOARD CONNECTION / 604 Alaskan Wy, Waterfront; 206/467-8545 Board sports for all seasons get ample representation at this 12-year-old store. Snowboards by K2, Burton, Ride, and more, plus tuning and great advice from experts who spend plenty of time on slopes, waves, and halfpipes; T-shirts, boots, and basic, functional warm clothing too. Also skateboards and surfboards. New products arrive daily. *Every day; www.snowboardconnection.com; map:N8*

SUPER JOCK 'N JILL / 7210 E Green Lake Dr N, Green Lake; 206/522-7711 or 800/343-4111 Pinpoint your footfalls' downfalls with analysis from the staff at Super Jock 'N Jill. These salespeople know their metatarsi and their merchandise and understand the mechanics of running and power walking. A podiatrist is in the store once a week to answer questions and help with problems. The selection of other merchandise (running gear, bathing suits) is smaller but carefully chosen. This is also a good source for race registration and info, fun runs, routes, and training. *Every day; sjnjill@uswest.net; www.jocknjill.com; map:EE7*

SWIFTWATER / 4235 Fremont Ave N, Fremont; 206/547-3377 Get rolling on a river with a craft from this little Fremont storefront, which specializes in rafts and inflatable kayaks. They'll rent you one, sell you one, or help you organize a trip on one (for fly-fishing). These guys know their waterways. *Mon–Tues, Thurs–Sat; map:FF7*

URBAN SURF / 2100 N Northlake Wy, Wallingford; 206/545-9463 The popular Burke-Gilman Trail, just steps from the door of this shop near Gas Works Park, yields plenty of walk-in customers here. In addition to windsurfing, in-line skating, surfing, and snowboarding equipment and apparel, the store bills itself as the area authority on kiteboarding—a sort of windsurf/parasail hybrid. In-line skate rentals, too. *Every day; usurf@ urbansurf.com; www.urbansurf.com; map:FF7*

WRIGHT BROTHERS CYCLE WORKS / 219 N 36th St, Fremont; 206/633-5132 Join the Wright Brothers cooperative and you'll get to tinker with your bike using their tools and space. Or if DIY repairs aren't your style, hand your cycle off to the reliable team here for fixing. Owner Charles Hadrann and his staff are known for wheel building, informative repair classes, and good advice. There's an ever-growing selection of tires, and prices on parts are fair. *Tues–Sun (summer), Tues–Sat (winter); map:FF7*

SEAFOOD

CITY FISH COMPANY / 1535 Pike Pl, Pike Place Market; 206/682-9329; 800/334-2669 The market's longest-running seafood vendor (open since 1917) boasts great quality and consistently knowledgeable service. This Main Arcade purveyor does a brisk business in local fish and shellfish, and also offers some exotics such as Louisiana crawfish. Dungeness crab and line-caught king salmon are specialties. Overnight shipping to anywhere in the country. *Every day; www.cityfish.com; map:J8*

JACK'S FISH SPOT / 1514 Pike Pl, Pike Place Market; 206/467-0514 It doesn't get any fresher: this fine seafood shop has the only live-shellfish tanks in the market's main arcade, with loads of live crabs, clams, lobsters, and oysters. They smoke their own salmon, run a walk-up oyster bar, and have great fish-and-chips and clam chowder. *Every day; jfish spot@aol.com; www.jacksfishspot.com; map:J8*

MUTUAL FISH COMPANY / 2335 Rainier Ave S, Rainier Valley; 206/322-4368 Mutual Fish fillets and steaks turn up on plates in many of Seattle's fanciest restaurants—and in the kitchens of the city's more discerning gourmets. This is the best in town: top quality and a dazzling selection are the result of the undivided attention of the Yoshimura family. Fresh tanks are full of several types of local oysters and crabs, and the seafood cases present the best from the West and East Coasts. Seattleites are pleased to find mahi mahi, tilefish, Maryland soft-shell crabs (in season), and other exotics. Prices are good, and they'll pack for air freight or carry-home. Just south of I-90, where Rainier Valley squeezes between Beacon Hill and the Mount Baker neighborhood. *Every day; www. mutualfish.com; map:II6*

PIKE PLACE FISH / 86 Pike Pl, Pike Place Market; 206/682-7181 or 800/542-7732 The fish-slinging antics and wisecracking commentary of this market stall draw hordes of gaping tourists wielding camcorders. At this Pike Place institution, there's also a good selection of fresh fish and shellfish, plus smoked and kippered seafood, and some local rarities such as the homely geoduck (a must-see). Pike Place Fish will pack and ship for the traveler. Located in the Main Arcade, next to the bronze pig. *Every day; pikeplacefish@pikeplacefish.com; www.pikeplacefish.com; map:J8*

QUEEN ANNE THRIFTWAY / 1908 Queen Anne Ave N, Queen Anne; 206/284-2530 / WEST SEATTLE ADMIRAL THRIFTWAY / 2320 42nd Ave SW, West Seattle; 206/937-0551 Yes, they're grocery stores, but not merely of the Wonder-bread-and-ground-beef variety. At the Queen Anne store, fish guru Rick Cavanaugh runs one of the best seafood departments in the United States (Julia Child orders from him): pristine stock and 20 to 30 kinds of fish and shellfish, from here and all over. He's also usually the first local to score the sought-after Copper River salmon, available only for a limited time each spring. Savvy cooks call ahead to tailor their menus to what's in that day. Special orders welcome; free packing for travel. The West Seattle Thriftway carries on the same fine tradition, with a stunning service counter. *Every day; map:GG8, II9*

SEATTLE CAVIAR COMPANY / 2833 Eastlake Ave E, Eastlake; 206/323-3005 The offerings at the pickup window of Seattle's only caviar importer put McDonald's to shame—as does the shop's regal interior. Owners Dale and Betsy Sherrow sell the finest beluga, osetra, and sevruga caviar from the Caspian Sea, in addition to Northwest fresh American malossol caviar and all the froufrou accoutrements of serious roe-eating (such as pretty mother-of-pearl spoons and caviar *presentoirs*). They'll gladly arrange beautiful gift packages and even handle shipping. Stop in for a Saturday caviar tasting, too. *Tues–Sat and by appointment; info@caviar.com; www.caviar.com; map:GG7*

UNIVERSITY SEAFOOD & POULTRY COMPANY / 1317 NE 47th St, University District; 206/632-3900 Although students, who make up the bulk of this neighborhood's population, aren't known for their culinary prowess, Dale Erickson's shop continues to thrive in the heart of the University District. The selection includes salmon, halibut, lingcod, seasonal treats such as local sturgeon, and an amazing array of caviars—from flying fish to Columbia River sturgeon to beluga. Hard-to-find game birds, free-run chickens, and the freshest eggs, too. Prices are not posted but, surprisingly enough, are in line with supermarket prices. The fishmongers at the counter are friendly, and are all good cooks with recipes to share. *Mon–Sat; map:FF6*

WILD SALMON SEAFOOD MARKET / 1900 W Nickerson St, Interbay; 206/283-3366 or 888/222-FISH This neighborhood fishmonger boasts personal service and fresh seafood in a dockside setting. In addition to tanks filled with live lobster, oysters, clams, and mussels, this small seafood specialist sells good-looking fish fillets, steaks, and whole fish and shellfish from its large service counter. Crab cakes and salmon cakes are usually available for impressive yet low-maintenance meals. *Every day; ask@wildsalmonseafood.com; www.wildsalmonseafood.com; map:FF8*

SHOES

CHURCH'S ENGLISH SHOES / 402 University St, Downtown; 206/682-3555 The selection of men's shoes in this Rainier Square shop is decidedly English: buttoned down and gleamingly proper. A variety of textures (lizard, suede) and styles (loafers, two-tones) punctuate the perfect-for-the-fancy-office footwear (in brown, black, and cream leathers). Also, more casual weekend wear from the notoriously comfortable Clark's of England. Prices are not scaled for the budget-conscious. *Every day; www.churchsshoes.com; map:J5*

DUNCAN AND SONS BOOTS AND SADDLES / 1946 1st Ave S, SoDo; 206/622-1310 Urban cowgirl or bona fide ranch hand: this family-run boot shop (around since 1898) outfits them all with more than 30 styles of Western boots for men, women, and children. Prices run from $90 to $350. Most of the boots are handmade in Texas. *Mon–Sat; map:P9*

EDIE'S / 319 E Pine St, Capitol Hill; 206/839-1111 One of the first stores in Seattle to carry Spanish cult-favorite brand Camper, Edie's stocks styles (for men and women) that are current and terribly chic. The selection here is minimal but alluring. Owner Erin Dolan is happy to special order, and also carries a few handbags and jewelry items. *Every day; map:K1*

J. GILBERT FOOTWEAR / 2025 1st Ave, Belltown; 206/441-1182 Leather soft enough to spread on your toast and candy colors (along with a healthy dose of black and brown) make the footwear at J. Gilbert irresistible. These are office-appropriate shoes for men and women who don't want to sacrifice hipness for professionalism. The mostly Euro inventory includes Camper, Immagini, Paul Green, Donald Pliner, and others. Prices are steep, but don't climb above $300. *Every day; jgilbert shoes@uswest.com; www.jgilbertfootwear.com; map:H8*

JOHN FLUEVOG SHOES / 1611 1st Ave, Downtown; 206/441-1065 or 800/568-DDFT This tiny store near the Pike Place Market is as much an avant-garde art gallery as a shoe shop. Styles for men and women are famously fashion forward: thigh-high lace-up boots, bright orange flare-heeled platforms, red cowboy/combat boots. The Canadian owner does the designs; the shoes are made in England, Poland, Mexico, and Spain. For club divas and daring souls. *Every day; seattle@fluevog.ca; www. fluevog.com; map:I7*

M. J. FEET / 1514 Pike Pl, Pike Place Market (and branches); 206/624-2929 The sturdy sandals that are a staple of the Northwest high-tech uniform can be found in many hues and styles here. The cheerful shops carry creative socks and tights, plus a small selection of clothing. They're also good places to get hard-to-find Ellington school bags. Great repair service. Other branches are on the Ave (4334 University Wy NE, University District; 206/632-5353; map:FF6) and in Old Bellevue (15 NE 103rd St; 425/688-9139; map:HH3). *Every day; mjfeet@aol.com; www.mjfeet.com; map:J8*

MAGGIE'S SHOES / 1927 1st Ave, Downtown; 206/728-5837 The fine footwear here is all Maggie's own label. The edgy designs and up-to-the-minute colors make Maggie's women's and men's shoes most desirable. Most pairs cost more than $100—average spending for fine footwear such as this. *Every day; map:I7*

PED / 1115 1st Ave, Downtown; 206/292-1767 Shoes from Ped are the make-the-outfit types. This footwear won't fade into the floor like ordinary loafers and mules, but stands out as expertly crafted, design-conscious showpieces. Styles for men and women from Giraudon, Cydwoq, and others range from strappy sandals to urban walking shoes. *Every day; www.pedshoes.com; map:L7*

SAN MARCO / 1631 6th Ave, Downtown; 206/343-9138 This tiny, trendy boutique flourishes even in the shadow of nearby giants Nordstrom and Pacific Place. You'll find Giofreddo Fantini, Arche, Espace, and other fine women's footwear. The store also carries clothing from Christian Lacroix and other haute shots. Watch for the end-of-summer and end-of-winter sales. *Every day; map:J5*

THE WOOLLY MAMMOTH / 4303 University Wy NE, University District; 206/632-3254 / 5 DOORS UP / 4309½ University Wy NE, University District; 206/547-3192 Most shoes in the original store are as rugged and weatherproof as their name. The Woolly Mammoth mostly carries sensible European comfort brands such as Josef Seibel, Ecco, and Naote. A second store up the street, called 5 Doors Up, carries trendier stuff—Steve Madden, John Fluevog, and the like. *Every day; map:FF6*

SPECIALTY SHOPS

ARCADE SMOKE SHOP / 1522 5th Ave, Downtown; 206/587-0159 Smoking may have lost its allure over the past few decades, but this shop, secreted away in an underground location next to a teriyaki joint, carries lacquered wooden humidors, Zippo lighters, and pipes (of briarwood and amber root, many by Dunhill). There are long glass counters of smooth cigarette and bulbous cigar cases made from leather, silver, and pewter. Cigars line the shelves of a separate, glass-walled room, while pipe tobacco blends fill hefty glass jars. The shop also sells hammered pewter and silver hip flasks, and thoughtfully provides Vicks cough drops. *Mon–Sat; map:J6*

ARCHIE MCPHEE / 2428 NW Market St, Ballard; 206/297-0240 Pop culture icons such as the boxing nun puppet and the wiggling hula girl dash ornament get center stage—instead of just a junk-near-the-checkstand nod—at this longtime purveyor of kitsch. Archie McPhee's is a great place to stock up on cheap toys and party favors or just to browse the memorable catalog. Plenty of grown-ups confess shameful inclinations to lose themselves among the windup toys and bendable plastic creatures. *Every day; www.mcphee.com; map:FF8*

DUSTY STRINGS / 3406 Fremont Ave N, Fremont; 206/634-1662 Flawless acoustic stringed instruments are crafted on-site at this folk-musician haven. Aside from carefully handmade hammered dulcimers and lever harps (as opposed to the classical pedal harp), Dusty Strings also sells high-quality guitars (many by Taylor), banjos, fiddles, mandolins (hourglass-shaped "mountain" and banjo-looking "walkabout" versions), hand drums, concertinas, and flutes. One room is devoted entirely to music, in sheet, lesson book, video, and CD form. Celtic, folk, bluegrass, traditional, and jazz musicians form the customer base, but if you ever wanted to learn Japanese *shakuhachi* flute or Hawaiian slack-key guitar, this is the place to look. Workshops are frequent and well attended. *Every day; musicshop@dustystrings.com; www.dustystrings.com; map:FF7*

METSKER MAPS / 702 1st Ave, Downtown; 206/623-8747 or 800/727-4430 In addition to the cartographic abundance here (shiny posters of satellite-image maps, thick Atlas Gazetteers, folding maps of Lebanon in German), Metsker carries a staggering assortment of worldwide travel guides, with a generous emphasis on the Northwest. Globes, including several that light up, sit underneath reproduction posters of antique maps and prints. Map tacks are boxed by color, and laminated Mac field guides, handy for flora and fauna identification on beach walks or mountain hikes, are tucked in a corner. The truly intrepid can purchase trail park passes for hikes into Washington's national forests. *Mon–Sat; sales@metskers.com; www.metskers.com; map:N8*

MICHAEL MASLAN HISTORIC PHOTOGRAPHS POSTCARDS & EPHEMERA / 214 1st Ave S, Pioneer Square; 206/587-0187 If you happen by Michael Maslan's store when he's open (his hours vary according to whim, so call first), stop in. You'll find vintage lithographs of jungle scenes, faded portraits of stiff-lipped Victorian-era families, and endless postcards from every location and era from the turn of the 19th century. The walls are covered with vintage maps, photographs, and posters, mostly elegant samples from the era of shipboard travel or kitschy ads from the post–World War II airline boom. Prices range from extremely reasonable to heirloom level. Infrequently open on weekends. *Mon–Fri; map:O8*

PAPERHAUS / 2008 1st Ave, Belltown; 206/374-8566 The shelves of sleek albums, portfolios, and (of course) paper at Paperhaus look like the organizational product of an obsessive-compulsive stationer—and we mean that in the best possible way. The neat-as-a-hospital-ward look of this Belltown shop shows off the selection of paper and leather or metal portfolios suitable for the most discerning designer's resumé. And the wares here are eco-conscious: paper products are made from recycled materials, leather items from by-products. *Every day; info@paperhaus. com; www.paperhaus.com; map:H7*

SCARECROW VIDEO / 5030 Roosevelt Wy NE, University District; 206/524-8554 This jam-packed two-floor store carries almost everything ever committed to celluloid anywhere in the world. Scarecrow's immense collection of videocassettes, DVDs, and laserdiscs is catalogued not just by New Releases and Top Rentals but by director (alphabetically), place of origin ("Balkan States") and unusual category (animé, blaxploitation, hip-hop, experimental, and so on). A revolving selection of new and used films is on sale at any given time, boosted by yearly blowouts and enhanced by a knowledgeable staff that not only order in-print movies but will search for out-of-print flicks as well. VCR (both American and PAL, a European VHS format) players and DVD players are available for nightly rental for under $10. There's even an espresso stand by the door for late-night video marathon fueling. *Every day; scarecrow@scarecrow. com; www.scarecrow.com; map:FF7*

SILBERMAN/BROWN FINE STATIONERS / 1322 5th Ave, Downtown; 206/292-9404 / 10220 NE 8th St, Bellevue; 425/455-3665 This shop does the lost art of letter-writing proud. Rows of richly colored pens (Waterman, Cartier) and shelves of fine stationery are just the beginning; handcrafted silver pen sheaths (to mask an unsightly ballpoint), floral painted stamp dispensers, and flat silver business card cases are a few of the elegant items attractive for their very lack of necessity. An ordering service can produce engraved announcements or invitations in (with luck) just a few days. Monogrammed stationery, seals and colored sticks of sealing wax, photo frames, tooled leather photo albums, and a Civil War chess set round out the eclectic, seductive wares. *Mon–Sat; map:K6, GG3*

YE OLDE CURIOSITY SHOP / 1001 Alaskan Wy/Pier 54, Waterfront; 206/682-5844 Some people revel in the kitschy clutter of this "world-famous" Seattle attraction (since 1899)—others bolt for the door. Either way, the Curiosity Shop is a novelty—it's even been immortalized with its own book (*1001 Curious Things*, University of Washington Press, 2001). This veritable kitsch museum houses a remarkable collection of Northwest Indian and Eskimo art, ivory, and soapstone, plus knick-knacks carved from Mount St. Helens ash, totem poles, and other curios. Among the curiosities, you'll find shrunken heads from the Jivaro tribe

of South America and creatively assembled animals. *Every day; www.*
yeoldecuriosityshop.com; map:L9

TOYS

AMERICAN EAGLES / 12537 Lake City Wy NE, Lake City; 206/440-8448
Planes, trains, and automobiles in miniature are among the models at this
largest hobby shop in the country. Owner George Edwards stocks more
than 87,000 different items, including a regiment of 22,000 miniature
soldiers, and lots and lots of models. *Mon–Sat; www.americaneagles*
hobbies.com; map:CC6

EASTSIDE TRAINS / 217 Central Wy, Kirkland; 425/828-4098 This Kirkland shop carries all the big names in little trains: Lionel, Atlas, Märklin,
and more. The business chugged along for years out of the owner's home.
Now it's full speed ahead in its Kirkland retail location. You'll also find
train-related videos here. *Mon–Sat; eastsidetrains@msn.com; www.east*
sidetrains.com; map:EE3

FAO SCHWARZ / 1420 5th Ave, Downtown (and branches); 206/442-
9500, Bellevue Square, Bellevue; 425/646-9500 Parents: prepare for
your children to go nuts. From the mechanical clock tower—a two-story-
high, singing, prancing toy sculpture that greets you at the door—to the
animal-stuffed jungle room with its talking tree, the preschool area with
toddler toys to interest one and all, and the Barbie room (a very pink display of all the Barbie dolls and accessories ever made), it's clear why FAO
is the biggest toy show in town. The Bellevue Square store is slightly less
ostentatious than the Seattle store in City Centre. *Every day; faoseattle@*
fao.net; www.fao.com; map:J5, HH3

THE GREAT WIND-UP / 93 Pike Pl, Pike Place Market; 206/621-9370
The buzz, whir, and chirp of the Great Wind-Up's mechanical menagerie
is audible from a few doors away. The shop is full of every kind of windup
(collectible tin items, too) and battery-operated animated toy imaginable.
Home to everyone's favorite nostalgia toys: Slinky, Sea Monkeys, Pez,
and Gumby. In the Economy Market Atrium. *Every day; www.great*
windup.com; map:J8

IMAGINATION TOYS / 1815 N 45th St, Wallingford; 206/547-2356 /
2236 NW Market St, Ballard; 206/784-1310 Sturdy classic toys, not
cheap, breakable plastic junk. Imagination is a great source for Brio,
Gund, and the ever-popular Lego. This family-run store also carries
activity toys by Playmobil, train sets, games, and puzzles. They feature a
wide assortment of musical instruments ranging from ukuleles to key-
boards, too. The Wallingford store is located in Wallingford Center.
Every day; map:FF7, FF8

MAGIC MOUSE TOYS / 603 1st Ave, Pioneer Square; 206/682-8097 Two large floors of top-of-the line diversions make this Pioneer Square shop at First Avenue and Yesler Way a favorite for Seattleites in search of playthings. Magic Mouse carries Steiff animals, Corolle dolls, Brio wooden train sets, and Märklin electric trains. The stuffed-animal collection includes more than 100 styles of teddy bears alone. There's a selection of developmental baby and preschool toys, art supplies, games and puzzles (for all ages), kids' books, windup toys, stocking stuffers, and literally hundreds of different decks of cards (including tarot cards). *Every day; map:N8*

PINOCCHIO'S TOYS / 4540 Union Bay Pl NE, University District; 206/528-1100 This store on the east side of University Village sells toys with a purpose: puzzles, interactive play media (such as Playmobil and Brio), nature-exploring aids (binoculars and science workbooks), a wide variety of paints (nontoxic watercolors and tie-dyeing kits), and Ty toys (stuffed animals by the makers of Beanie Babies). Books in stock are geared more toward adults reading bedtime stories to the little 'uns than toward older children who read on their own. *Every day; map:FF6*

TERI'S TOYBOX / 420 Main St, Edmonds (and branch); 425/774-3190 This is a great place to gift-shop (ask for wrap and they'll gladly tuck your purchase into a beribboned gift bag). Collectible dolls are handsomely displayed, and you're sure to find something for every kid on your list: art and jewelry-making supplies, educational toys, stuffed animals, building blocks, kiddy carpenter tools, cassette tapes and CDs, and more. There is one other Toybox, in the basement of the Bon at Northgate Mall (206/440-6753). *Every day*

THINKER TOYS / 10610 NE 8th St, Bellevue; 425/453-0051 Housed in a converted vintage gas station, this shop's intelligently chosen, upper-end inventory appeals to those with discriminating recreational tastes. There's a bit of everything: kites, games, trains, dolls, books, 3-D puzzles. Kids of all ages will go bonkers in the mind-boggler section. *Every day; map:HH3*

TOP TEN TOYS / 104 N 85th St, Greenwood; 206/782-0098 Barbie and her entourage don't get shelf space at this discerning store. Parents and kids love the sections of toys here devoted to toddlers, infants, and the "2's." Look for the tricycle and wagon section and the unexciting but most necessary Safety First line for parents (featuring electrical-outlet covers and cabinet safety locks). *Every day; map:EE8*

TREE TOP TOYS / 17171 Bothell Wy NE, Lake Forest Park; 206/363-5460 The big Brio train setup here in this Lake Forest Park Town Center store is directly responsible for the extension of many a visit. Kids can't get enough of it. Tree Top aims directly for a child's imagination, with a supply of dress-up clothes such as sequined ballerina outfits and Robin Hood garb. You'll also find lots of non-electronic toys, such as Playmobil, puzzles, Legos, and puppets. *Every day; map:BB5*

WOOD SHOP TOYS / 320 1st Ave S, Pioneer Square; 206/624-1763 Despite its name, traditional wooden toys make up only part of the inventory here (in the form of pull toys, trains, and the like). Wood Shop also carries high-quality stuffed animals, wall clocks, wind socks, and mobiles suitable for grown-up tastes. The Folkmanis puppets here come in wonderful animal shapes, and look like mere stuffed animals until a child's hand slipped inside brings them to life. *Every day; map:O9*

WINE AND BEER

BOTTLEWORKS / 1710 N 45th, Wallingford; 206/633-2437 A spotless Wallingford specialty beer seller that carries brews concocted everywhere from Alaska to Vietnam. The selection of more than 400 varieties is enough to quench the thirst of the most insatiable beer snob, and the case of Belgian chocolates provides a perfect accompaniment. *Tues–Sun; www.bottleworks.com; map:FF7*

CITY CELLARS FINE WINES / 1710 N 45th St, Wallingford; 206/632-7238 This small, approachable Wallingford shop carries a wide selection of European—especially Italian—wines. The wall of "100 wines for under $10" sets the budget-conscious at ease, and the selection of pricier vintages is comprehensive. The Bungalow Wine Bar and Cafe, run by former City Cellars owners Jeff Treistman and Polly Young, is located seven blocks east (2412 N 45th St; 206/632-0254) and, along with appetizers and desserts, offers tastings by the glass (with more than 60 selections from which to choose). *Tues–Sat; www.citycellar.com; map:FF7*

ESQUIN WINE MERCHANTS / 2700 4th Ave S, SoDo; 206/682-7374 or 888/682-WINE Close to 500 labels at Esquin boast many choices in the $5 to $15 range, and the store stocks close to 3,200 in all. Monthly specials reflect the best wines from all regions at some of the best prices in town. The owner seeks out the special or unique, occasionally acquiring wines no one else has. The French, Italian, Australian, and American selections are all good. You'll find case discounts, free twice-weekly tastings, and outstanding sales. *Every day; wine@esquin.com; www.esquin. com; map:II7*

LA CANTINA WINE MERCHANTS / 5346 Sand Point Wy NE, Sand Point; 206/525-4340 / 10218 NE 8th St, Bellevue; 425/455-4363 These two small specialty shops are separately owned but equally well stocked. Owners are knowledgeable and, by getting to know their regular customers, are able to make suggestions based upon the customers' tastes. With an emphasis on French bottlings, this is the shop for fine Burgundies and Bordeaux. The Bellevue store offers discounts through its buying club. *Mon–Sat (Sand Point); Tues–Sat (Bellevue); map:FF6, HH3*

LOUIE'S ON THE PIKE / 1926 Pike Pl, Pike Place Market; 206/443-1035 At a glance, Louie's is almost convenience store–like in appearance. But this all-purpose grocery at the north end of Pike Place Market has an extensive collection of wine and beer, especially the local stuff from small producers. Although service is at a premium—that is, there isn't much— the prices can be good enough that you won't care. *Every day; map:J8*

MARKET CELLAR WINERY AND HOME BREW SUPPLIES / 1432 Western Ave, Pike Place Market; 206/622-1880 The only winery in the downtown area, this shop (formerly Liberty Malt Supply) sells its own vintages exclusively, and also stocks an extensive array of supplies for home wine and beer brewing. *Mon–Sat; www.marketcellarwinery.com; map:J7*

MCCARTHY & SCHIERING WINE MERCHANTS / 6500 Ravenna Ave NE, Ravenna; 206/524-9500 / 2401B Queen Anne Ave N, Queen Anne; 206/282-8500 Dan McCarthy (at Queen Anne) and Jay Schiering (at Ravenna) are authorities on the nose, bouquet, and body of the wine world's rising stars. The pair seeks out the newest and most promising producers from Europe and the United States. Regular Saturday-afternoon in-store tastings, an informed staff, and a special rate for "Vintage Select" club members add appeal. A good place to find a rare bottle. California and the Northwest are as well represented as France. *Tues–Sat (Ravenna), Tues–Sun (Queen Anne); www.mccarthyandschiering.com; map:FF6, GG8*

PETE'S WINES / 58 E Lynn St, Eastlake; 206/322-2660 / PETE'S WINES EASTSIDE / 134 105th Ave NE, Bellevue; 425/454-1100 The small grocery and deli here are dwarfed by the vast array of wine overflowing into the store's narrow aisles (though they still answer the phone here, "Pete's Supermarket"). Pete's has the best deals in town on champagne, and also offers good values on Northwest, California, French, and Italian wines. The roomy Bellevue shop is devoted solely to wine, with the same good prices and special-order service. *Every day; map:GG7, HH3*

PIKE & WESTERN WINE SHOP / 1934 Pike Pl, Pike Place Market; 206/441-1307 Gathering the fixings for a meal at the market necessitates a visit to this sophisticated shop. Although this is still one of the best places to learn about Northwest wines, Pike & Western boasts a staff knowledgeable about wines from the rest of the world, too. They make a concerted effort to offer the best values and are especially adept at helping shoppers match wines to the dinner ingredients. Owner Michael Teer uses his knowledge of wine and food to help some of the city's best restaurants craft their wine lists. *Every day; map:J8*

PERFORMING ARTS

PERFORMING ARTS

Theater

Seattleites are extremely fortunate when it comes to theater. Okay, we'll grant that the seat-of-the-pants fringe explosion of a few years back isn't what it used to be. And yes, there is a proliferation of mediocre stuff in the *Waiter, There's a Slug in My Latte* school of buffoonery. But on any given night, there are plenty of innovative productions taking place on Seattle's numerous stages. Of course, New York drains off talent, but those who choose to stay do so to work on their craft rather than chase the higher salaries of Broadway or Hollywood. Seattle playwrights August Wilson and Steven Dietz tend to dominate the scene, although up-and-comers such as Elizabeth Heffron are starting to attract notice.

Seattle's biggest and brashest celebration of theater is the annual **SEATTLE FRINGE THEATRE FESTIVAL** (various venues; 206/342-9172; www.seattlefringe.org). Now scheduled in September to get in synch with the popular Canadian fringe theater circuit, the Fringe Festival offers a vertigo-inducing array of hundreds of shows presented over two weeks, filling up theaters, bars, and small performance spaces (most performances occur in the Capitol Hill neighborhood). Some of the Fringe Festival offerings are amateurish and tiresome, but buried in the dross are some interesting gems—you'll just need the patience of a saint and a little time on your hands.

Fringe theaters tend to come and go, but the following groups have established track records. Check the city's two weeklies, *Seattle Weekly* and *The Stranger*, for event listings and opinionated reviews. **ANNEX THEATRE** (various venues; 206/728-0933; www.annextheatre.org) is a solid fringe group that's still searching for a permanent home after suddenly finding itself homeless in 2001 when the company's longtime performance space on Fourth Avenue fell victim to the proliferation of condominiums erupting in Belltown. Performances are high-energy, and in that spirit, Annex produces an annual "Hot House" project in which four playwrights and four directors write and produce works in just two weeks. The **HOUSE OF DAMES** fringe troupe (various venues; 206/720-1729; www.houseofdames.com) creates luminous, mysterious, and sometimes outrageous music-theater works in unconventional settings. Director Nikki Appino's recent *Rain City Rollers*, for example, presented the myth of Orpheus and Eurydice in the guise of a 1930s roller derby and was staged in a former hangar at Sand Point. With more than 10 years of history, **ONE WORLD THEATRE** (various venues; 206/264-1735; www.oneworldseattle.org) is one of the grande dames of the fringe scene. Unfortunately, the company spends much of its time out of town playing the festival circuit, but it's definitely worth a visit when One World makes an appearance in its hometown. Offering a good mix of new and old, **PRINTER'S DEVIL THEATRE** (various venues; 206/860-7163; printersdeviltheatre@hotmail.com) stages everything from Ibsen to work by emerging local playwrights. Printer's Devil performs in a variety of venues around town, including the former hangar at Sand Point and the old streamlined ferry *Kalakala*. The multiethnic **REPERTORY ACTORS WORKSHOP** (various venues; 206/364-3283; www.reacttheatre.org), under the direction of David Hsieh, produces plays that heighten awareness of issues faced by minorities. The group can tackle everything from a musical about the Japanese-American internment (*Miss Minidoka 1943)* to the work of Italian surrealist Eugene Ionesco. Don't be put off by the flippant name of **THEATER SCHMEATER** (1500 Summit Ave, Capitol Hill; 206/324-5801; www.schmeater.org; map:K2), which takes the craft of drama quite seriously. Past shows have ranged from an adaptation of the poetry of Anne Sexton to late-night adaptations of *Twilight Zone* episodes. Tickets for those under 18 are free. Another quality fringe company with a goofy name, **A THEATRE UNDER THE INFLUENCE** (Union Garage Performance Space, 1418 10th Ave, Capitol Hill; 206/720-1942; map:HH6) performs a wide variety of material, including revivals of neglected classical plays and the occasional gory Grand Guignol spectacle.

If you're in the mood for Shakespeare in the sun (or perhaps a mild overcast), check out the annual **SEATTLE OUTDOOR FESTIVAL OF THEATER.** Three local companies—Greenstage, Theater Schmeater, and Wooden O Theater—jointly produce a free series of classic plays in Capitol Hill's Volunteer Park each July. Check arts listing in the local papers for dates and times.

For those looking for the latest touring Broadway musical, the **PARA- MOUNT THEATRE** (911 Pine St, Downtown; 206/292-ARTS tickets; soldout@theparamount.com; www.theparamount.com; map:J3) is the place to go. Jointly managed with the Moore Theatre by the nonprofit Seattle Theatre Group, the Paramount plays host to Broadway tours and

---

TICKET ALERT

Tickets to many local performing-arts events are available from **Ticketmaster** (various locations around town; 206/292-ARTS; www.ticketmaster.com), and some are also on-line at Tickets.com (www.tickets.com). The best deal in town is **Ticket/Ticket** (206/324-2744; www.ticketwindowonline.com), with three outlets that sell half-price, day-of-show tickets to theater, music, comedy, and dance performances: Broadway Market (401 Broadway Ave E, Capitol Hill; map:GG6), Pike Place Market Information Kiosk (1st Ave and Pike St, Pike Place Market; map:J7), and Meydenbauer Center (11100 NE 6th St, Bellevue; map:HH3). Ticket/Ticket is closed on Monday and accepts cash only. —*Andrew Engelson*

pop headliners of all descriptions. You can buy tickets through Ticket-master or in person at the Paramount box office. For some wacky musical dinner theater laden with awful Seattle jokes, your best bet is the **CRÊPE DE PARIS CABARET** (Atrium Level, Rainier Square, 1333 5th Ave, Down-town; 206/623-4111; map:K6). This modest stage in a downtown French restaurant is a showcase for all sorts of zany musical comedies. You can buy a ticket for the show only ($20), order the full three-course-meal-and-entertainment package ($49), or have a drink and/or dessert during the show.

A CONTEMPORARY THEATRE (ACT) / 700 Union St, Downtown; 206/292-7676 One of the big three theaters in town, along with Intiman and the Seattle Rep, ACT boasts a gorgeous facility containing three strikingly different performance spaces, an energetic artistic director (Gordon Edelstein), and a year-round program featuring some of the finest talent drawn from Seattle's pool of resident actors (as well as the occasional big name such as Julie Harris and Alan Arkin). ACT's Kreielsheimer Place downtown offers three stages: a theater-in-the-round, an intimate thrust stage, and the smaller Bullitt space. There's also Busters, a multi-use space that has served as home to the long-running one-nun show *Late Nite Catechism*. During the Christmas season, ACT presents its extremely popular adaptation of Dickens's *A Christmas Carol*. *www.acttheatre.org; map:K4* &

THE EMPTY SPACE THEATRE / 3509 Fremont Ave N, Fremont; 206/547-7500 An early pioneer of the Seattle alternative theater scene, the Empty Space has served up thought-provoking and entertaining the-ater for more than 30 years. A new rejuvenation comes with the arrival of artistic director Allison Narver, a local product who established a solid reputation as artistic director of Seattle's Annex Theatre and during brief stints in New York and at the Yale Drama School. The production mix at the Space was eclectic under former artistic director Eddie Levi Lee, and this should continue with Narver at the helm. At the company's Fre-mont performance space (which suffered minor exterior damage in the 2001 earthquake, but not enough to close the theater), you'll be treated to over-the-top adaptations (such as *Wuthering! Heights! The! Musical!*), trailer-park thrillers (*Killer Joe*), melodrama, and world premieres of important new works. *www.emptyspace.org; map:FF8* &

5TH AVENUE THEATRE / 1308 5th Ave, Downtown; 206/625-1900, tickets 292-ARTS Opened in 1926 as a venue for vaudeville, the fabu-lously ornate 5th Avenue (designed in its opulence to resemble the inte-rior of China's Forbidden City) is home to its own resident musical theater company that specializes in revivals of mainstream Broadway musicals, and an occasional world-premiere musical that the manage-ment hopes will make it to Broadway. One or two Broadway touring shows are thrown into the schedule to sweeten the mix for subscribers. Not the most adventurous house in town, but the 25,000 or so subscribers don't seem to mind. *www.5thavenuetheatre.org; map:L6* &

INTIMAN THEATRE / Intiman Playhouse, 201 Mercer St, Seattle Center; 206/269-1900 For a few years Intiman ruled the scene here, taking its *Kentucky Cycle* to Broadway for a Pulitzer, presenting the local premiere of *Angels in America*, getting the pick of serious new drama from New York and London. Now that ACT and the Seattle Rep are back in shape, Intiman has some competition for material, but the season lineup still includes plenty of high-powered drama. Artistic director Bartlett Sher's visually adventurous productions of Shakespeare offer some of the best opportunities to see inventive interpretations of the Bard's work in Seattle. Intiman is comfortable shifting from Northwest premieres of award-winning plays to the occasional commedia dell'arte revival. *www.intiman.org; map:A6* &

NORTHWEST ASIAN AMERICAN THEATRE / Theatre Off Jackson, 409 7th Ave S, Chinatown/International District; 206/340-1049 With a nearly 30-year history, NWAAT has a core mission to promote Asian-American plays, playwrights, and actors. But that doesn't mean that artistic director Chay Yew won't also produce plays on broader themes—particularly gay and lesbian subject matter. Every May, the theater produces the annual A-Fest, featuring Asian-American and Pacific Islander dance, solo theater, and music. Seeking to fill in gaps left by failed mid-level theaters, NWAAT's Black Box series produces new works by local playwrights of all ethnic backgrounds. *www.nwaat.org; map:Q6*

ON THE BOARDS / Behnke Center for Contemporary Performance, 100 W Roy St, Queen Anne; 206/217-9888 OTB occupies an intermediate place between fringe and mainstream theater, and has been offering an eclectic blend of dance, theater, and multimedia performance for nearly a quarter century (see also the Dance listing in this chapter). It's here you'll see both cutting-edge performance art from around the world (Japan, Croatia, Belgium, England, you name it) and new creations by Pacific Northwest artists (UMO Ensemble, Typing Explosion, and many other groups). Every spring the Northwest New Works Festival offers a kind of juried fringe festival for locally brewed experimental performance. *www.ontheboards.org; map:GG8*

SEATTLE CHILDREN'S THEATRE / Charlotte Martin Theatre, Seattle Center; 206/441-3322 Challenging Minneapolis's Children's Theater Company in size and prestige, SCT presents six beautifully mounted productions a year for young and family audiences. More than half the performances on the theater's two stages (the mainstage Charlotte Martin and more intimate Eve Alvord) are world premieres commissioned from leading playwrights and based on both classic and contemporary children's literature. The theater stages three evening and two matinee shows per week (with other daytime performances available to school groups), so sometimes tickets can be hard to come by. But they're worth the effort—for children and adults alike. SCT also sponsors a year-round youth drama school for ages 3½ through high school age, with performances staged in the summer. *www.sct.org; map:C7* &

SEATTLE REPERTORY THEATRE / 155 Mercer St, Seattle Center; 206/443-2222 Established in 1963, the Rep is the oldest and best-known theater in town. Under artistic director Sharon Ott, it's firmly in place at the center of the local theater solar system. With a reputation for lavish physical productions to live up to, the Rep always provides something to dazzle the eye, but under Ott the mind and heart get a workout as well. The Rep has the clout to score such crowd-pleasers as David Auburn's Pulitzer Prize– and Tony–winning play *Proof,* but at the same time the theater company isn't shy about using its influence to take risks. This can mean some intriguing productions, whether it's staging Marion Zimmerman's adaptation of *The Odyssey* or premiering the work of a Seattle playwright who *isn't* August Wilson or Steven Dietz—Elizabeth Heffron's *New Patagonia,* for example. *www.seattlerep.org; map:A6* &

UNIVERSITY OF WASHINGTON SCHOOL OF DRAMA / UW Arts Ticket Office: 4001 University Wy NE, University District; 206/543-4880 The nationally recognized UW School of Drama sometimes presents first-rate productions directed by jobbed-in big-name professionals and featuring students from the school's Professional Actor Training Program. Other productions are all-student work—some outstanding, others less so; inform yourself before you go. Performances are at four theaters on campus. *Map:FF6*

VILLAGE THEATRE / Francis J. Gaudette Theatre, 303 Front St N, Issaquah; 425/392-2202 Are you the very model of a modern major general? Even if you aren't, but happen to be in the mood for a little Gilbert and Sullivan, try venturing out to the Cascade foothills town of Issaquah, where the Village Theatre produces surprisingly elaborate and polished productions of all manner of musicals—modern, classic, and obscure. *www.villagetheatre.org* &

Classical Music and Opera

Classical music has a relatively large and devoted following here in the Emerald City. The symphony and opera are firmly on the national map, and chamber music is a local passion. Excellent early music and choral music groups abound. Several musicians of national and international reputation make their homes here and share their musical expertise generously. And Seattle is also a regular stop for major performers on tour.

The biggest change coming to Seattle's classical music landscape is the much-needed $125 million transformation of the Seattle Opera House into the **MARION OLIVER MCCAW HALL**, scheduled to be completed in August 2003. For all of the 2002 season, both the **SEATTLE OPERA** and **PACIFIC NORTHWEST BALLET** will be relegated to the challenging confines of the optimistically renamed **MERCER ARTS ARENA** (the exception being PNB's annual holiday *Nutcracker* performance, which will take place at the Paramount Theatre). Seven million dollars of temporary upgrades to the Mercer Arena, including an overhead reflective canopy and major shifts in seating and sight lines, will try to make the best of a marginal space. Despite the inconvenience, McCaw Hall should be worth the wait. In addition to providing essential seismic upgrading, it will offer a grand lobby, better sight lines, more rehearsal and wing space, a lecture hall, and, most importantly, double the number of women's rest rooms!

BELLE ARTE CONCERTS / Kirkland Performance Center, 350 Kirkland Ave, Kirkland; 425/893-9900 The Belle Arte Concerts series on the Eastside presents five superlative chamber music concerts per season. Director Felix Skowronek has attracted national and international groups of the highest caliber, along with the best that the Northwest has to offer. Recent performers have included the venerable Shostakovich String Quartet and the excellent Seattle-based Soni Ventorum Wind Quintet. *info@bellearte.org; www.bellearte.org; map:EE3* ♿

EARLY MUSIC GUILD / Various venues; 206/325-7066 Now celebrating its 25th anniversary, the Early Music Guild is credited with making Seattle a center of historically informed early music performance. EMG's popular International Series comprises five concerts of medieval, Renaissance, Baroque, or classical music, and features top international ensembles with such intriguing names as Chanticleer, Hesperion XXI, Bimbetta, and La Venexiana. The fine Recital Series, with three concerts, highlights performers whose art is best presented in an intimate venue, usually Town Hall Seattle (1119 8th Ave, Downtown; map:L4) or the Nordstrom Recital Hall at Benaroya (200 University St, Downtown; map:K7). EMG does a nice job of presenting performances of recognized composers (Handel, Bach, Corelli) as well as obscure music you never knew existed (Sephardic Jewish music of 13th-century Spain, for instance). EMG also gives concert assistance to many early music performers in the area. *emg@earlymusicguild.org; www.earlymusicguild.org*

GALLERY CONCERTS / Various venues; 206/726-6088 This plucky group has been performing Baroque and classical music on period instruments in a variety of intimate spaces for 11 years. Recent concert series, which have attracted increasing numbers of talented guest performers, have ranged in location among Town Hall Seattle (1119 8th Ave, Downtown; map:L4), the Seattle Asian Art Museum (1400 E Prospect St, Capitol Hill; map:GG7), the Frye Art Gallery (704 Terry Ave, First Hill; map:N3), and the Kirkland Performance Center (350 Kirkland Ave, Kirkland; map:EE3). The group is known to make some imaginative programming decisions, from staging a concert of music that might have been heard in the drawing rooms of Jane Austen's novels to presenting a sampling of works by 12th-century composer and mystic Hildegard von Bingen. *info@galleryconcerts.org; www.galleryconcerts.org*

MOSTLY NORDIC CHAMBER MUSIC SERIES AND SMÖRGÅSBORD / Nordic Heritage Museum, 3014 NW 67th St, Ballard; 206/789-5707

Sibelius and Meatballs! Grieg and Lutefisk! Begun in 1996 under the auspices of the Nordic Heritage Museum Foundation, Mostly Nordic presents five concerts per season, one for each of the Scandinavian countries. Contemporary and classical chamber music from Denmark, Finland, Iceland, Norway, and Sweden is performed by local (and occasionally Scandinavian) musicians, and is followed by an authentic smorgasbord—all for one reasonable ticket price. *nordic@intelistep.com; www.nordic museum.com; map:EE9* &

NORTHWEST CHAMBER ORCHESTRA / Benaroya Recital Hall, 200 University St, Downtown; 206/343-0445 Offering up small-scale classical works for more than 25 years, NWCO is one of the region's few professional chamber orchestras, and the group has masterfully adapted to the bright acoustics of Benaroya's small recital hall. Finnish pianist Ralf Gothoni was appointed music director in 2001, and there's no reason to

believe that the change in management should alter the orchestra's commitment to bold interpretations of works spanning the 17th to 20th centuries. Each season, NWCO performs seven mainstage concerts and five showcase events that have attracted such talents as pianists Richard Goode and Ian Hobson. The season's offerings also include five "Music in the Park" concerts at the Seattle Asian Art Museum (1400 E Prospect St, Capitol Hill; map:GG7). One child under 17 is admitted free with a ticket-buying adult. *nwco@nwco.org; www.nwco.org; map:K7* &

NORTHWEST MAHLER FESTIVAL / Meany Theater, University of Washington, University District; 206/667-6567 It takes a lot of bodies to perform the symphonies of Gustav Mahler. So during the summer, when amateur orchestra players around Seattle are looking for something to do outside of the regular performance season, they band together to play several symphonies by Mahler and other Late Romantic compositions requiring big, noisy orchestras. Sure, at a recent performance the festival wasn't able to come up with the requisite number of players for Mahler's Eighth Symphony (the "Symphony of a Thousand"), but the group makes up in quality what it lacks in quantity. *horndude1@yahoo.com; www.nwmahlerfestival.org; map:FF6* &

SEATTLE BAROQUE / Various venues; 206/322-3118 Seattle Baroque was founded in 1994 and, under the leadership of Baroque violinist Ingrid Matthews and harpsichordist Byron Schenkman, the group has been winning critical praise all around, scoring broadcasts on public radio and recording several acclaimed CDs. Soloists of national and international caliber return year after year—a local audience favorite is soprano Ellen Hargis—to join the brilliant young ensemble in historically informed performances, exploring familiar and unfamiliar literature of the era with panache. Seven concert pairs are presented between fall and spring at several venues both in Seattle and on the Eastside. SBO also sponsors the new Seattle Baroque Summer Festival, encompassing three days of 18th-century music performed at Town Hall Seattle (1119 8th Ave, Downtown; map:L4). *info@seattlebaroque.org; www.seattlebaroque.org*

SEATTLE CHAMBER MUSIC SOCIETY / Lakeside School, 14050 1st Ave NE, Haller Lake; 206/283-8808 Founded by University of Washington cello professor Toby Saks 20 years ago, the Seattle Chamber Music Society presents a popular monthlong series in July showcasing local and international talent as well as a brief "Winter Interlude" in January at Benaroya Hall (200 University St, Downtown; map:K7). The performances are spirited, oftentimes exceptional, and almost always sold out. Grace notes include preperformance dining on the lawn (bring a picnic or buy a catered meal) and a minirecital before each concert. More adventurous works are gradually creeping in to the programming, and the recitals feature the performers' own choices (and often rarely heard pieces). *scmfmail@scmf.org; www.scmf.org; map:CC7* &

SEATTLE CHAMBER PLAYERS / Benaroya Recital Hall, 200 University St, Downtown; 206/367-1138 An unusual grouping of flute, clarinet, violin, and cello, Seattle Chamber Players adds guests and high-quality out-of-town soloists, as needed, to perform chamber music of the 20th and 21st centuries (the latter being newly commissioned works). The players approach the series of six to eight concerts with style, imagination, and occasional humor (a piece entitled *Dead Elvis* featured a hip-swiveling bassoonist). The group also performs throughout the region, having taken the series to Olympia, Bellingham, and the San Juan Islands. *paultaub@dbug.org; map:K7* &

SEATTLE MEN'S CHORUS / Benaroya Hall, 200 University St, Downtown; Meany Theater, University of Washington, University District; 206/323-2992 Dennis Coleman, who directs the world's largest and most successful gay men's chorus, is one of the best choral conductors in this city of many choirs. SMC is also one of the country's busiest, with about

30 appearances a year at various events and a local subscription series of four concerts: an always-sold-out family-fun holiday concert in December, a popular-music spectacular during Gay & Lesbian Pride Week in summer, and two spring shows that vary in content. The chorus's Emerald City Arts production arm also brings in big-name performers, from Rosemary Clooney to Margaret Cho. *info@seattlemenschorus.org; www.seattlemenschorus.org; map:K7, FF6* &

SEATTLE OPERA / Mercer Arts Arena, Seattle Center; 206/389-7676 The show must go on. General director Speight Jenkins and the Seattle Opera had a difficult decision to make when it was clear that the Opera House needed major structural renovations: go into hibernation or find another venue. The second option has been the course of choice, with the hope that subscribers will patiently stick around during the interim. Maybe the $7 million spent on putting the "Arts" in Mercer Arts Arena will make things tolerable. While waiting for the new $125 million Marion Oliver McCaw Hall to open in August 2003, look for the opera to work extra hard to maintain its well-earned reputation as one of the more innovative companies in the country. Case in point: before its exile from the Opera House, the Seattle Opera staged its first new production of Wagner's 17-hour *Ring* cycle in six years—and sold out tickets one year in advance. SO stages five operas in its regular season—Jenkins always serves up an intriguing mix of old standbys and more obscure works. *www.seattleopera.org; map:B5* &

SEATTLE SYMPHONY / Benaroya Hall, 200 University St, Downtown; 206/215-4747 The Seattle Symphony approaches its 100th season (in 2004) as one of the most vital and stimulating orchestras in the nation, now well situated in the comfy confines of Benaroya Hall (the final piece—Benaroya's splendid 4,490-pipe concert organ—is now in place and under the talented hands of resident organist Carole Terry). SSO has an impressive track record of supporting classical works by contemporary composers—the late Alan Hovhaness, as well as David Diamond, Bright Sheng, David Stock, and, most recently, Samuel Jones, have all premiered work with the help of SSO's composer-in-residence program. As well as its 18 sets of season subscription concerts under longtime maestro Gerard Schwarz, the orchestra performs shorter series packaged for every kind of music lover: from pops to light classics to Baroque, from performances for children to programs for older adults to concerts with insightful commentary by the conductor, plus a distinguished artist series with international stars such as Jessye Norman. The symphony sponsors a host of community outreach and educational programs, including a new, popular interactive music center at Benaroya Hall. *info@seattle symphony.org; www.seattlesymphony.org; map:K7* &

SEATTLE YOUTH SYMPHONY / Benaroya Hall, 200 University St, Downtown; 206/362-2300 The largest youth symphony organization in the country, the Seattle Youth Symphony is looking for stability now that director Jonathan Shames has moved on to other projects. The talented young musicians give three usually dazzling concerts, plus a benefit performance, during the winter season. Five feeder orchestras train a large number of younger musicians, and perform during the summer. *info@ syso.org; www.syso.org; map:K7* &

UW INTERNATIONAL CHAMBER MUSIC SERIES—UW PRESIDENT'S PIANO SERIES—UW WORLD MUSIC AND THEATRE / Meany Theater, University of Washington, University District; 206/543-4880 or 800/859-5342 The University of Washington's 1,210-seat Meany Theater is home to three excellent music series that bring the world's finest performers to Seattle. The President's Piano series attracts pianists of international stature, including Garrick Ohlsson, Murray Perahia, András Schiff, and the winner of the prestigious Van Cliburn Gold Medal. The fascinating UW World Music and Theatre Series features seven famous ethnic performing-arts groups from around the world—you'll see an eclectic mix ranging from the Throat Singers of Tuva to the Guinean dance/music troupe WOFA and Turkish finger-drum master Burhan Öçal. The popular six-concert International Chamber Music Series, presented jointly by the University of Washington and the venerable Ladies Musical Club, brings to Seattle the best of the nation's chamber music ensembles (and an occasional group from abroad), with an emphasis on string quartets and trios. The Emerson String Quartet is a frequent visitor, as is the dynamic Ahn Trio. *www.meany.org; map:FF6* &

Dance

A new crop of choreographers is blossoming in this city known for exporting its best dance talent to New York and other environs. As a result, Seattle is no longer home to Merce Cunningham, Robert Joffrey, Trisha Brown, and wonderboy Mark Morris. But a second generation of talent is taking root—and the rest of the world is taking notice. At the top of the luminary list would have to be Pat Graney, who in 20 years has established herself as one of the most respected choreographers in the world. Emerging stars to keep an eye on are Amii LeGendre, 33 Fainting Spells, and the Maureen Whiting Company. One of the best opportunities to see these choreographers' work is to catch several performances during On the Boards' popular Northwest New Works Festival.

ON THE BOARDS / Behnke Center for Contemporary Performance, 100 W Roy St, Queen Anne; 206/217-9888 If you're looking for cutting-edge works that merge dance, music, theater, and visual media, strike a path for On the Boards. Now settled into two performance spaces at the Behnke Center for Contemporary Performance in Queen Anne (a 350- to 500-seat mainstage and a 100-seat studio theater), OTB offers a fine sampling of national genre-bending performance as well as a rich selection of local talent. The sellout New Performance Series (October to May) brings in internationally known contemporary artists such as Anne Teresa De Keersmaeker, Meredith Monk, and Ronald K. Brown, as well as local greats including Pat Graney, Maureen Whiting, 33 Fainting Spells, and Amii LeGendre. Every six weeks throughout the year, a series known as 12 Minutes Max showcases five to seven short performances of new and experimental work by regional composers, choreographers, and playwrights. The Northwest New Works Festival, which runs for several weekends in late spring, presents longer, more polished versions of similar work. *otb@ontheboards.org; www.ontheboards.org; map:GG8*

PACIFIC NORTHWEST BALLET / Mercer Arts Arena, Seattle Center; 206/441-2424 Under the guidance of artistic directors Kent Stowell and Francia Russell, former dancers with New York City Ballet, PNB has earned recognition as one of the top five regional companies in America. Even while the company is exiled to the temporary confines of the Mercer Arts Arena during the renovation of the Opera House (scheduled for completion in August 2003), audiences have the opportunity to see such greats as PNB ballerina Patricia Barker, one of the country's foremost dancers. Fueled by a strong, well-staged selection of classic and rare Balanchine repertory, a typical five-show PNB season also features large-scale classical works and story ballets by director Stowell, and contemporary offerings by the likes of Val Caniparoli, William Forsythe, Nacho Duato, and Mark Dendy. PNB's annual *Nutcracker* has become something of a cliché, but the Maurice Sendak sets and quality performances still make it an enjoyable spectacle. *www.pnb.org; map:B5*

SPECTRUM DANCE THEATER / Madrona Dance Studio, 800 Lake Washington Blvd, Madrona (and various venues); 206/325-4161 Spectrum, Seattle's only company dedicated solely to jazz dance, has been serving up energetic productions since 1982. The company isn't a big risk-taker, but artistic director and choreographer Dale Merrill has been building a solid and fun-loving repertoire over his 15-year tenure. The company, which is based out of the cozy Madrona Dance Studio on Lake Washington, offers two mainstage concert series at Meany Theater at the University of Washington every fall and spring, as well as informal "Dance in the Making" studio performances that include audience question-and-answer sessions with the dancers and a lecture on American jazz dance traditions. The company is very family-friendly and also runs a broad selection of instructional classes for kids and adults. *www.spectrum dance.org; map:HH6*

33 FAINTING SPELLS / Various venues; 206/568-8640 Founded in 1994 by Dayna Hanson and Gaelan Hanson (who both happen to share the same last name), 33 Fainting Spells is gaining national attention as one of the region's most original up-and-coming dance troupes. Along with co-member Peggy Piacenza, the two Hansons produce work that seamlessly moves between campy vaudeville and elegant solemnity. The group stages one or two performances per year in various venues. *33fs@33faintingspells.org; www.33faintingspells.org*

WORLD DANCE SERIES / Meany Theater, University of Washington, University District; 206/543-4880 or 800/859-5342 Six world-renowned dance groups come to town every year as part of Meany Theater's World Dance Series, and each year the programming seems to get more thrilling. The October-through-May series almost always includes such tried-and-true top draws as the Merce Cunningham Dance Company, the Alvin Ailey American Dance Theater, or Alonzo King's LINES Contemporary Ballet. The series works hard to keep the "world" in World Dance Series, and tends to add several non-Western dance groups to the mix to keep things lively. The World Dance Series also can be depended upon to offer an annual homecoming performance by Seattle-boy-done-good, choreographer Mark Morris. *www.meany.org; map:FF6* &

Film

In Seattle we may love to watch movies, but we don't make many of them here. Hefty tax credits and good exchange rates send most film production companies north of the border to Vancouver, BC. Despite the lack of a Hollywood presence, dedicated young filmmakers and video artists are shooting all sorts of experimental work in the city, much of which shows up on the screens of the burgeoning number of microcinemas. Local film impresario Joel Bachar (www.microcinema.com) helped spread this insurgency of small-screen un-dependent film across the country. At press time, his **INDEPENDENT EXPOSURE** film series (formerly screened in the backroom of Belltown's Speakeasy Café, until a fire shut it down) was showing films the fourth Thursday of every month at **VITAL 5 PRODUCTIONS** (2200 Westlake Ave N, Westlake; 206/322-0282; map:HH7). Another micro-film venue is the well-established **911 MEDIA ARTS CENTER** (117 Yale Ave N, South Lake Union; 206/682-6552; www.911media.org; map:F2), which maintains a busy schedule of documentaries and experimental work, as well as open screenings where anyone can show work in progress to an opinionated audience. The **ALIBI ROOM** near Pike Place Market (85 Pike St, Downtown; 623-3180; www.alibiroom.com; map:J7) is the place where "undie" film types meet and sip martinis. The Alibi occasionally screens films in the basement—call for details.

FESTIVAL CITY

Summertime in Seattle. It's no longer a secret to outsiders that summer in this city means balmy and mostly rain-free days. In order to take advantage of the fine weather, locals have developed a passion for outdoor events. Back in the old days, about the only big alfresco attraction was **Seafair** (206/728-0123; www.seafair.com), a bizarre amalgam of roaring hydroplanes, jets, and drunken bands of clowns and pirates. You can still do Seafair every August, but it's just one of many festivals filling up our calendar.

During Memorial Day weekend, the unofficial start of the summer season, **Northwest Folklife Festival** (206/684-7300; www.nwfolklife.org) rolls into action at Seattle Center. The event, which has been around for more than three decades, is free and crowded, but where else can you see local hip-hop, Polynesian drumming, Balkan dancing, and alternative country music all in one weekend?

Two neighborhood street fairs on the cusp of summer offer an amusing mix of food, music, crafts, and assorted antics by local eccentrics. The **University District Street Fair** (206/547-4417; www.udistrictchamber.org) invades the Ave every May, while the **Fremont Fair** (206/632-1500; www.fremontfair.com) has been dishing up zaniness (and nude bicyclists!) in the Republic of Fremont each June for more than 30 years.

In terms of sheer volume for your dollar, nothing beats the **Pain in the Grass** series of free outdoor rock concerts (Mural Amphitheatre, Seattle Center; www.paininthe grass.com; map:C6). The excellent **Summer Nights at the Pier** (Pier 62/63, Waterfront; 206/281-8111; www.summernights.org) series of pop-rock outdoor concerts

Seattle also hosts some seriously macro festivals and series. In mid-May through mid-June, the town goes slightly cuckoo for the SEATTLE INTERNATIONAL FILM FESTIVAL (Broadway Performance Hall, 1625 Broadway, Capitol Hill; 206/324-9996; mail@seattlefilm.com; www. seattlefilm.com; map:HH7) and its alter ego, the SATELLITES FESTIVAL OF FILM AND VIDEO (www.emeraldreels.com). A quarter-century old and one of the biggest fests in the country, SIFF is a juggernaut that seems overwhelming at first glance. But a seasoned staff at Cinema Seattle— SIFF's nonprofit umbrella organization—has made the event (staged at a handful of movie houses throughout the city) easy to navigate. Cinema Seattle also sponsors activities year-round that include the outstanding Women in Cinema Film Festival, which usually takes place in January; Talking Pictures, a series of movies screened with an après-film discussion hosted by critics and directors; and the Screenwriters Salon series, held July through April, which presents live readings of new scripts at stages shows next to the waters of Puget Sound. The **Summer Festival on the Green** series of concerts at Chateau Ste. Michelle (14111 NE 145th St, Woodinville; 425/488-3300; www.ste-michelle.com) serves up a mix of pop and acoustic sounds on its grounds. **Zoo Tunes** at the Woodland Park Zoo presents reasonably priced folk and pop performances on summer evenings; children under 12 are free (Woodland Park Zoo, Green Lake; 206/684-4800; www.zoo.org). Also free is the **Out to Lunch** series of jazz, classical, and R&B concerts at various locations downtown (206/623-0340; www.downtownseattle.com).

It's not exactly outdoors, but the new **UW Summer Arts Festival** (various venues, University District; 206/543-4880; www.summerartsfest.org), held every July in venues on the UW campus, lets Seattleites immerse themselves in a weeklong flood of dance, drama, film, music, and visual arts. The performances feature University of Washington students, faculty, and excellent touring performers.

Bumbershoot (various locations, Seattle Center; 206/281-8111; www.bumber shoot.com) is the biggest and best of Seattle's arts festivals, and its music programming has been called some of the best in the nation. About the only festival that rivals it in number and quality of musical acts is the New Orleans Jazz and Heritage Festival. Bumbershoot is held Labor Day weekend at Seattle Center, and lineups are usually announced a month in advance. Ticket prices have been inching up over the past several years, and the crowds can sometimes leave you feeling like cattle in a feedlot, but it's still the region's best entertainment bargain.   —*Andrew Engelson*

Capitol Hill's **RICHARD HUGO HOUSE** (1634 11th Ave; 206/322-7030; map:HH6), sometimes with the participation of noted actors, including local celebrity Tom Skerritt.

Curated for 30 years by the Seattle Art Museum film department's founder, Greg Olson, the quarterly **SEATTLE ART MUSEUM FILM SERIES** (100 University St, Downtown; 206/654-3100; www.seattleartmuseum. org/film; map:K7) usually focuses on the work of a renowned actor or director (Cary Grant, Alfred Hitchcock) or on a theme such as French comedy or American film noir. Frequent short programs are featured as well: a few weekends of Yasujiro Ozu, an evening of David Lynch, an afternoon with Marcel Pagnol. For less polished surroundings, the **FRE-MONT OUTDOOR FILM FESTIVAL** (3400 Phinney Ave N, Fremont; 206/781-4230; www.outdoorcinema.com; map:FF8) screens an odd mix of flicks, from *Fight Club* to *Casablanca*. Now situated in the parking lot across from the Redhook Trolleyman Pub, the festival requires that you bring your own seating—movie-themed costumes are optional.

At last tally, Seattle was also home to a Polish film festival, a Jewish film festival, a lesbian and gay film festival, an outdoor film festival, an Asian American film festival, a Scandinavian film festival, a human rights film festival, an Irish film festival, a children's film festival, a short-film film festival . . . well, you get the idea. Check the arts listings in local publications to find out which one is playing this week.

In between festivals, film nuts have plenty of other year-round viewing options. The city boasts a venue—from old movie houses with creaky character and smaller independent theaters to, yes, a good number of multiplexes—sure to fit nearly every genre of film fancier. Splashy first-run multiplexes include the roomy, three-screen **UPTOWN CINEMA** (551 Queen Anne Ave N, Queen Anne; 206/285-1022; map:A8), Lowes Cineplex Odeon's downtown **MERIDIAN 16** (1502 7th Ave; 206/223-9600; map:J5), and the upscale **PACIFIC PLACE 11**—decorated in a faux ski-lodge style—in downtown's tony Pacific Place shopping center (600 Pine St; 206/652-2404; map:J5).

The mini-chain **SEVEN GABLES/LANDMARK THEATRES** (www.land mark-theaters.com), which makes its living serving up a mix of select Hollywood films and foreign releases, currently operates an eclectic collection of theaters throughout the city. The **BROADWAY MARKET** (425 Broadway Ave E; 206/323-0231; map:K1) on Capitol Hill and the **METRO CINEMAS** (NE 45th St and Roosevelt Wy NE; 206/633-0055; map:FF7) near the University District both offer several screens of films. Capitol Hill's **HARVARD EXIT** (807 E Roy St; 206/323-8986; map:GG6), with its huge lobby and stately air, was founded ages ago by a pair of eccentric film fans. Also on Capitol Hill is the **EGYPTIAN** (801 E Pine St, Capitol Hill; 206/323-4978; map:HH6) was once a Masonic temple. The **GUILD 45TH** (2115 N 45th St, Wallingford; 206/633-3353; map:FF7) in Wallingford is actually two neighboring theaters, where one can usually find the latest Henry James adaptation. The small, dreamy **SEVEN GABLES** (911 NE 50th St; 206/632-8820; map:EE7), the anchor of the theater chain, makes for a very pleasant experience in the U District—even more so when the scent of delicious sauces from the Italian restaurant downstairs comes wafting up. In the U District, you'll also find the single-screen **NEPTUNE** (1303 NE 45th St; 206/633-5545; map:FF6) and the three-screen **VARSITY** (4329 University Wy NE; 206/632-3131; map:FF6), where one of the screens offers a repertory of one-night double features of classic and cult movies. In the far north, head to Shoreline for the **CREST** (16505 5th Ave NE, Shoreline; 206/363-6338; map:BB7), where second-run movies are screened at bargain prices ($3 for all shows).

The best place to see first-run movies, as well as occasional revivals of special effects classics, is on the giant screen of **CINERAMA** (2100 4th Ave, Belltown; 206/441-3080; www.seattlecinerama.com; map:H6).

Seattle mogul Paul Allen bought the landmark movie house in 1998 and stocked it with state-of-the-art digital sound, equipment to screen both 35- and 70-millimeter films, a digital projection system (ready for Hollywood's first digital movie), and innovative assistance tools for both blind and deaf moviegoers. The only place to catch the latest Hollywood blockbuster while tossing back a pint of hefeweizen and snacking on hot wings, pizzas, sandwiches, and other pub fare is at the **AURORA CINEMA GRILL** (130th and Aurora Ave N, Bitter Lake; 206/364-8880; www. cinemagrill.com; map:CC7), part of the Atlanta-based Cinema Grill chain.

Retro charm is the selling point of Ballard's new **MAJESTIC BAY THEATRE** (2044 NW Market St, Ballard; 206/781-2229; www.majestic bay.com; map:FF8), a three-screen gem filled with character—nautical themes in the lobby evoke Ballard's fishy history—and buoyed by digital sound and comfy chairs. The 35-year-old **GRAND ILLUSION CINEMA** (1403 NE 50th St, University District; 206/523-3935; www.nwfilm forum.org; map:FF7) and the multi-purpose **LITTLE THEATRE** (608 19th Ave E, Capitol Hill; 206/675-2055; map:GG6) offer a haven for little-shown underground, avant-garde, foreign, and locally produced films. And want to see the latest output of "Bollywood" (as Bombay's cinema is affectionately known)? Cruise down to Renton's **ROXY CINEMA** (504 S 3rd St, Renton; 206/587-7882; www.roxycinema.com; map:NN3), which screens first-run Indian movies Friday through Monday. The movies are in Hindi, without subtitles, you'll do fine if you just stick to the madcap musical comedies, where the plots are rather obvious and the song-and-dance numbers quite a spectacle.

Literature

Seattle is a city of bookworms. Whether they're curled up inside coffee-houses on drizzly days or splayed out with a mystery at Magnuson Park in the summer sun, it seems just about everyone in this town has their nose in a book. The Puget Sound area is home to a number of writers of diverse styles and talents, including Ivan Doig, Sherman Alexie, Charles Johnson, Rebecca Brown, mystery maven J. A. Jance, and Englishman-turned-Seattleite Jonathan Raban. Touring writers have made Seattle a mandatory stop on the book circuit, and local institution Elliott Bay Book Company practically invented the notion of the author tour. For better or for worse, Seattle-based **AMAZON.COM** introduced the world to on-line bookselling, even though it's still trying to prove that one can make a profit from it. Not surprisingly, this city of book lovers has page upon page of literary events on offer throughout the year.

ELLIOTT BAY BOOK COMPANY has probably the city's best reading series (see listing below). However, a multitude of other Seattle and Eastside bookstores (see Books and Periodicals in the Shopping chapter) also vie for visiting authors. Among the heavyweights are the **UNIVERSITY BOOK STORE** (4326 University Wy NE, University District; 206/634-3400; www.bookstore.washington.edu; map:FF6) and **THIRD PLACE BOOKS** (Lake Forest Park Towne Centre, 17171 Bothell Wy NE, Lake Forest Park; 206/366-3333; www.thirdplacebooks.com; map:BB5). On the smaller side, **BAILEY/COY BOOKS** (414 Broadway Ave E, Capitol Hill; 206/323-8842; map:HH6) caters to the alternative Capitol Hill crowd and holds several readings per month; **OPEN BOOKS: A POEM EMPORIUM** (2414 N 45th St, Wallingford; 206/633-0811; www.openpoetrybooks. com; map:FF7) also offers a first-rate reading series.

Scores of coffeehouses, cafes, and bars are host to open mikes, poetry slams, and oddball literary happenings. Open mike poetry generally ranges from execrable to mildly interesting, while the slam scene is either a kick in the pants or a desperate, alcohol-fueled battle of bellowing between audience and performer. **THE GLOBE CAFÉ** (1531 14th Ave, Capitol Hill; 206/324-8815; map:HH6) is home to the granddaddy of the recited poetry scene: Red Sky Poetry Theater, which has been around for more than a decade and gathers to perform on Sunday night. The Globe's Salon Poetry Series on Tuesday night appeals to the Hill's younger set. The Rendezvous Reading Series at **THE LITTLE THEATRE** (610 19th Ave E, Capitol Hill; 206/675-2055; map:GG6) offers a salon-style chance to chat with local authors over drinks. Local hipsters head for the open mike on Monday and Wednesday nights at **COFFEE MESSIAH** (1554 E Olive Wy, Capitol Hill; 206/861-8233; map:I1) and then give thanks by downing cup after cup of communal caffeine. More sedate is the Poets West open mike series at **WIT'S END BOOKSTORE & TEA SHOP** (770 N 34th St, Fremont; 206/682-1268; map:FF7). At the University District branch of Seattle Public Library (5009 Roosevelt Wy NE; map:FF7) the long-running **IT'S ABOUT TIME WRITERS' READING SERIES** (206/527-8875; eahelfgott@home.com) allows poets and writers of all experience levels to read from their work every second Thursday evening of the month. The peripatetic Seattle Poetry Slam seems to be settling its raucous butt down at **SIT & SPIN** (2219 4th Ave, Belltown; 441-9484; map:G6). Bring your laundry along to this bar-and-laundromat: even if the poetry stinks, at least you'll have the satisfaction of clean socks.

BUMBERSHOOT LITERARY ARTS / Northwest Rooms, Seattle Center; 206/281-8111 Even though it's somewhat lost in the shadow of Northwest Bookfest as a literary event, the Bumbershoot arts festival held during Labor Day weekend offers an impressive Literary Arts program packed with readings, performances, poetry slams, and panel discussions involving world-class authors. The festival's long-running Bookfair boasts the largest West Coast concentration of small presses, which come from around the country to promote and sell their collections of fiction, poetry, nonfiction, hand-set letterpress books, and zines. *www.bumber shoot.org; map:C6* &

ELLIOTT BAY BOOK COMPANY READING SERIES / 101 S Main St, Pioneer Square; 206/624-6600 Elliott Bay is a local literary landmark with a well-deserved national reputation for spotting talent: Amy Tan gave one of her first public readings here, as did Sherman Alexie. Elliott Bay's daily reading series, organized by bookseller extraordinaire Rick Simonson, brings more than 600 authors of national caliber—ranging from Chuck Palahniuk to Terry McMillan—into the cozy brick-walled cavern of Elliott Bay's basement reading room each year. The bulk of Elliott Bay's offerings are free; on rare occasions, typically for special benefit events, tickets cost $5–$10. *www.elliottbaybook.com; map:O8*

NORTHWEST BOOKFEST / Stadium Exhibition Center, 1000 Occidental Ave S, SoDo; 206/378-1883 The city's premier literary happening attracts more than 25,000 eager bibliophiles to the Stadium Exhibition Center every fall. This gigantic book-love-in brings to its stages a dizzying array of authors, and past years have seen appearances by Pam Houston, T. C. Boyle, Amos Oz, Ha Jin, and local guy David Guterson. There's plenty to do for the little ones as well: hands-on activities such as book making, a storyteller's stage, and those oh-so-cute costumed fictional characters. Other events include culinary demonstrations by cookbook authors and a book walk in Pioneer Square and Chinatown/International District. And what would a book festival be without books? Hundreds of mainstream and small-press titles are for sale at more than 200 booths. Admission to the fest, held during the third weekend in October, is free, though a $5 donation to support literacy organizations is recommended. *info@nwboofest.org; www.nwbookfest.org; map:Q9* &

RICHARD HUGO HOUSE EVENTS / 1634 11th Ave, Capitol Hill; 206/322-7030 Named in honor of the late Seattle poet Richard Hugo, this writers' resource center on Capitol Hill hosts writing classes, readings, book groups, screenwriters' salons, and other literary programs. The Hugo maintains a busy schedule of its own events, as well as hosting other organizations, including the Subtext Reading Series (a showcase of local avant-garde poetry readings throughout the year) and the Stage Fright open mike series for teenagers, held every other Wednesday night. The Seattle Poetry Festival (see listing below) stages many of its events here every April. Hugo House's biggest event, the Annual Inquiry symposium, takes place over three days in October and features a full schedule of readings and writers' panels centered around a common theme (past events have had such captivating titles as "Maps," "Disappearances," "Shelter," and "The Power of Place"). Most events at Hugo are free or low-cost. *www.hugohouse.org; map:HH6* &

SEATTLE ARTS & LECTURES / Benaroya Hall, 200 University St, Downtown; 206/621-2230 At the top of the local literary food chain is this evening lecture series, founded in 1987, which runs from fall through spring. Whether it be an evening of witty exchanges between a panel of top-drawer writers or strictly a solo affair, the lecturers always manage to surprise (resident writer Sherman Alexie caused a minor sensation with his assertion that writers peak at 25). The list of SAL guests reads like a veritable who's who of great modern writers: Don DeLillo, Salman Rushdie, Michael Ondaatje, Margaret Atwood, Philip Roth, Toni Morrison. Oftentimes the source of the best moments is the postlecture audience question-and-answer period. Tickets for the seven-event series range from $75 to $175; individual tickets cost $15–$18 and are half-price for students, though be warned: for popular lecturers, they can be as hard to come by as Mariners playoff tickets. *sal@lectures.org; www.lectures.org; map:K7* &

SEATTLE POETRY FESTIVAL / Various venues; 206/725-1650 Offering up a mixed bag of poesy—a bit of doggerel here, a splash of inspiration there—the Seattle Poetry Festival is held each spring. The festival tends to emphasize free verse, edgy alternative stuff, and aggressive poetry slams. Some of the offerings are good, some not. But lately, organizers have begun attracting bigger names from the world of renegade poetry, including Ishmael Reed and Michael McClure. *eleven@poetryfestival.org www.poetryfestival.org*

SEATTLE PUBLIC LIBRARY/WASHINGTON CENTER FOR THE BOOK / Temporary Central Library, 800 Pike St, Downtown; 206/386-4650 or 206/386-4184 When the Seattle Public Library selected Dutch architect Rem Koolhaas to design its new downtown library, they knew they'd be in for a wild ride. His dream of an oblong glass bookpile of a library, stocked with all sorts of interactive and user-friendly goodies (the slide into the entrance of the children's section had to be scrapped, unfortunately). While waiting for its new home (New Central Library, 1000 4th Ave, Downtown; map:L6) to open in 2003, SPL finds itself in temporary digs across from the Washington State Convention & Trade Center. During the intervening time, the library still offers a full plate of absolutely free events that include lectures, readings, storytelling, and workshops. Much of this programming happens thanks to the efforts of Nancy Pearl, the director of the Washington Center for the Book. Each year, the library and the Center for the Book undertake the ambitious "If All of Seattle Read the Same Book" program, in which one lucky author becomes the subject of numerous book groups, lectures, and radio discussions. *www.spl.org; map:J4* &

NIGHTLIFE

Nightlife by Feature

ALTERNATIVE
The Breakroom
Crocodile Café
Elysian Brewing Company
Experience Music Project
Graceland
I-Spy
The Old Firehouse
Paradox Theater
Re-bar
Showbox
Sit & Spin
Sunset Tavern
Tractor Tavern
The Vogue

BLUES
Bohemian Café
Dimitriou's Jazz Alley
Experience Music Project/
    Liquid Lounge
Larry's Blues Cafe
New Orleans Restaurant
Old Timer's Café
Rainbow
Scarlet Tree

COCKTAIL LOUNGES
Alibi Room
Axis
Backdoor Ultra Lounge
Ballroom in Fremont
Baltic Room
Capitol Club
Cloud Room
El Gaucho's Pampas Room
Experience Music Project/
    Liquid Lounge
Fireside Room
Five Point Café
Garden Court
Hattie's Hat
I-Spy
J&M Cafe and Cardroom
Kismet Bistro and Wine Bar
Larry's Blues Café
Last Supper Club
Linda's Tavern
Luau Polynesian Lounge
Manray
McCormick & Schmick's
Mecca Café
The Nitelite
Paragon Bar and Grill
Queen City Grill
Rainbow

Scarlet Tree
Shea's Lounge
Shuckers
Tini Bigs Lounge
Union Square Grill
Virginia Inn
Vito's Madison Grill

COUNTRY
Sunset Tavern
Timberline Spirits
Tractor Tavern

DANCING/DANCE
   FLOORS
Alibi Room
Arena
Backdoor Ultra Lounge
Ballard Firehouse
Ballroom in Fremont
Belltown Billiards
Century Ballroom
DV8
El Gaucho's Pampas Room
Garden Court
I-Spy
Last Supper Club
Manray
Neighbours
Polly Esther's
Re-bar
Showbox
Timberline Spirits
Tractor Tavern
The Vogue

DRINKS WITH A VIEW
Pescatore Fish Café
Salty's on Alki
Shea's Lounge
SkyCity at the Needle

FOLK/ACOUSTIC
Conor Byrne's Public House
Experience Music Project/JBL
    Theater
Fiddler's Inn
Grateful Bread Café
Hopvine Pub
Irish Emigrant
Kells
Latona by Green Lake
Murphy's Pub
Owl 'n' Thistle Irish Pub and
    Restaurant
Paragon Bar and Grill

Steel Sky Pub
Tractor Tavern
Two Bells Tavern
Zoka Coffee Roaster and Tea
    Company

GAY/LESBIAN BARS
Arena
Manray
Neighbours
Re-bar
Timberline Spirits
The Wild Rose

JAZZ
Baltic Room
Dimitriou's Jazz Alley
El Gaucho's Pampas Room
Elysian Brewing Company
Latona by Green Lake
New Orleans Restaurant
Old Timer's Café
Old Town Alehouse
Paragon Bar and Grill
Rainbow
Tula's

OUTDOOR SEATING
Axis
Capitol Club
Cloud Room
DeLuxe Bar & Grill
Fiddler's Inn
Harbour Public House
Kells
Kirkland Roaster & Alehouse
Leschi Lakecafe & GBB Bar
Linda's Tavern
Nickerson Street Saloon
Old Timer's Café
Pioneer Square Saloon
Red Door Alehouse
Roanoke Inn
Salty's on Alki
Wedgwood Ale House and
    Cafe

PIANO BARS
Baltic Room
Cloud Room
Fireside Room

POOL TABLES/
   BILLIARDS
Ballroom in Fremont
Belltown Billiards

Blue Moon Tavern
The Breakroom
The Buckaroo
College Inn Pub
Comet Tavern
The Duchess Tavern
Eastlake Zoo
Garage
Grady's Grillhouse
Linda's Tavern
Nickerson Street Saloon
The Old Pequliar
Owl 'n' Thistle Irish Pub and
  Restaurant
Red Onion Tavern
Roanoke Inn
Shark Club
Temple Billiards
The Wild Rose

PUBS/ALEHOUSES
The Attic Alehouse & Eatery
Big Time Brewery and
  Alehouse
College Inn Pub
Conor Byrne's Public House
Cooper's Alehouse
The Duchess Tavern
Elysian Brewing Company
Forecasters Public House
Grady's Grillhouse
Hale's Brewery & Pub
Harbour Public House
Hilltop Ale House
Hopvine Pub
Irish Emigrant
Issaquah Brewhouse
Kells
Kirkland Roaster & Alehouse
Latona by Green Lake
McMenamins Pub & Brewery
Murphy's Pub
Nickerson Street Saloon

The Old Pequliar
Old Town Alehouse
Owl 'n' Thistle Irish Pub and
  Restaurant
Pacific Inn Pub
Red Door Alehouse
Red Onion Tavern
Roanoke Inn
Roanoke Park Place Tavern
74th Street Ale House
Six Arms Brewery and Pub
Steel Sky Pub
Trolleyman Pub
Two Bells Tavern
Wedgwood Ale House and
  Cafe

ROCK
Ballard Firehouse
The Breakroom
Crocodile Café
DV8
Experience Music Project/Sky
  Church
Graceland
Paradox Theater
Showbox
Steel Sky Pub
Sunset Tavern
Tractor Tavern

ROMANTIC
Baltic Room
Dimitriou's Jazz Alley
El Gaucho's Pampas Room
Fireside Room
Garden Court
Shea's Lounge

SMOKE-FREE
Big Time Brewery and
  Alehouse
Experience Music Project

Fiddler's Inn
Hale's Brewery & Pub
Hilltop Ale House
Latona by Green Lake
McMenamins Pub & Brewery
Nickerson Street Saloon
Old Town Alehouse
Trolleyman Pub
Uptown Espresso and Bakery
Virginia Inn
Wedgwood Ale House and
  Cafe

SPORTS BARS
Big Time Brewery and
  Alehouse
Cooper's Alehouse
The Duchess Tavern
F. X. McRory's Steak, Chop,
  and Oyster House

SWING
Century Ballroom
Paragon Bar and Grill
Showbox

UNDERAGE/NO
ALCOHOL
The Breakroom (some all-
  ages shows)
DV8
Experience Music Project/Sky
  Church
Grateful Bread Café
I-Spy (some all-ages shows)
The Old Firehouse
Paradox Theater
Showbox (some all-ages
  shows)
Sit & Spin (some all-ages
  shows)

Nightlife by Neighborhood

BAINBRIDGE ISLAND
Harbour Public House

BALLARD
Ballard Firehouse
Conor Byrne's Public House
Hale's Brewery & Pub
Hattie's Hat
Mr. Spot's Chai House
The Old Pequliar
Old Town Alehouse
Sunset Tavern
Tractor Tavern

BELLTOWN
Axis
Belltown Billiards
Crocodile Café
El Gaucho's Pampas Room
Lava Lounge
Queen City Grill
Sit & Spin
Tula's
Two Bells Tavern
Uptown Espresso and Bakery

CAPITOL HILL
Arena
Baltic Room
B&O Espresso
Bauhaus Books and Coffee
The Breakroom
Café Dilettante
Caffe Vita
Capitol Club
Century Ballroom
Comet Tavern
DeLuxe Bar & Grill

NIGHTLIFE

Elysian Brewing Company
Garage
Green Cat Cafe
Hopvine Pub
Joe Bar
Linda's Tavern
Manray
Neighbours
Roanoke Park Place Tavern
Six Arms Brewery and Pub
The Vogue
The Wild Rose

DENNY REGRADE
DV8
Five Point Café
Graceland
Re-bar
Timberline Spirits
Tini Bigs Lounge

DOWNTOWN
Brooklyn Seafood, Steak, &
    Oyster House
Café Dilettante
Caffe Ladro
Cloud Room
Dimitriou's Jazz Alley
Garden Court
The Georgian
I-Spy
McCormick & Schmick's
McCormick's Fish House &
    Bar
The Nitelite
Showbox
Shuckers
Union Square Grill
Virginia Inn

EASTLAKE
Eastlake Zoo
Louisa's Bakery & Café

FIRST HILL
Fireside Room
Vito's Madison Grill

FREMONT
Ballroom in Fremont
The Buckaroo Tavern
Caffe Ladro
Nickerson Street Saloon
Pacific Inn Pub
Red Door Alehouse
Simply Desserts
Trolleyman Pub

GREENWOOD/GREEN LAKE
Diva Espresso
Kismet Bistro and Wine Bar
Latona by Green Lake
Luau Polynesian Lounge
74th Street Ale House
The Urban Bakery
Zoka Coffee Roaster and Tea
    Company

ISSAQUAH
Issaquah Brewhouse

KIRKLAND
Kirkland Roaster & Alehouse
Shark Club

LESCHI/MADISON PARK/MONTLAKE
The Attic Alehouse & Eatery
Grady's Grillhouse
Leschi Lakecafe
Red Onion Tavern

MAPLE LEAF
Cooper's Alehouse

MERCER ISLAND
Roanoke Inn

PIKE PLACE MARKET
Alibi Room
Kells
Procopio Gelateria
Shea's Lounge

PIONEER SQUARE
Backdoor Ultra Lounge
Bohemian Café
F. X. McRory's Steak, Chop,
    and Oyster House
J&M Cafe and Cardroom
Larry's Blues Cafe
Last Supper Club
New Orleans Restaurant
Old Timer's Café
Owl 'n' Thistle Irish Pub and
    Restaurant
Pioneer Square Saloon
Temple Billiards

QUEEN ANNE
Caffe Appassionato
Caffé Ladro
Caffe Vita
The Famous Pacific Dessert
    Company
Hilltop Ale House
McMenamins Pub & Brewery

Mecca Café
Paragon Bar and Grill
Uptown Espresso and Bakery

RAVENNA
The Duchess Tavern
Grateful Bread Café
Queen Mary

REDMOND
The Old Firehouse

ROOSEVELT
The Scarlet Tree

SEATTLE CENTER
Experience Music Project
Polly Esther's
SkyCity at the Needle

UNIVERSITY DISTRICT
Big Time Brewery and
    Alehouse
Blue Moon Tavern
Cafe Allegro
College Inn Pub
Espresso Express
Grand Illusion Espresso and
    Pastry
Irish Emigrant
Paradox Theater
Rainbow

WALLINGFORD
Diva Espresso
Murphy's Pub
Pacific Inn Pub
Teahouse Kuan Yin

WEDGWOOD
Fiddler's Inn
Wedgwood Ale House and
    Cafe

WEST SEATTLE
Caffé Ladro
Diva Espresso
Rocksport
Salty's on Alki
Steel Sky Pub
Uptown Espresso and Bakery

WOODINVILLE
Forecasters Public House

NIGHTLIFE

Music and Clubs

Clubs around Seattle shut down, change format, change names, or get crumbled by earthquakes at an amazing rate. For example, over the last 25 years the Showbox has been: a senior citizen bingo hall, a flea market, a punk club, closed down, a rock club, a comedy club, closed down again, a private club, a rock club desperately-in-need-of-work, and now, in its latest incarnation, a renovated multipurpose music hall. And the February 2001 quake took out three Pioneer Square clubs in 30 seconds of shaking—the Fenix and the OK Hotel have yet to recover, relocate, or reopen. A few of the clubs listed here will no doubt fade into history themselves (or change back into bingo halls). For the latest music listings, check the local daily newspapers (weekend goings-on listings appear on Friday), **SEATTLE WEEKLY** or **THE STRANGER** (the city's alternative weeklies, which come out on Thursday), or the on-line entertainment guide **CITYSEARCH** (www.seattle.citysearch.com).

ARENA / 925 E Pike St, Capitol Hill; 206/860-9500 In the past decade this space has had more names than an aspiring Hollywood starlet. In the '90s it was called Moe's Mo'Roc'n Cafe and was a rock club (before that, it was the Salvation Army's headquarters)—later it became aro.space and switched to electronic music with occasional live shows (Dido played her first Seattle show there). Beginning in 2001 it became Paradise Garage, which was plagued with bad press and financial problems. In its newest incarnation, Arena attracts a mostly gay crowd into whatever is the biggest dancing draw at the moment. *AE, MC, V; no checks; Wed–Sat; full bar; www.arenaseattle.com; map:L1*

BACKDOOR ULTRA LOUNGE / 503 3rd Ave, Pioneer Square; 206/622-7665 This venue began in the late '90s as a word-of-mouth phenomenon, and then slowly built a larger space around the crowds. Some of the best DJs in town spin here, drawing large, young audiences, particularly on the weekends. They also have an adjoining restaurant open Monday through Thursday afternoons. Enter the club through the alley off Yesler Way. *AE, MC, V; no checks; every day; full bar; www.backdoorlounge.com; map: O7*

BALLARD FIREHOUSE / 5429 Russell Ave NW, Ballard; 206/784-3516 The long-standing joke about this institution is to call it the Ballard Hellhouse. And that nickname isn't necessarily derogatory, since the club books mostly hell-raising hard-rock bands. Their typical weekend lineup looks like the schedule for VH1 *Behind the Music*. Despite legendarily smelly bathrooms and a ventilation system that needs work, this is still a fun place to rawk. They occasionally host all-ages shows. *AE, MC, V; no checks; every day; full bar; map:FF8*

BALTIC ROOM / 1207 Pine St, Capitol Hill; 206/625-4444 The Baltic Room wasn't where they filmed *The Fabulous Baker Boys,* but it could have been. This is as close as the city comes to a piano bar, though the musical lineup is much more diverse than simply piano. You can hear everything from Brit pop to drum 'n' bass combos to solo jazz bass players at this upscale room. The Baltic is tiny, however, so get there early if you want to concentrate on the music. *MC, V; no checks; every day; full bar; map:J2*

BOHEMIAN CAFÉ / 111 Yesler Wy, Pioneer Square; 206/447-1514 The lineup at this Pioneer Square stalwart runs from funk to reggae to hip-hop, with a few other stops in between, depending on what's hot at the moment. *AE, DIS, MC, V; no checks; Mon–Sat; full bar; map:N8*

THE BREAKROOM / 1325 E Madison St, Capitol Hill; 206/860-5155 When the much-missed club Moe closed down, the Breakroom gave life to the Capitol Hill rock scene again, and for half a decade it has rocked on. This is a great place to see an up-and-coming local band or to hear the hottest thing in Swedish punk rock from one of the many touring bands that come through here. The club has also begun early evening all-ages bookings. *MC, V; no checks; Mon–Sat; full bar; map:HH6*

CENTURY BALLROOM / 915 E Pine St, 2nd Floor, Capitol Hill; 206/324-7263 The Century is a beautiful old theater (formerly an Odd Fellows hall) that started booking music in 1999. Their schedule is erratic, so call first or look for ads, but this is one of the best places in Seattle to dance (wood floors!) or see bands. The room is big, airy, and fun, and since it is open only for performances, it doesn't attract lounge lizards—just people into music. Most of the bookings are salsa or swing related (they have lessons too), but the club has also hosted rock, jazz, singer-song-writers, and folk. *MC, V; no checks; every day; full bar; info@century ballroom.com; www.centuryballroom.com; map:GG6*

CROCODILE CAFÉ / 2200 2nd Ave, Belltown; 206/441-5611 The Croc is one of the few clubs in town where you can stop by almost any night of the week and find a band worth seeing—they've had the best bookers in town over the last decade. And speaking of decades, in 2001 the club celebrated its 10-year anniversary, almost unheard of in this business. They deserve the national attention they get—and the national bands—because they're both a well-run operation and a great room for music. The restaurant is also a fun place to hang, with reasonable prices and a lively community. And then there is always the back bar—more relationships have broken up or been formed in that room than in any other in the local music scene. *MC, V; no checks; every day; full bar; www.the crocodile.com; map:G7*

DIMITRIOU'S JAZZ ALLEY / 2033 6th Ave, Downtown; 206/441-9729
John Dimitriou's venue is not just the best jazz club in Seattle, it's one of the best in the nation. His reputation brings in international-caliber talent, and the club itself is perfectly designed—you can hear and see from every seat. Dimitriou has added more blues, Latin music, and big bands to the lineup over the past few years, and local artists frequently play during the week. Weekends are often packed, so call ahead to reserve tickets. You can guarantee yourself a seat by going early for dinner, although the food is not quite as good as the jazz. *AE, MC, V; checks OK; every day; full bar; www.jazzalley.com; map:H5*

DV8 / 131 Taylor Ave N, Denny Regrade; 206/448-0888 This is an 18-and-over club that does very well with young kids who can't legally drink yet but still want to go out and dance. The musical lineup is DJs spinning house, trance, R&B, and dance records. Occasionally the venue is used for live touring acts, but even those shows happen earlier than other clubs, so don't show up fashionably late—you might miss the entire show. If you're 20, you'll feel old most nights. *Cash only; Wed, Fri–Sun; no alcohol; map:D6*

EL GAUCHO'S PAMPAS ROOM / 90 Wall St, Belltown; 206/728-1140 The Pampas opened in early 1998 below the El Gaucho restaurant. Like its upstairs neighbor, it attracts a dressed-up crowd, but here the draw is the upscale jazz (and slow dancing) rather than the juicy steaks. *AE, DC, MC, V; checks OK; Fri–Sat; full bar; www.elgaucho.com; map:F8*

EXPERIENCE MUSIC PROJECT / 325 5th Ave N, Seattle Center; 206/EMP-LIVE or 877/EMP-LIVE EMP is actually three music venues in one since the site sports a trio of halls where live music is performed regularly. The main attraction is the **SKY CHURCH**, where several times a week a national act is scheduled. Though there's frequently a full bar attached, all Sky Church shows are all-ages, so feel free to bring the kids. It's a nice room for rock—for acoustic music, it lacks intimacy. For that, turn to the **JBL THEATER**, where EMP has special scheduled events: the acoustics here are phenomenal. And finally there's the **LIQUID LOUNGE**, which hosts music every night except Sunday and Monday. The lineup in the Liquid Lounge tends to be blues, but most of the bands are local. *AE, DIS, MC, V; no checks; every day; full bar; www.emplive.com; map:C6*

GRACELAND / 109 Eastlake Ave E, Denny Regrade; 206/381-3094 After five names in seven years, and many changes of management, this space is back to being a club where the rock is always loud, where the beer is always cheap, and where no one knows your name. Alternative rock, metal, and retro-grunge bands make up much of the billings here, so you'll always want to bring earplugs. *MC, V; no checks; every day; full bar; map:H1*

UP ALL NIGHT

Most of Seattle gets a little sleepy after 11pm, but its late-night entertainment includes options that will please indefatigable club-goers, sheep-counting bookworms, and every night owl in between.

Ballard's retro bowling alley, **Sunset Bowl** (1420 NW Market St; 206/782-7310; map:FF6), has hours that rival 7-Eleven for convenience—all day, every day—and a healthy karaoke scene on Wednesday, Friday, and Saturday nights. One word of caution: the diner closes at 8pm.

Those inveterate partiers who prefer to watch the sunrise through the haze of an all-night outing will find accommodating hours at **Contour** (807 1st Ave, Downtown; 206/748-9834; map:L7), where the last patrons bid the dance floor adieu around 9am Saturday and Sunday.

Midnight movies at the **Egyptian Theater** (805 E Pine St, Capitol Hill; 206/323-4978; map:HH7) are a weekend tradition. Every Friday and Saturday, this art house cinema, which is housed in a 1915 Masonic Temple, screens pop favorites and cult classics. In West Seattle, moviegoers toting bags of toast and rice convene on the first Saturday of each month at the **Admiral Theater** (2343 California Ave SW; 206/938-3456; map: I8) for a midnight screening of the mother of all cult flicks, The *Rocky Horror Picture Show.*

Capitol Hill's **Twice Sold Tales** (905 E John St; 206/324-2421; map:HH7) stays open all night every Friday, and rewards late-night literature seekers with 25 percent off books from 12am to 8am. The store is also open until 1am Monday through Thursday, until 2am Saturday, and until midnight Sunday.

The hunt for midnight (or 4am) snacking establishments often proves elusive in Seattle, where most restaurants shut down by 10pm. During the summer of 2001,

GRATEFUL BREAD CAFÉ / 7001 35th Ave NE, Ravenna; 206/525-3166 This little north-end bakery has turned into the city's best folk club. It's tiny, so get there early. Shows are held irregularly, and only during fall and winter; you'd be smart to call the club or the Seattle Folklore Society (206/782-0505) to check the schedule. *MC, V; local checks only; every day (music only occasionally); no alcohol; map:EE6*

I-SPY / 1921 5th Ave, Downtown; 206/374-9492 The lineup at this club is so eccentric, they began running a little legend in their ads with icons showing what kind of music each band plays. Most tend to be hip-hop or groove, or house. They also occasionally book all-ages shows, and some shows are licensed so that those 18 to 21 are allowed in part of the venue. They share a building with Nation (206/256-9667), a restaurant that also features DJ music. *MC, V; no checks; every day; full bar; map:I6*

13 Coins (125 Boren Ave N, Denny Regrade; 206/682-2513; map:G3), the Seattle standby infamous for long waits and pricey Italian and American fare, was joined in the 24-hour dining realm by **Jack's Roadhouse** (1501 E Olive Wy, Capitol Hill; 206/324-7000; map:HH7), an eatery that mimics classic roadhouse ambience. At Jack's, burgers and sandwiches cost about $6, a shark lolls about in a tank over the bar, and the menu includes a few Capitol Hill concessions, such as marinated tofu with mashed potatoes. **Charlie's on Broadway** (217 Broadway Ave E, Capitol Hill; 206/323-2535; map:GG7) is a favorite hangout for other food service folks since they don't close until 2am every day. **Tai Tung** in the Chinatown/International District (659 S King St; 206/622-7372; map:Q6) is open until 11pm weeknights and 1:30am on Friday and Saturday. **Pomodoro Ristorante** (2366 Eastlake Ave E, Eastlake; 206/324-3160; map:GG7), an Italian joint, doesn't kick folks out until midnight on weekdays and 2am on Friday and Saturday.

Those in search of a sugar fix should stop by the **Famous Pacific Dessert Company** (127 Mercer St, Queen Anne; 206/284-8100; map:A7) for tortes richer than a roomful of Microsoft founders. They're open until midnight Friday and Saturday, 11pm Tuesday through Thursday, and 10pm Sunday and Monday. Broadway's **Dilettante Chocolates** (416 Broadway Ave E, Capitol Hill; 206/329-6463; map:GG7) serves decadent treats and espresso until midnight on weekdays and until 1am Friday and Saturday.

For stain removal at any time of day, the **Five Point Café** near Seattle Center (415 Cedar St, Denny Regrade; 206/448-9993; map:E6) has a 24-hour laundromat.

And if your split ends give you nightmares, stylists at **Vain** (2018 1st Ave, Belltown; 206/441-3441; map:I7), the Seattle salon that has turned out many a red mohawk and blue fade, keep their shears snipping until 11pm Friday and Saturday nights. They also sponsor nighttime art or fashion shows and parties on occasion.   —*Marika McElroy*

IRISH EMIGRANT / 5260 University Wy NE, University District; 206/525-2955 Formerly the University Sports Bar (and, years before that, the Century Tavern), this U District landmark is now strictly Irish in both politics and music. They book mostly Irish bands six nights a week (Monday is a trivia contest). *AE, DC, DIS, MC, V; no checks; every day; full bar; www.irishemigrant.net; map:FF6*

LARRY'S BLUES CAFÉ / 209 1st Ave S, Pioneer Square; 206/624-7665 Larry's is a good venue for local blues (and for stiff drinks). *AE, DC, DIS, MC, V; checks OK; every day; full bar; map:O8*

LAST SUPPER CLUB / 124 S Washington St, Pioneer Square; 206/748-9975 The big attraction here are the DJs; many are cutting-edge and touring mixers. They also have salsa nights, hip-hop, and occasionally national acts booked in the large room. *AE, DC, DIS, MC, V; checks OK; Wed–Sun; full bar; map:O8*

NEIGHBOURS / 1509 Broadway Ave, Capitol Hill; 206/324-5358 Neighbours, the hottest gay dance spot in the city, is always packed on weekends. Music is almost always DJ-provided, but occasionally there is a live touring act (usually disco). Though the bulk of the patrons are gay, the club has a tolerant atmosphere and all are welcome. *MC, V; no checks; every day; full bar; www.neighboursonline.com; map:HH6*

NEW ORLEANS RESTAURANT / 114 1st Ave S, Pioneer Square; 206/622-2563 The New Orleans is one of the best venues in Pioneer Square because the owners support a booking policy that goes with the food: spicy, exotic, and classy. You'll find good Creole cuisine in the kitchen and zydeco, jazz, and blues in the showroom. They host music every night and provide the kind of Southern hospitality you won't find in many Pioneer Square joints. *AE, MC, V; local checks only; every day; full bar; map:N8*

THE OLD FIREHOUSE / 16510 NE 79th St, Redmond; 425/556-2370 Not to be confused with the Ballard Firehouse, this Redmond venue is an all-ages hot spot where teenagers go to hear alternative rock. There's no alcohol, but soda will cost you only 50 cents, and the bands playing here are some of the best in the region. Just because it allows underage kids doesn't mean hip adults have to skip it. Shows, when they are scheduled, are Friday and Saturday—make sure to call to see what the lineup is. *Cash only; Tues–Sat; no alcohol; map:EE1*

OLD TIMER'S CAFÉ / 620 1st Ave S, Pioneer Square; 206/623-9800 This used to be a jazz and blues club but now features salsa on weekends, as well as blues and karaoke other days. You do get classic Pioneer Square wood-and-brass decor. *AE, MC, V; no checks; every day; full bar; map:N8*

OWL 'N' THISTLE IRISH PUB AND RESTAURANT / 808 Post Ave, Pioneer Square; 206/621-7777 This Irish pub is hidden two blocks off the waterfront, just north of Pioneer Square, and it's worth the walk. The bookings usually are Celtic folk bands on weekends and other music during the week. There's also a small poolroom and a comfortable dining area up front. *AE, MC, V; no checks; every day; full bar; www.owlnthistle. com; map:M8*

PARADOX THEATER / 5510 University Wy NE, University District; 206/524-7677 This all-ages venue began in 1999 in an abandoned movie theater and has since become one of the most popular clubs in town. Their bookings are eclectic, including hard rock, metal, goth, industrial, pop, and punk. Most shows start at 8pm, but the club occasionally has matinee shows; however, if you're up for seeing punk rock at noon on

Sunday, you need help. *Cash only; Thurs–Sat (days vary according to bookings); no alcohol; www.theparadox.com; map:FF6*

PARAGON BAR AND GRILL / 2125 Queen Anne Ave N, Queen Anne; 206/283-4548 This Queen Anne nightspot features soft jazz, soft R&B, funk, solo guitar, and even a swing band on one night (Thursday). All of it is pretty sedate since the ambience is classy. Most nights of the week, there is some music, though the schedule varies, so call first. *DC, MC, V; no checks; every day; full bar; www.paragon-seattle.com; map:GG7*

POLLY ESTHER'S / 332 5th Ave N, Seattle Center; 206/441-1970 The name alone should help you understand this '70s-retro disco. Most of the crowd it attracts weren't born when the music they play was on the charts, but it still is a fun place—the crowds dress the part, so make sure to bring out your disco duds. *AE, DC, MC, V; no checks; every day; full bar; www.pollyesthers.com; map:C5*

RAINBOW / 722 NE 45th St, University District; 206/634-1761 This U District nightspot has had more format changes than Jackie O had hats. The latest is a variety of live acts including blues guitar, jazz, DJ, drum 'n' bass, and funk jams. It is a nice room—and how many clubs can say they once hosted both the Ramones and the Neville Brothers in one week? *MC, V; local checks only; every day; full bar; www.therainbow. cc; map:FF6*

RE-BAR / 1114 Howell St, Denny Regrade; 206/233-9873 Re-bar books live music only occasionally, but it does attract musicians, who either hang out in the bar or get funky and dance. Thursday, which was Queer Disco night for years (though the crowd is always sexually diverse), has been renamed Hot Rocks. The DJs here are topnotch, as are the live performances. Cross street is Boren. *MC, V; no checks; Tues–Sun; beer and wine; www.re-bar.com; map:I2*

ROCKSPORT / 4209 SW Alaska St, West Seattle; 206/935-5838 The West Seattle beer hall now has a full bar and usually books bands at least one night a week: like a lot of West Seattle, it's the kind of place that takes you back about 10 years. The bookings tend to be rock, so don't expect any of that DJ hip-hop here. *AE, MC, V; no checks; every day; full bar; map:JJ8*

SCARLET TREE / 6521 Roosevelt Wy NE, Roosevelt; 206/523-7153 The Scarlet Tree may be best known as a place where you can get a hard drink at 6:30am (and don't think people aren't doing just that), but it also consistently draws crowds for the hard-driving blues bands, as well as the R&B and funk it books. *AE, MC, V; local checks only; every day; full bar; map:EE7*

SHARK CLUB / 52 Lakeshore Plaza, Kirkland; 425/803-3003 This club, known locally as the Shark, draws a mostly Bellevue crowd who want a little dose of Seattle rock in Kirkland. Actually, make that Seattle funk, since most of the bookings are dance-oriented '70s, '80s, and '90s cover bands. The venue itself is well designed, and it's a good place to see a show if you can handle the beer buddies next to you. The club books music Thursday through Saturday. *AE, DIS, MC, V; no checks; every day; full bar; www.thesharkclub.com; map:EE3*

SHOWBOX / 1426 1st Ave, Downtown; 206/628-3151 This is the grande dame of Seattle music venues—how many clubs can say they've hosted shows by both Captain Beefheart and Pearl Jam? If you haven't been to the club recently, you may not recognize it since it is much improved— more room, more air, more bar space. The Showbox also occasionally has all-ages shows, so even youngsters can see the inside of an institution. *MC, V; no checks; every day; full bar; www.showboxseattle.com; map:K7*

SIT & SPIN / 2219 4th Ave, Belltown; 206/441-9484 Sit & Spin once was simply a laundromat that also had a coffee shop. Then it became a cafe, and for several years now it's also been a nightclub. Why anyone would want to wash their clothes in the middle of a nightclub is hard to answer, but you'll find a brave few folding their panties at 1am. The music room is tiny, but it's also a fun place to see bands; it is intimate enough that you won't be more than 20 feet away from the stage. It's one of the few places that takes chances with younger pop bands, and they also book more all-ages shows than any other mixed-use nightclub in town. *MC, V; no checks; every day; full bar; map:G7*

STEEL SKY PUB / 3803 Delridge Wy SW, West Seattle; 206/935-2412 Formerly Madison's Café, this pub began in 1995 as one of the first local clubs to book the growing number of singer-songwriters who aren't quite folk and aren't quite rock. It also boasts a decent cafe. It's somewhat hard to find (take the Delridge Way exit from the West Seattle Bridge, and look for it on the right before the first stoplight) but worth the trip. Entertainment is booked only on weekends and occasionally on Monday. *DC, DIS, MC, V; no checks; every day; full bar; map:KK8*

SUNSET TAVERN / 5433 Ballard Ave NW, Ballard; 206/784-4880 This small Ballard hole-in-the-wall started booking music a few years back and is now one of the best places in town to see a show. There's live music every night, and the caliber of national acts they bring in might surprise you if you just looked at the outside of the place. The lineup ranges from country, western, or singer-songwriter to punk and metal. The crowd is always friendly and the beer very cold. *AE, MC, V; no checks; every day; beer and wine; www.sunsettavern.com; map:EE8*

TIMBERLINE SPIRITS / 2015 Boren Ave, Denny Regrade; 206/883-0242
Shake a leg to country and western music at this lively, popular gay and
lesbian disco. Don't know how to two-step? Show up Tuesday and they'll
teach you for free, and give you line-dancing lessons as well. Karaoke is
on Thursday, and Saturday night is strictly country and western. You can
shake your thang on Sunday afternoon to classic '70s disco (a Seattle tradition), which the Timberline calls "Sunday Church." *MC, V; no checks;
Tues–Sun; full bar; www.timberlinespirits.com; map:G3*

TRACTOR TAVERN / 5213 Ballard Ave NW, Ballard; 206/789-3599
Almost everyone onstage at the Tractor has that windblown look of alternative country—and so do many members of the audience. It's one of the
few clubs in Seattle where you can wear cowboy boots, a plaid shirt, and
Levi's and fit in. The booking is consistently excellent (rock, rockabilly,
bluegrass, and folk are featured in addition to alt country), and the venue
itself is intimate without being claustrophobic. *MC, V; no checks; every
day (varies according to bookings); full bar; www.tractortavern.com;
map:FF8*

TULA'S / 2214 2nd Ave, Belltown; 206/443-4221 Tula's has quietly
grown into a noted jazz club. They book mostly local musicians, but their
jam sessions attract top-rate talent and it's a great room for music. They
don't advertise much, so make sure to call to check on bookings. *AE,
DIS, MC, V; no checks; every day; full bar; map:G7*

THE VOGUE / 1516 11th Ave, Capitol Hill; 206/324-5778 In 1999, the
Vogue left Belltown and moved to Capitol Hill, which was more appropriate anyway for a club where "fetish night" is the most popular event.
Most of the music is DJ, but occasionally goth and industrial bands play.
If you don't know what goth sounds like or what "fetish night" might
be, you don't want to go. *MC, V; no checks; Tues–Sun; full bar; www.
vogueseattle.com; map:L1*

Bars, Pubs, and Taverns

ALIBI ROOM / 85 Pike Pl, Pike Place Market; 206/623-3180 Opened
and owned by local Hollywood types (including the ubiquitous Tom
Skerritt), the Alibi was conceived of as a watering hole for Seattle indie
filmmakers, complete with film-related decor. On weekends, the nicely
restored space hidden in cobblestoned Post Alley is packed with drinkers
of the hip and single variety, film literacy not required. Lunch and dinner
menus offer sandwiches and seafood. The club also has DJs playing on
most weekend nights, and draws a young and peppy crowd for that. *AE,
MC, V; no checks; every day; full bar; www.alibiroom.com; map:J8*

THE ATTIC ALEHOUSE & EATERY / 4226 E Madison St, Madison Park; 206/323-3131 From Madison Park old-timers to fresh-faced UW grads, everyone comes to the Attic for a good selection of microbrews, Guinness on tap, and consistently tasty nightly dinner specials. Great value for your dollar. *AE, MC, V; checks OK; every day; beer and wine; map:GG6*

AXIS / 2214 1st Ave, Belltown; 206/441-9600 Delectable snacks and an endless parade of well-dressed (or badly dressed, depending on your point of view) professionals make the lounge at Axis one of Belltown's liveliest. Order a glass of wine from the thoughtfully chosen list, and indulge in some deep-fried pickles—if you can find a table. *AE, DC, MC, V; no checks; every day; full bar; map:G8*

BALLROOM IN FREMONT / 456 N 36th St, Fremont; 206/634-2575 This nightclub in Fremont has nine pool tables, but most people come for the liquor and ambience, which is funky but chic. They have music on weekends—always DJ—and the dance floor really does turn it into a ballroom. *MC, V; no checks; every day; full bar; map:FF7*

BELLTOWN BILLIARDS / 90 Blanchard St, Belltown; 206/448-6779 Belltown Billiards is a mishmash—part high-tech bar and dance floor, part high-class pool hall, part high-gloss Italian restaurant—but everyone is having too much fun to mind the confusion. The food takes a backseat on weekend nights, when the crowds descend and the crush of bodies turns pool into a true spectator sport. *AE, MC, V; no checks; every day; full bar; http://belltown.citysearch.com; map:G8*

BIG TIME BREWERY AND ALEHOUSE / 4133 University Wy NE, University District; 206/545-4509 Antique beer ads clutter the walls at the U District's most popular alehouse, where the brews are made on the other side of the wall. The place is hopping with students and faculty, some burrowed into booths with piles of books, others looking for love or entertaining visiting friends and colleagues. The front room is nonsmoking; in the back there's a shuffleboard game, though it's the off-the-floor variety. *MC, V; no checks; every day; beer and wine; www.bigtimebrewery. com; map:FF6*

BLUE MOON TAVERN / 712 NE 45th St, University District; 206/633-6267 It's seedy, it's smoky, and it's beloved: when this lair of legends and gutter dreams appeared to be in the path of the wrecking ball, a cry of protest went up, books on its shady history were quickly printed, and demonstrations were organized. A yearlong battle with developers produced a 40-year lease and a collective sigh of relief from the neighborhood pool players, Beat ghosts, living poets, and survivors of the U District's glory days. Tom Robbins put in his time in this crusty joint, and no wonder; the graffiti-covered booths are filled with strange characters who seem to be in search of a novel. Blue Moon funds the literary journal

Point No Point and holds an annual poetry and fiction contest. *Cash only; every day; beer and wine; map:FF7*

BROOKLYN SEAFOOD, STEAK, & OYSTER HOUSE / 1212 2nd Ave, Downtown; 206/224-7000 If you're looking to meet a lawyer, this is the place: after work, the Brooklyn crawls with suits. On summer weekends tourists replace lawyers, oohing and aahing at the fresh oyster selection. There's plenty of seating at the wraparound bar and a good choice of beers, although this is more of a single-malt Scotch crowd. *AE, DIS, MC, V; checks OK; every day; full bar; www.thebrooklyn.com; map:K7*

THE BUCKAROO TAVERN / 4201 Fremont Ave N, Fremont; 206/634-3161 Upper Fremont's legendary roadhouse sports one of the city's finest displays of neon—the lassoing cowboy out front. The helmet rack is always full, as bikers from miles around pile in for a brewski and a game of pool. One doesn't come here for MENSA meetings, though. The place can get a bit rowdy; women heading out for an evening alone might better drink elsewhere. *No credit cards; checks OK; every day; beer and wine; map:FF7*

CAPITOL CLUB / 414 E Pine St, Capitol Hill; 206/325-2149 Seattle's own Casbah, this stylish second-floor den is a favorite with hip young professionals, who crowd the outdoor terrace and cozy up at candle-lit tables with martinis and plates of Middle Eastern noshes, including fragrant olives, pita, and hummus. The restaurant occupies the main level, and its adjacent Blue Room serves as an intimate gathering place for special occasions, but the comfortable yet exotic bar is the place to make the scene. *AE, MC, V; no checks; every day; full bar; map:J2*

CLOUD ROOM / 1619 9th Ave (Camlin Hotel), Downtown; 206/292-6206 Kitty-corner from the Paramount, this dark, clubby place is a great spot for pre- or post-show sipping. The piano bar seems straight out of New Jersey. The well-mixed drinks are strong and expensive, and you can count on the tickler of the ivories to know "our song." No views of the water—those have been obscured by surrounding buildings for decades. Nonetheless, in fine weather the rooftop terrace is a pleasant spot to while away an evening, with city lights a-twinkle. The Cloud Room is now legendary for the time Elvis Costello played there. *AE, DIS, MC, V; local checks only; every day; full bar; map:I4*

COLLEGE INN PUB / 4006 University Wy NE, University District; 206/634-2307 The dark, cozy basement of the College Inn is the closest thing hereabouts to a campus rathskeller, since any such is strictly verboten at the university a block away. Students who've reached the age of majority drink microbrewed ales by the pitcher, attack mounds of nachos, play pool (free on Sunday) to loud music, and convene for more serious symposia in the private room in back. *MC, V; no checks; every day; full bar; map:FF6*

COMET TAVERN / 922 E Pike St, Capitol Hill; 206/323-9853 The scruffy Comet is a Capitol Hill institution, packed on the weekends with ripped-jean types of both genders who keep the pool tables and dart boards in active use. The bar now even occasionally books music, which is as loud and raucous as the patrons. *Cash only; every day; beer and wine; map:L1*

CONOR BYRNE'S PUBLIC HOUSE / 5140 Ballard Ave NW, Ballard; 206/784-3640 The former site of the long-beloved Owl has aged into the most authentic-feeling Irish pub in town, where the Guinness flows freely, loosening the silver tongues of the (real and pseudo) Irishmen sitting at the bar. Celtic music on weekends. *MC, V; checks OK; every day; beer and wine; www.conorspub.com; map:FF8*

COOPER'S ALEHOUSE / 8065 Lake City Wy NE, Maple Leaf; 206/522-2923 A mecca for serious brew lovers and home to postgame soccer and rugby bacchanals, this neighborhood pub aims to please in a straight-forward, no-nonsense manner. Patrons can opt for darts or for sports on TV, but the beer's the main thing, and Cooper's offers 25 taps, most of them dispensing Northwest microbrews. The Ballard Bitter–battered fish-and-chips (say that fast after a couple of pitchers) are terrific. *MC, V; no checks; every day; full bar; map:EE7*

DELUXE BAR & GRILL / 625 Broadway Ave E, Capitol Hill; 206/324-9697 The time-honored DeLuxe is where the more mainstream Broadway boulevardiers go for stuffed baked potatoes and electric iced teas. The bar is often crammed, although the retractable wall in front lets you sit on the sidewalk in nice weather and watch the steady stream of passersby. Nightly drink specials. *AE, DIS, MC, V; no checks; every day; full bar; map:GG6*

THE DUCHESS TAVERN / 2827 NE 55th St, Ravenna; 206/527-8606 This is the kind of neighborhood tavern that former university students remember fondly decades after graduation. Today's Duchess has cleaned up its act considerably, it's more open and airy than in the past, and there are 20 beers on tap (more than half are microbrews). The darts, the pool table, and the '60s rock make it the perfect place to stop for a pitcher after the game. The pizza is remarkably tasty. *AE, MC, V; local checks only; every day; beer and wine; map:FF6*

EASTLAKE ZOO / 2301 Eastlake Ave E, Eastlake; 206/329-3277 One of the city's most venerable and beloved neighborhood tavs, the Zoo is equally popular with young pool hustlers and older barflies, including regulars who've made this their home away from home for more than two decades. Plenty to do besides drink beer: play pool, shuffleboard, darts, or pinball (no video games). Free pool until 5pm. *Cash only; every day; beer and wine; map:GG7*

ELYSIAN BREWING COMPANY / 1211 E Pike St, Capitol Hill; 206/860-1920 This spacious Capitol Hill club is best known for its beer (excellent, and brewed on the premises), but it's also become a live music venue on Saturday night for jazz and other genres. *AE, DC, MC, V; no checks; every day; beer and wine; www.elysianbrewing.com; map:HH6*

F. X. MCRORY'S STEAK, CHOP, AND OYSTER HOUSE / 419 Occidental Ave S, Pioneer Square; 206/623-4800 There's plenty of old-world charm here, as well as more Gilded Age bravura and bourbon than you can imagine. F. X. McRory's is a favorite among the town's sports fans, and it lives and dies by the success of the teams. Fresh oysters and a solid beer collection, too. Go with a Seattle Prep grad who talks sports—loudly. *AE, DC, DIS, MC, V; checks OK; every day; full bar; www.mickmchughs.com/fx.html; map:P9*

FIDDLER'S INN / 9219 35th Ave NE, Wedgwood; 206/525-0752 Under new ownership in Wedgwood since 1995, this affiliate of the Latona by Green Lake pub has the look and feel of a log cabin in the woods. It's a one-room, nonsmoking establishment, with picnic tables set on an outdoor patio. There's acoustic music on weekends. *MC, V; checks OK; every day; beer and wine; www.fiddlersinn.org; map:DD6*

FIRESIDE ROOM / 900 Madison St (Sorrento Hotel), First Hill; 206/622-6400 The clubby lounge in the lobby of the Sorrento evokes a leisurely world of hearthside chats in overstuffed chairs, an unrushed perusal of the daily newspaper, a hand of whist. Most pleasant for a late-evening drink, particularly on Thursday through Saturday nights, when the piano accompanies the music of many and varied conversations. Appetizers are available until midnight on weekends, 11 on weekdays. *AE, DIS, MC, V; checks OK; every day; full bar; www.hotelsorrento.com; map:M4*

FIVE POINT CAFÉ / 415 Cedar St, Denny Regrade; 206/448-9993 Stuffed fish on the wall, nuts in the chairs, rocks in the jukebox—you never know what you'll find here, except extra-strong drinks that have minimal impact on your wallet. With a friendly clientele that ranges from bluehairs and gays to suburban babes and Rastafarians, the place—despite its divey decor and perma-nicotined walls—gives hope that world peace may be achievable after all. *AE, MC, V; no checks; every day; full bar; map:E7*

FORECASTERS PUBLIC HOUSE / 14300 NE 145th St, Woodinville; 425/483-3232 The bustling, cheery pub at Redhook's Woodinville brewery is a hub for tourists and Sammamish River Trail cyclists in warm weather, and a cozy spot for beer- and food-lovers of all stripes to linger in winter. Take a tour of the brewery, or just enjoy several Redhook varieties while munching on appetizers or heartier sandwiches and seafood entrees. Live music is played on Friday and Saturday nights. *AE, MC, V; checks OK; every day; beer and wine; www.redhook.com; map:BB1*

GARAGE / 1130 Broadway Ave E, Capitol Hill; 206/322-2296 Just what Seattle needed—another pricey pool hall. Fortunately, this one's oozing with amiable character and outfitted with 18 good tables plus plenty of neon in the bar. Local celebrity owners include Pearl Jam's Mike McCready. Come during happy hour for $2 beer and $3 well drinks, and order a designer pizza or a plate of fries. Cigar smokers are free to light up. *AE, MC, V; no checks; every day; full bar; map:M1*

THE GARDEN / 411 University St (Four Seasons Olympic Hotel), Downtown; 206/621-1700 Spacious and grand, the Garden is the pièce de résistance of the Four Seasons Olympic. You come here to celebrate with expensive champagne, to dance on a parquet floor to the strains of a society combo, to hobnob with the pearls-and-basic-black set (although of late we've seen an influx of blue jeans too). Have a drink and hors d'oeuvres, or coffee and a slice of torte, among the palm fronds. *AE, CB, DC, DIS, JCB, MC, V; no checks; Tues–Sat; full bar; www.fourseasons.com/seattle; map:L6*

GRADY'S GRILLHOUSE / 2307 24th Ave E, Montlake; 206/726-5968 Grady's is a convivial neighborhood pub, comfortable and clean. Come for the good selection of micros on tap and the food, which is a cut above the usual pub fare, but stay away on Husky game days unless you're a die-hard fan. Nonsmokers beware. *MC, V; local checks only; every day; full bar; map:GG6*

HALE'S BREWERY & PUB / 4301 Leary Wy NW, Ballard; 206/782-0737 This gleaming, spacious brewpub, a showcase for locally renowned Hale's ales, also serves as an oasis of sophistication in the Fremont-Ballard industrial neighborhood. Grab a booth, or bring along enough of the gang to fill one of the long tables in the high-ceilinged back room, where live music is performed on weekend nights. At least nine varieties of Hale's pour year-round, as well as a selection of rotating seasonal varieties. Salads, sandwiches, and nicely crafted pizzas make up the menu, and the entire place is nonsmoking. *MC, V; checks OK; every day; beer and wine; www.halesales.com; map:FF8*

HARBOUR PUBLIC HOUSE / 231 Parfitt Wy SW, Bainbridge Island; 206/842-0969 This friendly pub on Bainbridge's Eagle Harbor is an easy stroll from the ferry dock. In winter it's cozy and amber-lit; in summer, sunlight slants through loft windows and onto the airy waterside deck. There's a connoisseur's selection of lagers and ales along with a broad list of wines, ports, and sherries. And there's an enlightened menu of food, from traditional pub fare to pasta. *AE, MC, V; local checks only; every day; beer and wine; www.harbourpub.com*

HATTIE'S HAT / 5231 Ballard Ave NW, Ballard; 206/784-0175 Hattie's Hat is an old-time place that underwent a major renovation several years ago, and now lives on as a hybrid: it's got both young hipsters and old Ballard fishermen. The food is excellent and the bar is lively even early in the morning. *MC, V; local checks only; every day; full bar; map:FF8*

HILLTOP ALE HOUSE / 2129 Queen Anne Ave N, Queen Anne; 206/285-3877 The 74th Street Ale House's sister establishment atop Queen Anne shares many of its excellent qualities: a healthy selection of beers, tasty pub food, and a convivial atmosphere, making the Hilltop a great contribution to the neighborhood. *MC, V; checks OK; every day; beer and wine; map:GG7*

HOPVINE PUB / 507 15th Ave E, Capitol Hill; 206/328-3120 Another seedy tavern transformed into a clean pub featuring lots of microbrews. There are hop vines stenciled and sculpted on the walls, wooden booths and tables stained in bright colors, and a smoking area in back. With pizza on the menu and acoustic music a couple of nights each week, this is a welcome addition to the Capitol Hill neighborhood. *MC, V; checks OK; every day; beer and wine; map:GG6*

ISSAQUAH BREWHOUSE / 35 W Sunset Wy, Issaquah; 425/557-1911 The only marked difference between Issaquah Brewhouse, now owned by Oregon's Rogue Ales, and its cousins across Lake Washington is that the room is filled with crying children instead of smoke (though smoking is permitted at the back bar). Still, it's a nice place to stop for a pint—try the on-site-brewed Bullfrog, a tasty wheat ale with hints of citrus and honey. *MC, V; checks OK; every day; beer and wine; www.rogue.com*

J&M CAFE AND CARDROOM / 201 1st Ave S, Pioneer Square; 206/292-0663 Pioneer Square's beloved historic saloon has a long front bar, plus another in the former card room that you can escape to when the crowds get thick, as well as a decent menu of *hofbrau* sandwiches and burgers. Sold and saved from eviction in 1995, the J&M is the place to meet someone before or after a sporting event—if the packs of roaring fraternity brothers don't drive you away. *AE, DC, MC, V; no checks; every day; full bar; map:O8*

KELLS / 1916 Post Alley, Pike Place Market; 206/728-1916 Rousing sing-alongs to live Celtic music boom throughout the licensed pub side of this Irish restaurant every day. Good coddle, good soda bread. *AE, MC, V; local checks only; every day; full bar; map:I8*

KIRKLAND ROASTER & ALEHOUSE / 111 Central Wy, Kirkland; 425/827-4400 Serving microbrews long before the rest of the Eastside caught on, the Kirkland Alehouse is entering its second decade of operations with no signs of slowing. The bar celebrates its raison d'être—the dispensing of quality beer—in its decor. Beer barrels, taps, and bottles line walls covered with microbrew-label murals. Everything seems to shout of beer. Why resist? *AE, DC, MC, V; checks OK; every day; full bar; map:EE3*

KISMET BISTRO AND WINE BAR / 7311 Greenwood Ave N, Greenwood; 206/706-5430 This funky wine bar and bistro is in Greenwood, not a place known for the exotic. But the food and drink here are worth a detour. *AE, DC, MC, V; checks OK; Tues–Sun; full bar; map:EE7*

LATONA BY GREEN LAKE / 6423 Latona Ave NE, Green Lake; 206/525-2238 The Latona is a light, woody, microbrew-and-cheese-bread-lovers kind of place, a favorite with its residential neighbors and lake lizards alike. Things can get cozy in this small but thankfully smoke-free space, which seems more expansive due to high ceilings. Service is extra friendly and accommodating. Most Friday and Saturday evenings, the pub hosts local jazz and folk musicians. *MC, V; local checks only; every day; beer and wine; map:EE7*

LAVA LOUNGE / 2226 2nd Ave, Belltown; 206/441-5660 This long, skinny Belltown bar sports a tiki-hut theme in spades, from Lava lamps to velvet paintings of bare, busty maidens. Don't expect any froufrou drinks with little umbrellas, however; this is a beer bar (beers are available both bottled and on tap). A standard stop on the Belltown watering-hole circuit, it's a great place to meet friends, grab a booth, and get down to serious gabbing and gulping. Pinball and shuffleboard provide added amusement, along with Wednesday-night live music. *MC, V; no checks; every day; beer and wine; map:G8*

LESCHI LAKECAFE & G.B.B. BAR / 102 Lakeside Ave, Leschi; 206/328-2233 Ah, the sporting life. The Lakecafe serves the jogging-sailing-cycling constituents of the Leschi neighborhood with a vast selection of beers and booze. It's best in summer, when the umbrellas in the courtyard shade the hottest tables around Lake Washington. *AE, DC, DIS, MC, V; no checks; every day; full bar; map:HH6*

LINDA'S TAVERN / 707 E Pine St, Capitol Hill; 206/325-1220 There might be a stuffed buffalo head over the bar, a wagon-wheel chandelier, and other Wild West decor, but Linda's ain't no place to go two-steppin'. The crowd here is a multiethnic mix of Gen-Xers, with a smattering of just plain folks. They all come to drink or play pool to the strains of alternative music blaring from the stereo, to watch films on the back porch in summer, or to listen to DJ music (Monday and Tuesday nights). Everyone is made to feel welcome—and that's another nice alternative. *MC, V; no checks; every day; full bar; map:GG6*

LUAU POLYNESIAN LOUNGE / 2253 N 56th St, Green Lake; 206/633-5828 This new spot just north of Green Lake has bizarre drinks, great food, and a hip crowd. Drink something with rum and you can't go wrong. *AE, DC, DIS, MC, V; local checks only; every day; full bar; map:EE6*

MANRAY / 514 E Pine St, Capitol Hill; 206/568-0750 This nightclub primarily attracts a gay crowd. The ultrawhite, modern expressionist decor complete with TV screens inset above the bar is not to be missed. *AE, DC, DIS, MC, V; no checks; every day; full bar; www.manrayvideo. com; map:K2*

MCCORMICK & SCHMICK'S / 1103 1st Ave, Downtown; 206/623-5500 Bankers like it because it looks like a bank. Dark-stained mahogany and beveled glass provide just the right atmosphere for stockbrokers and lawyers sipping Irish coffees and stiff well pours. Good downtown location; great happy-hour and late-night specials on both drinks and snacks. *AE, CB, DC, DIS, JCB, MC, V; no checks; every day; full bar; www. mccormickandschmicks.com; map:L8*

MCCORMICK'S FISH HOUSE & BAR / 722 4th Ave, Downtown; 206/682-3900 Polished wood and brass, stand-up counters, and fresh oysters make this the closest thing to a high-class San Francisco bar. McCormick's crawls with attorneys and bureaucrats after 5pm, as well as tourists in season. Excellent meal deals at happy hour. *AE, CB, DC, DIS, JCB, MC, V; no checks; every day; full bar; www.mccormickand schmicks.com; map:N6*

MCMENAMINS PUB & BREWERY / 200 Roy St, Queen Anne; 206/285-4722 This brewpub—Seattle's first venture for the Portland-based McMenamin brothers—has settled quite nicely into its Lower Queen Anne neighborhood, hosting local residents and Seattle Center visitors alike with characteristic low-key amiability. There's a great selection of McMenamins brews, plus great fries and other reasonably priced pub grub, and the place is smoke-free. *AE, DIS, MC, V; no checks; every day; beer and wine; www.mcmenamins.com; map:A6*

MECCA CAFÉ / 526 Queen Anne Ave N, Queen Anne; 206/285-9728 The narrow bar alongside this cafe was formerly home to many a geriatric drinker. The clientele is now young, cool, and prone to take advantage of the hit-heavy jukebox in the corner. Dark and snug, this hideaway lined with cardboard coasters can barely hold a dozen, but it's a festive place to end a rollicking night on Queen Anne. *AE, MC, V; no checks; every day; full bar; map:GG7*

MURPHY'S PUB / 1928 N 45th St, Wallingford; 206/634-2110 As Irish pubs go, Murphy's is a pretty classy place (fireplace, antiques, and stained glass). Wallingfordians and others pile in to play darts (real, of course, not electronic) or to catch the Wednesday open mikes and weekend music (often Celtic). The 'tenders are kindly, the comfort food tasty. More than a dozen local brews and stouts are poured on draft, and there's a nice collection of single-malt Scotches and single-barrel bourbons, but no well drinks. It's a zoo on St. Paddy's Day. *AE, MC, V; local checks only; every day; beer and wine; map:FF7*

NICKERSON STREET SALOON / 318 Nickerson St, Fremont; 206/284-8819 Alas, the legendary burgers that made the former tenant at this site (the 318) famous are no more, but you can enjoy a wide selection of beers on tap (including some lesser-known varieties) and some decent pub grub. The place has been cleaned up and the outdoor seating is nice—but we still miss those 318 burgers! On the north side of the ship canal, next to the bridge. *AE, DC, MC, V; no checks; every day; full bar; www. nickerstonstreetsaloon.com; map:FF7*

THE NITELITE / 1926 2nd Ave, Downtown; 206/443-0899 A favorite of the hip, young bar-hopping crowd, the Nitelite could well be the king of kitschy Seattle lounges. The original decor is from the '40s, with a mind-bending compendium of objects spanning the decades through the '70s. The place was used as a set in the movie *Dogfight* in 1991, and most of the props were kept firmly in place. Check out the train set encased in plastic under the bar. Cheap beer specials, stiff martinis, and syrupy libations for the Cap'n Crunch crowd are what's pouring. *MC, V; no checks; every day; full bar; map:I7*

THE OLD PEQULIAR / 1722 NW Market St, Ballard; 206/782-8886 It's part scruffy tavern, part Old English pub, and the folks on the Ballard bar circuit seem to eat it up. Play pool, shoot some darts, listen to live music, or test your brainpower at the Tuesday-night quiz contests. There's always a congenial crowd quaffing microbrews and imports. Just snag a table in the comfy pub corner and you're set. *DIS, MC, V; no checks; every day; beer and wine; map:FF8*

OLD TOWN ALEHOUSE / 5233 Ballard Ave NW, Ballard; 206/782-8323 The Old Town evokes the look of Old Ballard, with an ornate antique bar and icebox, exposed-brick walls, and old black-and-white photos. Tuesdays are devoted to live jazz. The Ballard Wedge sandwiches are tasty—and the fries that come alongside are out of this world. Smoke-free. *MC, V; local checks only; every day; beer and wine; map:FF8*

PACIFIC INN PUB / 3501 Stone Wy N, Fremont/Wallingford; 206/547-2967 Should you come for the brew (a dozen on tap, a couple of dozen in bottles and cans) or for the fab cayenne-spiked fish-and-chips? Most regulars enjoy both at this workingman's mainstay where Wallingford and Fremont merge. Old-timers know the PI's owner, Robert Julien, as the wonderful singing bartender at long-gone-but-not-forgotten Jake

O'Shaughnessy's. *AE, DIS, MC, V; no checks; every day; full bar; map:FF7*

PIONEER SQUARE SALOON / 77 Yesler Wy, Pioneer Square; 206/628-6444 This is one of the few bars in Pioneer Square that doesn't offer live music—and thus doesn't slap on a cover. The clientele ranges from slackers to corporate types, the taped tunes are good, and there's a dart board in the back. In summer, the patio tables—where you can survey the tourists wandering by—are packed. Between the kindly bartenders, the good (and cheap) wines by the glass, and the unaffected air, this could be the best spot in the city for making new friends. *AE, DC, MC, V; no checks; every day; beer and wine; map:N8*

QUEEN CITY GRILL / 2201 1st Ave, Belltown; 206/443-0975 Fluted lights, flowers, and a rosy glow that bathes the room make this one of Belltown's classiest options. On weekends it gets packed with artists, yuppies, and off-duty bartenders pretending they're in New York or San Francisco; we much prefer Queen City on weeknights, when sitting at the curved bar can be quietly lovely. *AE, DC, DIS, MC, V; no checks; every day; full bar; http://queencitygrill.citysearch.com; map:G8*

RED DOOR ALEHOUSE / 3401 Evanston Ave N, Fremont; 206/547-7521 They had to move the entire building one block west, but the Red Door remains the same even in its new location. During the day, suits, salesmen, and salty dogs stop in to down a cold one with a burger and fries. At night it's so crowded with the fraternity/sorority crowd, you could mistake the place for a J Crew catalog shoot. There's a wide selection of beers, predominantly Northwest microbrews, to complement some terrific (inexpensive) pub grub. Order a bowl of mussels and eat 'em in the beer garden. *AE, MC, V; local checks only; every day; beer and wine; map:FF7*

RED ONION TAVERN / 4210 E Madison St, Madison Park; 206/323-1611 Perfect in winter, when you can drink a beer beside the huge stone fireplace, this Madison Park institution is also known for its pool tables and its pizza. Mellow local crowd, except on Thursday night in summer, when the Red Onion is invaded by the overflow of party-hearty students from the Attic down the street. *MC, V; local checks only; every day; beer and wine; map:GG6*

ROANOKE INN / 1825 72nd Ave SE, Mercer Island; 206/232-0800 The Roanoke Inn isn't the kind of place most people will just happen upon. It resides on secluded Mercer Island, which is usually a destination only for its inhabitants. However, die-hard pub-crawlers may want to seek this one out for its history alone. It's known for its somewhat checkered past—apparently the upstairs rooms once housed a brothel of sorts, and the main room was the site of many bloody barroom brawls. Today its biggest draw is the outdoor seating on a generous front porch reminiscent of a Southern estate. *AE, MC, V; local checks only; every day; beer and wine; map:II4*

ROANOKE PARK PLACE TAVERN / 2409 10th Ave E, Capitol Hill; 206/324-5882 A gathering ground where the junior gentry of north Capitol Hill can feel like just folks. Good burgers and beers, but loud music often drowns out conversation. And the place is packed after Husky games. *MC, V; local checks only; every day; beer and wine; map:GG6*

SALTY'S ON ALKI / 1936 Harbor Ave SW, West Seattle; 206/937-1600 The spacious West Seattle bar spills over onto the bay-level patio (warmed, thankfully, by high-rise heat lamps), where you can order from a lengthy menu of seafood appetizers and gaze at the twinkling lights of Seattle. *AE, DC, DIS, MC, V; local checks only; every day; full bar; www.saltys.com; map:II9*

74TH STREET ALE HOUSE / 7401 Greenwood Ave N, Greenwood; 206/784-2955 An alehouse it is, with regulars lingering at the bar and taps pouring nearly two dozen brews. The food, however, is more than a cut above pub grub, including a delectable gumbo and several sandwiches and main dishes worthy of a "real" restaurant. It's a great place to meet after work, or to while away a rainy Sunday afternoon. *MC, V; checks OK; every day; beer and wine; map:EE8*

SHEA'S LOUNGE / 94 Pike St, Pike Place Market; 206/467-9990 Don't let the near-hidden location (on the top floor of the Corner Market building) keep you from ferreting out this charming little offshoot of Chez Shea. Seven small tables and a minuscule bar are set in a slender, elegant, dimly lit space with enormous casement windows looking out over market rooftops to Elliott Bay beyond. A nice selection of Italian and Spanish wines is complemented by a short but tasteful, mainly Mediterranean menu. Utterly romantic. *AE, MC, V; no checks; Tues–Sun; full bar; www.chezshea.com; map:J8*

SHUCKERS / 411 University St (Four Seasons Olympic Hotel), Downtown; 206/621-1984 Here you'll find Establishment and celebrity hotel guests enjoying Northwest oysters and shrimp or talking to the friendly bartenders. Afternoons there's a light menu of seafood and good local beers. *AE, DC, DIS, JCB, MC, V; no checks; every day; full bar; www.fourseasons.com/seattle; map:L6*

SIX ARMS BREWERY AND PUB / 300 E Pike St, Capitol Hill; 206/223-1698 Sister to McMenamins on Lower Queen Anne, this outpost offers a bit more funky character, albeit the same menu of tasty pub food and the fabulous brews for which the Portland brothers McM are known.

Grab a window seat for primo people-watching. Service can be mellow to a fault. *AE, MC, V; no checks; every day; beer and wine; www. mcmenamins.com; map:K2*

SKYCITY AT THE NEEDLE / Space Needle, Seattle Center; 206/443-2100 or 800/809-0902 If enjoying a truly sensational view means sipping one of the most expensive drinks you'll ever have in your life, cough up $11 for the hop to the top (only restaurant patrons ride free)—and then drink slowly. *AE, DIS, MC, V; checks OK; every day; full bar; www.spaceneedle.com; map:C6*

TEMPLE BILLIARDS / 126 S Jackson St, Pioneer Square; 206/682-3242 It's not as glossy as Belltown Billiards, but that's just fine with the youngish crowd that shoots pool at the Temple. Word has it the regulars here include certain local band members, so keep your eyes peeled if celebrity-spotting thrills you. There's a decent selection of beer and wine, and some tasty sandwiches. *AE, MC, V; no checks; every day; full bar; map:O9*

TINI BIGS LOUNGE / 100 Denny Wy, Denny Regrade; 206/284-0931 Located on the jumpin' corner of First and Denny, Tini's adds casual elegance to the KeyArena area. Perch at the bar or grab a more intimate table, and dish over a bracingly cold martini (Tini's offers 20 variations). Prices aren't cheap but the standard's a double; be forewarned: these babies go down smooth. Tini's is also a purveyor of fine cigars and tasty little plates: specialty pizzas, quesadillas, and such. Weeknights are considerably less frantic than Friday, Saturday, and Sonics game nights, when the place packs out in elbow-to-elbow fashion. *AE, MC, V; no checks; every day; full bar; map:C9*

TROLLEYMAN PUB / 3400 Phinney Ave N, Fremont; 206/634-4213 Couches and upholstered chairs abound in this renovated turn-of-the-19th-century trolley barn. It was once attached to the Redhook Brewery, and the pub stayed even when the brewery moved east. The fireplace can make one forget it's pelting outside. The doors close earlier than legality dictates: around 11pm on weekdays. There's also a light snack menu. No smoking. *AE, MC, V; no checks; every day; beer and wine; map:FF7*

TWO BELLS TAVERN / 2313 4th Ave, Belltown; 206/441-3050 Even the most self-conscious hipster lets it all hang out at Two Bells. Good selection of local microbrews and imported gems, plus sporadic but always creative bookings of solo guitar acts, unusual art exhibits, and poetry readings. Great burgers and sausage plates, and a late-night happy hour. *AE, DIS, MC, V; no checks; every day; beer and wine; map:F7*

UNION SQUARE GRILL / 621 Union St, Downtown; 206/224-4321 One of the best after-work downtown bars, where drinks go down easy with an au jus sandwich. The barroom is long and narrow, with lots of dark wood. You may have to scramble for a table, but you'll be comfortable once you get settled. *AE, DC, DIS, MC, V; local checks only; every day; full bar; map:K5*

VIRGINIA INN / 1937 1st Ave, Downtown; 206/728-1937 What do you get when you mix arty Belltown dwellers, chic-seeking suburbanites, and babbling pensioners in a historic, brick-tile-and-avant-garde-art tavern on the edge of Pike Place Market? You get the VI, a very enlightened, very appealing, vaguely French-feeling tav with a fine list of libations (including pear cider) and character to burn. You'll have to burn your cigs elsewhere, though. *AE, MC, V; local checks only; every day; full bar; map:I8*

VITO'S MADISON GRILL / 927 9th Ave, First Hill; 206/682-2695 If you like a well-constructed cocktail (such as a gigantic martini) and enjoy watching a professional bartender in action, this old-timey joint is the place to go. All dark wood and maroon leather, it attracts police detectives, lawyers, the sports crowd, and judges on the road to intemperance, as well as a contingent of younger drinkers-in-training. They now even have DJs providing music. *MC, V; no checks; every day; full bar; map:M4*

WEDGWOOD ALE HOUSE AND CAFE / 8515 35th Ave NE, Wedgwood; 206/527-2676 This congenial neighborhood pub draws a low-key local crowd that comes for the decent burgers and the good sampling of micro-brews. The outdoor tables in front are the draw in summer, and there's a new nonsmoking family dining room. *MC, V; local checks only; every day; beer and wine; map:EE6*

THE WILD ROSE / 1021 E Pike St, Capitol Hill; 206/324-9210 The center of the universe for the Seattle lesbian scene, the Wild Rose has served as community center, coffeehouse, music venue, pool hall, and just plain great tavern since 1984. Now that cocktails have been added, it's a great bar, too. Tables are just as likely to be filled with women reading alone as those dining with friends or drinking in uproarious groups. There's an extensive, serviceable menu of mostly comfort food. The other sex is gladly welcomed. *MC, V; no checks; every day; full bar; map:HH6*

Coffee, Tea, and Dessert

Coffee has become synonymous with Seattle for many people, thanks to the multiple branches of Starbucks, Seattle's Best Coffee (SBC), and Tully's, which you can find on almost every corner in town. Though many of the chain espresso bars are open late, and some even feature occasional live music, we've concentrated here on independent tea- and coffeehouses.

B&O ESPRESSO / 204 Belmont Ave E, Capitol Hill; 206/322-5028 / 401 Broadway Ave E, Capitol Hill; 206/328-3290 Legendary for espresso, extraordinary desserts, and serious conversation, this vigorous Capitol Hill coffeehouse buzzes from morning to 1am (on Friday and Saturday). It's a peaceful place for breakfast, for a steaming latte and a tart, or for a plate of fried new potatoes with peppers and onions. Lunches are thoughtful, out-of-the-ordinary creations such as Thai crab cakes and Egyptian lentil soup, there are full dinners here, and lighter fare is available for the later hours. Desserts and coffee are where the B&O really shines; these are some of the best (though they're not the cheapest) homemade desserts in town. The Broadway Market branch is a coffee bar with limited seating. *MC, V; no checks; every day; beer and wine; map:GG6*

BAUHAUS BOOKS AND COFFEE / 301 E Pine St, Capitol Hill; 206/625-1600 At Bauhaus, function follows form. It's a high-ceilinged place with a wall of bookshelves stocked with used art books (Bauhaus doubles as a used-book store—though we suspect the books actually look better than they sell). Big windows afford a view of the Pike/Pine corridor and the Space Needle, which appears oddly inspiring and appropriate in this context. The wrought-iron fixtures and greenish walls lend stylishness, as does the clientele. Sweets are typical—with the exception of single Ding-Dongs, served with reverence on a plate for a mere 56 cents. Kool-Aid is available; the vintage cold-cereal boxes displayed by the counter, unfortunately, are not. This is a nonsmoking establishment. *No credit cards; local checks OK; every day; no alcohol; map:J2*

CAFE ALLEGRO / 4002 University Wy NE, University District; 206/633-3030 People who got into the Allegro habit while they were at the UW still find themselves gravitating back. It's hard to pin down the cafe's appeal. Perhaps it's the moody, dark-wood decor and often smoke-saturated air; or the cachet of the location (it's not easy to find, set in a U District back alley); or the serious and interesting conversations among its wonderfully international crowd of students. You may feel as if you've been left out of a private joke on your first few visits, but it doesn't take long to become a regular. *No credit cards; local checks only; every day; no alcohol; map:FF6*

CAFÉ DILETTANTE / 416 Broadway Ave E, Capitol Hill; 206/329-6463 / 1603 1st Ave, Downtown; 206/728-9144 The name of this Seattle institution is derived from the Italian word *dilettare,* "to delight." And that's exactly what its sinfully rich truffles and buttercream-filled chocolates do. No chocoholic is safe here—gift-boxed chocolates are available to go. In any case, be prepared to splurge. The Broadway location inevitably bustles (till 1am on weekends), and the First Avenue storefront acts as a retail shop only. Pssst . . . there's a small retail outlet at the candy factory (2300 E Cherry St, Central District; 206/328-1530; map:HH6), with

333

ESPRESS YOURSELF

Seattle is bean obsessed. The town spawned Starbucks, espresso bars and pushcarts (now in nearly every conceivable location, from gas stations to doctors' offices), and a nationwide caffeine habit. A specialized vocabulary has developed around ordering espresso—the high end of the coffee continuum. And, as at the Soup Nazi's place immortalized on *Seinfeld*, precise language is required. Woe to the person who gets to the front of the espresso line and asks for a "small" latte. An eye roll from the barista is sure to follow. It's a "short," "tall," or "grande," if you please. To help the espresso-ignorant fake their way through, here's a cheat sheet of espresso lingo. And remember, half the trick is ordering with confidence.

THE BASICS

Americano: your basic cup of coffee (except for the price), prepared with the espresso method—a shot of espresso with hot water

barista: espresso bartender

breve: with steamed half-and-half instead of milk

cappuccino: shot of espresso with steamed milk, topped with foamed milk

double (or doppio): a drink with a double shot of espresso

drip: regular brewed coffee, just like Folger's used to make

latte: a shot of espresso with steamed milk, capped by foamed milk; also called caffe latte (Italian) or café au lait (French)

mocha: espresso, steamed milk, and chocolate

THE SLANG

lid nerd: someone who can't attach an espresso lid

no form: no foam

no fun: a latte made with decaffeinated espresso

rocket fuel or red eye: drip coffee with a shot of espresso

schizophrenic: half decaf, half regular espresso

tall skinny: a tall latte made with nonfat milk

thunder thighs: double tall mocha made with whole milk, capped with extra whipped cream

why bother?: nonfat decaf latte

with room: not filled to the brim

Now that you've got all the terms down, there's one last thing. The various components of an espresso drink must be strung together in a specific order: (1) amount of espresso (single or double); (2) size of cup; (3) type of milk; (4) foam; (5) whipping cream (if any); (6) beverage type (including with or without caffeine). So a "double tall skinny formless no fun latte" is a latte with a double shot of decaf espresso made with lowfat milk and no foam served in a "tall" cup.

Now, what could be simpler?   —*Shannon O'Leary*

seconds at reduced prices. *AE, DIS, MC, V; checks OK; every day; beer and wine; map:GG6, I8*

CAFFE APPASSIONATO / 1417 Queen Anne Ave N, Queen Anne (and branches); 206/270-8760 Perched on the top of Queen Anne, this sleek cafe offers outdoor seating and excellent people-watching opportunities. Visitors can sip espresso drinks made from beans roasted locally at the Caffe Appassionato Fisherman's Terminal location. The signature coffee beans are also available in bulk. If the weather takes a turn for the worse, slip inside and warm up in front of the fireplace. *MC, V; no checks; every day; no alcohol; map:GG7*

CAFFÉ LADRO / 2205 Queen Anne Ave N, Queen Anne (and branches); 206/282-5313 You won't confuse Caffé Ladro with Starbucks, though the local chain now has five locations. Most of their cafes have plum mottled walls adorned with the work of local artists and photographers. The food is also notable and includes quiche, soup, and sandwiches. The sweets and baked goods are way above average. There's a second location on Queen Anne (600 Queen Anne Ave N; 206/282-1549), one in Fremont (452 N 36th St; 206/675-0854; map:FF7), one downtown (801 Pine St; 206/405-1950; map:J4), and one in West Seattle (7011 California Ave SW; 206/938-8021; map:JJ8). *MC, V; checks OK; every day; no alcohol; map:A7*

CAFFE VITA / 813 5th Ave N, Queen Anne; 206/285-9662 / 1005 E Pike St, Capitol Hill; 206/709-4440 Locals are rabid about this little cafe tucked in the unlikely neighborhood just north of Tower Records and another located on Capitol Hill in the old Café Paradiso location. All the beans are roasted to perfection, including the well-rounded Del Sol, the Caffe Luna (French roast), and the organic Papua New Guinea. Beware: all espresso drinks are made with double *ristretto* shots. *No credit cards; checks OK; every day; no alcohol; info@caffevita.com; www.caffevita. com; map:A3, GG6*

DIVA ESPRESSO / 7916 Greenwood Ave N, Greenwood (and branches); 206/781-1213 This local fave has three locations—it's in West Seattle (4480 Fauntleroy Ave SW; 206/937-5225; map:JJ8) and Wallingford too (4615 Stone Wy N; 206/632-7019; map:FF7)—and all have excellent coffee and nifty pastries. *No credit cards; local checks OK; every day; no alcohol; map:EE7*

ESPRESSO EXPRESS / 6500 15th Ave NE, University District; 206/524-6326 Believe it or not, this was one of the very first espresso joints in town, here on the cusp of the U District and Ravenna, and it's consistently remained one of the finest. Though the ambience isn't fancy, Espresso has consistently used some of the finest beans around (shipped from Los Angeles, actually) and the quality of their pulls beats Starbucks hands down. If you want nonfat milk, forget it: they don't think it tastes as good, so they offer only low-fat. Kind of like a small piece of Italy in Seattle. *No credit cards; checks OK; every day; no alcohol; map:FF6*

THE FAMOUS PACIFIC DESSERT COMPANY / 127 Mercer St, Queen Anne; 206/284-8100 Their motto says it all: "Eat dessert first; life is uncertain." This is the place that introduced us to the ultimate indulgence, Chocolate Decadence, and for that we'll be forever indebted. On any given night, fewer desserts may be available than you might expect—considering the massive product line and reputation. But we have had some wonderful concoctions here: rich, incredibly silky cheesecakes; a custardy ice cream laden with chunks of chocolate; a chocolate hazelnut cake. *MC, V; local checks only; every day; no alcohol; map:A7*

THE GEORGIAN / 411 University St (Four Seasons Olympic Hotel), Downtown; 206/621-1700 All sparkles and cushioned elegance, the Georgian is where you can linger over a large selection of loose-leaf (and some wrapped) teas while nibbling on a petit four. A winter holiday package includes tea and your choice of scones, sandwiches, or petit fours, with sorbet for dessert. *AE, CB, DC, DIS, JCB, MC, V; no checks; 2:30–4pm Tues–Fri, 1:30–3pm Sat; full bar; www.fourseasons. com/seattle; map:L6*

GRAND ILLUSION ESPRESSO AND PASTRY / 1405 NE 50th St, University District; 206/525-2755 Attached to the last independent movie theater in town is the Illusion, where UW students (and their professors) rendezvous at the small tables, near the fireplace, or, on warm afternoons, in the tiny courtyard outside. Light lunch selections such as quiche and soup change daily, and the scones, cookies, and fruit pies are favorites; however, most customers come for post-film conversation or late-afternoon quiet. *MC, V; no checks; every day; no alcohol; map:FF6*

GREEN CAT CAFE / 1514 E Olive Wy, Capitol Hill; 206/726-8756 The Green Cat was a neighborhood favorite from the moment it opened. There's a heavy sidewalk-society scene here, where people coming up from Fallout Records run into friends having lunch (good vegetarian and vegan menu choices) outside, but the crowd is not all mod; lots of joggers and casual types stop in for morning coffee and a pastry. *MC, V; checks OK; every day; beer and wine; map:GG6*

JOE BAR / 810 E Roy St, Capitol Hill; 206/324-0407 Owner Wilie Bush stocks baked goods from the Hi-Spot Cafe in Madrona at this comfortable bilevel space across the street from the Harvard Exit movie theater. The desserts and good espresso drinks add to the we're-all-friends-here atmosphere, fostered by the closely spaced tables and the eager après-film conversation. *Cash only; every day; no alcohol; map:GG6*

LOUISA'S BAKERY & CAFÉ / 2379 Eastlake Ave E, Eastlake; 206/325-0081 Even the three bears would crawl out of winter hibernation to nuzzle up to Louisa's raspberry oatmeal, served in a Papa Bear–size bowl. The long lines along the display cases—especially during weekend breakfast hours—give you time to select one of the mouthwatering baked goods. Whatever you choose, it'll be worth the wait. Make yourself comfortable; the friendly staff will bring your order to your table. *No credit cards; checks OK; every day; no alcohol; map:GG7*

MR. SPOT'S CHAI HOUSE / 2213 NW Market St, Ballard; 206/297-2424 This mellow-to-the-marrow Ballard spot specializes in spectacular chai creations, such as the Morning Glory chai spiked with astragalus, galungal, cardamom, coriander, and a host of other ingredients. They also book music—from rock to Afro-Cuban jazz—and sell herbs, incense, candles, and soap. *MC, V; checks OK; every day; no alcohol; map:FF7*

PROCOPIO GELATERIA / 1501 Western Ave, Pike Place Market; 206/622-4280 Seattle's original gelateria still serves the most civilized Italian ice cream in town, in a stylish little nook right off the Hillclimb. At least 16 flavors of freshly made ice cream are always displayed (they're rotated daily from the repertoire of more than 200), and if you can get past these positively first-class ices, you can choose from an assortment of luscious desserts. Beverages include a great wintertime hot spiced cider, and espresso drinks. *No credit cards; checks OK; every day (summer), Mon–Sat (winter); no alcohol; map:J9*

QUEEN MARY / 2912 NE 55th St, Ravenna; 206/527-2770 This little gem may never be a major stop on the coffee-tea-dessert circuit, but that doesn't diminish the teahouse's appeal as a refuge on gray Seattle days. Baked goods are the house specialty, along with a reassuringly proper pot of tea, correctly brewed and served in fussy china. Tea with a capital T is available from 2 to 5pm every day. Breakfast and lunch are served between 9am and 2pm every day. *MC, V; checks OK; Wed–Sun; wine only; www.queenmarytearoom.com; map:FF6*

SIMPLY DESSERTS / 3421 Fremont Ave N, Fremont; 206/633-2671 Simply Desserts cooks up a selection of classic pastries: chocolate espresso cake, berry and fruit pies, a white-chocolate strawberry cake that wins raves from everyone, and countless variations on the chocolate cake theme—the most popular being the chocolate Cognac torte and the Bailey's Irish Cream cake. This small spot with an enormous reputation gets plenty busy in the evenings, when chocolate-cake fans from across the city sip espresso and enjoy what may be simply the best desserts around. *No credit cards; checks OK; Tues–Sun; no alcohol; map:FF7*

TEAHOUSE KUAN YIN / 1911 N 45th St, Wallingford; 206/632-2055
Depictions of Kuan Yin, the Buddhist goddess of mercy, preside over the serene atmosphere of "Seattle's first teahouse." Kuan Yin offers a full spectrum of teas, including plenty of blacks and greens, a few oolongs, and some herbals. Complementing these is a multiethnic assortment of panini, piroshkis, and croissants, as well as desserts such as green tea ice cream, pies, and scones. You're invited to sit in leisurely and lengthy contemplation (quilted tea cozies keep your tea warm for up to 2 hours). Be sure to chat with the staff: instruction in the ways of tea drinking is dispensed generously and with a philosophical air. *MC, V; local checks only; every day; no alcohol; map:FF7*

UPTOWN ESPRESSO AND BAKERY / 525½ Queen Anne Ave N, Queen Anne (and branches); 206/285-3757 This topnotch coffee hangout turns out a range of superb muffins, scones, and other sweet-and-semihealthy treats. All three locations of the Uptown—it's also in West Seattle (3845 Delridge Wy SW; 206/933-9497; map:JJ8) and downtown (2504 4th Ave, Belltown; 206/441-1084; map:F6)—are always busy, whether with the quiet post-movie or post-theater crowd at night or with friendly tête-à-têtes throughout the day. Rightfully so, as these are some of the best espresso drinks you'll find in Seattle, and the morning treats are on their way to matching that claim. No smoking. *No credit cards; checks OK; every day; no alcohol; map:GG7*

THE URBAN BAKERY / 7850 E Green Lake Dr N, Green Lake; 206/524-7951 Morning, noon, and night you'll find Green Lake's urban yuppies hanging inside or out of this popular corner spot near the Green Lake shore. Enjoy excellent soups and vegetarian chili, the usual sandwiches and salads, and a world of freshly baked breads, pastries, pies, cakes, and cookies that taste as good as they look. All the requisite coffee drinks, too. *MC, V; checks OK; every day; no alcohol; map:EE7*

ZOKA COFFEE ROASTER AND TEA COMPANY / 2200 N 56th St, Green Lake; 206/545-4277 Owners Tim McCormack and Jeff Babcock bring more than 20 years of experience in the specialty coffee business to this spacious community coffee- and teahouse. Leather couches and tables with high-backed chairs invite neighborhood locals and visitors to settle in and read or challenge each other to a game of Scrabble. Zoka roasts its own signature coffees, with the roaster serving as an appropriate backdrop for live acoustic music on Friday and Saturday nights. A variety of loose teas are available by the cup, by the pot, or in bulk. Complement your drink of choice with a selection from the sandwiches, salads, and baked goods, all made here. *MC, V; checks OK; every day; no alcohol; map:FF7*

ITINERARIES

ITINERARIES

Exploring a city and making your own discoveries is half the fun, but when you've got only a few days to do it, a little advice is invaluable. That said, here's a three-day introduction to the best of Seattle, with day-by-day activities to entertain almost everyone, young or old, visitor or resident. We've also created a few themed days geared to those with special interests. More information on most of the places in boldface may be found in other chapters (Restaurants, Lodgings, Exploring, Shopping, and so on) throughout this guide.

Three-Day Tour

DAY ONE

On your first day in Seattle, concentrate on the city's heart: **PIKE PLACE MARKET**. Ideally you're staying in a view room at the **INN AT THE MARKET** (86 Pine St; 206/443-3600 or 800/446-4484)—if you've been savvy enough to secure a reservation months in advance. The inn is close to downtown and the waterfront, and has a reputation for excellent service—and some think the views of Elliott Bay from the rooftop deck alone are worth the relatively lofty room rates. If you're looking for less expensive digs near the market, check out **PENSIONE NICHOLS** (1923 1st Ave, Downtown; 206/441-7125), but note that some rooms have shared baths.

MORNING: Watching the market come to life is worth setting your alarm for, even on vacation. Grab a fresh croissant from **LE PANIER VERY FRENCH BAKERY** (1902 Pike Pl; 206/441-3669) and a latte from the original **STARBUCKS** (1912 Pike Pl; 206/448-8762), and wander among the farmers and craftspeople as they set up their wares. Arrive before 9am, and you'll experience this most beloved of Seattle landmarks without the crowds that flock here on the weekends and every day in summer. You'll also get first pick of a wonderful array of produce—including berries, peaches, and apples, in season—to snack on as you wander. Head into the depths of the market to explore an unusual array of shops, including the **MARKET MAGIC SHOP** (206/624-4271) and **GOLDEN AGE COLLECTABLES** (206/622-9799).

AFTERNOON: If weather permits, have lunch on the terrace at **THE PINK DOOR** (1919 Post Alley; 206/443-3241), a favorite of local office workers and couples opting for a little Italian-style romance. If it's raining, **CAFE CAMPAGNE** (1600 Post Alley; 206/728-2800), a French-inspired bistro, makes a cozy retreat. After lunch, shoppers may want to head for the main **DOWNTOWN SHOPPING DISTRICT**, between 3rd and 6th Avenues and Stewart and University Streets. Here you'll find upscale malls, boutiques, and chain stores, including the flagship **NORDSTROM** (500 Pine St; 206/628-2111).

Those wanting to explore more of the city and get a glimpse of local history in the bargain should hop a **METRO** bus (206/553-3000)—ride free on Metro until 7pm throughout the downtown core—or take the short walk down First Avenue to **PIONEER SQUARE**. This is the oldest part of the city, dating back to before the Great Fire of 1889, and you can learn about the early days by joining the **UNDERGROUND TOUR** (610 1st Ave; 206/682-4646), an informative, if somewhat campy, look at the city's early days. Literary devotees won't want to pass up a visit to the **ELLIOTT BAY BOOK COMPANY** (101 S Main St; 206/624-6600); in a city full of rabid readers, it's considered by many to be the best bookstore, and art lovers will find plenty of galleries to peruse in the immediate neighborhood.

EVENING: After freshening up at your hotel, enjoy the Pacific Northwest's bounty with dinner at intimate little **MATT'S IN THE MARKET** (94 Pike St, 3rd floor, Pike Place Market; 206/467-7909), then wander next door and bring the evening to a close at romantic **SHEA'S LOUNGE** (206/467-9990) overlooking **ELLIOTT BAY**.

DAY TWO

On your second day in the city, take in the 74-acre Seattle Center; originally built for the 1962 world's fair, it was expanded and improved in recent years. This is also a great day for kids.

MORNING: Grab breakfast at your downtown hotel, then catch the **MONORAIL** (206/441-6038) from **WESTLAKE CENTER** (5th Ave and Pine St, Downtown) for a quick ride above the city streets to **SEATTLE CENTER**. Locals may scoff, but visitors are invariably drawn to the 605-foot **SPACE NEEDLE** (206/443-2145). If it's a clear day, take a ride to the top, where you can literally get the lay of the land. (Or opt to dine in the revolving restaurant, **SKYCITY AT THE NEEDLE** (206/443-2150); the elevator fee—$11 for adults—is waived for restaurant patrons.) After breakfast, explore the rest of the center. If you've got young companions, visit the **CHILDREN'S MUSEUM** (Center House; 206/441-1768); kids of all ages enjoy the hands-on exhibits and two IMAX screens at the **PACIFIC SCIENCE CENTER** (200 2nd Ave N; 206/443-2880). Later, have a seat on a bench by the **INTERNATIONAL FOUNTAIN** and watch the dancing water.

AFTERNOON: The **CENTER HOUSE** has plenty of ethnic fast food options, but you'll find better multicultural eats just off the center grounds in the Queen Anne neighborhood. Try **TUP TIM THAI** (118 W Mercer St; 206/281-8833) for Thai fare, **MCMENAMINS PUB AND BREWERY** (200 Roy St, Ste 105; 206/285-4722) for pub grub, or **CHUTNEYS** (519 1st Ave N; 206/284-6799) for Indian curries. Then return to the center and enter the eccentric-looking **EXPERIENCE MUSIC PROJECT** (EMP) museum (325 5th Ave N; 206/EMP-LIVE or 877-EMP-LIVE; www.experience.org). The building, designed by Frank Gehry and said to resemble a gigantic smashed guitar, is a monument to rock 'n' roll, featuring a gallery on Northwest artists as well as great hands-on opportunities to play instruments or perform. Another worthy attraction at the center is the two-stage **SEATTLE CHILDREN'S THEATRE** (2nd Ave N and Thomas St; 206/441-3322; www.sct.org), known for its excellent performances of old favorites and future classics, afternoons and evenings, September through June.

EVENING: Head back downtown on the Monorail, then hop a cab to **BELLTOWN** to enjoy the imaginative pan-Mediterranean cuisine at **BRASA** (2107 3rd Ave; 206/728-4220) for dinner. If EMP whetted your appetite for local music, check out the nightlife in this boisterous part of town. Try **TULA'S** (2214 2nd Ave; 206/443-4221) for jazz or the **CROCODILE CAFE** (2200 2nd Ave; 206/441-5611) for local or national alternative rock, folk, and blues acts.

DAY THREE

Use your third day to explore some of the neighborhoods that make up the soul of Seattle; it's easiest to do this with a car.

MORNING: From downtown, head north to **FREMONT,** a colorful, quirky commercial-and-residential district bordering the northwest end of Lake Union and the inland end of the Lake Washington Ship Canal. Have breakfast at the **STILL LIFE IN FREMONT COFFEEHOUSE** (705 N 35th St; 206/547-9850), a funky spot with mismatched tables and healthy food that epitomizes the spirit of old Fremont. The neighborhood is fast being mainstreamed (the high-tech offices of Adobe, alongside the canal, are one indication), but still offers unusual shopping—check out the crafts at **FRANK & DUNYA** (3418 Fremont Ave N; 206/547-6760); some good dining—try the Tex-Mex at **EL CAMINO** (607 N 35th St; 206/632-7303); and unique public art—favorite examples are *Waiting for the Interurban* (Fremont Ave N and N 34th St) and the *Fremont Troll* (on N 36th St, under Hwy 99), which clutches a VW Bug.

AFTERNOON: East (and north) of Fremont is **GREEN LAKE**, where you can have a picnic—grab some basic supplies at a grocery store on the way, or pick up food to go from local favorite **TAQUERIA GUAYMAS** (6808 Green Lake Wy E; 206/729-6563). If you prefer being served, try the **GREENLAKE BAR & GRILL** (7200 E Green Lake Way N; 206/729-6179) for casual pub fare or **ROSITA'S MEXICAN RESTAURANT** (7210 Woodlawn Ave NE; 206/523-3031) for old-fashioned Tex-Mex food; or sit by the windows at **SIX DEGREES** (7900 E Green Lake Dr N; 206/523-1600), where you can watch walkers, runners, skaters, and bike riders jostle for space on the path.

Feeling inspired? Rent a bike or a pair of in-line skates at **GREGG'S GREENLAKE CYCLE** (7012 Woodlawn Ave NE; 206/729-5102) and head out for a lake loop. The park's public swimming pool, wading pool (in summer), basketball courts, playground, soccer fields, tennis courts, and more will keep everyone busy for the afternoon.

EVENING: For dinner, head through **BALLARD,** the city's Scandinavian center—it's west of Fremont—and on to **SHILSHOLE BAY. RAY'S BOATHOUSE** (6049 Seaview Ave NW; 206/789-3770) is a bit touristy, but it also has one of the city's best waterside views of the Olympics and the endless boat traffic heading through the locks. After your meal, stop in at historic Ballard's **OLD TOWN ALEHOUSE** (5233 Ballard Ave NW; 206/782-8323) for some acoustic jazz or blues, or see what's playing at the nearby **TRACTOR TAVERN** (5213 Ballard Ave NW; 206/782-3480), where the fare could be rock, country, Celtic, or zydeco.

Family Fun Day

If you're traveling with children, Seattle is an easy place to amuse them. Many of the itineraries suggested on these pages will please visitors of all ages, but here's a day planned with families in mind. You'll need a car to get around—but assure the young ones that it won't involve any long rides on freeways.

MORNING: Breakfast at **MAE'S PHINNEY RIDGE CAFE** (6412 Phinney Ave N; 206/782-1222), a Seattle morning institution in the **GREENWOOD** neighborhood, featuring giant cinnamon rolls and a whimsical atmosphere. Then head south for the nearby **WOODLAND PARK ZOO** (5500 Phinney Ave N; 206/684-4800; www.zoo.org) to watch the animals have their morning meals. Many of the creatures are most active in the morning (the zoo opens at 9:30am), and weekday morning crowds are sparse. This is a good time to observe the penguins swimming, or to catch a glimpse of the elusive snow leopards. Woodland Park measures 188 acres, and has trails to walk and a nice play area on Phinney Avenue. The zoo's baby elephant, born in November 2000 and named Hansa (it means "supreme happiness" in Thai), is one of the most popular attractions. Forgo the snacks at the zoo and convince the kids to save their appetites for burgers, fries, and shakes at **RED MILL BURGERS** (312 N 67th St; 206/783-6362), about 10 blocks north of the zoo.

AFTERNOON: Hop in the car and head for the **WATERFRONT** for your next stop, the hands-on fun at **ODYSSEY, THE MARITIME DISCOVERY CENTER** (Pier 66; 206/374-4000). At this interactive museum, you can simulate kayaking, fishing, or navigating a freighter, as well as learn about the natural and commercial uses of Seattle's marine environment. Then take the **WATERFRONT STREETCAR** (206/553-3000)—a real

1927 trolley, originally from Australia—south to the busier part of the waterfront and the **SEATTLE AQUARIUM** (Pier 59; 206/386-4320). Here, say hello to the otters, admire the saltwater creatures in the underwater dome, carefully handle starfish in the touch tank, and learn about water pollution. A little farther south is **YE OLDE CURIOSITY SHOPPE** (Pier 54; 206/682-5844), where kids love—or love to hate—the mummies and other oddities.

EVENING: Finish the day with dinner at **SAZERAC** (1101 4th Ave, Downtown; 206/624-7755), where the bright colors, plush purple upholstery, and playful decor provide a distraction before the appetizers—hush puppies and molasses dipping sauce—show up. Then tuck in the whole family at the luxurious **FOUR SEASONS OLYMPIC HOTEL** (411 University St, Downtown; 206/621-1700 or 800/821-8106), which has a pool and makes a special effort to cater to children (though prices reflect the Olympic's four-star rating).

Pacific Rim Day

Seattle's geographic position on Puget Sound gives it an important role on the world's "Pacific Rim." The Pacific Ocean links the city's port—and our culture—with several Asian nations. Their influences can be found throughout the city, especially in the places on this itinerary. Plan on driving for parts of the tour.

MORNING: Skip breakfast at the hotel and head straight for the **CHINATOWN/INTERNATIONAL DISTRICT** (it's accessible via bus or the waterfront streetcar.) Those expecting a Chinatown like that in other West Coast cities may be surprised by the influences of Japanese, Filipino, Korean, and Southeast Asian cultures. The newly remodeled **UWAJIMAYA VILLAGE** (600 5th Ave S; 206/624-6248) opens at 9am and offers a wide range of Asian specialties, tanks of live fish and rare imported produce, a Japanese bookstore, and wonderful cooking accessories. Your first stop should be the deli and food court, where you'll find hot and cold entrees plus Asian pastries (cream-filled buns, Hawaiian pineapple-coconut bread) and an espresso counter.

After breakfast, stroll the streets and admire the fresh produce and wares at shops such as **HOVEN FOODS** (502 6th Ave S; 206/623-6764) and **HIGO VARIETY STORE** (604 S Jackson St; 206/622-7572). Then visit **KOBE TERRACE PARK** and the **DANNY WOO INTERNATIONAL DISTRICT COMMUNITY GARDENS** (Maynard Ave S and S Main St; 206/624-1802). The **WING LUKE ASIAN MUSEUM** (407 7th Ave S; 206/623-5124), named for the city's first Chinese-American City Council member, displays a permanent collection as well as rotating exhibits that document the Northwest Asian-American experience. When you get hungry again, head for spacious **HOUSE OF HONG** (409 8th Ave S; 206/622-7997), where the dim sum is popular.

AFTERNOON: You'll need a car for the next leg of your journey, though it isn't far north to **VOLUNTEER PARK** and the **SEATTLE ASIAN ART MUSEUM** (1400 E Prospect St, Capitol Hill; 206/654-3100). Here, the original Seattle Art Museum building holds an extensive collection of Asian art; be sure to check out its **ASIAN ART LIBRARY**. Next, head north again to the **BURKE MUSEUM OF NATURAL HISTORY AND CULTURE** (17th Ave NE and NE 45th St, University District; 206/543-5590) to check out its *Pacific Voices* exhibit highlighting the cultures of the Pacific Rim using historic and contemporary artifacts. At the nearby **WASH-INGTON PARK ARBORETUM,** visit the **JAPANESE GARDEN** (1502 Lake Washington Blvd E, Madison Valley; 206/684-4725), March through November. The authentic garden was constructed under the direction of Japanese landscape architect Juki Iida in 1960. Plan ahead to attend a tea ceremony in the garden's teahouse, performed on the third Saturday of the month, April through October.

EVENING: Just around the corner from the arboretum, on Madison Street, you'll find one of the city's best sushi restaurants: **NISHINO** (3130 E Madison St, Madison Valley; 206/322-5800). Or cap your day with food inspired by travels in Asia, at **WILD GINGER ASIAN RESTAURANT AND SATAY BAR** (1401 3rd Ave, Downtown; 206/623-4450). If you've got time, head back to Chinatown/International District to catch a program at the **NORTHWEST ASIAN AMERICAN THEATER** (409 7th Ave S; 206/340-1445; www.nwaat.org).

Seattle by Water

Seattle is a city almost surrounded by water: Puget Sound on the west, Lake Washington on the east, and Lake Union to the north of downtown. Here's an itinerary that lets you explore those waterways. Unless you've got your own boat, you'll need a car for this day's touring.

MORNING: Wake up at **THE EDGEWATER** hotel (Pier 67, Waterfront; 206/728-7000 or 800/624-0670) overlooking Puget Sound, then drive northwest to **FISHERMAN'S TERMINAL** and **CHINOOK'S AT SALMON BAY** (1900 W Nickerson St, Interbay; 206/283-4665) for breakfast. You'll get a preview of the day ahead by gazing out at a large portion of the city's fishing fleet. Drive north across the Ballard Bridge, then head west to the **HIRAM M. CHITTENDEN LOCKS** (3015 NW 54th St, Ballard; 206/783-7059), where you can watch the boats rise and fall as they move between Puget Sound and the inland waterways. In season, watch the salmon move through the fish ladder on the south side of the locks.

Drive east to the **UNIVERSITY DISTRICT** and seek out the **AGUA VERDE CAFE & PADDLE CLUB** (1303 NE Boat St; 206/545-8570). Below the cafe, the paddle club rents kayaks, and you can slip into a boat built for two (the attendant will give you some basic instructions and steer you in the right direction). Shove off for the Washington Park Arboretum through the Montlake Cut, painted with the inspirational slogans of local crew teams. When your arms are tired of paddling, head back to Agua Verde and fortify yourself with tasty halibut or yam tacos, or a mangodilla, a quesadilla made with spicy chicken and cooling mangos.

AFTERNOON: After lunch, head back to the downtown **WATERFRONT,** park the car, and take a break from powering your own boat. Settle in for an **ARGOSY CRUISES** (Piers 54, 55, and 57; 206/623-1445 or 800/642-7816; www.argosycruises.com) harbor tour of the working waterfront—or one of the company's other tours. Afterward, head to Colman Ferry Dock (Pier 52) and hop aboard a **WASHINGTON STATE FERRY** (206/464-6400, 800/84-FERRY or 888/808-7977; www.wsdot.wa.gov/ferries/) for the 35-minute crossing to **BAINBRIDGE ISLAND.** You can get off there and spend an hour or so strolling Winslow before the next return sailing—stop in at the **BAINBRIDGE ISLAND BAKERY** for coffee and a pastry, or just stay aboard the ferry, watching the cars unload and reload, then return to Seattle. Take a seat on the south side of the boat for clear views of **MOUNT RAINIER** in the distance, and watch the seagulls keep pace with the boat.

EVENING: Drive north to South Lake Union to check into your hotel, the **MV CHALLENGER** (1001 Fairview Pl N; 206/340-1201), a bunk-and-breakfast on a real red-and-white tugboat. You can walk to nearby **DANIEL'S BROILER** (809 Fairview Pl N; 206/621-8262) for one of the city's best steak dinners, or cross yet another body of water—Lake Washington—driving across a floating bridge for dinner at Kirkland's waterside **YARROW BAY GRILL** (1270 Carillon Pt, Kirkland; 425/889-9052). Then return to your bunk on Lake Union to tuck in for the night and fall asleep to the gentle movement of the water.

DAY TRIPS

DAY TRIPS

South Puget Sound

BAINBRIDGE ISLAND

Take the Washington State Ferry from Colman Dock (Pier 52) in downtown Seattle to Bainbridge Island; the crossing is approximately 35 minutes.

Bainbridge Island's downtown, parks, and attractions make it well worth the 35-minute ferry ride (see the "Ferry Rides" sidebar). Downtown Bainbridge (formerly Winslow) may be a small town, but it has a thriving cultural scene with many nationally known writers in residence, great restaurants, an art theater, and its own vineyard. For information about visiting the area, contact the Bainbridge Chamber of Commerce (590 Winslow Wy E; 206/842-3700; www.bainbridgechamber.com).

From the ferry dock on Bainbridge, head north to the first traffic light and take a left—and you're in downtown Bainbridge, where you could shop for hours. Start with breakfast at **STREAMLINER DINER** (397 Winslow Wy E; 206/842-8595) or get a tasty orange sweet roll at **BLACKBIRD BAKERY** (210 Winslow Wy E; 206/780-1322). Don't miss the great selection of new and used books (and author readings) at **EAGLE HARBOR BOOKS** (157 Winslow Wy E; 206/842-5332) or the whimsical works at **BAINBRIDGE ARTS & CRAFTS** (151 Winslow Wy E; 206/842-3132), an artists' cooperative that began when two women decided to sell local art at a garage sale in 1948. **WINSLOW HARDWARE & MERCANTILE** (240 Winslow Wy E; 206/842-3101) is a great place to chat, get visitor information, and, oh yeah, buy tools.

There are plenty of excellent eateries in Bainbridge, but the folks at the hardware store swear by the blackened snapper sandwich at **HARBOUR PUBLIC HOUSE** (231 Parfitt Wy SW; 206/842-3132). **BISTRO PLEASANT BEACH**'s (241 Winslow Wy W; 206/842-4347) Mediterranean food is a hit, as are **CAFÉ NOLA**'s (101 Winslow Wy W; 206/842-3822) hearty soups and sandwiches. You can also pick up picnic fixings at **TOWN & COUNTRY MARKET** (343 Winslow Wy E; 206/842-3848) and visit a local park.

FORT WARD STATE PARK (2241 Pleasant Beach Dr NE; 206/842-4041) on the island's south end is good for picnicking, beach walking, or fishing. It can be hard to find but, fortunately, Bainbridge is a great place for exploring. Or opt for the easier-to-find park: from downtown Bainbridge, take SR 305 north to the turnoff at Day Road E and follow signs to the small beachfront **FAY-BAINBRIDGE STATE PARK** (15446 Sunrise Dr NE), complete with playground, picnic shelters, and Bainbridge's only

348

campground. On the way, visit **BAINBRIDGE ISLAND VINEYARDS AND WINERY** (682 Hwy 305; 206/842-WINE) for wine tastings and a self-guided tour of the vineyard. The **BLOEDEL RESERVE** (7571 NE Dolphin Dr; 206/842-7631) is the island's best stop. Plan to spend at least 2 hours perusing the former home of timber magnate Prentice Bloedel. The 150-acre estate features woods, landscaped gardens, and a bird sanctuary. Reservations required; open Wednesday through Sunday.

Farther north, on the Kitsap Peninsula just north of the island, it's a short drive on the Highway 305 bridge over Agate Passage and up Suquamish Way (the first street on the right after the bridge) to **CHIEF SEATTLE'S GRAVE** and a view of the Seattle skyline. For more information about the chief, head back to Highway 305 and visit the **SUQUAMISH MUSEUM** (15838 Sandy Hook Rd; 360/598-3311; www. suquamish.nsn.com).

Reward yourself with dinner and a movie off the beaten path in Lynwood Center, on the southwest end of Bainbridge Island. Try the Asian/seafood restaurant **MOONFISH** (4738 Lynwood Ctr Rd NE; 206/780-3473) or **RUBY'S ON BAINBRIDGE** (4569 Lynwood Center Rd; 206/780-9303), then take in the show at the retro **LYNWOOD THEATRE** (4569 Lynwood Center Rd NE; 206/842-3080). Appealing tuck-in options for the night are the **BUCHANAN INN** (8494 NE Oddfellows Rd; 206/780-9258), a renovated 1912 B&B, or **GAYLE BARD'S OLD MILL GUEST HOUSE** (6159 Old Mill Rd; 206/842-8543), a tiny but charming getaway.

VASHON ISLAND

Take the Washington State Ferry from Fauntleroy dock in West Seattle to Vashon Island; crossing is approximately 15 minutes.

Sometimes the best places to get away are closer than you think. Artsy little Vashon Island is only 15 minutes away from West Seattle's southwest shore, but its serene countryside and Baker-to-Rainier views make it seem hundreds of miles away. The island is 12 miles long and 6 miles wide including Maury Island, joined to Vashon by a mudflat. For information on visiting, contact the Vashon–Maury Island Chamber of Commerce (206/463-6217; www.vashonchamber.com).

Its long country roads through forests and peaceful pastures make it great for biking—once you make it past the killer hill near the ferry dock. Rent bikes at **VASHON BICYCLES** (9925 SW 178th; 206/463-6225), 4 miles from the ferry dock, accessible by **METRO** bus (206/553-3000).

Most Vashon beaches are private, but **MAURY ISLAND'S DOCKTON COUNTY PARK** (Stuckey Rd and SW 260th St), facing Vashon's southeast shore across Quartermaster Harbor, is a nice rest stop. A circa 1915 Coast Guard lighthouse stands sentry over the lonely beach and loop walking trail at **POINT ROBINSON** on Maury's easternmost tip, facing

WINERY TOURS

Until fairly recently, Washington vintners traveling abroad or to the East Coast were used to being asked which side of the Potomac was better for growing their grapes. Now Washington State is regularly included in any survey of the world's best wine-producing regions. With 90-some wineries, Washington is second only to California in U.S. wine production.

Although the first European grape varieties were planted here in the late 1800s, fledgling winemaking efforts were hurt by icy winters and limited demand, and Washington vintners resigned themselves to producing safe, sweet dessert wines from winter-hardy vines instead. It wasn't until the late 1960s that the potential of Washington's soil and climate was fully appreciated and the first real premium wines were made. Washington's initial fame came from its full-flavored whites; only in recent years have reds equaled and surpassed the whites in reputation. Though most of the grapes are grown in the sun-soaked Yakima River and Columbia River Valleys east of the Cascades, the Seattle-area oenophile can find plenty of tastings close to home. Most of the wineries in the greater Seattle area are located on the Eastside.

Chateau Ste. Michelle (14111 NE 145th St; 425/488-3300; map:CC2), 2 miles south of Woodinville off State Route 202, is the state's largest winery, occupying showplace headquarters on the 87-acre former estate of industrialist Henry Stimson. This is a popular destination for locals and visitors alike, since it offers the region's most comprehensive tour and, in summer, a lively outdoor concert series on its beautifully manicured grounds, which also provide lovely picnicking opportunities (you can buy picnic food to go with your wine in the gourmet shop on the premises). The single-vineyard wines are the winery's most exciting, but its winemakers also produce consistently well-

Des Moines on the mainland. It's an ideal spot to watch the sunset over Mount Rainier. Hikers also get access to a bit of beach along the forest trail at **BURTON ACRES PARK** (on a southeast Vashon peninsula east of Burton that extends into Quartermaster Harbor), where reasonably warm inner-harbor waters make it good for swimming. You can rent kayaks from **VASHON ISLAND KAYAKS** (206/463-9257) at the Burton Acres boat launch and paddle the inner harbor; staff also lead tours.

You could spend an entire day just visiting island-based companies that market their goods locally and nationally. One that offers tours (call ahead) is **SEATTLE'S BEST COFFEE** (19529 Vashon Hwy SW; 206/463-3932), known as SBC, which offers fresh organic coffees and a 50-cent cup of fresh java. The island also boasts coffee-making monks at the **ALL MERCIFUL SAVIOUR MONASTERY** in Dockton on Maury Island (SW 268th St; 206/463-5918). The monks don't roast their Monastery Blend

made whites and reds with the Columbia Valley appellation. The winery has also collaborated with top Italian and German wineries to make great Washington wines including Eroica and Col Solare.

You'll get a different perspective across the street at **Columbia Winery** (14030 NE 145th St, Woodinville; 425/488-2776; map:BB2). Originally located in Bellevue, this is one of the region's pioneer wineries. Its varied picnic facilities, where you can sprawl out after a wine-tasting, are open daily and offer a pretty view of Ste. Michelle's grounds. The winery has an annual calendar of concerts and events. To reach both wineries, from I-405 take the NE 124th Street exit, proceed east across the valley, then turn left at State Route 202/Redmond-Woodinville Road and left again on NE 145th Street.

Smaller wineries provide an interesting counterpoint to the giants. To taste the wines made by Chateau Ste. Michelle alum Cheryl Barber Jones, stop by **Silver Lake Winery** (15029 Redmond-Woodinville Rd, Ste A, Woodinville; 425/486-1900; map:CC2). There's not much to see here, but you can taste daily, noon to 5pm. **Facelli Winery** (16120 Redmond-Woodinville Rd NE, Ste 1, Woodinville; 425/488-1020; map:BB2), inconspicuously tucked into an industrial office park, is worth a visit if only to meet one of the area's most exuberant (and entertaining) winemakers, Lou Facelli. Open Saturday and Sunday, noon to 4pm.

Other worthwhile winery stops in the area include **Bainbridge Island Vineyard and Winery** (682 Hwy 305, Bainbridge Island; 206/842-WINE) for estate-grown wines in the European style, with a picnic area (open Wednesday through Sunday). To see a wine glass museum and wine-related antiques for sale, or to buy wines or sample them in the tasting room, visit **Hedges Cellars** (195 NE Gilman Blvd, Issaquah; 425/391-6056).

Coffee here, but you can get a tour of the grounds if you call in advance. **WAX ORCHARDS** (22744 Wax Orchards Rd SW; 206/463-9735) doesn't do tours, but it does sell preserves, syrups, and apple cider. Many island products are available at the **COUNTRY STORE AND GARDENS** (20211 Vashon Hwy SW; 206/463-3655), a general store with potted herbs, gardening supplies, outdoor clothing, and 10 acres of fields, flowers, and U-pick filberts, blueberries, and Asian pears. Nearby **MINGLEMENT MARKET** (20316 Vashon Hwy SW; 206/463-9672) offers organic foods, specialty teas, herbs, and local crafts.

BLUE HERON ARTS CENTER (19704 Vashon Hwy SW; 206/463-5131) has an art gallery with rotating exhibits and is home for the live arts events of **VASHON ALLIED ARTS** (206/463-5131; vashonalliedarts. com), including literary readings, dance, folk music, and plays on weekends September through June. It also holds kids' programs, classes, and works in progress. The Blue Heron's crafts gallery and its pottery, wood-work, and textiles are available at **THE HERON'S NEST GALLERY** (17600 Vashon Hwy; 206/463-5252), in the center of the town of Vashon.

There aren't many strawberry farms left, but early July's **STRAW-BERRY FESTIVAL** is the island's biggest event, with a parade, music, and crafts. Don't miss the Thriftway Marching Grocery Cart Drill Team. Maury Island's **FIELD DAY FARM** (23720 Dockton Rd; 206/463-9032) is the area's best U-pick place: strawberries, cherries, pears, vegetables, dahlias, walnuts, chestnuts, filberts, and apples.

For dinner, Vashon Islanders favor **EXPRESS CUISINE**'s (206/463-6626) superbly prepared pastas, curries, salads, and stews; it's located in the town of Vashon on the Vashon Highway. In-store diners share tables. Vashon's most formal eatery is the **BACK BAY INN** (24007 Vashon Hwy SW; 206/463-5355), a renovated turn-of-the-century landmark serving Northwest cuisine. Four rooms upstairs are available should you be charmed into spending the night. Island B&Bs range from remote farm-houses to restored Edwardians; for information, call the Central Reser-vation Service (206/463-5491).

To continue a tour of South Puget Sound, you can leave the island via Vashon's southern ferry terminal at Tahlequah (Tahlequah Rd, on the south end of the island), which drops you off at Tacoma's Point Defiance Park (see Tacoma and Gig Harbor, below).

TACOMA AND GIG HARBOR

Take Interstate 5 south of Seattle 30 miles to exit 133, approximately 45 minutes. Gig Harbor is about 10 miles northwest of Tacoma via State Route 16 (exit 132 off I-5).

Snickering Seattleites forget that **TACOMA** once earned the nickname "City of Destiny" by beating out the Emerald City in the race to win a major rail line. Seattle still became bigger and more glamorous, while Tacoma became labeled a blue-collar mill town. All that's been changing in the last decade as the city discovered historic preservation. Downtown cleaned up its act, a branch of the University of Washington moved in, moviemakers discovered the stately homes of the north end, and history and architecture buffs fell in love with Tacoma's classic buildings. Their favorites include the Renaissance clock and bell tower of City Hall, the Romanesque First Presbyterian Church, and the coppered **UNION STA-TION** turned **FEDERAL COURTHOUSE** (1717 Pacific Ave). Union Station's interior is also worth a visit because its rotunda is graced by glass artist Dale Chihuly's works. Free; open to the public during business hours.

The Federal Courthouse isn't the only improvement near Union Sta-tion. The **WASHINGTON STATE HISTORY MUSEUM** (1911 Pacific Ave; 888/238-4373) sits just south of the once long-neglected depot in a building that was designed to blend into its surroundings and complement the 90-year-old station. Inside are interesting permanent and visiting exhibits on two floors, a museum store, a cafe, and an auditorium. Although the **TACOMA ART MUSEUM** (12th St and Pacific Ave; 253/272-4258) is slated to move into a new building north of Union Station in early 2003, it is currently housed in a former downtown bank. The new stainless-steel building designed by Antoine Predock will be oriented toward Mount Rainier. The museum features paintings by Renoir and Degas plus a collection of contemporary American prints.

Classic old theaters have also become part of downtown Tacoma's renaissance. The lovingly restored **PANTAGES THEATER**, a 1,186-seat moviehouse designed by B. Marcus Priteca, now hosts dance, music, and stage presentations; the refurbished 742-seat **RIALTO THEATER** is the site of smaller performance groups. Both often feature shows mounted by the **BROADWAY CENTER FOR THE PERFORMING ARTS** (901 Broadway Plaza; 253/591-5890, www.broadwaycenter.org). The **TACOMA ACTORS GUILD** (253/272-2145), Tacoma's popular professional theater, draws an audience from throughout the Puget Sound to performances at Theatre on the Square, next to the Pantages.

On Tacoma's northwest side, **POINT DEFIANCE PARK** has 500 acres of pristine forest jutting out into Puget Sound, one of the most dramatically sited parks in the country. The 5-mile drive and parallel hiking trails provide amazing views of Vashon Island, Gig Harbor, and the Olympic Mountains. This treasure also includes Japanese and Northwest native gardens, a railroad village with a working steam engine, a reconstruction of Fort Nisqually (originally built in 1833), a swimming beach, the Tahlequah ferry dock for sailings to and from Vashon Island, and the **POINT DEFIANCE ZOO AND AQUARIUM** (253/591-5335). Don't miss watching seals, sea lions, and the white beluga whale from an underwater vantage point. The **RUSTON WAY WATERFRONT**, a 6-mile mix of parks and restaurants filled with people in any weather, connects Point Defiance Park with downtown. **WRIGHT PARK** (Division Ave and S "I" St) is a serene in-city park with many trees, a duck-filled pond, and a beautifully maintained conservatory, built of glass and steel in 1890.

One of the area's largest estates is **LAKEWOLD GARDENS** (12317 Gravelly Lake Dr SW; 253/584-3360), a beautiful 10-acre site about 10 minutes south of Tacoma (off I-5 at exit 124) that has been recognized as one of the outstanding gardens in America. It has one of the country's largest rhododendron collections, and its design was influenced by park planner Frederick Olmsted and landscape architect Thomas Church. Both men helped Eulalie Wagner design the landscaping.

Many Seattleites also know about the **TACOMA DOME** (253/272-6817) because so many television commercials advertise events that are "*Live! Live! Live! At the Tacoma Dome!*" It is the country's largest wooden dome, hosting trade shows, concerts, and sporting events, including Tacoma Sabercats hockey games. When it comes to sporting events, nothing beats going to **CHENEY STADIUM** in west Tacoma (from Seattle, take I-5 south, exit 132/Hwy 16 west) to watch the Tacoma Rainiers (253/752-7707), the Seattle Mariners' Triple-A affiliate.

Nightlife options include **ENGINE HOUSE NO. 9** (611 N Pine St; 253/272-3435) near the University of Puget Sound, a smoke-free beer-lover's neighborhood tavern, and the **SPAR** in Old Town (2121 N 30th St; 253/627-8215). If it's food you're after, **ALTEZZO** (1320 Broadway; 253/572-3200) at the top of the Sheraton has a great view of downtown, serves some of Tacoma's best Italian cuisine, and has to-die-for tiramisu. The **CLIFF HOUSE** (6300 Marine View Dr; 253/927-0400) survives on its commanding view of Commencement Bay and its formal airs. Masahiro Endo's stylish downtown Japanese restaurant, **FUJIYA** (1125 Court C, between Broadway and Market; 253/627-5319), attracts a loyal clientele from near and far with the best—and most consistent—sushi and sashimi around, feathery-crisp tempura, and delicious *yosenabe* (seafood stew).

Other top Tacoma eateries include **STANLEY & SEAFORT'S STEAK, CHOP, AND FISH HOUSE** (115 E 34th St; 253/473-7300), with a panoramic view of the city, harbor, and the Olympic Mountains; **BIMBO'S** (1516 Pacific Ave; 253/383-5800), an Italian restaurant serving hearty pasta dishes; **EAST & WEST CAFE** (5319 Tacoma Mall Blvd; 253/475-7755), a charming Asian restaurant; and **THE DASH POINT LOBSTER SHOP** (6912 Soundview Dr NE; 253/927-1513) and the **LOBSTER SHOP SOUTH** (4015 Ruston Wy; 253/759-2165).

Tacoma accommodations include fine B&Bs and hotels. Among the former is **CHINABERRY HILL** (302 Tacoma Ave N; 253/272-1282; chinaberry@wa.net; www.chinaberryhill.com). This 1889 Victorian mansion in Tacoma's historic Stadium District has been restored as a garden retreat with bay views and fireplaces. **THE VILLA BED & BREAKFAST** (705 N 5th St; 253/572-1157; villabb@aol.com; www.villabb.com), in the heart of the historic north end, is an Italian Renaissance mansion exuding Mediterranean style and the opulence of the roaring '20s with a lavish interior including rare hardwoods. The **SHERATON TACOMA HOTEL** (1320 Broadway Plaza; 253/572-3200) is considered the best hotel in town. Adjacent to the Tacoma Convention Center, most rooms look out over Commencement Bay or have Mount Rainier views.

To visit nearby **GIG HARBOR** (253/851-6865 Chamber of Commerce), take SR 16 west across the Tacoma Narrows Bridge about 60 minutes. Once a fishing village and still home port for an active commercial fleet, Gig Harbor is part suburbia, part weekend getaway. Boating remains important, with the town's good anchorage and various moorages attracting gunwale-to-gunwale pleasure craft. When the clouds break, Mount Rainier dominates. It's also a picturesque spot for browsing the numerous interesting shops and galleries lining Harborview Drive. Traffic is congested and parking limited because the city was built for boats, not cars, but it's still a good place for festivals, including an arts festival in mid-July and the Maritime Gig in mid-June. A **FARMERS MARKET** features local produce and plants on Saturday, May through October.

Its seafood with a French accent and outdoor dining on a deck overlooking Gig Harbor make the **GREEN TURTLE** (2905 Harborview Dr; 253/851-3167) the best restaurant in town. **MARCO'S RISTORANTE ITALIANO** (7707 Pioneer Wy; 253/858-2899) is a favorite, with fare ranging from traditional Italian to more original specials. Both are owned by members of the same family. The **TIDES TAVERN** (2925 Harborview Dr; 253/858-3982) is a popular watering hole perched over the harbor—boaters like to tie up at its dock—that is often packed to capacity, especially on the deck on sunny days. Originally a general store, it's a full-service tavern with pool table, Gig Harbor memorabilia on the walls, and live music on weekends.

Gig Harbor's **PARADISE THEATER** (9916 Peacock Hill Ave NW; 253/851-7529) has a full season of dinner shows from mid-September to June and offers outdoor shows during the summer. Bring a picnic and a blanket for this summer tradition. There's also an improv group on Friday nights. The recently remodeled **MARITIME INN** (3212 Harborview Dr; 253/858-1818) is downtown, across from the waterfront. Now each of its 15 rooms has a theme, such as the Canterwood Room's golf motif.

KOPACHUCK STATE PARK west of Gig Harbor is a popular destination (follow signs from SR 16), as are **PENROSE POINT** and **ROBERT F. KENNEDY STATE PARKS** on the Key Peninsula farther west (SRs 16 and 302 to Longbranch Rd). All have beaches for clam digging. At **MINTER CREEK STATE FISH HATCHERY** (12710 124th Ave; 253/857-5077), also on the Key Peninsula, you can watch the developmental stages of millions of salmon, daily.

OLYMPIA

Take Interstate 5 south of Seattle 60 miles, approximately 1½ to 2 hours.
The Nisqually Earthquake may have left Olympia shaken and stirred in February 2001, but life has returned to normal. This capital town with three colleges still closes up shop in late spring and early summer after the students and legislators go home—unless there's a special legislative session. The best time to visit is late winter, when the legislature, schools, and businesses are in full swing.

If you schedule carefully, you can see a great deal of the lawmaking process, including debates, speeches, and hearings. The **LEGISLATIVE BUILDING** (14th Ave SW and Capital Wy; 360/586-8687) houses the chambers of the Senate and House of Representatives and the governor's office. Visitors' galleries on the fourth floor allow you to sit in on legislative debates. **THE WASHINGTON STATE VISITOR INFORMATION CENTER** (14th Ave SW and Capitol Wy; 360/586-3460) has plenty of additional information about the campus. The grounds themselves, marked by well-manicured lawns, a sunken garden, and a conservatory (currently closed due to earthquake damage), are beautifully strollable. There are also free daily guided tours of the capitol buildings (360/586-8687), including the **GOVERNOR'S MANSION** (Wednesday afternoons only). Just south of campus, the **STATE CAPITOL MUSEUM** (211 W 21st Ave; 360/753-2580) has an outstanding collection of Native American baskets and memorabilia from the state's founding and its territorial government's early days. The capital isn't just for adults, though. Kids will love the **HANDS ON CHILDREN MUSEUM** (106 11th Ave SW; 360/956-0818), filled with interactive exhibits that will entertain (and educate) them for hours.

Olympia's downtown has a variety of galleries, offbeat shops, cafes, and entertainment venues. **BATDORF AND BRONSON COFFEE ROASTERS** (513 Capital Wy S; 360/786-6717) boasts the best coffee in town and a large following of folks who would never even consider going to Starbucks. A large blackboard lists all of the coffees, teas, and espresso drinks. Just up the street, **SYLVESTER PARK** is the perfect place to escape the mad rush of the legislative session. Once legislators and students return, this usually peaceful park hosts outdoor concerts and demonstrations. A nearby boulder at the corner of Capital and Legion Ways marks the end of the Oregon Trail. Olympia's best-known restaurant, the **URBAN ONION,** is right across the street in the **OLYMPIAN HOTEL** (116 Legion Wy; 360/943-9242). Its signature sandwich, the Haystack—sprouts, tomatoes, guacamole, olives, and melted cheese piled high on whole-grain bread—draws crowds for lunch; breakfast and dinner are also served. There's also the venerable **SPAR** (114 E 4th Ave; 360/357-6444), which features Saturday night jazz, a cigar smoking room in back of the lounge, historic photos, and lots of character.

Downtown doesn't fold up its sidewalks after business hours. The **WASHINGTON CENTER FOR THE PERFORMING ARTS** (512 Washington St SE; 360/753-8586) offers a wide range of performances, including dance, symphony, and theater. **THE CAPITOL THEATRE** (206 E 5th Ave; 360/754-5378) is a showcase for locally produced plays, musicals, and Olympia Film Society–sponsored screenings, including an October film festival. The activity continues into the weekend with the **OLYMPIA FARMERS MARKET** (700 Capitol Wy N; 360/352-9096), selling produce, flowers, and South Sound crafts Thursday through Sunday during the growing season. Not far away is **PERCIVAL LANDING** (at the foot of State

Street), a waterfront park with a tower providing views from Budd Inlet and the capitol dome to the snowcapped Olympic Range. One of the country's top liberal arts colleges, **THE EVERGREEN STATE COLLEGE** (Evergreen Pkwy; 360/866-6000) to the west of town on Cooper Point has a woodsy campus with an organic farm and 3,100 feet of beachfront property. It also hosts a range of cultural events throughout the year.

There are a number of side trip options nearby as well. The **MILLER BREWING COMPANY** (100 Custer Wy; 360/754-5000) in Tumwater offers free tours Monday through Saturday; nearby are Tumwater Falls and Capital Lake. Five miles farther south off Pacific Highway SE is **WOLF HAVEN** (3111 Offut Lake Rd, Tenino; 360/264-HOWL), a nationally renowned conservation organization that teaches wolf appreciation, invites the public to join its wolves in a "howl-in" Saturday night, June through September (reservation required), and gives hourly tours Wednesday through Monday year-round except February. Nature lovers will also enjoy the **NISQUALLY WILDLIFE REFUGE**'s 5.5-mile bird-watching hike through its wetlands sanctuary (100 Brown Farm Rd; 360/753-9467; nisqually.fws.gov), 10 miles north of Olympia just off I-5.

Snoqualmie Valley

Take Interstate 90 east of Seattle approximately 30 miles to exit 27, Snoqualmie–Fall City, about 40 minutes.

Seattle's eastward-oozing suburbs have caused the loss of many sleepy farm hamlets of yesteryear, but Snoqualmie Valley's relatively bucolic stretch of cow country just west of the Cascades is still great for weekend biking or driving, especially if you like U-pick berry farms, roadside stands, and local cafes.

From the town of Snoqualmie off I-90, State Route 202 heads south to North Bend and north to Fall City, then State Route 203 takes over heading north through Carnation and Duvall—both highways are criss-crossed by a web of backroads leading to dairy farms, quiet lakes, beaches along the Snoqualmie River, and tree-lined drives. Cyclists should stick to backroads to avoid weekend traffic. Mountain bikers, hikers, and horseback riders can hit the Snoqualmie Valley Trail, an old railroad right-of-way connecting Stillwater (between Carnation and Duvall) and Tokul (south of Fall City); the trail continues north to the Snohomish County line just north of Duvall, and south to Snoqualmie.

Head into downtown **SNOQUALMIE** and climb aboard the **SNO-QUALMIE VALLEY RAILROAD** (38625 SE King St; 425/888-3030 fares and schedules; www.trainmuseum.org) for a scenic upper valley tour. That's just one part of the "living" Northwest Railway Museum; there's also a Santa Train during early December weekends (reservations required) and numerous railroad artifacts. If you're hungry, head to **ISADORA'S** (8062 Railroad Ave SE; 425/888-1345), a funky shop with a little bit of everything in country collectibles as well as a cozy cafe. Not far to the south, North Bend's main attraction is the **FACTORY STORES OF NORTH BEND** (exit 31 off I-90; 425/888-4505), an outlet mall with everything from kitchenware and clothes to sporting goods and luggage.

Continue north on SR 202 to the region's 268-foot-high natural wonder, **SNOQUALMIE FALLS**. The **SALISH LODGE** (6501 Railroad Ave SE; 425/888-2556 or 800/826-6124; salishlodge.com) is adjacent to the falls and is a high-end stay-over spot. You can look out at the nearby gorge from the restaurant—where you can gorge yourself on its famed four-course breakfast—but you can't see the falls. You can see them from a cliffside gazebo or hike down to the bottom for a closer look.

Continue northwest to **FALL CITY**. For lunch, the perfect place to fuel up for an active day on the Snoqualmie is **SMALL FRYES** (4225 Preston–Fall City Rd; 425/222-7688), a burger stand with seasoned French fries and tasty milk shakes (try banana or mocha malt). From Fall City, take SR 203 north (SR 202 heads west to Redmond).

South of Carnation, **TOLT RIVER–JOHN MACDONALD PARK** (31020 NE 40th St; 206/296-2964), at the confluence of the Tolt and Snoqualmie Rivers, is a fine place for a barbecue in a reservable picnic shelter. Throw a Frisbee on the grass, ride an inner tube where the Tolt empties into the Snoqualmie, camp, or watch teenagers dive from the Tolt Hill Road Bridge. Mountain bikers can hit the 7.4-mile Snoqualmie Valley Trail here, meander over the Snoqualmie River into the Tolt River Campground and through part of the Snoqualmie Valley, and see eye-popping views of the Cascades and Mount Si along the way.

CARNATION is home to **REMLINGER FARMS** (32610 NE 32nd St; 425/333-4135 or 425/451-8740; www.remlingerfarms.com), one of the biggest, best produce markets around. You can buy their farm-grown fruits and veggies (U-pick or not), baked goods, gift items, and canned foods. Its restaurant out back serves lunch, desserts, and candy. Kids love it in summer because it has a petting zoo, pony rides, puppet shows, and a small theme park with rides. Open May through October.

From Carnation, SR 203 follows the Snoqualmie west, then north, to **DUVALL**, which has preserved its small-town storefronts despite commercial growth. **DUVALL BOOKS** (15635 Main St NE) has a remarkable range of used books, fascinating old photos, and other collectibles. **GARDENS AND SUNSPACES MAIN STREET GALLERY** (15611 Main St; 425/788-9844) is an indoor sanctuary of fountains, sundials, garden statuary, and fine art. End your day on the Snoqualmie at the **DUVALL CAFE** (15505 Main St NE; 425/788-9058), which offers surprisingly upscale dinners (as well as humongous big-ass breakfasts and fresh lunches). Don't pass up dessert, especially the pie.

An option for returning to Seattle is to continue north on SR 203 to US Highway 2 at Monroe, from which you can head west toward Everett on US 2 or southwest to Seattle on SR 522 for a loop tour.

North Puget Sound

WHIDBEY ISLAND

Take Interstate 5 north about 25 miles, past Lynnwood, then take State Routes 526 east and 525 north about 5 miles to Mukilteo; driving time is about 45 minutes. Take the Washington State Ferry from Mukilteo to Clinton; crossing is approximately 20 minutes.

You don't have to go to the San Juans to get away from it all when the pretty villages, viewpoints, sandy beaches, and rolling farmland of Whidbey Island are so close. The island is ideal for a family outing of sightseeing, beachcombing, and clam-digging. And the long island's roads are good for biking.

The ferry lands at **CLINTON** on Whidbey's south end. Drive north on State Route 525 and Langley Road to **LANGLEY,** about 10 minutes north. First Street is a browser's dream filled with shops and galleries. Swap stories with Josh Hauser of **MOONRAKER BOOKS** (360/221-6962). **THE COTTAGE** (360/221-4747) sells adornments and elegant clothing; **VIRGINIA'S ANTIQUES** (360/221-7797) features Asian and American wares; and **WHIDBEY ISLAND ANTIQUES** (360/221-2393) is a two-in-one shop with both restored and unrestored pieces. The **STAR STORE** (360/221-5222) is a genuine mercantile outpost with a grocery and deli, gifts, and gadgets galore; upstairs, the **STAR BISTRO** (360/221-2627) specializes in seafood, Northwest cuisine, and martinis.

Langley is also home to a number of fine galleries. More than 40 island artists and craftspeople sell their wares at the **ARTISTS' GALLERY COOPERATIVE** (360/221-7675). **MUSEO** (215 1st St; 360/221-7737; www.museo.cc) offers work by local and regional glass artists as well as rotating exhibits from artists nationwide; **HELLEBORE** (360/221-2067) features glass art made in the studio. Many of the galleries in the area are open late on the first Saturday of the month. **GALLERIO** (111 Anthes St; 360/221-1274) is hard to miss—just look for a turquoise stucco building with a giraffe on the side of it—to see Kathleen Miller's hand-painted silk and wool clothing and enamel jewelry, as well as husband Donald Miller's art photography. **GASKILL/OLSON** (302 1st St; 360/221-2978) is a highly respected local gallery that specializes in original Northwest art and fine crafts. And don't miss the **CLYDE THEATRE** (360/221-5525), host to live theater productions and regularly scheduled films.

If you want to stay in downtown Langley, try Linda Lundgren's retreat, the **GARDEN PATH INN** (360/221-5121; www.whidbey.com/gp), with two handsomely furnished suites. The interior designs are also on display at her adjoining shop, Islandesign. Excellent B&Bs abound. **HOME BY THE SEA** (2388 E Sunlight Beach Rd; 360/321-2964; www.homebytheseacottages.com) is right on the beach, ideal for beach walking and bird-watching because the tide goes out three-quarters of a mile every day. You can sleep on a (moored) stern-wheeler houseboat at **LONE LAKE COTTAGES AND BREAKFAST** (5206 S Bayview Rd; 360/321-5325; www.lonelake.com). Or you can try for a room at the idyllic **INN AT LANGLEY** (400 1st St; 360/221-3033).

CAFÉ LANGLEY (113 1st St; 360/221-3090) is a busy eatery specializing in Mediterranean dishes. Join native islanders for a microbrew, along with a burger and fries, at the classically dumpy **DOG HOUSE BACKDOOR RESTAURANT AND TAVERN** (230 1st St; 360/221-9825). Or take a picnic to **DOUBLE BLUFF BEACH** northwest of Langley—the perfect place to fly kites, spot bald eagles, watch a sunset, or stroll an unspoiled beach. When the tides are right, this is also one of the Sound's best clam-digging beaches. **WHIDBEY ISLAND VINEYARDS AND WINERY** (5237 S Langley Rd; 360/221-2040), a mile south of town, specializes in small bottlings of rhubarb wine, estate-grown grapes, and a full line of Eastern Washington–grown varietal grapes.

Continuing west and north on SR 525, you'll pass Freeland at Holmes Harbor and, just beyond, the road west to South Whidbey State Park. Halfway up the island on its narrowest section is Whidbey's **GREENBANK FARM** (360/678-7700), famed for its loganberry products including jams, jellies, and liqueurs (all available for sampling). Greenbank doesn't make its famous liqueur anymore (Chateau Ste. Michelle does, and the farm is run by a local nonprofit), but it has plenty for sale. You can also sample and buy 36 regionally produced wines in the store. The farm is a fun picnic spot, especially during the two-day **LOGANBERRY FESTIVAL** in July.

Continue north to Keystone, where SR 525 ends and SR 20 begins; follow it north into **COUPEVILLE**, the state's second-oldest incorporated town. It started as a farming community in 1852, and a fort was added after Indian scares. Part of the fort, the **ALEXANDER BLOCKHOUSE**, remains on Alexander Street and is open for tours. The **ISLAND COUNTY HISTORICAL MUSEUM** (908 NW Alexander St; 360/678-3310) recalls Whidbey Island's past. Despite the pressures of development, the town is dedicated to historic preservation. Downtown is made up of souvenir and antique shops and a few restaurants. Stop by the **JAN MCGREGOR STUDIO** (19 Front St; 360/678-5015), which specializes in Japanese antique furniture, hand-woven silks, and the pottery McGregor makes using rare porcelain techniques (Thursday through Sunday in winter, every day in summer). Drop by **TOBY'S 1890 TAVERN** (8 NW Front St; 360/678-4222) for Penn Cove mussels, burgers, beer, and pool. The **KNEAD & FEED** (4 Front St; 360/678-5431) offers homemade breads, pies, and soups, or you can join the locals for coffee and a slice at **GREAT TIMES ESPRESSO** (12 Front St; 360/678-5358). Annual community events include the **PENN COVE MUSSEL FESTIVAL** the first weekend in March and the **COUPEVILLE ARTS & CRAFTS FESTIVAL** the second weekend in August (360/678-5434).

You can ride in the bike lane on Engle Road 3 miles south to **FORT CASEY STATE PARK,** a decommissioned fort with beaches and commanding bluffs. The Washington State Ferry (206/464-6400 or 888/808-7977; www.wsdot.wa.gov/ferries) to Port Townsend leaves from Admiralty Head in Keystone, just south of Fort Casey.

Other good places to explore include the bluff and beach at 17,000-acre **EBEY'S LANDING** and **FORT EBEY STATE PARK** northwest of Coupeville. SR 20 winds north around Penn Cove to Oak Harbor. The Whidbey Island Naval Air Station, an air base for tactical electronic warfare squadrons, dominates **OAK HARBOR,** making it a home for active and retired military folk. Check out **LAVENDER HEART** (4233 N DeGraff Rd; 360/675-3987), which makes topiaries at a working studio in a remodeled barn on what the owner says is one of the Northwest's oldest holly farms. Old and young alike will enjoy **BLUE FOX DRIVE-IN THE-ATRE** and **BRATTLAND GO-KARTS** (1403 Monroe Landing Rd; 360/675-5667; www.bluefoxdrivein.com). You can get good Mexican food at **LUCY'S MI CASITA** (31359 SR 20; 360/675-4800), then have a 27-ounce Turbo Godzilla margarita in the lounge upstairs.

At the north end of the island is pretty Deception Pass State Park with 2,300 acres of prime camping land, forests, and beach. Here the beautiful, treacherous gorge of **DECEPTION PASS** has highly hazardous currents—don't go in the water. You can cross the bridge over Deception Pass that links Whidbey to Fidalgo Island and the mainland via SR 20 to I-5; or take the Whitney–La Conner Road south to La Conner in the Skagit Valley.

SKAGIT VALLEY

Take Interstate 5 north of Seattle 60 miles, then take exits 221, 226, or 230 west to La Conner; approximately 1 hour.

The Skagit Valley may be little more than a blur to northbound tourists most of the year, but during early spring the area blossoms into color worth slowing down for. In fact, if you pull off the highway during the annual **TULIP FESTIVAL,** you'll have to slow down because the roads are gridlocked most weekends in early April. Many of the country roads are level, making biking an ideal way to get around the traffic. There's also plenty of parking at several I-5 exit ramps, where travelers can hop shuttles. You can also avoid traffic hassles by taking a **VICTORIA CLIPPER** boat/bus tour (206/448-5000 or 800/888-2535; www.victoriaclipper. com); tours leave Seattle's waterfront every morning during the festival, boats dock in La Conner, and buses take visitors throughout the countryside. There's still plenty to see after the tulips are cut. Tourists swarm U-pick farms during the June strawberry season, continuing with raspberries, blueberries, and sweet corn, and ending in October with pumpkins. A wide range of vegetables, fruits, and honey are also available at fresh fruit stands throughout the area.

Right off I-5 at exit 226, **MOUNT VERNON** is the "big city" to folks in Skagit and Island Counties. It's a rural town where good restaurants outnumber taverns and video stores, it's a college town (even if **SKAGIT VALLEY COLLEGE** is only a small community college), and it's a major shopping center thanks to the **OUTLET MALLS** between Mount Vernon and Burlington that feature such stores as J. Crew, Liz Claiborne, and Tommy Hilfiger.

If you take I-5 exit 230 to **LA CONNER** instead, you'll cruise through Conway, where locals meet to eat panfried oysters, charbroiled burgers, and onion rings at the classic **CONWAY PUB** (360/445-4733). Five miles west of town, don't miss **SNOW GOOSE PRODUCE**, a huge roadside stand (open late February to mid-October) worth its own day trip. Get a waffle cone, a wide range of local produce, fresh-caught Hood Canal shrimp, and specialty foods including cheese and pasta.

Although La Conner was founded by trading post operator John Conner in 1867, much of the town remains unchanged today. In those days, the area's fishing and farming communities traded by water—the Skagit River, the Swinomish Channel, and many small streams and sloughs. The arrival of trains and interstate highways made the town a backwater and haven for different drummers and artists, including Guy Anderson, Morris Graves, Mark Tobey, and writer Tom Robbins. The result is a culturally rich town—made more so by the contributions of the nearby Swinomish Indians. Adding to the town's atmosphere is an American bazaar on First Street with **SHOPS** such as Cottons, Nasty Jack's Antiques, and Ginger Grater. Try **HUNGRY MOON DELI** (360/466-1602) for soup and a sandwich.

TILLINGHAST SEED COMPANY (623 Morris St; 360/466-3329), at the southern entrance to town, is the oldest retail and mail-order seed store in the Northwest (since 1885), complete with seeds bred specifically for the Northwest, plus a nursery, florist shop, and general store. **GO OUTSIDE** (111 Morris St; 360/466-4836) is a small garden and garden-accessories store. **GACHES MANSION** (703 S 2nd St; 360/466-4288) is an example of American Victorian architecture, with a widow's walk that looks out on the Skagit Valley. It's filled with period furnishings and houses the Northwest's only quilt museum (open Wednesday through Sunday). Don't miss the **MUSEUM OF NORTHWEST ART** (121 S 1st St; 360/466-4446), featuring the work of Northwest artists. At the town's edge, the **HERON** in La Conner (117 Maple St; 360/466-4626) has pretty-as-a-picture rooms and a tempting hot tub out back.

Kitsap and Olympic Peninsulas

BREMERTON
Take the Washington State Ferry from Colman Dock (Pier 52) in downtown Seattle to Bremerton; crossing is approximately 1 hour.

It's not easy to make an industrial area look pretty, especially if that industrial center is in the heart of a city's downtown, as Bremerton's U.S. Naval Shipyard is. One local wag says the retail core looks like a nuclear bomb hit it; others say it's a good place to pass through . . . headed somewhere else. A few attractions in the area near the ferry terminal make downtown Bremerton worth a stop, and an art scene is slowly emerging.

Start at the promenade along the shore from First to Fourth Streets with picnic tables, benches, a shipworker statue, and views south to Sinclair Inlet. The walkway ends near the **USS TURNER JOY,** a destroyer that played a pivotal role in U.S. involvement in Vietnam. The ship, open for self-guided tours (daily in summer, Thursday through Sunday in winter), has a POW memorial featuring a reproduction of a cell from Vietnam's infamous "Hanoi Hilton." Get tickets at the Ship's Store Gift Shop. The shop also sells tickets for **KITSAP HARBOR TOURS'** (360/377-8924) narrated 45-minute trip around the harbor (daily in summer), providing close-up views of battleships, nuclear subs, the carrier **USS CARL VINSON** (when it's not at sea), and the eerie mothball fleet. The company also offers a cruise to **TILLICUM VILLAGE'S** salmon dinner and stage show on **BLAKE ISLAND** (also accessible from Seattle; see Boat Tours under Organized Tours in the Exploring chapter). The naval theme continues at the free **BREMERTON NAVAL MUSEUM** (130 Washington St; 360/479-7447), open daily in summer, Tuesday through Sunday in winter; 10am to 5pm. Two doors south, the comfortable **FRAICHE CUP COFFEEHOUSE** (360/377-1180) offers pastries and espresso drinks.

The **AMY BURNETT FINE ART GALLERY** (412 Pacific Ave; 360/373-3187) started the growth spurt, but the arts district on Fourth now includes **COLLECTIVE VISIONS** (360/377-8327), **VIEWPOINTS GALLERY** (360/4400-3843), **METROPOLIS GALLERY** (360/373-4709), and a **GALLERY TOUR** the first Friday of the month. (The corner of Fourth and Pacific also boasts a plaque commemorating the origin of Harry S. Truman's campaign slogan, "Give 'Em Hell, Harry," which was shouted by a bystander in the crowd.) Plays at the art deco **ADMIRAL THEATRE** at Fifth and Pacific are also adding life to downtown.

Just a five-minute drive north of downtown on Washington Avenue, across Port Washington Narrows on the Manette Bridge, the Manette district boasts a few antique stores, a used-book shop, and three good restaurants. The ever-popular **BOAT SHED** (101 Shore Dr; 360-377-2600) is much loved for its seafood, clam chowder, and view from its deck, but the intimate Northern Italian restaurant just down the street, **FISCHIARE LA FERMATA** (2204 E 11th St; 360/373-5927), is gaining a following. If you're in a rush, go to **PETE'S JERSEY SUBS** (2100 E 11th St; 360/377-5118) for subs and an excellent vegetarian cheesesteak sandwich.

At the Bremerton Ferry Dock you can hop a **HORLUCK TRANSPORTATION COMPANY** (360/876-2300) foot ferry for the 10-minute crossing of Sinclair Inlet to **PORT ORCHARD**. The ride ends at the Sidney Dock, a block from Bay Street's antique stores, taverns, and cafes. (The ferry runs until 8:30pm weekdays, 7pm Saturday, closed Sunday; $2 for adults.) Must-sees include the **OLDE CENTRAL ANTIQUE MALL** (801 Bay St; 360/895-1902) and the **WATERFRONT FARMERS MARKET** on Saturday, April to October.

From Bremerton you can skip the ferry and drive 7 miles around the west end of Sinclair Inlet via State Routes 3, 16, and 166 and make a few additional stops at places including **SPRINGHOUSE DOLLS AND GIFTS** (1130 Bethel Ave; 360/876-0529), with its huge collection of modern dolls and teddy bears as well as the flouncy **VICTORIAN ROSE TEAROOM**. Attend a monthly Victorian High Tea and keep your floral china teacup as a souvenir (reservations required). On State Route 16 just beyond milepost 28, don't miss **ELANDAN GARDENS** (3050 W SR 16; 360/373-8260), an open-air art gallery/nursery/gift shop along the shore specializing in priceless bonsai (closed Monday and in January).

Head the other direction from Bremerton, north on SRs 3 and 308 to Keyport at the north end of Dyes Inlet, and you'll see the free **NAVAL UNDERSEA MUSEUM** (610 Dowell St; 360/396-4148; num.kpt.nuwc.navy.mil), with exhibits on naval history, undersea technology, and the submersible that helped explore the *Titanic*. Stop at the sandwich shop in **KEYPORT MERCANTILE** (Washington and Grandview; 360/779-7270) for a post-museum snack.

You can return via Poulsbo and continue south on SR 305 to the Bainbridge ferry. Or you can return to Bremerton on SR 3, continuing south to explore Hood Canal.

HOOD CANAL

Take the Washington State Ferry from Colman Dock (Pier 52) in downtown Seattle to Bainbridge Island; crossing is approximately 35 minutes. From the Bainbridge ferry dock, take State Route 305 north across Agate

Passage and through Poulsbo to State Route 3 (driving time approxi-mately 45 minutes). North leads to the Hood Canal Bridge at the mouth of the canal, with its crossing to State Route 104 and US Highway 101, which leads south along the west shore of the canal—your return route. Near Poulsbo, take State Route 3 south to explore the east shore of Hood Canal first.

Hood Canal, a 65-mile-long, fishhook-shaped inland waterway, lies west of Puget Sound, between Kitsap Peninsula and the Olympic Penin-sula to the west. The eastern arm of Hood Canal extends from Belfair southwesterly along State Route 106 to Union. The area is filled with mansions and homes built by urbanites seeking summer getaways with Olympic views. From Union, the canal turns north at the Great Bend; US 101 follows the west shore of the less domesticated western arm, which has long stretches of forested slopes and accessible beaches. Three rivers that plunge down from the Olympics to Hood Canal's western arm offer trail access to the mountains: the **DUCKABUSH**, the **HAMMA HAMMA**, and the **DOSEWALLIPS**. US 101 and SR 104 lead north and west to the mouth of Hood Canal, closing the loop tour described below.

From SR 3 just outside Poulsbo, head south toward Silverdale and follow signs west to Seabeck. On the peninsula's west shore, tiny **SEABECK** is home to the **SEABECK CONFERENCE CENTER** (360/830-5010), which may be rented by nonprofit groups. Just to its west is **SCENIC BEACH STATE PARK**, with picnicking, campsites, and a view of the Olympics. On the way to Seabeck (via Seabeck Highway), stop to watch a play at the **MOUNTAINEERS' FOREST THEATER** (206/284-6310). To reach the southern tip of the peninsula, follow back roads south through Holly and Dewatto to reach the Belfair-Tahuya Road, or return to SR 3 south to Belfair and take State Route 300 southwest, which fol-lows the north shore of the east arm. At the tip of the peninsula, over-looking the canal's Big Bend, sprawling **TAHUYA STATE PARK** embraces beach and forest and is sought out by mountain and motor bikers, hikers, and horseback riders.

Returning north on State Route 300, **BELFAIR STATE PARK**, 3 miles south of Belfair, is one of the peninsula's busiest parks. Campers must reserve in summer (800/452-5683). You can swim, fish, or dig clams. Just north of the state park, South Belfair's **HOOD CANAL–THELER WET-LANDS** (E 22871 SR 3; 360/275-4898) features 3.8 miles of wheelchair-accessible trails through marshes, woods, and the Union River estuary. A wooden causeway over a tidal marsh provides a view of the head of the canal's expanse. The interpretive center gives insight into the value of wetlands.

From Belfair, continue south on State Route 3 a short way to State Route 106 and follow it southwest. The big, safe, shallow pool and fast-food concession makes **TWANOH STATE PARK**, on the south shore of

FERRY RIDES

No activity better captures the spirit of Seattle than a ferry ride—both for commuters who use them for transportation and for sightseers who want to simply enjoy the sunset or the city skyline from an ideal vantage point.

Most of the ferries on Puget Sound are run by **Washington State Ferries** (206/464-6400 or 888-808-7977; www.wsdot.wa.gov/ferries). The largest ferry system in the country, it operates 10 routes serving 20 terminal locations and transporting 27 million passengers a year. On weekend and evening runs, ferries often don't have room for all the cars, so be prepared to wait unless you walk on or ride your bike (fare is much cheaper for pedestrians and cyclists). Food service is available on almost all routes, beer and wine on some. (However, in all cases you'll do better dining at your destination.) Rates range from $2.90 one way for foot passengers traveling from West Seattle to Vashon to $62.25 for a car and driver going from Anacortes to Sidney, British Columbia. The bike surcharge is 90 cents from Seattle to Bainbridge, Vashon, or Bremerton. Passengers pay only on westbound ferries (so if you're island-hopping, head to the westernmost destination first and work your way back).

Three ferry routes leave downtown from the main Seattle terminal at Colman Dock (Pier 52, Alaskan Wy and Marion St; map:M9). A small, speedy walk-on ferry takes mostly commuters to **Vashon Island** (Monday through Friday only; 25 minutes) or to the Navy town of **Bremerton** (60 minutes). The car-ferry trip to Bremerton takes an hour. The **Seattle–Bainbridge Island** run takes 35 minutes. If sightseeing is your objective, take the Bremerton trip. It's a bit longer, but the scenic ride crosses the Sound, skirts the south end of Bainbridge Island, and passes through narrow Rich Passage into the Kitsap Peninsula's land-enclosed Sinclair Inlet.

In recent years, the population of Bainbridge and Vashon Islands has increased and more folks are commuting by ferry. As a result, drive-on ferry passengers should arrive early, especially when traveling during peak hours (mornings eastbound, evenings westbound; summer weekends: Friday and Saturday westbound, Sunday eastbound). Schedules vary from summer to winter (with longer lines in summer); credit cards are not accepted. Americans traveling to Canada should bring a passport or other proof of U.S. citizenship. Other major Puget Sound routes are listed below.

Edmonds-Kingston (30 minutes)

Kingston, close to the northern tip of the Kitsap Peninsula, is reached from Edmonds (about 15 miles north of Seattle; take the Edmonds/Kingston Ferry exit, exit 177, from I-5 and head northwest on State Route 104).

Fauntleroy–Vashon Island–Southworth (15 minutes to Vashon plus 10 minutes to Southworth)

Vashon, an idyllic retreat west of Seattle, can be reached via passenger ferry from downtown Seattle Monday through Friday, or via car ferry from the Fauntleroy ferry dock in West Seattle every day (15 minutes). Vashon is the first stop on a trip from the Fauntleroy terminal in West Seattle (exit 163 off I-5; map:LL9) to Southworth on the Kitsap Peninsula (10 minutes by ferry from Vashon); see Vashon Island in this chapter.

Vashon-Tacoma (15 minutes)

At the southern end of Vashon Island is the Tahlequah ferry dock, from which the ferry departs for Point Defiance Park, on the northwest edge of Tacoma.

Mukilteo-Clinton (20 minutes)

From Mukilteo, 26 miles north of Seattle (take exit 189 from I-5), a ferry goes to Clinton on pretty Whidbey Island (see Whidbey Island in this chapter).

Keystone–Port Townsend (30 minutes)

From Keystone, 25 miles up Whidbey Island from Clinton, a ferry reaches Port Townsend on the Olympic Peninsula, one of the most enchanting towns in the state (see Port Townsend in this chapter). This route subject to cancellation due to extreme tidal conditions.

Anacortes–San Juan Islands–Sidney, BC (crossing times vary)

The remote San Juan Islands are reached by ferry from Anacortes (82 miles northwest of Seattle, exit 230 off I-5). There are 743 islands at low tide, but only 172 have names, and only four have major ferry service: the boat stops on Lopez, Shaw, Orcas, and San Juan Islands. Once a day (twice a day in summer), the ferry continues on to Sidney on British Columbia's Vancouver Island, just 15 minutes north of Victoria by car. It returns in the early afternoon. During the summer, you can reserve space for your car on this crowded run.

Seattle-Victoria, BC (2 hours)

The *Victoria Clipper* fleet (206/448-5000, 250/382-8100, or 800/888-2535; www.victoriaclipper.com) offers the only year-round ferry service to Victoria from Seattle. The waterjet-propelled catamarans carry foot passengers only between Seattle and Victoria four times a day from mid-May to mid-September, and once or twice a day the rest of the year. Reservations are necessary (see Victoria in this chapter).

Port Angeles–Victoria, BC (1½ hours)

The privately run Black Ball Transport's (360/457-4491) *MV Coho* makes two runs daily in winter and spring and four daily runs in summer from Port Angeles, on the Olympic Peninsula, to Victoria, on Vancouver Island.

Hood Canal's eastern arm, popular with families. Farther southwest, the **UNION COUNTRY STORE** (E 5130 SR 106; 360/898-2641) offers exotic groceries, produce, wines, and wonderful fresh-daily dips (free tastings) plus calzone, lasagnes, and fettuccines. Barbecued pork ribs smoked in peach wood is the weekend special. Continue west to cross the Skokomish River and meet US 101, where you turn north to follow the canal's west shore.

Stop at **POTLATCH STATE PARK**, 3 miles south of Hoodsport, for a picnic or a refreshing dip. At low tide, you can gather oysters on the beach. **HOODSPORT WINERY** (360/877-9894), a mile south of Hoodsport, will match its wine to your oysters. Sample one of the four fruit wines, white varietals, or such reds as the legendary Island Belle, made from grapes grown on nearby Stretch Island (to the east in Case Inlet), as you look out on the canal.

Hoodsport serves as the gateway to the Lake Cushman area. Just west of the lake's development, the Olympic National Park boundary has a ranger station, campground, picnicking, and trailheads. The short **STAIRCASE RAPIDS TRAIL** along the upper Skokomish River is a pleasure. From Hoodsport to Quilcene, Hood Canal's west arm boasts many recreational areas in the **OLYMPIC NATIONAL FOREST** and **OLYMPIC NATIONAL PARK**; the many ranger stations along US Highway 101 provide all the information you need to visit them. Hoodsport Ranger Station (just off Hwy 101 on Lake Cushman Dr; 360/877-5254) has single-sheet maps for a range of hikes along the canal's southern sector.

Public beaches where **OYSTERING** is permitted along the canal's west reach include Cushman Beach, Lilliwaup Recreational Tidelands, Pleasant Harbor State Park (near the mouth of the Duckabush River), Dosewallips State Park (a choice stop, with 425 acres of meadows, woodlands, and beach), and Seal Rock Campground. Most have clam beds. North of Seal Rock, Bee Mill Road heads eastward from US 101 to the Point Whitney State Shellfish Laboratory, with an interpretive display and a good oyster and swimming beach. Check the state hotline (800/562-5632) for red-tide warnings. North of Hoodsport, and just south of the Hamma Hamma River, shucked **OYSTERS** may be purchased at Hamma Hamma Oyster Company Seafood Store (35959 N Hwy 101; 360/877-5811). Call ahead to check hours.

Gardeners will find a paradise of their own at **WHITNEY GARDENS** (306264 Hwy 101; 360/796-4411) in Brinnon, which is between Dosewallips State Park and Seal Rock. You can see the rainbow of colors from blooming rhododendrons, azaleas, and camellias in early spring or stroll the 7-acre retreat's leafy corridors of weeping spruces, colorful maples, and magnolias. The gardens are open every day (small fee). There's a nursery and small picnic area. You can also eat at the folksy, unassuming **HALFWAY HOUSE** (US 101 at Brinnon Ln; 360/796-4715), where tourists and locals mingle.

Just 5 miles south of Quilcene off US 101, 2,750-foot **MOUNT WALKER** is one of the canal's most spectacular viewpoints, providing views of Seattle, Mount Rainier, and the Cascades. You can reach it by driving up a 5-mile dirt road that snakes around the mountain (summer only) or hiking the 2-mile trail up. Bring a picnic. Also worth a stop is the **WALKER MOUNTAIN TRADING POST** (near the Mount Walker turnoff from Hwy 101; 360/796-3200), which crams a variety of antiques and collectibles into a pioneer home. On the highway's west side, north of the Mount Walker turnoff, **FALLS VIEW CAMPGROUND** is a short hike from a lovely waterfall on the Quilcene River.

The Quilcene Ranger Station (360/765-2200 or 360/765-3368), just south of Quilcene, has information about outdoor recreation at the canals' north end, including advice on shellfishing. **QUILCENE** has the world's largest oyster hatchery and possibly the purest salt water in the West. The mellow **WHISTLING OYSTER** (360/765-9508) is where knowing locals go for food, darts, and shuffleboard. In the heart of town, the **TWANA ROADHOUSE** (360/765-6485) features fresh soups, sandwiches, homemade pies, hand-dipped ice cream, and quick, cheery service.

North of Quilcene, just before the junction of US 101 with State Route 104, the **OLYMPIC MUSIC FESTIVAL** (206/527-8839; www.music fest.net) holds forth at 2pm on Saturday and Sunday, June through mid-September, in a turn-of-the-century barn/concert hall. Listeners sit inside on hay bales or church pews, or outside on the grass. Bring a picnic, or buy dinner at the well-stocked deli on site. It's a real farm, and youngsters are encouraged to pet the animals. The music is sublime, performed by the Philadelphia String Quartet with guest artists from around the world. Reservations advised.

Head east on State Route 104 and cross the Hood Canal Bridge to close the loop at State Route 3 south of Port Gamble. Or continue north on US 101 to Discovery Bay and State Route 20 north to Port Townsend.

PORT TOWNSEND

Take the Washington State Ferry from Colman Dock (Pier 52) in downtown Seattle to Bainbridge Island; crossing is approximately 35 minutes. From the Bainbridge ferry dock, head northwest on State Route 305 to State Route 3. Follow State Route 3 north to the Hood Canal Bridge and cross it to continue west on State Route 104; at US Highway 101 head north to State Route 20. Follow State Route 20 north into Port Townsend, 50 miles northwest of Seattle (approximately 2 hours).

Port Townsend may now be known for its Victorian architecture and beautiful waterfront, but the atmosphere was far more raucous not that long ago. In the mid-1800s whiskey flowed free, brothels flourished, and sailors were often shanghaied, facts that are fun to remember as you wander through town. Parking can be tight in summer, especially during festivals. Avoid the hassle by stopping at the Park & Ride at Haines Place, near Safeway as you enter town, and riding the shuttle, which runs every half hour to uptown (Lawrence Street) and downtown (Water Street). Hidden away near the Park & Ride, **KAH TAI LAGOON PARK** is favored by birders, walkers, bikers, and waterfowl.

Downtown, stroll along Water Street and soak up the town's mix of 19th-century charm and quirky, modern-day shops, galleries, and restaurants. Downtown also has a few good parks: **JACKSON BEQUEST TIDAL PARK** is behind Elevated Ice Cream (see below) on Water Street; compact **POPE MARINE PARK** at the end of Adams Street has picnic tables, logs, and playground equipment; and the 130-year-old **UNION WHARF** has a pavilion with views of Mount Baker and Mount Rainier.

In addition to downtown's miniparks, picnic tables, and piers, there's a nice variety of shops to visit. **EARTHENWORKS** (702 Water St; 360/385-0328) houses crafts and fine art. The **ANTIQUE MALL** (802 Washington St; 360/379-8069) houses 35 little shops offering the standard mix of old stuff plus Port Townsend's answer to Underground Seattle, a display of artifacts from the area's old Chinatown. The Chinese Colony was destroyed by fire at the turn of the 19th century, and the items were discovered when the mall basement was excavated. **PACIFIC TRADITIONS,** in the Waterstreet Hotel lobby (637 Water St; 360/385-4770), sells masks, Salish blankets, and jewelry created by artists from the Olympic Peninsula. A superior bookshop, **IMPRINT BOOKSTORE** (820 Water St; 360/385-3643), is stocked with classics, contemporary works, and a fine selection of regional guidebooks. **WILLIAM JAMES BOOKSELLER** (360/385-7313) across the street sells used and rare books. **APRIL FOOL & PENNY TWO** (725 Water St; 360/385-3438) specializes in collectibles, dollhouses, and whimsical greeting cards. **THE WINE SELLER** (940 Water St; 360/385-7673) offers a large selection of wines, beers, and coffees.

ELEVATED ICE CREAM COMPANY (627 Water St; 360/385-1156) has the best ice cream in town, plus a sundeck overlooking the bay. Have soda in a nostalgic setting at **NIFTY FIFTYS** (817 Water St; 360/385-1931). Newcomer **FIN'S COASTAL KITCHEN** (1019 Water St; 360/379-5244) at Flagship Landing has a fresh daily menu prepared by European-trained chefs, plus a balcony view. **BREAD & ROSES BAKERY** (230 Quincy St; 360/385-1044) is known for great breads, pastries, light lunches, and open-air seating. **SALAL CAFÉ** (634 Water St; 360/385-6532) has breakfast and innovative meals, served in the dining room or the atrium overlooking Franklin Court, where concerts are held. The classic **ROSE THEATRE** (235 Taylor St; 360/385-1089) has daily showings of contemporary American and foreign films.

You can go uptown by ascending the stairway at Taylor and Washington Streets or driving past the old Episcopal church and rusty-red **OLD BELL TOWER**. From here you can see venerable mansions a few blocks away from Lawrence Street's pizzerias, cafes, and galleries. **ALDRICH'S** (940 Lawrence St; 360/385-0500), the old general store, has quality wines, produce, a deli, and a bakery. Stock up for a picnic, then head for the emerald lawns, rose arbors, playground, and beach access of **CHETZEMOKA PARK** at Jackson and Blaine Streets. You can dig clams if the tide's right.

Or visit **FORT WORDEN STATE PARK**, once an army base and now inexpensive lodgings (great for families) and the headquarters of the Centrum Foundation, which puts on summertime concerts, plays, festivals, and workshops. The **COMMANDING OFFICER'S QUARTERS** (360/379-9894) at the end of Fort Worden's Officers' Row faithfully reproduces the life of a turn-of-the-19th-century officer and family. **BLACKBERRIES** (in the heart of Fort Worden; 360/385-9950) serves appetizing meals in a rustic dining room. The beach's **MARINE SCIENCE CENTER** (360/385-5582) has touch tanks and aquaria that allow children to tickle a seastar (closed in winter; call for hours). Up on Artillery Hill, visit the bunkers and gun emplacements from the fort's heyday.

You can gain insight into Port Townsend's tawdry past at the **JEFFERSON COUNTY HISTORICAL SOCIETY MUSEUM** in City Hall (540 Water St; 360/385-1003; jchsmuseum.org), which includes the city's original courtroom, jail, and a replica of a Victorian bedroom. The 130-year-old **ROTHSCHILD HOUSE** (360/379-8076 group tour reservations) at Jefferson and Taylor Streets features original furnishings and beautiful herb and rose gardens. Every September, Port Townsend holds a **HISTORIC HOMES TOUR** (Port Townsend Visitors Information Center, 360/385-2722; ptchamber.org). To experience Port Townsend's quaint history more fully, stay at the exquisitely turreted, Victorian **F. W. HASTINGS HOUSE/OLD CONSULATE INN** (313 Walker St; 360/385-6753).

The city has two marinas downtown and a Washington State Ferry dock. From here, you can take a short ferry ride across Admiralty Inlet to the Keystone ferry dock on Whidbey Island. Port Townsend's annual **WOODEN BOAT FESTIVAL** (360/385-3628), on the first weekend after Labor Day, is centered at Point Hudson at the end of Water Street. Attractions include concerts, entertainers, and, of course, boats.

And don't miss the annual Kinetic Sculpture Race in early October, when locals race anything they can get to move.

Mount Rainier and Mount St. Helens

MOUNT RAINIER

Take Interstate 5 south from Seattle to exit 142; then take State Route 161 south through Puyallup, Graham, and Eatonville; head east on State Route 7 to Elbe. Take State Route 706 east through Ashford to the park's southwestern (Nisqually) entrance; 100 miles southeast of Seattle (approximately 2½ hours).

Before there was the Space Needle, there is and always was Mount Rainier, the dominant element of the skyline on a sunny day in Seattle. It is the way Seattleites measure the quality of a summer day. If it's sunny and the mountain is "out," it is a great day indeed. Originally called Tahoma, this volcano defies simple description. It isn't just a majestic geological landmark that has become associated with Washington, it is a moody Native American god and a magnetic force of nature that creates its own weather and draws admirers from all over the world.

On your way to the park, 55 miles south of Seattle off State Route 161, you can visit **NORTHWEST TREK WILDLIFE PARK** (11610 Trek Dr E, Eatonville; 360/832-6117; www.nwtrek.org), a natural habitat 60 miles from the Nisqually entrance to the national park. Bison, caribou, moose, elk, and deer roam in pastures, peat bogs, ponds, and forests, while visitors watch from trams. Naturalists narrate the hour-long, 5.5-mile trip. Admission is $8.75 for adults, less for children and seniors, free for kids under 3. The steam-powered trains of the **MOUNT RAINIER SCENIC RAILROAD** (schedule varies seasonally; 360/569-2588), based in Elbe on State Route 7, provide mountain views, but don't get close enough.

The closest accommodations near the park's Nisqually entrance are around Ashford. **WELLSPRING** (54922 Kernahan Rd, Ashford; 360/569-2514) has two spas surrounded by evergreens. If your massage or sauna (or hour-long hot tub soak for $10) has you too relaxed to travel, consider spending the night. **ALEXANDERS COUNTRY INN** (37515 SR 706 E, Ashford; 360/569-2300 or 800/654-7615) offers bed-and-breakfast–style rooms (with free, full-course breakfasts) with modern-day comforts in a turn-of-the-19th-century inn. Make reservations for a fine meal, including panfried trout—caught out back in the holding pond. Six large guest rooms and a private outdoor 23-jet Jacuzzi spa are available at **MOUNTAIN MEADOWS INN B&B AT MOUNT RAINIER** (28912 SR 706 E, Ashford; 360/569-2788; www.mt-rainier.net). The 24-room **NISQUALLY LODGE** (31609 SR 706 E, Ashford; 360/569-8804; www.escapetothe mountains.com) offers reasonably-priced respite to those willing to trade charm for a phone, TV, and air conditioning.

A mile past **MOUNT RAINIER NATIONAL PARK**'s Nisqually entrance (entry fee $10 per car; 360/569-2211; www.nps.gov/mora) is Sunshine Point Campground (open year-round); 6 miles farther is the village of Longmire, home to the simple **NATIONAL PARK INN** (360/569-2275), a wildlife museum, a hiking information center, and a cross-country skiing rental outlet. The 235,625-acre park is a lushly forested reserve with the 14,410-foot-high volcano as its centerpiece. Tour the mountain by car, hike or snowshoe it, ski nearby, or climb to its summit. The most popular summer-time option is to drive a loop around the mountain: follow the road from Longmire to Paradise (you can use it during daylight hours in winter, but it's best to carry tire chains and a shovel and check conditions beforehand on the 24-hour information line (360/569-2211) to State Route 123 over Cayuse Pass to State Route 410 just west of Chinook Pass (both passes are closed in winter), then take the road west to Sunrise (open only when it's snow free, usually July 1 through Labor Day).

The park road winds past Cougar Rock Campground (reservations required: 800/365-2267), many scenic viewpoints, and waterfalls as it climbs to **PARADISE**. At 5,400 feet on the mountain's south side, it is the park's most popular destination because it offers the most complete services in the park, including rustic accommodations at **PARADISE INN** (mid-May to October; 360/569-2275 reservations; www.nps.gov/mora), the **JACKSON MEMORIAL VISITORS CENTER**'s 360-degree view, and a network of spectacular hiking trails that are ideal for cross-country skiing, snowshoeing, or inner-tubing in the winter; Paradise has a guided snowshoe walk in winter.

The park road continues east to State Route 123 at the Stevens Canyon entrance; head north over Cayuse Pass to State Route 410, then continue north to the Sunrise Road at the White River entrance; White River Campground is on the way up to Sunrise. About 1,000 feet farther up, the **SUNRISE** visitor area offers a view of the peak from the northeast. It's the highest point open to cars and is open only in summer. A number of naturalist talks will enhance your experience. They range from a half-hour slide show (at Paradise) or a 2-mile geologic walk (at Sunrise) to a 6-mile alpine ecology hike (at Paradise).

There are also 305 miles of trails within the park, including the 93-mile Wonderland Trail, which circles the mountain. Backcountry permits are required for camping and are available at ranger stations and visitors centers. The campgrounds at Ohanapecosh (just south of the Stevens Canyon entrance) and Cougar Rock require reservations (800/365-2267), while sites at White River, Ipsut Creek (on the park's northwest corner), and Sunshine Point are first-come, first-served.

It's also possible to ski the area in winter and spend the night at a hut-to-hut ski trail system south and west of Mount Rainier National Park. **MOUNT TAHOMA SKI HUTS,** run by the Tahoma Trails Association (PO Box 206, Ashford, WA 98304; 360/569-2451; skimtta.com), has more than 75 miles of trails, three huts, and one yurt. Rooms at **WHITTAKER'S BUNKHOUSE** (30205 SR 706; 360/569-2439; www.welcome toashford.com) are basic and cheap. Near the Sunrise Road on State Route 410 is **CRYSTAL MOUNTAIN** (360/663-2265; www.crystalmt. com), said to have the state's best skiing (see Skiing in the Recreation chapter).

Or you can climb the mountain, either with a concessioned guide service such as **RAINIER MOUNTAINEERING** (summer: Ashford, WA 98304, 360/569-2227; winter: 535 Dock St, Ste 209, Tacoma, WA 98402, 253/627-6242) or in your own party. For the latter, you must register at one of the park's ranger stations and pay $15 per person ($25 for an annual pass). The guide service offers a one-day training session that teaches all you'll need to know to make the two-day climb. It can be done year-round, but late May to mid-September is the best time to go. It's best to climb with a guide service unless you're qualified to do it solo.

To complete your loop around Mount Rainier, continue north and west on State Route 410 through Enumclaw back to State Route 161. Or return to Elbe on State Route 7 and turn south to Morton on US Highway 12 to reach Mount St. Helens from the north.

MOUNT ST. HELENS

Take Interstate 5 south from Seattle to exit 49, then follow signs east via State Route 504; approximately 150 miles south of Seattle (2–3 hours).

As if Mardi Gras riots and earthquakes weren't enough, worrywarts remain concerned about temperamental Mount St. Helens, which last blew its top on May 18, 1980. The 8,365-foot simmering remains are worth the trip. It's best to go on a clear day when you can see the regrowth on the mountain.

 Just off I-5 at exit 49/Castle Rock, where SR 504 begins, start your visit at the **CINEDOME** (360/274-8000; mtsthelenscinedome.com), where you can see *The Eruption of Mount St. Helens* on a three-story-tall, 55-foot-wide screen. The seat-rattling rumble alone is worth the $5 (adult) admission.

As you travel east along State Route 504 (the Spirit Lake Memorial Highway), there are five interpretive centers, each of which complements the others. First is Washington State Park's **MOUNT ST. HELENS VISITORS CENTER** (milepost 5; 360/274-2100; www.fs.fed.us/gpnf/mshnvm/). Built shortly after the eruption, it commemorates the blast with exhibits, a walk-through volcano, hundreds of historical photos, geological/anthropological surveys, and a film documenting the destruction and rebirth.

Cowlitz County's **HOFFSTADT BLUFFS VISITORS CENTER** (milepost 27; 360/274-7750; www.mtsthelens.com) is second. It features a restaurant, a gift store, and a memorial to those who died in the blast. Helicopter tours are available here.

Third is the Weyerhaeuser-operated **FOREST LEARNING CENTER** at North Fork Ridge (milepost 33; 360/414-3439; www.weyerhaeuser. com/sthelens), covering the eruption's impact on tree farms and how wood was salvaged after the blast. Next is the Forest Service's **COLD-WATER RIDGE VISITOR CENTER** (milepost 43; 360/274-2131), a multi-million-dollar facility with a billion-dollar view of the black dome resting in the middle of the 2-mile-wide steaming crater and of Coldwater and Castle Lakes (both formed by massive mud flows). This center focuses on the landscape's amazing biological recovery. The final stop is the Forest Service–run **JOHNSTON RIDGE OBSERVATORY** (milepost 52; 360/274-2140; www.fs.fed.us/gpnf/mshnvm/), providing a view directly into the crater. This center's focus is the eruption itself, how geologists monitor volcanoes, and what we have learned since the eruption.

It costs $3 per adult to visit one of the Forest Service visitor centers ($6 for more than one center, free for children under 4). There are other viewpoints lining roads approaching the mountain (from the south, State Route 503 via Woodland and Cougar; from the north, US Highway 12 east to Randle, then Forest Roads 25 and 99), but all the visitors centers are on State Route 504. Those who enter from Randle via Forest Road 99 will get a dramatic view of the blowdown destruction. Although there is no camping in the Mount St. Helens National Monument, there is in the 1.3 million-acre **GIFFORD PINCHOT NATIONAL FOREST** (360/891-5000) surrounding the monument, with its more than 50 campgrounds and excellent fishing. Call ahead for road and campground conditions.

To climb the mountain, budget at least six or seven hours. Registration can add another day, however, because you must get a permit ($15 per person) well in advance—call monument headquarters (360/247-3900) for the procedure—and you must register at **JACK'S STORE AND RESTAURANT** (23 miles east of Woodland on SR 503 just west of Cougar; 360/231-4276). It's best to climb in May and June (when there's still enough snow to tame the ash). Bring good hiking boots, drinking water, sunscreen, sunglasses, crampons, and an ice ax. There are still glaciers on the crater's rim, so only the experienced should make the climb.

You can extend your mountain sojourn by staying at the moderately priced, 50-room **SEASONS MOTEL** (200 Westlake Ave, Morton; 360/496-6835; www.whitepasstravel.com/seasons.htm), located about halfway between Mount St. Helens and Mount Rainier on US 12.

British Columbia

VANCOUVER

Take Interstate 5 north from Seattle to the U.S.–Canada border, then continue north on Highway 99; 145 miles (approximately 3 hours).

Although Seattle is among the country's top 10 most expensive cities to live in, not far away there's a city that's even more cosmopolitan but far less expensive—beautiful Vancouver, British Columbia. A topnotch dinner and night at the theater costs about $175 (U.S.), and you can stay at a luxury hotel in the off season for around $100 (U.S.). Perhaps that's why everything is booked far in advance during summer. Best of all, it's close. A commuter flight takes 25 minutes, cars three hours, and Amtrak four hours. (The oft-discussed lineups at the border tend to occur heading back into the United States.)

Vancouver itself has a European flavor. The city proudly claims that its West End along Denman Street is the most densely populated urban district in North America. The result is a vibrant, ethnically diverse, always-bustling neighborhood filled with apartments, condos, shops, cafes, and restaurants. It's a city made for walking, as well as the distinctive brand of businesses that accompany pedestrian-friendly surrounds. To get the full-on Euro effect, book into the oh-so-proper **SUTTON PLACE HOTEL** (845 Burrard St; 604/682-5511) or, for less expensive B&B-style accommodations, the **KINGSTON HOTEL BED & BREAKFAST** (757 Richards St; 604/684-9024).

Denman Street is one of the best places to experience the variety. It's also near one of Vancouver's best places, **STANLEY PARK**. A walk or bike ride around the seawall at the city's biggest urban park is a quintessential Vancouver experience. Go for lunch at **BOJANGLES** (785 Denman St; 604/687-3622), then spend the afternoon browsing shops along Denman and the Robson shopping district. Chain stores have been moving in on Robson Street, but interesting shops remain. **LUSH** (1025 Robson St; 604/687-LUSH) is an aromatic soap and lotion emporium. One of the world's best tea stores, **MURCHIE'S** (970 Robson St; 604/669-0783), has a tea that sells for $25 (Can.) per ounce (most are cheaper). You can buy an even more expensive Cuban cigar to accompany your tasty beverage at **LA CASA DEL HABANO** (980 Robson St; 604/609-0511) next door.

The famed shopping/dining district of **GASTOWN** is just a five-minute walk east. A few additional blocks farther, you can marvel at **SIKORA'S CLASSICAL RECORDS** (432 W Hastings St; 604/685-0625), a store that specializes in classical music, with thousands of CDs, used vinyl, and a staff that know their stuff. The **INUIT GALLERY** (206 Canby St; 604/688-7323) offers topnotch First Nations artwork. Designer

DOROTHY GRANT (1656 W 75th Ave; 604/681-0201; www.dorothy grant.com) may have moved out of Gastown, but she still turns First Nations patterns into exquisite clothing.

West of downtown, overlooking the Strait of Georgia, the University of British Columbia's **MUSEUM OF ANTHROPOLOGY** (6393 NW Marine Dr; 604/822-3825; www.moa.ubc.ca) is a stunning glass and concrete affair filled with totem poles and one of the world's most comprehensive collections of Northwest Coast Native artifacts.

There are plenty of distinctive dining options downtown. Among the best: **C RESTAURANT** (1600 Howe St; 604/681-1164), a contemporary seafood restaurant using classical French technique married with Asian influences and West Coast style; **DIVA,** in the Metropolitan Hotel (645 Howe St; 604/602-7788), a famed, glitzy shrine of West Coast cuisine; and **BACCHUS** (845 Hornby St; 604/608-5319), French haute cuisine two blocks away at the exceptionally charming **WEDGEWOOD HOTEL** (845 Hornby St; 604/689-7777). Budget-minded travelers will find all they can eat at **STEPHO'S GREEK TAVERNA** (1124 Davie St; 604/683-2555), but long waits are typical.

For more information on Vancouver, contact **TOURISM VANCOUVER** (604/683-2000; tourismvancouver.com) or visit the information center in the **WATERFRONT CENTRE** (200 Burrard St; 604-683-2000) across from Canada Place. Also, check out *Best Places Vancouver*.

VICTORIA

Take the passenger-only Victoria Clipper *from Pier 69 in downtown Seattle; crossing is 2½ hours.*

Victoria may have a reputation as a city of British charms and romance, but many people are beginning to see it as a soft adventure destination as well. Ever since the Cousteau Society rated it as home to the second-best winter diving in the world, it's become a big diving destination. Biking and whale watching are also popular.

First, you have to get there. Ferries range from under $20 up to $125, depending on carrier, season, embarkation point, and whether you're driving or afoot. (Victoria is very walkable.) The waterjet-propelled catamaran of the **VICTORIA CLIPPER** (206/448-5000 Seattle, 250/382-8100 Victoria, or 800/888-2535 outside Seattle and BC; www.clippervacations.com) takes foot passengers from Seattle, with four trips a day between May and September ($109 round trip in summer), once or twice a day off season. You can also fly **KENMORE AIR** (425/486-1257; kenmoreair.com) from Lake Union to the Inner Harbor for $168 round trip; **HELIJET AIRWAYS** (800/665-4354; www.helijetairways.com) from Boeing Field south of Georgetown; or **HORIZON AIR** (800/547-9308; www.horizonair.com) from Sea-Tac Airport.

Visit **TOURISM VICTORIA** (812 Wharf St; 250/953-2033; www.tourismvictoria.com) for useful information on where to go biking, diving, hiking, and whale watching, and on dozens of other activities. Victoria has an extensive system of biking trails, and **CYCLE BC RENTALS** (950 Wharf St; 250/385-2453) is just a block away. The 78-mile (125-kilometer) **GALLOPING GOOSE TRAIL** is just across the Johnson Street Bridge. If diving is your thing, it's a quick **KABUKI CAB** (bicycle cab) ride or 10-minute walk to the **OGDEN POINT DIVE CENTER** (199 Dallas Rd; 888/701-1177; www.divevictoria.com), where the experts can outfit you and have you out diving in the breakwater in no time flat.

For more traditional touring, hop on one of **TALLY HO**'s (250/383-5067) horse-drawn carriages for a fun city history lesson. The one-hour narrated tour, with humorous historical asides, starts at the **PARLIAMENT BUILDINGS** (Belleville and Menzies) and winds through Beacon Hill Park to the waterfront and James Bay. The company also offers private tours. The **ROYAL BRITISH COLUMBIA MUSEUM** (Belleville and Government Sts; 250/387-3701; www.rbcm.gov.bc.ca) has dramatic dioramas of natural landscapes and reconstructions of Victorian storefronts, as well as a Northwest Coast Indian exhibit of spiritual and cultural artifacts (open every day). The **ART GALLERY OF GREATER VICTORIA** (1040 Moss St; 250/384-4101; www.aggv.bc.ca) features a world-class Asian art collection, including North America's only Shinto shrine, and engaging contemporary exhibits throughout the year (open every day). It's in the Rockland neighborhood, a five-minute walk from downtown. Also nearby is **CRAIGDARROCH CASTLE** (1050 Joan Crescent; 250/592-5323; www.craigdarrochcastle.com), built by coal tycoon Robert Dunsmuir in the 1890s to compensate his wife for having to live in the then wild hinterlands. Open every day.

Want to see more homes? There are five **VICTORIA HERITAGE HOMES** (250/387-4697 information) downtown, including Helmcken House (behind Thunderbird Park, east of the Columbia Museum), Point Ellice House (Bay and Pleasant Sts), Craigflower Manor (110 Island Hwy), Craigflower Schoolhouse (Admirals Rd and Gorge Rd W), and painter Emily Carr's childhood home, Carr House (Government and Simcoe Sts). (Admission to each is $5; seasonal closures.)

Another grand old building worth a visit is **THE FAIRMONT EMPRESS** (721 Government St; 250/384-8111 or 250/389-2727 tea reservations; www.fairmont.com). The turn-of-the-19th-century Edwardian edifice isn't just a landmark, it's still an operating hotel. Afternoon tea at 12:30pm (summer only), 2pm, 3:30pm, and 5pm is a Victoria tradition. The hotel's Bengal Lounge is known for its curry buffet and martinis. Also still in use is the **MCPHERSON PLAYHOUSE** (3 Centennial Sq; 250/386-6121), another classic building. The former Pantages vaudeville house offers evening entertainment throughout the year. The free *Monday Magazine* contains the city's best weekly calendar of events.

Victoria has more than just old buildings. Just south of downtown, the 177-acre **BEACON HILL PARK** provides spectacular water views and beautiful landscaping (some of it wild). The **BEACON HILL CHILDREN'S FARM** is a kid-friendly minizoo that includes a turtle house, aviary, and petting corral (admission fee; closed in winter). **CRYSTAL GARDEN** (713 Douglas St; 250/381-1213) is a turn-of-the-19th-century swimming-pool-building-turned-glass-conservatory with a tropical theme, a fine place to spend a rainy day (admission fee; open daily). Just across the street is the **VICTORIA CONFERENCE CENTRE**, linked to the Empress Hotel by a beautifully restored conservatory. Also within walking distance of the park is **ABIGAIL'S HOTEL** (1906 McClure St; 250/388-5363), a four-story, 22-room Tudor manor.

What would a trip be without shopping? The area around the Empress Hotel is a great place to browse. **W & J WILSON CLOTHIERS** (1221 Government St; 250/383-7177) sells European-style clothing and Scottish cashmere sweaters; **SASQUATCH TRADING COMPANY** (1233 Government St; 250/386-9033) offers Cowichan sweaters and Native art; **OLD MORRIS TOBACCONIST** (1116 Government St; 250/382-4811) carries fine pipes, tobaccos, and Cuban cigars; and **MUNRO'S BOOKS** (1108 Government St; 250/382-2464), an early-20th-century bank-building-turned-bookstore, is one of Canada's largest independent bookstores. Don't forget the Victoria creams at **ROGERS' CHOCOLATES** (913 Government St; 250/384-7021); the **ENGLISH SWEET SHOP** (738 Yates St; 250/382-3325) for chocolates, black-currant pastilles, and Pontefract cakes; or **BERNARD CALLEBAUT CHOCOLATERIE** (621 Broughton St; 250/380-1515) for beautiful Belgian chocolates.

MARKET SQUARE (between Wharf and Store Sts on Johnson St) is a restored 19th-century courtyard surrounded by three floors of shops and restaurants. A few blocks farther north at Fisgard Street is **CHINATOWN**, marked by the Gate of Harmonious Interest. A growing number of upscale boutiques, non-Chinese bistros, and lofts are now encroaching on the area's original mix of Chinese restaurants and greengrocers, however. Walk through **FAN TAN ALLEY**, the country's narrowest thoroughfare, which originally was a discreet passageway into the area's opium dens and gambling parlors. Visit **PANACEA, THE FURNITURE ART COMPANY** (532 Fisgard St; 250/391-8960) and have a bubble tea—a concoction of green or red tea and fruit flavorings poured over tapioca pearls. On Fisgard Street, enjoy an unpretentious Chinese dinner at **WAH LAI YUEN** (560 Fisgard St; 250/381-5355). A block north of Chinatown you can stop in at the Victoria institution **HERALD STREET CAFFE** (546

Herald St; 250/381-1441) for tasty West Coast cuisine, a great wine cellar, and walls festooned with funky art.

Antique hunters should head east of downtown, up Fort Street, to **ANTIQUE ROW**—the 800 to 1100 block—which boasts block after block of shops, ending with **FAITH GRANT THE CONNOISSEUR SHOP** (1156 Fort St; 250/383-0121). Visit **BASTION SQUARE** (bounded by View and Fort Sts and Wharf and Government Sts) for sidewalk restaurants, galleries, and the **MARITIME MUSEUM OF BRITISH COLUMBIA** (250/385-4222; www.mmbc.bc.ca), the location of Victoria's old gallows. The museum has apparently become a hotspot for ghost sightings. If you want to learn about others, take the **GHOSTLY WALKS** (250/384-6698) tour. Held nightly in July and August and weekends during October's Ghosts of Victoria Festival, the tours start at the Visitor Info Center and visit alleys, squares, and many of Olde Town's happy haunting grounds. Admission is $10 for adults. Don't miss Bastion Square's great gardeners' shop, called **DIG THIS** (250/385-3212).

Located 13 miles (21 kilometers) north of town is one of Victoria's most impressive landmarks, the **BUTCHART GARDENS** (250/652-5256; www.butchartgardens.com). The result of Jenny Butchart's mission to relandscape her husband's limestone quarry is now a mecca for gardening enthusiasts, with 50 acres of beautifully manicured gardens. It's best to go early in the morning, when the dew is still on the grass, or late afternoon in summer, after the busloads of tourists have departed. Afternoon tea and light meals are served in the garden's teahouse. Entertainment and fireworks are featured on Saturday night in July and August. (Admission fee; open daily.)

The **ESQUIMALT AND NANAIMO RAILWAY** (450 Pandora Ave; 800/561-3949 or 800/561-8630) has a morning run from a mock-Victorian station near the Johnson Street Bridge to up-island resorts. It's a slow, scenic trip and there's no food served aboard. The **PACIFIC WILDERNESS RAILWAY** (250/381-8600; www.pacificwildernessrailway.com) also offers a variety of narrated sightseeing tours on restored vintage 1950s diesel electric locomotives.

RECREATION

RECREATION

Outdoor Activities

Seattleites are an active lot. We ski, sail, run, row, and in-line skate—and then we go on vacation and take up new sports. It's part of why people come here: you can drive to Snoqualmie Pass and ski the slopes in the morning, then be home in time for an afternoon sail on Puget Sound. If you're unfamiliar with the region, a good place to start planning your activity is at one of the five local branches of **REI** (Recreational Equipment Inc.), the largest of which is at its flagship store downtown (222 Yale Ave N, Denny Regrade; 206/223-1944 or 888/873-1938; www.rei. com; map:H2). REI has a generous stock of guidebooks for all outdoor sports, as well as U.S. Geological Survey maps and other equipment (see Outdoor Gear in the Shopping chapter). The U.S. Forest Service/ National Park Service **OUTDOOR RECREATION INFORMATION CENTER** located in the downtown REI (206/470-4060; map:H2) offers trail reports, maps, guidebooks, and weather information. Its staff can also direct you to a ranger station near your destination. For some basic information on some of the city's best—or most accessible—outdoor activities, read on. And please remember, if you lack skills or experience, get training and guidance before you start.

BASKETBALL

While pro basketball doesn't hold locals' attention as raptly as does baseball, there are 58 public courts around the city upon which to practice your jump shot. Beyond those listed here, you can get more information on-line from the **SEATTLE PARKS DEPARTMENT** site (www.ci.seattle.wa. us/parks/athletics/basketba.htm).

DENNY PLAYFIELD / Westlake Ave and Denny Wy, Denny Regrade The benches, greenery, and quiet make the full court at Denny Playfield a good spot to watch a pickup game or play one. No need to bring a ball, really. Across the street is the Athletic Supply Company (224 Westlake Ave N; 206/623-8972). *Map:F4*

GREEN LAKE COMMUNITY CENTER / 7201 E Green Lake Dr N, Green Lake; 206/684-0780 There is a full lighted outdoor court, as well as a full indoor court, at Green Lake Park, which has a rep as being a hot spot for a pickup game. *Map:EE7*

NATE MCMILLAN BASKETBALL COURT / 5th Ave N and Republican St, Seattle Center; 206/281-5800, ext 1781 Bearing the name of the Sonics' head coach and the team's perky green and yellow colors, this lighted outdoor full court across from Memorial Stadium is open to anyone who wields a ball. For some seriously fun spectating, check out the annual

Sonics and Storm 4-on-the-Floor Basketball Tournament, for boys and girls ages 10 and up, usually held in August. *Map:C5*

UNIVERSITY HEIGHTS COMMUNITY CENTER / 5031 University Wy NE, University District; 206/527-4278 It's a little rough around the edges, but the public outdoor court at this former grade school draws a lot of weeknight and weekend hoopsters. *Map:FF7*

BICYCLING

Despite Seattle's large amount of rainfall and fairly hilly terrain, cycling—from cruising to commuting to racing—is all the rage in and around the city. Many bicycle shops **RENT BIKES** for the day or week, from mountain to tandem to kids' bikes. Some even include helmets for free. Al Young Bike & Ski (3615 NE 45th St, Sand Point; 206/524-2642; map:FF6), Bicycle Center (4529 Sand Point Wy NE, Sand Point; 206/523-8300; map:FF6), and Gregg's Greenlake Cycle (7007 Wood-lawn Ave NE, Green Lake; 206/523-1822; map:EE7) are all near major bicycle trails. Downtown, you can rent bikes from Blazing Saddles (1230 Western Ave; 206/341-9994), near the waterfront.

CASCADE BICYCLE CLUB organizes group rides nearly every day, ranging from a social pace to strenuous workouts. Check out the hotline (206/522-BIKE; www.cascade.org) for current listings, information about cycling in the Northwest, and upcoming events. The legendary **SEATTLE-TO-PORTLAND CLASSIC** (STP) is a weekend odyssey in which approximately 10,000 cyclists pedal from the University of Washington to downtown Portland in late June or early July. Late February's **CHILLY HILLY**, a 33-mile trek on the rolling terrain of Bainbridge Island, marks the beginning of cycling season. Cascade's hotline has information on both rides.

The Seattle Parks and Recreation Department (206/684-4075; www.pan.ci.seattle.wa.us/td/satsun.asp) sponsors monthly **BICYCLE SATURDAYS/SUNDAYS** (generally the second Saturday and third Sunday of each month, May through September) along Lake Washington Boulevard, from Mount Baker Beach to Seward Park (map:II5–JJ5), which closes to auto traffic. Anyone with a bike is welcome to participate. This great activity offers a serene look at the boulevard and provides a haven for little cyclers who are not yet street-savvy.

The city **BICYCLE AND PEDESTRIAN PROGRAM** (206/684-7583) provides a biker's map of Seattle. (See also the trails listed under Running in this chapter.) Following are some of the area's favored rides.

ALKI TRAIL / Harbor Ave SW at Fairmount Ave SW to Fauntleroy Wy SW, West Seattle This 8-mile West Seattle route from Seacrest Marina to Lincoln Park has great views of downtown and Puget Sound. The first half is on a paved bike/pedestrian path along Alki Beach Park to the Alki Point lighthouse; the remainder is along roads (primarily Beach Drive

SW) wide enough for both bikes and cars. On sunny weekend days, it is often crowded. *Map:II9–KK9*

BAINBRIDGE ISLAND LOOP / Start a bike expedition on the island by taking your bicycle on the ferry—porting a bike costs only 90 cents more than the walk-on fee and allows you to avoid waiting in long car-ferry lines. The signed, hilly 30-mile route follows low-traffic roads around the island. Start on Ferncliff (heading north) at the Winslow ferry terminal (avoid Highway 305) and follow the signs.

BLUE RIDGE / **NW 105th St at 8th Ave NW to 32nd Ave NW near NW 85th St, Crown Hill** The view of Puget Sound and the Olympic Mountains is spectacular on this less-than-2-mile ride. From NW 105th Street at Eighth Avenue NW (just south of Carkeek Park), head west onto NW Woodbine Way, where the Blue Ridge neighborhood begins. Stay on the ridgetop roads all the way south to Golden Gardens Park at 32nd Avenue NW, near NW 85th Street. *Map:DD8–DD9*

BURKE-GILMAN TRAIL / **8th Ave NW and Leary Wy, Fremont, to Kenmore** A popular off-street route for Seattle cyclers commuting to downtown or the U District, this 12.5-mile path is also great for the bicyclist who wants great views of the city, waterways, and Lake Washington. The Burke-Gilman Trail, built on an old railway bed, has a trailhead on the Fremont-Ballard border, from which it meanders along the ship canal and Lake Union in Wallingford, through the University of Washington and Sand Point, along the west shore of Lake Washington, and ends at Kenmore's Logboom Park (Tracy Owen Station Park). From here cyclists can continue east a couple of miles to Bothell Landing and the start of the Sammamish River Trail. *Map:FF7–BB5*

ELLIOTT BAY TRAIL / **Pier 70 to Elliott Bay Marina, Waterfront** You get a grand view on this brief ride along Puget Sound. The 1.5-mile-long trail skirts the waterfront, passes between the grain terminal and its loading dock, winds its way through a parking lot of cars right off the ship, and continues to the Elliott Bay Marina. It's full of runners and in-line skaters at noontime. *Map:HH8–GG8*

LAKE WASHINGTON BOULEVARD / **Madrona Dr, Madrona, to Seward Park Ave S, Rainier Valley** There are great views along this serene 5-mile stretch between Madrona and Seward Parks. The road is narrow in spots, but bicycles have a posted right-of-way. On Bicycle Saturdays and Sundays, the southern portion (from Mount Baker Beach south) is closed to cars (see intro above). On other days, riders may feel safer using the asphalt path that follows this portion of the road. Riders can continue south, via S Juneau Street, Seward Park Avenue S, and Rainier Avenue S, to the Renton Municipal Airport and around the south end of Lake

Washington, then return via the protected bike lane of I-90. This makes for a 35-mile ride. Take a map with you. *Map:HH6–JJ5*

MERCER ISLAND LOOP / Martin Luther King Jr Wy on I-90 lid, Central District, to E and W Mercer Wy, Mercer Island From Seattle, a bicycles-only tunnel (entrance in I-90 lid park at Martin Luther King Jr Wy) leads to the I-90 bridge on the way to Mercer Island. Using E and W Mercer Way, you'll ride over moderate rolling hills the length of this 14-mile loop. The roads are curving and narrow, so avoid rush hour. The most exhilarating portion of the ride is through the wooded S-curves on the eastern side of the island. *Map:II4–KK4*

SAMMAMISH RIVER TRAIL / Bothell Landing off Hwy 522 to Marymoor Park, Redmond This flat, peacefully rural route follows the flowing Sammamish River for 9.5 miles. Stop for a picnic at parklike Chateau Ste. Michelle Winery, just off the trail at NE 145th Street (bring your own lunch or buy one there), or visit Columbia Winery or the Redhook Brewery. Bike rentals are available at Sammamish Valley Cycle (8451 164th Ave NE, Redmond; 425/881-8442; map:EE2). *Map:BB3–FF1*

SEWARD PARK LOOP / S Juneau St and Lake Washington Blvd S, Rainier Valley Take this paved and traffic-free 2.5-mile road around the wooded Bailey Peninsula in Seward Park, which juts out into Lake Washington. The peaceful ride offers a look at what may be the only old-growth forest left on the shores of the lake, and occasional eagles soaring overhead. *Map:JJ5*

GOLFING

There are a number of fine public golf courses in Seattle and environs, many in wonderfully scenic surroundings.

BELLEVUE MUNICIPAL GOLF COURSE / 5500 140th Ave NE, Bellevue; 425/452-7250 This course (5,547 yards), the busiest in the state, is fairly level and easy. Eighteen holes, PNGA 66.5. *Map:FF2*

GOLF CLUB AT NEWCASTLE / 15500 Six Penny Ln, Bellevue; 425/793-GOLF The rates here are steep, but the view from the two 18-hole courses (6,011 yards) at this hilltop club is impressive; it also has an 18-hole putting course. PNGA 74.6. *www.newcastlegolf; map:JJ2&*

INTERBAY FAMILY GOLF CENTER / 2501 15th Ave W, Interbay; 206/285-2200 The best par-3 course in the city, Interbay is conveniently located and has a driving range and an 18-hole miniature golf course. *Map:GG8*

JACKSON PARK MUNICIPAL GOLF COURSE / 1000 NE 135TH ST, LAKE CITY; 206/363-4747 An interesting—but crowded—course over rolling hills, Jackson Park has a huge, well-maintained putting green, a nicely secluded chipping green, and a great short nine, which is sparsely played.

Eighteen holes, 5,878 yards, PNGA 66.8. *www.jacksonparkgolf;* *map:*CC7

JEFFERSON PARK GOLF COURSE / 4101 Beacon Ave S, Beacon Hill; **206/762-4513** You get great views of the city from the hilltop fairways of this enormously popular course, which has a driving range. Eighteen holes, 5,857 yards, PNGA 67. *www.jeffersonparkgolf; map:*JJ6

RIVERBEND GOLF COMPLEX / 2019 W Meeker, Kent; 253/854-3673 The complex includes an 18-hole course (6,266 yards), a nine-hole par-3 course, and a driving range. PNGA 68.6.

WEST SEATTLE MUNICIPAL GOLF COURSE / 4470 35th Ave SW, West Seattle; 206/935-5187 A good but forgiving course just west of the Duwamish River, tucked into an undulating valley, which makes for some surprising lies. Tee times are the easiest to come by in the city, views of which are spectacular on the back nine. Eighteen holes, 6,175 yards, PNGA 68.9. *www.westseattlegolf; map:*JJ8

HIKING

The hiking in Washington is superlative. Alpine lakes, rain forests, ocean cliffs, mountain meadows—all are within easy access of Seattle, and day hikers can count on reaching any of a score of trailheads within an hour or two. For this reason, the national parks, state parks, national forests, and wilderness areas nearby are heavily used, but conservation efforts have managed to stay a small step ahead of the impacts.

Like any other outdoor activity, hiking requires a marriage of caution and adventurous spirit. Always carry water and bring extra clothing (wool or synthetics such as polypropylene—not cotton) and rain gear, even if it's 80 degrees and sunny when you set out and you plan only a short hike. Remember, it can rain here almost anytime. Permits may be required for hiking or camping. Check with the local ranger station before setting out, and buy a trailhead parking permit at a ranger station or outdoor equipment store if necessary; a Northwest Forest Pass, good at Forest Service trailheads in Oregon and Washington, is $30 per year or $5 per day. In general, national forests require free backcountry permits for hiking, and national parks usually charge fees to enter the park but none to hike.

Good hiking guides are published in association with **THE MOUN-TAINEERS** (300 3rd Ave W, Queen Anne; 206/284-6310 or 800/573-8484 in Western Washington; www.mountaineers.org; map:A9), a venerable and prominent outdoors club whose bookstore—open to the public—has the largest collection of climbing, hiking, mountain biking, and paddling books in the Pacific Northwest. Another reliable information tap to the outdoors is the Seattle branch of the **SIERRA CLUB** (8511 15th Ave NE, Ste 201, Maple Leaf; 206/523-2147; www.sierraclub.org;

map:EE6). The **WASHINGTON TRAILS ASSOCIATION** (1305 4th Ave, Ste 512, Downtown; 206/625-1367; www.wta.org/wta; map:K6), a non-profit outreach group, welcomes telephone inquiries about hiking. A good source of information in book form is *Inside Out Washington* by Ron C. Judd. Here are some popular nearby hiking areas, described broadly by region.

The most easily accessible hiking area from Seattle (20 miles east of Seattle via I-90), the comely Cascade foothills called the **ISSAQUAH ALPS** have dozens of day trails frequented by both hikers and horseback riders. The Issaquah Alps Trails Club (PO Box 351, Issaquah, WA 98027; 206/328-0480; www.issaquahalps.org) organizes day hikes through the hills, ranging from short and easy to strenuous—a good way to introduce children to hiking.

The best hiking near Seattle is in the **CENTRAL CASCADES** between Snoqualmie Pass (via I-90 due east) and Stevens Pass (via Highway 2 to the north), one to two hours from the city. The Central Cascades are mainly national forest and wilderness areas, including the **ALPINE LAKES WILDERNESS,** a scenic marvel. A gorgeous section of the Pacific Crest Trail cuts through the wilderness along the mountain ridges.

Good hiking can also be found farther from the city in the **NORTH CASCADES** (between Stevens Pass and the Canadian border via State Route 20), with glaciers, summer alpine flowers, and blazing fall colors; part of this area is in remote and rugged **NORTH CASCADES NATIONAL PARK** (360/856-5700, visitor info). The **OLYMPIC MOUNTAINS** (on the Olympic Peninsula; see the Day Trips chapter) feature **OLYMPIC NATIONAL PARK** (visitors center: 3002 Mount Angeles Rd, Port Angeles, WA 98362; 360/452-0330; www.nps.gov) and striking Hurricane Ridge. In the **SOUTH CASCADES** (between Snoqualmie Pass and the Oregon border via US Highway 12 and others), the highlight is **MOUNT RAINIER NATIONAL PARK** (see the Day Trips chapter).

KAYAKING/CANOEING

In a city that is girdled by water, one of the best ways to explore is by boat. Several locations around Seattle rent canoes and kayaks for day excursions. A good general resource is *Boatless in Seattle: Getting on the Water in Western Washington Without Owning a Boat!* by Sue Hacking. For those who want instruction on kayaking, perhaps in preparation for a whitewater trip, one of the oldest kayaking clubs in the nation is the **WASHINGTON KAYAK CLUB** (PO Box 24264, Seattle, WA 98124; 206/433-1983; www.wakayakclub.com), a safety- and conservation-oriented club that organizes swimming-pool practices, weekend trips, and sea- and whitewater-kayaking lessons in the spring. Several companies rent kayaks by the hour year-round, and some will set you up with a cartop rack for longer trips or those farther afield, spring through fall. Here are some favorite places to paddle.

From Tukwila (where the Green River becomes the Duwamish) to Boeing Field (map:QQ5–JJ7), the scenic **DUWAMISH RIVER** waterway makes for a lovely paddle. North of Boeing, you pass industrial salvage ships, commercial shipping lanes, and Harbor Island, where the river empties into Elliott Bay. Rent a canoe or a kayak at **PACIFIC WATER SPORTS** (16055 Pacific Hwy S, SeaTac; 206/246-9385; map:OO6) near Sea-Tac Airport—the staff can direct you to one of several spots along the river where you can launch your craft. The current is strong at times, but not a serious hazard for moderately experienced paddlers.

GREEN LAKE's tame waters are a good place to learn the basics. **GREEN LAKE BOAT RENTALS** (7351 E Green Lake Dr N; 206/527-0171; map:EE7), a Seattle Parks and Recreation Department concession on the northeast side of the lake, rents kayaks, rowboats, paddleboats, canoes, sailboards, and sailboats. Open daily, except in bad weather, March through October.

If you've always wanted to get an up-close look at houseboats, kayaking or canoeing on **LAKE UNION** is a great way to do it. You'll also find great views of the city and, if you're ambitious, you can paddle west from the lake down the Lake Washington Ship Canal, past the clanking of boatyards and the aroma of fish-laden boats to Elliott Bay, or east into Lake Washington. Rent sea kayaks at **NORTHWEST OUTDOOR CENTER** (2100 Westlake Ave N, Ste 1, Westlake; 206/281-9694 or 800/683-0637; www.nwoc.com; map:GG7). NWOC also offers classes and tours. **MOSS BAY ROWING & KAYAKING CENTER** (1001 Fairview Ave N, South Lake Union; 206/682-2031) rents kayaks hourly, as does **AGUA VERDE CAFE & PADDLE CLUB** (1303 NE Boat St, University District; 206/545-8570; www.aguaverde.com; map:FF6). Reservations are recommended on summer weekends for these Lake Union rental outlets.

On a typical hot August day, drivers sitting in bumper-to-bumper commuter traffic on the Evergreen Point Bridge gaze longingly at canoeists in the marshlands of the **WASHINGTON PARK ARBORETUM AND MONTLAKE CUT** (map:GG6). Rent a canoe or a rowboat at low rates at the University of Washington **WATERFRONT ACTIVITIES CENTER** (206/543-9433; map:FF6) behind Husky Stadium, February through October. Here the mirrorlike waters are framed by a mosaic of green lily pads and white flowers.

Seattle's proximity to the open waters and scenic island coves of **PUGET SOUND** makes for ideal sea kayaking. Bainbridge Island's **EAGLE HARBOR** is a leisurely paddle in protected waters. Tiny **BLAKE ISLAND**, a state park, is a short trip from Vashon Island, Alki Point, or Fort Ward State Park on Bainbridge Island. Bird-watchers can head for the calm waters of the **NISQUALLY DELTA** and Nisqually National Wildlife Refuge off I-5 between Tacoma and Olympia. And the **SAN JUAN ISLANDS** to the north provide endless paddling opportunities, though the currents can be strong, and unguided kayaking here is not for novices.

The trip up the gently flowing **SAMMAMISH SLOUGH** (map: BB5–FF1) is quiet and scenic. Ambitious canoeists can follow the slough from the north end of Lake Washington at Bothell all the way to Lake Sammamish, about 15 miles to the southeast, passing golf courses, the town of Woodinville, wineries, and Marymoor Park. In Redmond, you can rent from **AQUASPORTS PADDLE CENTER** (7907 159th Pl NE; 425/869-7067; map:EE1).

MOUNTAIN BIKING

Though all of the aforementioned trails are great jaunts for those with mountain bikes, the advantage of mountain bikes is that they can be taken off-road.

Unfortunately, the booming popularity of mountain biking in the past few years presents something of a dilemma to environmentalists as well as bikers. The very trails that provide an optimum off-road experience—ones that were once quiet, remote, untouched—are those that often end up closed by the Forest Service because of the damage caused by increasing numbers of bikers. The **OUTDOOR RECREATION INFORMATION CENTER** (206/470-4060) provides information on trail closures. The **BACKCOUNTRY BICYCLE TRAILS CLUB** (206/283-2995; www.bbtc.org) organizes local rides and is adamant about teaching "soft-riding" techniques that protect trails from the roughing-up that can eventually cause closures. The best local guidebook is *Kissing the Trail: Greater Seattle Mountain Bike Adventures* by John Zilly, available at bookstores and biking and outdoor retail outlets.

For downhill rides, ski areas such as Crystal Mountain and the Summit at Snoqualmie open their trails to bikes in summer—complete with lift rides up the mountain (see Snow Sports in this chapter). Below are some other options.

DECEPTION PASS STATE PARK / South of Anacortes off Hwy 20 on Whidbey and Fidalgo Islands; 360/902-8844 An hour and a half northwest by car from Seattle, Deception Pass is without doubt one of the most beautiful wild spots in Washington. And it has more than 16 miles of bike trails that rise and fall over 1,000 feet of elevation. Trails climb to high rocky bluffs with views of the San Juan Islands, then descend to sandy beaches. The trails are single-track, and not all of the park is open to mountain bikes.

ST. EDWARDS STATE PARK / Off Juanita Dr NE, Kirkland; 360/902-8844 Up to 12 miles of varied terrain make this park great for all skill levels. Located in the Juanita neighborhood of Kirkland, it is the largest undeveloped area on Lake Washington and has 3,000 feet of shoreline. Be wary as you ride among the tall trees and up and down the 700 feet of elevation: the park's trails interweave, and it's easy to get lost if you don't pay attention. *Map:CC4*

ROCK CLIMBING

In Seattle and its environs, several indoor climbing walls—or manmade outdoor structures—allow you to get vertical for after-work relaxation or for a good rush on the weekend.

MARYMOOR CLIMBING STRUCTURE / East end of Marymoor Park off Hwy 520, Redmond; 206/296-2964 Otherwise known as Big Pointy, this 45-foot concrete-brick-and-mortar "house of cards" just south of the Velodrome was designed by the godfather of rock climbing, Don Robinson. It features climbing angles up to and over 90 degrees. *Map:FF1*

REI PINNACLE / 222 Yale Ave N, Denny Regrade; 206/223-1944 or 888/873-1938 This 65-foot freestanding indoor climbing structure (inside the REI flagship store), with more than 1,000 modular climbing holds, is very popular—waits can be as long as an hour, and you get only one ascent. You're given a beeper, however, so you can peruse the store while you wait your turn, and the climb is free. For gear, to rent and to purchase, and occasional free lectures about climbing, browse the store. *www.rei.com; map:H2*

SCHURMAN ROCK AND GLACIER / 5200 35th Ave SW, West Seattle; 206/684-7434 The rock was recently closed due to damage, but the glacier at West Seattle's Camp Long offers good—though unsupervised—climbing forays for the beginner and is a child's dream structure with deep foot- and handholds. *Map:KK8*

STONE GARDENS / 2839 NW Market St, Ballard; 206/781-9828 One section of this indoor climbing gym consists of low overhangs; the rest of the gym offers faces that can be bouldered or top-roped, with climbs for beginners to advanced. Staff members offer helpful advice, or you can take classes ranging from one-on-one beginner instruction to several levels of advanced techniques. *www.stonegardens.com; map:FF8*

VERTICAL WORLD / 15036-B NE 95th St, Redmond; 425/881-8826 / 2123 W Elmore St, Interbay; 206/283-4497 The Redmond location of this rock gym offers 7,000 square feet of textured climbing surface, while the newer, equally striking Seattle club sports 35-foot-high walls and a whopping 14,000 square feet of climbing area. The walls are fully textured, making the more than 100 routes varied and interesting. Lessons are offered at both gyms. *www.verticalworld.com; map:DD2, FF8*

Once you've attained the highest pinnacles indoors and in controlled outdoor settings, take your hardened hands and clenching toes to the great outdoors. But first stop at **THE MOUNTAINEERS** (300 3rd Ave W, Queen Anne; 206/284-6310 or 800/573-8484; www.mountaineers.org; map:A9), the largest outdoor club in the region and a superb resource, offering group climbs, climbing courses, and general information.

ROLLERSKATING/IN-LINE SKATING/SKATEBOARDING

Roller skaters and in-line skaters compose an ever-widening wedge of the urban athletic pie. In fair weather, they are found anywhere the pavement is smooth, including the downtown waterfront, along Lake Washington Boulevard, and north on the tree-shaded **BURKE-GILMAN TRAIL** that connects with the **SAMMAMISH RIVER TRAIL,** which you can follow all the way to Redmond's **MARYMOOR PARK** (see Bicycling and Running in this chapter). Note: Skate-rental shops won't let you out the door if the pavement is damp.

GREEN LAKE / E Green Lake Wy N and W Green Lake Wy N This is the skate-and-be-seen-skating spot in town, where hotdoggers in bright spandex weave and bob past cyclists, joggers, walkers, and leashed dogs. The 2.8-mile path around the lake is crowded on weekends, but during the week it's a good place to try wheels for the first time. When the wading pool on the north shore of the lake isn't filled for kids or commandeered by rollerskating hockey enthusiasts, it's a good spot to learn to skate backward. Rent or buy skates, as well as elbow and knee pads, at nearby Gregg's Greenlake Cycle (7007 Woodlawn Ave NE; 206/523-1822). *Map:EE7*

NATIONAL OCEANIC AND ATMOSPHERIC ADMINISTRATION / 7600 Sand Point Wy NE, Sand Point Another urban skating site excellent for practicing is the NOAA grounds next to Magnuson Park. This facility can be reached via the Burke-Gilman Trail, and offers a quiet workout along a smooth 1-kilometer loop, with one low-grade hill and some exciting turns. *Map:EE5*

SKATE PARK / 5th Ave and Republican St, Seattle Center Situatied across from the Space Needle, this is the only authorized skate park in the downtown area for both skateboards *and* in-line skates. Smooth concrete dips and ridges and lots of space make a great diversion when the family trip to the Needle just isn't your bag. Open every day, dawn to dusk. *Map:D5*

ROWING

In a city graced with two major lakes, many people have discovered an affinity for sleek, lightweight rowing shells and the calm silver-black water of early morning. Seattle has one of the largest populations of adult rowers in the country, and has numerous women-only, men-only, and age-specific clubs. For a full list, contact **US ROWING** (800/314-4ROW; www.usrowing.org).

The Seattle Parks and Recreation Department runs two rowing facilities: one on Green Lake, out of the **GREEN LAKE SMALL CRAFT CENTER** (5900 W Green Lake Wy N; 206/684-4074; map:EE7), and the other on Lake Washington, through the **MOUNT BAKER ROWING AND SAILING CENTER** (3800 Lake Washington Blvd S, Rainier Valley; 206/386-1913; map:JJ6). Both operate year-round, offer all levels of instruction, and host annual regattas.

The **LAKE WASHINGTON ROWING CLUB** (910 N Northlake Wy, Fremont; 206/547-1583; lakewashingtonrowing.com; map:FF7), the **POCOCK ROWING CENTER** (3320 Fuhrman Ave E, Eastlake; 206/328-0778; www.scn.org/gprf; map:FF7), and **LAKE UNION CREW** (11 E Allison St, Eastlake; 206/860-4199; www.lakeunioncrew.com; map:GG7) have competitive rowing teams, as well as introductory rowing programs. Some clubs allow experienced oarspeople to row once or twice without paying fees. Ask individual boathouses about guest policies.

RUNNING

Step out just about any door in the area and you're on a good running course, especially if you love hills. Flat routes can be found, of course, especially along bike paths (see Bicycling in this chapter). The mild climate and numerous parks make solo running appealing, yet the city also has a large, well-organized running community that provides company or competition. Club Northwest's *Northwest Runner* (pick it up in any running-gear store) is a good source for information. Racers, casual or serious, can choose from a number of annual races (at least one every weekend in spring and summer). Some of the biggest are the 4-mile **ST. PATRICK'S DAY DASH** in March, the 6.7-mile Seward-to-Madison **SHORE RUN** in July, the 8-kilometer **SEAFAIR TORCHLIGHT RUN** in August, October's 5-kilometer **RACE FOR THE CURE**, the **SEATTLE MARATHON** in November, and December's 5-kilometer **JINGLE BELL RUN**. One of the finest running outfitters in town, **SUPER JOCK 'N JILL** (7210 E Green Lake Dr N, Green Lake; 206/522-7711; www.superjock njill.com; map:EE7), maintains racing news on its web site. Listed below are some popular routes.

The 2.8-mile marked path around **GREEN LAKE** (Latona Ave NE and E Green Lake Wy N; map:EE7) has two lanes: one for wheeled traffic, the other for everybody else. On sunny weekends, Green Lake becomes a recreational Grand Central—great for people-watching, but slow going. Early mornings or early evenings, though, it's lovely, with ducks, geese, red-winged blackbirds, mountain views, and rowers and windsurfers on the lake. The path connects with a bikeway along Ravenna

Boulevard. A painted line establishes the cycling lane; runners can follow the boulevard's grassy median.

The Eastside's high-visibility running path stretches along the **KIRK-LAND WATERFRONT** (along Lake Washington Blvd, Kirkland; map:FF3–EE3) from Houghton Beach Park to Marina Park—a little over a mile one way.

Various paths cut through thickly wooded **LINCOLN PARK** (Fauntleroy Wy SW and SW Trenton St, West Seattle; map:KK9), overlooking Vashon Island and Puget Sound. The shoreline is tucked below a bluff where auto traffic can no longer be heard.

A striking run in clear weather, the **MAGNOLIA BLUFF AND DIS-COVERY PARK** route (along Magnolia Blvd W, Magnolia; map:GG9–EE9) offers vistas of the Olympic Mountains across Puget Sound. From the parking lot at Magnolia Boulevard W and W Galer Street, run north along the boulevard on a paved pedestrian trail. Magnolia Park ends at W Barrett Street; continue north for four blocks to Discovery Park, which has numerous paved and unpaved trails.

Formerly part of the Naval Air Station at Sand Point, **MAGNUSON PARK** (Sand Point Wy NE and NE 65th St, Sand Point; map:EE5) has many congenial running areas, including wide, paved roads and flat, grassy terrain, all overlooking Lake Washington. On clear days, the view of Mount Rainier is superb.

MEDINA AND EVERGREEN POINT (along Overlake Dr and Evergreen Point Rd, Bellevue; map:FF4–HH4) offer a scenic run along nicely maintained roads with views of Lake Washington and of some of the area's most stunning homes. Two and a half miles each way.

In **WASHINGTON PARK ARBORETUM** (Arboretum Dr E and Lake Washington Blvd E, Madison Valley; map:GG6), you can stay on the winding main drive, Lake Washington Boulevard E, or run along any number of paths that wend through the trees and flowers. (The main unpaved thoroughfare, Azalea Way, is strictly off-limits to joggers, however.) Lake Washington Boulevard connects with scenic E Interlaken Boulevard at the Japanese Garden and then winds down to the lake. The northern lakeside leg, from Madrona Drive south to Leschi, is popular for its wide sidewalks; farther south, from Mount Baker Park to Seward Park, sweeping views make for a pleasing run.

SAILING

Seattle has a great deal of water but, in the summer at least, precious little wind. Thus many sailors hereabouts reckon that sailing season runs from around Labor Day to the beginning of May (although in summer, late afternoon winds sometimes fill the sheets). Looking toward Seattle from its bodies of water will give you perspectives you can't get from your car.

The wannabe sailor can find classes or chartered tours. **SAILING IN SEATTLE** (2000 Westlake Ave N, Ste 46, Westlake; 206/298-0094; www.sailing-in-seattle.com; map:GG7) offers three different staffed cruises on a 33-foot sailboat: on Lake Union, through the **HIRAM M. CHITTENDEN LOCKS,** or on **LAKE WASHINGTON.** Sit back and enjoy the sights or, even if you've never sailed before, try your hand at sailing with instruction from the on-board crew. Reservations are a must. Sailing in Seattle also offers courses from beginning to advanced.

For beginners who want to learn to sail in a smaller boat and have a few days to pick up the essentials, the **GREEN LAKE SMALL CRAFT CENTER** (5900 W Green Lake Wy N, Green Lake; 206/684-4074; map:EE7), at the southwest corner of the lake, offers classes. Green Lake, no more than a mile across in any direction, is the perfect place to learn: it's free from motor cruisers, floatplanes, and barge traffic. **MOUNT BAKER ROWING AND SAILING CENTER** (3800 Lake Washington Blvd S, Rainier Valley; 206/386-1913; map:II6), on Lake Washington, also offers sailing lessons in small boats.

Salty dogs who want to be their own skipper should try a classic wooden boat at the **CENTER FOR WOODEN BOATS** (1010 Valley St, South Lake Union; 206/382-2628; www.cwb.org; map:D1). Call and schedule a free checkout to show them you know how to tack, jibe, and dock under sail (takes about 25 minutes), and then access to the fleet of rental boats is yours; rowboats require no skills demonstration. Rates range from $10 to $37.50 per hour; viewing exhibits is free. Visitors are encouraged to touch the center's approximately 100 historic boats and to ask questions of the volunteers.

SNOW SPORTS

The rain that falls on Seattle turns to snow at higher elevations in the winter—making for wonderful skiing. And although some call the rain-thickened, heavy snow of the region's skiing areas "Cascade concrete," most mornings a new layer of white has blanketed the slopes. Several ski areas have weekend shuttle buses leaving from Seattle. If you plan to drive, carry tire chains and a shovel, and inquire ahead about **ROAD CONDITIONS** (800/695-7623; www.wsdot.wa.gov/traveler). All local downhill ski facilities rent skis, snowboards, and other gear. Many rental outlets are available in the city as well.

Though commercial downhill ski areas have ski patrols, skiers in unpatrolled areas or in the mountainous backcountry should heed the constant danger of avalanche. Conditions change daily (sometimes hourly), so always call the Forest Service's **NORTHWEST AVALANCHE INFORMATION HOTLINE** (206/526-6677) before setting out. Finally, if you are heading off into the backwoods, most plowed parking areas near trailheads and along state highways require a Sno-Park permit (800/233-0321), which costs $20 per vehicle for the winter season (using groomed trails requires an additional $20 grooming sticker). A one-day Sno-Park permit is $8 for all areas. These can be purchased at local retail outlets.

Below are the ski areas most accessible to Seattleites, with information about downhill and cross-country skiing. For daily updates on conditions in downhill areas, call the **CASCADE SKI REPORT** (206/634-0200 winter only).

CRYSTAL MOUNTAIN RESORT / 1 Crystal Mountain Blvd, Crystal Mountain, WA 98022; 360/663-2265, 888/754-6199 snow conditions Nine chairlifts lead to 55 groomed trails of more than 3,300 skiable acres of snow. On a clear day, the 7,002-foot vantage point at the top of Green Valley affords a tremendous view of Mount Rainier and Mount St. Helens. A six-person chairlift makes getting up the mountain easy for the beginner or the expert, and there's weekend night skiing all winter long. Nordic skiers will be charmed by Silver Basin's big, broad open area. The ski patrol here monitors your whereabouts if you check in and out, and for 50 cents they supply area topographical maps. *www.skicrystal.com/; 76 miles southeast of Seattle on SR 410*

I-90 CORRIDOR / Exits 54 to 71; 800/233-0321 The U.S. Forest Service offers a wide variety of marked cross-country trails here, which are free and close to Seattle, but you must have a Sno-Park pass to use the parking lots (see intro above). At **CRYSTAL SPRINGS/LAKE KEECHELUS** (top of Snoqualmie Pass off exit 54), Sno-Parks are at either end of a 11.2-kilometer trail that runs along the shores of Lake Keechelus. Crystal Springs has a concession stand with hot drinks and snacks. **CABIN CREEK** (10 miles east of Snoqualmie Pass, off exit 63) has 12 kilometers of trails (some of them groomed); the ones on the south side are easy, and the ones on the north side are intermediate, with plenty of turns. At **IRON HORSE SNO-PARK** (off exit 71), about 10 miles of easy, flat trails around Lake Easton and Iron Horse State Park are combined with a 12-mile trek from Easton to Cle Elum (not always accessible). For more trails, call the state for a brochure, or contact local outdoor retailers to learn which trails are at their best. *76–91 miles east of Seattle off I-90*

METHOW VALLEY / Methow Valley Sport Trails Association: PO Box 147, Winthrop, WA 98862; 800/682-5787 One of the top Nordic ski areas in the country, the Methow Valley offers the charm of Vermont, the snow conditions of Utah, and the big sky of Montana. Too far from Seattle for a day trip, its 175 kilometers of groomed trails make for a great weekend getaway. The valley towns of Mazama, Winthrop, and Twisp offer an ample number of lodges, guides, lessons, and rental shops. Contact Central Reservations (800/422-3048; www.mvcentralres.com) for hut-to-hut skiing or housing/rental reservations. *www.mvsta.com; 250 miles northeast of Seattle off SR 20*

MOUNT BAKER SKI AREA / 1019 Iowa St, Bellingham, WA 98226; 360/734-6771, 360/671-0211 snow conditions The first area to open and the last to close during the ski season, Mount Baker—which has the highest average annual snowfall (595 inches) in North America—is a terrific weekend destination, though most of the lodgings are in Glacier, about 17 miles to the west. The view is remarkable; the runs are varied but mostly intermediate, with one bowl, meadows, trails, and wooded areas. Snowboarders (welcome on all runs) test their mettle in the Legendary Banked Slalom Race, held on the last weekend in January. No night skiing. On the northeastern flank of Mount Baker, Nordic skiers find sporadically groomed trails. Rentals and lessons are available in the main lodge. *www.mtbakerskiarea.com; 56 miles east of Bellingham off I-5 on SR 542*

MOUNT RAINIER NATIONAL PARK / Ashford, WA 98304; 360/569-2211 ext 3314 See the Day Trips chapter for details on Mount Rainer. *www.nps.gov/mora/; 86 miles southeast of Seattle off SR 706*

STEVENS PASS / PO Box 98, Skykomish, WA 98288; 206/812-4510, 206/634-1645 winter conditions, 800/695-7623 road conditions Challenging and interesting terrain makes Stevens Pass a favorite for many skiers. Ten chairlifts lead to a variety of runs and breathtaking Cascade views. Snowboarders, welcome on all runs, tend to congregate near the Skyline Express and Brooks lifts, where nearby is a half-pipe and a roped-off terrain park. For Nordic skiing, head farther east on Highway 2 to the full-service Stevens Pass Nordic Center, complete with rentals, instruction, hot food and drink, and 25 kilometers of groomed trails over a variety of terrain. The Nordic Center is touted as having the best white stuff within 90 minutes of Seattle, but it's open only Friday through Sunday and holidays. *www.stevenspass.com; 78 miles northeast of Seattle on Hwy 2 (Nordic Center, 5 miles east)*

THE SUMMIT AT SNOQUALMIE / PO Box 1068, Snoqualmie Pass, WA 98068; 425/434-7669, 206/236-1600 snow conditions Now consisting of four neighboring sections along I-90—Alpental, Summit Central (formerly Ski Acres), Summit West (formerly Snoqualmie Summit), and Summit East (formerly Hyak)—this complex offers many options for skiers of all abilities. Linked by a free shuttle-bus service (three are also linked by ski trails), all four honor the same lift ticket, but each has its own appeal. Alpental, for example, boasts high-grade challenges, including a nationally recognized run. Summit Central offers intermediate-to-expert runs, and most of the mountain is open for night skiing. Summit West's gentler slopes are ideal for children, beginners, and intermediate skiers. Dozens of ski and snowboard classes operate here. Summit East, the smallest, caters to intermediate skiers. The new Summit Nordic Center at Summit East has 50 kilometers of trails—some accessed by two chairlifts—to please skiers of any ability level. The center also offers lessons and ski rentals, a yurt, and a warming hut. *www.summit-at-snoqualmie.com; 47 miles east of Seattle off I-90 at exit 52*

TENNIS

Tennis is popular here, but not so much so that it's impossible to get a public court. There's only one indoor public tennis facility in the city: **SEATTLE TENNIS CENTER** (2000 Martin Luther King Jr Wy S, Rainier Valley; 206/684-4764; map:II6), with 10 indoor courts (there are also four unlighted outdoor courts). Most public outdoor courts in the city are run by the Seattle Parks and Recreation Department and are available either on a first-come, first-served basis or by reservation for $6 per hour. Players can make phone reservations up to two weeks in advance (206/684-4077) with a major credit card (AE, MC, or V). Otherwise, reservations must be made in person at the scheduling office of **SEATTLE PARKS AND RECREATION** (5201 Green Lake Wy N, Green Lake; map:EE7). If it rains, your money is refunded.

The Eastside has a similar facility, **ROBINSWOOD TENNIS CENTER** (2400 151st Pl SE, Bellevue; 425/452-7690; map:II2), which has four lighted outdoor (two covered) and four indoor courts. Eastside outdoor public courts cannot be reserved in advance. The best time to play is early in the day; in spring and summer, the lines start at about 3pm.

Most private Seattle tennis courts do not sell weekly or daily memberships. Following is a list of the best outdoor public courts in the area.

BRYANT: two unlighted courts. *40th Ave NE and NE 65th St, View Ridge; map:EE5*

GRASS LAWN PARK: six lighted courts. *7031 148th Ave NE, Redmond; map:EE2*

HILLAIRE PARK: two unlighted courts. *15731 NE 6th St, Bellevue; map:HH1*

HOMESTEAD FIELD: four unlighted courts. *82nd Ave SE and SE 40th St, Mercer Island; map:II4*

KILLARNEY GLEN PARK: two unlighted courts. *1933 104th Ave SE, Bellevue; map:HH3*

LINCOLN PARK: six lighted courts. *Fauntleroy Ave SW and SW Webster St, West Seattle; map:KK9*

LOWER WOODLAND PARK: 10 lighted courts. *W Green Lake Wy N, Green Lake; map:FF7*

LUTHER BURBANK PARK: three unlighted courts. *2040 84th Ave SE, Mercer Island; map:II4*

MAGNOLIA PLAYFIELD: four courts (two lighted). *34th Ave W and W Smith St, Magnolia; map:GG9*

MARYMOOR PARK: four lighted courts. *6046 W Lake Sammamish Pkwy NE, Redmond; map:FF1*

MEADOWBROOK: six lighted courts. *30th Ave NE and NE 107th St, Lake City; map:DD6*

MONTLAKE PARK: two unlighted courts. *1618 E Calhoun St, Montlake; map:GG6*

NORWOOD VILLAGE: two unlighted courts. *12309 SE 23rd Pl, Bellevue; map:II2*

RAINIER PLAYFIELD: four lighted courts. *Rainier Ave S and S Alaska St, Columbia City; map:JJ5*

RIVERVIEW: two unlighted courts. *12th Ave SW and SW Othello St, West Seattle; map:KK7*

VOLUNTEER PARK: four courts (two lighted). *15th Ave E and E Prospect St, Capitol Hill; map:GG6*

WINDSURFING

Definitely not for landlubbers, windsurfing takes athleticism, daring, and a lot of practice. The **COLUMBIA RIVER GORGE** (about 200 miles south of Seattle) is the top windsurfing area in the continental United States (and second only to Maui in the entire country), thanks to the strong winds that always blow in the direction opposite the river's current—ideal conditions for confident windsurfers. Here are some popular locations closer to home.

GREEN LAKE (E Green Lake Dr N and W Green Lake Dr N; map:EE7) is the best place for beginners; the water is warm and the winds are usually gentle, though experts may find it too crowded. You can take lessons and rent equipment at **GREEN LAKE BOAT RENTALS** (7351 E Green Lake Dr N; 206/527-0171) on the northeast side of the lake.

LAKE UNION has fine winds in the summer, but you'll have to dodge sailboats, commercial boats, and seaplanes. To launch, head to **GAS WORKS PARK** (N Northlake Wy and Meridian Ave N, Wallingford; map:FF7). You can rent equipment and catch a lesson from **URBAN SURF** (2100 N Northlake Wy, Wallingford; 206/545-9463; map:FF7).

Most experienced windsurfers prefer expansive **LAKE WASHINGTON**. Head to any waterfront park—most have plenty of parking and rigging space. **MAGNUSON PARK** (Sand Point Wy NE and 65th Ave NE, Sand Point; map:EE5) is favored for its great winds. At **MOUNT BAKER PARK** (Lake Park Dr S and Lake Washington Blvd S, Rainier Valley; map:II6), you can take lessons at **MOUNT BAKER ROWING AND SAILING CENTER** (3800 Lake Washington Blvd S, Rainier Valley; 206/386-1913). Choice Eastside beaches include **GENE COULON BEACH PARK** (1201 Lake Washington Blvd N, Renton; map:MM3), where you can also rent boards and get instruction, and **HOUGHTON BEACH PARK** (NE 59th St and Lake Washington Blvd NE, Kirkland; map:FF4), with rentals nearby at **O. O. DENNY PARK** (NE 124th St and Holmes Point Dr NE, Juanita; map:DD5).

On **PUGET SOUND**, windsurfers head for **GOLDEN GARDENS PARK** (north end of Seaview Ave NW, Ballard; map:DD9) or Duwamish Head at **ALKI BEACH PARK** (Alki Ave SW, West Seattle; map:II9).

Spectator Sports

Mere decades ago, Seattle was seen as a nonplayer when it came to big-time professional sports. The city nostalgically clung to the memory of the Seattle SuperSonics' NBA championship in 1979, but it was a long time between celebrations.

Fortunately, as with any good sports story, it was only a matter of time before Seattle's losing streak was reversed. Things began looking up in the late '80s and early '90s, when some all-star athletes brought Seattle national media attention and a much-needed injection of hometown pride. A couple of division-winning seasons and a sports-facility spending spree helped the city regain its sports swagger (see "We Got Game" sidebar). Today, a tonsil-ringing enthusiasm makes itself heard in all three houses of the city's pro teams, as well as at the University of Washington and other local venues.

EMERALD DOWNS RACETRACK / 2300 Emerald Downs Dr, Auburn; 253/288-7000 or 888/931-8400 Emerald Downs, a sweet little track in Auburn, 25 minutes south of downtown Seattle, brought the sport of kings back to Western Washington when it opened in 1996. There's plentiful indoor and outdoor seating, cuisine that goes beyond the usual hot dogs and beer—yakisoba, anyone?—and about 700 color television monitors to ensure that race fans won't miss a thing, plus a sports bar, a gift shop, and an attractive paddock area. Besides the on-site action, Downs visitors can wager on races at tracks around the country. Racing season runs from mid-April to mid-September, Thursday to Sunday (plus Wednesday, mid-July and August). General admission is $4, free for children 17 and under; grandstand seating is $6, clubhouse seating is $6.50. Free general parking is available (catch one of the parking shuttles); preferred spaces (a shorter walk) are $4; valet parking (no walk) is $7. *www.emeralddowns.com; I-5 south to 272nd St exit; east to West Valley Hwy and south to 37th St N*

EVERETT AQUASOX / 39th and Broadway, Everett; 425/258-3673 or 800/GO-FROGS in Washington Real grass, real fans, real hot dogs—the AquaSox have it all, including a lime-green frog mascot, Webbly, that is a hot collector's item around the world. Watching this Class-A farm team of the Seattle Mariners is always worth the drive to Everett's 4,500-seat Memorial Stadium, where the baby M's take their first steps toward major-league careers. The AquaSox attract a loyal cadre of fans from

WE GOT GAME

With a few notable exceptions—such as the gold rush of the 1890s and the Grunge Rock of the 1980s—Seattle has traditionally maintained a low profile. In recent years, however, as the city has moved increasingly into the international spotlight (translation: WTO riots) and absorbed a diverse collection of residents (translation: New Yorkers), a decidedly pluckier persona has emerged. About as good an indicator as any of this change of face is the city's newly supercharged professional sports culture.

The initial spark was the **Mariners** winning Seattle its first major-league division title in 1995. Our boys of summer parlayed a citywide case of pennant fever into a sparkling new ballpark, Safeco Field. Then Paul Allen, already owner of the Portland Trail Blazers, finagled a new home for his latest franchise acquisition, the **Seattle Seahawks.** One imploded Kingdome—and nearly $1 billion—later, two side-by-side stadiums physically—and, more importantly for sports fans, psychologically—dominate our southern waterfront.

Now fans formerly dogged by an almost comical inferiority complex exude an almost comical self-confidence. When upper-deck talents Ken Griffey Jr. and Alex Rodriguez defected, Mariners fans adopted a defiant "Don't love our city? Don't let the door hit you" attitude. They even learned to sing the boos (an astonishing development for spectators known in the past for routinely applauding good plays by the opposition). Just ask A-Rod. After he signed a $252 million contract with division rival Texas, the shortstop was treated to a bum's rush of operatic scale—complete with caustic rain showers of dollar bills and banners dubbing him "A-Fraud"—when he returned to the Safe in Ranger colors in 2001. M's fans instead rallied around their new imports Ichiro Suzuki and Kazuhiro Sasaki (and the subsequent influx of Japanese tourists) and, in between nibbling on sushi and sipping microbrews, cheered the Mariners on to their history-making tie for the most wins in one season. Unfortunately, while records fell, the New York Yankees would not—ending the Mariners' 2001 World Series dreams with a crushing loss in the American League Championship series.

And what about the prospects for the playoff-plagued **Seattle SuperSonics?** Starbucks owner Howard Schultz headed a group of investors who purchased the basketball team in 2001. In keeping with Seattle's newfound sporting spunk, expectations are high. Besides, considering what the latte king has managed with just a coffee bean, another championship for the Sonics should be a slam dunk.   —*Shannon O'Leary*

mid-June through the first week of September. Tickets can usually be bought at the gate (the popular "Chicken Night" sells out fast, however) and are also available through Ticketmaster outlets. Tickets are $5 for adults, $4 for kids 12 and under; reserved seats are $6–$10. *www.aqua sox.com; 30 miles north of Seattle on I-5 at exit 192*

HUSKY BASKETBALL / Bank of America Arena at Hec Edmundson Pavilion, University of Washington, University District; 206/543-2200 Around here, real women play hoops—and they play them well. The members of the University of Washington's strong Husky women's basketball team often put on a better show than their male counterparts, but the men are gaining ground, and both teams are fun and affordable to watch. The Dawg teams start play in early November and continue through March. General seating costs $6; reserved seats are $10 for women's games, $16–$18 for men's. The Husky-Stanford women's games are always a hot ticket. *www.gohuskies.com; map:FF6*

HUSKY FOOTBALL / Husky Stadium, University of Washington, University District; 206/543-2200 Beginning in September, the UW's beloved "bad-to-the-bone Dawgs" play top-drawer football in the 73,000-seat Husky Stadium. Tickets are tough to get, so plan ahead, especially for big games; when the Huskies are home, the games are on Saturday. Be sure to pack rain gear, carpool (just follow the cars with the Husky flags), and wear purple. Also, plan to watch game highlights later on TV, as the lovely lake views from the stadium will likely distract even die-hard fans from some of the gridiron action. General seats are $16–$18, reserved seats are $32–$36. *www.gohuskies.com; map:FF6*

SEATTLE MARINERS / Safeco Field, between Royal Brougham Wy and S Atlantic St, SoDo; 206/346-4000 Since the team's thrilling foray into the playoffs in 1995, the Mariners have become the undisputed darlings of local sports fans—and even converted a few non-sports types. That stellar '95 season helped catapult attendance through the Kingdome roof and the M's right into an open-air ballpark. Safeco Field borrows from the classic design of other new ballparks, such as Baltimore's Camden Yards, but adds a state-of-the-art retractable roof and a menu sporting Pacific Rim offerings such as California Rolls. Other amenities include an open barbecue pit, several shops offering Mariners merchandise, and a baseball museum. The season lasts from early April through the first week of October. Individual ticket prices range from $6 for center-field bleachers to $36. The $15 upper-deck seats may be the best in the park, with unobstructed vistas of Mount Rainier, Elliott Bay, and downtown Seattle. *www.mariners.org; map:R9*

SEATTLE SEAHAWKS / Occidental Wy S and S King St, SoDo; 888/NFL-HAWK When Microsoft co-founder and Northwest sports mogul Paul Allen (who also owns basketball's Portland Trail Blazers) purchased the Hawks in 1997, the deal was contingent upon building a new stadium to replace the much-maligned Kingdome. The new facility opens on the old Dome site in summer 2002. The best bet is to take a free Metro bus from downtown—parking near the stadium is an expensive nightmare. The Hawks' regular season starts in September (preseason games in August) and runs through December. Ticket prices range from $10 to $52. *www.seahawks.com; map:Q9*

SEATTLE SOUNDERS / Memorial Stadium, Seattle Center; 800/796-KICK While some American cities are still discovering the world's most popular sport, professional soccer has been kicking around Seattle off and on since 1974, when the Sounders were founded. The 1995–96 A-League champions play at the cozy 10,000-seat Memorial Stadium, north of the Space Needle, from April through September. Tickets range from $7 to $15. *www.seattlesounders.net; map:B6*

SEATTLE STORM / KeyArena, Seattle Center; Ticketmaster: 206/628-0888 Seattle acquired a Women's National Basketball Association franchise in 2000 when this fledgling team blew into town. Games are held during the short NBA off season (late May through mid-August), but the team already has a loyal contingent of fans. Tickets are a comparatively affordable $8–$55 (courtside). *www.wnba.com/storm/; map:B7*

SEATTLE SUPERSONICS / KeyArena, Seattle Center; Ticketmaster: 206/628-0888 Since winning it all in the '70s, the Sonics have been an uneven team, especially when it comes to the playoffs. On the other hand, unpredictability is part of the team's charm, and the Sonics are a consistent winner when it comes to drawing the home crowd—known as one of the loudest in the nation. The team tears up the courts from early November to late April, and tickets (ranging from $9 to $110 for near-courtside) often sell out early. *www.nba.com/sonics/; map:B7*

TACOMA RAINIERS / Cheney Stadium, 2502 S Tyler St, Tacoma; 800/281-3834 On clear days at the M's Triple-A farm club's Cheney Stadium facility, spectacular views of Mount Rainier play background for these boys of summer. The Rainiers play 72 home games, from early April to September. Tickets are very affordable, ranging from $5 to $10. *www.tacomarainiers.com; about 34 miles south of Seattle on I-5, take exit 132 (Hwy 16) west*

THUNDERBIRDS HOCKEY / KeyArena, Seattle Center; 206/448-7825 or 425/869-7825; Ticketmaster: 206/628-0888 Arguably the best ticket buy in local sports, the 1996–97 Western Hockey League champion Seattle Thunderbirds take to the ice in September and play through March—or early May if they make the playoffs. No one could mistake these young icemen for the NHL, but what they lack in finesse (and years) they make up for with sheer energy and some of the most vocal, loyal fans in the region. The T-birds' 36 home games are mostly on weekends; tickets are $8–$20. *www.seattle-thunderbirds.com; map:B7*

Index

We Stand By Our Reviews

Sasquatch Books is proud of *Best Places Seattle*. Our editors and contributors go to great lengths and expense to see that all of the restaurant and lodging reviews are as accurate, up-to-date, and honest as possible. If we have disappointed you, please accept our apologies; however, if a recommendation in this 9th edition of *Best Places Seattle* has seriously misled you, Sasquatch Books would like to refund your purchase price. To receive your refund:

1. Tell us where and when you purchased your book and return the book and the book-purchase receipt to the address below.
2. Enclose the original restaurant or lodging receipt from the establishment in question, including date of visit.
3. Write a full explanation of your stay or meal and how *Best Places Seattle* misled you.
4. Include your name, address, and phone number.

Refund is valid only while this 9th edition of *Best Places Seattle* is in print. If the ownership, management, or chef has changed since publication, Sasquatch Books cannot be held responsible. Tax and postage on the returned book is your responsibility. Please allow six to eight weeks for processing.

Please address to Satisfaction Guaranteed, *Best Places Seattle*, and send to:

Sasquatch Books
615 Second Avenue, Suite 260
Seattle, WA 98104

Best Places Seattle Report Form

Based on my personal experience, I wish to nominate the following restaurant, place of lodging, shop, nightclub, sight, or other as a "Best Place"; or confirm/correct/disagree with the current review.

_____

_____

_____

_____

(Please include address and telephone number of establishment, if convenient.)

REPORT

Please describe food, service, style, comfort, value, date of visit, and other aspects of your experience; continue on another piece of paper if necessary.

_____

_____

_____

_____

_____

_____

_____

I am not concerned, directly or indirectly, with the management or ownership of this establishment.

_____

SIGNED

_____

ADDRESS

_____

_____

PHONE   **DATE**

Please address to Best Places Seattle and send to:
SASQUATCH BOOKS
615 SECOND AVENUE, SUITE 260
SEATTLE, WA 98104
Feel free to email feedback as well: **BESTPLACES@SASQUATCHBOOKS.COM**